HISTORY OF
ANCIENT INDIA

OUR PUBLICATIONS ON HISTORY

THE MIDDLE AGES	*K C Chowdhury*
HISTORY OF GREECE	*K C Chowdhury*
BRITISH HISTORY	*K C Chowdhury*
HISTORY OF MEDIEVAL INDIA	*K C Chowdhury*
HISTORY OF MODERN INDIA	*K C Chowdhury*
H.S. HISTORY OF EUROPE AND THE WORLD	*K C Chowdhury*

HISTORY OF ANCIENT INDIA

Dr Kiran Chandra Chaudhuri

MA, LLB, PhD

To be had of

New Central Book Agency (P) Ltd

LONDON

HYDERABAD ERNAKULAM BHUBANESWAR

NEW DELHI KOLKATA PUNE GUWAHATI

NCBA

REGD OFFICE

8/1 Chintamoni Das Lane, Kolkata 700 009, India
email: ncbapvtltd@eth.net

OVERSEAS

NCBA (UK) Ltd, 149 Park Avenue North, Northampton, NN3 2HY, UK
email: ncbauk@yahoo.com

EXPORT

NCBA Exports Pvt. Ltd, 212 Shahpur Jat, New Delhi 110 049
email: ncbaexports@ncbapvtltd.com

BRANCHES

2/27 Ansari Road, 1st Floor
Daryaganj, **New Delhi** 110 002
email: ncbadel@ncbapvtltd.com

Shop Nos. 3 & 4, Vinayak Towers
681/B Budhwar Peth, Appa Balwant Chowk
Pune 411 002
email: ncbapune@ncbapvtltd.com

Shop No. 15, Bharati Towers, Ground Floor
Forest Park
Bhubaneswar 751 001
email: ncbabub@ncbapvtltd.com

House No. 3-1-315, 1st Floor
Nimboliadda, Kachiguda, **Hyderabad** 500 027
email: ncbahydb@ncbapvtltd.com

GSS Shopping Complex, 1st Floor
Opposite College Post Office, Convent Road
Ernakulam 682 035
0484-4021054/53

Radhamayee Complex (Second Floor)
Opp. SBI, Panbazar, Jaswanta Road
Guwahati 781 001
email: ncbaguwahati@ncbapvtltd.com

HISTORY OF ANCIENT INDIA • KIRAN CHANDRA CHAUDHURI

First Published: 1983
Reprinted: 1993, 2002, 2011, 2015

PUBLISHER
Central Educational Enterprises (P) Ltd
54B Patuatola Lane, Kolkata 700 009

PRINTER
New Central Book Agency (P) Ltd
Web-Offset Division, Dhulagarh, Sankrail, Howrah

ISBN: 978 81 7381 420 4

Price: ₹ 350.00

FOREWORD

History of Ancient India is written in conformity with B.A. Honours standard of Indian Universities, particularly, the University of Calcutta. Special emphasis has been put on the socio-economic, religious and cultural history of different phases of the Ancient Indian History.

I hope the B.A. Honours students and students who follow an advanced course of study in Ancient Indian History, particularly, those preparing for competitive examinations will find the book useful.

15th August, 1982
Calcutta

K. C. CHAUDHURI

CONTENTS

CHAPTER ONE : **Introduction** 1—17

•Geographical situation: Physical characteristics p. 5, Influence of Physical geography on the Indian History p. 7, People of India p. 8, Unity in Diversity p. 9, Sources of Ancient Indian History p. 13.

CHAPTER TWO : **Pre-history and Proto-history of India** 18—22

Palaeolithic age p. 20, Mesolithic age p. 21, Neolithic age p. 22, Chalcolithic culture p. 22, Iron age p. 23, Proto-historic age p. 24.

CHAPTER THREE : **The Indus Civilisation** 23 — 34

Economic life p. 27, Date of the Indus Civilisation: Its relation with other civilisations p. 30, Architects of the Indus Civilisation p. 31, Decline and Disappearance of the Indus Civilisation p. 32, Survivals of the Indus Civilisation p. 35.

CHAPTER FOUR : **The Aryans and the Aryan Civilisation** 35 – 56

Original home of the Aryans p. 37, The early Vedic age: Early Aryan Settlements p. 39, The Vedic literature p. 40, The Religion of the Aryans p. 42, Society: Varna-srama, i.e. Four-fold division of Society p. 43, Four Asramas, i.e. Four stages of life p. 43, Economic life of the Aryans p. 44, Arts and Sciences of the Aryans p. 45, Political life of the Aryans p. 45, Position of women in the Vedic society p. 47, Social life in the later Vedic age p. 48, Economic life in the later Vedic age p. 49, Political condition in the later Vedic age p. 49, Impacts of the Non-Aryans on the Aryan society p. 51, The age of the Epics p. 52, The Mahabharata p. 54, The Ramayana p. 55, Historical importance of the Mahabharata and the Ramayana p. 55, The Dharma-Sutras p. 57, The Puranas p. 58.

CHAPTER FIVE : **Age of Sixteen Mahajanapadas** 57—64

Sixteen Mahajanapadas p. 59, Kasi p. 59, Kosala p. 60 Anga p. 60, Magadha p. 60, Vriji or Vajji p. 60, Malava or Malla p. 60, Chedi p. 61, Vamsa or Vatsya p. 61, Kuru p. 61, Panchala p. 61, Matsya p. 62, Surasena p. 62, Asmaka p. 62, Avanti p. 62, Gandhara p. 62, Kamboj p. 63, Political conditions during the period of the Sixteen Mahajanapadas p. 64, Social conditions during the period of the Sixteen Mahajanapadas p. 65, Economic and Religious conditions during the period of the sixteen Mahajanapadas p. 66.

CHAPTER SIX : **The Post-Vedic Religious and Political Evolution** 65—82

Reaction against Vedic Brahmanism p. 67, Mahavira

Vardhamana p. 68, Gautama Buddha and Buddhism p. 70, Buddhism, Jainism and Hinduism compared p. 72, The Jaina and Buddhist Religious Organisation p. 73, Spread of Jainism and Buddhism: Extinction of Buddhism in India p. 76, The Rise of Magadha p. 77, Ajatasatru p. 80, Successors of Ajatasatru p. 81, Sishunaga dynasty p. 81, The Nandas p. 82, Mahapadmananda p. 82, Successors of Mahapadmananda p. 83.

CHAPTER SEVEN : **Foreign Invasion of India** 83 – 94

The *Persian Invasion* p. 85, Cyrus p. 85, Darius p. 86, Xerxes p. 86, The *Macedonian Invasion* p. 87, Political condition of Uttarapath (North-Western India) on the eve of Alexander's invasion p. 87, Indian compaign of Alexander p. 88, Ambhi p. 89, Poros p. 89, Battle of Hydaspes p. 89, Nature of Indian resistance to Alexander p. 91, Motive behind Alexander's Indian conquests: his administrative arrangement p. 91, Impact of the Persian and Macedonian invasion p. 93.

CHAPTER EIGHT : **The Mauryas** 95 —153

Chandragupta's Ancestry p. 97, Dhanananda p. 99, Early life and rise to power of Chandragupta p. 99, Conquests of Chandragupta p. 101, Seleukos p. 104, Chandragupta's administration p. 106, Statements of Megasthenes p. 112, Bindusara (300-273 B.C.) p. 117, Kautilya's Arthasastra: Date and Authorship p. 118, Asoka: his birth and early life: Accession p. 121, Asoka's family and family life p. 124, The Kalinga War p. 125, Extent of Asoka's empire p. 127, Administration of the empire under Asoka p. 130, Character of Asoka's government p. 132, Asoka's conversion into Buddhism p. 132, Asoka's administrative reform p. 134, Change in Foreign Policy under Asoka p. 135, Asoka's Dharma p. 137, Nature of Asoka's Dharma p. 138, Propagation of Asoka's Dharma within his dominion p. 139, and outside his dominion p. 141, Effects of Asoka's Missionary Activity p. 142, Character and Estimate of Asoka p. 145, Asoka and Akbar p. 148, Asoka's place in History p. 149, Successors of Asoka p. 150, Decline and Fall of the Maurya Empire p. 152, Pushyamitra p. 153, Taxila p. 154.

CHAPTER NINE : **Post-Maurya Dynasties (in Northern India)** 154 — 161

The *Sungas* p. 156, Divyavadana p. 156, Yajnasena p. 157, Pushyamitra p. 157, Agnimitra p. 157, Vasumitra p. 158, Successors of Pusyamitra Sunga p. 160, Importance of the Sunga Period in Indian History p. 161, The *Kanvas* p. 162, Devabhuti Sunga p. 162, Vasudeva p. 163, Magadha after the Kanvas p. 163.

CHAPTER TEN : **Post-Maurya Dynasties (in Southern India)** 162—188

Kalinga under Kharvela p. 164, Mahameghavahana p. 164, Kharvela: his date: his career p. 165, Kharvela's career and achievements p. 167, Bahasatimita p. 168, ***The Satavahanas*** p. 170, Satavahana chronology—a puzzle p. 171, Satakarni I p. 172, Rise of the Satavahana p. 172, *Andhras* or *Andhra-bhrityas* p. 172, Original home of the Satavahana p. 173, *Aitareya Brahmana* p. 173, Political and Administrative of the Satavahanas p. 174, Simuka p. 175, Krishna p. 175, Satakarni I p. 175, Successors of Satakarni I p. 176, Hala p. 177, The later Satavahanas p. 178, Gautamaputra Satakarni p. 178, Kardamakas p. 179, Nahapana p. 179, *Vasisthiputra Pulumayi* II p. 179, Sivasri p. 180, Satakarni p. 180, Yajnasri Satakarni p. 180, Satavahana decline p. 181, Political, Social, Economic, Religious and Cultural life under the Satavahanas p. 181, The Deccan after the Satavahanas p. 186, The Vakatakas p. 186, Vindhyasakti p. 187, Madhavavarmana I p. 187, The Abhiras p. 188, The Bodhis p. 188, Sribodhi p. 188, The Ikashvakus p. 189, Santamula I p. 189, Mathuraputra p. 189, Virapurushdatta p. 190, Santamula II p. 190, The Brihatphalayanas p. 190, Jayavarman p. 190.

CHAPTER ELEVEN : **The Yavanas (Bactrian Greeks)** 189 - 200

Antiochus I p. 191, Antiochus II p. 192, Diodotus I: Diodotus II p. 192, Euthydemus p. 192, Antiochus III p. 192, Demetrius p. 193, Eucratides p. 196, Helioctes p. 177, Indo-Greek Rulers—Apollodotus p. 197, Menander p. 198, Strato I: Strato II p. 200, Antialcidas p. 200, Hermaeus p. 200.

CHAPTER TWELVE : **The Scythians (The Sakas)** 201—205

Yue-chi p. 203, Mithridates I p. 205, Vonones p. 205, Spalahora p. 205, Spaladagama p. 205, Spalirises p. 205, Maues or Moga p. 206, Liaka Kusuluka p. 206, Azes I p. 206, Azilises or Azes II p. 207.

CHAPTER THIRTEEN : **The Parthians (the Pahlavas)** 206 — 214

Gondophernes p. 208, Successors of Gondophernes p. 209, Abdagases p. 209, Pacores p. 209, The Saka Satrapies p. 209, Satraps or Kshatrapas p. 209, Mahakshatrapa p. 209, Northern Satrap of Taxila p. 209, Laika Kusalaka p. 209, Mahadanapati Patika p. 209, Mevaki Miyika p. 209, Northern Satrap of Mathura p. 210, Kshatrapa p. 210, Mahakshatrapa p. 210, Sodasa p. 210, Sivadatta p. 210, Sivaghosa p. 210, The Western Satrapies p. 210, The Western Satraps of Maharashtra p. 211, Nahapana p. 211, Western Satraps of Ujjaini p. 212, Yasamalika p. 212, Chastana p. 212, Jayadamana p. 213, Rudradamana I p. 213, Successors of Rudradamana p. 214, Damaghsada I p. 214, Jivadaman p. 214, Rudrasimha I

p. 214, Rudrasena I p. 214, Rudramana II p. 214, Rudrasimha III p. 214, Administrative Machinery of the Scynthian Parthian Period: its cultural achievements p. 214.

CHAPTER FOURTEEN : **The Kushanas** 215 —236

Sources p. 217, Origin and rise of the Kushanas p. 218, Han dynasties p. 218, *Tsian Han-shu* and *Hou Han-shu* p. 218, Yue-chi p. 218, Kiu-tsiu-kib (Kujula Kadphises) p. 219, Ta Yue-chi p. 219, The Kushana Kings: Kujula Kadphises p. 219, Kadphises II p. 221, Kanishka: his date p. 222, Kanishka's conquests: Extent of his empire p. 225, Kanishka's administration p. 226, Kanishka's religion p. 227, Buddhist council during the reign of Kanishka p. 228, Hinayana and Mahayana p. 228, Art and Learning during the reign of Kanishka p. 229, Estimate of Kanishka p. 229, Kanishka's successors p. 230, Vasiska p. 230, Vajishka p. 230, Jushka p. 230, Kanishka II p. 231, Vasudeva I p. 231, Kanishka III p. 231, Vasudeva II p. 231, The downfall of the Kushana Empire p. 231, Huvishka p. 231, Yaudheyas p. 232, The Maghas of Kausambi p. 232, Sassanian Power p. 233, Ardeshir I p. 233, Achievements of the Kushanas—A review p. 233, Administration, Society, Religion, Art, Sculpture and Architecture, Literature and Economy during the reign of Kushanas pp. 233-38.

CHAPTER FIFTEEN : **The Gupta Empire** 237 —294

Disintegration in the Post-Kushana Period p. 239, The Nagas p. 239, Ganendra or Ganapa p. 239, Nagasena p. 239, The Maghas of Kausambi p. 240, Kautsiputra Pothasri p. 240, The Foundation of the Gupta Dynasty p. 241, Epigraphic and Numismatic evidence of the Gupta Dynasty p. 241, Monuments and Literature as sources of the Gupta Dynasty p. 242, Accounts of Foreign Travellers as sources of the Gupta Dynasty p. 243, Origin of the Gupta Dynasty p. 243, Ghatotkacha p. 245, Chandragupta I p. 246, Samudragupta p. 248, Samudragupta's foreign relations p. 251, Meghavarna p. 251, Personal Accomplishment of Samudragupta: his estimate p. 252, Successors of Samudragupta—Ramagupta p. 254, Chandragupta II p. 255, Rudrasimha III p. 256, Accounts of Fa-hien p. 258, Estimate of Chandragupta II Vikramaditya p. 260, Kumaragupta I p. 261, Skandagupta p. 263, Problem of succession p. 263, Skandagupta's successors p. 266, Purugupta p. 266, Narasimhagupta Baladitya p. 266, Kumaragupta II p. 266, Budhagupta p. 267, Tathagatagupta p. 268, Baladityagupta p. 268, Narasimhagupta p. 268, Vinayagupta and Bhanugupta p. 268, The Huns p. 269, Toramana p. 269, Mihirgula or Mihirkula p. 270, Yashodharman p. 272, Other Feudatories p. 273, Vanga p. 273,

Gauda p. 273, The Gupta Administration p. 274—Central Government: king p. 274, Limitation to the power of the king p. 275, State officials p. 276, Administrative divisions p. 277, Provincial administration p. 277, The Gupta culture p. 280, The Gupta Art and Architecture p. 284, Socio-Economic condition under the Gupta p. 287, Slaves p. 288, Marriage: Position of Women p. 288, Religion under the Gupta p. 291, The Later Guptas p. 293, Causes of the Downfall of the Gupta Empire p. 293, Foreign impacts on the Guptas p. 296.

CHAPTER SIXTEEN : **The Maukharis and the Pushyabhutis** 295—320

Maukharis of Kanauj p. 297, Pushyabhutis of Thaneswar p. 298, Prabhakarvardhan p. 298, Rajyavardhan p. 299, Harshavardhan p. 300, Harshavardhan's conquests p. 302, Extent of Harshavardhan's Empire: A clique p. 305, Administration under Harsha p. 306, Revenue system under Harsha p. 307, Penal system, character of the administration and religion under Harsha p. 308, Kanauj assembly p. 309, Prayag assembly p. 310, Religious condition during the reign of Harsha p. 310, Authorship and Patronage of learning of Harsha p. 311, Estimate of Harsha p. 312, Relation with China p. 314, Accounts of Hiuen T-Sang p. 315-320, Banabhatta's Harshacharit p. 320, Nalanda p. 320.

CHAPTER SEVENTEEN : **General Review** 321—352

Economic factors in Political History p. 323, Economic factors in the growth and decline of Magadhan Imperialism p. 323, Trade and Industry p. 326, Economic factors in the history of the Imperial Kushanas p. 329, Chief features of the Society (4th Century B.C. to 6th Century A.D.) p. 331, Caste system p. 334, Slavery p. 337, Foreign elements in population p. 339, Family life p. 340, Marriage p. 342, Status of women p. 344, Education p. 346, General life p. 350.

CHAPTER EIGHTEEN : **Economic Condition (4th Century B.C. to 6th Century A.D.)** 353—376

Agriculture p. 355, Industry p. 357, Trade: Inland and Maritime p. 359, Organisation of Trade and Industry p. 364, Labour and Wage p. 366, Medium of Exchange: Currency and Banking p. 367, State control over Trade and Industry p. 370, Problem of the origin of Feudalism in Socio-Economic set-up p. 371, Problem of the origin of Feudalistic elements in India p. 373.

CHAPTER NINETEEN : **Art and Architecture (3rd Century B.C. to 7th Centurv A.D.)** 377—415

Cities and Architecture, Palaces, Stupas, Chitya, Hall and Caves, Pillars, Sculpture, Printing and Terracotta under Maurya-Sunga-Kanva Period pp. 379-385, The Gupta

Art, Sculpture, Architecture, Temples, Painting under Indo-Bactrian-Saka-Pahlava-Kushana Period pp. 385-393, Buddhism, Jainism, Vaishnavism and Saivism during the period of 3rd century B.C. to 6th century A.D.) pp. 393-411, Other religious sects: Bhahma, Surya, Uma or Durga, Lakshmi, Naga Cult, Secular literature: Gupta Renaissance pp. 411-417.

CHAPTER TWENTY: **Bengal from Earliest Times till 1202 A.D.** 416 — 422

Vangas p. 418, Bhima of the Mahabharata, 418, Suhmas p. 418, Kingdom of Gauda p. 420, Sasanka p. 421, Estimate of Sasanka p. 424.

CHAPTER TWENTY-ONE: **Bengal under the Palas and Senas** 423 - 440

Matsya-nyaya in Bengal p. 425, The Palas—Gopala p. 426, Dharmapala p. 426, Devapala p. 427, Vigrahapala p. 428, Narayanpala p. 429, Rajyapala p. 429, Gopala II p. 429, Vigrahapala II p. 429, Kambojas's invasion in Bengal p. 429, The Second or the Revived Pala Empire p. 429, Mahipala I p. 429, Nayapala p. 430, Vigrahapala III p. 430, Mahipala II p. 430, Kaivarta rebel p. 430, Dibyok p. 430, Surapala p. 430, Ramapala p. 430, The Senas-Samanta Sena p. 431, Hemanta Sena p. 431, Vijoy Sena p. 431, Vallal Sena p. 432, Lakshman Sena p. 432, Administration, Society, Economic condition under the Palas and the Senas pp. 433-442.

CHAPTER TWENTY-TWO: **South Indian Kingdoms: The Rastrakutas: Chalukyas: The Great Pallavas and the Cholas** 441 - 452

The Rastrakutas p. 443, The Chalukyas—Chalukyas of Batapi p. 445, Chalukyas of Kalyani p. 446, The Pallavas of Kanchi p. 447, Pallava Art p. 448, Pallava Literature p. 449, Religion of the Pallava p. 449, The Cholas p. 449, Rajendrachodevagogai-konda p. 451, Chola administration p. 451, Chola art p. 452, Pandya kingdom p. 452, Chera Kingdom p. 453, Maritime activities of the Tamil Kingdoms p. 453.

HISTORY OF ANCIENT INDIA

CHAPTER ONE

INTRODUCTION

No land on earth possesses a civilisation so distinctive for its antiquity and continuity as India. Although there were other ancient civilisations, notably in Egypt, Mesopotamia etc. yet it is difficult, if not impossible, to identify those civilisations in the modern life of their peoples. But in case of India the Hindus repeat in their daily worship as well as in their ceremonies like marriage, sraddha etc. the Vedic hymns composed more than three thousand years ago. In a lesser degree, only China can claim such continuity.

The vitality of the Indian civilisation, its ability to adapt to alien ideas, harmonise contradictions and mould new ideas into its own thought pattern gave it a life and a soul which kept its continuity through ages.

The origins of the Indian civilisation are traced to the pre-Vedic and highly advanced Harappan culture. History of such a civilisation and land is bound to be fascinating, at the same time difficult to reconstruct.

Man is more ancient than civilisation and what we have been able to know of our remote past constitutes only a fraction of the history of the ancient times. Comparatively recent discipline of archaeology is opening by and by the vista of history extending to thousands of years backwards although some of the links still remain missing.

Man is one of the weakest of animals, yet it was man alone that was capable of adapting himself to environment, controlling it to his own requirements. It is man's genius to control his environment, his ability to deal with other men and adjust himself into a working relationship with other groups of human beings that lay at the roots of progress of human civilisation. Two elements, therefore, lay as the bases of human civilisation, namely: man's genius and his environment. Man's environment again depends on the nature and specialities of his country. These apart, history ceases to be history without chronology; it becomes unconnected stories. It has, therefore, been rightly said that chronology and geography are the Sun and the Moon, right eye and the left eye of History.

Of the four territorial areas where first signs of civilisation emerged Indus Valley was one and the others were the Nile Valley, Tigris and Euphrates Valleys and the Yangtse Valley. These civilisations were almost contemporaneous.

Indian civilisation has certain specialities peculiar to her own. These are: *First*, the unparalleled continuity of her civilisation. Whether in religion, society, economy, language or literature the ancient lives in the present. The Yogin, i.e. the Pasupati and the Mother Goddess of the Harappan civilisation are still worshipped today as Siva and Parvati. The Vedic hymns chanted by the Vedic Aryans on the banks of the Indus are repeated by the Hindus on ceremonial occasions from Kashmir to Cape Comorin. Despite different waves of foreign invasions at different periods of Indian history, the main structure of the Hindu civilisation continues to exist even today. Like a snow-ball the Indian civilisation has added to its body whatever has been acceptable to it from the different peoples and different civilisations that entered into India in different waves. Yet its soul remains unchanged. 'She was like some palimpsest on which layer upon layer of thought and reverie had been inscribed yet no succeeding layer had been completely hidden or erased what had been written previously.'[1]

Secondly, adaptability of the Indian civilisation did not lose her individuality. While India kept her door open for whatever was conducive to her well-being and progress she did not hesitate to shun whatever was likely to usurp her individuality. This can be noticed when the Indian civilisation faced the challenge of the Islamic civilisation or when the three cultures, namely, the Islamic, English and Hindu cultures were poised against one another in India. Integrity and individuality characterise the Indian civilisation.

Thirdly, the western civilisation had its origin in the civilisations of Greece and Rome which were urban in nature due to the peculiarities of their geography. The Western civilisation established itself and made progress by conquering Nature. Conquest of Nature seems to be the main theme of the western civilisation. Even today the idea of conquest is the motivation behind that civilisation. But the Indian civilisation which was established in the midst of Nature saw relationship with nature and its elements as the greatest truth. Conquest of Nature, therefore, was absent here, rather adjustment with Nature and environment was the main theme of the Indian civilisation. "The West seems to take pride in thinking that it is subduing Nature, as if we are living in a hostile world where we have to wrest everything we want from an unwilling and alien arrangement of things......But in India the point of view was different; it included the world with the man as one great truth. India put all her emphasis on the harmony that exists between the individual and the Universe."[2]

---

[1] Jawaharlal Nehru ; *The Discovery of India.*

[2] *Discourses delivered by Rabindranath Tagore at Chicago and Harvard Universities,* 1912-13.

Fourthly, every civilisation has its own message and purpose. That of the Indian civilisation is adjustment. To bring about unity in diversity, to develop tolerance and brotherliness among the wider human world are among the purposes of the Indian civilisation. If better understanding between the human world be the ultimate goal of civilisation, then it may be said with emphasis that this has been the perennial feature of the Indian civilisation.

Some of these special features of the Indian civilisation may have been the source of political weakness of India and prejudicial to her interests yet it is these features that have helped India and the Indians to retain the Indian character which has not been lost under external influences.

Geographical Situation : Physical Characteristics

The largest peninsula in the southern part of the Asiatic Continent is India. It is almost a Continent by itself. It is as large as the whole of the European Continent except Russia. Before August 15, 1947, India had a total area of 4,095,000 sq. kilometers with a length of 2,900 kilometers and breadth of 2,190 kilometers. The boundary of this vast land is covered by nearly nine thousand six hundred kilometers of mountains and eight thousand kilometers of sea coasts.

The Himalayan range stands like a wall towards the north, north-west and north-east of India. The southern portion gradually tapers and juts out into the Indian ocean. Its north eastern shores are washed by the Bay of Bengal and south western coast by the Arabian sea.

In ancient literature mention is found of five natural divisions of India. These were : (i) *Madhyadesa,* i.e. Indo-Gangetic plain stretching from the valley of the river Saraswati to the Rajmahal Hill. This *Madhyadesa* has been known as *Aryavarta* from the ancient times. (ii) *Uttarapatha or Udichya* i.e. North-west India. (iii) *Pratichya or Aparanta,* i.e. western India. (iv) *Dakshinapatha or Dakshinatya,* i.e. the area south of *Madhyadesa.* (v) *Prachya or Purvadesa,* the region east of Madhyadesa. As all the different regions were defined with reference to their situations in relation to the Madhyadesa, i.e. Aryavarta, it shows its importance and eminence.

Apart from the above five natural divisions two other names were found in the Puranas. These were the Himalyan region and the Vindhya region. It may be mentioned here that from the ancient past India was broadly divided into *Aryavarta* and *Dakshinatya.*

Considered from the geo-physical peculiarities India may be divided into four major regions. From the point of view of political history this division is more reasonable. The four divisions are : (i) *Parbatasrayin,* i.e. the hilly countries of the north, (ii) The plains watered by the Indus, the Ganges and the Brahmaputra,

(iii) The Central Indian and the Deccan Plateaus, (iv) The long tapering region of far south.

(i) The Hilly Countries of the North : In the north of India the Himalayan mountain range stands almost like a wall of defence. This mountain range extends from Kashmir to Assam, and it has separated India from China, Tibet and Burma. The Suleiman and the Hindukos mountain ranges have separated India from Russia, Iran and Baluchistan. From the Himalayan Terai to the top of the mountain range, the ascending heights comprise Kashmir, Nepal, Sikim and Bhutan. The physical geography of these countries preclude easy communicotion. This was primarily the reason for which the political vicissitudes of the Indian plains did not influence these hilly countries to any large extent. Naturally, these countries retained their independence for ages.

(ii) The Indo-Gangetic-Brahmaputra plain : This vast plain comprises the valley of the Indus, Sind, the desert of Rajputana and the fertile valleys of the Ganges and the Jumna. This area is the most important in the whole of India. The fertility and the natural wealth of this area had attracted the Aryans in the ancient past and had also attracted foreign invaders in different stages of history. The facility of internal transport due to the numerous rivers transpiercing this area, its rich natural resources and population helped the rise of different empires. One aim of the Indian emperors and the foreign invaders was to occupy the whole of this plain. This was exactly the reason why five decisive battles of Indias history, namely, the first and the second battles of Terrain, three battles of Panipath were fought in this vast plain.

(iii) The Central Indian and the Deccan Plateaus : The Central Indian plateau extends from the southern limits of Aryavarta to the Vindhya-Satpura mountains. The area comprising the peninsula south of Vindhya-Satpura mountains is called the Deccan Plateau. Although from the point of view of the Indian history no differentiation is possible between the two parts, called Aryavarta and Dakshinatya, and although both the parts are essential constituents of India, yet from the political point of view of the Aryavarta enjoyed greater consideration and importance.

The history of the ancient times of the Deccan is the history of the Dravidas, but this history cannot be said to have been complete. Much of the ancient history of the Deccan is still to be known. That Aryavarta always had enjoyed greater importance relatively to the Deccan is borne out by the fact that no ruler of the Deccan had ever succeeded in extending his authority over Aryavarta, but many a ruler of the Aryavarta had extended his domination over the Deccan even though for temporary periods.

(*iv*) *The Narrow Tapering Region of the Far South*: The gradually tapering peninsula from the Eastern and the Western Ghats to the Indian Ocean is known as Far South of India. This region exemplified the political and cultural excellence of the ancient Dravidian civilisation. No Hindu or Muslim conqueror succeeded in establishing unquestioned authority for long in this region.

Influence of Physical Geography on the Indian History

Egypt is said to be the gift of the Nile. Similarly India may be regarded as the gift of the Himalayas. But for the Himalayas the history of India would have been different. The Himalayas has given India a strong natural frontier towards the north. From the hoary past it has been protecting India like a lofty wall of defence. By separating India from the northern part of Asia it helped India to retain the distinctive character of her civilisation and culture. The Himalayas is the watershed of India. Many of the Indian rivers have their source in the Himalayas and water flowing down these rivers has made India fertile and full of luscious green. The riverine country of ours is rich in agriculture and forests. India is equally rich in mineral resources. Nature has bestowed her blessings in the abundance of every kind of natural resources. In ancient India there was no problem of livelihood. This, while made the life of the Indians easy-going and somewhat indolent on the one hand, it made the Indians turn their attention more towards religion, philosophy, poetry and literature. This was also the reason why the Indians in the ancient times became shy of physical labour and prone to religious, artistic and literary pursuits.

The diversity of physical geography in the vast country of ours made life full of diversities. Sky high mountains, vast plains, raised plateaus, wide expanse of deserts, and the net work of rivers have contributed to impart the different regions of the country certain local specialities.

Although the high mountain ranges have separated India from the rest of Asia, yet this separation did not prevent intercourse with other countries of the world. In the north-west of India the Khyber Pass, Gomal and Bolan Passes facilitated the entry of outsiders into India from the time of the Aryan invasion till the invasion of Ahmad Shah Abdali. The Persians, the Greeks, the Sakas, the Huns, the Turks, the Afghans and the Mughals entered into India through these mountain passes. In the north, India had contacts with Nepal through the land routes via Tibet, in the east with Burma through land routes via Assam. India had religious, cultural and commercial contacts with Nepal, China, Burma and the neighbouring regions from the earliest times of her history. In ancient times Afghanistan was within the Indian empire. Through Afghanistan the Indians of ancient times had set up colonies in Central Asia, Khotan, Kashgarh, Kucha, Turfan, Yarkhand etc. The relics of ancient Indian religion, culture and civilisation have been found in these areas as a result of excavation.

The long sea coasts of India facilitated the growth of maritime trade and a large number of harbours were established through which trade relations with Rome, China, Malaya, South East Asian archipelago were set up. Through commercial relations were spread the cultural influences of India in these countries. Not only that, the commercial relations helped the establishment of political supremacy of India in the south-east Asian countries. It was again through these trade routes and commercial relations that the English established their political dominance in India in later history. Even in commercial and political history the physical geography played an important part.

The people of northern India living as they did far away from the seas, naturally developed no attraction for the sea or for maritime activities. There were, however, maritime activities among the Bengalees and through some of the ports on the sea coasts of Bengal maritime trade was conducted. But real urge for sea and maritime trade grew among the people of south India from the ancient times. Nearness to sea was particularly responsible for creating this urge among the people of south India. The influence of physical geography is also noticeable in the political history of India. The plain of Aryavarta was most suitable for imperial expansion. As a result all the Indian empires grew up in this vast plain. The Vindhyas standing almost in the middle of India hindered the political unity of northern and southern India. The domination of the north over the south was at best partial and short-lived.

Natural and commercial wealth of India excited both jealousy and greed of foreigners. The result was repeated invasions of India from outside. Thus we find that the political, religious, economic, social and cultural life of the Indians had been directly and indirectly influenced by the physical geography of India.

People of India

India is the home of a large part of the vast population of the world. It is a curious meeting place of diverse religions, races, manners and customs. Rabindranath Tagore's poem *"Hethay Arya, hethay Anarya, hethay Dravid Chin, Sak, Hun dal, Pathan, Mughal ek dehe holo leen"*, that is, here the Aryans and the non-Aryans, the Dravidians and the Chinese, the Sakas, Huns, Pathans and the Mughals lost their identity in one vast sea of humanity, is a very apt description of the racial diversity of the Indian people. From the point of religion India is the home of the Hindus, Muslims,

Buddhists, Christians, Jainas, Sikhs and the Persians,. Diversity is also to be seen in the languages of the Indian people. From the points of view of race, religion, language, manners and customs the Indians constitute a composite population.

Considered from the racial point of view anthropologists have divided the Indians into different ethnic groups. In 1901 the British Indian government had divided the Indians into seven racial groups. In 1933 Dr. J. H. Hutton divided the Indians into eight racial groups. But the eminent Indian anthropologist Dr. B. S. Guha divided the Indians into six racial groups on well reasoned arguments. Dr. Guha's opinion has been almost universally accepted. These six racial groups are: (i) Negrito, (ii) proto-Australoid, (iii) Mongoloid, (iv) Mediterranean, (v) Western Brachycephallous and (vi) Nordic.

The Negrito population in India is almost extinct. Traces of the people of this racial group are found in the Andamans and Nicobar islands, among the Angami Nagas of Assam, and among the Kadars, Palayans, Irullas, Kurumbas of south India. Their complexion is dark, hairs woolly. nose flat and stature short.

The Proto-Australoid, that is, people with similarity with the original people of Australia, may be seen among the people of Sree Lanka, South-East Asian countries and in some of the lower castes in India.

People of Mongoloid racial group are largely to be found in hilly tracts of Chittagong, Sikim, Bhutan etc.

People of the Western Brachycephallous racial group live in Bengal, Orissa, Bihar, Uttar Pradesh, in Gangetic plains, Kanada, Tamil, Gilgit, Chitral etc.

Mediterranean type people are seen in parts of the Gangetic plain, Sind, the Punjab, Rajputana and parts of Uttar Pradesh.

Nordic or Aryan types are largely found in north-western limits of India. People of this racial group are also found in the Punjab, Rajputana and Maharastra.

It may be noted here that there is no rigidity about the distribution of the above racial groups in India. There has been a great intermixing of the different races and it is impossible to claim any racial purity by any of the above racial groups. Ethnically the Indians constitute a composite population and the Indian culture and civilisation are also composite in nature.[1]

Unity in Diversity

Nature has, as if, chosen India for her diverse and multifarious manifestations. In no other land perhaps Nature has been so playful. India has in consequence been a land of diversities. These diversities

---

[1] "It must be clearly understood that no rigid separation is possible as there is considerable overlapping of types." Dr. B. S. Guha vide: *The Vedic Age*, p, 145.

relate to physical geography, race, religion, colour, language, dress, manners and customs and what not! From the point of view of geographical diversities mention may be made of the abundance of water supply through a net work of rivers and their tributaries on the one hand and total lack of rainfall and water in vast desert areas on the other, Bengal, the Punjab, the Deccan etc. intersected by rivers and their tributaries are fertile and full of luscious green, but Rajputana is dry and arid, and for want of rains and water unsuitable for thick population. Even in rainfall the diversity is manifest. Cherpunji in Assam records the highest rainfall in the world every year; again Sind, Rajputana regions are greatly handicapped for lack of required minimum rainfall. In matters of altitudes the Mount Everest is the highest peak in the world, yet again there are deep gorges much below the sea level. Diversities in climate are seen in the cold, hot and temperate zones within the country. There are places where there are perpetual snows, e.g. parts of Kashmir, there are again places which are rather warm all the months of the year, e.g. south India; there are places which are bracing throughout the year, e.g. Shillong, Darjeeling, Simla etc. and yet other places which are cold in winter and hot in summer months, e.g. Bengal, Bihar, Orissa etc.

India is the home of one-fifth of the total population of the world. Rabindranath has rightly called India an *Ocean of humanity.* People of innumerable races, castes and sub-castes live in India, speaking diverse languages, wearing different dresses and professing different religions. From the racial point of view India is an *ethnological museum* as Dr. Smith has rightly remarked. In ancient times the Aryans, Dravidas, Persians, Greeks, Sakas, Kushanas, Huns; in the medieval age the Arabs, Turks, Afghans and the Mughals and last of all the Portuguese, Dutch, French and the English came to India leading to a great admixture of races and formation of a composite population and a composite culture in India.

Natural resources also vary from place to place. Diversities of fauna and flora are more remarkable in India than in any other land of the world.

The political effects of geographical diversities were manifest in the political disunity that had characterised the early history of India and the division of India into numerous politically independent regions.

To a casual observer the diversities of so many different natures are certainly bewildering. But on a closer examination it will be evident that despite these diversities India possesses a deep underlying fundamental unity. This unity in diversity, this harmony despite differences reveal the soul of India, in fact, this is the message of the Indian civilisation.

Turning to the bonds of unity that bind the Indians despite

numerous diversities, it may be mentioned at the outset that India is separated from the rest of the world by a well-defined geographical boundary. As we think of India we become conscious of a political and geographical entity that India represents. The very name 'India' gives us a picture complete and whole well protected in the north by the Himalayas and on other sides by the seas. This unity of the land from the geographical concept helped to foster a feeling of union among the Indians living in different parts of the country. Despite political disunity there is an emotional unity among the Indians. This unity was not the result of victory of one upon the other, it was the result of mutual adjustment. Rabindranath said that the one aim of India was to bring about unity in diversity, to make different ways and opinions converge towards fulfilment of the same ideal; to realise oneself in many; to emphasise and possess the internal unity without effacing the apparent separatism.[1] Thus it may be pointed out that the Indian unity did not, nor does it to-day, depend on the success of any ruler to conquer the whole of India.

Although the Indian unity was not dependent on the political unity, yet it cannot be denied that political ideals of the ancient kings and emperors to become Ekarat, i.e. Emperor of emperors, Rajchakravartin etc., in other words to become universal sovereign helped to generate an idea of oneness of the country and the people. Under the Mauryas, the Guptas and under the Mughals almost the whole of India came under the same political organisation. The economic and social history of the people of India under one or the other emperor was more or less the same. This naturally generated a feeling of oneness among the Indians.[2]

No doubt India is inhabited by people of diverse racial origins, of different religions, languages, literature and culture as well as manners and customs, yet all this has contributed to the emergence of a composite culture distinctive in itself. The Indian civilisation has a special character which distinguishes it from the civilisations and cultures of other lands of the world. When we say 'European civilisation' it gives us an impression of a civilisation common to the Germans, the French etc.; in fact, all the countries of the west. But when we say 'Indian civilisation' or 'Indian culture' it denotes a civilisation or culture which is peculiar to India and India alone and does not represent the civilisations or cultures of other countries of the East. The Indian civilisation can be expressed by the expression 'Indian civilisation' and by no other words, because it has a distinctive character of its own.

Considered from the point of view of culture the fundamental

---

[1] Vide Rabindranath : *Discourses at Chicago and Harvard Universities.* 1912-13.
[2] Vide Sir J. N. Sarkar's article : *Unity in India,* Modern Review, Nov. 1942.

unity of the Indians will become all the more manifest. Different peoples had entered into India in different stages of history no doubt, but none succeeded in altering the basic Hindu character of the Indian civilisation. On the contrary the different groups of people who had entered India in different waves of time with their own civilisation and culture got lost in the vast corpus of the Indian civilisation. The only exception is perhaps the Muslims.

Despite differences of religion, manners and customs, race and language the same nature of life and living indirectly fostered a sense of unity among the Indians of different parts.

Under the British rule and even under the Mughals, the unity of administration, use of the same state language, same currency helped to develop a sense of unity among the Indians.[1]

The struggle for Indian independence generated the feeling of unity among the Indians in a very great degree. During the struggle for freedom Indian patriots from different parts of India had one and one aim only, that is, the independence of India as a whole. Patriots of different parts did not join the freedom struggle against the British imperialism to free their own local areas. This unity of ideal gave a sense of profound unity among the people of India.

In the freedom struggle again, the people of India from whatever part of the country they had come had one slogan: *Bandemataram*. People of different parts, of distant and unknown villages, laid their lives down in the cause of the country's freedom with the *mantra* Bandemataram in their lips. This sense of patriotism, this boldness to lay everything down on the altar of mother India had undoubtedly fostered a deep sense of unity among the Indians.

In 1947 India was divided into Bharat and Pakistan ignoring the age old unity of India, and on the artificial basis of two-nation theory—the Hindus and the Muslims. This division might have satisfied the political obstinacy and communal jealousy but it had cut across the traditional unity of the people of India.

From the political point of view India, i.e. Bharat, has achieved complete political unity due to the statesmanly efforts of Sardar Ballav Bhai Patel who played the part of Bismarck in India. What the British government could not achieve during their nearly two hundred years of rule, he achieved.

From the above discussions it is not difficult to conclude that despite apparent diversities, a deep fundamental emotional unity binds the Indians. V. A. Smith's remark is an apt conclusion of the discussion about the Indian unity in diversity. "India beyond all doubt possesses a deep underlying fundamental unity far more profound than that produced either by geographical isolation or political suzerainty. That

[1] Vide: Majumdar; *Ancient India*, p. 3.

unity transcends the innumerable diversities of blood, colour, language, dress, manners and sect.[1]

Sources of Ancient Indian History

The history of any ancient people is largely conditioned by the authenticity of the source materials. Where the sources are indirect, historians' job is beset with great difficulty and it is on their ability to choose the important ones leaving out those which are not of consequence that the quality of history writing will depend.

The absence of chronological historical writing about the ancient times of the Indian history has made it necessary to cull historical materials from indirect sources. In ancient India there was no dearth of literary works, but there was no attempt at writing history. There were certainly rulers in ancient India who must have been fond of getting the events of their reigns recorded by court panegyrists, but as Smith points out their writings did not survive the ravages of moths, insects and climate. But when we find that many literary works had survived despite ravages of moths, insects and climate, it is somewhat unintelligible why the moths, insects and climate should have chosen historical writings for destruction. Smith's remark, therefore, is not much valid. True that the ancient Indians were not devoid of historical sense and not unconcerned about the need of chronology. This is proved from the Vedas, Jaina and Buddhist literature. Hiuen Tsang noticed the system of recording of events of specially auspicious and inauspicious nature in every province of India that he had visited. Thus one thing is certain that there was no lack of historical sense or historical materials in ancient times in India but dearth was in respect of historical writers who could effectively use these materials to write authentic history. Although the ancient Indians showed their talent in various literary works, India lacked men like Herodotus, Thucydides, Livy or Tacitus who could write history. The source materials of the history of ancient India are, therefore, indirect mostly, and to certain extent direct as well.

(1) *Literary Evidence*: The ancient Indian literature is an indirect but important source of the history of the ancient period. The Vedas give us an idea of the political, social and religious life of the Indians of that age. The Puranas, the Ramayana and the Mahabharata contain lists of kings dynastically. Such lists as also the traditions and legends found in these works give us some historical materials for the reconstruction of the history of ancient India. But extreme care has to be taken in sifting the historical materials from the traditions and legends.

---

[1] Vide Smith: *Oxford History of India*, p. 10.

Apart from the Vedas, Puranas, the Ramayana and the Mahabharata, the Jaina and the Buddhist religious texts contain much important historical materials. Jaina *Parisistapravana,* Buddhist *Dwipavamsa* and *Mahavamsa* contain traditions which supply us some historical materials. *Gargi Samhita,* a book on Astronomy, the Grammar of Panini and Patanjali also contain materials that help us in the reconstruction of the history of the ancient period of India.

From the second half of the ancient period of Indian history, that is from the Gupta Age, although there was no abundance of historical literature, yet the genealogy of the local ruling dynasties and the panegyric and biographical sketches of rulers are replete with historical materials. These are entirely different from the traditions and legends and there is no doubt about the existence of their authors in those days. Among these writings there are not only panegyrics of kings and emperors but also political treatises dealing with the principles of administration. Kautilya's *Arthasastra* may be mentioned in this connection. It was a work of the Maurya period. Among the historical works of ancient period, Banabhatta's *Harsha-Charit,* dealing with the character and achievements of Harshavardhana as also history of his times, Bakpatiraja's *Gaudabaho* describing how Jasovarman conquered Gauda deserve special mention. Poet Bilhana described the history of the reign of Chalukya king Vikramadity VI in his *Vikrmanka Charita.* Sandhyakar Nandi's *Ramcharita* is a description of the reign of Rampal, a king of the Pala dynasty of Bengal. Kalhana's *Rajatarangini* is a valuable book on history of the kings of Kashmir. Likewise Padmagupta's *Nabasahasanka Charit* is a valuable historical work. These apart, Jai Sinha's *Kumarapal Charit,* Hem Chandra's *Dwasraya Kavya,* Nyaya Chandra's *Hampir Kavya,* Ballal's *Bhoja Prabandha,* Chand Bordoi's *Prithwiraj Charit,* and *Prithwiraj Vijay* by an annonymous writer contain important historical materials. Although these works may not be regarded as historical works in the conventional sense, yet these contain enough materials for the reconstruction of the history of ancient India.

In literary work containing the details of the ruling dynasties, Kalhana's *Rajatarangini* is of great importance. It gives the chronological history of the ruling dynasties of Kashmir and is the only work of the ancient period of Indian history which may be called truly historical literature. Even though this work is not so much important insofar as the historical details of the ancient period of the history of Kashmir is concerned, yet it is of particular importance in respect of the history of Kalhana's contemporary times. *Rajatarangini* also contains critical observations about the events of the time, description of the life of the common people etc. and the dispassionate manner of writing gives it a character which is particularly needed in history. Kalhana's impartial attitude in writing history was followed by subsequent writers like Jainul Abedin, Sreedhar, Prajyabhatta etc. who wrote the history of Kashmir.

If Kashmir has its *Rajatarangini*, Gujarat has its *Kirti Kaumudi* by Someswar, *Prabandhakos* by Rajshekar which contain chronological description of the royal dynasties of Gujarat. Even in Nepal, Sind etc. there were writers who left dynastic history of their own localities. From these works on dynastic history the remark of Hiuen Tsang that the Indian rulers of ancient times were fond of getting their dynastic history written gets corroboration. Historical materials for the reconstruction of the history of ancient India are also found in the writings of the Tibetan historian Taranath.

(2) *Archaelogical Evidence*: Without archaeological researches and patient examination of ancient inscriptions the history of ancient India would have remained largely unknown. It is true that the archaeological research is comparatively new in India yet due to the enthusiasm of some European scholars much of the details about the history of ancient India have come to our knowledge. The names of Dr. Buchanon, Hamilton, James Princep, Sir Alexander Cunningham, James Burges, Sir John Marshall, Aurel Stein—all Europeans, and names of the Indians like Rakhaldas Banerjee, K. N. Dikshit deserve special mention. The archaeological evidences which have helped to reconstruct the history of ancient India fall under three main heads, namely, Inscriptions, Coins, Monuments.

(a) *Inscriptions*: The most important source of historical materials which has come to us as a result of patient and painstaking efforts by scholars is the mass of inscriptions. Inscriptions are the most reliable evidence on the basis of which ancient Indian history can be written. Inscriptions are of various types and related to various matters. Inscriptions on stone, gold, silver, iron, copper and bronze plates are unchallengeable historical materials because these were not liable to be changed at any subsequent time. Some of the inscriptions have, however, not yet been deciphered, for instance, the seals discovered at Mohenjodaro, Harappa etc. But those which have been deciphered have given us important data like dates, events etc. which are unquestionably authentic. Inscriptions again are mainly of three types: royal eulogy, official documents like royal rescripts, boundary marks, deeds, gift etc. and private records of votive, donative or dedicative type.

Inscriptions in Prakrit, Pali, Sanskrit, Telegu, Tamil and other languages have been discovered. But most of the inscriptions are in Brahmi and Kharosti scripts. Brahmi scripts are written from left to right whereas Kharosti script is written from right to left. Inscriptions belonging to pre-Gupta Age were almost wholly (95%) written in Prakrit. But Sanskrit got eminence from the Gupta period.

From the various types of inscriptions the political history of ancient India has been known. Although these inscriptions give us greater details about the political history, yet enough materials about the social, economic and religious history have been found in them. In some cases materials important for the reconstruction of the history of India have been found in inscriptions in foreign countries. From the inscriptions discovered at Boghaz-Koi some indirect materials have been found about the coming of the Aryans in India. Inscriptions discovered at Behestan, Parsepolis. Naks-i-Rustam contain references to the contacts between India and Persia.

Not long back it was supposed by the historians that the inscription discovered at Piprawa was the oldest of the Indian inscriptions. But as a result of archaeological research this theory has been proved incorrect. Sohgor inscription is now held to be the oldest of the Indian inscriptions. This inscription is supposed to be about fifty years older than the inscription of Maurya Emperor Asoka.

Among the inscriptions of ancient past those of empror Asoka, his rock-cut edicts, pillar edicts etc. are by far the best historical evidence about his reign. Inscriptions of Kharvela, king of Kalinga, Saka ruler Rudradamana, Allahabad Prasasti by Harisena, the court poet of Samudragupta, inscriptions found at Khalimpur and Bhagalpur of the Gupta Age are important evidences for the reconstruction of the history of India.[1]

(b) *Coins*: From coins of ancient times it has been possible to gather some very important data for the reconstruction of the Indian history of the ancient times. Thousands of ancient Indian coins have been discovered from which idea about the contemporary economic condition, currency system, development of the metallurgical art has been obtained. From the figures embossed or inscribed on the coins it has been possible to understand the nature of the development of the artistic skill as well as the tastes of the kings and emperors. For instance, from the image of Samudragupta playing on a lyre gives us an idea of his love of music. From the dates on the coins it has been possible to understand the contemporary political history. Synchronistically we may fix the time of other kings from such dates. From the find spots of coins we may get an idea of the expanse of the

---

[1] "It is almost from a patient examination of the inscriptions that our knowledge of the ancient political history of India has been derived. But we are also ultimately dependent on the inscriptions in every other line of Indian research. Hardly any dates and identifications can be established except from them."—Fleet; vide Sinha & Banerjee: *History of India*, p. 17.

"Inscriptions have proved a source of the highest value for the reconstruction of the political history of ancient India." Vide *The Vedic Age*, p. 52.

"Inscriptions have been given the first place in the list of the sources of Ancient Indian History, because they are, on the whole, the most important and trustworthy source of our knowledge." Smith: *Oxford History of India* (3rd Edition), p. 13.

"Unquestionably the most copious and important source of Indian history is the epigraphic." Smith: *Early History of India*, p. 16.

empire or kingdom of the ruler whose coins these are. Samudragupta's Aswamedha coins, Lion-slayer coins give us an idea of Samudragupta's ambition and love of hunting.

After the fall of the Maurya Empire when the Bactrian Greeks occupied the north-western parts of India, they used to issue coins with their names and dates as well as the images of the rulers. But even before the coming of the Bactrian Greeks, Indian rulers used to issue coins with their images and certain unintelligible marks. In certain cases, however, there were inscriptions on the coins. From the coins of the Saka, Pahlava, Kushana and the Gupta rulers some historical materials relating to the contemporary times have been found. The coins of these rulers were made in imitation of the coins of the Greek and the Roman coins.

(c) *Monuments*: Palaces, tombs, massoleum, buildings, temples etc. are important sources of the history of architectural and artistic development in ancient India. The ornamental work on the walls, pillars, sculptural remains on the walls of palaces, temples etc., give us an idea of the artistic skill of the time. From the ruins of towns and cities, for instance, of Harappa and Mohenjo-daro we have not only been able to know about the town planning of the time but also the architectural excellence and the municipal amenities made available to the people of the time. The remains of the Indus valley civilisation have borne testimony to the antiquity of the Indian civilisation. Taxila, Sarnath, Nalanda etc. have revealed as a result of excavation, the cultural and religious history of the contemporary times. Yet it may be said that what we have been able to know of the ancient history from the relics excavated in different sites is not the whole of what can be known. For, more relics still await excavation and attention of scholars.

(3) *Accounts of the Foreigners*: Materials of considerable historical value in respect of the ancient times of India may be had from the accounts of the foreign travellers. There are writings of the foreigners, not travellers, which contain observations on Indian subjects. The earliest foreign notice of India is to be found in the inscriptions of Daurius. Herodotus who wrote late in the fifth century B. C. contributed valuable information concerning the relation between India and Persia. The fragments of the works of Ktesias, physician of Artaxerxes are, however, of meagre value. Both Herodotus and Ktesias had written about the relation between India and the Persian empire by hearing from the travellers who came to India. Whereas the account of Herodotus contains some valuable historical materials, that of Ktesias contains much of which was imaginary, hence not of much value.

Quite a number among the Greeks who accompanied Alexander had left their accounts about India. It was from their accounts that the Europeans came to know of India. These writers had lifted the veil of India. About a score of years after the death of Alexander, came Megasthenes to the court of Chandragupta Maurya. He was sent by Seleukos. His work called *Indica* has not survived but the fragments of his work are to be found in the writings of the subsequent Greek writers from which it has been possible to know much of what he had written about India. From the Greek authors it is known that the king of Syria had sent Deimachos to the Maurya court. Dionysius was another Greek who visited India after Megasthenes. From the writings of both Deimachos and Dionysius corroboration of the observations of Megasthenes has been found.

An anonymous Greek writer was responsible for writing a book named *Periplus of the Erythrean Sea* in which a very interesting and important account of the Indian sea ports and harbours as also of the maritime commerce of ancient India has been found. The date of the book is 80 A.D.

The account of the journey from India to Greece left by Nearchos, an admiral of Alexander, contains much about the Indian geography of the time. Similar account is also found in the writings of Ptolemy who wrote in the second century A.D. But as he had depended on the stories told by travellers his work contains many geographical inaccuracies. Account of the Roman writer Pliny about the mineral and forest resources of India as well as the animals to be found in India in ancient times, is also full of inaccuracies as he also did not write from his own knowledge and experience. Yet all these works contain valuable materials for the reconstruction of the history of India.

Apart from the above Greek and Roman writers, the works of Quintus Curtius, Diodorus, Arrian, Strabo, Plutarch etc. and other Greek and Roman writers supply us with important historical materials about ancient Indian history. Philostratos, an Athenian, wrote a philosophical romance in honour of Apollonois of Tyana in which interesting observations about north-western India are found.

Next to the Greeks were the Chinese travellers. Of course, most of the Chinese travellers came to India on pilgrimage, as such, their writing contained more of religious descriptions than social, political or economic. But occasional references to political, social, economic condition of India, manners and customs of the Indians are of great historical value. Suma-Chien, the *Herodotus of China,* who completed his work in the first century B.C. threw a flood of light on the annals of ancient India. He was called the father of Chinese history.

A stream of Chinese pilgrims who continued to visit India for several centuries, began with Fa-Hien. Fa-Hien visited India during the reign of Chandragupta Vikramaditya, during the years 399-414

A.D. His account is a very reliable source of the history of the Gupta Age. The most important Chinese pilgrim was Hiuen Tsang. He visited India during the reign of Harshavardhana. His travel described in the work entitled *Record of Western World* is a storehouse of accurate information about India. Hwui-li, a friend of Hiuen Tsang, wrote the biography of Hiuen Tsang in which materials for the history of India are also found. In the seventh century A.D. I-Tsing, another Chinese traveller, visited India. He also left a very interesting account about the Indian Buddhism. Indirect references to the political, social and economic condition of the Indians of the time are also found in his work.

In the eighth century A.D. the Arabians came to India and occupied some parts of Sind. From that time some Arab writers wrote about India. Among the Arab writers the learned mathematician and astronomer Alberuni came to India, mastered Sanskrit language and literature and wrote a book entitled *Tahkik-i-Hind,* i.e. an enquiry into India. Important details of the Hindu manners and customs, literature, philosophy, mathematics, astronomy, sciences of the contemporary India were recorded in this book. Alberuni's book is an indispensable source for the writing of the history of that period. Apart from Alberuni, Al Biladuri, Hasan Nizami, Al Masudi, Ibn-ul-Athir and other Arab writers also supply us with materials for the history of this period.

Chapter Two

PRE-HISTORY AND PROTO-HISTORY OF INDIA

Pre-history and Proto-history are terms which according to Prof. M. C. Burkitt are misnomers, for as he observes, "there is no *period* before history begins". Long unknown vista of human history cannot be bound by term like *Pre-history* or *Proto-history,* and what we have been able to know of man before history begins, is only a fraction of the unknown vast to admit of any such nomenclature. However, these terms have come to stay in the vocabulary of history and historical writings. These have come to represent something which almost every body understands.

Prof. Stuart Piggott remarks that "the distinction between history and pre-history in India is a peculiarly elusive one". The reasons for his remark are, while the Pre-history of Western Asiatic countries like Mesopotamia, Egypt etc. ended immediately after 3000 B. C. when records of dynasties, King-lists came to be written which can be interpreted to form the outline of a fairly reliable chronology in terms of years before the Christian era, in India although writing was known in the third millennium B.C. as is evident from the Indus seals these have not yet been deciphered to help us in preparing an outline of a reliable chronology in terms of years. Further, there is a big gap between the 3rd millennium B. C. and 650 B. C. during which no written historical materials have been found. As Dr. Smith says, "Definite chronological history begins about 650 B. C. for northern India", absolutely certain and precise date of the beginning of the historical period of India, however, is 326 B. C., the date of Alexander's invasion.

All the same, like the Pre-Historic period of Europe, India had also passed through Palaeolithic, Mesolithic and Neolithic Ages.[1]

Palaeolithic age

According to Prof. Basham, India like Europe of the Pre-historic age had passed through Ice Ages. After the second Ice Age, a hundred thousand years before Christ, men left traces of their stone tools, discovered in the bed of the river Soan or Sohan in the Punjab. These were Palaeolithic Stone, rough, blunt and crude. The stone used was quartzite, hence the Palaeolithic men in India were known as Quartzite men.

---

[1] **Greek** Palaeo = Old + *lithos* = Stone ; *Meso* = middle + *lithos* = Stone ; Neo = New + *lithos* = Stone. Hence Palaeolithic is Old Stone, Mesolithic Middle Stone, and Neolithic is New Stone.

Not only in the north but in the South India also, stone implements of the same period, *i.e.*, of the Sohan men, have been discovered which the archaeologists call 'Madras Industry'. In the Gangetic valley similar old Stone Age implements have been discovered.

From the rough, crude stone tools used by the people of the Palaeolithic period, *i.e.*, Old Stone Age, we can at best form a vague, general idea of their life and living. "Palaeolithic man was a hunter and food gatherer and lived in very small communities" with no fixed homes. They were nomads, although a few might have made huts of shrubs and leaves. In course of time they learnt to produce fire, protect their body against cold by use of tree-barks. leaves or animal skins and domesticated the dogs. They had no idea of agriculture. Their food was flesh of animals and birds they would hunt or fruits and vegetables they would gather. They were then food-gatherers. From modern point of view, the Palaeolithic men were savages not far removed from animals. However, it was on their culture and civilisation that further improvements were made down the ages and we have reached our civilisation today. About the people of the Palaeolithic Age of India, it is suggested that they belonged to negrito race and were of dark complexion, woolly hair, flat nose and of short stature.

About the culture of the Palaeolithic men we must remember that a sparsely populated world without any systematic communication, every region developed of its own and thousands of years must have passed before some very simple improvement in shaping a stone could be made. Naturally the pace of development in different regions was not the same. Further, the only evidences available to us are the imperishable stone materials. These are not a fair index of the cultural progress or cultural pattern. It is also difficult to determine whether the hand-axes found in Madras and in Abbvile on the river Somme in Europe, although almost of the same workmanship belonged to the same period of time.

The Palaeolithic people of India, as all over the world, lived in this age for many thousands of years. But their knowledge and skill were imperceptibely improving through the ages.

Mesolithic age

With the progress of time, the Palaeolithic man acquired greater knowledge and skill in mastering the forces of nature. Prof. Gordon Childe says that man developed "an aggressive attitude to his environment" and gradually entered into the Neolithic *i.e.*, New Stone Age. But midway between the Old Stone and the New Stone Age, scholars speak of a Mesolithic Period which was characterised by the making and use of small stone implements, instead of quartzite. Chelcedony and Silicate varieties of stone were used. Archaeologists regard this mesolithic phase as one in which men lived by hunting and fishing with the help of implements of bones and flint, the latter being of minute size. Fish hooks made of bones and flint, pottery etc. were in use in that age. The small delicate stone implements, made during this age were called microliths *i.e.*, small stones. Microliths appear to have been in use even during the Neolithic Age in the Deccan and did not go altogether out of use till iron replaced them.

Neolithic age

The chief characteristic that distinguishes men from animals is their ability to think and move from progress to more progress. As time passed, men naturally acquired more knowledge than what they possessed during the mesolithic phase and gradually entered into the Neolithic culture. The development was gradual and down through ages, but the pace of progress is difficult to estimate.

The tools and implements of the Neolithic Age were very different from those of the preceding ages, *i.e.*, the Palaeolithic and Mesolithic. The people of this age used stones other than quartzite and the tools and implements they made were far better grooved, ground and polished. For different types of work, they had different types of highly finished tools and these can be very easily distinguished from the rough, crude tools of the Palaeolithic Age. As the name Neolithic denotes, it was the New Stone Age, metals except gold being then unknown.

The tools and implements left by the Neolithic people of India have been found all over India. A stone factory of the time has been discovered in the Bellary district of Madras where traces of the various stages of the making of the tools and implements can be still seen.

The life and living of the Neolithic men showed a distinct advance from those of the previous ages. Agriculture became known to them, domestication of animals like ox, goat etc., production of fire by friction of bamboos or pieces of wood or flint, making of painted pottery were all known to them. They lived in caves, decorated their walls by painting scenes of hunting, dancing etc. They knew spinning and weaving, as also making of boats.

Some tombs of the Neolithic men which have been discovered show that they used to bury their dead in large earthen urn. There were also tombs with stone-slab roof on stone pillars.

The period of thousands and thousands of years covered by the Palaeolithic and Neolithic ages is called Pre-historic. Whether the Neolithic people were descendants of the Palaeolithic predecessors is not known for certain.

Chalcolithic culture

Although scholars are not unanimous in regarding the Palaeolithic men as the ancestors of the Neolithic men, there is a general agreement that the Neolithic men were the predecessors of the next stage of men who knew the use of metals. However, the transition from use of stone to the use of metals is slow and longdrawn. There is no doubt that there was an overlapping period when both stone and metals were used. This is proved by the close resemblance of metallic tools and implements with those made of stone. It must, however, be remembered that use of metals in different parts of India was not uniform. While in Northern India copper was the metal that came to be used after stone, in Southern India iron replaced stone without the intermediate stage of use of copper. Bronze which is an alloy made of copper and tin was in use in India simultaneously. The Chalcolithic age of India was a period of copper-bronze. Bronze implements of India have been found along with those of copper. Thus in India there was no separate Bronze Age as we find in some of the countries of Europe.

It was centuries later that iron appeared as a substitute of copper or bronze in Northern India. The Chalcolithic, *i.e.*, Copper-Bronze Age of India produced a splendid civilisation in the Indus Valley which spread in the neighbouring regions. A detailed treatment of this Chalcolithic civilisation of the Indus Valley will be made in a separate chapter.

Iron age

We have already seen that in different parts of India there was no systematic succession of stone by copper-bronze or copper-bronze by iron. In Southern India use of iron came after the use of stone. In any case there were periods of overlapping in the use of stone, copper, bronze, and iron.

Our only evidence of the transition from copper-bronze age to the iron age is the monuments like dolmens, cairns, cromolechs etc. These have been found in wide areas all over India, such as Assam, Bihar, Orissa, Central India, Gujarat and Kashmir. But by far the largest number has been found in south India, in Karnataka and the Deccan. These iron monuments appear to have belonged to both pre-historic and historic periods.

Some of these monuments have been found at Ranchi which are supposed to have been the work of the Asuras, that is, the ancient predecessors of the present day Mundas. But these were found along with polished stone tools, wheel-made pottery, copper and bronze materials. It is, therefore, impossible to determine the date of the beginning of iron age in this area.

Monuments discovered in Hyderabad, Mysore, Tinnevelly district, Coimbatore, Malabar, Penumbur etc. also show varied stages of development. Neolithic, Microlithic tools along with copper, bronze and iron implements have been discovered, making it difficult to identify the actual period of transition from copper-bronze age to the iron age. At this stage of our limited knowledge, no definite conclusion in this regard can be arrived at.

Proto-historic period

Proto-historic period is the age nearest to the historical period. In so far as India is concerned the civilisation of the Vedic period is the proto-historic period. The hymns composed by the Vedic priests had perfected a poetic technique. These hymns were praise of their gods and were sung at sacrifices. These were not reduced to writing but were handed down by words of mouth. Even when the art of writing was widely known to the Indians, hymns were not committed to writing. "The period of the Vedas, Brahmanas and Upanishads", says Prof. Basham, "is a sort of a transition from prehistory to history". Naturally it falls in the proto-historic period of Indian history, that is nearest to the historical period. But as Prof. Basham points out, "If history, as distinct from archaeology, is the study of the human past from written sources, then Indian history begins with the Aryans. The *Rig Veda*, and the great body of oral religious literature which follow it in the first half of the first millennium B.C. belong to the Hindu tradition. The Vedic hymns are still recited at weddings and funerals, and in the daily devotion of the brahman. Thus they are part of historical India, and do not belong to her buried pre-historic past."

But it cannot be denied that the Vedic period is not within the really historic period of India, for it is only the matter of religion about which we are fully informed. About other matters or events we have only indirect and vague references. Thus the Vedic Age of Indian history has to be regarded as the period immediately preceding the historical period ; hence it belongs to the proto-historic period of India, a period which marks the transition from pre-historic to historic period of the Indian History.

CHAPTER THREE

THE INDUS CIVILISATION

In the third millennium before Christ a civilisation flourished in north-west India which derived its name from the Indus, the main river of the region. It is known as the Indus Civilisation or Harappa Culture as archaeologists call it from modern name of the site of one of its two great cities—Harappa. In 1924 scholars in history were roused by the announcement of Sir John Marshall that his Indian aides, particularly R. D. Banerjee, discovered (1922-23) at Mohenjo-daro in the Larkana district of Sind now in Pakistan, the remains of a civilisation, one of the oldest of the world. A few hundred miles towards the north of Mohenjo-daro four or five superimposed cities were excavated at Harappa in the Montgomery district of the Punjab, now in Pakistan. Recently, excavation carried out on the site of Kalibangan has revealed a third city as large as Harappa and Mohenjo-daro. That the civilisation was not confined to the limits of the Indus valley can be understood from the finds of relics of the same civilisation at Sutkajen-dor on the sea board of south Beluchistan, in the west of Alamgirpur in the Uttar Pradesh in the east ; and from Ropar in the Himalayan foot hills in the north to Bhagatrav on the river Kim in between the Narmada and Tapti in the south. This civilisation belonged to the Chalcolithic, *i.e.*, Copper-bronze age of history ; no trace of iron has been found.

Until the discovery of the remains of the Indus civilisation it was believed by scholars that the history of India practically began with the coming of the Aryans. But this theory is an exploded one and the pre-historic civilisation of India, that is, the Indus civilisation is contemporaneous with the civilisations of Mesopotamia, Egypt etc.

Towns and Town Planning : The first thing that strikes us is the town planning. Mohenjo-daro, Harappa, Lothal or Surkotada were built according to a set plan. Two cities, Mohenjo-daro and Harappa, were built on similar plan. To the west of each was a citadel built on a high platform. It was defended by wall and on it were constructed the public buildings. Below this citadel was the town proper. Everywhere the main streets ran from north to south and other streets ran at right angles to the main streets. Houses, residential or others, stood on both sides of the streets. Both at Harappa and Mohenjo-daro houses were built of Kiln-burnt bricks. At Lothal and Kalibangan residential houses were made of sun-dried bricks, the drains, wells, bathing platforms were made of kiln-burnt bricks. An average house had, besides kitchen and bath, four to six living rooms. Large houses with thirty rooms and staircases suggest that there were large two or three storeyed buildings. Most of the houses had wells within them and a drainage system carried the waste water to the main underground drain of the street. There were also public baths with wells. The covered drains of the streets had soak-pits and manholes for clearing. There were also arrangements for street lighting.

Of the places where the relics of the Indus civilisation have been discovered, the towns of Mohenjo-daro and Harappa are the most important. These two towns were connected also by land and their town planning was similar. Stuart Piggott is of the opinion that the towns of Mohenjo-daro and Harappa were the two capitals of the Indus civilisation. But in absence of more reliable evidence it will not be proper, as Sir Mortimer Wheeler observes, to regard them as two capitals of the time of the Indus civilisation.

The city of Mohenjo-daro had, besides numerous dwelling houses, a few very spacious buildings of elaborate structure and design. There were nine phases of rebuilding of this city on the same site. The lowest strata under sub-soil water have not been reached by archaeologists for obvious difficulties. But what is peculiar is that different strata do not show any sign of modification. Some of these buildings contained large pillared halls One of the halls was as large as 24 meters square. Although the exact nature and the purpose of such buildings with spacious halls are not known, they are supposed to have been either palaces, temples or municipal halls. The most noteworthy structure the remains of which have been found was a large swimming enclosure with rooms and galleries on all sides. The water was supplied by a well situated in one of the rooms. The water was discharged by a huge drain.

At Harappa a great granary has been discovered. It was built on a raised platform to protect it from floods. The granary was divided into storage blocks for storing of corn collected from the people as land tax. "We may assume", writes Prof. Basham, "that it had its counterpart at Mohenjo-daro".

The make of the buildings was so strong that it had withstood the ravages of five thousand years. Kiln-burnt bricks were used for buildings in places which were ravaged by floods and sun-baked bricks in other places. The ruins of Mohenjo-daro, Harappa and other towns and cities leave us in no doubt that the cities were largely populated and the inhabitants enjoyed municipal advantages of a very high order unknown to the people of the contemporary world. The ruins also give us an impression that the people lived in luxury and developed a culture of a very high order.

Economic life

From the relics discovered at Mohenjo-daro in particular, and in other towns and cities we get a comprehensive idea of the economic life of the people. As in most of the other contemporary civilisations, agriculture was the backbone of the Indus economy. Although Mohenjo-daro is an arid zone today, at the time when the Indus civilisation had developed, there was adequate rainfall as can be imagined from the making of kiln-burnt bricks which needed abundant supply of wood. There must have been vast forest areas, and forests attracted rains. Further, the Indus, Ravi, Ghaggar, Sutlej, and Bhogavo ensured adequate water supply to Harappa, Kalibangan, Ropar and Lothal. The main agricultural crops were wheat, barley, besides bananas, peas and melons. Cultivation of cotton was perhaps the most remarkable of all agricultural produces of the Indus people. People ate besides cereals, fish, vegetables, mutton, fowl, beef and pork. Cat, dog, elephant, humped bulls also called *Brahmani bulls,* buffaloes, pigs, camels etc, and the bullock, the main beast of burden, were the domesticated animals. Whether horse was known to the Indus people is not known for certain. But Harappa people may have known the use of horse. This is deduced from the find of a few horses' teeth at the lowest stratum of Baluchistan site of Rana Ghundai dating from several centuries earlier than the foundation of Harappa.

Dress : *Ornaments* : *Household Articles* : For dress cotton fabrics were mostly used. From the portrayal of a man in Harappa it is supposed that people used something like a dhoti. Shawl was used as an upper garment. For warm textiles wool was used. Finding of buttons and needles among the relics shows that some of the clothes were stitched. Ornaments were used both by men and women. Some of the ornaments, such as neck-chain, fillets, fingure rings, armlets and bangles were used by both men and women, but girdles, nose-studs, ear-rings, anklets were used only by women. The variety of ways in which the women dyed their hair and the ornaments that they wore from head to foot leave us in no doubt that the life of the women folk was not all work.

The elaborate hair style as seen in the female figurines, find of a vanity bag and toilet jars at Harappa with remains of face-paints and cosmetics indicate that the women folk of the time were fond of personal elegance as their modern counterparts.

Among the household articles earthenwares of various shapes and sizes were made with the help of the potter's wheel. These were both plain and painted. Vessels were also made of copper, silver, bronze and porcelain. The Indus civilisation belonged to a perfect Bronze Age. There was, however, not a trace of iron. Among other articles of household use mention may be made of spindles, spindle whorl, sickles, razors, fish hooks etc. For the purpose of weighing blocks of stone were used. Discovery of dice-pieces shows that the game of dice was known to the Indus people. Toys of the children included small chairs, wheeled cart, etc. These show that chairs, wheeled carts were in actual use at that time.

The Harappa people manufactured lifelike miniatures of animals, specially interesting being the tiny monkeys climbing up and down a string and squirrels used as pinheads and beads. Little toycarts, cattle with movable heads, whistles in the shape of birds, indicate their use in daily life. In one respect the Harappa people were technically in advance of their contemporaries, they devised a saw with teeth which allowed saw dust to escape from the cut automatically. This shows that in carpentry the people acquired a great skill.

The Indus people had weapons of war like spears, axes, daggers, maces, slings but defensive armours like shield, helmet etc. were not found to be in use.

Seals : Terracotta seals, more than five hundred in number have been discovered in the ruins of the Indus civilisation. Some of them have representations of animal figures as also pictorial inscription on them. Animal features on the seal show a high degree of artistic excellence. A few stone images found at Harappa are of such high degree of artistic excellence that these may be compared with Greek statues. Needless to remark that the art of sculpture was highly developed.

The seals discovered in the Indus valley have not yet been deciphered. It has, therefore, not been possible to get any idea of the nature of the political life and organisation of the Indus people. Some of the seals were used for commercial purposes. The Indus people had trade relations with other parts of India as also with countries beyond India. Finds of seals of Indus style in west Asian sites such as Ur, Lagash, Susa, Umma and Tell Asmar prove that there must have been trade contacts between the Indus people and those of West Asian countries. In recent years a seal of the Persian Gulf areas has been discovered at Lothal. The remains of a dockyard at Lothal have also been discovered. From these it is reasonable to conclude that there were both overland and maritime trade relations with the west Asian countries and the Indus people. Finds of precious stones like lapis lazuli, jade, turquoise etc. which were not found indigenously, suggest trade with Iraq, Iran, Afghanistan, Tibet and Central Asia. The chief merchandise was most probably cotton, which had always been one of India's main exports.

Weights and Measures : A large number of weights belonging to a uniform system have been found at Mohenjo-daro and Harappa as well as in Chanhudaro and other smaller towns. The unit was ratio 16, as we even today calculate 16 annas to a rupee or 16 chittacks to a seer. The find of a broken scale engraved on a shell at Mohenjo-daro shows a decimal scale of inches rising to a foot which was, however, 13.2 inches long.

Society : *Professions* : That the agricultural class constituted the largest section of the Indus population cannot be gainsaid. Among the industrial classes, potters, carpenters, weavers, blacksmiths, masons, goldsmiths, ivory-workers, stone-cutters, sculptors, jewellers etc. need special mention. That there was a great technical advance can be understood from the use of the potter's wheel, kiln burnt bricks, highly aesthetic designs in ornaments, execution of metallic and stone statues and figurines.

The People : The Indus people, particularly the city dwellers were of a cosmopolitan nature. The population included Proto-Australoid, Mediterranean, Alpine and Mongoloid types. A few skulls of the Aryans have also been found which may have been of the Aryan invaders.

Religion : As it happens with mixed population it is supposed that there was a variety of religious practices among the Indus people. Several seals have been found with a three-horned Yogin surrounded by wild and domesticated animals which naturally denote the early conception of *Pasupati Siva*. Phallic form of Siva cult is supposed to have been there in the Indus people because of the find of *lingas*. Rituals with the use of fire places, suggested by find of such relics, presuppose the religious practices of the nature of Yajna. From the finds of articles of daily use in the graves it is supposed that the Indus people probably believed in life hereafter as did the Egyptians. The Indus people also worshipped a Mother Goddess which must have been the early form of Sakti. Traces of worship of primitive religious cult which is called animism have been found in Mohenjo-daro. Worship of stones, trees, animals, Nagas and Yakshas in Mohenjo-daro is clear from the traces of these found there. Indication of the existence of *Bhakti* cult has been found at Mohenjo-daro. It may, therefore, be concluded that modern Hinduism was largely indebted to the Indus people.

The seals and the inscriptions on them bear testimony to the fact that the Indus people were literate. Inscriptions have also been found on pottery and other household articles. This indicates that the literacy was not confined to select classes. The organised system of weights and measures testifies to the knowledge of arithmetic among the Indus People.

From the above discussion it is clear that the Indus people had developed a civilisation of very high order which was one of the earliest on earth.

Date Of The Indus Civilisation : Its Relation With Other Civilisation

The Indus Valley civilisation had its distinctive characteristics no doubt and developed in its own way. But this did not preclude its contacts with other sister civilisations of Elam, Sumer, Mesopotamia etc. There are several outstanding common features among Indus civilisation and these contemporary civilisations. As no trace of iron has been found in any of the sites of the Indus civilisation it was in chalcolithic age of development which shows remarkable similarity with culture of Elam, Mesopotamia and Proto-historic Period of Sumer which was about 2750 B.C. This gives us the lowest limit of the Indus civilisation

Due to the difficulty in exploring the lowest strata of the cities, below the sub-soil water the earliest time when the civilisation had begun cannot correctly be determined. The upper limit of the civilisation remains more or less conjectural.

Until recently the period of the Indus civilisation was determined by reference to the discovery of the Indus seals at Elam and Mesopotamia and a cuneiform inscription at Mohenjo-daro. These apart, seal of late Mohenjo-daro period was found at Eshnunna in layers belonging to 2600 to 2500 B.C. This naturally pushed the early period of Mohenjo-daro further backwards, about 2800 B.C. This is also borne out by the finds of a cylinder seal of Indian origin at Tell Asmar discovered by Dr. Frankfort and a vase depicting a *Brahmani bull* at Tell Agrab which push back the Indus civilisation to 2800 B.C. Dr. Gadd and Dr. Fabri indicate the upper limit of the Indus civilisation as 2800 B.C. A comparison of the plain and painted pottery of the Indus civilisation with similar specimens at Sumer, Elam and Egypt shows that the Indus civilisation must have flourished not later than 2500 B.C. Ceramic evidence shows that the earliest stage of the Indus civilisation was 3000 B.C. Recently carbon test carried out on the materials from Mohenjo-daro, Lothal, Kalibangan and Surkotada determines the dates of the Indus civilisation from 2400 B.C. to 1700 B.C. But the scientists working on the subject are of the opinion that carbon activity was not constant in the past and observe that the likelihood of 4000 B.C. as the upper limit of the Indus civilisation cannot be ruled out.

It must be mentioned in conclusion that the Indus civilisation must have had a long history of anterior development before it reached the stage at which we find it. It is difficult to fix the dates of the civilisation particularly because the lowest layer of the cities of Mohenjo-daro, Harappa, Chanhu-daro, Junkar cannot be reached because of sub-soil water. The civilisation from what has been known till now, may well reach beyond 3500 B.C.

In any case, "the culture period of the Indus Valley civilisation, as revealed by its finds seems to have lasted roughly from B.C. 2800 to 2200 B.C."

Architects of the Indus Civilsation

In determining the authorship of the Indus civilisation the only definite and reliable materials available are the human skeletal remains and the skulls which have been discovered in the ruins of the cities of the Indus civilisation. From an examination of the skulls it has been found that the Indus people was a heterogeneous people and comprised Proto-Australoid, Mediterranean, Alpinoid and Mongoloid racial types. In certain cities, however, one or the other racial type was more predominant than the others. For instance, the Mohenjo-daro people were mainly of Mediterranean type. Evidence supplied by the sculptured pieces also confirms the composite nature of the Indus people. The anthropological and statuary evidences while confirm the composite character of the Indus people, they by no means help us to venture any definite conclusion as to the authorship of the civilisation and there has been a good deal of speculation among the anthropologists and scholars as to the naming of the people of any particular race as the author of the civilisation. The authorship has been variously ascribed to the Dravidians, Brahuis, Sumerians, Panis, Asuras, Dasas, Nagas, Aryans etc.

Most of the anthropologists and scholars prefer to name the Dravidians as the author of the Indian civilisation. But when we consider the fact that the Dravidians buried their dead we cannot say that the Indus civilisation was their work, for the number of the graves discovered does not justify this conclusion. Further, excavation in south has not revealed any trace of the Indus civilisation.

Some are of the opinion that the Brahuis who spoke Dravidian language were racially different from the peoples speaking Dravidian language in Central and South India. The Brahuis were of Turko-Iranian origin.

As to the opinion that the Sumerians were the author of the Indus civilisation it may be said that although there were close contacts between the people of Sumer and those of the Indus Valley, there is no definite evidence in support of their authorship of the Indus civilisation.

As to the Panis, Dasas, Asuras, Nagas etc. there are no materials to help us in placing them in any racial category.

Turning to the theory advanced by a number of scholars that the Indus civilisation was the work of the Aryans we have to deal with a good deal of counter arguments. Sir John Marshall after a careful comparison of the Vedic civilisation with the Indus civilisation has come to the conclusion that these two civilisations were clearly distinct. Further, he is of the opinion that the Rig Vedic times were posterior to 15000 B.C. and had been about a thousand years subsequent to the disappearance of the Indus civilisation. Naturally, as he opines, there could not be any connection between the Aryan and the Indus civilisations. But here again, we have a different opinion. Some scholars point out that the Rig Veda was certainly composed quite a long time after the advent of the Aryans in India. Again, there is no certainty as to the date of the Indus civilisation. From the skeletal remains it is also held by some scholars that the Aryans were also a part of the composite population of the Indus civilisation. One of their main arguments is that the Siva-Sakti cult of Mohenjo-daro was borrowed by the Aryans in later time. Another argument is that the Indus people did not know the use of horse and they also worshipped images. Dr. Mackay refutes the argument that horse was not known to the Indus people by pointing out a model of animal looking like horse and says that horse was known to the Indus people. It is also pointed out that the Siva cult of Mohenjo-daro might as well have been borrowed from the Rig Veda period.

The opinion of Sir John Marshall is, however, generally accepted but it may be pointed out that some scholars still hold that the Vedic civilisation was anterior to the Indus civilisation. In the maze of arguments and counter arguments it is not possible in the present state of our knowledge to come to any conclusion suggestive of the fact that the authors of the Indus civilisation were the Aryans. In fact, the authorship of the Indus civilisation cannot be ascribed to any particular race.

Decline and Disappearance of the Indus Civilisation

Our knowledge about the decay and decline of the Indus civilisation is still in a conjectural stage more or less. Nothing, therefore, can be said with certainty at this stage of our knowledge. Archaeologists have, however, tried to find out from the available evidences the factors that were very likely to have caused the decay and disappearance of the civilisation. The problem is a controversial one, there is no doubt.

Most of the archaeologists are of the opinion that the climatic change in the Indus region was by and large responsible for the decay and disappearance of the Indus civilisation. As Sir Mortimer Wheeler says, 'The rainfall in the Indus zone was somewhat more ample and equable than it is today. Except the riverine strips and areas artificially irrigated, the whole terrain is now sandy. Yet it was in these mountainous and desert areas the earliest agricultural communities of India have been identified.'

It is imposible to believe that the people of Mohenjo-daro or Harappa or for that matter the people of the Indus region could develop a culture as they did in an arid, inhospitable desert. There are evidences that Indus region was marshy and jungle infested. The vivid representations by the artists of the time, of tiger, buffalo, rhinoceros, elephants with whom they were obviously familiar, bear out this fact. The extreme scarcity of evidence of camel indicate that the area was not dried, arid desert. Adequate water supply from rainfall and rivers made the region fertile and suitable for agriculture which was the main stay of the economic life of the Indus people.

But the climate began to undergo a gradual but sharp change. Aurel Stein observes that evidence "distinctly pointed to the local climate having undergone a great change since the Chalcolithic times in its effect on agriculture". While there was less of rainfall and consequently more of heat, the moisture contained in the soil was brought to the surface as a result of evaporation. The crust of the soil became white, arid and brittle. This process of "desiccation was far advanced by the time Alexander the Great, whose returning army was decimated in the cheerless wastes of Makran. And it may be said that an increasing aridity had already contributed to the downfall of the Indus cities".[1]

Now, what were the causes of the desiccation of the Indus zone? It is variously suggested that the northward movement of the Atlantic cyclones which deflected southwards to north Africa and extended to Arabia, Persia and India. It has also been suggested that the south-western monsoon touched the Indus Valley. But these are mere suggestions.

But as Wheeler points out, the basic climatic change is unlikely to have been the sole or even the main cause in the deterioration of the agricultural conditions in the Indus Valley and its environs. True that a basic change in the climatic conditions may be reasonably argued but human neglect or interference was no less an important contributory factor.

Millions of kiln-burnt bricks must have required fuel which the forests could yield. Excessive deforestation that resulted in consequence of drawing timber for the kiln from the forest led to decrease in rainfall. Human neglect was also evidenced in inadequate maintenance of such dams and irrigation canals as may have been found necessary, a falling off in agricultural standards etc. are factors which resulted in the reduction in the precipitation of moisture which led to progressive desiccation.[2]

Besisdes these domestic potentials for the decay and disappearance of the Indus Civilisation, must be added the invasion of the nomadic outsiders in the second millennium B.C. which broke up the organised

[1] Sir Mortimer Wheeler : *Cambridge History of India, The Indus Civilisation Supplement*, p. 6.

[2] *Ibid.* p. 8.

agriculture altogether. It is likely that the invaders were none other than the Aryans who entered India during the middle of the second millennium B.C. (B.C. 1500), When Harappa was first built the citadel was defended by a great turret wall. In course of time it was refaced more strongly than before. Towards the later history of Harappa its defences were further strengthened and one of its gateways towards the west was wholly blocked. All this was certainly because the city was threatened by invaders. In Mohenjo-daro also there was a walled citadel, the town was in the lower level.

The first to suffer were the Beluchistan villages. When gradually the barbarians, i.e., the outsiders had conquered the outlying villages, people flocked within the cities. The Indus cities must have suffered great strain. In order to accommodate more people large rooms at Mohenjo-daro were divided into smaller rooms. Potters' kilns were built within the city. Jewelleries were buried to secure them against the invaders. The city became over-crowded and full of new-comers upon whom the city fathers could not enforce the age old pattern of its culture. Naturally, the high civic standard fell and the towns and cities became derelict, decadent settlements hastening to their end. "Later day Mohenjo-daro and by inference Harappa and the rest" remarks Wheeler "were poor shadows of former selves". The end of the Indus civilisation was a mere question of time.

Besides progressive desiccation, the growing danger of floods was certainly responsible for the evacuation of Mohenjo-daro, although flood was only one of the causes. The rising water level due to the immense quantity of silt brought down annually by the Indus water had caused devastating floods that swept over the city at least on three occasions.[1] A mud brick embankment or bund, 43 feet high, was constructed to protect the city from the devastation of flood and had to be reinforced externally. A large drain made of kiln-burnt bricks which lay along the foot of the embankment had to be rebuilt at a level 14 feet higher denoting that the water level was rising up as a result of silting. Houses were also rebuilt on higher level in order to make them secure against flood.[2]

When the end came, it would seem that most of the citizens of Mohenjo-daro had fled. But from a group of huddled skeletons in one of the houses, one skeleton of a woman lying on the steps of a well suggests that a few stragglers were overtaken by the invaders.

Thus numerous causes, both natural and human, were responsible for the end of the Indus civilisation. About the invaders who gave the ultimate blow for the disappearance of the civilisation opinions vary. Sir John Marshall is of opinion that a period of nearly two

---

[1] *Ibid.* p. 41.
[2] *Ibid.* p. 27.

centuries elapsed between the end of the Indus civilisation and coming of the Aryans. This indicates, according to him, that the fall of the Indus civilisation was due to invasion by people other than the Aryans.

But recent excavations at Harappa and elsewhere, indication of the Rig Veda itself, have tended to reduce the gap suggested by Sir John Marshall. "Many competent scholars led by Sir Mortimer Wheeler, now believe that Harappa civilisation was overthrown by the Aryans. The skeletal remains excavated in the later cemetery at Harappa are those of the true Vedic Aryans and that the forts or citadels, the Vedic War-God Indra is said to have destroyed, included Harappa in their number."[1]

Survivals of the Indus Civilisation

The question which appears to be the most pertinent is how far did the Indus civilisation contribute to the sum-total of human achievement ? While the civilisation of Mesopotamia may be easily related to the general development of civilisation of the West, the Indus civilisation cannot claim that much of continuity. At the first sight the Indus civilisation does not seem to have any claim on the subsequent cultural development of the Indian sub-continent itself. Their cities decayed, and were obliterated in their decadence by an insurgent barbarism. "Slaughtered Harappans lay unburied amid their streets and drains. Did all that they represented perish with them ?"

Their system of plumbing and drainage, and their special artistry they could not bequeath to later ages. About their thoughts and ideas, their philosophy and their beliefs, the archaeology is not of much help. But there are reasons to believe that later Hinduism did in fact retain a non-Aryan Harappan mentality. The recurrent figures of a Proto-Siva, that is *Pasupati Yogin* in seated posture, or dancing as *Nataraja* are beyond doubt, bequeathed to Hinduism by the Indus people. Likewise the Indus Mother Goddess bequeathed to later ages the Hindu concept of *Parvati*.

The evidence of phallic worship, reverence to animals, particularly the cult of the bull are the contributions of the Indus people to Hinduism.

Further, the punch-marked coins, with their symbols embossed on them are reminiscent of the Indus Valley scripts and with their standard of weight conforming to the weight system of Mohenjo-daro, constitute an important survival of the Indus Valley Civilisation.

Some of the designs, motifs, shapes and forms found in the pottery and terracotta articles at Mohenjo-daro and Harappa have

---

1 Prof. A. L. Basham : *The Wonder that was India*, p. 29.
Prof. Wheeler : *The Indus Civilisation*. p. 95.

their counterparts in objects discovered in the Punjab and the North-West belonging to period shortly before the Christian era.

It is something paradoxical that while the Indus civilisation failed to transmit its physical aspects to the later times, it succeeded in transmitting its philosophy, its religion to its successors. Therefore, it is certain that there was no break or hiatus after the Indus civilisation. The successor civilisation, i.e., the Aryan, was enriched in some measures by the influences of the Indus culture and the continuity of the Hindu Civilisation from the third millennium B.C. cannot be questioned.

Chapter Four

THE ARYANS AND THE ARYAN CIVILISATION

Original home of the Aryans

Our knowledge about the original home of the Aryans is still in a speculative stage. There has been a great divergence of opinion in the matter of identification of the place wherefrom the Aryans came into India. No firm conclusion is, therefore, possible in this regard.

The problem of identification of the original home of the Aryans has to be approached from both linguistic and racial points of view. As early as the sixteenth century Filippo Sassetti, a Florentine, during his long stay in India noticed a definite relation between Sanskrit and some of the principal languages of Europe. But it was Sir William Jones who in 1786 showed that Sanskrit and the European languages such as Greek, Latin, German, Celtic, Gothic, as also the Persian, had a common origin. The scholars have named this language group as Indo-European or Indo-German language group. Max Muller also emphatically pointed out that scientifically speaking, Aryan means language and not race. From this language affinity it is argued that the Indo-European languages, at least a large number of them, are crowded in Europe and some of them are found to stretch out in a narrow length reaching upto the region of the Punjab in the early Rig Vedic time. This has led many a scholar to conclude that the original home of the Aryans was Europe rather than India. They support their conclusion by pointing out that comparative philology has shown that the Lithuanian language is the only language that retains the basic Aryan idioms even to-day.

Penka and his school of thought, particularly Kossuna, approached the problem of the Indo-Aryans from racial point of view and concluded that Germany was the original home of the Indo-Aryans.

From the above approaches the claim that India was the original home of the Aryans becomes untenable. However, some scholars, such as Gananath Jha, D. S. Triveda, L. D. Kalla, are advocates of the theory of indigenous origin of the Aryans. While Jha seeks to prove that Brahmarshi-Desha was the original home of the Aryans, Triveda mentions the region of the Devika river in Multan, and Kalla claims Kashmir and the Himalayan regions as the original home of the Aryans. In support of the theory of the indigenous origin of the Aryans it has been pointed out that there is a mass of literary evidence to show that Sapta-Sindhu was regarded by the Vedic Aryans as their original home. Further, there is no reference to their coming into India from any outside country and it is not possible that the Aryans had forgotten all about their original home if it were anywhere out of India. In fact, there is an emotional association with the land of the origin of all migrating people. But no such evidence has been found in the literature of the Vedic Aryans.

It has also been pointed out that linguistic affinity cannot be regarded as positive proof of immigration of the Aryans from any outside country. For in the Sanskrit language largest number of vocables of the Aryan languages is found. But in parts of Europe, if it were the original home of the Indo-Aryans, it is inexplicable why only very few vocables are found in the languages of the European countries. This is argued to be a pointer to the fact that India was the original home of the Aryans and from India the Aryan language and other languages of Aryan affinity came into existence due to the contacts between the migrating Aryans and non-Aryans out of India.

Another argument in support of this view is that the Vedic literature was the expression of the highly developed thoughts of the Aryans. If the Aryans had come to India from outside it would be natural to find some traces of their thoughts and literary activities in some of the places through which they had travelled. But no such record has been discovered at any place. To suggest that the Aryans had attained the highly developed literary and intellectual acumen after coming into India does not justify the absence of any record whatsover in any of the places through which they had travelled into India.

Another argument is that the original home of the Aryans was Lithuania on the basis that the language of the Lithuanians is archaic and has the greatest resemblance to the original Aryan language. But this by itself does not conclusively prove that the Aryans migrated into India from Lithuania.

Absence of the mention of tiger in the Rig Veda and the reference to *Mrigahastin* meaning elephant have been pointed out to be good grounds for the belief that tigers were actually not known to the Aryans when they came from outside and that *Mrigahastin* was anything but a poetic name. But the geographical data in Rig Veda show that the Punjab and the neighbouring regions were the home of the people who had composed the Rig Vedic hymns. Such arguments have been put forward in support of the contention that the Vedic Aryans did not come from outside but were original inhabitants of India. But as we have already discussed before, the overwhelming majority opinion is in favour of regarding the Aryans as a people who had migrated into India.

The Early Vedic Age : Early Aryan Settlements

The territories which the Aryans had occupied by the time that they composed the Rig Veda, can be defined from the references to the names of the rivers and the geography of the areas mentioned in the Rig Vedic hymns. The rivers referred to in the Rig Vedic texts are the Indus, and its main tributaries, the five rivers of the Punjab, namely, the Satadru, Bipasa, Ravi, Chenab, and the Jhelum. From the Rig Vedic texts it has been possible to get a fair idea of the early Aryan settlements as well as of their centres of activities. Yet it must be remembered that the Rig Veda is not a book on Geography and absence of the names of places or rivers in the Rig Vedic texts does not mean that other places, not mentioned in the texts, were not included in the early Aryan settlements. It may also be pointed out that reference to rivers, hills and mountains, races, territories, kingdoms in the Rig Veda cannot be regarded as conclusive proofs of the extension of the Early Aryan settlements.

There is reference to the Himalayas in the Rig Veda. That the influence of rivers on the religion and life of the Vedic Aryans was tremendous can be realised the mention of as many as twenty-five rivers in the Rig Veda itself out of a total of thirty-one rivers mentioned in all the Vedas. Apart from the rivers already mentioned above, the names of the rivers Ganges, Jumna, Saraju and Saraswati are also found in the Rig Veda. From all this, we may generally conclude that the early Aryan settlements extended in the valleys of the rivers mentioned above. Reference to Sapta-Sindhava in the Rig Veda is taken to mean the territories along the courses of the five rivers of the Punjab, the Indus and the Saraswati. Historians like Ludwig, Lassen and Whitley are in favour of including the river Oxus in the place of Saraswati. Mention of the rivers Krumu (Kurram), Gomati (Gomal) and Kubha (Kabul) and Suvastu (Swat) in the Rig Veda shows that the Aryan settlements extended to territories within the boundaries of present Afghanistan. Naturally the Oxus region was not unknown to the early Aryans. The main area of the early Aryan settlements was the Punjab ; but there has been difference of opinion in this regard. It is supposed that the early Aryans had not extended their settlement into Bengal. Absence of reference to tiger in the Rig Veda leads to the conclusion that Aryan expansion in Bengal, Assam and the Deccan took place in later times.

There are references in the Rig Veda to constant conflict between the Aryans and the Dasas, that is, the non-Aryans. In these conflicts the non-Aryans were progressively defeated and the Aryans extended their settlements towards the east. This movement of the Aryans from the Punjab towards the east naturally reduced the importance of the Punjab eventually. This is borne out in the Brahmanas. During 1500 to 800 B.C., that is the period when the Brahmanas were written the Aryan settlements had extended from the valley of the river Saraswati to the Gangetic doab. This vast plain became the main settlement of the Aryans. During that period Kurukshetra, Magadha, Kasi, Videha, Anga etc. acquired importance as Aryan kingdoms. During the Brahmana period the Kurus and the Panchalas were the most important and powerful Aryan kingdoms. From Videha or North Bihar to South and East Bihar, Bengal etc. were not brought under the Aryans before 800 B.C. This area was known as Prachi or Prachya. In course of time the Aryan settlements were also extended to the Brahmaputra and Irawdy valleys. It took a little longer time before Saurastra, Avanti, i.e., present Malwa and Saubir came under the Aryans.

By 200 B.C. the Aryans spread all over the vast area from the Himalayas to the Vindhyas and from the Arabian sea to the Bay of Bengal. It has been from that period of history that this vast area came to be known as Aryavarta.

In course of time the Aryans crossed the Vindhyas and moved into the southern parts of India. The story of Agastya Muni's crossing the Vindhyas and Ram Chandra's expedition to Ceylon (Lanka) are supposed to be instances of the Aryan penetration into the south. It may, however, be mentioned that the Aryans did not succeed to bring the whole of the south under their control. There were a large number of non-Aryan tribes which existed by the side of the Aryan settlements in the southern India. The Andhras, Pulindas, Nishads may be mentioned as instances in point. In the Vindhya region reference to the existence of a non-Aryan tribe called the Sabars has been found. In the far south the Tamil, Malayalam and Kanada speaking Dravidians continued to live.

The Vedic Literature

The literature of the Aryans is called the Vedas. The word Veda is derived from the root *Vid* meaning knowledge or to know. The Aryans produced four Vedas: the Rig, Sham, Yayu and Atharva Vedas. Rig Veda was the oldest of the Vedas and it contains more than a thousand hymns. Description of Nature and hymns to the Nature gods and goddesses are the subject matter of the Vedas. The hymns contained the Sam Veda were mostly adapted from the Rig Veda. These were sung at the time of Yajna. In the Yayurveda mantras and rituals for the Yajna are incorporated. The Atharva Veda was the last of the Vedas. It contained the mysteries of creation, mantras for the cure of diseases, and many kinds of mysterious signs and mantras. From the earliest times the Hindus believed the Vedas to be the words of God and as such these were divine, eternal and not of human authorship. As the Vedas were received from God's mouth through hearing the other name of the Vedas is *Sruti*. But the Vedangas which were composed later were not the words of God. These were descended from generation to generation through memory and as such came to be called *Smriti*.

Each of the Vedas is divided into four parts, namely. Samhita, Brahman, Aranyak and Upanishad. Samhita is hymns which were sung and written in rhymes. Each Veda has its own Samhita. Likewise each Veda has its own Brahman. In the Brahmanas the ritualistic side of the Yajna is described. These were mostly written in prose. In later time the Aranyakas and the Upanishads were written. According to the Aryan social rule people had to renounce their household and live in the forest after having attained the age of fifty. As it was not possible for such people to follow the intricate rituals of Vedic Yajna, Aranyakas were composed for them. The philosophical thought that emanated from the essence of the Aranyakas came to be known as Upanishads. As the Upanishads had been the result of the philosophical speculations at the last and ultimate stage of the Vedic literature these are also known as Vedantas, i e., *Veda Anta,* end of the Vedas. For correct reading and comprehension of the Vedas and following the very essentials rituals during the Yajnas six Vedangas and six Darshana (philosophies) were written in later times. Both the Vedangas and the Saradarshana together came to be known as Sutra Sahitya.

The six Vedangas were : (i) Siksha. Study of this would enable correct pronunciation of the Vedic texts. (ii) Chhanda. The rhymes of the Vedic hymns could be correctly understood by study of Chhanda. (iii) Vyakaran or Grammar would enable use of language correctly. (iv) Nirukta dealt with the roots of words, (v) Jyotish dealt with the knowledge of the stars and sky, and (vi) Kalpa was the study of duties of the householders, and the rules to be followed in social behaviour among the Aryan Society. Kalpa or Kalpasutra was again divided into Srautasutra, Grihyasutra and Dharmasutra. While Srautasutra was a compilation of the rituals to be followed in times of Yajnas, the Ghriyasutra dealt with the duties of the householder, the method of living, christening of children, sacred thread investment, marriage etc. Dharmasutra contained the social discipline, administration of the state etc. It was on the basis of the Dharmasutra that Manusamhita and similar other samhitas were composed. Apart from Dharmasastras the Aryans also had written treatises like Arthasastra, Sangit Sastra, Natyasastra, Dharmavéd, Hastisastra, Aswasastra, Sthapatya Vidya, etc. In Sulvasutra details of the construction of the Yajna Vedi, i.e., fireplace for the Yajna was narrated. It was from Sulvasutra that the knowledge of geometry developed among the Hindus of the past.

From the philosophical speculations, explanations and discussions on the Upanishads the Hindu Philosophy had developed. Hindu Philosophy has six distinct parts: (i) Kapila's Samkhya Philosophy, (ii) Patanjali's Yogasastra, (iii) Gautam's Nyaya Philosophy, (iv) Kanad's Vaisesik Philosophy, (v) Jaimine's Purba Mimamgsa, (vi) Vedavyasa's Uttar Mimamgsa as Vedanta Philosophy.

The ancient Hindus used to memorise the Vedic slokas and handed them down from generation to generation. The Vedas were not reduced to writing at that time. The faultless manner in which the ancient Hindus held the Vedic texts in their memory showed the great reverence they had for the Vedas. The Hindus are even today deeply reverential to the Vedas. In their daily life the Vedic influence can be noticed. For instance, in the saying of prayers (Ahnik) Pujas, Sacred thread investment, marriage and Sraddha the Vedic mantras are chanted.

The Religion of the Aryans

The Aryan civilisation developed amidst Nature, and it was Nature that had influenced all the different aspects of their life and living, including their religion. The Aryans worshipped the forces of Nature as gods and goddesses, thus we see them worshipping the god of light–Sun, also called Mitra, the god of the vast blue sky–Dyau, god of rain and thunder–Varuna, god of air–Marut, as also gods and goddesses like Agni, Usha, Prithivi, Saraswati etc. Indra and Varuna were the greatest of the gods of the Aryans There is some similarity between the religious beliefs of the Aryans and the ancient Greeks and Romans. The Greek God Apollo, was the Sun God, Zeus was their god of the sky. Likewise Jupiter was the god of the sky of the Romans. The Aryans worshipped various gods and goddesses no doubt yet they believed in the unity of the god head, the different gods and goddesses being but various emanations of the same.

The Aryans used to light sacrificial fire for Yajna and would pour ghee, milk and cakes in the fire with the chanting of the mantras. Animal sacrifice, drinking of *soma rasa* were parts of the rituals. Soma rasa was a kind of intoxicant liquor. It may be noted that animal sacrifice, worship of images were non-Aryan religious customs which gradually entered into the religious practice of the Aryans. Hinduism, as a matter of fact, developed as a result of the mixture of the religious customs of the Aryans and the non-Aryans.

In course of time the Vedic religious practices like Yajna and the chanting of the mantras became so elaborate and complex that the common people relegated the religious duties to a class of experts who came to be known as Purohits, i.e, priests. In course of time the priests became the guardians and protectors as also the guides of the religion of the common people.

Society : Varnasrama, i.e., Four-fold Division of Society

When the Aryans entered into India they had no class distinction between themselves. They were fair complexioned, tall, sharp-nosed and handsome. But the original inhabitants of India on the other hand were dark complexioned and short. When the Aryans defeated the non-Aryans and established their settlement in India, there arose two classes in the society, namely, the Aryans and the non-Aryans on the basis of their complexion, i.e., *Varna*. To begin with, the social division was based on *Varna*, i.e , complexion. But with the growth of population and complexities of social life the society came to be divided into four *classes* on the basis of division of labour. The division was with reference to one's *guna*, i.e., quality and *karma*, i.e., nature of work. Those who were given to worship, Yajna, and study of the Sastras were called the *Brahmanas*. Those who knew the art of warfare and had ability to defend the country and carry on administration were called the Kshatriyas. Persons who were expert in trade and commerce, animal husbandry etc. came to be known as *Vaisyas*. Manual workers who worked for the first three classes and mainly did physical labour came to be called the *Sudras*. In this way there arose a furfold division in the Aryan society, viz., the Brahmanas, Kshatriyas, Vaisyas and Sudras. But there was no rigidity in the division, for one could improve his quality and ability and get into the next higher class. These four classes were not castes. It was permissible for a person of one class to marry in any other class. But in the latest Vedic Age rigidity in the class division began to develop and the classes were gradually being transformed into castes. Intermarriage between different classes was being gradually looked upon with disfavour and was eventually prohibited. Change over from one class to another was also not permissible.

Four Asramas, i.e., Four Stages of Life

The life of the Vedic Aryans of the Brahmana, Kshatriya and Vaisya classes was divided into four stages or *Asramas*. For each of these *asramas* or stages there were a set of rigid rules and practices which had to be meticulously followed. The first asrama was *Brahmacharya*, i.e., continence, the second was *Garhasthya*, i.e., householders's life, the third *Vanaprastha*, i.e., staying in the forest, and the fourth *Sannyas*, i.e., life of a recluse.

In the first stage, i.e., Brahmacharyya, every young man of the first three classes—the Brahmana, Kshatriya and Vaisya—had to live in the house of the preceptor, i.e., Guru. It was a stage of studentship and training. Every male had to be invested with sacred thread, i.e., Upanayana and had to be sent to the house of Guru, i.e., the preceptor. He has then to be a Brahmachari and become a member of the preceptor's household. The idea was that he should live a simple and austere life identifying himself with his preceptor in sharing the vicissitudes of the preceptor's life and studying the sastras. When the study of the sastras would be complete he had to return to his own house and live the life of a grihi, i.e., householder with his wife and children. It was the stage called *Garhasthya Asrama* where all worldly affairs had to be looked after.

On the attainment of the age of fifty, the *grihi* had to live in forests separately from the household, that is, take to *Vanaprastra* and prepare himself for the final stage of life. The fourth or the final stage was that of the *Sannyasin* when the person had to renounce the world and take to the life of a recluse and bide his time in meditation and sustaining himself with whatever he would receive as gifts. The entire life of the Vedic Aryans was but religion in practice.

Economic Life of the Aryans

The Aryan, i.e., the Vedic civilisation was based on village life. In the Rig Veda there is reference to *Puras* as military citadels but no reference to towns or cities. Later on, however, we came across cities like Asandhibat, Kampila etc. In the later Vedic Age although towns and cities had grown up yet the Vedic civilisation continued to be rural in character. Village was the unit of political, social and economic life of the Vedic Aryans. Naturally, the basis of the economic life was agriculture and animal husbandry. Every family of the village had a plot of agricultural land. Apart from this, every village had a large area of pasture land. Every villager had equal right to graze his cattle in this pasture land.

Among the domestic animals mention may be made of the cattle, horse, dog, sheep, goat etc. Cow's milk was one of the most important and indispensable food. Land was ploughed by bullocks. The Jumna Valley was particularly noted for cow's milk and Gandhara for wool.

Agriculture and animal husbandry were the main stay of economic life but trade and commerce were no less important. The Vedic Aryans knew the art of manufacturing various articles of daily use. Trade and commerce were, however, in the hands of the non-Aryans. Manufacture of textiles, potteries, painting, metallurgy and various other articles was the source of income of a large section of the Vedic Aryans. In those days, coins were not in use. Cow was the medium of exchange. A gold piece called *Niska* was also used as medium of exchange besides cow. In the Rig Vedic times, there is reference to the use of *Mana,* a piece of gold, as the medium of exchange. Some scholars think that the Rig Vedic *Mana* was the copy of the Babylonian *Mana* and *Latin Mina*.

The transport during the Vedic Age consisted of chariots and bullock carts. Chariots were drawn by horses. Whether the Vedic Aryans carried on sea-borne trade and commerce is not very sure and there has been considerable controversy among scholars in this regard. But if we agree that the Rig Vedic *Mana* was the Indian version of the Babylonian *Mana* and Latin *Mina* then we will have to agree with the view that the Rig Vedic Aryans must have had commercial relations by sea with those countries.

The early Aryans took wheat, barely, milk, fruits, fish and meat as food. Sura or Soma rasa, i.e. intoxicant liquor was very popular drink of the Aryans. Soma rasa was particularly used in times of Yajna.

The dress of the Aryans were made of both cotton and wool. In certain cases dress was also made of animal skin. The dress of the Aryans comprised three parts—the *Nivi*, a sort of an underwear, above which there was the *Paridhan*, i.e., cloth and *Adhivasa*, i.e., a flowing upper garment. Both male and female would use ornaments. Gold was mainly used for the manufacture of ornaments but other metals were also used for the purpose.

Arts and Sciences of the Aryans

It is generally supposed that the Aryans did not know the art of writing. It was because of this that they used to memorise the Vedic texts and hand them down from generation to generation. Yet, that the Aryans were adept in composing poetry goes without saying. The *Rik Samhita* was the finest expression of the art of poetry of the Aryans.

The Aryans were highly developed in the art of house building. Reference to large palace with a thousand pillars and doors testifies to the highly developed knowledge of architecture on the part of the Aryans. They were also expert in the science and medicine. The medical men used to rely on mantras, besides medicines, for the cure of diseases. Reference to iron leg pressupposes the knowledge of science of surgery among the Aryans.

The Aryans were also expert astronomers. The Science of Astronomy had been very much developed at that time. This can be realised from the naming of some of the stars and planets by the Aryans.

Political life of the Aryans

The basis of the political life of the Aryans was family. Each family was under a head of the family called the Grihapati who was the eldest male member of the family. His orders were law unto the members of the family. A number of families would constitute a village which was under the administration of the *Gramani*. The *Gramani* exercised both civil and military functions. A group of villages would constitute a *Vish* or *Jana*. The ruler of a *Vish* or *Jana* was *Vishpati* or *Rajan*, that is monarch. As a general rule monarchy was the system of government prevailing in the early Vedic Age. There are references to a large number of kings in the Vedic texts. This was obviously because the country which the Vedic Aryans had occupied was split up into numerous tribal principalities. The king occupied a position of high dignity and his supremacy was emphasized by a formal consecration and laudatory hymns. The lines of kingly succession that we come across in the Rig Veda presupposes hereditary kingship to be the normal system. Theoretically the king was supreme and repository of all powers of the state. Yet in practice the king had to consult the opinions of two assemblies called *Sabha* and *Samiti*. The *Sabha* was a select body usually believed to be a Council of Elders. The Samiti was a more comprehensive body more popular and political in character. The Samiti discharged the political business of the tribe and was presided over by the king. Although the exact nature of the functions of the *Sabha* and *Samiti* cannot be defined yet it is generally believed on the basis of the reference to the *Sabha* and *Samiti* in the Rig Vedic texts that the Sabha was a council of the Brahmanas and the rich patrons which came into session for administrative purposes. From references to the game of dice in the hall in which the *Sabha* met it is clear that non-political business could as well be transacted by the *Sabha*. It, however, gave decisions on matter of public importance and as we find in later literature, it became particularly prominent in matters of the administration of justice.

The *Samiti* which was practically the assembly of the people was attended by the members of the royal family as well as the people. It met for transacting political business of the tribe.

That both the *Sabha* and *Samiti* exercised considerable authority and acted as healthy checks of the powers of the king goes without saying. This is also borne out by a hymn in the Rig Veda which stresses the importance and the need of unity among the members of the assembly and concord between the king and the assembly.

The authority of the king was also curbed by the power and prestige of the *Purohita* who not only helped the king and the people of the tribe by spells and prayers, but actually accompanied the king to battle where he invoked God's blessings for the king's victory. The cases of Vashista and Viswamitra are noteworthy in this regard. It may be mentioned here that the tribal kings of the Rig Vedic times were constantly at war and naturally they needed God's blessings which the Purohita would invoke for them.

Although the prevailing system of government in Rig Vedic times was monarchy, yet references to *Gana, Ganapati* or *Gana Jyestha* show the existence of tribal republics. *Ganapati* and *Gana Jyestha* were names for the administrative head of a *Gana*, *i.e.*, republic.

Protection of the people, their properties etc. was the primary duty of the king. He had to defend the Kingdom against attacks from without, to wage war for expansion of territory to attend to the complaints of the subjects and mete out justice. In order to administer the country efficiently and effectively, the king would be assisted by a body of royal officers. The *Purohita* and the *Senani*, i.e. the commander of the royal forces, were the most important of all officers. The king was the supreme commander but below the king the highest commander was the *Senani*. In times of war the *Senani* had to go to battle, but in times of peace he would discharge civil functions. The army comprised infantry, cavalry and chariotry. Bows and arrows, swords, axes, spears etc. were the weapons of war. The king used to fight from chariot.

Spies were engaged for gathering secret information about the kingdom and the people, in order to keep the king always aware of what was happening in the country. *Dutas*, messengers and emissaries were appointed to carry information to the different parts of the country.

In return for all that the king did, he received the loyalty and obedience of the people. He also received takes like *bali, sulka* and *bhaga*. *Bali* was perhaps the tribute received by the king from the tribe brought under his sway by conquest. *Sulka* was tax on goods and *bhaga* must have been king's share of the produce.

Position of Women

Families were patrilineal, as such, people desired larger number of male children than female. Birth of daughters was not desired but this did not mean any maltreatment of the daughters and for the matter of that of the women. In fact, in the early Vedic period women were held in high esteem, women's education was not neglected and some of the women of the time had acquired such eminence as to be ranked with the great scholars in sastras. Women like Visvavara, Ghosa and Apala were experts in sastras and composed hymns and verses and belonged to the rank of seers. Girls were given in marriage on their attaining puberty. Although polygamy was not unknown yet the general practice was that a man married only one wife. Women were not independent persons in the eye of law but they had to depend on their parents before marriage, on their husbands after marriage, on their sons in old age. But position of women in the household was of honour and she was not only the mistress but also the master of the house. Wife not only managed the domestic life of the family but also participated in the religious activities of her husband. From references in the Rig Veda that women trooped to festal occasions decked in shining clothes, we may conclude that the Rig Vedic women were not kept in life of seclusion.

Widow remarriage was permissible and girls were given in marriage through negotiations by their parents or they might choose their own husband i.e. have *Swayamvara.*

Social Life in the Later Vedic Age

In the later Vedic Period the society underwent considerable changes. The four *Varna,* i.e., classes, were now taken in the sense of castes. The period witnessed gradual hardening of the caste system and deterioration of the position of the *Vaisyas* and *Sudras* in relation to the Brahmans and the Kshatriyas. The Brahmans now became a well-organised priesthood given to study and teaching of the Vedas, offering sacrifices for themselves and others and receiving gifts. The Brahmans, however, could not become kings nor could the Kshatriyas become priests. Certain degraded Sudras like the Bratyas and Nishadas were forced to reside outside the limits of the village or town. The nation consisted of the upper class castes—the Brahmans, Kshatriyas and the Vaisyas, the Sudras being excluded from it.

The position of women did not improve during the later Vedic Period, rather their status marked a positive deterioration. Women could no longer attend the Assembly, i.e., the *Samiti.* They had no right to inherit properties. As marrying more than one wife was permissible among the upper classes, married women of these classes had often to suffer the presence of rival wives. The lot of the queens was rather unenviable in this regard and although there was the practice of naming one of the queens as *Rajmahisi* or Chief Queen yet the lot of the other queens was one of neglect and lack of honour due to queens. But they were allowed to participate in religious rites. Some of the women, such as, Gargi, Maitrayi, Lopamudra, Mamata, received education of high order and even took part in philosophical disputations in royal courts. Rule of marriage underwent a great change and there was much rigidity in matters of marriage. Intercaste marriage was permissible but was not looked upon with favour.

The Upanishads are by themselves a living testimony to the high intellectual attainments during the later Vedic Age. That a very high standard was maintained in education is clear from the stories of Svetaketu and Satyakama and the instruction given to the student at the end of his studies as contained in the *Taittiriya* Upanishad. The subjects of study included the Vedas, Itihasa, Purana, grammar, mathematics, astronomy, military science, ethics, dialectics, science of snakes etc. Personal purity and good health were regarded as essential conditions for study. After the completion of the whole course of studies came the ceremony called *Samavartana,* i.e., convocation, and the students could become *Snataka,* i.e. one who took ceremonial bath after the completion of studentship. Teacher, that is the preceptor, was the pivot of the educational system and the State had nothing to do with education. Pupils had to show great respect to the teachers who had also to observe certain rules of conduct towards the pupils.

Economic Life in the Later Vedic Age

It may be mentioned at the outset that most people lived in villages and the village agriculturists were the true representatives of ancient India. Importance of agriculture in the economy of the period is also denoted by the rites for putting the bullocks to the plough and for honouring the goddess of agriculture. Sacrifices were also offered to *Kshetrapati* i.e. the Lord of the agricultural field.

Rice and barley were, as before, the staple food of the later Vedic people. Cattle were an invaluable possession and all the upper three classes were engaged in cattle-keeping. Cows were not merely a property and source of milk, but a great reverence to them was gradually growing.

The Vaisyas were engaged in trade and commerce and several forest products, besides articles of food, clothing, figured as items of trade and commerce, e.g. Kutaja, Vamsa, Madhya, Ikohu etc.

From Panini we know that a system of currency was in use although a large part of trade and commerce was managed by system of barter. Pinini mentions coins like *Pana, Karshapana, Pada, Vaha* etc.

Implements and vessels of copper, iron, stone, and earthenware are mentioned. These were manufactured by skilled artisans. Gold and silver were also used for manufacture of cutleries, such as spoons, dishes etc. Clothes made of cotton, wool, silk and hemp were in use. From the above discussions it is clear that various occupations, professions, arts, crafts and industries were there. That the transport system was highly developed during this period is clear from references to bridges, roads, cross-roads, light two-wheeled wooden carriage etc. Horses, oxen were common draught animals. Horses, asses, camels, elephants were used for travels by land and raft and boats for travel by water.

Political Condition

In the later Vedic Age a vast change had taken place in the political condition of the country. Many of the former tribal kings who were mutually at war had in the process developed into emperors by conquering the weaker kingdoms. The emperors took the honorifics like *Ekrat, Samrat, Rajchakravartins* etc. These denoted the expansion of the territories and powers of the kings who had grown into emperors. But a highly intellectural and moral discipline was prescribed for the king. "He must be fully instructed in threefold sacred sciences, and in logic, and learn the management of chariot and the use of bow, he shall be holy in acts and speech, pure and of subdued senses". His essential duties and functions were to protect the castes and orders in accordance with justice. He must support the learned Brahmins and the poor and the needy of all classes, and none in the realm must suffer from hunger, sickness, cold etc. He must be impartial to his subjects. The *Sabha* and *Samiti* of the Early Vedic Age do not figure in the later Vedic Age. In any case the powers of the *Sabha* and *Samiti* to regulate the affairs of the State and to control the powers of the king must have been very much reduced if not totally absent. Despite the increase in the powers of the king, it must be mentioned that he did not become despotic since he had to take an oath for doing his duties as narrated above and failure to do his duties would be visited with adequate penalties in this world and the world hereafter. This was considered to be a sufficient deterrent. The Brahmanas and the *Purohita* still exercised same political control over the king.

The kingship became normally hereditary in the period. For the efficient administration of the country, the king would appoint a regular hierarchy of officers for the three upper classes, i.e. the Brahmanas, Kshatriyas and the Vaisyas, but they must be pure, truthful. These officers would appoint subordinate officers under them, who must also possess the same quality.

Collection of taxes was one of the most important branches of administration. One-sixth, one-eighth, or one-tenth of the produce of the soil would be variously charged as land taxes. This variation was perhaps due to the variation in the quality of the soil. One twentieth of merchandise, one-sixtieth of roots, fruits, flowers, medicinal herbs, honey, meat, grass and fire wood would be payable as tax. Artisans and other manual workers had to do a day's work for the king every month. One-tenth of the imports had to be handed to the king.

The king was to remain always prepared for war. He should lead his fighting forces in the battle. He must be brave and fearless in the battle field. Ethics of war prevented the use of poisonous weapons in fighting. As in the former times, the army consisted of the infantry, cavalry, charioteers, elephants etc.

The king was the highest civil and criminal judge but there is reference to a Chief Judge who was next to the king in matters of judicial authority. The Senani who was the commander-in-chief below the king did both executive and judicial functions in peace time. Killing a Brahmana was the greatest crime. Punishments ranged from death to physical disablement and expulsion from the country. Penalty of death might be commuted by gift of cows to the relation of the murdered.

Impact of the Non-Aryans on the Aryan Society

It was by defeating the non-Aryan population that the Aryans established their settlements. This process of conquest went on for long after which some of the non-Aryans came to be reconciled to their fate and lived under their conquerors while many others moved away to other parts of the country. Long stay side by side gradually removed the original feeling of mutual hostility between the Aryans and the non-Aryans. This naturally led to mutual understanding and influence. The Aryan society gradually accepted and assimilated many of the social and religious customs and rites of the non-Aryans. The mixture of the Aryan and non-Aryan customs and rites etc. gave rise to the Hindu culture of India. It may be mentioned here that although the non-Aryans were less developed in civilisation and culture compared to the Aryans, yet there is no reason to believe that they were uncivilised. In fact, the Dravidian civilisation among the non-Aryan civilisation was highly developed. The term non-Aryans meant nothing more or less than those who were not Aryans. It was not a term of contempt.

It is, however, difficult to determine the quantum of contributions made by the Aryans and the non-Aryans to the Hindu culture and civilisation. Yet it is possible to refer to certain special impacts of the non-Aryans upon the Aryan society and religion.

When the Aryans came to India, their main stay of life was animal husbandry but when they settled in India they took to agriculture and adopted the method of cultivation followed by the non-Aryans. Cultivation of food grains, fruits, sugarcanes etc. were learnt by them from the non-Aryans. Preparation of molasses from juice of the sugarcanes, building of houses, making of pottery with various paintings and decorations, boat-making and boat plying, manufacture of dresses, use of bricks etc. are supposed to have been learnt by the Aryans from the non-Aryans. Use of horses, manufacture of articles from iron, use of milk products, and liquor, sewing of garments and charioteering etc. were also learnt by them from the non-Aryans.

The Aryans originally did not worship any image. They only worshipped different forces of nature as gods and goddesses. The non-Aryans, on the other hand, worshipped images of gods and goddesses. The image worship is supposed to have been adopted by the Aryans from the non-Aryans.

Impact of the non-Aryans is also noticeable in the food habits of the Aryans. Meat and butter were used by the Aryans as their main food. But gradually they began to take rice, pulses, curd, ghee, oil, fish etc. as food as did the non-Aryans. In ceremonies like marriage etc. use of vermillion, cocoanut, betel leaf, incense etc. and animal sacrifice in certain religious ceremonies were learnt by the Aryans from the non-Aryans.

The civilisation and culture that developed in India in the ancient times had been the product of the mixture of the Aryan and non-Aryan manners, methods and habits, the main ethical bases of which were brotherliness, non-violence and mutual tolerance. The Indian civilisation acquired a potency incomparable to many other civilisations due to the mixture of the Aryan and non-Aryan cultures. The basic structure of the Indian culture is, therefore, the joint contributions of the Aryans and the non-Aryans.

The Age of the Epics

Many writers have referred to an Epic Age in the history of India. But modern historians are definitely against such a view. According to them the period during which the Indian Epics, the Ramayana and the Mahabharata, were composed, belonged to the Vedic Age. As such what is usually called as the Epic Age, in fact, is a part of the later Vedic Age.

In the *Sutra-Sahitya* which was written in the later Vedic Age there is reference to the Epics. It was from the *Gatha* and *Narasangshi,* i.e. the folk songs that the epic like the Mahabharata emerged. The Ramayana and the Mahabharata are not the songs of the court poets, nor the composition of any individual[1] at any particular time, but the collection of diverse poems of unequal value which had been sung through centuries and had continued interpolations and additions. Naturally, the Mahabharata or the Ramayana does not represent the life or events of any particular period. Thus two things that have to be remembered are: the epics, the Mahabharata and the Ramayana, belonged to the greater body of the Vedic literature,[2] and that they do not represent the life and conditions of any particular period. In fact, during the period the Vedic Brahmanas were composed, the kings like Janmenjaya, Parikshit etc. mentioned in the Mahabharata were actually ruling princes. Historians like R. D. Banerjee and

---

[1] "....the Mahabharata and the Ramayana are not the old heroic songs as those singers and travelling minstrels of ancient India sang them, compiled into unified poems by great poets or at least by clever collectors, but accumulation of very diverse poems of unequal value, which have arisen in course of centuries owing to continual interpolation and additions." Winternitz(*vide* Sinha Banerjee pp. 46-47

"The Mahabharata could not have been the work of any single person, and in order to be brought upto its present size, the process of interpolation must have gone on for several centuries. It cannot, therefore, be said that the Mahabharata depicts the state of India at any particular period", R, D, Banerjee : *Prehistoric Ancient and Hindu India,* p. 47.

[2] "The majority of writers or history of India have been obsessed with the idea of an epic age following the later Vedic Age. It is now quite clear that there is no epic age proper in India. The Mahabharata is a story or a hero-laud belonging to the later Vedic period" *Ibid,* p. 47.

others, therefore, consider the naming of any period as the *Epic Age* to be erroneous.

As to the question which of the two epics, the Ramayana and the Mahabharata, was composed first and the time these two epics were composed cannot be said with certainty. When the greater excellence[1] of the poetic expression in the Ramayana compared to that of the Mahabharata is considered, it may be concluded that the Mahabharata was composed first and the Ramayana was composed subsequently at a time when the poetic genius had registered a great improvement. This is also borne out by the fact that the main theme of the Mahabharta has been mentioned in the Vedic Sutras.

The socio-economic condition of the people during the time of the Mahabharata and the Ramayana do not show any remarkable difference. But it is certain that the cultural condition that we come across in the Ramayana is superior to that of the time of the Mahabharata. But in the Advanced History of India, it has been remarked that of the two epics, the Ramayana and the Mahabharata, the Ramayana preceded the Mahabharata.[2] This view is based on the ground that reference to the Ramayana is found in the Mahabharata. It is also argued that while the Mahabharata was known to Asvalayana, Panini etc. there is no reference to the Ramayana.

It may, however, be pointed out that when it is considered that if both the Ramayana and the Mahabharata had been sung as folk songs for long before they were put into writing and in that process there had been interpolations extended over long period, it will be difficult, if not impossible, to decide which of the two epics had been composed first. But from the references to the Mahabharata found in the Vedic literature it will be logical to conclude that the Mahabharata was composed before the Ramayana.

From the historical point of view, however, the Mahabharata is more important than the Ramayana, for its narration is based on historical matters. But the Ramayana, on the other hand, is entirely

---

1 "The verses of the Mahabharata are less polished than those of the Ramayana. There are many tales in both the epics which depict similar economic conditions, and the social usages recorded are identical but the Ramayana betrays a later or more advanced stage of civilisation," Ibid p, 47, also vide *Camb, History of India,* Vol. I', p. 264,

2 "Of he two ancient Sanskrit epics the Ramayana is alluded to in, and was probably completed before, the extant Mahabharata, But while the Mahabharata was known to Asvalayana and Panini, there is no similar early reference to the Ramayana." *Advanced History of India,* p, 92,

"While the Ramayana is solely the production of a poet's brain, the Mahabharata possesses a solid substratum of historical truth. Most of its heroes were real men and women and the framework of the story is historically correct," R, D, Banerjee : *Prehistoric Ancient and Hindu India,* pp. 47-48,

the result of poetic imagination.[1] Many of characters of the Mahabharata were historical persons but that cannot be said with regard to the most of the characters in the Ramayana.

The Mahabharata

The main theme of the Mahabharata is the conflict between the Pandavas and the Kauravas and the eventual defeat of the Kauravas by the Pandavas being assisted by Sreekrishna. In the olden times there was a kingdom called Hastinapura, now included within the Meerut district. Its king was Vichitravirya. Dhritarastra and Pandu were his two sons. As Dhritarastra was born blind the younger brother Pandu succeeded Vichitravirya. Pandu predeceased Dhritarastra leaving Yudhisthir, Bhim, Arjuna, Nakul and Sahadeb—his five sons. They were known as the Pandavas after the name of their father Pandu. On the other hand, Dhritarastra had Duryodhan, Dushasan etc. hundred brothers. The Pandavas married Draupadi, the duaghter of the king of Panchala. Arjuna was also married to Subhadra, the sister of Sreekrishna, the leader of the Mathura-Dwaraka Jàdava federation.

On the death of Pandu, his sons naturally sought to succeed to their father's estate. Dhritarastra, their uncle, divided the kingdom between the Pandavas and his own sons, giving the Khandava forests to the Pandavas and Hastinapura to his own sons. The pious Pandavas were satisfied with what they received and built their capital at Indraprastha near modern Delhi. They also added to their territories by defeating Jarasandha, the king of Magadha, and extended their kingdom on all four sides. Indraprastha acquired a great prestige as a powerful kingdom. They also arranged for *Rajasuya Yajna* in order to acquire the status of Samrat. All this excited the jealously of the Kauravas, that is, the sons of Dhritarastra and they sought to devise a plan for grabbing the kingdom of the Pandavas. On the advice of their maternal uncle, Sakuni, who was a past master in machination the Kauravas, that is, Duryodhan and his brothers invited Yudisthir to the game of dice on stake. In the game which was unfair due to the manipulation of Sakuni, Yudhisthir lost his kingdom and everything that he could call his own including Daupadi, the common wife of the Pandavas. It was also a condition of the game of dice that the party which would be defeated would have to go into exile in the forests for twelve years to be followed by one year's living *in cognito*. The Pandavas did all that was stipulated as the stake in the game which the eldest of the

[1] "The Ramayana is in truth, artificial in both senses, for one cannot believe the tale ; whereas the Mahabharata makes its tale real." *Cambridge History of India*, Vol. I, p. 264.

Padavas, i.e., Yudhisthir, had lost and returned to demand their kingdom. Duryodhan and his brothers refused to return the kingdom of the Pandavas which they acquired and enjoyed for long thirteen years. The Pandavas at last asked for only five villages for five of them but this was also not conceded by the Kauravas. This ultimately led to the Bharata War in the field of Kurukshetra. Visma, Drona, Karna etc. joined the side of the Kauravas while Sreekrishna sided with the Pandavas. He became the charioteer of Arjuna. For eighteen days the war went on unabated and ultimately the Pandavas were victorious. This is the theme of the Mahabharata.

The Ramayana

In the Faizabad district of Oudh in modern Uttarpradesh, Dasaratha, the king of Ikshaku Dynasty, was the ruler. His eldest son was Ramchandra. Ramchandra married Sita or Janaki, daughter of Janaka, king of Videha, who ruled over his kingdom in modern North Bihar. Due to the selfish plan of the step-mother Kaikei Ramchandra had to go to exile for fourteen years. Ramchandra was accompanied by Sita and Lakshman. When in exile they were living in the forest called *Panchabati*. At that time the Dravida King, Ravana of Lanka (Ceylon), kidnapped Sita, resorting to a stratagem. With the help of leader of monkeys—Hanuman of Kishikindhya kingdom—and many other local leaders, Ramchandra with his brother Lakshmana crossed over to Lanka and defeating Ravana rescued Sita. During the period of Ramchandra's exile, Bharata, his step-brother, ruled over Ayodhya as his regent since in the mean time old King Dasaratha had died of the shock of the departure of Ramchndra, Sita, and Lakshmana into exile.

The people of Ayodhya objected to the consecration of Sita on the throne along with Ramchandra as Queen on the ground that she had been a captive at the hands of Ravana. Ramchandra obeyed the desire of the people and eventually forsook Sita.

Historical Importance of the Mahabharata & the Ramayana

Considered from the point of view of history while considerable historical materials can be gathered from the Mahabharata, not much materials are available from the Ramayana. However, from both the epics, particularly from the Mahabharata it has been possible to glean political, social, and economic conditions of the contemporary period of history. From the story of Ramchandra's living on the Godavari and his invasion of Lanka, historians think that these were significant in the Aryan expansion in the South.

Both from the Mahabharata and the Ramayana it appears that kingship was the usual form of government. Ability to rule the kingdom efficiently and ministering to the well-being of the subjects were the criteria for occupying the throne, although kingship was normally hereditary. There are instances of overriding the claims of the eldest son due to inability to rule. The case of Dhritarastra is an instance in point. In tribal states, kings were elected in times of war. Needless to say, the strongest person of the tribe would be elected as king.

The king was theoretically the repository of all powers but in reality the king used to take counsel of the people of his own caste and his ministers. There are references to the royal court or Rajsabha in the Mahabharata but in that age it was nothing more or less than a military advisory council. The capital of the kingdom and the chief towns and cities of the kingdom were protected by walls and moats. The army, in those days, comprised the archers, catapult throwers, charioteers, cavalry and elephants. Provisions were made for payment of allowances to the family of those soldiers who died in battle. In times of war it was customary to form military coalitions. The kings who would be victorious in wars would perform *Rajasuya* or *Asvamedha Yajna* and adopt imperial titles like *Samrat, Ekarat, Rajchakravartin* etc.

In the royal palace there were spacious halls for holding royal court, pleasure halls for games of dice, and also open arenas for fight among beasts. King would go out of the palace in accompaniment of dancing girls, women attendants etc.

In both the Ramayana and Mahabharata we notice the dominance of the Kshatriyas in the political field. The villages enjoyed self-government. In the society the caste system had been solidified and the intermingling and inter-marriage between the four classes of the society were prohibited. The Aryans—the Brahmanas, Kshatriyas and the Vaisyas and the non-Aryans the Sudras were solidified into four water-light compartments of social castes.

In that period a section of the society lived on animal husbandry and hunting. The rest earned their livelihood by agriculture. Villages were set up on all sides of fortresses or protected cities and towns. In times of war the villagers would take shelter within the protected place.

Custom duties had to be paid in fixed places for transportation of goods from one area to another. There were numerous guilds of producers of different kinds of articles. These guilds played very important part in the economic life of the country. They set up the standard of the manufactured goods, protected the members of their respective guilds from exploitations. There were also merchant guilds. The importance of the guilds can be realised from he eagerness of the kings to enlist the support of the guilds. Cheating by using lesser weight and measure was not unknown. The king would arrange for a class of overseers to look after the interests of the consumers by preventing use of shorter weight or measure by sellers.

Revenue could be paid by the produce of the soil or any other commodities. But when any body would be punished by a court to pay a fine, the payment had to be made by copper coins.

Eating of meat, drinking of liquor were in vogue. But the social life as a whole was simple, unostentatious and easy. Showing respect to the elders, obeying the parents, etc. were the normal values of the time. Voluntary exile of Ramchandra in order to redeem the promise of his father, king Dasaratha, was illustrative of the moral attitude of the time. Respect of the women, special place of honour for the mothers of heroes were the specialities of the time. Polygamy was not unknown, but not polyandry. The same woman could have more than one husband. Draupadi, wife of the five Pandavas may be cited as an instance. Women had the liberty of choosing their husbands but the normal practice was marriage by negotiating through parents of both sides.

Worship of Brahma, Vishnu and Maheswara as also worship of Sreekrishna as gods were the main characteristics of the religious life of the time.

The Dharma-Sutras

During the period when the Dharma-Sutras and Samhitas were written the society had undergone further change. The caste system had not only become extremely rigid but had outstripped its proper limits and influenced the legal system. The law of manslaughter shows that the system of wergild was in force but the quantum would vary according to the caste to which the murdered belonged. The crime of murder of a Brahamana could not be expiated by payment of wergild but one thousand cows would be the wergild for the murder of a Kshatriya, one hundred cows for a Vaisya and ten cows for a Sudra. In other crimes as well comparatively light punishment would be meted out to people of higher castes. Existence of mixed castes is borne out by Dharma-Sutra and Ghriya-Sutra. The mixed castes arose out of marriage where the husband belonged a lower caste than the wife (Pratiloma marriage) offspring of a Sudra male and a Brahmana female became *Chandals*.

In this period only the Brahmanas were required to follow the fourfold *asramas,* i.e. *Brahmacharya, Garhasthya, Banaprastha* and *Sannyasa*. The liberty formerly enjoyed by women was drastically reduced during this period. According to Manu women had to be under the control of the father during childhood, of the husband in youth, of the son in old age. From the period of Dharma-Sutras widow remarriage and inheritance to property by women had been prohibited.

The Puranas

In the Puranas the genealogy of the Aryan kings have been elaborately mentioned. There are altogether eighteen Purnas and almost the same number of Upa-Puranas. The Puranas have the following five chapters, namely the *Sarga, Pratisarga, Vamsa, Mannantar* and *Vamsa charita.* The theory that the Puranas represent Kshatriya tradition as distinct from the Brahmana tradition contained in the Vedic texts is regarded as incorrect by the modern historians. The Puranas follow the Vedic religion and take pride in calling themselves as the *fifth Veda.*

A composition or compilation in order that it may be called Purana must contain all the above chapters or divisions. But strangely enough in none of the eighteen Puranas this has been followed. The Puranas, like the Vedas, are regarded as divine revelation by the Hindus. To begin with the Puranas contained only genealogical accounts of the kings but subsequently hymns relating to the worship of Siva, Vishnu and traditions concerning the religious places were included. In this way each of the Puranas had two broad divisions, in the first were recorded the historical traditions and genealogical accounts of the kings and in the second, the narratives and traditional accounts relating to the religious places of the Hindus. Most of the Puranas were reduced to the existing form either during the Gupta period or immediately after that. The Upa-Puranas contain the traditions and accounts of the local gods or goddesses and their worship.

The Puranas contain although in somewhat desultory fashion, the traditions and the genealogical tables of the kings, these have recorded correctly the genealogy of the contemporary kings. But the different Puranas contain contradictory traditions and genealogy of the same kingly dynasty. Yet, the Puranas contain certain important historical materials. The *Matsya Purana* and the *Vishnu Purana* may be mentioned in this regard. The Vishnu Purana contains the genealogy of the Andhra kings and the Matsya Purana contains the genealogy of the Maurya dynasty. Their historical importance is great. The Buddhist and Jaina traditions bear out many of the traditions contained in these Puranas.

CHAPTER FIVE

AGE OF SIXTEEN MAHAJANAPADAS

Sixteen Mahajanapadas

The period from the fall of the kingdom of Videha early in the sixth century B.C. till the rise of the kingdom of Magadha in the middle of the same century is known as the Age of sixteen Mahajanapadas. Reference to the Age of sixteen Mahajanapadas is to be found in the Buddhist Angauttara Nikaya. Reference is also to be found in the Jaina Bhagabati Sutra but the lists of Mahajanapadas in the Buddhist and the Jaina sources differ in respect of certain names. But both the lists contain the names of the comparatively large kingdoms. Dr. Roychaudhuri is, however, of opinion that of the two books Buddhist Angauttara Nikaya and Jaina Bhagabati Sutra the former was written at a time nearer to the Age of Sixteen Mahajanapadas than the latter. He, therefore, thinks that the list of the sixteen Mahajanapadas given by the Buddhist Angauttara Nikaya is more reliable. The names given by the Buddhist source are: (1) Kasi, (2) Kosala, (3) Anga, (4) Magadha, (5) Vriji or Vajji, (6) Malla or Malava, (7) Chedi, (8) Vamsa or Vatsya, (9) Kuru, (10) Panchala, (11) Matsya, (12) Surasena, (13) Asmaka, (14) Avanti, (15) Gandhara, and (16) Kamboja.

Kasi

In the Age of the sixteen Mahajanapadas the kingdom of Kasi was first to rise into prominence. Its capital was Baranasi which was more prosperous than the capitals of other kingdoms. Dr. H. C. Roychaudhuri is of opinion that the kingdom of Kasi reduced the kingdom of Videha and not only that the kings of Kasi dreamed of conquering whole of Jambudwipa, that is, India. The Buddhist and Jaina texts also testify to the power and greatness of the kingdom of Kasi. Kings of Kasi attacked the kingdom of Kosala more than once. King Manoj of Kasi is said to have conqured Kosala, Anga and Magadha. The Jatakas testify to this achievement of King Manoj. The power and prosperity of Kasi particularly its capital Baranasi roused the jealousy of the neighbouring kingdoms. Once as many as seven of the neighbouring kingdoms jointly besieged the kingdom of Kasi.[1] The power, prestige and predominance of the kingdom of Kasi did not last long.

[1] "Benares in the respect resembled ancient Babylon and medieval Rome, being the coveted prize of its more warlike but less civilised neighbours." Roychoudhuri : *Political History of Ancient India*, p. 98.

Kosala

The kingdom of Kosala comprised Keshputra and Kapilavastu regions and was surrounded by the rivers Gomati, Sarpika and Sadanira and the Nepal hills. In the middle of the sixth century B.C. the small kingdom of Kapilavastu was compelled to accept the suzerainty of Kosala. Ajodhya, Saketa, Sravasti etc. were very prosperous cities of the kingdom of Kosala and showed how great was the kingdom of Kosala. The kings of Kosala belonged to the Ikshaku dynasty. Sravasti was the capital of Kosala.

Anga

The kingdom of Anga was situated in the west of the Rajmahal mountain range and east of Magadha. This kingdom acquired great power and prestige for a time and conquered a number of neighbouring countries. This is borne out by the Aiteriya Brahman. The capital of Anga was Champa which was on the confluence of the rivers, the Ganges and the Champa (modern Chandan). Anga was one of the six great kingdoms of India till the demise of Gautama Buddha. The capital of Anga—Champa, was particularly noted for the great volume of trade and commerce it had with other countries as also for its great prosperity. Many a businessman would sail to the Suvarnabhumi for commercial purposes from Champa. It was after the name of Champa, the capital of Anga, that the Hindu colony of Annam in Indo-China was named Champa.

Magadha

The kingdom of Magadha in the Age of sixteen Mahajanapadas comprised the modern districts of Patna and Gaya in Bihar. Magadha was encircled by the rivers, the son and the Ganges. Giribraja was the original capital of Magadha. Later, however, its new capital was set up at Pataliputra. Of the different dynasties that ruled over Magaddha the Sishunaga dynasty was the most noteworthy. At the time of Gautama Buddha Bimbisara was the King of Magadha He belonged to Haryanka dynasty.

Vriji or Vajji

The kingdom of Vriji or Vajji extended from the north of the Ganges to the Nepal Hills. It was a federation of eight tribal principalities. Among these tribal principalities Videha, Licchavi, Yatrika and Vriji or Vajji were particularly important. The capital of Vriji was Vaisali.

Malava or Malla

The kingdom of Malla or Malava was divided into two parts, each having its own capital. Pava was the capital of one and Kushinara was that of the other. It was at Kushinara that Gautama Buddha breathed his last. Wilson, Cunningham and other archaeologists are of opinion that modern village called Kasai was the site of Kushinara or Kushinagara. Pava was situated ten miles away from Kushinagara towards the east. Malla or Malava was originally a kingship but later it adopted republican form of government. When Alexander invaded India Malava or Malla was a republic.

Chedi

Chedi kingdom was near the Jumna. Its capital was Shuktimati. Reference to the inhabitants of Chedi are to be found in the Rig-Veda. The kingdom of Chedi was on close friendly terms with the kingdoms of Kasi and Matsya. There was a highway connecting Chedi with Benaras. But journey along this road was very unsafe in those days.

Vamsa or Vatsya

The kingdom of Vamsa or Vatsya was on the south of the Ganges and its capital was Kausambi. Many historians are of opinion that the kings of Vamsa or Vatsya belonged to the royal dynasty of Kasi. But in *Swapna Vasabadatta*, a work of Bhasa, King Udayan of Kausambi is described as a scion of the royal dynasty called Bharatakul. Udayana, Gautama Buddha, Pradyot, King of Avanti and Bimbisara and Ajatasatru of Magadha were contemporaries.

Kuru

The kings of Kuru according to Pali texts belonged to *Yudhisthira Gotra*.[1] The capital of the kingdom was Indrapath or Indraprashtha. It was a vast city extending over seven *Yojana*. According to Pali texts the scions of Yudhisthira ruled over Kuru in the sixth century B.C. In the Buddhist Jataka reference is there of Dhananjay Kauravya, Suttasoma etc. as the kings of Kuru. In any case the real identity of the royal dynasty of Kuru cannot be ascertained properly.

Panchala

The kingdom of Panchala comprised parts of the Central Indian Duab and Rohilkhand. The northern bank of the river Bhagirath was called *Uttar Panchal* or North Panchal and the southern bank was known as *Dakshin Panchal* or South Panchal. The king of Kuru attempted to occupy North Panchal and this led to a war

---

[1] "The reigning dynasty according to Pali texts belonged to the *Yudhisthilas Gotta*, that is the family of Yudhisthira", Roychaudhuri, *Political History of Ancient India*, p, 153.

between the kingdoms of Panchal and Kuru. The capital of North Panchal was Ahichhatra and that of South Panchal was Kampilya.

Matsya

The ancient kingdom of Matsya comprised the area in the middle of the forests on the banks of the rivers Chambal and Saraswati, covered by modern Jaipur. For a time, Matsya was conquered by the king of Chedi after which again, it became a part of the Magadhan Empire. Asokan inscriptions have been discovered in the middle of the Matsya kingdom. The capital of Matsya was Viratnagara.

Surasena

The kingdom of Surasena was situated on the bank of the river Jumna and its capital was Mathura. The kingdom of *Sourasenoi* referred to by the Greeks has been identified with the kingdom of Suraseana. The Jadu or the Jadavas used to rule over this kingdom.

Asmaka

On the bank of the river Godavari was situated the kingdom of Asmaka with its capital at Potali, Potan or Podan. In the Vayu Purana, the kings of Asmaka were mentioned as have been scions of the Ikshaku clan. In the Asmaka Jataka there is mention of the supremacy of the kingdom of Kashi on the Asmaka kingdom for a time.

Avanti

The kingdom of Avanti included Ujjain and a part of the Narmada valley. The kingdom was divided into two parts by the Vindhyas, each of which had a capital of its own. The upper part, that is, the northern part had its capital at Ujjain or Ujjaini and its most important river was Sipra. The capital of the southern part was Mahiswati or Mahisamati and its main river was Narmada. In the Puranas the kings of Avanti are referred to as belonging to the Jadu dynasty.

Gandhara

The Kashmir valley and Taxila formed the kingdom of Gandhara. In the middle of the sixth century B.C. Pukkasati was the king of the Gandhara kingdom. He sent an emmissary to the court of Bimbisara, king of Magadha. He had defeated Pradyut, king of Avanti but towards the end of the sixth century B.C. his kingdom was occupied by the Emperor of Persia. Reference to the conquest of Gandhara by the Persian Emperor Darius is to be found in the Behestan incription. The capital of Gandhara was Taxila, modern Rawalpindi.

Kamboj

In north-west India, not far from the kingdom of Gandhara was situated the kingdom of Kamboj. Its capital was Rajpur. In the post-Vedic period Kamboj grew into a very important centre of the study of Brahmanical religion. There was friendly relations between the kingdom of Kamboj and Gandhra. Several centuries afterwards, the Chinese traveller Hiuen Tsang referred to the cordial relations between these two kingdoms. It may be mentioned here that the manners and customs of Kambojas were far different from the Aryans of other parts of India. There was a remarkable political development in the kingdom of Kamboj. Originally it was a kingship but later on the administration of the country was carried on by a corporate body comprising the peasants, businessmen, soldiers etc.

Apart from the Mahajanapadas mentioned above which were ruled over by kings, there were also tribal states ruled by tribal Chiefs in full independence. Reference to the Sakyas of Kapilavastu may be made in this connection. The Moriyas or the Mauryas of Pippalivana, the Kolias of Ramgram were also independent tribal Chiefs. Reference to the Vaggas, a similarly independent tribe, is to be found in Aiteriya Brahman, Mahabharata and Harivamsa. These tribes were originally under kingship but later on they passed under Aristocracy or Republican form of government. Megasthenes also referred to this change in the political system of the above tribes.

The reason for the decay of kingship and rise of Aristocratic or Oligarchic and republican forms of government was almost similar to that which had led to the decay of monarchical form of government in ancient Greece or Rome. The lack of capable successors of kings led to lack of efficiency in rule but repression of the subjects remaining unchanged led to the downfall of kingship. Having lived under kingship for long years, the people did not lose initiative nor did they lose the power of self-assertion. This was certainly due to political liberty enjoyed by the people under kingship. Political liberty helped the growth of mental and moral liberty which was exemplified in the rise of Mahavira and Buddha from autonomous tribal states.

The Age of the Sixteen Mahajanapadas was not very long. In the fifth century B.C. the Mahajanapadas were deeply engrossed in mutual warfare and in the process the smaller ones were occupied by the larger ones, eventually giving to a vast empire.

Of the sixteen kingdoms that of Kasi was first to fall. Kasi and Kosala were mutually at war for long and at the initial stage although Kasi fared well but ultimately Kosala became victorious. After Kosala, Magadha rose into prominence. King Bimbisara of Magadha was a contemporary of the king Mahakosala of Kosala. It was Magadha which embarked on a career of imperial conquests and ultimately grew into a vast empire.

Palitical, Social, Economic and Religious conditions during the period of the Sixteen Mahajanapadas

That the whole of India was not covered by the Sixteen Mahajanapadas is evident from the names of the kingdoms. Major portion of southern India remained separate from the Sixteen Mahajanapadas. We have scanty knowledge about the political social, economic and religious life of the people of the Sixteen Mahajanapada period. But from the Ramayana, the Mahabharata, the Puranas, Jatakas, the Buddhist and the Jaina texts, some information is, however, available. A general view of the different aspects of the life at that period can be taken on the basis of the above sources.

POLITICAL

During the period of the Sixteen Mahajanapadas, the political administration in different parts of India varied widely. The names of the heads of states or administration also necessarily varied. These were King, Samrat, Virat, Swarat etc. The person who ascended the throne after holding *Rajasuya Yajna* was called King. He might assume the title of Emperor by performing *Rajasuya Yajna* again. The king who would receive Indra's unction would assume the title of *Virat*. Every king would try to conquer territories in the neighbourhood and if he would succeed, he would become an *Ekarat*. Kingship in the Age of the Sixteen Mahajanapada was generally hereditary, but in certain cases the king used to be elected by the people. A king could take as many as four wives. The chief queen was called *Rajamahishi*.

Theoretically and legally the power of the king was unlimited. But in practice the king had to carry on administration with the advice of the Brahmanas, the Ministers, the Rajasabha and the villagers. The king had to do obeisance to the Brahmanas in the open Court by descending from the throne. It may be mentioned that the Brahmanas of that time were the repositories of culure and education and were held in highest esteem.

The kings were Kshatriyas by caste but their ministers were Brahmanas. In all matters of administration the opinion of the Ministers was consulted. *Samiti* that is, the Assembly of the people had also to be consulted. Politically speaking the opinion of the Assembly was of great importance. There are instances where a despotic rulers had to abdicate according to wishes of the Assembly.

In extreme cases the king could be sentenced to death by the Assembly of the people.

Besides kingship, there were also republican states at that time. The Lichhavi, the Vriji, Bhoga, Kaurava, Ikshaku etc. were republican states.

SOCIAL

With the spread of the Aryans all over India the social system naturally was reorganised. But there was no uniformity in social customs and manners all over India. The customs and manners of the people of the Gangetic valley were not acceptable to the people of the south, nor even in the other parts of northern India. In the Gangetic valley, the women had practically no liberty, but in other parts of India the women enjoyed enough liberty in social life and were held in high esteem.

In north-west India the rite of *Sati,* that is, burning of the widow in the funeral pyre of the deceased husband was prevalent but was not followed in the Gangetic valley except in very rare cases. In the Vedic times it was permissible for a male to take more than one wife and this practice was followed in some areas during the Epic age but during the period of the Sixteen Mahajanapadas the practice was looked down upon. *Svayambara,* that is choosing the husband by the girl herself, was prevalent during the Sixteen Mahajanapada period. Although in certain cases the women were not allowed to go out of the family yet speaking generally the women enjoyed fullest liberty.

As the society was largely agricultural, most of the people lived in villages. Only the king, the Ministers, the members of the royal Court, the officers of the state used to live in the well protected and walled up city which was the capital of the country. The walled capital had observation towers at places. These were defensive measures. Within the city there were wide roads, pleasure halls where game of dice used to be played, pleasure garden, hall of justice, dancing hall etc. The royal palace was made of wood. The royal princess and the daughters of high officials used to play the game of *Kunduk* that is foot-ball. Young men liked to play *Kunduk* and *vita,* that is foot-ball and hocky. Hunting, game of dice, sword play, listening to tales of warfare and of heroes were the prevalent pastimes.

The dress of the males had three parts, namely, *Abharan,* that is, cloth to cover the body from waist downwards, *Orna,* that is a piece cloth to cover the upper part of the body and *Shirabharan,* that is, the head dress. The dress of the females consisted of two parts, the lower garment and the garment for the upper part of the body. Men used to grow beard and use certain types of ornaments. Women, particularly of the higher classes would use neck-chain, bangles, girdles, nose-studs etc. Use of umbrella and shoes was known at that time.

The caste system was prevalent and was gradually hardening into extreme conservatism, but during the period of the Sixteen Mahajanapadas the caste division did not give rise to any class animosity. Although marriage within one's own caste was generally preferred, yet there was no bar to inter-caste marriages. But towards the end of the period inter-caste marriage was strictly prohibited. The authority of the Brahmanas during this period was turning towards autocratic control over the society.

Economic

The basis of the economic life of the period was agriculture. One-tenth of the produce of the soil had to be paid as land revenue. The agricultural land was divided into small plots and for the purpose of irrigation, cultivation and conservation of water co-operative system was followed. Famine was not altogether uhknown but it was of very rare occurrence.

Besides agriculture, animal husbandry was an important source of economic life. Arts and industries like ivory work, mural painting, stone-carving etc. were highly developed at that time. Business was carried on both within and without the country. Bharuch, Tamralipti, Sopara etc. were the important ports of the time through which water-borne trade with Burma, Ceylon, Malaya, Babylonia etc. was carried on. Silk, gold, embroidered cloth were the principal merchandise. There are proofs of co-operative system in the trade and commerce of the period. The medium of exchange was copper and silver *Karshapana*. The silver *Karshapana* was also known as *Dharan*. A silver *Karshapana* was one-tenth in value of the Vedic *Niska*.

Religious

In religion there was a great change during that period. Worship of new gods and goddesses as also the cult of Devotion prevailed during the period. Animal sacrifice was made to some gods and goddesses but there was a strong feeling against the practice. Some religious-minded people also preached against animal sacrifice as a part of religion. The most important characteristic of the religious life of the time was the belief in *Karmafal* and rebirth. The worship of Brahma, Vishnu and Mahesvar was taking shape during this period. The Vedic religion had by that time become observance of certain rituals which were practically meaningless to the people. The Brahmanas were exercising a tremendous control over the social and religious life of the people of the time. The complexities of the Vedic religion and the autocratic control of the priestly class, that is, the Brahmanas, made thoughtful people to seek for a simpler, intelligible religion.

CHAPTER SIX

THE POST-VEDIC RELIGIOUS AND POLITICAL EVOLUTION

Reaction against Vedic Brahmanism

Towards the end of the Vedic Age, particularly when the Vedic Brahmanas were being written, the Vedic Brahmanism became meaningless observance of a series of religious rites and performances which were both complex and unintelligible to the common people. Religious formalities were prized above devotion, honesty, truth and real faith. The complexities of religious observances, not within the comprehension of the common people, naturally made the priestly class, that is, the Brahmanas the sole trustees of common man's religion. It was believed that if the priests would perform religious rites on behalf of a person or a family it would be free from sins, and prosperity would follow. This common belief naturally gave the priests an autocratic control over the society. This is also borne out in the Vedic Brahmanas.

While submission to the Brahmanas, performance of *Yajna* through the priests, animal sacrifice etc. were considered to be the best method of following religion, hatred towards the lower classes of the society was not considered to be wrong. In fact, violence to life, hatred towards men went on side by side with the performance of elaborate religious rites and *Yajnas*. But man's inherent sense of truth and justice, religion and humanity naturally revolted against prevalent Brahmanism. Animal sacrifice and mere formalities of religious rites and holding of *Yajnas* were not regarded by the thoughtful people to be the correct way to attain the knowledge about God, i.e. Brahma. The independence of thought that the sages had roused in the Upanishads became the basis of the protest against the prevalent Brahmanical religion. As the Renaissance in Europe had initiated independence of thought which led to the protest against the immorality, corruption and the worldliness of the Catholic priests and the Church, similarly the independence of thought initiated by the Upanishads and the Aranyakas led to the rise of protestant religions called Jainism and Buddhism. Both Jainism and Buddhism have much in common and both were revolts, not against Hinduism itself, but against diverse polytheism and in as arrogant claims of the Brahmanas. The time was propitious in as much as the Vedic religion had lost its appeal with the masses.

The sixth century B.C. was particularly noted for the rise of a number of new and simpler religions, but Jainism and Buddhism were the most important two. The leadership of these two important protestant religions, namely, Jainism and Buddhism, was not in the hands of the priestly class but in those of the Kshatriyas. The *Sramanas* and the *Parivrajakas* of the time had helped in the preparation of the ground for new religions by preaching against animal sacrifice and the prevalent worldliness.

Jainism and Buddhism are, some times, called anti-Vedic religions, but it will be a mistake to regard them so. Both these had originated from the philosophical thoughts contained in the Upanishads. It will, therefore, be correct to regard both Jainism and Buddhism as continuation of the Vedic religion although in course of time the religious ideals, worship and rituals of these two religions became inconsistent with Vedic philosophy and worship.[1]

Dr. Smith is, however, of opinion that Mahavira and Gautama were of Mongolian origin like the Tibetans, Gurkhas, Bhutiyas etc. As there were divergence between the Hindu and the Mongolian religions, Mahavira and Gautam ventured to protest against the Vedic Brahmanical religion. But the opinion of Smith has been rejected by the modern historians because both Jainism and Buddhism had originated from the philosophy contained in the Upanishads.

Mahavira Vardhamana

Mahavira Vardhamana to whom Jainism owes its establishment as a religion probably lived from 540 to 468 B.C. According to Jaina tradition there were altogether twenty-four *Tirthankaras* that is, ford-makers or prophets, Mahavira being the twenty-fourth. The religious sect which came to be known as Jainism after the name of Mahavira Jina seems to have been in existence from some time before the advent of Mahavira. The twenty-third *Tirthankar* Parsvanath was a historical person and was the real founder of the sect which later came to be known as Jaina. As Mahavira had conquered human passions he was called *Jina* i.e. Conquerer, and from the epithet Jina the religion came to be known as Jainism.

Mahavira whose name was originally Vardhamana, was the son of Siddhartha the tribal Chief of Kundapura. His mother was Trisala. Siddhartha was a Kshatriya by caste and Trisala was connected by blood relationship with the royal dynasties of Magadha and

[1] "It would be a mistake to regard the rise of Jainism and Buddhism as a breach with the Vedic view of life, although in course of time these religions developed certain ideals and rituals inconsistent with Vedic philosophy and worship." Sinah & Banerjee, p. 50.

Vaisali. Although the date of the birth of Mahavira is not known for certain, yet it is doubtless that he was a senior contemporary of Gautama Buddha.

Our knowledge about the early life of Mahavira is meagre. From the Svetambara Jaina traditions it is known that he married a princess named Yasoda and having lived the life of a householder till the age of thirty, he renounced the world. He spent six years as a *Digambar* i.e. naked mendicant given to extreme austerity and penance but could not attain Divine knowledge. He then became a disciple of Gossala Mankhaliputta and spent long six years with him in rigid practice of penance but with no effect. After which he started meditation independently on the bank of the river Rijupalika in eastern India. After one year, that is, in the thirteen year of his renouncing the world he obtained Supreme Knowledge or *Kaivalya* and became a *Kevalin* that is, he became omniscient and conquerer of passions. He came to be variously known as *Jina* that is, conquerer of passions, *Nirgrantha,* that is, one who is free from bondage of the world. He preached Jainism for long thirty years in Magadha, Mithila, Anga, Kosala etc. and died at the age of seventy two in Pawapuri. It is said that he was very closely known to Bimbisara.

It has already been mentioned that the real founder of Jainism was Parsvanath. He had left four tenets namely, *non-violence, non-lying, non-stealing and non-attachment.* Mahavira added *continence* to the above four tenets. Mahavira carried the tenet of non-attachment to the extreme and recommended giving up everything, even clothes. Those who followed this recommendation came to be known as *Nirgranthas* or *Digambar* Jainas. In the third century B.C. there arose among the Jainas a sect known as the *Svetambara* who wore cloth. Later on the Digambar Jains also began using cloth although the name of the sect remained *Digambar* as before.

The highest ideal before the Jainas is to attain *Siddhasila* i.e. blissful abode or *Nirvana* which meant freedom of the soul from rebirth and its attendant sorrows and miseries. According to Jainism one has to practice three-fold virtues for attaining Nirvana. These are good behaviour, honest work and real wisdom.

The Jainas while believe in rebirth of the soul, do not believe in the divine character of the Vedas. Violence to life in any form is strictly prohibited in Jainism. They extend the principle of non-violence to stones, metals, trees etc. since they believe that these also have life. The Jainas do not believe in the existence of God, to them a perfect human soul is divinity. Accordnig to them good work, austere life and continence can lead to improvement of the soul and when the soul become perfect by following all that Jainism enjoins, the soul will attain *Nirvana,* which is their ideal.

From the Jaina traditions it is learnt that the teachings of

Mahavira had been preserved in fourteen *Purvas* that is volumes. In the fourth century B.C. a terrible famine stalked the whole of south Bihar. A large number of the Jainas left for Mysore under the leadership of Bhadrabahu. The fourteen Purvas must have been lost during this exodus. Those who remained in Bihar summoned a religious convention at Pataliputra in order to re-introduce Jainism in Bihar where it was almost non-existent then. The decisions arrived at the meeting were put in twelve volumes and are known as *Angas*. In the fifth or the sixth century A.D. another religious convention was summoned at Gujarat where the entire Jaina religious principles and tenets were compiled under the heads *Anga, Upanga, Mula* and *Sutra*.

Jainism at first was limited to south Bihar only but gradually it spread to west and south India. The Maurya Emperor Chandragupta became a Jaina and in old age left for Sravana Belgola where he died of fasting and penance. This we have from the Jaina literature *Rajbalikathe*. Bhadrabahu's going to Mysore with a large number of Jainas and Chandragupta Maurya's leaving for Mysore in the old age are good grounds for the belief that Jainism also had spread to south India by the fourth century B.C.

Gautama Buddha & Buddhism

Siddhartha, Gautama or Sakyamuni, who was known as Buddha after his attainment of Enlightenment probably lived between 560 and 480 B.C. He was the son of Suddhodan, Chief of Kshatriya caste who ruled in Kapilavastu in the foothills of the Himalayas on Nepal border. Traditionally he was said to have been born in Lumbini Park while his mother Mayadevi was on her way to her father's house. The discovery of Ashoka's Pillar in the Lumbini Park with the inscription 'Here was born Buddha, Sankyamuni' leaves no doubt in the truth of the traditional belief about Gatama's birth place. Mayadevi died at the time of the birth of the child and was reared up by his aunt and step-mother Gautami after whose name he was called Gautama. Though born in a royal family Gautama did not find pleasure in the princely pursuits of hunting, warfare, riding etc. He became somewhat introvert in nature. At the age of sixteen he was married to a princess variously known as Gopa, Bimba, Yasodhara, Subhadraka etc. A few years were passed by him in the pleasures of the royal palace. But human sorrow, disease and death made him disconsolate. He felt increasingly disturbed in mind. All the pleasures of the palace life could not bring any peace of mind for him. He became busy in the thought of finding way to salvation of human soul. At the age of twenty-nine a son was born to him. He was christened Rahul. The birth of the son made him feel that he was being drawn more into worldly life. Soon after, he renounced the world leaving wife, child and all the pleasures of the royal palace.

As a recluse he tried many of the disciplines and doctrines current at that time, followed the precepts of many a Sannyains, exercised every conceivable austerity and penance but failed to attain the truth he was seeking after. He also travelled far and wide and had been to Uruvilla and Rajagriha. At Uruvilla near Gaya Gautama practised severest of penances which reduced his body to all bone and skin. But Truth still eluded him. He then took bath in the Niranjana river, modern Nilajan or Lilajan and sat under a pipal tree in fresh meditation. Here he ultimately received what he believed to be the Truths of life and death. The place where he attained the Truth came to be known as Bodhgaya and the tree under which he had sat in meditation is known as Bodhi tree. After getting the Englightenment he came to be known as Buddha. He then gave his first sermon in the Deer Park near Sarnath and initiated five disciples. For next forty-five years he peached his religion in Bihar and Ayodhya and set up Buddhist Samgha. In the course of his peaching he came into touch with Bimbisara, king of Magadha and Presenjit, king of Kosala. He is said to have converted Bimbisara into Buddhism. At the age of eighty he breathed his last at Kushinara or Kushinagara, modern Kasiari. Demise of Buddha is called *Mahaparinirvana* and it is supposed to have taken place at 486 B. C. Some put the date at 480 B. C. According to Sinhalese Buddhist texts, Buddha's Parinirvana is placed in the year 544 B. C.

Essence of the teaching of Buddha is based on four great truths: the Truth of Pain, that is, human beings are subject to sorrow, disease and death; Truth of the Origin of Pain, that is, every pain has its cause and it is greed or desire; Truth of the End of Pain, that is, pain must be ended by elimination of desire, Truth of the Elimination of Desire, that is, the path to be followed for the elimination of desire. Buddha, therefore, recommended the Noble Eightfold Path. Buddha was neither in favour of extreme austerity in religion nor extreme enjoyment of worldly life. His was a *Middle Path* which could be followed by the householders. His Noble Eightfold Path was a middle path. The eight virtues recommended by Buddha in his Eightfold Path are: Right Speech, Right Conduct, Right Views, Right Aspirations, Right Efforts, Right Mindfulness, Right Contemplation and Right Livelihood. The Noble Eightfold Path, if followed would 'open the eyes, bestow understanding, lead to peace of mind, to higher wisdom, to full enlightenment, to Nirvana'. Nirvana was extinguishment of cravings and of desires and the consequent end of suffering. On the eve of his death Buddha in his last exhortation to his disciples pointed out that decay was inherent in things and one has to work for salvation with diligence. Working for salvation requires observance of moralities such as non-violence, continence, non-lying, non-stealing and abandonment of luxury, slander, hankering for wealth, animal sacrifice and similar other practices. Other requisities for salvation are *Samadhi*, i.e. deep concentration, which will lead to *Prajna* i.e. insight which in its turn will lead to *Sambodhi*, i.e. Enlightenment and *Nirvana*. Buddhism does not recognise the existence of God and other gods and goddesses. The Divine character of the Vedas is also not recognised by Buddhism. Like the Jainas, the Buddhists do not believe in caste system. Gautama Buddha established a *Samgha* with all his disciples. Gradually Samgha became an inseparable part of Buddhism.

Buddha did not reduce the principles of his religion to writing. He had exhorted his disciples verbally in Pali language. After his death his disciples summoned a Buddhist Council at Rajagriha and divided Buddha's teachings into three *Pitakas* i.e. Baskets, and reduced them to writing. The Three Pitakas were *Sutra Pitaka* wherein Buddha's sermons and activities were compiled. In *Benoya Pitaka* the rules of conduct to be followed by the Buddhist monks and nuns were written down. In *Abhidhamma Pitaka* the philosophy of Buddhism was put into writing.

In later times there arose difference of opinion about the sermons of Buddha to resolve which three more Buddhist Councils were convened. The Second Council was held at Vaisali after almost a hundred years from the death of Buddha. The third Council was held at Pataliputra during the reign of Asoka and the fourth and the last Council was held at Kashmir or Jullundar which was called by Kushana king Kanishka.

Buddhism, Jainism & Hinduism compared

Both Jainism and Buddhism are protestant Hinduism as both had their origin in the philosophical speculations of the Upanishads. While there are certain things in common between Jainism and Buddhism they have differences also. Both Jainism and Buddhism do not believe in the existence of God, the ultimate aim of both is attainment of *Nirvana* or *Moksha*. Both have non-violence as the basic principle. Both believe in *Karma* i.e. retribution of the work done and rebirth of the soul. Both do not believe in the divine character of the Vedas.

Despite the above smilarities, there are differences between them. While Buddhism can be followed by householders, Jainism which lays too much stress on austerity, penance etc is fit to be followed by recluses. Buddhism is more or less pragmatic whereas Jainism is extremely idealistic. The doctrine of *Ahimsa* i.e. non-violence is carried too far in Jainism and stones, metals etc. are also believed to have life by the Jainas.

The Buddhists do not recognise any relation with Hinduism but the Jainas have adopted worship of Lakshmi, Ganesh etc. of the Hindu gods and goddesses. *Samgha* is an inseparable part of Buddhist organisation but the Jainas have no *Samgha*.

Ostensibly, Buddhism and Jainism are at variance with Hinduism no doubt, yet there are certain similarities between the three. All the three believe in *Karma* and rebirth. Further, non-violence is not the sole characteristic of Jainism and Buddhism. Non-violence is also a recognised and highly prized tenet of the Hindus. The Hindus regard Buddha as an *Avatar* i.e. incarnation of God. It may, however, be mentioned here that similarity between the Hindus and the Jainas is much greater by the way that gods and goddesses like Lakshmi, Ganesh etc. are common to both.

Dissimilarity between Hinduism, Buddhism and Jainism is no less. While the Hindus believe in the existence of God, neither Buddhism nor Jainism believes in the exsistence of God. The Hindus believe in caste-system but not the Buddhists nor the Jainas.

The Jaina & Buddhist Religious Organisations

Although *Samgha* is not an indispensable part of the Jaina religious organisation yet, the Jainas have innumerble monasteries. Jainism is essentially a religion of the people who have forsaken the world, for, it was not possible to follow the tenets of the Jaina religion by the householders. As such there had to be *maths, viharas* and *sangharams* that is, monasteries of various kinds for the Jainas. The Jainas had to follow *Chaturjama* i.e. four kinds of self-control, such as non-violence, truth, non-stealing and non-attachment. Mahavira had added the vow of continence to these four-fold self-control. These five principles had to strictly followed by the Jaina monks and nuns in their speech, work and behaviour.

In the Buddhist religious organisation *Samgha* is an indispensable organ. The Buddhist recluses who renounced the world would live in Buddhist Samghas. But those who lived in the *Samghas* had to follow certain rules of conduct. At first they had to shave off their hair and take initiation from the *Guru,* wear saffron coloured dress and show greatest self-control in speech, behaviour and activities. If they would satisfy their superiors in the hierarchy of the Buddhist monks they would be called *Vikshus* or *Vikshunis* that is, monks or nuns. It was obligatory for the *Vikshus* and *Vikshunis* to live in *Samgha* or monastery. They could receive food and drink, dress and medicines from their disciples among the house holders. The kings would also supply the daily requirements of the Buddhist monks and nuns within their respective kingdoms.

Strict discipline of conduct had to be observed within the *Samgha* or monastery. Twice everymonth, the monks would meet to judge the cases of transgressions on the part of the monks or nuns. The punishment would depend on the nature of the offence of the monk whose case would be adjudicated by the general body of the monks. In administration of the Samgha democratic principles had to be strictly followed and decision had to be taken after consulting the entire body of the monks. To begin with there was no provision for the entry of nuns in *Samgha*. Later, however, the nuns were also admitted to *Samghas*. With spread of Buddhism all over India, a huge number of *Samghas, Viharas* and *Chaityas* were built.

Jaina & Buddhist Arts

From the ancient times till the rise of the Muslim State in India art and architecture in different parts of India had developed under the influence of Buddhism. In sculpture and paintings also the influence of Buddhism was noticeable. In Bodhgaya, Sanchi, Bharut, Sarnath, Amaravati and many other places excellent proofs of the Buddhist art, architecture and sculpture still exist. Speciality of the Buddhist architecture is to be seen in monasteries, stupas, railings round the stupas, gates of monasteries and stupas etc. The Sanchi Stupa, its railing and the gate are still in existence as best specimens of Buddhist art and architecture. The speciality of the Buddhist sculpture is that ornamenal work on the walls of the stupas, railings, gates depict the events and incidents of the life of Buddha as well as the stories of the *Jatakas*. Gandhara, Amaravati, Mathura etc. were specially noted for Buddhist sculpture depicted in life-like statues of Buddha. In the sculpture at Gandhara a mixture of the Graeco-Roman-Buddhist schools can be seen.

In the Buddhist *Sutra-Sahitya* description of cities of similar architectural features lead many to think that in those cities the Buddhist architectural methods were followed. In the Buddhist architecture use of stone, bricks and wood were made according to climatic conditions of different places. In *Milindapanho* and Megasthenes' description, references to the influence of the Buddhist architecture on the buildings and palaces are found. In the description left by the Chinese travellers reference to the wooden *Chaitya* of 400 feet in height made by Kanishka at Peshwar is found. Caves cut out of standing rocks is another speciality of the Buddhist architecture. The caves in Barabar hills and in the Nagarjun Mountains may be referred to in this connection. Making of stone pillars with animal capitals had been another noteworthy characteristic of the Buddhist sculpture. Even after hundreds of years these pillar force our admiration.

The Buddhist art had also expressed itself in different kinds of paintings. The pleasure Hall of king Prasenjit was beautifully decorated by wall paintings. This we have from the *Benoy Pitaka.* Buddhist art of painting was of three different kinds, such as, *Lepya Chitra, Lekhya Chitra* and *Dhuli Chitra.*

Stupas, Maths and *Viharas* were also constructed under the influence of Jaina religion. But as Jainism did not receive the royal patronage as did Buddhism, the Jaina art and architecture did not develop to the extent that the Buddhist art and architecture did. There are, however, some specimens of Jaina art, architecture and sculpture in the caves of Udaigiri and Khandagiri in Orissa, Ellora Jaina temple, Jaina temples at Junagar and at Mount Abu. In painting on paper, the Jainas were the pioneers in India.

It may be mentioned here that the commercial and cultural relations that subsisted between India and Afghanistan, Central-Asia, China, Indo-China, Java, Sumatra and the Malayan archipelago in ancient times led to the spread of the Indian, particularly the Buddhist art and architecture as also sculpture in these regions. Archaeological excavations in Kashgar, Khotan, Kucha, Turfan, Yarkhand etc. in Central Asia has brought to light many Indian temples, images of gods and goddesses and mural paintings of Indian origin. These were particularly of Buddhist origin. The *Stupas, Viharas* etc. in these areas were also constructed in imitation of the Buddhist architecture. The Gomati Vihara at Khotan was the finest specimen of Buddhist Vihara in Central Asia. Buddhist *Stupas.* and *Maths* were also constructed in China, Tibet, Ceylon, Indo-China and Sumatra. The Buddhist sages Kashyapa Matanga and Dharmaratna were invited by China to preach Buddhism there. A great *Vihara* named *Sveta Asva Vihara* was constructed for them. The Buddhist temple and the images of Buddha at Nanking were built after the Indian Buddhist architecture. In Tonkin as many as twenty Buddhist Biharas were constructed.

In Ceylon Asoka had sent Mahendra, his son according to some, and his brother according to others, for preaching Buddism, through which was spread the Buddhist art and architecture there. In Tibet, Burma, Sumatra, Java, Borneo etc. temples and images made in imitation of the Indian art and architecture are to be seen even now.

Importance of Jainism & Buddhism in the Indian History

The simple and easy life which have been the basic character of the Indian society was particularly stressed by the Jaina and the Buddhist preachers. Formation of moral character, peace, charity and brotherhood were the essence of both the Jaina and Buddhist religions. In place of extreme conservatism of caste-system, most complex system of Vedic religion both Jainism and Buddhism had preached casteless, simple and most human type of religions. Both Mahavira and Buddha had placed all men on the same footing of equality. True that the Buddhism had received greater patronage from the kings and emperors than Jainism did, yet from the point of view of basic truth and social ideal, both these religions had preached most liberal outlook of life. The Buddhist *Samgha* by doing away with caste-system had served as an asylum for many an unfortunate man and woman besides devout Buddhists. Buddha's religion drew in its fold both high and low, rich and poor. Bimbisara, king of Magadha, Prasenjit, king of Kosala, Ajatasatru, son of Bimbisara, middle class men like Sariputta, Moggalana and Anathpindada of the business community, low born people like Ananda and Upali, all were drawn within its fold by Buddhism.

Marching through the vicissitude of history, through rise and fall, Buddhism has lost its hold in the country, of its origin since long, yet the basic ideals of Buddhism, namely peace, charity and brotherhood, and the principle of live and let live, have not been lost in India.

Spread Jainism & Buddhism: Extinction of Buddhism in India

Lack of royal patronage to Jainism as well as the extreme extension of non-violence etc. were mainly responsible for very limited spread of this religion in India. But compared to Buddhism the number of the followers of Jainism in India is quite large even today. It was mainly because the Jaina religion gradually adjusted itself to Hinduism to some extent. For instance the Hindu gods and goddesses were accepted by them. The result was that there did never develop any intolerance between Hinduism and Jainism. The reason why Jainism is existing side by side with Hinduism in different parts of India is this pragmatic adjustment. Today the number of the Jainas in India is a thousand times greater than that of the Buddhists.

Buddhism continued to exist as a local religion for a few centuries after the demise of Gautama Buddha. It was in the third century B. C. when Asoka extended his patronage to Buddhism and began to preach Buddhism both within India as well as to near and far off countries like Burma, Ceylon, Sumatra, Egypt, Macedonia, Syria, Cyrene, Epirus etc. that Buddhism was made a world region from a local one. In the second century B. C. the Kushana king Kanishka, following the foot-steps of Asoka extended his patronage to Buddhism which spread into China, Tibet and Central Asia.

During the period from the time of Asoka till the Gupta rule, Buddhism had also spread in different parts of India. The Chinese traveller Fa-Hien testifies to the fact that during the rule of the Guptas the Indian society was deeply influenced by Buddhism. Even during the seventh century A.D. the influence of Buddhism was largely seen on the Indian society and Buddhism received the patronage of Harshavardhana. Under the Palas of Bengal Buddhism received royal patronage and it was during that period that the Bengalee savant Atisa Dipankar was invited to Tibet to effect some reformation of Buddhism there.

Later on, however, Buddhism began to lose its grip on the people and society in India. The reasons behind this gradual loss of appeal of Buddhism with the Indians were, *first,* the Buddhist religion had spread due to the royal patronage. In later times when it lost this patronage it naturally began to lose its appeal with the people. After all, in those days the religion of the king was more or less the religion of the people.

Secondly, with gradual growth of *Tantrikism* in Buddhist religion as well as formal worship of the image of Buddha in imitation of the Hindu worship, it became easier for Hinduism to bring back the Buddhists within the Hindu fold.

Thirdly, Sankaracharya, Kumaril Bhatta etc. had brought about a Hindu revival which the decadent Buddhism could not resist.

Lastly, the greatest blow to the decadent Buddhism was dealt by the Turkish invasion. As a result of the Turkish invasion whatever remained of Buddhism in India became extinct. The conservative Hinduism became a greater and stronger force to resist the invasion of Magadha and the Magadhan royal dynasties can be found. But it may be mentioned here that although Buddhism has lost its grip upon the people of its land of birth, yet a very large part of the population of the world profess that religion even today. In China, Japan, Korea, Ceylon (Sri Lanka), Burma etc. Buddhism is the main religion of the people.

The Rise of Magadha

During the Sixteen Mahajanapadas period (6th century B.C.) the small kingdoms were often at war amongst themselves. The war between Kasi and Kosala may be referred to in this connection. But of all the kingdoms it was Magadha that had launched upon a career of imperial conquest. This is borne out by ancient Hindu, Jaina and Buddhist literature. In the Puranas elaborate description of the Turks in so far as religion and society were concerned. But the dynastic lists contained in Ceylonese Buddhist writing Mahavamsa are regarded as more reliable by the modern historians.

Bimbisara

In the Puranas it has been mentioned that *Barhdratha* dynasty ruled first at Magadha to be followed by the Pradyot dynasty which was in its turn followed by Sishunaga dynasty. It has also been mentioned that Bimbisara was the fifth ruler of Sishunaga dynasty. But modern researches have proved that the Pradyot dynasty did never rule in Magadha. It was the ruling dynasty of Avanti. It is also proved that Bimbisara ascended the throne immediately after the rule of the last king of the Barhadratha dynasty named Ripunjay. Thus the Puranic version that Bimbisara was the fifth ruler of Sishunaga dynasty is erroneous. Sishunaga was a ruler posterior to Bimbisara.

Asvaghosa, the author of Buddha Charit refers to Bimbisara as a scion of Haryanka dynasty. Modern historians like H. C. Roy chaudhuri and others consider the Buddhist source to be more reliable and accept the view that Bimbisara was a scion of Haryanka dynasty. Nothing is, however, known about the rise of this dynasty.

According to Ceylonese Buddhist literature Mahavamsa, Bimbisara was consecrated to the throne by his father at an early age of fifteen. Bimbisara's father was Mahapadma.[1] Mahapadma was once defeated by Brahmadatta, king of Anga. But his son Bimbisara after ascending the throne introduced into Magadha a revolutionary instrument—a new type of army without tribal basis, loyal only to the king. With this army he defeated the kingdom of Anga and thereby avenged the defeat of Mahapadma and launched Magadha upon a career of imperial conquest. Matrimonial alliances also played an important part in his career of imperial expansion. His first wife was a sister of Prasenjit king of Kosala. This marriage brought him a dowry of a village in Kasi with a revenue of one lakh while his second wife Chellana, daughter of the Lichchavi Chief Chetaka, third wife Vaidehi Vasavi and fourth wife Khema daughter of the king of Madra brought him much power and prestige.[2] He maintained friendly relations with king Pukkasati of Gandhara and Pradyot, king of Avanti. By his organised system of taxation, diplomatic and matrimonial relations Bimbisara proceeded on his policy of imperial aggression with success.

From the Buddhist literature detailed description of the administrative system of the Magadhan empire may be had. Villages used to enjoy considerable autonomy. The Chief of the village was called *Gramaka*. The Gramakas used to administer the villages with the

[1] "Turnover, N. L. Dey and others mention Bhatiya or Bhattiya as the name of the father. Tibetans on the otherhand call him Mahapadma." Roychaudhuri : *Political History of Ancient India*, p. 117 (f. n 5).

[2] According to Mahavagga Bimbisara had 500 wives. *Age of Imperial Unity*, p. 19.

help of the village Council. The Central Government was divided into three distinct parts, namely, (i) *Sarbarthak* that is, the Executive Department, (ii) *Voharika*—the Judicial Department, and *Senanayaka*—the Military Department. Bimbisara used to look after all the three departments personally. The method of punishment at that time was rather very cruel. Besides imprisonment, amputation of hands or legs was often resorted to.

Bimbisara was tolerant in his religious views. The Jainas and Buddhists received equally liberal treatment at his hand. In Jaina *Uttaradhyana Sutra,* Bimbisara is claimed to have been a Jaina convert and the meeting of Mahavira and Bimbisara is described in details. But on the other hand the Buddhist literature refers to the meeting of Bimbisara and Gautama seven years before latter's attainment of Enlightenment and to a second meeting after he had become Buddha. The Buddhist texts refer to the conversion of Bimbisara into Buddhism by Gautama Buddha himself. Bimbisara appointed his own physician Jivaka to treat Buddha as well as the inmates of the *Samgha*.

Both Jaina and Buddhist literature contain numerous stories about the death of Bimbisara. In the Buddhist literature Bimbisara is said to have been killed by his son Ajatasatru at the instigation of Devadatta, a cousin of Gautama Buddha. According to the Jaina literature, however, Ajatasatru kept Bimbisara imprisoned and during this period he had a bad sore in his fingure which was cured due to the nursing of queen Chellana. This instance of Chellana moved Ajatasatru and he felt remorse for his earlier conduct and proceeded to free his father whom he had kept confined. But Bimbisara at the sight of Ajatasatru thought that the latter had come to kill him and to avoid the disgrace committed suicide. Whatever might have been the truth in the Buddhist or Jaina stories, it may not be wrong to suppose that Ajatasatru was responsible for Bimbisara's death.

Ajatsatru

Bimbisara was succeeded by his son Ajatasatru in 490 B.C. He was a very powerful king and following the foot-steps of his father, he began to expand his empire by conquests. He declared war against Prasenjit, king of Kosala although the royal house of Kosala was related to him, for Bimbisara had married Kosaladevi, sister of Prasenjit. Kosaladevi did not survive the shock of the death of Bimbisara at the hands of Ajatasatru. The death of Bimbisara at the hands of Ajatasatru and also Kosaladevi's death due to the shock of the death of her husband were sufficient grounds for Prasenjit's anger and he proceeded to punish Ajatasatru. At the initial stage Ajatasatru was victorious in the war against Prasenjit but ultimately the latter compelled Ajatasatru to surrender along with his huge army. A peace treaty was, however, signed between the parties and to mark the friendliness between them Ajatasatru married Vajira, daughter of Prasenjit.

Ajatasatru then proceeded to conquer the greatest republican federation of eastern India. This federation comprised nine Mallaka, nine Lichchavi and eighteen Kasi and Kosala republics. The real reason for the war, according to the Buddhist literature was that on the Ganges a mine of precious stones was discovered. It was agreed that the produce of the mine would be divided equally between Magadha and the Lichchavi republic. But when the Lichchavis began to violate the agreement Ajatasatru declared war against the entire republican federation. In the Jaina literature, however, the story is different. It is said that Bimbisara had made a gift of an elephant named *Sethanka* and a very highly priced jewel necklace to his sons Halla and Behalla born of his second queen, daughter of the Lichchavi Chief Chetaka. Ajatasatru wanted to grab the necklace and the elephant. Halla and Behalla took shelter with their maternal grandfather to avoid despoliation by Ajatasatru. Ajatasatru demanded surrender of Halla and Behalla which Chetaka refused to do. This led to declaration of war against Chetaka by Ajatasatru. But it was not easy to defeat Chetaka, for all the republican states stood by him. In the circumstances Ajatasatru began to follow a double course of action. On the one hand he began to strengthen his army and on the other to have recourse to create divisoin among to the republican states through diplomacy. He strengthened the fortification at Rajagriha and established a second capital at Pataliputra at the confluence of the rivers Son and the Ganges. He sent his minister Varsaka or Bhasmakar to Lichchavi republic. There by machination and secret propaganda Bhasmakar succeeded in creating division among the Lichchavis which ultimately created division among the republican states of eastern India. This made it possible for Ajatasatru to conquer the republican federation of eastern India. It, however, took long sixteen years to do so. In this war Ajatasatru is said to have used two new weapons of war called *Rathamul* and *Mahasilakantaka*.

Ajatasatru had added two hundred leagues to the already three hundred leagues in the extent of the Magadhan empire. At the growth of the power and prosperity of Ajatasatru, Chanda Pradyot of Avanti became jealous and made preparations for invading Rajagriha, capital of Magadha but ultimately did not venture to do so. Ajatasatru enlarged his empire by occupying Vaisali and a part of Kasi as also by maintaining friendly relations with the King of Kosala, thus laying the foundation a vast empire.

Both the Jaina and the Buddhist literature claimed Ajatasatru to be their convert. In the Jaina literature it is also claimed that Mahavira was often visited by Ajatasatru along with the members of his family. It is also said that originally Ajatasatru was inimical to the Jaina religion, but after killing his father there was deep remorse in him and he got himself converted into Jainism. That Ajatasatru was also on visiting terms with Gautama Buddha is borne out by carved scene on stone at Barhut. It is also claimed that great change had come upon him as a result of his meeting with Buddha. On hearing the news of the death of Buddha Ajatasatru hurried to Kushinagara and brought some of the physical relics of Buddha for ceremonial burial. He rennovated eighteen *Mahaviharas* in and arround Rajagriha and constructed metal *Chaityas* on all the four sides of Rajagriha. In the first Buddhist Council that was convened at Rajagriha after the death of Buddha, Ajatasatru played an important role. Five hundred Buddhist monks are said to have attended the Council, Ajatasatru arranged for their stay, food, drink, medicine, clothe etc.

Successors of Ajatasatru

According to Buddhist literature Ajatasatru was succeeded by Udayabhadra who in his turn was succeeded by Anuruddha. Anuruddha was followed by Munda and Nagadasaka. Udayabhadra was none other than Udayabhadra referred to in the Buddhist texts who had ascended the throne by killing his father Ajatasatru. According to the Buddhist source all kings of Bimbisara line from Ajatasatru were all patricides. From Udayabhadra to Nagadasak, a period of fifty-six years the patricide kings ruled over Magadha. It was the people of Magadha who in order to get rid of the patricide king's rule elected Minister Sishunaga to the throne. This story is to be found in the Celonese chronicle Mahavamsa.

Sishunaga dynasty

After accession to the throne Sishunaga maintained the power and prosperity of Rajagriha, the capital of the Magadhan Empire. He protected the Magadhan Empire by warding off the invasions by Avanti, Kasi and Kosala. Not only that he defeated Avanti and having put an end to the rule of the Pradyota dynasty attached Avanti to the Magadhan Empire. Vatsya and Kosala kingdoms also probably had been annexed by him. Sishunaga made Magadha the greatest empire of northern India.*

* 'Probably both the kingdoms of Vatsya and Kosala were also annexed and thus Magadha absorbed almost all the important states in North India that flourished at the time of Gautama Buddha,' *The Age of Imperial Unity*, p. 30.

Sishunaga was succeeded by Kalasoka or Kakavarna. It was during his reign that the Second Buddhist Council was convened. On the evidence of Bana and the Greek writer Quintus Curtius we learn that Kakavarna was stabbed to death by a barber. This barber killed all the ten sons of Kakavarna and himself occupied the throne. In this conspiracy tht queen of Kakavarana is said to have played a secret role.

The Nandas

That the founder of the Nanda dynasty was low born is mentioned in the Jaina *Parisistaparvana*, the Purnanas and the Buddhist literature. But the name of the founder of the Nanda dynasty mentioned by the Puranas is Mahapadmananda. There is also reference to Ugrasena of the Mahabodhi dynasty as the founder of the Nanda dynasty. Some modern historians think that the reference to Agrammes as the ruler of Magadha by the Greek writers when Alexander invaded India, might have been a corruption of Augrasenya, i.e. son of Ugrasena. Thus it is possible that Ugrasena was the founder of the Nanda dynasty. There were altogether nine kings of this dynasty who ruled over Magadha, the last of whom was Dhanananda.*

In the Puranas Mahapadmananda is mentioned as the founder of the Nanda dynasty and he is also called the *Second Parasuram* as he was responsible for the extirpation of many a Kshatriya royal dynasty. Ikshaku, Panchala, Kasi, Kalinga, Asmaka, Haihaya, Kuru, Mithila, Surasena, Bitihotra and other Kshatriya dynasties were defeated by Mahapadmananda and the Magadhan Empire was extended over their territories. In the *Kathasaritsagar* the Nandas have been described as the kings of Ayodhya. From this, it may not be wrong to conclude that Kosala was also included in the Magadhan Empire. In the Hatigumpha Inscription of Kharvela reference is found of the conquest of Kalinga by the Nanda king. There is a place named *Nabananda Dera* on the river Godavari from which some historians think that the empire of Magadha under the Nanda kings extended to certain parts of the Deccan. Further, from the find of certain inscriptions in Mysore it is supposed that the Nanda rule had extended upto Kuntala in Mysore.

Mahapadmananda was the master of a vast empire no doubt, bus it was not simply the vastness of the empire that was the contribution of Mahapadmananda; he gave it both consolidation and a

---

* "They are named in Mahabodhivamsa as follows : (i) Ugrasena, (ii) Panduka, (iii) Pannugati, (iv) Bhutapala, (v) Rashtrapala. (vi) Govishanka, (vii) Dasasiddhaka, (viii) Kaivorta, and (ix) Dhana". *The Age of Imperial Unity*, p. 31.

strong administration. On the foundations laid by Bimbisara and Ajatasatru, Mahapadmananda built a vast and strong empire.

The sixth and the fifth centuries B.C. marked a novelty in the political and religious history of India. It was a period during which the Kshatriya kings and princes were attracted to religion and quite a few of them became founders of new religious sects. On the other hand, contrary to the age long custom Sudras were emerging as rulers. For instance, Sudra king Mahapadmananda not only founded a royal dynasty but acquired unprecedented importance as a ruler by defeating a number of Kshatriya rulers.

Successors of Mahapadmananda

The life and history of the seven rulers of the Nanda dynasty who succeeded Mahapadmananda are obscure. Some details about the personality and rule of the ninth and the last Nanda king Dhananada are, however, available from the writings of the Greeks and *Kathasaritsagar*. Dhanananda is said have been very greedy for which he earned the name *Dhananada*. His empire extended as far as the borders of the Punjab and on the evidence of Quintus Curtius we know that he had an army comprising 2 lakh infantry, 20 thousand cavalry, 2 thousand chariots and 4 to 6 thousand elephants. But despite the vastness of his empire and largeness of his army he could not earn the love of his people because of the excessive burden of tax that he had levied on the people due to his greed for money. Besides, he was looked down upon because of his low birth. In this connection Chandragupta Maurya's suggestion to the Greeks that it would be easy for Alexander to defeat Dhananada because he had forfeited the confidence and love of the people because of his worthlessness as a ruler and his low birth may be mentioned. Poros is also said to have made similar remarks about Dhanananda. Dhanananda had, however, escaped the invasion of Alexander as the latter's army refused to proceed further after reaching the Beas, but retribution came from another quarter. He had insulted Chanakya in the open court for which the latter vowed to avenge the insult by uprooting the Nanda dynasty. He kept his promise by defeating and removing Dhanananda from the throne of Magadha with the help of Chandragupta.

The fall of the Nanda dynasty did not mean the end of the empire of Bimbisara. On the contrary, at the hands of Chandragupta Maurya, who had founded a new dynasty called the Mauryas, the empire received extension almost all over India. There were some special reasons for the continuance of the Magadhan Empire : *First*, the geographical situation of Magadha, and particularly of Pataliputra, was largely responsible for it. Pataliputra was situated on the confluence of the rivers Son and the Ganges and was protected by the rivers Gogra and Gandak in the north and by Son in the south. Further, these rivers provided good outlets for northern India into the sea. The old capital Rajagriha was equally protected by Nature. It was surrounded by seven hills.

Secondly, Magadha was cosmopolitan in nature and was the mingling place of diverse races, religions and cultures. The Vedic culture and conservatism did not strike deep roots here as in some other parts of India. Magadha which was the meeting ground of Brahmanical Hinduism, Jainism and Buddhism naturally had become suitable for political liberalism. This liberalism was largely responsible for the continuance of the Magadhan Empire for a very long time since its foundation from the time of Bimbisara.

CHAPTER SEVEN

FOREIGN INVASIONS

The Persion Invasion

The Iranians or the Persians and the Indians of the Aryan stock were bifurcated in ancient past, one entering into Persia and the other into India. But relations between them were not forgotten. In those days the boundaries of India and Persia were not well defined and naturally in the bordering areas of the two countries a mixture of Persian and Indian languages and manners and customs took place. In the period of the Sixteen Janapadas the people of Kamboja used to speak the Iranian Aryan language. Further, the Oxus valley is described in ancient Sanskrit literature as a part of India. Similarly in the ancient Persian literature the same area has been described as part of Persia. This was obviously because the boundary between Persia and India was not well demarcated.

In the sixth century B.C. the north-western region of India (now in Pakistan) was divided into a number of small independent states. The most noteworthy of these states were Gandhara, Kamboj and Madra. When Bimbisara was expanding Magadha into an empire, the north-western parts, i.e. *Uttarapatha* was still divided into small independent states with no political unity among them. It became, therefore, easy for the Achaemenid emperors of Persia to conquer these small states. It is said that in the Persian religious epic Zendavesta there is reference to the inclusion of some places of Uttarapatha in the Persian Empire long before the sixth century B.C. But this is not acceptable to historians for the lack of corroboration by any other source.

However. from the Greek historians and writers like Herodotus, Ktesias, Xenophon etc. we know that the Persian emperors after having established their sway over Western Asia, proceeded towards India. Cyrus is said to have conquered Gandhara. But it is doubtful. It is also said by Ktesias that Cyrus died of a wound inflicted by an Indian soldier. Xenophon refers to the sending of an emissary by an Indian king to the Court of Cyrus with some money. But in the writings of Nearchus, an admiral of Alexander who came to India with him we know that Cyrus' Indian invasion was a failure. There is also no reference to Cyrus' invasion of India by Megasthenes. On the other hand, Pliny, a Roman writer, refers to the conquest of Kapisa, i.e. Gandhara by Cyrus. From these conflicting evidences although it is difficult to come to any definite conclusion yet the historians feel that Cyrus might have conquered the area between Kabul and the Indus.

Next emperor Cambyses was too much occupied in quelling rebellion in the empire to think of any invasion of India. He was also unbalanced and ultimately became completely mad.

Darius who came to the throne (522-486 B.C.) seems to have extended the Persian empire upto northern Punjab. About his reign we have reliable evidence. In his Behistun inscription a list of twenty-three provinces of the Persian Empire is found, but it does not include the name of India. But in two later inscriptions at Persepolis and Nakshi-Rustam mention of northern Punjab as a part of his dominion is found. This leaves us in no doubt that northern Punjab was included by him in the Persian Empire (518 B.C.). This part of India was the twentieth Province of the Persian Empire and the annual revenue earned from this province was gold dust of the value of ten lakh pound-sterlings. One-third of the total revenue of the Persian Emperor came from Indian province. In order to have a better idea of the course of the river Indus, Darius is said to have appointed Scylax to explore the Indus. This we get from Herodotus.

It may, however, be mentioned here that in the Behistun inscription of Darius there is reference to one place called Gadara. It is also mentioned in the Susa palace inscription of Darius that teak was brought from Gadara for the construction of the palace. From these references to the place called Gadara historians suppose that Gadara might have been Gandhara and it might have been conquered by him.

Darius was succeeded by his son Xerxes (under whom the Indian province continued to be a part of the Persian Empire. This is attested by his claim that he obtained the military services of an Indian contingent in his war against Greece. The Indian recruits were called the *Gandharians and Indians*. Thus it was in such a remote past that the Indian soldiers fought on the European soil. The fighting ability of the Indians impressed the Persians and later Darius III had also recruited Indian soldiers for his army. From Arrian we know that the Indian soldiers fought for Darius III against Alexander in the battle of Gaugamela. Herodotus gives an interesting account of the Indian soldiers: "The Indian clad in garments made of cotton, carried bows of cane and arrows of cane, the latter tipped with iron; and thus accoutred the Indians were marshalled under the command of Pharnazathres, son of Artabates." With the final defeat of Darius III at the hands of Alexander, the Persian dominance over the Indian province came to an end (330 B.C.)

MACEDONIAN INVASION

Political condition of Uttarapath (North-Western India) on the eve of Alexander's invasion

Alexander, son of Philip of Macedon, succeeded to throne at an early age of twenty and undertook to finish his father's unfinished task of conquering the rest of Greece and the entire civilised world. He avenged the insult of the Persian invasion of Greece by conquering the whole of the Persian Empire after which he advanced towards India in 327 B.C. North-Western India at that time was politically divided into several small states. There was no sovereign power in that area at that period. Between the Jhelum (Hydaspes) and the Beas (Bipasa) there were seven different independent tribes living at that time.* Most of the states were kingship but there were some republican states as well. From the Greek source we come to know of the following peoples who lived in that area at that period of time. These were (i) The Asvayanas (Aspasians) in the hilly tract on the northern bank of the river Kabul, (ii) Nikia (Nicaea) in the land between the rivers Kabul and the Indus, (iii) Goureanas (Garaeans) in the valley of the river Gouri or Panjkora. (iv) Asvakas (Assakenos) the people of the Swat or Bunar area, (v) Puskaravati (Peukelaotis) in the modern Peshwar district, (vi) Taxila, modern Rawalpindi, (vii) Ursa (Arsakes) in modern Hazara district, (vii) Abhisara in the hilly tracts north of Taxila, (ix) kingdom of Poros between the rivers Jhelum and Chenub, (x) Gandhara (Gandaris) the eastern part of the Gandhara of the Sixteen Mahajanapada period. (xi) Katha (Kathaioi), (xii) Kingdom of Saubhuti (Sophytes), (xiii) Kshudraka (Oxydrakaoi), (xiv) Malava (Malloi), (xv) Sudra (Sodrai) and many other states.

For want of political unity among these kingdoms as well as republican states there was no end of mutual jealousy and war between them. Ambhi, king of Taxila, was at constant conflict with the kingdoms of Abhisara and of Poros. He was also in conflict with the neighbouring republican states like Malava, Kshudraka etc. In the circumstances there was no willingness nor capability to stand against the foreign invader among these states. There was also no good relation between Poros of the kingdom of Paurava and his nephew Junior Poros, king of Gandhara. Other smaller states were

---

* Vide Smith: *Oxford History of India* (3rd Edn.) p. 91.

also disunited and mutually jealous. The political condition of Uttarapatha, i.e. North-West India, having been a picture of disunion it naturally became easy for Alexander to subdue many of them by mere show of force.

Indian campaign of Alexander

We have detailed information about Alexander's Indian campaign from the writings of Arrian, Quintus Curtius, Plutarch, Diodorus. Justin etc. Within three years of the defeat of Darius III in the battle of Gaugamela Alexander completed his conquest of the eastern and the north-eastern parts of the Persian empire as well as the western part of the Hindukos. It was in 327 B.C. he conquered Bactria, Bokhara, Syr Daria region and Nikia and proceeded towards India. From Nikia Alexander sent his emissary to Ambhi, king of Taxila to ascertain whether it would be possible to obtain the allegiance of the Indian princes without war and invited him to come to Nikia for discussion in this regard. But before Alexander's emissary had reached Txila Ambhi had already sent information to Alexander that he (Ambhi) was prepared to assist Alexander in his Indian campaign on condition that Taxila would be spared. Besides this offer of help he sent 65 elephants, 3.000 oxen and a large number of sheep as a sort of tribute to Alexander. In this way craven hearted Ambhi played the part of the first traitor in the history of India to his country.* It is supposed that it was his unsatisfied jealousy of Poros that made Ambhi to do so. Ambhi failed to defeat Poros and was intolerant of the power and prestige of Poros and his kingdom. Alexander's invasion gave him an opportunity to feed fat his grudge. There were other cowards besides Ambhi who purchased Alexander's neutrality by timely surrender. They were Kofius (Cophaeus), Sanjaya (Sangaeus), Asvajit (Assagetes), Sashigupta (Sisikottos) etc. Thus without any resistance Alexander entered India with his thirty thousand soldiers.

But Uttarapatha, i.e. north-western India, did not have only cowardly kings. Kings of smaller kingdoms and the republican states stood firmly against the foreign invader. King Astak (Astes) of Pushkaravati with his small army stood against the advancing army of Alexander. For long thirty days he was in a state of siege by the Greek army but he was unrelenting. He died fighting for the defence of his country. Two tribal republics Asvayan and Asvakayan (Aspasio and Assakeni) tried their utmost to prevent the progress

* "This is the first recorded instance of an Indian king proving a traitor to his country; what is worse, his treachery was instigated by a petty spirit of local hostility to his powerful neighbour Poros" *Age of Imperial Unity*. p. 44.

of the invading army but not with success. But the two cities Massage and Andaka gave heroic defence and Alexander could occupy them with great difficulty. When the republic of Asvakayana was defeated, 7,000 heroic soldiers of the republic were put to death at the order of Alexander. This cruelty towards the defeated enemies who had done their best for their mother land somewhat tarnished the character of Alexander.

This was followed by conquest of the city-state of Nysa, the region between the Indus and Puskaravati and the hilly fort of Varan (Aronus). It was in the Spring of 326 B.C. that Alexander set his foot on the soil of India proper.*

With a contingent of 5,000 soldiers sent by Ambhi Alexander's army crossed the Indus and held a Council at Taxila. The local chiefs of the surrounding areas pledged their loyalty to Alexander. But king Poros whose kingdom lay between the rivers Jhelum and Chenub was a person of different mettle. The lack of the sense of patriotism and self-respect on the part of other Indian kings shocked and dismayed but not frightened him. The king of Abhisara initially promised to stand by Poros but prevaricated and sent his brother as an emissary to Alexander to purchase his neutrality.

Surrounded on all sides by cowards, traitors and unpatriotic Indian rulers Poros determined to defend, at all costs, the independence of his kingdom and the honour of his family. When Alexander sent his envoy to Poros summoning him to meet the proud invader, Poros' dauntless reply was that he would certainly meet him near his own frontier and in arms.

Alexander now marched against Poros. He was informed that Poros with his whole army was waiting on the other side of the river Hydaspes 'having determined either prevent him from making the passage, or to attack him while crossing'. Alexander at once sent for his vessels which he had left in the Indus, which were dismantled and carried by land to the bank of the Hydaspes and reassembled.† Alexander camped on the Hydaspes and on the other side Poros kept his army which 'Arrian estimates 30,000 foot, 4,000 horse, 300 chariots and 2,000 elephants'. From the two banks the two armies watched each other. Alexander then had recourse to a stratagem. He divided his army into many parts and moved them into various directions. He also conveyed food from different quarters thereby giving an impression to Poros that he would wait for the end of the rainy season when the river would become fordable at various points. His vessels also sailed up and down the Hydaspes. A report

* "It was in Spring of 326 B.C, that the Macedonian invader first set foot on Indian soil proper," *Ibid*, p. 47.

† *Classical Accounts of India, Majumdar*, pp 29-33.

was also spread by Alexander that he would wait for the winter season. All this had confused the camp of Poros. At last after a night of torrential rains Alexander crossed the river at dawn at a point seventeen miles up stream by a bridge made of boats.

Poros was taken unawares and when surprised by the Macedonian army he hurriedly sent a contingent of 2000 soldiers and 120 chariots under his son who was defeated and killed in action. Soon Poros proceeded with 50,000 foot, 4,000 cavalry, 200 elephants and 300 chariots and engaged the invader. From the point of view of the military strength victory of Poros was more than certain but unfortunately in the rain-soaked earth the end of the long bows of the cavalry could not be fixed on earth for releasing the arrows, nor could his chariots move because their wheels got stuck in the mud. Alexander charged the army line of Poros with picked Macedonian cavalry and his Central Asian mounted archers and soon made breaches in the army and the cavalry line of Poros and threw the whole of Poros' army into confusion. From Plutarch we know that even in that great confusion in his own army Poros gave battle to the enemy for long eight hours and it was possible to take him prisoner when all was over and there were nine bleeding wounds in the body of the valiant defender of freedom. Thousands of his soldiers were slain and all his great generals including his two sons lost their lives in the battlefield. Poros was conducted to Alexander who asked him how would he like to be treated, his reply which became classic was: *Act as a king.** Alexander had nothing but admiration for the valiant Indian enemy who fought for the defence of the freedom of his country. He reinstated Poros in his kingdom to which he added fifteen republican territories towards the east. Alexander next conquered the republic of Glauganikai and annexed it to the kingdom of Poros. He then crossed the Chenub and conquered the king Poros II (nephew of Poros) who fled and took shelter in the territories of the Nanda king. The kingdom of Poros II was also annexed to the kingdom of Poros.

Alexander then marched upto the river Hydraotes, i.e. Ravi and defeated the small, weak republics of Kathaioi etc. as also the kingdoms of Sophytes. and Phegelas (Saubhuti and Bhagala). Alexander's unbroken success in conquests whipped up his ambition for more conquests. But when he reached the Beas his army refused to advance further. Alexander's address to his men reminding them of their glorious achievements failed to persuade them to proceed further.* He was obliged to begin his return journey homewards in the month of November, 326 B.C. by water route through Jhelum. Near the confluence of Jhelum and Chenub the

* *Vide Age of Imperial Unity*, p. 49,

republican tribes, the Malloi, Oxydrakai, Agalassci (i.e. the Malavas, Kshudrakas, Arjunayana) attacked him but were defeated. They had to accept Alexander as their overlord. The republic of Sibae (i.e. Sibi), however, submitted to Alexander without a fight.

In 325 B.C. Alexander was attacked by the tribes called the Sudra (Sogdre), Musika (Musicanus), Partha (Oxycanus or Porticanus) but were defeated and had to accept him as their overlord. The last country to be defeated by him was Pattala, after which he crossed through Baluchistan (Gedrosia) for Babylon in September, 325 B.C. On reaching Babylon he fell sick and died there in 324 B.C.

Nature of Indian resistance to Alexander.

Fighting ability, sense of unity as well patriotism and above all determination to defend independence at all costs always determine the nature of resistance to foreign invaders. India at the time of Alexander's invasion was ruled over by small cowardly rulers in the north-west, called Uttarapath. Lack of their unity in the face of foreign invasion, on the contrary their mutual jealousy and recrimination made them weaker than what they actually had been. True they were inferior to the invading Macedonian forces in so far as their military strength and equipment were concerned but with a sense of unity and patriotism and with determination to face the invader unitedly could have worked miracle. After all, a brave and patriotic breast was the greatest weapon of defence. The rulers of north-west India lacked all this and most of them proved traitors to their own country and the people. But there were exceptions indeed. Poros and a number of small republics and republican tribes did their best to defend their countries against Alexander and put him to no inconsiderable difficulty. Poros and republican tribes like the Malavas, Kshudrakas, Aryunayanas, Sibis, Musikas etc. fought against Alexander knowing full well that their defeat was a foregone conclusion. But an independent breast fears not the consequence of such noble task, the task of defending his freedom and doing his duty to his country and the people.

Motive behind Alexander's Indian conquests: his administrative arrangement

Alexander is sometimes represented as 'a mad man dazzled by wild and whirling visions of dominion and glory, impelled by an insatiable lust of conquest for conquest's sake'.* But judging by his schemes it has to be pointed out that he was ambitious indeed, but ambition did not blind him and he was capable of distinguishing between shine and substance. His advance to the Indus 'was no

* *History of Greece*, Bury, p. 809

mere wanton aggression, but was necessary to establish secure route for Indian trade, which was at the mercy of the wild hill tribes; and the subjugation of the Punjab was a necessity for securing the Indus frontier. Solid interests of commerce underlay the ambitions of the Macedonian conqueror. It is not without significance that the Phoenician merchants accompanied his army'.*

Apart from interests of commerce personal megalomania was no less a motive behind his Indian conquests. for he thought his conquest of the Persian Empire would not be complete and his adoption of the title of King of Persia would be somewhat truncated, Indian satrapy being the most populous and wealthy of the Persian Empire paying a proportionately larger tribute—360 talents of gold dust, valued at more than a million pound-sterling if India was not annexed. 'Vanity conspired with curiosity to lead him into such distant territory' although his generals advised against it, his army obeyed unwillingly.**

The proposition that one of the major considerations behind the Indian invasion of Alexander was but an extension of his wider plan of Hellenising the East was an over statement. What Alexander aimed at was at best to graft Greek culture on the Eastern civilisation, not to effect wholesale Hellenisation of the East. This is borne out by his adoption of Persian costume and Persian ceremonies in his court. marrying a Persian Princess and giving Persian wives to many of his followers. His wearing of Persian costume and adoption of Persian court ceremonies and his preference to the society of the Persian grandees roused the indignation of many of his followers. 'His soldiers saw in this change the conquest of Alexander by the Orient; they felt that they lost him.'† In India his policy naturally could not be on any count one of Hellenisation.

It may be recalled that completion of Philip's unfinished work, namely, conquest of the parts of Greece which still remained outside Macedonian rule and the conquest of the civilised world, had been the last instruction left by Philip at the time of his premature death, for his son Alexander. Smith's observation that Alexander's ambition was to out-shine the heroism of the legendary Greek heroes was more or less a legacy left for him by his father Philip.

Alexander's plan for consolidation of his conquests was extensive. Unlike the barbarian invasions of Tamerlane or Nadir Shah who were intent on plunder, Alexander intended to divide the Indus plain into provinces and to build at strategic points strong, walled cities with Greek inhabitants with a view to turning them into permanent colonies.

All the same Alexander had really no chance of permanent

---

* *Idem*

** *Life of Greece*, Will Durant, p. 548.

† *Idem*

success against the difficulties of the Indian situation. His administrative arrangements show a correct apprehension of the situation. He therefore divided his Indian conquests into seven satrapies two of which were outside India proper. Two of these comprised the land between the Hindukos and the Indus. The Hindukos region was formed into a satrapy under Oxyartes, father-in-law of Alexander and the Kabul valley into another which was placed under Philip. Within India proper the region round the confluence of the Punjab rivers was formed into a satrapy under Philippus, Sind under Pthon. These four satrapies were placed under Macedonian or Persian Satraps, i.e. Governor in some cases assisted by the Indian Chiefs like Sasigupta of Varnavati (Aornos) and Ambhi of Taxila. The territories further north of the Punjab were left to the Indian Chiefs. The satrapy of Txila under Ambhi, that of Paurava under Poros and of Kashmir region under Abhisara. The last three satrapies, namely those of Taxila, Paurava and Kashmir were in the nature of protected states acknowledging nominal vassalage of the Macedonian conqueror. Although Macedonian garrisons were stationed at strategies centres such as Pushkaravati, Taxila and others, it was inevitable that the Indian satraps were *de facto* sovereigns from the very beginning and it would not be long before they would overthrow the nominal suzerainty of Macedon. New cities, mostly on great rivers, were built with a view to establishing firmly conqueror's authority in the acquired territories as well as to stimulate maritime trade and navigation of great rivers of India and communication by water between India and the west.

Impact of the Persian and Macedonian Invasion

Neither the Persian nor the Macedonian invasion succeeded in making any deep dent in the political system of India, but cannot be said to have been in vain or altogether meaningless.

The Persian conquest had for the first time unveiled India to the western world and established contact between the Indians and the peoples of the Levant. Indian soldiers, particularly Indian archers and spearmen, were drafted into the Persian forces and they fought for the Persians on the European soil in the fifth century B.C. The dresses of the Indian struck strange to the Greeks and quickened the interest of the people of the Hellas in the homeland of these strange folks and its fabulous wealth. Persian officials found employment in the Indus provinces and naturally they made their presence felt in diverse ways. The introduction of the *Aramaic* and *Kharosti* scripts and the *Yavanani* alphabet so called by Panini are supposed to have been the result of this contact. According to some writers use of certain phrases in the Asokan inscriptions and certain features in the Maurya architecture betray Persian influence. But this is highly debatable.

Macedonian

The invasion of Alexander was in itself no more than an episode in the Indian history; its significance lying only in the establishment of a simple medium of communication between the Indian and the western cultures. The claim that Alexander had opened India to the West is untenable, for opening of India to the West can be traced to earlier times. The Persian invasion and conquest of a part of India had already unveiled India to the West and the Greeks had seen with amazement the strange dresses of the Indian soldiers who fought for the Persians on the European soil.

The Indian body politic was dented no deeper than mere surface by Alexander's invasion and the scar took no long time to be healed up and eventually totally forgotten. This is borne out by the fact that no where in the Indian literature there was any reference to the invasion. Even the Indian army did not adopt any of the tactics of the Macedonian army at whose hands it was defeated. The conservative Indian society did not permanently accept anything of the Greeks beyond the very transient Greek ideas and practices which were found in the Greek occupied parts of north-west India. All this leaves us in no doubt that Alexander's invasion was a passing phase in the history of India.

The Indian society had reasons to be hateful to the Macedonians because of the atrocities perpetrated on the people of the small republics who boldly stood against Alexander. 'In one of their towns the citizens numbering 20,000, after a brave resistance, cast themselves with their wives and children into flames, anticipating the Rajput *Jauhar* of later days'* in order to escape the brutalities of the Greek soldiers. One may agree with Michael Edwardes that Alexander's invasion was unlike those of the barbarian invasions of Tamerlane and Nadir Shah which had plunder as their aims yet the brutalities of Alexander's army experienced by the people of the small republics which made the Arjunayanas to immolate themselves with their wives and children did not certainly show Alexander in any better light. Even if we agree that Alexander contemplated a westernisation of the East, and that he brought with him historians and engineers intent not on narrow mechanics of war but on the permanencies of an active occupation, his contemplation remained at best an unfulfilled dream. 'His grandiose conception remained merely a scratch on the palimpsest of Indian history'† Simith's fond

* Vide : *The Age of Imperial Unity*, p. 51.
† Michael Edwardes : *A History of India*, p. 19.

hope that spared some more years Alexander might have been successful in Hellenising India, remains, to say the least, in the realm of conjectures.

Alexander's invasion had fewer direct results than the indirect. Among the direct results were the establishment of a few *Yavana,* i.e. Greek settlements in the Uttarapatha, i.e. north-west India. These were the cities of Alexandria in the Kabul region, Boukephala on the spot from where Alexander had started to cross the Hydaspes (Jhelum), Nikia where the battle with Poros took place a second Alexandria on the confluence of the Indus and the Chenub, and Sogdian Alexandria below the confluence of the Punjab rivers.

The second direct result was the removal of the barrier between the Indian and the Mediterranean civilisations and opening up of four lines of communication, three by land and one by sea. The land routes were through Kabul, Baluchistan and Makran and that by water was through the Persian Gulf. India had, no doubt, communication with the western world long before Alexander's Indian campaign, but route was circuitous and indistinct. Alexander was accompanied by historians and geographers, voyagers and engineers and this helped in the acquisition of knowledge historical and geographical, about India by the West. The name of the voyager Nearchus needs particular mention. Under orders of Alexander Hephaestion a general-cum-engineer built a naval station and constructed dock-yards at Patala on the mouth of the Indus where the river divides itself into two.

The indirect results of Alexander's invasion were, however, more far-reaching and enduring. Through the lines of communication opened up as a result of the Indian campaign and exploration by Alexander's men a long process of cultural intercourse between India and the West, particularly with the Greek world, began. The Greeks of post-Alexandrian ages learnt lessons in philosophy and religion from the Indian Buddhists and Bhagavatas, the Indians on their part imitated the Greek coinage, learnt Greek astronomy, honoured Greek astronomers and appreciated and learnt Greek art. The Gandhara art was the result of adaptation of the Graeco-Romano-Buddhist schools of art into one unified form.

The Macedonian empire in the Indus valley no doubt collapsed within less than five years of Alexander's death but his arduous campaigns had welded the political atoms in north-west India into one unit and thereby paved the path for the more permanent unified India under the Mauryas.

The colonies set up by Alexander in the Indian border land were brought under the Magadhan kingdom no doubt, and the *Yavana,* i.e. the Greek officials continued to serve under the Magadhan king.

The indirect results of Alexander's invasion, if somewhat beneficial to both India and the West, were of a fortuitous nature. These were not the main purpose of Alexander's Indian campaigns. The military success of his campaigns was of a very limited nature and brought in their train the harrowing tales of ravages, ruthless killing and bestial revenge. The only success, if it can be reckoned as any success, was the reduction of the Confederacy of the republican tribes led by Malloi (Malavas) and Oxydrakai (Kshudrakas). Every town of the Malavas became a citadel of resistance and in one of them five thousand Brahmins left their religious and literary pursuits and took swords for the defence of the country and laid their lives down in the battlefield leaving a few to be taken prisoners. In taking another town Alexander was severely wounded and although it was captured it had cast a gloom in Alexander's camp. The Macedonians 'were also in a state of perplexity how to get back in safety to their own country, being quite enclosed by so many warlike nations, some of whom had not yet submitted, and who they conjectured, would fight stoutly for their freedom'* When the city was taken the infuriated soldiers put to sword every one irrespective of age and sex. The heroic resistance by the small republics had no doubt redeemed the honour of the Indians which was tarnished by Ambhi of Taxila and a few other craven hearted Indian rulers. Alexander's invasion gave an opportunity to the otherwise peace-loving Indians to prove their mettle and it may be pointed out that retreat of Alexander was not solely due to the unwillingness of his soldiers, as some Greek writers would have us believe, but caused by the terror of the mighty power of the Nandas as many more Greek writers have pointed out.†

* Vide: R. C. Majumdar: *Ancient India*, pp. 101-2.

† *Classical Accounts of India*, pp. 69-71, by the same author,

Chapter Eight

THE MAURYAS

Alexander had overrun the Punjab and while withdrawing from India left the areas west of the Indus in charge of the Greek satrap Philippos. The civil government east of the Indus was virtually left in the hands of the Indian princes. There was no intention to give up the conquered territories in India but to incorporate them permanently to the Macedonian empire. Soon after Alexander had left India Philippos was done to death and was succeeded by another Greek officer Eudemos. On Alexander's death his empire was partitioned between his generals after long struggle between themselves but there was no desire to withdraw from the territories on the Indian border land. There was no quiet in those territories, in fact, even before Alexander left India disaffection against foreign rule had appeared in the Indian border land. The Brahmins of the lower Indus Valley had fomented a formidable rising which was however crushed and retribution fell heavily on the instigators. But the Indian avenger was a Taxilan Brahmin variously named Kautilya, Chanakya, Visnugupta who through his chosen pupil Chandragupta freed the parts of the country 'long harassed by outlanders'. The imperial crown of Magadha at that time was worn by a Nanda ruler who was universally 'detested and held cheap'. Chandragupta overthrew the Nanda ruler thereby freeing the country from the tyrranical Nanda rule. But whether the overthrow of the Nanda ruler, Dhananada, preceded the ouster of the vestiges of the Greek rule in north-west India is still controversial.

Chandragupta's Ancestry

The rise of the Maurya Empire was a political phenomenon of great consequence in the history of India. It is as remarkable as captivating. The hero who ushered in this new age of unity and imperial rule was Chandragupta Maurya.

Chandragupta's ancestry is not known for certain. In the maze of conflicting literary traditions it is difficult to arrive at any definite conclusion yet on the basis of modern researches it is possible to arrive at conclusions which stand to reasonable analysis.

The Brahmanical, Buddhist and Jaina traditions are at great variance. The same is true of the Greek source. The earliest available Brahmanical traditions which refer to the origin of the Mauryas are to be found in the Puranas. In the Puranas there is simple mention that the Nandas were uprooted by the Brahmana Kautilya who anointed Chandragupta as King. It was a commentator on Vishnupurana who for the first time suggested by way of explaining his title *Maurya* that Chandragupta was base-born.* According to this commentator Chandragupta was the son of Mura, a wife of the Nanda King. From *Mura* the title Maurya was derived. But according to Panini *Mura* is the name of a *gotra* and the word is a masculine word. It has, therefore, been held that the Commentator of Vishnu Purana was "guilty both of fictitious history and bad grammar". **This Commentator, however, did not cast any aspersion on the mother of Chandragupta and unlike other writers did not call *Mura,* a Sudra or a mistress of the Nanda King.

It was in a later drama *Mudrarakshasa* by Vishakhadatta, Chandragupta had been called a *Vrishala, Kulahina* which were taken by some writers to mean *Sudra* and social outcaste. But it has been suggested that epithet *Vrishala* applied to Chandragupta meant that "in regard to certain matters he (Chandragupta) did deviate from strict orthodoxy" † This has also been borne out, by implication, by the Greek evidence that Chandragupta was a follower of sacrificial religion. Further, the Puranic text applies the epithet *Vrishala* to the Andhra Dynasty which was Brahmin.†† The expression Kulhina, it has been suggested, means that Chandragupta was only of lowly, i.e. humble origin is not necessarily low born.*† A Commentator on Mudrarakshasa, Dhundiraja**† by name mentions that "Chandragupta was the eldest son of Maurya who was the son of Nanda King Sarvarthasiddhi by Mura, daughter of a Vrishala". But when we remember that the expression *Vrishala* meant no more than 'unorthodoxy' then there is no ground to take it to mean Sudra.

It may be pointed out that nowhere in the Purana texts, the Mauryas have been called Sudra or base born; no slur has as well been cast on the Mauryas. Further, reference to Chandragupta's consecation as king by Brahmin Kautilya, in the Puranas, leaves us in no doubt that Chandragupta was not a Sudra but a Kshatriya, for it was then the prerogative of the Kshatriyas to be rulers. This is also in conformity with claim made by the Buddhist Tradition recorded in *Mahavasmsa,* Jaina Traditions recorded in *Parisistaparvana* that the Mauryas belonged to the Kshatriya class. In Jaina *Parisistaparvana* Chandragupta is represented as the son of a daughter of the Chief of a village of peacock-tamers (Mayuraposaka). In the

---

* *The Age of Imperial Unity*, p. 55.
** *Idem*.
† H. C. Roychaudhuri : *Political History of Ancient India*, p, 295,
†† *Ibid.* pp. 355-56 fn.
*† *The Age of Imperial Unity*, p. 55.
**† H. C. Roychaudhuri : *Political History of Ancient India*, p. 260

Divyavadana, Bindusara, son of Chandragupta has been called Kshatriya *Murdhabhisikta,* i.e. an anointed Kshatriya. As H. C. Roychaudhuri points out the Moriyas were the ruling clan of the republic of Pippalivana during the sixth century B.C. In the fourth century B.C. they were reduced to great straits and Chandragupta grew up among the peacock-tamers in the Vindhya forest. From the name Mayuraposaka, therefore, was derived the epithet Mauryas. All this will lead to the conclusion that Chandragupta was a Kshatriya who originally belonged to a humble station of life but not of low or base origin.*

The Greek source based on the contemporary Indian tradition also points to the same conclusion and fits in well to the story of the rise of Chandragupta. According to Justin Chandragupta was a "man of humble origin, but was stimulated to aspire to regal power".** Justin's reference to 'humble origin' at best means humble station of life not low born or base-born. This is in agreement with H. C. Roychaudhuri's observation that during the fourth century the Mauryas were reduced to great strait and Chandragupta grew up among the Peacock-tamers in the Vindhyas. We may, therefore, conclude that Chandragupta Maurya was a Kshatriya and originally belonged to the ruling clan of the little republic of Pippalivana. This is also borne out by *Mahaparinirvana Sutra,* a Buddhist composition almost contemporaneous with the Mauryas of Pippalivana and the oldest of our evidences in this regard.

Early Life and Rise to Power

Alexander's campaigns had dislocated the Political Organisation of north-west India. This part of India had already passed under the grip and stranglehold of foreign rule. The Eastern India was under the tyrannical rule of the Nanda King Dhanananda. The atmosphere was full of frustration and depression. A battle of India's independence was the only way to shake off the yoke of foreign rule as well as to bring an end to the tyrannical rule of the Nandas. All this called for a leader of exceptional ability and vision who could infuse life and enthusiasm among the Indians and organise a national resistance. Fortunately, such a leader emerged in the person of Chandragupta.

The story of Chandragupta's early life and rise to power is of absorbing interest. On the evidence of the Buddhist traditions Chandragupta's father who was the Chief of Pippalivana was defeated and killed in a battle with the ruler of the neighbouring kingdom.

* H. C. Roychaudhuri : *Political History of Ancient India,* pp. 265.
** *Idem.*

This had reduced Chandragupta's mother to great straits. Poverty and lack of personal security compelled her to seek shelter in Pataliputra, the Magadhan capial. She was then an expectant mother. In Pataliputra Chandragupta was born. He was adopted by a cowherd of a nearby village and Chandragupta began to grow among the cowboys. Here Kautilya saw the boy Chandragupta and having been impressed by certain signs in the boy that promised future greatness Kautilya purchased him from the cowherd on payment of one thousand *Karshapanas*. There are, however, minor discrepancies in the details given in different works.* Kautilya then took the boy to his native city of Taxila, the most famous seat of learning of the time and "had him educated in the humanities and the practical arts and crafts of the time including the military arts".† This confirms Plutarch's statement that Chandragupta as a young man met Alexander in his camp in the Punjab to seek Greek help for ousting the tyrannical Nanda rule in Magadha. Chandragupta was then, evidently, living in Taxila with Kautilya. It is also said that Kautilya or Chanakya went to the Imperial Court at Pataliputra but received insulting treatment at the hands of the Nanda reigning King. He then returned to the Vindhyas where he met Chandragupta‡ who had fled from Alexander's Camp because of his outspokeness which incurred Alexander's wrath and who ordered his men to kill the precocious, intrepid youth. It was while living in the Vindhyas as a tramp that a lion licked his sweat while he was asleep. This and some other good omens portended his rise to royal dignity.

The minor discrepancies in details apart, the fact, however, remains that it was the famous Taxilan Brahmin Chanakya or Kautilya who taught and trained boy Chandragupta to grow into the hero of India and first man who thought of independence from the foreign yoke as well as from that of Nanda Tyranny. It was Kautilya who infected his pupil Chandragupta with his hatred of foreign rule as an unmitigated evil and to avenge his personal insult at the hands of the infamous Nanda ruler, 'detested and held cheap by his people'.

Chandragupta with the assistance and guidance of Chanakya who came upon some treasure trove underground, raised an army of 'robbers' as Justin characterised it. But as McGrindle points out, they were the republican peoples of the Punjab who played a prominent part in resisting Alexander. But that the army raised by

* "Kautilya discovered Chandragupta in a village as the adopted son of a cowherd from whom, seeing in him the sure promise of his future greatness, he bought the boy paying on the spot 1000 *Kanhapanas* (Karshapanas)".
A Comprehensive History of India, Vol. II, p. 2.
"The boy was brought up first by a cowherd, and then by a hunter."
The Age of Imperial Unity, p. 56.

† R. K. Mookerjee ; *Chandragupta Maurya and his Times*, pp. 25-26.

‡ Vide : *An Advanced History of India*, p. 92.

Chandragupta included the *Choras,* or *Pratirodhakas,* i.e., the robbers and the outlaws, is borne out by Kautilya himself. The reason for their recruitment was that they were most heroic fighters, obviously because of their habitual daring activities. But the main strength of Chandragupta's army was derived from the heroic republican military clans whose heroic resistance Alexander had to face and whom Curtius calls "fierce nations resisting Alexander with their blood".*

Chandragupta's war of liberation had two distinct parts, namely, to free the north-western India from the Greeks and Eastern India from the tyrannical rule of the Nandas. According to Justin Chandragupta after having raised an army solicited the Indians to overthrow the existing government. The use of the expression 'existing government' necessarily meant the Nanda government and his appeal was to *all* Indians also point to this conclusion. Any way, according to Nilkantha Sastri, R. K. Mukherjee and Thomas, Chandragupta directed his attention first to the overthrow of the Greek rule. But H. C. Roychaudhuri is of the opinion "Chandragupta's appeal to the Indians to overthrow the existing government meant overthrow of the Nanda rule" and he concurs with the view of Smith that "Sometimes after his acquisition of sovereignty Chandragupta went to war with the prefects or generals of Alexander and crushed their power".† It stands to reason that Chandragupta and for the matter of that any other hero in the circumstances would seek to strengthen his position by overthrowing and thereby getting hold of the indigenous royalty before attempting to overthrow the foreign rule in small parts of India. Nilkantha Sastri places the accession of Chandragupta to sovereignty in 323 B.C., the year of the death of Alexander. It is, therefore, more reasonable to conclude that overthrow of the Greek Governors took place after the death of Alexander and the overthrow of the Nanda rule preceded that of the Greek Governors.

His Conquests

We have seen that Chandragupta raised a formidable army drafting recruits from the heroic republican clans such as the Kshudrakas, Malavas etc. According to *Mahavamsa Tika* both Kautilya and Chadragupta set out to collect recruits from different places. Chandragupta strengthened his position by an alliance with the Himalayan Chief Parvataka as mentioned in Sanskrit Drama *Mudrarakshasa* and

* *Comprehensive History of India,* Vol, II, p. 3. *Also vide The Age of Imperial Unity,* p. 57,

† H. C. Raychaudhuri : *Political History of Ancient India,* p. 269. Also vide : *Comprehensive History of India,* Vol. II. p. 5.

Jaina text *Parishistaparvana.* Thus military strength and statesmanship lay at the bottom of success of Chandragupta. The astute diplomacy of Chanakya and bravery of Chandragupta made the formidable army raised by both of them invincible in every battle field.

The liberation of the Punjab and the overthrow of the infamous Nandas were not the only achievements of Chandragupta. According to Plutarch Chandragupta overran and subdued the whole of India with an army of 600,000 men. But his mission of conquests was aided materially by the prevailing internal condition.

Leaving aside the controversy whether Chandragupta had dealt with the Greek rulers or the Nandas first, it may be pointed out that in both cases his success was aided by the then internal situation. The Nanda ruler 'was a man of quite worthless character and held in no respect' as Diodorus puts it. Plutarch also mentions that young Chandragupta reported to Alexander about the hatred of the people to the Nanda ruler for his wickedness and meanness of origin. But the Nanda ruler whom the name *Dhana* Nanda was given in the Pali Texts, was immensely rich—'a sovereign of untold wealth' and was very strong in military power. In *Kathasaritsagara* there is mention of Dhana Nanda's having kept 990 millions of gold pieces buried in a rock in the bed of the Ganges. The Buddhist sources compute his wealth at 80 crores. His greed for wealth led him to levy taxes on "Skins, gums, trees and stones". His army as Curtius estimates stood at 600,000 infantry, 20,000 cavalry, 2,000 four-horsed chariots and 3,000 elephants. He was the sole sovereign (*Ekrat*) of numerous states such as Aikshakus, Panchalas, Kasis, Haihayas, Kalingas, Asmakas, Kurus, Maithilis, Surasenas, Kosala and others. It was, therefore, not an easy task to defeat such a king in an encounter. Even Alexander did not venture an engagement with the Nanda ruler.

From the Buddhist and the Jaina texts we come across some details about the initial defeats of Chandragupta because of the wrong military strategy followed by him. At first Chandragupta dashed victoriously from the borders of the Nanda Empire towards its centre without caring to leave any garrison to protect him from the rear. Because of this mistake in strategy Chandragupta met with defeat at the initial stage of the conquest of the Nanda Empire. Then he corrected the strategy and as he marched ahead, he left garrisons in, conquered Janapada and besieged Pataliputra, the capital of Magadha, defeated and killed Dhana Nanda. A different version is given by Parisisthaparvana where it is said that Chandragupta forced Dhana Nanda to capitulate and his life was spared and he was allowed to leave

Pataliputra with his two wives and one daughter with as much as he could carry in one single chariot.

According to tradition Chandragupta had to engage all his military strength, even Greek mercenaries from the Punjab in his conquest of the Nanda King. In *Milindapanhs* it is stated that one crore of soldiers, ten thousand elephants, one lac horses and five hundred charioteers were killed in the encounter between Chandragupta and the Nanda ruler whose army commander was Bhadrasala. This leaves us in no doubt that the battle between Chandragupta and the Nanda King was one of the bloodiest battles of India and Chandragupta had to strain his every nerve to win the victory.

Conquest of the Nanda Empire made Chandragupta master of a vast empire to which was jointed the land of the Punjab which he conquered from the Greek Governors. While the universal hatred towards Dhana Nanda, the greedy, tyrannical ruler of the Magadhan Empire made the internal fabric of the empire weak and incoherent making it comparatively easy for Chandragupta to eventually conquer the empire, the local Greek rule in the Punjab fell into disarray since the murder of Necanor and Philippos in 325 B.C. The process of Conquest of the Greek ruled areas of the north-west had begun even before the death of Alexander in 323 B.C. It was on the news of Alexander's death reaching India that *Sandrakottas*, as the Greeks called Chandragupta, shook off the yoke of servitude from the neck of India and put Alexander's governors to death.

By 321 B C. when Alexander's generals after a continued struggle for sharing Alexander's empire agreed to a second partition treaty of Triparadisus, we find no mention of Indus. Obviously, Indus, then had ceased to be a part of the Greek dominion. This is further borne out by the fact that the Greek Satraps in the Punjab in 321 B.C. lamented that unless strong reinforcement of Greek contingents were sent, it would be impossible for them to withstand the pressure of the Indian rulers. This leaves us in no doubt that the Indian King of the north-west must have made a common cause with the Kings of the area and furthered the cause of freeing the Punjab from the foreign rule. Had it not been the case how do we explain the absence of any campaign of conquest of the territories of the Indian rulers of the area. The Indian Rajas of the north-west must have accepted the overlordship of Chandragupta. In any case there is no evidence of any resistance on the part of the Indian rulers of this part to Chandragupta.

After the death of Alexander his empire was partitioned between his generals after a long struggle. The eastern part of the empire fell to Seleukos, one of Alexander's generals. He became the King of Syria. He carried on several wars to recover other eastern parts of the empire of Alexander. He took Babylon, subdued the Bactrians and then made an expedition into India to recover the territories now lost to the Greeks. Seleukos reached the Indus about 305 B.C. The Greek writers such as Appianus, Plutarch, Strabo, Justin, etc. curiously enough do not give us any detail of the encounter between Seleukos and Chandragupta but merely record the result of the encounter. Even when viewed from the results, there can be no doubt that Seleukos could not make much head way and was obliged to conclude an alliance with Chandragupta ratifying it by a matrimonial contract between the two sides. R. C. Mazumder's observation that "Seleukos was worsted in his fight with Chandragupta", therefore, is the only conclusion that one can arrive at. It is generally accepted that the martimonial contract was a marriage between a daughter of Seleukos and Chandragupta and the cession of Herat (Aria), Kandahar (Arachosia), Makran (Gedrosia) and Kabul (Paropanisadai), can be rightly regarded as dowry to the bridegroom. But all this is not warranted by known facts. The only reasonable conclusion that we may arrive at is that Seleukos had to purchase peace by ceding to Chandragupta the territories, namely, Herat, Kandahar, Makran and Kabul.

Chandragupta reciprocated by presenting Seleukos 500 war elephants. Several scholars including Tarn have entertained doubts as to the cession of Herat, Kandahar, Makran and Kabul in their entirety to Chandragupta by Seleukos. According to Tarn "The Indians occupied a larger portion of Ariana which they have received from the Macedonians".* But from the inscriptions of Asoka, Chandragupta's grandson proves the inclusion of the Yonas and the Gandharas as vassals of the Maurya Empire. This means that empire of the Mauryas received extension upto Kabul under Chandragupta due to the cession of the territories mentioned above by Seleukos to Chandragupta Maurya because there is no evidence of conquest of these areas either during the reign of Bindusara or that of Asoka.

Chandragupta did not rest content with the overthrow of the Nanda rule, he ousted the Greeks from the Punjab and warded off the invasion of Seleukos. As Plutarch remarks he "overran and subdued the whole of India". Justin also observed that Chandragupta was "in possession of India". Such remarks leave us in no doubt that Chandragupta brought under his sway almost the whole of India and built up the first all India Empire. That his empire had extended

* Vide : H. C. Roychaudhuri : *The Political History of Ancient India*, p. 269. *The Age of Imperial Unity*, p. 61.

upto Podiyil Hill in the Tinnevelly district in the South is borne out by Mamulanar, a Tamil author.

Certain Mysore inscription refers to Chandragupta's rule in Northern Mysore and Nellore. Thus when we take together the statements of Plutarch, Justin, Mamulanar and the Mysore inscription we may safely conclude that Chandragupta Maurya had conquerred a considerable portion of the Trans-Vindhyan India.

That Saurashtra in Western-India was a province of the Maurya Empire under Chandragupta and was ruled over by his Governor Pushyagupta is borne out by Junagarh inscription of Rudradamana I.

Smith is, however, of the opinion that Chandragupta's all out effort to emerge from obscurity to imperial throne in North India left him no time to turn his attention to the South and it was more probable that the South was brought under the Maurya rule by Chandragupta's son Bindusara. Obviously Smith relies on the evidence of Taranatha that Bindusara destroyed "the nobles and kings of sixteen towns and made him master of all territories between the eastern and the western seas". This has been taken not only by Smith but also by some other scholars such as Hemchandra, Jayaswal, etc, to mean the annexation of the Deccan.* But H. C. Roychaudhuri points out that at the Chandragupta's time the Maurya Empire extended from Surashtra to Bengal (Gangaridae), i.e., from the western to the eastern seas. There is no early evidence of the conquest of the Deccan by Bindusara. The only reference to military activity under Bindusara was the suppression of the revolt at Taxila where Prince Asoka was sent for the purpose. It goes without saying that extension of the Maurya Empire to the south was the work of Chandragupta. This is also in conformity with the view that Nau-Nander-Dera on the Godavari testifies to the extension of the Nanda Empire upto the Godavari. This will mean that Chandragupta Maurya who occupied the Nanda Empire had *ipso facto* became the ruler upto the Godavari wherefrom it was not difficult to extend the boundary further southward upto Mysore and Nellore. Jaina tradition is that towards the end of his reign when there was a terrible famine in north India Chandragupta became a Jaina and renounced the world and took a band of Jaina Monks with him and went to Sravana Belgola in Mysore.

The Maurya Empire under Chandragupta extended towards the north-west upto the borders of the Persia, towards the east upto Bihar, in the west upto the seas bordering Saurashtra and the south

---

* Smith : *Early History of India*, p. 139. Jayaswal : *The Empire of Bindusara*, Journal of Bihar & Orissa Research Society, ii, pp. 79

upto the Chital Durg and Nellore districs of Mysore. Thus the whole of India from the borders of Persia upto parts of the Deccan, comprising Uttarpatha, Avanti, Dakshinapatha and Prachya was under Chandragupta. This is in consonance with remarks of Plutarch that Chandragupta "subdued whole in India" and Justin's statement that Chandragupta was in "possession of India".

Chandragupta's Administration

For Chandragupta's administration we have the unique evidence of the Greek ambassador Megasthenes, deputed to his Court at Pataliputra. Megasthenes's observations on the working of the Maurya administration acquired through personal knowledge have been confirmed in many respects by Arthasastra attributed to Chandragupta's minister Kautilya. This work although not definitely dated is generally regarded as a document of Maurya history and Prof. Thomas remarks that the work "clearly falls within or near the Maurya Period".

The account of Megasthenes containing the details of the geography, products, social and political institutions of India of that period is lost but many extracts from it have been preserved in the writings of the later classical writers. The information obtained from these later classical writers like Strabo, Arrian, Diodorus and others, although fragmentary, is highly interesting and of immense historical value being recorded by an eye witness. These fragments of information quoted in the writings of the later classical writers were collected by Schwanbeck and translated into English by Prof. McGrindle. True that Megasthenes *Indica,* as his account was called, contained some mistaken statements. As Prof. Rhys Davids observes, Megasthenes possessed very little critical judgement and was often misled by wrong information received from others or by his lack of understanding of the Indian System, for example, his misunderstanding of the Indian caste-system. But he is unquestionably a truthful witness in respect of matters which came under his personal observation. In such matters we have corroboration in Kautilya's Arthasastra and Asokan Edicts.*

The King was the supreme head of the state and had fourfold functions: military, judicial, executive and legislative. According to Megasthenes Chandragupta was a very hard-working official. He remained in court whole day, did not sleep at day time and even

* Vide: H. C. Roychaudhuri: *Political History of Ancient India,* pp. 273-74, *The Age of Imperial Unity,* p. 62, *Comprehensive History of India ii,* p. 10.

when he would have his body massaged or his hair combed and dressed he attended to public business and gave audience to his ambassadors.

As the highest military commander he would consider plans of operation with his *Senapati*, i.e., the Commander-in-Chief. Chandragupta maintained a vast standing army of more than 600,000 men. He had an effective control over the military through a War Office comprising thirty members, obviously experts in different branches of military art and science. It was divided into six Boards of five members each ; such as the (i) Board of Admiralty, Boards of (ii) Infantry, (iii) Cavalry, (iv) War-Chariots, (v) War Elephants, and (vi) Transport and Commissariat and Army service.

This scientific division and control of the military administration stood Chandragupta in good stead and while made his army invincible in the battle field spoke elonquently of his efficiency and ability as the supreme head of the military administration.

At the head of the judiciary stood the king himself. He personally adjudicated the cases that came before him. Judging of cases consumed a great part of his time in the court. He would never keep his petitioners waiting. He obviously followed the exhortations of Kautilya, his minister, who observed in his Arthasastra that 'when in the court, he (the king) shall never cause his petitioners to wait at the door, for when a king makes himself inaccessible to the people and entrusts his work to his immediate officers, he may be sure to invincible in the battle field spoke eloquently of his efficiency and himself a prey to his enemies'.*

In his capacity as the head of the executive government, Chandragupta appointed all the high officials of the state such as, the *Sachivas* or *Amatyas, Mantrins* or the High Ministers, the *Purohita* or the High Priest, Spies, *Adhyakshas,* maintained correspondence with the Mantriparishad, received envoys Governors and Viceroys, etc.

His legislative functions comprised issuing of rescripts, maintenance of *Porana pakiti,* i.e., ancient rules and customs. Kautilya calls the King *Dharmapravartaka* and this could be done by the king by issuing *Rajasasana,* i.e., royal rescripts.

Chandragupta's government was divided into two parts, namely, the Central and the Provincial Governments. In the Centre there was the King who was the sovereign head of the state, and the Mantriparishad, Councillors and Assessors, that is the *Mantrins* or High Ministers, *Sachivas* or *Amatyas.*

The empire was divided into a number of provinces which were

---

* Vide Majumdar's Political History of Ancient India, p. 279.

subdivided into districts. The exact number of provinces under Chandragupta, is not known but we know that there were five provinces under Asoka, grandson of Chandragupta, including Kalinga. The last named province Kalinga was conquered by Asoka. Therefore, if we leave out Kalinga then we may arrive at the conclusion that under Chandragupta there were altogether four provinces. This may be regarded as conclusive as we know that no additional territory was conquered by Bindusara, son of Chandragupta. The four provinces under Chandragupta were Uttarapatha with its capital at Taxila, Avanti with Ujjayini as its capital, Dakshinapatha with its capital Suvarnagiri, and Prachya, the Prasii of the Greeks, with its capital at Pataliputra.

Prachya and the Madhyadesa, that is, Eastern and Mid-India, were directly ruled by Chandragupta himself. The provinces were under Governors or Viceroys who were princes of the royal blood. Besides imperial provinces, there were a number of territories which enjoyed some measure of autonomy.

At the centre, the king was assisted and advised by the *Mantrins*, the High Ministers and the *Mantriparishad*. Members of the Mantriparishad occupied an inferior position, this is borne out by the fact that while the Mantrins received 48,000 panas as salary per annum, the members of the Mantriparishad received only 12,000 panas per annum. Under the High Ministers there were various officers of varied grades who looked after water supply, maintenance of roads and putting milestones along the road, agriculture, forests, mines, metal industries, etc. The Magistrates who looked after towns and cities were called *Nagaradhyakshya* and those looking after the military were called *Baladhyakshas*.

According to Megasthenes and later Greek writers like Diodorus, Starbo, Arrian etc. the *Mantriparishad* was very influential. Besides advising the King in matters of administration, it exercised great influence in the appointment of Governors, Viceroys, Deputy Governors, Treasurers, Generals, Admirals, Judges, Chief Magistrates and other High Officials.*

Kautilya's *Arthasastra* laid down certain specific tests to determine the suitability of appointment of persons as different *Amatyas*. In order that the *Amatyas* in charge of civil and criminal justice might be sufficiently religious-minded to adjudicate cases impartially they had to be purified by religious tests. Likewise those to be appointed as Chancellor of the Exchequer (Samahartri) had to be purified by money test, i.e., *Arthopadhasuddha*; those appointed to the Pleasure Gardens had to be purified by love-test, i.e., *Kamopadhasuddhas*,

* The Age of Imperial Unity, p. 63.

those who had to be employed in work which needed bold, immediate step had to be purified by fear test, i.e., *Bhayopadhasuddha.* Sufficiently qualified persons were appointed Ministers plempotentiary, Ministers of correspondence and *Adhyakshas,* i.e., Superintendents.

The meeting of the Mantriparishad was also attended by the Maha-Mantrins or the High Ministers. The King would consult the *Mantriparishad* in all matters of importance and emergency. Although the *Mantriparishad* was an advisory Council, and the King was at liberty either to accept or reject its advice, yet it is easy to understand that King would honour the decision of the *Mantriparishad* remembering as we do that it was attended by no less a person than Kautilya.

The municipal administration of Pataliputra, the capital city of Chandragupta, was of a unique character. From Megasthenes, corroborated by Arthasastra, we know that the Municipal Board comprised thiity members of six Boards of five members each. Each of these Boards was in charge of a particular type of function. The First Board was in charge of Industrial Art. It had to look after production of commodities, keep watch on the quality of raw materials used, decide the fair value of the articles produced and stamp the finished articles as evidence of their suitability to be marketed.

The Second Board was in charge of looking after the foreigners. Strabo, Diodorus state that the Maurya Government took special care of the foreigners. "Among the Indians officers are appointed even for foreigners, whose duty is to see that no foreigner is wronged. Should any one of them lose health, they send Physicians to attend him and take care of him otherwise, and if he dies they bury him and deliver over such property as he leaves to his relatives".*

The Third Board was in charge of vital statistics. This Board would enquire how deaths occurred and register every birth and death. "The third Body consists of those who enquire when and how births and deaths occur, with a view to not only levying a tax, but also in order that birth and deaths among both high and low may not escape the cognizance of Government".**

The Fourth Board looked after trade and commerce. It kept watch over the weights and measures and saw to it that commodities were sold out before their quality did not deteriorate. It also saw that seasonal products were sold by public notice. No one was allowed to deal in more than one commodity but one could do so by paying

---

* McCrandle : *Megasthenes and Arrian,* p. 42. Also vide H. C. Roychaudhuri : *Political History of Ancient India,* p. 292. *The Age of Imperial Unity.* p. 63,

** *The Age of Imperial Unity.* pp. 63-64.

double or three times the tax as according to the number of commodities dealt with.

The Fifth Board supervised the manufactured articles. Public notice had to be given for the sale of manufactured articles. This Board kept strict watch so that newly manufactured articles were not mixed or piled with the old stock.

The Sixth Board was in charge of collection of one-tenth of the prices of the articles or produce sold, as tax. Any fraud in payment of this tax was punishable with death.

Megasthenes referred to the Municipal Board of the capital city of Pataliputra where he stayed, but it may not be unreasonable to conclude that similar Municipal Councils and Boards were there in other cities of the time such as Taxila, Ujjaini, Kaushambi, Pundranagar, etc. which were important cities under Chandragupta.

The Arthasastra calls officials of the Military and Municipal Boards as *Adhyakshas* whom Megasthenes called *Astynomoi*, the Magistrates of Strabo. Smith is of opinion that Boards described by Megasthenes were unknown to Kautilya and the creation of the Boards might have been an innovation made by Chandragupta. But Roychaudhuri points out that Smith's confusion is due to his ignoring nagaradhyakshas and other officials referred to in the Arthasastra.

We have already noticed that at the top of the judiciary stood the King. But besides the Royal Court which was the highest in the State there were tribunals of justice both in cities and the country sides. The city tribunals were presided over by *Vyavaharika Mahamatras* and the coventry tribunals were presided over by *Rajukas*. From the classical source we know that the judges also decided cases in which foreigners are concerned, with greatest care and would come down sharply on those took unfair advantage of them.

Punishment to persons held guilty by the court were very severe, Decapitation, amputation of limbs, fines and forfeitures were the different types of punishment prevalent at that time. Inhuman torture was resorted to for extorting confession from the criminals.

The revenue of the State was mainly of two kinds : *Bhaga* and *Bali*. Bhaga was the King's share of the produce of the soil which was normally one-tenth. In special cases is was one-fourth or reduced to one-eighth. All lands were property of the Crown and the husbandmen paid, according to the Greek source, a land tribute besides one-fourth of the produce of the soil. *Bali* was originally this land tribute. In any case *Bali* was an extra import over and above Bali. one-tenth of the prices of the commodities sold is another important source of revenue. In certain areas, the main sources besides tithes on the sale of commodities were birth and death duties, fines and forfeitures, etc.

A considerable part of the revenue was spent for the maintenance of the army, the war horses, war elephants and war-chariots. The artisans also received maintenance from the royal exchequer. Herdsmen were paid grains from the royal granary for their labour in clearing the land of wild beasts and fowls. The Philosophers, i.e., the Brahmanas and the Sramanas received royal bounty. Constuction of roads, buildings, forts, repairs of the existing constructions, etc. claimed a good part of the expenditure during the rule of Chandragupta.

The land tax was collected by a class of officials called *Agranomoi* by Megasthenes. He also refers to various other classes of officials "who superintended the rivers, measure the land, inspect the sluices by which water is let out from the main canals into their branches so that every one may have an equal supply of it". Apart from such officers Megasthenes also mentions others who were in charge of Agriculture, Forestry, Timber Works, Metal Foundries, Mines, Roads, etc.

Chandragupta maintained a body of spies called Overseers—the *Episkopoi* of the Greek writers who kept watch on what was going on throughout the country and the cities and report to the King. Strabo says that the *Ephori* i.e., the Inspectors (Spies) were appointed from the most faithful persons. Appointment of different classes of spies is also borne out by *Arthasastra* which refers to stationary spies (Samsthah) who are posted permanently at places and wandering spies (Sancharah) who wandered from place to place for collecting secret information.

At the head of the Provincial administration was the Governor. During the rule of Chandragupta there were four Provinces into which the Maurya Empire was divided. These were Uttarpatha. Dakshinapatha, Prachya and Avanti. Both Kautilya and the classical writers mention the existence of autonomous tribes and cities during Chandragupta's time. Thus it may be said that the Maurya system of Government was a combination of monarchy and autonomy.

Besides the Governor or Viceroy who was at the head of the provincial administration and who would almost invariably be the Prince of the royal blood, there were a hierarchy of officials. The province was divided into Janapadas each under a *Pradestri* and a *Samahartri*. One-fourth part of a Janapada was put under an officer called *Sthanika*. A group of five to ten villages would be placed under an officer called the *Gopa*. Every village again was under an officer elected by the villagers and was responsible for the village administration. This officer was called *Gramika*. The Maurya administration was thus structurally in the nature of a pyramid with the *Gramika* at the bottom and the Emperor at the top.

According to the Jaina traditions, Chandragupta became a Jaina convert in his old age Towards the end of his reign a terrible famine stalked the land. According to the Hindu belief, famine or such other calamity was then regarded as the Divine visitation for the sin of the reigning King. Chandragupta Maurya abdicated his throne in favour of his son Bindusara when the famine overtook the land and repaired to *Sravana Belgola* in Mysore where he is said to have laid down his life by voluntary starvation as prescribed in the Jaina religion, in the year 300 B.C.

Megasthenes : After the Salenkdian War an era of peace and friendly relations began between the Maurya Emperor Chandragupta and the Syrian Court. Megasthenes was sent to the Court of Chandragupta by Selencos as an ambassador. Megasthenes was originally working at Arachosia with the Satrap Sibytrios where from he was sent to Pataliputra where he stayed in Chandragupta's Court and left an account of the Indian affairs of the time. The work of Megasthenes has been lost but fragments of his work survive in the works of later classical writers such as Strabo, Arrian, Diodorus, and others which have been collected by Schwanbeck and translated into English by McGrindle.

Although in certain aspects of his statements Megasthenes betrayed lack of critical judgement in cases of his secondary information, as Prof. Rhys Davids puts it, yet in matters which came under his direct observation he has been truthful.

The most important piece of information that we have from Megasthenes is the description of the capital city of Pataliputra. Megasthenes' *Palimbothra*, i.e Pataliputra stood on the confluence of the rivers Son and the Ganges, and was nine and half miles (80 Stades) in length and one and three-fourths miles (15 Stades) in breadth. The city was surrounded by a wooden wall and by a ditch 606 feet wide and 30 cubits in depth. The wooden wall of the city had 570 towers and 64 gates.

Pataliputra was not the only city of the Maurya Empire. Arrian remarks that "It would not be possible to record with accuracy the number of the cities on account of their multiplicity. Those which were situated near the river or the sea were built of wood ; for if they were built of brick they could not long endure on account of rain and because the rivers overflowing their banks fill the plains with water. But those which have been founded on commanding places are of mortar." The most important cities of Chandragupt's time were Taxila, Kausambi, Ujjaini and Pundranagara (in North Bengal).

The account of Aelian based on Megasthenes contains descriptions of the royal palace. Chandragupta's palace within the city of Pataliputra was, according to Megasthenes, the finest in the whole world and forced admiration. Neither Susa nor Ekbatana—the Persian Palaces could vie with the royal palace in Pataliputra. The palace had gilded pillars adorned with golden vines and silver birds. In the Palace park tamed Peacocks, Parrots and domesticated Pheasants were kept. There were shaded groves and trees deftly interwoven by the woodmen. Artificial ponds were dug within the palace grounds which contained fishes of enormous size. The imperial palace is supposed to have stood near to the modern village of Kumrahar where ruins of Maurya pillar-hall have been unearthed.

From Strabo we learn that the King had female guards for his protection within the palace and it was on four occasions only, namely in times of war, while sitting as a judge in the royal Court, to offer religious sacrifice and while going on hunting expeditions that the King would go out of the Palace.

Megasthenes left us a detailed description of both Municipal and Military Councils of Chandragupta's time. "Each of the councils had six Boards with well-defined functions to perform.[1] This gives us an impression of the highly developed urban administration as also scientific military administration prevalent during Chandragupta's time Some details of the equipment of the army are also given by the Greek ambassador. The foot soldiers carried a bow equal in length to the man who bears it. There is nothing which can resist an Indian archer's shot. Some are equipped with Javelins instead of bows, but wear a sword which is broad in the blade".[2]

About the peace and prosperity of the people Megasthenes observes that the inhabitants having abundant means of subsistence grew taller than the ordinary stature as might be expected of people who inhale pure air and drink the finest of water. They are well-skilled in various arts. Referring to the fertility of the soil Megasthenes mentions that profusion of rivers and streams facilitates growth of cereals and plants of various kinds. Abundant rainfall enables harvesting of two crops. Megasthenes was so much impressed by the contentment and prosperity of the people that he made the sweeping remark that "famine has never visited India and that there has never been a general scarcity in the supply of nourishing food". Megasthenes, however, justifies this remark by stating that even in times of war the Indians would never ravage the cultivated soil as was done by other nations but would fight their battles away from agricul-

[1] See *ante*, p.

[2] McCrindle : *Megasthenes and Arrian*, pp. 220-1.

tural fields allowing the tillers of the soil to carry on cultivation even when battles were raging. The Indians regarded the husbandmen as sacred and inviolable. Besides, they neither ravage an enemy's land with fire nor cut down its trees".[1]

It may be pointed out here that Megasthenes' observation regarding absence of famine is factually incorrect, for there are references in literary works to the occurrences of famine in India. A terrible famine stalked the land within years of Megasthenes' departure from India.

Due to agricultural prosperity by far the most numerous class in the society was formed of the husbandmen. But they did not prevent the growth of towns and cities. Megasthenes observed that the number of cities was so large that 'it cannot be stated with precision'. Cities near rivers or seas were built of wood in order to save them from destruction by flood and rains, but those built on heights and away from rivers or seas were built of bricks and mud.

Megasthenes refers to the frugal nature of the Indians but remarks that they were fond of fineries and jewelleries which fostered growth of trade and industry. A large number of persons were employed in production of weapons of war, ships for the navy as well as maritime trade and human transport. Sailors of state owned ships, and skilled persons appointed for building of war ships and manufacture of weapons were paid from the State coffers.

Megasthenes mentioned existence of *Seven Castes* in the then Indian Society which was contrary to the traditional fourfold division of the Caste-System then prevalent. In fact, Megasthenes' division of the people into the Seven Castes, viz. : Philosophers, Husbandmen, Hardsmen, Artisans, Soldiers, Overseers and Councillors, obviously was a division with reference to the professional pursuits of different sections of the society. Megasthenes perhaps did not realise the import of the fourfold division of the society into Brahmins, Kshatriyas, Vaisyas and Sudras. He, in all probability, was led by his knowledge of the division of the 'Egyptian Society into Seven Castes, on professional basis'. Prof. Rhys Davids observes that Megasthenes betrayed lack of critical judgment. This was one such instance.

Megasthenes notices a general contentment among the people and the treatment of the underdogs of the society then must have been so liberal that he observed that slavery was unknown to India. Even the foreigners were not converted into slavery by the Indians. But here again, there is a factual error. Obviously it was the benignity of treatment of the slaves, their right to private property and source freedom

---

[1] *The Age of Imperial Unity*, p. 68.

unlike those of the Greek Slaves who were no better than chattles of their master that must have been responsible for this error in observation but the fact remains that slavery existed in India at that time. This is borne out by the Arthasastra which says that no Arya or freeman could be reduced to slavery. Reference to *Dasas,* i.e., the slaves in Asokan inscriptions also bear testimony to the existence of the institution of slavery in Maurya India.

That Megasthenes' account although available to us in fragments referred to by later classical writers, is, to say the least, a unique document and the good words that he said about the administration, people and the political, social economic and cultural life of the Indians under the first Maurya redounds to the credit of our fourbears of the time. It is particularly gratifying to read praises of the country and the people in the account of a foreigner.

Chandragupta: His Personality and Estimate

Alexander's invasion of India in the last quarter of the fourth century before Christ brought out in bold relief two diametrically opposite characters of the Indian rulers of the time, one of craven heartedness and betrayal to the cause of the country, and the other of intrepidity, patriotism and defence of the cause of the country and the people. If Ambhi of Taxila and many others had betrayed the cause of the country by buying Alexander's overlordship, without any compunction, there were kings like Poros, republican tribes like the Malavas and Kshudrakas, who preferred death to dishonour and offered stubborn resistance to the Macedonian conqueror. But by far the greatest defender of freedom was the intrepid Chandragupta Maurya who rising from an obscure station of life won double freedom for the country and successfully defended it from one of Alexander's generals who possessed all knowledge of Alexander's military strategy. He freed the parts of the country from the Greek rule, overthrew the tyrannical Nandas bringing liberty to the people and warded off the invasion Seleukos.

As a youth of no much experience he thought of invoking Alexander's help in overthrowing the vicious Nandas of Magadha and unknowingly was about to play the part of Sangram Singha who invited Babur to put an end to the rule of Ibrahim Lodi. But fortunately the plan did not materialise and in the bargain he gave offence to the proud Macedonian conqueror and had to flee for life.

All this did not damp his spirit. He organised an army with the assistance of his mentor Kautilya and eventually put an end to the foreign rule in the Punjab and overthrew the infamous Nanda ruler. Likewise attempt of Seleukos to recover the Greek conquests in India was foiled by inflicting a crushing defeat on him. All this shows Chandragupta as an intrepid soldier, a military organiser, a patriot and a great defender of the freedom of the country and the liberty of the people. With his vast army Chandragupta has extended his empire from Afghanistan to Mysore. But if he had created the first politically United Indian Empire he did not fail to give it an efficient administration, profusely praised by Megasthenes, the Greek ambassador sent to Pataliputra by Seleukos. Chandragupta's military prowess and the friendly relations that had ushered in with the Greek world after Seleukos's defeat opened up a long and continuous process of friendliness with the West in general and the Greeks in particular.

Chandragupta's government was a commendable compromise between autocracy and democracy capitalism and State socialism. Theoretically the king was the sovereign head of the State and his powers comprised legislative, executive, judicial and military decisons of ultimate nature. But although not bound theoretically by the advice of the Mantriparishad, in practice he could not flout it, remembering as we do that person of Kautilya's eminence was a member of the Mantriparishad. Further, from the Arthasastra we know that the king had to be guided by the majority opinion (*Bhuyishthah*). In matters concerning war or army development the king would consult the Commander-in-Chief (*Senapati*). It is needless, therefore, to say that Chandragupta's government was personal in character but not despotism, it was autocracy without authoritarianism, it was tampered by democracy. Well-being of the people was the fundamental principle of the Government.

Kautilya's administrative scheme what must have been the basis of Chandragupta's administration provided for a large measure of nationalisation of industries. The state-owned vast estates and forests held State monopoly of mines and marketing of produce of the mines. The Government established factories for turning raw materials into finished goods; it also dealt in vast quantities of agricultural products and maintained a central reserve of food grains for current needs and for meeting natural calamities like famine etc.[1] Chandragupta's government, therefore, had a very modern outlook and economically it was a mixture of capitalism and State Socialism—as some writers hold.

The elegance of the court life, the wonderful decorations in the gilded pillars studded with golden vines and silver birds, the palace garden with tamed peacocks and pheasants, artificial ponds with large fishes, trees and shrubs deftly done into beautiful shapes by woodmen betray a great artistic and aesthetic sense on the part of Chandra-

[1] *Comprehensive History of India*, Vol. III, p. 14.

gupta. Evidences are there that Chandragupta held discourses with Brahmana and Jaina Philosophers and folk lores (gathas), Sutras (sullas) etc. were composed during his time.

Chandragupta spent long hours in attending to the business of the Court and administration. He showed both knack and ability to keep an administrative control over the different branches of the government. He was rightly considered to be the greatest of all kings of the country by Aelian.

BINDUSARA (300–273 B.C.): Chandragupta Maurya was succeeded by his son Bindusara in 300 or 299 B.C. According to *Rajavalikathe,* a Jaina text, name of Bindusara was Simhasena. In Hemchandra's Parisisthaparvana, Bindusara was the son of Chandragupta's queen named Duradhara. But historians like H. C. Roychaudhuri are of opinion that the name cannot be accepted as genuine.[1] Bindusara was also known by his epithet *Amitraghata* or *Amitrakhada* i.e., killer of enemies or devourer of enemies. Obviously this epithet was earned by him because of his success against enemies, but details are lacking. But whether the title or epithet *Amritraghata* or *Amitrakhada* was added to his name due to any spectacular success against any enemies is doubtful, for in Patanjali's Mahabhasya the word *Amitraghatin* occurs as an epithet of princes and warriors in respect of their success against enemies. The Greeks called Bindusara *Amitrachates* or *Allitrochates* which Dr. Charpentier rendered into *Amitraghata* as well as *Amitrakhada*.[2] In *Arya-Majusri-Mula-Kalpa* as also in the works of Hemchandra and Taranatha there are references to Chanakya's outliving Chandragupta and serving as Bindusara's minister and procuring destruction of 16 towns and making the "master of all the territory between the Eastern and Western Seas". This was taken by some scholars such as Smith to mean Bindusara's conquest of the Deccan but from Rudradamana's inscription we know that Chandragupta's empire had already extended from *Surashtra* to Bengal, i.e., from the Western to the Eastern Seas. From *Divyavadana* we know that Taxila revolted during the reign of Bindusara and Prince Asoka was despatched to put it down. We may, therefore, conclude that at least one town was restored to the empire under Bindusara. That Bindusara was not of soldierly habits and was rather of a happy-go-lucky disposition, given to ease and luxury is corroborated by contemporary evidence.[3] At best Bindusara succeeded in keeping the Maurya empire as he succeeded from his father Chandragupta in tact, but he can hardly be credited with making any addition to the empire.

---

1 *Pol. History of Ancient India,* p. 295 fn.
2 *Ibid*. p. 296.
3 *Comprehensive History of India.* Vol. II, p. 19.

Bindusara maintained friendly relationship with the Greek rulers initiated during his father's time. From Greek writer, Hegesender, we know of the most cordial relation between Bindusara and Antiochos, Greek King of Syrian to Diodoros. Bindusara has great love for the Graecians.[1] Bindusara once asked Antiochos I, Soter, son of Seleukos to send some 'sweet wine, figs and a philosopher'. Antiochos complied with the request by sending sweet, wine and figs but expressed regret that law of his country did not permit deporting any Philosopher from the country. Antiochos sent Deimachos to the Court of Bindusara to succeed Megasthenes as ambassador. Pliny mentions that another Greek King Ptolemy Philadelphos of Egypt sent Dionysius as ambassador to the Court of Bindusara. The period of Ptolemy's rule was from 285 to 247 B.C. from which some historians think that Dionysius was accredited to Bindusara's Court, although there is no clear evidence to dispel the doubt whether Dionysius presented his credentials to Bindusara or his son Asoka.

We have no details about the administration or reign of Bindusara. We have noticed that he had sent Asoka, his ablest son to quell the rebellion at Taxila which was caused by the tyrannical conduct of the local officials (Dustamatyas). Asoka was also placed as his Viceroy at Ujjaini, capital of Avanti. Bindusara placed his eledest son Susima also called Sumana as Viceroy at Taxila and when rebellion broke out there and situation went out of Susima's control, Asoka was sent to quell the rebellion. Bindusara appears to have followed Chandragupta's system of appointing princess of royal blood as Viceroys and governors of imperial provinces.

Arthasastra : Date and Authorship

Science of Polity in ancient India was called by various names such as *Arthasastra, Nitisastra, Rajniti, Dandaniti* etc. which included political theory and organisation and matters related to State and Society.

Kautilya's *Arthasastra* was regarded as the standard work on the subject and had cast into shade all the previous works of as many as thirteen individual writers due to masterly treatment and well-deserved reputation of Arthasastra.

The book was somehow completely lost and it was not till the beginning of the present century that a copy was discovered by Dr. Sham Sastri from a pandit in Tanjore district. Two other manuscript of Arthasastra was later found in the Munich Library and another "Seems to exist in Calcutta".[2]

---

[1] *Ibid.* p. 299.
[2] Smith : *Early History of India*, p. 160.

Translation of some extracts of the manuscript of Arthasastra was published by Sham Sastri in 1905, a second edition in 1908. Translation of the book in full-fledged form appeared in 1915.

The traditional Indian view is to regard the book as the work of Kautilya, also known as Chanakya and Vishnugupta, the minister of the first Maurya ruler. Keith is the foremost among the scholars who place the treaties in C. 300 A.D. According to him "That the work was a product of C. 300 A.D. written by an official attached to some Court is at least plausible, if it cannot be proved". But Keith's view suffers from infirmity because elsewhere he himself assigned the work "to the first century B.C. while the matter, very probably, is older by a good deal than that".[1]

But in the Puranic text there is a passage which refers to the revolution effected by Chandragupta with the help of Brahmin Kautilya who consecrated him.[2] The dynastic change that took place as a result of the revolution is also referred to in Kautily's Arthasastra, Kamandaka's *Niti Sastra*, the *Mudrarakshasa*, the *Chanda Kausika*, and the Ceylonese chronicles.[3]

Johnston, however, remarks that Kautily's *Arthasastra* is not separated by a great interval from Asvaghosa and is distinctly earlier than Jatakamala of Aryasura who flourished in the fourth Century A.D. This naturally means that the Arthasastra was a work of a period later than the time of the First Maurya.

An earlier date is also suggested because there is reference to Denarius in Book II, Chapters 12 and 19 of *Arthasastra*. But mention of the *Chinapatta* and *Chinabhumi* in Book II, Chapter XI, precludes the possibility of a date earlier than the middle of the third century B.C. 'The great silk-producing country (China) was clearly out of the horizon of the early Mauryas. Further, the imperial title *Chakravarti* mentioned in the Arthasastra is not found before the inscriptions of Kharvela.[4]

The researches of the German scholars, however, clearly established that the *Arthasastra* is a genuine ancient work of the Maurya period and rightly attributed to Chanakya or Kautilya, minister of Chandragupta Maurya. Hermann Jacobi remarks that the *Arthasastra* "is the work of the famous minister of Chandragupta, as established by both external and internal proofs".[5]

It may also be pointed out that many passages in the text of the *Arthasastra* expressly describe it as the composition of Kautilya who uprooted the Nandas, thereby clearly identifying him with the Prime

[1] Vide Singhal : *India and the World Civilisation*, Vol. I, p. 76.
[2] Raychaudhuri : *Political History of Ancient India*, p. 238.
[3] *Ibid.* p. 238 fn.
[4] *Ibid.* p. 10 fn.
[5] Smith : *Early History of India*, p. 161.

Minister of Chandragupta. Roychaudhuri, however, remarks that "Nevertheless a critical examination of the contents has convinced some sholars that the text as it were not the work of a single individual but of a school of politics, and that it could not be composed in the third century B.C. but probably received its present from three or four centuries later. Although the view is now greatly accepted some distinguished scholars still regard the text as genuihe and long lost work of Kautilya".[1]

Although the German scholars, on the basis of their researches are more categorical about the authenticity of the work and its composition by Kautilya, the Prime Minister of Chandragupta Maurya, Smith points out that "The German verdict, of course, does not exclude the possibility, or probability that the existing text may contain certain interpolations of later date, but the bulk of the book certainly dates from the Maurya period".[2]

But certain points have to be considered before any positive conclusion is reached. (1) The language used in *Arthasastra* is Sanskrit and not Prakit which was used by the Mauryas. (2) The wall of Kautilya's fort (Durga) was to be made of bricks and Kautilya had horror of wooden structure as "fire finds a happy abode in it" but from Megasthenes we learn that such cities as were situated on the banks of rivers or sea coasts were built of wood instead of brick. Pataliputra was girded by wooden walls. (3) There is reference to the royal titles adopted by the Mauryas in the *Arthasastra*. On the contrary title like *Indra-Yama-Sthanametat* mentioned in the *Arthasastra* is very much akin to the titles referred to in the *Allahabad Prasasti*. (4) Some of the official designations were found to be in use under the Mauryas but two important designations, viz., *Samahartri* and *Sannidhatri* were found in inscriptions of later times. (5) *Chinapatta*, *Chinabhumi* and *Kambu*, i.e., Cambodia wherefrom silk came into India, referred to in the *Arthasastra* shows that the treatise did not belong to the early Mauryas since China and Cambodia "were outside the horizon of the earliest Mauryas". India's contact with China before the Han Dynasty (206 B.C. to 200 A.D.) is not indisputable. In view of these points raised about the date of the composition of the *Arthasastra* remains still controversial and awaits solution.[3]

We may, therefore, conclude that although, it is generally accepted that the work was of Kautilya the Prime Minister of the First Maurya, Chandragupta, it contained references to contents of earlier works on the subject now lost, as well as certain later interpolations. In

---

[1] Raychaudhuri : *Ancient India*, p. 140.
[2] Smith : *Early History of India*, p 161
[3] *Age of Imperial Unity*, pp. 285-87.

any event the treatise contains to be controversial and a subject matter for further researches.

ASOKA

Birth and Early Life : Accession

The romantic hypothesis based on Seleukos entering into a matrimonial alliance with Chandragupta Maurya, Asoka's grandfather, which according to Sylvain Levi "introduced a Greek Princess in the Mauryan harem" that Asoka was either the grandson or son of the Greek Princess remains unproved. That he was not the son of the Greek Princess is proved on the evidence of *Asokavadana*, *Divyavadana* and *Vamsatthapakasini*. While both *Divyavadana* and *Asokavadana* give the name of Asoka's mother as Subhadrangi, daughter of a Brahman of Champa *Vamsatthapakasini* gives her name as Darma. There is a legend behind the name 'Asoka'. It is said that Queen Subhadrangi could not enjoy her rightful position of the royal consort due to some palace intrigue. When she ultimately gained her position as royal consort and a son was born to her she named him *Asoka*, i.e., no sorrow and when second son was born she called him *Vitasoka*, i.e., end of sorrow.

Two points, however, emerge for consideration: (i) If the mantrimonial alliance between Seleukos and Chandragupta means a marriage between a Greek Princess and Bindusara, then the palace intrigue in keeping the princess separate from the King (Bindusara) may have some meaning as the princess was of an outlandish origin. (ii) This may as well somewhat explain the opposition of some of the brothers of Asoka to latter's succession to the throne which led to a struggle accounting for the interregnum of four years from 273—269 B.C.

On Bindusara's death his son Asoka succeeded him and with him begins a memorble chapter of the history of India. He has been called the 'Greatest of Kings' by H. G. Wells and by common consent he has been given the highest place of honour among the Kings and Emperors of the World.

Our knowledge of the history of his reign is based on inscriptions left by him engraved on rocks and pillars which from the very nature of permanence stand unaltered and without any interpolation till today. But although his inscriptions are an excellent source of our information of his reign they do not throw any light on his early life. We have to depend solely upon the Buddhist texts like *Divyavadana* and the Ceylonese chronicles like *Dipavamsa*, *Mahavamsa* etc.

According to *Mahavamsa* Asoka while a Prince was appointed as Viceroy at Ujjain. Two later Buddhist texts, the *Asokasutra* and *Kunalasutra* state that Asoka was the Viceroy at Taxila. But according to *Asokavadana* we know that a revolt took place at Taxila during the reign of Bindusara due to the oppressive rule of the local officials and Asoka was sent there to put it down. This fact is also corroborated by an Aramic inscription found in a house at Sirkap in Taxila. It may be that after the revolt had been quelled Asoka continued to stay at Taxila for sometime. This might have led to the confusion in the Buddhist texts *Asokasutra* and *Kunalasutra* where Asoka has been stated as the Viceroy of Taxila. Most of the evidences bear out that Asoka was the Viceroy at Ujjain before he became the King.

From *Dipavamsa* we have information regarding the personal life of Asoka when he was a viceroy at Ujjain. There he fell in love with a daughter of a merchant, named Devi or Vidisamahadevi whom he is said to have married and had two children through her : Mahendra and Samghamitra. Devi continued to remain at Vidisa, when Asoka ascended the throne at Pataliputra, obviously because, she was not of an appropriately high rank to become the Queen.

The Buddhist texts depict Asoka in his early career as a cruel, blood thirsty tyrant for which he earned the epithet of *Chandasoka* (ferocious Asoka), but after his conversion he became a *Dharmasoka* (religious Asoka). Asoka is said to have seized the throne on his father's death by slaying his ninety-nine brothers born of different wives of Bindusara. These are hardly credible and were introduced to glorify Buddhism by drawing a glaring contrast between Asoka's career before and after conversion into Buddhism.

There is, however, a general agreement on the point that Asoka was not the heir-apparent and that there was a fratricidal struggle after the death of Bindusara and his sons. On the evidence of *Divyavadana* we know that Bindusara before his death desired to appoint his oldest son Susima as King. But his ministers, particularly his Chief Minister Radhagupta placed Asoka on the throne.

At the time of Bindusara's death Asoka was the Viceroy of a province, according to some sources Taxila, according to others Ujjain. *Mahavamsa* mentions Asoka's slaying of his eldest brother and elsewhere the same work as also *Dipavamsa* mention that Asoka killed his ninety-nine brothers sparing only Tishya or Tissa the youngest of all.

Asoka's slaying of his ninety-nine brothers born of different wives of Bindusara can be, without hesitation, dismissed as imaginary. There is no independent evidence of such a struggle. The story must have been introduced by the Buddhist writers to glorify the influence of Buddhism on Asoka showing the contrast between his nature before his becoming a Buddhist and after. This story is refuted by his inscriptions which mention of not only one brother, but several of them living in the thirteenth year of his reign both in Pataliputra and other towns of his empire whose household were of Asoka's most anxious care. In his 5th Rock Edict Asoka mentions officers who besides their other duties, had the special function of superintending the welfare of the families of his brothers, sisters and others relatives.

However, from historical standpoint what the Buddhist stories suggest has two distinct matters to be considered, viz. (i) that there was a fratricidal struggle on the death of Bindusara and Asoka was involved in it and he had to remove all his brothers who opposed his accession to the throne, and (ii) that the delay that occurred between the year of the death of Bindusara, 273 B.C. and Asoka's coronation in 269 B.C. was due to the fratricidal struggle and this explains the period of interregnum of four years.

As to the first, it may be pointed out that there is no independent evidence to show that there was such a fratricidal struggle in which so many of his brothers had been done to death by Asoka. This must have been a fabrication of the Buddhist writers to show the contrast of Asoka's wickedness and piety before and after his conversion into Buddhism. Only point that has emerged as a historical fact is Asoka's supersession of the claim of his eldest brother Susima.

With regard to the delay between the accession and coronation, most scholars have accepted it as historical, particularly in view of Asoka's dating of the events of his reign from his coronation in all his inscriptions. But no satisfactory explanation has been given for this unusual course, "and it is a mere gratuitous assumption that the long delay may have been due to disputed succession involving much bloodshed" as Smith suggests. The Ceylonese chronicles simply state that Asoka's coronation took place four years after he "had won for himself the undivided sovereignty". This naturally raises a presumption that his sovereignty might have been disputed in parts of the empire. Asoka's grandson Dasarath also dated the events of his reign from the date of his coronation. Most of the scholars except Dr. D. R. Bhandarkar accept the view that there was a gap between Asoka's accession and coronation although no valid reasons have been adduced for it.

The whole controversy over the legend of slaying of ninety-nine brothers and all that, boils down to one probability that there was a contest for the throne in which Asoka had succeeded against the claims of his step-brother Susima, the eldest of the sons of Bindusara, with the help of Radhagupta the Chief Minister of Bindusara.

On his coronation Asoka assumed the title of *Piyadasi,* i.e., Priyadarshi, meaning of gainly looks. The fullest appellation by which Asoka styled himself is *Devanampriya Priyadarsi Raja.* He did not call himself Asoka, his personal name, except in the Maski Edict which sets at rest the question of identity of the Priyadarsi.

Asoka's Family and Family Life

Some members of Asoka's immediate family have been mentioned in various sources. Asoka had several queens, the exact number is not known to us.

There are references to at least three queens in chronicles and Buddhist texts like *Mahavamsa, Divyavadana,* etc. Asoka's Chief Queen for most of his reign was Asandhimittra who died four years before Asoka's death. On the death of Asandhimittra, Tissarakkha was raised to the position of the Chief Queen. It is said that this queen had a very great influence on Asoka, wherefrom a modern scholar suggests that she might have been married by Asoka late in his life, obviously on the assumption that young wives have always exercised undue influence on aged husband. The second queen of Asoka was Karuvaki, mother of Trivara mentioned in the Queen's edict. Another Queen referred to in the *Divyavadana* as his third wife was Padmavati who was the mother of the crown prince Kunala also called Dharmavivardhana. Fa-Hien also mentions Dharmavivardhana as the son of Asoka who was the Viceroy at Gandhara. From *Rajatarangini* we have the reference to another son of Asoka, named Jalauka, and a third Tivara born of queen Karuvaki.

Asoka had two daughters, Samghamitra and Carumati. Fa-Hien's writing in the fourth century A.D. and following him Hiuen-Tsang two centuries later mentions Mahendra as brother of Asoka. But as we have already seen, Mahendra was the son of Asoka born of Devi of Vidisa, the beautiful daughter of a merchant. From all this, it is reasonable to believe that although a Buddhist he had a number of queens as well as 'left handed' wives as is evidenced from his mention of *avarodhana,* i.e., harem. Asoka's reference to devikumaras besides his sons *Aryaputras* as distinguished from *devikumaras,* though his queens might have been born of his wives other than his queens.

About Asoka's private life and habits we have very little information. From Rock Edic VI we have some indirect reference to how he would abide his time when he had no official business to attend to. "Evidently, therefore", remarks Dr. Bhandarkar in analysing the information found in the Rock Edict VI "when Asoka had no business to dispose of, and of course, was not asleep, he was to be found at his capital either regaling in the dining hall, engaged with the inmates of his harem, chatting in his retiring cabin, or inspecting the royal stud, or enjoying a horse ride or beguiling his time in the orchard".[1] About his tastes and fascinations, we have a little bit of information from his first Rock Edict whereform we know that even when he was carrying out his programme of stopping slaughter and injury to living beings he permitted only two peacocks and one deer to be killed for his royal dish, the killing of deer was not being very regularly done. This gives us an idea of the food that gratified his royal palate.

As a King, before his conversion into Buddhism, Asoka seems to have done what the kings of ancient India would do. He feasted and amused his subjects, for which purpose he followed the celebration of *Samajas*. The *Samajas* were of two kinds, one for entertaining the people in a banquet, the chief item of food was meat. The other *Samaja* was one in which dancing, music, wrestling etc. were performed in an amphitheatre. Hunting was also a part of the entertainment in this kind of *Samajas*. The *Samajas* as Nilkanta Sastri mentions were unquestionably a diplomatic mode of keeping the people pleased and satisfied. But such *Samajas* were all stopped after Asoka began to preach his *Dhamma*.

The Kalinga War

Asoka had given ample evidence of his ability as a soldier and a statesman even before becoming the king. He was the Viceroy of Ujjain and when there was a rebellion in Taxila and the situation went out of hands of Susima, his eldest brother, who was the Viceroy there, Asoka was sent there to quell the rebellion. To begin with Asoka followed the footsteps of his illustrious grandfather Chandragupta Maurya and launched upon a career of conquest and aggression. The Buddhist text Divyavadana mentions his conquest of Svasa (Khasa) country. But the only conquest referred to in his edicts took place in the ninth year of his coronation.

In the thirteenth year of his reign and eight years after his coronation Asoka made war against Kalinga, modern Orissa including Ganjam and included it into the Magadhan Empire. The conquered country was formed into a viceroyalty with its headquarters at Tosali. Parts of Kalinga were within the dominions of the Nanda Kings, the reconquest of Kalinga, therefore, was necessitated by its having severed connection with Magadha after the fall of the Nandas. If we go by

1. R. D. Bhandarkar : *Asoka,* pp.14-15.

the story of a general revolt under Bindusara during which Taxila revolted, it is not "unlikely that Kalinga like Taxila" remarks Dr. H. C. Raychaudhuri "threw off the allegiance of Magadha during the reign of that monarch." But Dr. Raychaudhuri also mentions the evidence of Pliny, who based his work on Megasthenes' *Indika*, that at the time of Chandragupta Kalinga was an independant kingdom with an army of 60,000 foot soldiers, 1,000 horsemen and 700 elephants which was in "Procint of War". Thus the evidence of Pliny belies the presumption of a revolt by Kalinga during the time of Bindusara for it was already independent during Chandragupta's time.

We now turn to the probability of Kalinga becoming independent after the fall of the Nanda rule in Magadha. According to R. S. Tripathy confusion occasioned by the overthrow of the Nanda rule by Chandragupta was taken advantage of by Kalinga and became independent. Dr. Tripathy remarks that Chandragupta Maurya's pre-occupation in setting the newly acquired soverigntly and building up the administration left no time at his disposal to turn to the conquest of Kalinga.

A pertinent question that still remains is why Asoka instead of trying to conquer the Chola and the Pandya countries which his father tried to subdue proceeded to conquer Kalinga. Andhra which lay South of Kalinga had been conquered by Bindusara but when he proceeded to conquer the Chola and the Pandya countries, Kalinga an ally of the Cholas and the Pandya's attacked Bindusara from the rear and became the cause of Bindusara's failure. Thus Kalinga was an enemy of the Mauryas both because its breaking away from the Magadhan empire and particularly because of the turning into an ally of the countries Bindusara wanted to conquer. Kalinga as Nilkanta Sastri remarks became "a thorn in the body politic of his (Asoka's) dominions". "It was, therefore, perhaps supremely imperative to reduce Kalinga to complete subjection". This reasoning of Dr. Bhandarkar is, however, regarded as speculative by Nilkanta Sastri.[1]

The major cause for the conquest of Kalinga was its military strength. We have seen how Pliny described the military strength of Kalinga. R. C. Majumdar remarks that Kalinga was a populous and powerful state. It had thrived on maritime trade. Thus wealth both human and material accounted for the strength of the country and her spirit of independence has been demonstrated by her assuming independent status after taking advantage of the confusion consequent upon the overthrow of the Nandas and her jealous guarding of independence by not allowing Bindusara to conquer her allies, the

[1] *Vide* Nilkanta Sastri : *Comprehensive History of India*—ii p. 23, also fn.

Cholas and the Pandyas. The huge casualties of the war as described in the Rock Edict XIII with one hundred fifty thousand taken prisoners, hundred thousand slain and as many number dead bear out hugeness of the army of Kalinga and its highly populousness. Obviously, the Kalinga King must have added to his army strength between the time of Megasthenes and that of the Kalinga War. For such a strong country remaining in procint of war on the border of his dominions could certainly not be a matter of indifference to any emperor. Asoka, therefore, felt the need of subjugating Kalinga. The conquest and annexation of Kalinga left Asoka free to carry out his policy of conquest of Chola and Pandya countries to complete the conquest of the whole of the Indian peninsula. But soon after the Kalinga War Asoka became a Buddhist. For a year Asoka was lukewarm but thereafter he began strenuous efforts for promoting the *Dhamma* for his mind was fired by ennobling aspiration of becoming supreme on earth not through territorial conquests but through conquest of Dhamma and which stood for love, humanity, and nonviolence.

Extent of Asoka's Empire

The conquest of Kalinga marks the end of an era in the history of Magadha as also of India. It closed the career of imperial conquests begun with Bimbisara's conquest of Anga. While it ended the era of Magadhan imperial expansion, it marked the beginning of an era of peace and social progress, of brotherliness and religious propaganda, and consequent military inefficiency and political stagnation. The era of *Digvijaya* was over and the era of *Dhammavijaya* was to begin.

It is worthwhile to consider the final expansion that the Maurya Empire had reached Asoka's conquest of Kalinga. We have a fair idea of the extent of the Maurya Empire under Chandragupta and his son Bindusara. It extended from Herat in the north-west to Mysore and Nellore district of Madras. Under Bindusara Andhra was annexted to the Maurya Empire. It was under Asoka that Maurya Empire reached its apogee in expanse.

About the extent of Asoka's empire we have more precise knowledge than we had about the Maurya Empire under his predecessors. Our knowledge is derived from two sources, namely, the find spots of Asoka's edicts and the references in the inscriptions themselves.

The peculiarity with Asoka's Rock Edicts is that they are found on or about the frontiers of his dominions. Again, whereas the Rock seems to be engraved in the capitals of outlying provinces, the Minor

Rock Edicts are mostly found at places which separate his territory from those of independent or semi-independent neighbours. Thus the find spots of his Rock Edicts and Minor Rock Edicts give us almost a full picture of the extent of his empire. Now as we move from the east and proceed westwards noting the findspots of his edicts we first come across that near the Bay of Bengal engraved in a village called Dhanli Bhuvaneswar. One version of this edict is found inscribed in the town of Jaugada in the Ganjam district of the Madras Presidency. Both these versions of the Rock Edicts were put up in the newly conquered province of Kalinga which was the south-eastern limit of Asoka's empire. Towards the north a third copy of Asoka's Ronk Edicts has been found near Kalsi in the Dehra Dun district. Two versions of the Rock Edicts have been found inscribed one at Mansera in the Hazara district and another at Shahbazgarhi in the Peshwar district in the North-Western Frontier Province. Moving towards the South along the Western coast one version has been discovered at Junagarh in Kathiawar and another at Sopara in the Thana district. One set of the fourteen Rock Edicts of Asoka has been found at Yerragudi in the Kurnool district of the Madras Presidency. Mr. Lewis Rice discovered three copies of the Minor Rock Editcs of Asoka at three places in the Chitaldurg district in Mysore.

From the find spots of the Rock Edicts of Asoka on the bordering areas of his dominions we get a fairly precise idea of his empire extending to the Bay of Bengal in the east, the northern districts of Mysore in the south, the Ganjam in the South-east, to the North-Western Frontier Province, to the Himalayan region in the north and to Kathiawar and Bombay towards the West. Thus we may say that the empire of Asoka extended from the Himalaya in the north to Madras in the south and from the North-Western Provinces in the west to Bay of Bengal in the east.

Now turning to the evidence contained in the body of the Edicts we may find out what places have been named therein as within the dominions of Asoka. Asoka's Rock Edicts II and XIII give us the names of his frontager kings. Towards the north-west outside India reference is to *Anitiyoka Yoṇa Raja,* i.e., the Yavana King Antiochus II of Syria whose kingdom bordered on the limits of Asoka's empire towards the north-west. This quite fits in with the indigenous and the Greek evidences that Seleukos made over Kabul, Kandahar, Makran and Herat to Chandragupta Maurya.

Towards the south the Kingdoms on the borders of Asoka's empire were those Cholas, Pandyas, Keralaputra and Satiyaputra, and beyond India towards the south *Tambapamni* i.e., Ceylon.

Asoka mentioned the following places as within his empire: *Magadha, Pataliputra, Khalatikaparvata, Kosami, Lumminigama, Kalinga, Atavi, Suvarnagiri, Isila, Ujjaini, Takshasila.*

From the Greek source we know that *Gangaridae,* i.e., Bengal was within the empire of Asoka. From Hiuen-Tsang's record and Kalhana's *Rajatarangini* it is known that Kashmir was included in the dominions of Asoka.

In Rock Edicts V and XIII Asoka refers to the outlying provinces of his kingdom. These are Yonas, Kambojas, Gandharas, Rastrika-Petenikas, Bhoja-Petenikas, Nabhaka-Nabhapamtis, Andhras and Parimdas. Except Nabhapamtis and Parimdas, it has been possible to identify all these places. Yonas have been identified with the Greek Colony of Nysa which lay between the Kabul and the Indus. Kambojas have been identified with the province to the South of Kashmir. Gandhara was a province of Asoka's empire with Taxila as its capital. The Rastrikas were the occupants of Nasik and Poona districts, and the Bhojas the occupants of Thana and Kolaba districts of Bombay and parts of Madhya Pradesh and Hyderabad. According to Senart the names mentioned in the Edicts have been placed in a definite order. If this is accepted then Nabhaka-Nabhapamtis were somewhere in Baluchistan, and Parmidas as the name follows Andhras, it must have been somewhere in the easternmost part of Asoka's empire. This view is taken by both Hultzch and N. K. Sastri.

In the Cambridge History of India (Vol. I) Rapson mentions the above areas to be under the sphere of influence of Asoka's empire. Some Scholars take these to be feudatory (Hida raja) states under Asoka. But as Dr. Bhandarkar points out, it was due to a misreading and misinterpretation of a phrase in Rock Edict XIII that they were regarded as feudatory chiefs. But the Girnar version of the same edict has proved beyond doubt that these were all subject peoples of Asoka. Dr. Roychaudhuri also points out that the fact of Asoka's appointing Dhamma Mahamatras in these places and peoples prove beyond doubt they were the subjects of his empire.

If we compare the extent of Asoka's empire as we understand from the external evidence, that is the evidence of the find spots of Asoka's Edicts, with the internal evidence, that is, the evidence furnished by the inscription and other recorded sources, we get a dear and precise idea of the extent of Asoka's empire. It comprised whole of India except Kamrupa, i.e., Assam in the east and the Tamil States in the extreme south and upto the borders of the kingdom of Antiochos of Syria towards the north-west.

Administration of The Empire under Asoka

The empire of the Mauryas even under Chandragupta was vast enough to admit its being easily administered. Under Asoka the empire reached its utmost expansion covering almost the whole of the Indian sub-continent. An empire so vast and made up of parts so widely separated as Herat, Orissa and Mysore need a Hercules to administer it effectively and keeping it together in those days of distant past. Asoka, therefore, continued the policy of decentralisation of the administration as it existed under his grandfather and father making certain changes in its functioning.

Asoka perhaps had a Deputy or *Uparaja* like his brother Tissa to assist him. Besides the *Uparaja* there were the *Yuvaraja,* i.e., the Crown Prince and *Agramatya,* i.e., the Chief Minister Radhagupta to help him in carrying out the administration of the empire. He also shared his administration with the Princes, the *Kumaras* or *Aryaputras* as they were called, who were appointed viceroys in the outlying provinces of the empire. Asoka's inscriptions mention four such viceroys ruling at Ujjaini, Taxila, Suvarnagiri and Tosali. The Buddhist text Divyavadana mentions Prince Kunala as viceroy at Taxila. Kunala was also known as Dharmavivardhana, referred to in the Chinese traveller Fa-hien's account.

The empire was divided into viceroyalties under which were governorships. Obviously the Viceroyalties were divided into divisions, called Pradeshas and the Governors called *Pradeshikas* in the inscriptions.[1] According to N. K. Sastri the empire was divided into a number of *Janapadas* or Provinces which were subdivided into *Pradesas* or divisions, each *Pradesa* was again divided into *aharas* or districts and *aharas* into *Visayyas* or talukas.[2]

There was hierarchy of officials beginning from the Viceroy downwards such as governors or *Pradeshikas,* and *rajukas,* or district officers ; below the Rajukas came the *Purushas,* who were of three different ranks. *Yuktas* were district officers who kept accounts assisted by the Upa-Juktas. In the separate Kalinga Edicts there has been refernece to three *Kumaras* one in charge of each of the provinces such as *Janapadas* of Ujjaini, Taxila and Tosali (in Kalinga). In the fourth province with Suvarnagiri as its capital, the Viceroy is called *Aryaputra* in the Minor Rock Edict I. The word *Aryaputra,* as N. K. Sastri says refers to Yuvaraja or the Crown Prince in this case. All the viceroys did not have same measure of autonomy. N. K. Sastri remarks "we notice some differences with regard to the degree of authority they exercised in their provinces". Whereas the Kumara of Tosali

---

[1] *Age of Imperial Unity,* p. 79.

[2] N. K. Sastri : *Comprehensive History of India.* Vol. II, p. 27.

ruled over Kalinga jointly with *mahamatras* subject to the control of the King himself. Mahamatras were high officials who worked under the Kumaras as in the cases of the Kumaras of Ujjaini and Taxila but were joint rulers with Kumara at Kalinga.[1]

Asoka's inscriptions mention a few other categories of Officers such as *Stryadhyaksha-Mahamatras, Vajrabhumikas* and *Anta-mahamatras*. According to N. K. Sastri *Anta-mahamatras* appear to be high officials who accompanied Asoka's envoys to foreign countries.

It is worthwhile to mention that the Viceroys had an official hierarchy modelled on that of the imperial government at the centre and were enjoined by the emperor to follow the same procedure in regard to circuit as was followed by the central government.

Asoka had a Parishad or Council which he refers to in two of his edicts. In the 3rd Rock Edict the Council appears to act in a subordinate way, for it was being merely expected to order the *Yuktas* to register the new administrative measures adopted by Asoka. In the 6th Rock Edict the Council appears to have much greater authority. It appears empowered to discuss King's policy in his absence and suggests change or it may discuss emergent matters referred to it by the King. In such cases the decisions of the Council had to be reported to the King without loss of time. But the final decision rested with the King; this shows that the Council was more or less an advisory body. It may, however, be mentioned that the Council in which powerful minister like Radhagupta would be present its decision could not possibly be altogether ignored by the King. It may also be mentioned that King's control over the Council was gradually inceased with appointment of new Councillors who were chosen by the King himself and such they were persons who were in favour of his policy.

In provincial administration the Council of Minister had much greater power than its central counterpart and it acted, in fact, as a check on the power of the Prince and when occasion would demand, they could have direct contact with the King. At times the King would send direct orders to the ministers bypassing the Prince. The Mahamatras in the viceroyalties would be appointed by the King himself on occasions.

Asoka took punctilious care to see that justice was meted out to the people without any delay or injustice. In his separate Edict addressed to the *mahamatras*, Asoka emphasised the importance of just behaviour and impartial justice and cautioned them against weaknesses like anger, fatigue, laziness, impatience, etc., which might prejudice a judgment. The jurisdiction in the urban areas was in the

---

[1] *Comprehensive History of India*, Vol. II. p. 28.

charge of the *mahamatras* and that in the rural area in the hands of the *rajukas*. In the Maurya penal system fine was the prevalent punishment Those who could not pay the fine might accept bondage in lieu. Capital punishment was also practised. In spite of Asoka's conversion to Buddhism in extreme cases death penalty would be given. Although Asoka was not in favour of capital punishment he did not do away with the practice. This was obviously an instance of Asoka's prudent statecraft which triumphed over his ideals.

Asoka kept himself informed of everything that was going within his dominions through *Pulindas* and *Pativedakas*, i.e., the special reporters who had access to the king at all places and all hours. Asoka's system of espionage was not so complex as to be found in Kautilya's *Arthasastra*. His reporters were not secret people, they were known to the population and the administration and they went from place to place and made reports to the king.

Character of his Government

In one way Asoka's administration ushered in a new form of administration. Till we reach the Maurya period the system of government in India was of diverse nature comprising in it kingship, small republics and confederation of smaller states. But it was under the 1st Maurya king that a centralised monarchy based on political union of a vast area of the country had emerged. Under Asoka this unity was further extended. Asoka desired a complete control over the country and it was under him that a centralised empire on such a vast scale was established in India. As set forth in the political treatise *Arthasastra* every detail of the organisation and administration of the State was aimed at giving the final control into hands of the king. According to the traditional concept of Indian kingship of the time the supremacy of the king's authority was meant for protection of social usages and for the welfare of the people. To serve these purposes king's law might even supersede sastra. This gave a tremendous increase in the power of the king but under Asoka this centralised authority took the shape of paternalism. "The previously held idea of the king being a protector, remote from the affairs of his subjects, gave way to the belief that he had complete control over all spheres of social and political life." "All men are my children" defined Asoka's attitude to his subjects and welfare of the subjects became the basic character of his government.

His Conversion into Buddhism

Asoka till his conversion into Buddhism had the traditional devotion of the Hindu kings to gods and goddesses. The Kashmir

Chronicler Kalhana identifies his favourite deity as Siva. Born and brought up in the splendour of the Maurya imperial atmosphere, he took pleasure in hunting, gambling and war. He had no scruple in slaughter of men and animals. Like other Princes of royal blood he had no hesitation in defeating the claim of his eldest brother to the throne. Even if we reject the claim of the Buddhist texts and Ceylonese traditions that he had killed his ninetynine brothers except the youngest as a fabrication, his struggle for the throne with the help of the Chief Minister cannot be brushed aside. All this shows him in the true colour of the section of an imperial house. Even his war of conquest of Kalinga was in complete conformity with his imperial ambition.

But the Kalinga War which took place in the ninth year of his coronation and terrible carnage that it resulted in, and the untold miseries that it brought in its train appalled Asoka. The sight of miseries and bloodshed in the sanguinary campaign touched him too deep in his heart and roused in him a deep feeling of remorse and sorrow. In his own words in his inscription (R. E. XIII) he says: "Thus arose His Sacred Majesty's remorse for having conquered the Kalingas, because the conquest of a country, previously unconquered, involves the slaughter, death and carrying away captive of the people. That is a matter of profound sorrow and regret to His Sacred Majesty."

Acting upto his feelings of remorse and sorrow, Asoka abstained from aggressive war for the rest of his life. To seathe the sword at the moment of success which would have definitely led to further success by way conquest of the Tamil countries which his father had attempted but failed, is a unique experience in history of imperialism. It was at this time that Asoka came under the influence of Buddhism which stood for peace and non-violence.

For about two years and a half Asoka remained a lay disciple after which he formally joined the Buddhist Order and became a *Bhikshu*. He then began to exert himself strenuously for the propagation of Buddhism in which he found solace and peace of mind.

As a monk he visited the holy places connected with the life of Buddha. He first visited *Sambodhi,* i.e., Bodhgaya the place where Buddha became *Sambuddha* or enlightened one. Later he visited Lumbini Park, the Bethelhem of Buddhism, the birth place of Buddha, where an inscribed pillar still stands to commemorate the emperor's visit.[1] In these visits he was led by his preceptor Saint Upagupta.

---

1 "Upagupta addressed Asoka and said: 'Here, the great King! was the Venerable One born'. A pillar inscribed with these words, still as legible as when they were incised, was set up by Asoka to preserve the memory of his visit". V. A. Smith, *The Early History of India,* p. 167.

In due course Upagupta led his royal disciple to Kapilavastu, Sravasti and Kushinagar.

Asoka combined the functions of an emperor and a Buddhist zealot. He even dressed himself in the robe of a monk and at times retired to a monastery after making suitable arrangement for the administration of his empire. "What with the elevating intercourse with the *Samgha,* i.e., monastery and the enthralling sanctity attaching to this place, he became completely transformed and forthwith developed into a zealot." Almost like Charlemagne of the Holy Roman Empire of Europe Asoka also adopted the position of the head of both Church and State during the last twenty years of his reign.

His Administrative Reform

Asoka's conversion had its effects both upon internal and external policies of the government. In the fourth Rock Edict and the Kalinga Edict Asoka expressed his unhappiness about several matters in which maladministration in the provinces was a major one. To remove the maladministration Asoka adopted some measures of administrative reforms.

He instituted two kinds of circuits (anusamyana), quinquennial and triennial of state officials like *Yutas, Rajukas, Pradesikas* and *Mahamatras*. The *Yutus, Rajukas* and the *Pradesikas* had to go on tour of the different parts of the country every five years. According to H. C. Raichaudhuri their circuit or tour was mainly for propaganda work. But they had also to look after, supervise and check the work of administration in different parts of the country. The circuit (*Anusamyana*) of the *Mahamatras* was triennial and was specially instituted for the purpose of checking miscarriage of justice, arbitrary imprisonment and torture in the outlying provinces like Kalinga, Ujjaini and Taxila.

Asoka also created a number of new posts such as *Dhamma Mahamatras* and *Dhamma-Yutas.* The *Dhamma-Mahamatras* were given the protective mission among the people of all sects, the Brahmanas, Jainas, Yavanas, Kambojas, Gandharas, Rastikas and all Aparantas. They were also appointed among the servants, masters, wealthy, the helpless, and the aged for freeing them from the wordly cares and propagation of the Law of Piety.

They were also employed to grant remission of penalties or execution on the merits of the case. They were also to consider the motive behind the crime and if they found sufficient grounds might even release the convicted person. If the person was of advanced age, or committed the crime on instigation or had dependent children they might as well be released by such Officers.

Dhamma-Mahamatras were further engaged everywhere in the imperial dominions "or indeed in the whole world (*Prithivi*) as known to the Mauryas, among the *Dhamma-Yutas* with regard to the concerns of the Law, the establishment of the Law and the business of alms giving". This shows that Asoka appointed a new class of officers called *Dhamma-Yutas* for looking after the Law of Piety and alms giving. The border countries were placed under the special care of the *Avutikas*, a new class of officials.

Asoka who was anxious to keep himself fully informed of the affairs of the State, whether there was any delay in public affairs, specially in the work of the *Mahamatras*, gave special direction to the *Pativedakas*, i.e., reporters to report to him immediately whenever any urgent or important matter was committed to the *Mahamatras* or discussed in the *Parishad*.

From the Kalinga Edicts and the Sixth Rock Edict it is clearly understood how Asoka himself kept an watchful eye on the *Mahamatras*, especially on those who were entrusted with the administration of justice in cities.

He granted much freedom to the *Rajukas* in their function of awarding honours or penalties so that they might perform their duty with fullest freedom and without any fear. The *Rajukas* were placed over many hundred thousands of people. Grant of this freedom of action was made only to the *Rajukas* who obviously enjoyed much respect and confidence of Asoka.

In order that there might be uniformity in penalties and procedure, he ordered that all condemned prisoners awaiting capital punishment must be given a respite of three days during which they might appeal to the higher authorities for pardon or prepare themselves for the other world.

Asoka also issued regulations legally restricting the slaughter or mutilation of animals on certain occasions. He also effected jail deliveries almost once in every year. Twenty-five jail deliveries were ordered upto twenty-seventh year of his coronation.

Change in Foreign Policy

Asoka's conversion to Buddhism had its immediate effects on the foreign policy of the country. He declared that it would be a matter of great regret to him if a thousandth part of the sufferings, death and maiming that took place in the Kalinga War were to come upon his people. Asoka assured the unsubdued peoples of the countries on the frontiers of his dominions that they should not be afraid of him, they should trust him and would receive happiness and not sorrow (Kalinga Edict I). He even assured them that he would bear any wrong done to him, so far as it could possibly be borne with. He eschewed war and declared that the chiefest conquest was not the conquest by arms (*Digvijay*) but conquest by righteousness (*Dhamma-Vijaya*). Thus traditional Maurya policy of imperial expansion through wars of conquests was reversed and a policy conquering the hearts of the frontagers through friendliness, love, and peace was adopted instead. In pursuance of his policy of no-war Asoka declared with a feeling of exultation that the reverberation of his war drums (*Bherighosa*) has been converted into reverberation of Law of Piety (*Dhammaghosa*). Not content with eschewing war himself, he banned war of conquests by the sons and grandsons even. He declared : "From now my sons and grandsons should not go in for any conquests (*Putre papotra me asu navam vijayam ma vijetavyam*).

In strict conformity with his profession Asoka in practice as well made no attempt to annex the frontier kingdoms of the extreme south such as Chola, Pandya, Satiyaputra, Keralaputra, Tambapamni (Ceylon) which he could have done in a trice should he so desired. The same policy he pursued in regard to the realm of Amtiyoko Yonaraja who has been identified with Antiochos II Theos, King of Syria and Western Asia. On the contrary, he followed a policy of extreme friendliness in his relations with them. Asoka's friendly relations were not confined to the frontagers only, but also kingdoms beyond. He had cordial friendly relations with Ptolemy II Philadelphos of Egypt, Magas of Cyrene in North Africa, Antigonas Gonatas, King of Macedon and Alexander of Epirus.[1] He sent his envoys to these countries for propagation of the Law of Piety and as H. C. Raichaudhuri remarks, "Buddhism doubtless, made some progress in Western Asian countries. But the Greeks apparently were not much impressed by the doctrine of non-violence. They seemingly remained friendly towards India for they were aware that Asoka's strong arm, in spite of his repentance, possessed the power to punish and as soon as Asoka was dead the Yavanas once more pounced upon the Kabul Valley, the Punjab, and Madhyadesa and threw these areas into confusion."

Asoka's missions seem to have attained greater success in the South. In the Tamil countries of the South, Ceylon as well as in *Suvarnabhumi* the Law of Piety and through it the culture of India had an abiding influence.

---

[1] *Turumayo* = Ptolemy, *Amtekina* = Antigonas, *Maka* = *Magas*, Alikasundaro = Alexander (R.E. XIII).

Asoka's Dhamma

We have a clear and precise idea about the constituents of Asoka's *Dhamma* from the attributes he mentions that fall under the term as well as the specific practices thereof.

In the 2nd and seventh Pillar Edicts Asoka mentions the qualities that constitute his *Dhamma.* These are : *Sadhave* or *bahukayane,* i.e., much good, *apasinave,* i.e., freedom from depravity, *daya,* i.e., mercy, *dane*, i.e., liberality, *Sache* i.e., truthfulness, *Sochaye* i.e., purity and *madave,* i.e., gentleness. Asoka also left indication of how these virtues could be practised or put into action. The enumeration of duties in this connection which vary slightly in difference inscriptions are as follows : Daya means *anarambha prananam* and *avihisa bhutanam,* i.e., non-slaughter of animate beings and non injury to creatures. *Dane* means liberal behaviour towards friends, acquaintances and relatives, also towards Brahmanas and Sramanas. *Madave* means hearkening to parents, elders, seemly behaviour to friends relatives, acquanintances, Brahmanas and Sramans. By *Sadhava* or *Kayana* he means work of public utility and refers to his own doings in this regard, such as planting of trees by roadside, digging of wells and inns for travelling public. Establishment of healing arrangements for both men and animals, etc. also fall under *Sadhava* or *Kayana.* These are all on the positive side of Asoka's *Dhamma* which one had to perform but there is also a negative side where one has to refrain from doing certain things. These are *apasinava* which mean freedom from *asinava,* i.e., sins like cruely, anger, conceit and envy.

Asoka also recommended self-examination and introspection to the followers of his *Dhamma.* He discouraged religious intolerance and stressed the virtue of *Samavaya,* i.e., concord among peoples of different religions. He clearly pointed out that "those who out of attachment to their own religion disparage the religion of others, in fact, do much harm to their own religion". Thus Asoka's *Dhama* is a comprehensive moral code, comprising positive as well as negative duties as well as warnings against falling victim to normal weakness such as religious bigotry or intolerance.

Now let us turn to the *summum bonum* or the ultimate end for which the *Dhamma* was to be practised. Even here his Edicts come to our help. In the 6th Rock Edict Asoka says that all his efforts are directed towards making his people happy in this world and in order that they may attain *Svarga* heaven in the next world. He also compares this world and the world hereafter by use of the terms *hidata, palata* or *hida-lokika, pala-lokika.* In one place he mentions that performance of *Dhamma* begets endless merit in the next world and enables men to attain *Svarga,* i.e., heaven.

Nature Asoka's Dhamma

The very simple character of the *Dhamma* taught by Asoka was not in full comformity with Buddhism to which he had been converted. This has led Prof. Fleet to remark that Asoka's *Dhamma* was *Raja-dharma*, that is a code of conduct and duties prescribed for the kings. We have seen from what we have discussed about Asoka's *Dhamma* that is not the duties prescribed for the kings and rulers but a code of conduct and duties for the people to follow for the leading righteous life and to attain happiness in this world and heavenly bliss in the life hereafter.. V. A. Smith is of the opinion that Asoka's *Dhamma* had few, if any, distinctive features. The doctrine he preached was essentially common to all Indian religions. Smith also points out that the only difference of Asoka's *Dhamma* with Hindu religion is a tinge of Buddhism, rather saturation with ethical thought which lies at the basis of Buddhism. Prof. F. W. Thomas also does not regard Asoka's *Dhamma* to be Buddhism as it does not mention the "Four Grand Truths" or the "Eightfold Path or the word *Nirvana*". Thus these scholars, namely, Smith and Thomas think the non-sectarian and the non-distinctive are not reconcilable with Buddhism. But scholars like Sinart are of the opinion that teachings of Asoka were in some points consistent with Buddhism and his inscriptions reveal the Buddhism of the time of Asoka which was purely moral doctrine and without dogmas or abstract theories. Dr. Bhandarker, however, does not agree to this view and observes that Asoka's inscriptions do not portray those of Buddhism of his time. A modern scholar says, "if Dhamma was an attempt at preaching Buddhism it would have been inevitable for Asoka to have added that lay person should also pay special attention to the words of Buddhist monks and preachers. But Asoka's explanation of what he means by the *Dhamma* indicates that it was a secular teaching. For Asoka's *Dhamma* was a way of life, the essence of which he had called from the teachings of various thinkers known to him and probably his experience of life". Bhandarkar is of the opinion that most scholars do not remember that Buddhism always consisted of two parts—one for the monks and the nuns and the other for the householder and what Asoka taught was the latter form of Buddhism. Prof. B. M. Barua pointed out the institute called *gihi-vinaya*, i.e., institute for the householder and that Asoka was preaching the duties of the householders. The virtues like *daya, dane, sache, sochaye*, etc. are also found in the *Digha-nikaya* of the Buddhist scriptures. Even Asoka's *Dhamma-mangalas* have been taken from Buddhist *Sutta-nipata*. In the twelfth Rock Edict Asoka's exhortation to the people not to disparage other's religions is a development that is found in *sutta-nipata.* Prof. R. K. Mookerjee thinks that in his personal religion, Asoka was a Buddhist and the one he preached was different from Buddhism. Dr. Bhandakar refutes the opinion of Prof. R. K. Mookerjee and concludes that Asoka's *Dhamma was Buddhism* and he was a Buddhist.

About the nature of *Asoka's Dhamma* it must be mentioned that "he never discussed any metaphysical doctrines nor did he refer to God or Soul but simply asked people to have control over their passion, to cultivate purity of life and character in inmost thoughts, to be tolerant to others' religion, to abstain from killing and injuring animals and to have regard for them, to be charitable to all, to behave with decorum to parents, teachers, friends and ascetics, to treat slaves and their servants kindly, and aboveall to tell the truth".[1] N. K. Sastri is of the opinion that Asoka was a Buddhist and the *Dhamma* he preached was not that simple piety which is common to all religions, as Smith thinks, but specific code of moral duties laid down for the lay followers of Buddhism. It was Buddhism for the householders simplified and made practical for the common people to follow.

A modern scholar observes that from a study of Asoka's *Dhamma* it is clear that the ideas that he tried to communicate were socio-religious. Tolerance and humanism, non-violence and concord were the virtues that he wanted his subjects to inculcate. Long period of thirty years free from war was no mean achievement of Asoka and its peace permitted the realisation of the values of *Dhamma* he sought to settle in the minds of his people.

PROPAGATION OF DHAMMA

Within his Dominions

History bears testimony to the propagation of religion by kings and emperors, and the method almost invariably followed by them was the use of the sword. Wars have been fought for propagation of religion, untold numbers died by the sword of proselytising monarchs. Constantine and Charlemagne forced Christianity on their unwilling subjects. But Asoka's *Dhamma* taught him to seathe his sword for all time and made him a combination of a saint and a ruler. Whatever might have been the true character of his *Dhama* Asoka propagated for the loftiest end in view. He began with a feeling of indebtedness to his subjects, nay, to the entire living world, and whatever effort he made, he says in his 6th Rock Edict, he made in order to be free from his debt to the creatures and in order that he might render some happy in this world and they might gain heaven in the next world. Such were the lofty ideas he had set as his ideal and purpose of the propagation of Dhamma. Non-violence to life as such was the basic principle of his *Dhamma* and was in fullest conformity with his ideal of service to all living creatures. He took certain practical steps that ensured application of the principle of non-violence in a practical, though in a limited way. (i) He stopped *Viharajatra,* i.e., pleasure tours which involving killing of animals by way of hunting, feasting, etc. Instead he instituted *Dhamma-Yatra,* that is pilgrimage to Buddhist holy places on which occasions gifts were given to the brahmanas and sramanas. (ii) He also stopped killing of animals and fowls in the royal kitchen restricting the killing to two peacocks and one deer, but these were also to be given up within a short time as he announced. (iii) The offensive *Samajas* where public feasts and entertainment were held and which involved killing of animals for meat were ordered to be discontinued and instead *Dhamma-Samajas* in which the Law of Piety was practised. (iv) Asoka substituted the ordinary *mangalas* in which superstitious and worthless rites were performed, by *Dhamma-mangalas* which comprised practice and fulfilment of Dhamma. (v) Asoka in his 7th Rock Edict confesses that he was not the first king to think of propagating *Dhamma,* there were many others who tried to do so but with no success. He therefore gave this matter most serious and anxious thought. He clearly understood, whatever effort he might put for diffusing his *Dhamma* far and wide his mission was not likely to succeed if the missionary work was limited to himself. He, therefore, in the twelfth year of his reign commanded the district officials, the Yutus, the Rajukas and the Pradesikas wherever they would go on circuit every five years, to deliver instruction in *Dhamma* to people in the discharge of their official duties. Obviously, it was a novel and ingenious method of reaching all people of his realm. (vi) Preaching by the royal officials would not have gone very far if Asoka did not devise another method of impressing upon the people his religious instruction. He took his cue from the Buddhist work called *Vimanavathu.* In this work the rewards for virtuous men in the life hereafter were described. These rewards were *Viman*—column supported palace, *hastin,* a celestial elephant, all white and well-caparisoned. *Agikhandani,* Gods with resplendent complexion compared to fire, lighting, star etc. Asoka devised to show these spectacles to the people in the *Dhamma-Samaja* in order to impress upon them the heavenly reward that awaited the virtuous. Such spectacles must have had much influence upon the common people. (vii) Asoka appointed a new class of officials whom he called *Dhamma-Mahamatras,* appointed among all classes of people even including his brothers' families to see to the establishment, inculcation and increase of the *Dhamma,* i.e., the Law of Piety as well as for the welfare and happiness of those devoted to *Dhamma.* In the 8th Pillar Edict Asoka says "The same (object) being in view, I have set up *Dhamma-Stambhas*, appointed *Dhamma-Mahamatras* and made *Dhamma-Sravanas*", i.e., proclamation of *Dhamma* and *Dhammanusati*, i.e., instruction in *Dhamma.* K. N. Sastri points out that *Dhamma-Stambhas* are not pillars in the material sense, it meant public utility work. (viii) The ideal of his *Dhamma* having been making the life of men and animals happy in the world, Asoka planted trees by the road sides, dug wells and set up inns for the benefits of both men and animals. He also made healing arrangements for both men and beasts. (ix) Asoka had much respect for the monkish Buddhism and in order to preserve the *Samgha* and to prevent Schism in the Buddhist Church he summoned a Council at Pataliputra and the decisions arrived at that Councils were embodied in his Sarnath Edict. Heresy was suppressed as a result of the Pataliputra Council. Asoka's missionary zeal did not make him inattentive to the growth of heresy in the Buddhist Church. (x) One of the most unique methods ever followed for propagation of *Dhamma* was Asoka's inscribing Edicts with *Dhamma-lipi* on rocks and pillars so that people might read them and follow the qualities and virtues enumerated there. The edicts were placed in such places that, as Asoka mentions, even foreigners might see them and inculcate the doctrines laid down therein.

Outside his Dominion

Asoka did not rest content by propagating his *Dhamma* within his dominions. He maintained friendly relations with his frontagers as also with countries beyond taking advantage of the friendliness with those countries. Asoka sent his envoys there for the purpose of propagating his *Dhamma.* He also established charitable institutions in the countries of his frontagers. The Ceylonese Chronicles *Dipavamsa* and *Mahavamsa* refer to Asoka's sending as many as nine missions for the propagation of *Dhamma.* Of these nine, seven were sent to "the countries lying between the Himalayas and Peshawar in the north and southern portion of the Mysore State" in the south. Two remaining missions are said to have been sent to countries outside India, one to *Suvarnabhumi* or lower Burma and the other to *Lanka* or Ceylon (modern Sri Lanka). The mission to Ceylon was a complete success. King Tissa of Ceylon was a friend of Asoka and the mission was sent on his initiative either in 251 or 250 B.C. Mahendra who has been variously described as a brother and son of Asoka was the leader of the mission. Mahendra was aided by his sister Sanghamitra.

The conquest through *Dhamma* that is Law of Piety was according to Asoka was considered by him to be the chiefest of conquests. The 13th Rock Edict says with confidence that this "has been achieved by the Beloved of the Gods here and in the bordering dominions even as far as six hundred *Yojanas* where dwell the Yavana King Amtiyoka, and beyond this Amtiyoka, the four kings called Turamaya, down below, where we the Chodas, the Pandyas, as far as Tamraparniyas—likewise here in the king's dominions among the Yavanas, Kambojas, the Nabhakas and Nabhapamtis, the hereditary Bhoja rulers, Andhras and Parimdas—every where they follow the teaching of the Beloved of the Gods in respect of Dhamma". Asoka also mentions that the conquest he achieved everywhere was a conquest flavoured with love.

It goes without saying that Asoka's sending of missions to the countries enumerated in the 13th Rock Edict attained much success and although the effects on the Greek countries were less permanent than elsewhere.

Prof. Rhys Davids, however, regards Asoka's claims of success of him *Dhamma* over whole of India, Ceylon, independent Greek States of Western Asia, Eastern Europe and Northern Africa were a "mere royal rodomontade". But when we consider certain important features in Christianity which are common with Buddhism such as confession, fasting, rosaries etc. and remember Asoka's sending of his envoys (dutas) in the Courts of the contemporary rulers we realise that Asoka's missions contributed in some measures in shaping the tenets of Christianity when infant Christianity met the full-grown Buddhism in those countries later. On Pre-Christian Judaism there was definite and noticeable influence on Christianity. According to J. K. Saurers "The mission of King Asoka are amongst the greatest entered countries for the most part barbarous and full of superstition, and among these animistic peoples Buddhism spread as a wholesome heaven".

In the 6th. Rock Edict Asoka's declaration that there was no higher duty than welfare of the whole world and his efforts were all for freeing him from debt to the creatures seem to have been a well fulfiilled duty. He obviously had taken his ideal from the Buddhist Pali-Sutta which mentions the ideal to be followed by one who is aspiring to become a *Chakravarti Dharmika Dharmaraj* and Asoka had certainly become one such ruler by his righteousness, humanitarianism and his conquest through *Dhamma* of the world known to him.

Effects of Asoka's Missionary Activity

The Maurya empire even under the first Maurya emperor Chandragupta extended from the Hindukush to the frontiers of the

Dravidian kingdoms of the extreme south of the Indian peninsula. Under Asoka it received further extension by inclusion of the kingdom of Kalinga. Had not Asoka been influenced by the ideal of *Chakraborty Dharmika Dharmaraja*, the centripetal force that had been organised from the time of Bimbisara would have absorbed the entire Indian sub-continent within the Magadhan empire under the Mauryas making whole of India one nation and even making Pataliputra, like Rome, the Capital of a world power. Here Asoka's policy of conquest through *Dhamma* stood in the way and "India was lost to nationalism and political greatness". If India, due to the missionary activity of Asoka, gained in cosmopolitanism and humanitarianism which have become characteristic of the Hindu Society, India lost politically.

We have already noticed how Asoka's missionary efforts, his sending out of missionaries to countries like Suvarnabhumi and how through these countries Buddhism spread into China, Korea, Japan etc. in subsequent periods of history.

In the West Asian countries under the Greeks the influence of the *Dhamma* did not leave much permanent marks, yet the infant Christianity when came in contact with the mature Buddhism in those countries after two more centuries it came to be influenced in some of its aspects. Particularly, the gnostic Christianity was deeply influenced by Buddhism. The Pre-Christian Judaism, namely, the Essenes and Therapeutal sects had been influenced by Buddhism.

But one of the most important effects of the missionary activity of Asoka "was the immense stimulus it imparted to Indian art".[1] Indian architectural material till the time of Asoka was wood, but it was he that made it lithic. The art of stone-cutter was not unknown before the time of Asoka, in fact, it was already at a developed stage. Asoka's rock-cut inscriptions also was not altogether a novel thing, for the Persian monarch Darius had done so long time before Asoka. What Asoka's workmen did in a novel way was to bring stone columns for his inscriptions with artistically sculptured capitals. Asoka was responsible for the construction of 84,000 *Chaityas*. The Sarnath Lion capital and the Dharma Chakra are excellent specimens of the lithic art of Asoka's time.

The walls of the hall within the rock-cut caves in the Barabar and Nagarjuni hills have a mirror-like glass even today. Asoka's pillars are specimens of the perfection in the cutting, dressing, chiselling and shaping stones at the time of Asoka. Travellers like Tom Coryate and Whittaker mistook them as brass pillars and Chaplin Terry thought them to be marble pillars, and Heber took them to

---

[1] N. K. Sastri, *Comprehensive History of India*, Vol. II, p. 41.
Bhandarkar, *Asoka*, p. 252.

be cast metal. Sir John Marshall remarks that Asokan pillars with figures of bulls and lions on the Crown are "masterpices in point of both style and technique, examples of finest carving".

The Pillars of Asoka which were on an average 30 feet in height weighing 50 tons must have been an engineering problem with regard to their transportation from the quarries where they were shaped to distances of five to six hundred miles which the people of the time must have solved easily. As late as the second half of the fourteenth century A.D., Sultan Firuz Tughlaq transported one Asoka pillar to Delhi. First 4,800 men and a 42-wheeled cart were engaged to carry the Pillar to the bank of the Jamuna where 20,000 men were needed to place it on boats. The re-erection of the Pillar at Delhi was another strenuous job. One more Pillar from Meerut was also shifted by Firuz Tughlaq to Delhi. The engineers of Asoka's time transported them by some other easier method obviously. "The Fabrication, conveyance and erection of these pillars bear eloquent testimouy to the skill and resources of the stone-cutter and engineers of the Maurya age." Another remarkable act of the Maurya engineers was the construction of the Sudarsana lake by artificially damming up some of the streams of the mountains Raivatak and Urjayat.

One of the most noteworthy effects of Asoka's missionary acivity as Saunders remarks was the humanising and civilising influence his missions had spread in countries outside India. Within India the contribution of Asoka's missionary activity was the abiding influence of non-violence and humanitarianism which remain even today as the basic principles of Hindu Society.

What Asoka achieved by his missionary activity was to turn a local sect into a world religion and "More living men cherish his memory today than have ever heard the names of Constantine or Charlemagne".[1]

Two other boons that India enjoyed were (1) the communication between the Indian provinces became more frequent and brisk. This led to (2) the universal desire for a common language—a language that would be studied and understood in all provinces for both religions and secular purposes. "This led to the acceptance of Pali or monumental Prakrit as the *lingua franca* of India", and both secular and religious scriptures came to be written in Pali. Buddhist scriptures which were originally written in Magodhi dialect were now translated into Pali. This effected a sort of a cultural integration of India under Asoka.

---

[1] H. G. Wells: *Outlines of History*, p 212.
Also vide Bhandarkar: *Asoka*, p. 249.
Ibid, pp. 209, 251.

Character and Estimate of Asoka

Our knowledge about the early life and character of Asoka is derived from Buddhist texts like *Divyavadana* and the Ceylonese chronicles such as *Dipavamsa* and *Mahavamsa*. But for his later life we have excellent sources, namely, his Rock Edicts, Minor Rock Edicts, Pillar Edicts and other minor inscriptions from which we can form a clear idea about his personality and character.

Difficulty about the Buddhist sources of information about his early life and character is that there has been deliberate fabrication in order to portray Asoka as an Ogre transformed into a saint by the magical effect of his conversion to Buddhism. We may easily ignore such exaggeration.

Asoka was born in an imperial family and imbibed all its traditional characteristics. His love of hunting, love of feasting and merry-making, skill in fighting battles, quelling rebellion and administering provinces as viceroy and all that were but normal predilections one may expect in a progeny of an illustrious imperial house. He did not hesitate to put to death his brothers who were opposed to his aspiration to ascend the throne. He superseded the claims of his elder brother to the throne and in doing so he enlisted the support of his father's ministers. He had the normal princely weakness of marrying more than one wife, to have some left-handed wives in different points of the realm. His taste was no less royal and dishes were prepared for his table as suited to his palate.

But the real man in Asoka was awakened by the shock of the Kalinga War. What more nobility did any of the great monarchs of the world demonstrate than Asoka's sheathing of his sword at the moment of his great victory? There are innumerable instances in history of monarchs who had been feeding their sword with blood and more blood and one victory leading them to anonther. Asoka is the solitary instance of an emperor who shrank from war after victory which opened up opportunity for more victories.

What was most peculiar about his character is that he was great both at war and peace. He knew how to field his men in a battle and to wrest victory from his most determined and powerful enemy, Kalinga, he knew no less how to follow the policy of peace and love, humanitarianism and non-violence. An able administrator, an impartial judge, a ruler solicitous of the well-being of his subjects, nay of all men, and animals both in this world and the world hereafter, a stateman par excellence, Asoka sought to gather the treasures of wisdom not the trash after which thousands and thousands of rulers ran.

Whether as a man or a ruler Asoka stands pre-eminently first among the myriads of rulers of the world that crowd the pages of history. Scholars have compared him with other rulers, ancient, medieval and modern, Hindu, Moslem, Christian and Pagan and have most ungrudgingly given him the highest place of honour.

To estimate the achievements of such a monarch is bound to be of absorbing interest and no uniformity of opinions can reasonably be expected.

Asoka's achievements divide themselves into two parts, viz., before his conversion, i.e., upto the Kalinga War and after his conversion to Buddhism.

As a Prince Asoka assisted his father in the administration of the country as the viceroy at Ujjain and for a time at Taxila where he was sent to quell a rebellion and proved his worth both as an administrator and a general. He succeeded against his eldest brother's claim to the throne on the death of his father. But there can be no doubt that he was the ablest of the sons of Bindusara to ascend the throne.

As a monarch he began his career with all the traditions of Maurya imperialism, taking pleasure in hunting, waging war and loving all the royal paraphernalia and liking royal delicates. It is not a little curious that such a monarch was transformed into an apostle of non-violence, peace and common well-being. It was as if by a magic that he was metamorphosed into a new man and a new soul. The diabolism of the Kalinga War in which hundred thousands of people were done to death, many left wounded and many more carried away as prisoners changed monarch Asoka into Saint Asoka. The horrors of one war of conquest were enough to touch him at the very core of his heart, and the change came upon it, marked a new chapter in the history of the Maurya Empire and of India. The prospect of becoming a world conqueror which would have lured any other monarch and would have possibly turn Pataliputra into Rome of the East did not have any appeal to him. He turned to the service of his people, nay all men, and not only men again, but of all living creatures. The ideal that he wanted to subserve was to make them happy both in this world and the world hereafter. He himself practised what he professed and through administrative changes as well as by sending of missions both to countries within the Indian peninsula and to outside countries of Western Asia, South East Asia etc., he preached the Law of Piety, i.e., his *Dhamma*. It was no religion in the metaphysical sense of the term, but a code of love, righteousness and humanitarianism. Quinquennial and Triennial circuit of officials, appointment of *Dhamma-mahamatras*, *Dhamma-Yutas*, etc., for the establishment, inculcation and increase of *Dhamma* were the steps that he took within his dominions for the spread of of his Dhamma. Both in the material and spiritual aspects of the human life, Asoka brought about a change that transformed the whole concept of Kingship and the Maurya government was converted into a theocracy, tolerant of all lives and beliefs. In his personal life he practised what he professed and he became an ardent devotee of Buddhism and practised the most rigorous injunctions of a Saint's life avoiding the least transgression from what he believed and sought to preach. With regard to foreign countries he pursued the policy of love and friendliness. He transformed the reverberation of the war-drum into the reverberation of the drum of peace and he issued injunction to his future generations against territorial conquests. He assured his frontagers not to be afraid of him, for they would receive nothing but love and peace from him. He made healing arrangements for both men and beasts within his own countries as also in the realms of his frontagers.

He revolutionised the concept of the kingly duties by declaring *Sabe munise paja mama,* i.e., all men are my children and thinking that the king is indebted to his people and could be free from the debt by doing their welfare.

If Europe could produce enlightened despots only in the eighteenth century, India produced one and the very best ever produced who placed the welfare of his subjects above everything, and it was Asoka.

All the same Asoka has been held responsible for the rapid decline and fall of the Maurya empire. "The martial ardour of imperial Magadha had vanished with the last cries of agony uttered in the battle fields of Kalinga. Asoka had given up the aggressive militarism of his forefathers and had evolved a policy of Dhammavijaya which must have seriously impaired the military efficiency of his empire."[1] The military weakness of India in the post-Asokan period is also testified by the *Yuga Purana* section of the *Gargi Samhita.* In pursuance of his policy of propagation of *Dhamma* and total withdrawal from the path of militarism and war he turned his civil administration into religious propagandists and "entrusted the fierce tribesmen of the North-Western Frontier and in the wilds of the Deccan to the tender care of the Superintendents of piety and did not rest till the sound of the war-drum was completely hushed".[2] Dr. Bhandarkar also holds the same view when he says : "Asoka's new angle of vision, however, sounded a death-knell to the Indian aspiration of a centralised national State and World-wide empire. The effects of his policy became manifest soon after his death."[3]

1 H. C. Raichaudhuri : *Political History of Ancient India,* p. 365.
2 *ibid.* p. 347,
3 Bhandarkar ; *Asoka,* pp. 258—259.

Religiosity of Asoka was, of course, responsible for the total loss of martial spirit of the Indians and the consequent loss of independence to the foreign invaders, yet it is time that we judged the intrinsic merit of his policy in the political set up of the present world and realised the great success the monarch achieved not only in the contemporary world of the third century B.C., but in the direction left for the posterity to follow in the war-torn, intolerant, selfish and irreligious world of today.

But, the question is whether the Maurya empire would have survived even if Asoka pursued the policy of aggressive militarism. It would perhaps been possible to bring the Tamil Kingdoms of the south within his empire after the victory at Kalinga, knowing as we do that Bindusara's attempt to conquer the Tamil countries of the south was frustrated by the support rendered to those countries by Kalinga. Asoka's assurance to the frontagers that they had nothing to fear from him also bears out the position of strength that Asoka had in relation to the frontagers. If we hold for argument's sake that Asoka conquered the remaining independent Kingdoms and tribes within the Indian sub-continent would it have ensured permanence to his empire? Had his successors been not those capable of keeping the reigns of such an empire in their grip, the empire would have definitely fallen into pieces sooner or latter. "But the moral ascendancy which Asoka was mainly instrumental in bringing about, remained for centuries as monument to his glory and has not altogether vanished even now after a lapse of more than two thousand years."[1]

History is replete with instances of mighty empires dwindling into nothingness, thrones eaten up by moths, sceptre kissing the dust, swords consumed by rust and monarchs forgotten in the moth-eaten chapters of history, but in India there was a monarch, Asoka, who instead of all earthly treasures, gathered the treasures of wisdom, peace, love and non-violence which have ever since been the proud heritage of India.

Asoka and Akbar

It has been customary to compare Asoka with great monarchs of history, particularly Akbar the Great. True both Asoka and Akbar are the most conspicuous in the long roll of Indian monarchs, yet there are more things to be contrasted than compared between them. If one war was sufficient to change the heart of Asoka, Akbar remained all throughout his life a man of inordinate ambition eager to earn the fame of a conqueror. Again while Akbar conquered by the

---

[1] *Age of Imperial Unity*, p. 92.

sword, Asoka conquered by love and humanitarianism. Akbar was a diplomat but Asoka was peculiarly and obviously sincere. While both were zealous in the discharge of kingly duties, yet their concept of kingly duties and ideals were different. Both were men of good taste and both spared no pains to choose the best of men for their services and both did honest work. Both were also preachers of religion, but while Asoka's success as a preacher turned a local sect into a world religion, Akbar's Din-Ilahi, a political religion, proved a total failure. But above all both were solicitous of the well-being of their subjects, both were Catholic in their views and tolerant of others' religions and both left their impress indelibly on the canvass of history and deserve the epithet 'Great'.

His place in History

To determine Asoka's place in history, it is necessary to remember the ideals that guided him and the motives that impelled him. From his different edicts it is possible to get a clear idea of the ideals that he had set before him. Prof. Charpentier's contention that Asoka's inscriptions concealed rather than expressed his own personality and his ideas and ideals, are not accepted by scholars.

Welfare of the whole world was his ideal and he thought himself indebted to the creatures and what little effort he made was to make them happy in this world and that they might gain heaven in the next world. (R. E. VI). Such were his ideals. His idea of welfare of the creatures comprised men, animals and creatures. The temporal as well as the spiritual well-being of the whole animate world were his concern. Again his welfare measures for the happiness of the men and beasts were not confined within his own empire but were spread to the countries of his frontagers. He declared "all men are my children"—*Saba munise paja mama.*

Asoka's motive was to become *Chakkavatti Dhammika Dhammaraja.* It was through spiritual conquest, that is through love and humanism and not through terrestrial conquests that one might become a Chakravarti Dharmika Dharmaraja. He, therefore, eschewed war for good, geared his entire administrative machinery to the propagation of Dhamma, i.e., Law of Love and Piety. He set up edicts so that people might inculcate the moral virtues set forth therein. He sent envoys to foreign countries for the spread of his message of love and humanism. For temporal happiness of men and beasts he constructed roads flanked by trees, dug wells and rest-houses for the travellers, made curative arrangements for both men and beasts. Curative arrangements were made by him even in the countries of his frontagers. By this policy of *Dhamma Vijaya* he seemed to have attained what he had in his mind and the Buddhist Text *Divyavadana* actually calls him *Chaturbhaga Chakravarti Dharmiko Dharmarajo*.

Now what place could Asoka be assigned in history? According to Prof. Rhys David Asoka's conversion to Buddhism and his munificent endowments to the Samgha were the first step towards on the downward path of Buddhism, the first step to its expulsion from India, just as the religious benefactions of Constantine were the cause of the spiritual decay of the Christian Church. But Dr. Bhandarkar points out that decay of Buddhism at a remote subsequent period of time could not be due to Asoka and also asks where is the proof of Asoka's misdirected endowments to the Buddhist Church. We must not forget that Constantine spread Christianity with the help of the sword, Asoka spread his Dhamma through love and humanism. If Constantine tolerated other religions, it was for political reasons but Asoka's toleration was inherent in his *Dhamma*.

Asoka has also been compared to Marcus Aurelius, Charlemagne, Omar Kaliff I, etc. There were others who might have been great warriors or administrators like Asoka. Some might as well have been superior to Asoka in mental culture (e.g. Marcus Aurelius) but in the totality of temporal and spiritual good done to the animate world, in humanism and toleration no prince is worthy of being compared to Asoka. In the estimation of the European Scholars Alexander, Caesar, and Napoleon are world's greatest monarchs. But H. G. Wells pertinently questions "what were their permanent contribution to humanity—these three who have appropriated to themselves so many of the pages of our history?" But Mr. Wells gives Asoka the first place of honour when he says "amidst the tens and thousands of monarchs that crowd the columns of history, their majesties and graciousness and serenities and royal highnesses and the like, the name of Asoka shines, and shines almost alone a star. From the Volga to Japan his name is still honoured. China, Tibet and even India, though it has left his doctrine, preserve the tradition of his greatness. More living men cherish his memory today than have ever heard the names of Constantine or Charlemagne". Dr. Copleston says, "Asoka was not merely the Constantine of Buddhism, he was Alexander with Buddhism for Hellas, an unselfish Napoleon..." Dr. Macabhail thinks that Saint Paul is the only historical character that can be rightly compared to Asoka.

Successors of Asoka

The vast empire of Asoka extending from the foot of the Hindukush to the borders of the Tamil countries in the extreme South was incapable of being ruled over by any weaker kings. When after an eventful reign of thirty years Asoka died in 236 B.C. his sceptre which was "the bow of Ulysses" could not be drawn by any weaker hands.

Unfortunately, after the wealth of historical materials for the period of the earlier Mauryas, particularly for that of Asoka, we enter into a period of obscurity and the genealogy after Asoka cannot be drawn up with certainty. We have to depend on scanty data supplied by one or two inscriptions and on the genealogical lists given in the Brahamanical, Jaina and Buddhistic works which are both confusive and discrepant. The Brahmanical, i.e., the Puranic source, however, gives us more or less correct names of the later Maurya rulers as also the total span of the period they ruled (137 years).

Asoka had many sons of whom the name of only one, Tivara, is found in the inscriptions, but the names of three other sons, Mahendra, Kunala also known as Dharma-Vivardhana, and Jalauka are referred to in literature. Tivara does not seem to have ascended the throne either because he predeceased Asoka or for any other reason we are not aware of. According to Vayu Purana Kunala succeeded Asoka, ruled for eight years and was succeeded by five rulers the last of whom was Brihadratha. *Matsya Purana*, however, gives a different list of the successors of Asoka and his immediate successor being Dasaratha—*Vishnu Purana* again gives a third list. The last king Brihadratha's name appears in all these lists and that of Dasaratha in more than one. Kalhana in his *Rajatarangini* mentions Jalauka as Asoka's successor in Kashmir. It is, therefore, difficult to reconcile the divergent versions given by different sources.

From three brief dedicatory inscriptions on the walls of the rock-cut caves on the Nagarjuni hills, dedicated to the Ajivikas we come across the name of Dasaratha who adopted the epithet *Devanampiya*, who ruled for eight years and who was according to the Puranas was Asoka's grandson. Dasaratha's name was Kunala who was also known as Dharmavivardhana and probably also as Suyasas. From the Buddhist legend it is known that Kunala was the heir apparent of Asoka but he blinded himself "on account of the intrigues of his step-mother Tishyarakshita" thus his son Dasaratha became the immediate successor of Asoka. According to *Vayu Purana* Kunala's son was *Bandhupalita*. Bandhupalita may have been Dasaratha himself and Indrapalita who succeeded Dasaratha may have been Samprati.

According to Dr. V. A. Smith Dasaratha and Samprati were brothers reigning simultaneously in two parts of the empire, Dasaratha over the eastern part while Samprati ruled over the western part. Dr. H. C. Raichaudhuri points out that Dr. Smith's hypothesis is incorrect in-as-much as Samprati, according to the Jaina writers, ruled over both Pataliputra and Ujjaini.[1] According to the Puranas also Dasaratha was succeeded by his son Samprati. The Jaina records speak highly of Samprati's efforts for the propagation of the Jaina faith. Smith's view, therefore, has been rejected by the modern writers. In Acharya Jinaprabhusuri's Pataliputrakalpa it is stated that "In Pataliputra flourished the Great King Samprati, son of Kunala, lord of Bharata with its continents".[2]

Samprati was succeeded by Salisuka. This is proved by the *Vishnu Purana, Gargi Samhita* and *Vayu Purana*. He is supposed to be identical with Vrihaspati, son of Samprati referred to in the *Divvavadana.*

The last of the imperial Mauryas was Brihadratha mentioned by the *Puranas* as well in Bana's *Harshacharita.* He was assassinated by his general Pushyamitra. With the assassination of Brihadratha the Maurya imperial line of Magadha came to an end after 137 years of rule in 187 B.C.

During the half century following the death of Asoka the Maurya empire was fast passing through a process of disintegration. According to Rajatarangini Jalauka, one of the sons of Asoka set up an independent Kingdom in Kashmir, with himself as the ruler and conquered Kanauj. He is said to have crushed off the invading "Mlechcha Horde". This is perhaps a reference to the invasion by the Bactrian Greeks which was to become a formidable menace in future. On the evidence of Taranath we come to know of another successor of Asoka who set up an independent Kingdom at Gandhara. Poet Kalidasa in his drama Malavikagnimitram refers to Vidarbha as independent Kingdom. On the north-western frontier that a King named Sophagasenus, i.e., Subhagasena was ruling independently is referred to by Greek writer Polybius who wrote about 206 B.C.

That the disintegration of the Maurya empire was speeded up by the centrifugal forces after Asoka's death and the *Yavana* invasion i.e., the invasion of the Bactrian Greeks. The final blow was administered by Pushyamitra, Commander-in-Chief, who assassinated his royal master Brihadratha and established a dynasty known as the Sunga Dynasty.

Decline and Fall of the Maurya Empire

The vast empire of the Mauryas that comprised practically the whole of the Indian Sub-Continent and beyond, and reared on the political theories of Kautilya, reached its tragic end with the assassination of the last of the imperial Mauryas, Brihadratha, at the hands

[1] H. C. Raichaudhuri : *Political History of Ancient India,* p, 353,
[2] *Comprehensive History of India,* p. 44.

of the traitor regicide Pushyamitra, Commander-in-Chief. The end came within barely fifty years of Asoka's death. That within half a century from the time when Asoka had to assure his frontagers that they had nothing to fear from him, the empire became extinct, has given cause to scholars to identify the factors that speeded up the decline and fall of the Maurya empire.

According to one school of thought, Asoka's religious policy mainly accounts for the debacle. The Chief exponent of this school of thought is Mahamahopadhyaya Haraprasad Sastri who is of the opinion that the reaction prompted by the Brahmanas against Asoka's policy of patronising Buddhism and deliberately humiliating the Brahmanas led to this reaction. He and others of his way of thinking see the hands of the Brahmanas in the revolution headed by Pushyamitra. Haraprasad Sastri thinks that Asoka's edicts were directed against the Brahmanas and these were specially offensive as these were promulgated by a Sudra. Asoka's prohibition of animal sacrifice enjoined by Brahmanical religion, his appointing of *Dhamma Mahamatras* as superintends of morals among the Brahmanas thereby infringing the privilege of the Brahmanas, his introduction of *Vyavasharasamata* and *Danda-samata* i.e., equality in treatment as well as punishment of the Brahmanas with all other castes infringing the special consideration always shown to the Brahmanas have been enumerated as the causes prompting the Brahmanical reaction.

Dr. H. C. Raichaudhuri argues at length that prohibition of animal sacrifice was not specially directed to the Brahmanas, for long before Asoka, non-violence had been recommended in *Sruti*. Further it has been proved beyond doubt that Asoka's Grand-father, Chandragupta was not of *Sudra* extraction, but was a *Kshatriya* of the village Mayuraposaka in Pippalivana. Further, the *Dhamma-mahamatras* were no more superintendents of morals. They were entrusted with the duties of the promotion of welfare also of the Brahmanas and the establishment of the Law of Piety which included liberality to the Brahmanas. Again, there is nothing to show that *Dhamma-mahamatras* were all appointed from the non-Brahmanas. It has also been pointed out by Dr. Raichaudhuri that Brahmanas were not immune from principle of equality before Law and in punishment. In *Brihadaranyaka Upanishad* it is clearly laid down that a priest, i.e., Purohita (Brahmana) might be punished with death for treachery towards his master. Pandit Sastri's contention that as soon as the strong arm of Asoka was withdrawn the Brahmanas revolted against his successors. This is not borne out by history. In *Rajatarangini* we come across definite evidence that Jalauka and the Brahmanical Hindus of Kashmir were on most friendly terms.

About Pushyamitra's revolt it cannot be said that he being a

Brahmana his revolt was an expression of Brahmanical reaction. We must not forget that his revolt can be better accounted for his hold over the army rather than his leadership of a band of discontented Brahmanas.

According to another school of writers the root cause of the fall of the Maurya empire was Asoka's policy of non-violence which he had adopted as state policy and which totally sapped the martial ardour of imperial Magadha. He gave up the aggressive militarism of his forefathers and disabanded his army. He not only eschewed all wars but also enjoined upon his sons and grandsons to do so. All this had the natural effect of imparing martial spirit and military efficiency of the empire. But it was not, by itself, the only cause of the downfall of the empire. We must seek for other causes as well.

The Maurya empire was ruled by a central authority, and it is no wonder that such a vast empire could not be kept together from the centre, particularly when weaker rulers succeeded to the throne. Empires rose and fell not only in India but also in other parts of the world and nearly one and half centuries that the Mauryas empire endured cannot be considered too small a span of time. The Maurya empire had certain natural causes, also traceable in the factors of the downfall of other empires. These were the spirit of autonomy, oppressive nature of rule by the royal officials, rebellious disposition of the governors of outlying provinces, official treachery, palace intrigues and difficult communication with distant parts of the empire.

Taxila was in repeated revolt. The oppressive rule of the local officials led to the revolt of Taxila once under Bindusara when Asoka had to be sent to put it down. Even under Asoka it once revolted. This attempt at repeated revolts was symptomatic of what were happening elsewhere of the empire. Even if there were no open revolts the willingness was definitely there. The Kalinga Edicts show that oppression by his officials was very much known to him and he did not hide his displeasure in this regard. If even under Asoka there was cause for anxiety at the neglect of duty, one can simply imagine what happened under Asoka's weak successors. That there were intrigues and treachery in the imperial court is evident from the treacherous conduct of Pushyamitra. Such treacherous conduct could not be the result of momentary impulse or short-time preparation.

There are also grounds to believe that the Maurya Court after the death of Asoka was gradually divided into two factions one headed by Pushyamitra, the Commander-in-Chief, and other by the minister. The minister managed to place his son as governor at Vidarbha and the Commander-in-Chief his son as governor at Vidisa.

To the above weaknesses should be added the invasion of the Bactrian Greeks from the north-west. From Syria to whole of Western

Asia upto the borders of Hindukush were under Seleukos. About 250 B.C. two provinces of Bactria and Parthia revolted against the Selencidan dynasty and became independent. Attempt to reconquer them by Antiochos III, King of Syria, failed and in 208 B.C. independence of Bactria and Parthia was recognised. Soon afterwards, the Bactrian and Parthian Kings turned their eyes towards India. About 190 B.C. Demetrius invaded India, when Brihadratha was the Maurya emperor and wrested considerable portion of his empire in the north-west. The revolt of the Andhras, success of the raid of the Bacterian Greeks and loss of north-western part of the empire dealt a severe blow to the prestige of the empire and confusion reigned supreme in the country. Obviously, Pushyamitra, the Commander-in-Chief of the Maurya army, took advantage of the situation and killed his master Brihadratha while he was reviewing his army and thus put an end to 137-year old dynasty founded by Chandragupta Maurya.

Yet, there need be no regret, for empire of Asoka would have gone the way of many more mighty empires of the world even if he had pursued the policy of aggressive militarism; it would be only a question of time. But the moral ascendancy of the Indian culture over a large part of the civilised world which Asoka's policy had brought about has not vanished even today, after a lapse of two milleniums.

CHAPTER NINE

POST-MAURYA DYNASTIES (IN NORTHERN INDIA)

I. The Sungas (187[1]–75 B.C.)

With the fall of the Mauryas we enter into a broken, desultory period of Indian history the unity of which is lost for the time being, through the north-western gates of India hordes of outlanders poured in and established aggressive monarchies in Gandhara, Western Malwa, and the Punjab. The Andhras and the Kalingans had tore off from the empire. The connection of *Madhyadesa,* i.e., Central India with the valleys of the Indus and the Godavari had been snapped.

The continuity of the history of India would have been broken but for our sources of information such as the *Puranas, Gargi, Samhita,* the *Mahabhasya* of Patanjali, the Vedic Literature, the *Divyavadana,* the *Mahavikagnimitra* of Kalidasa and the *Harshacharit* of Bana etc.

The story given by the Puranas of the assassination of the last of the imperial Mauryas, Brihadratha by Pushyamitra, while the former was inspecting the muster of the imperial army is corroborated by Bana in his *Harshacharit,* a work about eight centuries later. Lack of direct evidences, such inscriptions, etc., has made the lineage of Pushyamitra a subject of controversy among scholars. The origin of the regicide family is wrapped up in mystery.

Panini traces the origin of Pushyamitra Sunga to the Brahmana class of *Bharadwaja.* The association of the Sungas with the ancient priestly families is proved by the Vedic literature. In the *Brihaaranyaka Upanishad* the Saungayani., i.e., the descendant of the Sungas, is mentioned as a teacher in the *Vamsa Brahmana.* This view is also held by Keith and Macdonell. Kalidasa in his *Malavikagnimitra* refers to Pushyamitra as belonging to the Baimbaka family of Kashyapa clan. This also supports the view that the Sungas were Brahmanas.

Divyavadana, however, calls Pushyamitra a scion of the Maurya family. One writer even goes to the extent of calling the Sungas as Iranians because their names ended with 'Mitra' i.e., worshippers of Mithra (the Sun) like the Iranians. The Puranas mention Pushyamitra as belonging to the Sunga family. The balance of opinions is definitely in favour of the Brahmanical origin of the Sungas.

[1] The date is variously mentioned as 187, 185 and 184 B.C.

The assassination of Brihadratha in the very presence of the army and there being no reaction on the latter proves that Pushyamitra was preparing for the event from some time back and had the tacit support of the army behind. Pushyamitra's accession does not seem to have led to any mentionable opposition and the people seem to have acquiesced in the change of Dynasty as the later Mauryas had proved unworthy of rule and incapable of stemming the tide of the Greek invasion and keeping the parts of the empire together. Yet the "astute statesman took adequate measures to ensure against all eventualities".[1] It was as a part of the scheme that a minister of late King Brihadratha was imprisoned. The Crown-prince Agnimitra was appointed Viceroy at Vidisa. Another Viceroy at Kosala was probably a relation of Pushyamitra. Agnimitra's brother-in-law Virasena (wife's brother) was placed in charge of a fortress on the frontier of the Kingdom on the bank of the Narmada.

From Malavikagnimitra it is learnt that Yajnasena, brother-in-law (Sister's husband), a minister of Brihadratha established an independent kingdom in Vidarbha when there was the overthrow of the Maurya rule by Pushyamitra. This made him a natural enemy of Pushyamitra. Yajnasena arrested and imprisoned his cousin Madhavasena who was the governor of the frontier and a personal friend of Agnimitra. The latter asked Yajnasena to release Madhavasena but Yajnasena agreed on condition that his relation, a former minister of Brihadratha, who had been imprisoned by Pushyamitra must also be released. This enraged Agnimitra who marched against Yajnasena who surrendered. Vidarbha was divided between Yajnasena and Madhavasena and both acknowledged the suzerainty of Pushyamitra. This extended the sphere of influence of the Sugna King upto the Narmada region.

Pushyamitra's dominions comprised only the central portions of the Murya empire. The north-western boundary was ill-defined but tradition credits the house of Pushymitra with having exercised con-
Madhavasena and both acknowledged the suzerainty of Pushyamitra.
was still the capital of the Sungas. Vidisa formed one of the vice-royalities under the Crown-Prince Agnimitra.

Pushymitra was now the undisputed master of Northern India and in order to proclaim his sovereignty he undertook the performance of the *asvamedha*, i.e., horse sacrifice. In Ayodhya inscription of Dhanadeva, Pushyamitra is said to have performed two horse-sacrifices. No ruler can let loose the sacrificial horse unless he was sure of its safe return and any ruler or monarch who would feel himself stronger might catch hold of the horse which would lead to war

[1] N. K. Sastri : *Comprehensive History of India*, Vol. II, p. 96.

with the King who has let loose the sacrificial horse and naturally no king aspires after a horse-sacrifice ceremony if he were not sure of his strength and supremacy. The second horse sacrifice seems to have taken place at an advanced age of Pushyamitra, for his grandson, Prince Vasumitra, son of Agnimitra, was an already grown up Prince to lead the escorting force along with a hundred princes who guarded the sacrificial horse. While the horse was wandering on the right banks of the Indus it was seized by a squadron of Greek horsemen of Menander, a relative of the Bactrian monarch Eukratides and King of Kabul and the Punjab who having formed a design to emulate Alexander, advanced with a formidable force into the interior of India. The horsemen who seized the sacrificial horse of Pushyamitra must have been an advance column of Menander. In a hotly contested battle between the Greeks and Vasumitra, the former were completely routed and the Greek King was obliged to retire to his own country. The sacrificial horse was brought back to Pataliputra and the horse-sacrifice was held. This means, that the territories of Pushyamitra extended upto the *Sindhu,* i.e., the Indus.

There is a sharp difference of opinion with regard to the identity of this river *Sindu* referred to in *Malavikagnimitra*. Prof. Rapson identifies it with *Kali Sindhu,* a tributary of the river Chambal near Chitor. But Dr. H. C. Raichaudhuri adducing strong arguments has conclusively proved that the river referred to is the Indus.[1]

Pushyamitra is, however, supposed to have met with two reverses. According to Prof. Rapson, he lost Ujjaini to Andhra King *Satakarni*. He has come to this conclusion by identifying Sata with Satakarni. But recent discoveries have proved Prof. Rapson's identification Sata with Satakarni as incorrect, since Sata is an abbreviation of Satavahana and not Satakarni.

On the basis of a statement in the Hatigumpha inscription of Kharvela of Kalinga, it has been suggested that Kharvela attacked Magadha and defeated Bahasatimita who is identified with Pushyamitra. But R. P. Chanda and Allan have demonstrated the incorrectness of the suggestion on the basis of epigraphical and Philological grounds. According to Allan the name cannot be read as Bahasatimita.

Again Prof. Rapson's suggestion that Sakala, i.e., Punjab was wrested by Menander during Pushyamitra's life-time is untenable on the ground that reference to Greek invasion in the *mahabhasya* and *Yugapurana* mut have been the invasion of Demetrius.

Pushyamitra ruled for 36 years (187—151 B.C.). According to Dr. Smith, his horse-sacrifices with all formalities of Brahmanical

[1] *Comprehensive History of India,* Vol. II, p. 97, fn.

worship, marked the early stage of Brahmanical reaction. The exaggerated regard for the sanctity of animal life and prohibition of bloody sacrifice during Asoka's reign led to this Brahmanical reaction under Pushyamitra, which developed fully after a few centuries under Samudragupta.

On the basis of semi-mythological stories of the Buddhist writers, Pushyamitra was not content with the peaceful revival of Hindu rites, but indulged in a savage persecution of Buddhism. He is said to have burnt Buddhist monasteries and put to death monks from Magadha to Jalandhar. Many Buddhist monks who escaped his sword took shelter in the Kingdoms of other rulers. Dr. Smith observes that "It would be rash to reject this tale as wholely baseless, although it may be exaggerated".[1] N. N. Ghosh as also K. P. Jayaswal are of the opinion that Pushyamitra cannot be exonerated from the blame attributed to him about persecution of the Buddhists. Jayaswal mentions the pitiless policy pursued by Pushyamitra against the Buddhists in the north. At Sakala Pushyamitra set "a price of 100 gold pieces on the head of every Buddhist".[2]

N. K. Sastri is, however, of the opinion that religious persecution in ancient India was an exception and when it is kept in mind that Buddhist writers have a general tendency to distort facts, for example, in characterising Asoka, we cannot give same credence to their stories as some writers have done "while it may be conceded that some Buddhists, particularly the monks, may have suffered from certain disabilities the story of a general persecution of all and sundry is evidently the invention of frustrated minds which found that the State patronage was rapidly being shifted to the Brahmins, and were aghast at the revival of ancient Vedic ritual of the *asvameda*".[3]

It is also suggested by N. K. Sastri that the overthrow of the Maurya Dynasty which was a bulwark of Buddhism made the Buddhist irreconciled to the rule of Brahman Pushamitra and this may have been political cause of their discomfiture.

From K. P. Jayaswal's reference to pitiless persecution of the Buddhists at Sakala which was a base of Menander, raises the presumption that the Buddhists there may have allied themselves with the Greeks and thereby earned the punishment all traitors deserve.

Had it been a policy of senseless persecution, how one can account for the survival of Sanchi *Stupas*, Bharut from Pushyamitra's fury? On the contrary some of the beautiful railings of these monuments were made during the Sunga rule, and a donation was made to a *Stupa* at Bharut.

---

1 V. A. Smith : *Early History of India*, p. 213.
2 Vide Comprehensive History of India, Vol. II. p. 99.
For N. N. Ghosh and K. P. Jayaswal's remarks, *ibid*, p, 99 fn,
3 *Comprehensive History of India*, Vol. II, p. 99.

Dr. H. C. Raichaudhuri points out that Pushyamitra Sunga did not dispense with the services of his Pro-Buddhist ministers and the Court of his son was graced by Pandit Kausiki. *Mahavamsa* testifies to the existence of numerous monasteries in Bihar, Oudh, Malwa and adjacent provinces between 101—77 B.C. Dr. Raichaudhuri observes that "Though staunch adherents of orthodox Hinduism, the Kings of the line of Pushyamitra do not appear to have been as intolerant as some writers represent to be".

Successors of Pusyamitra Sunga

There is divergence of opinion about the date of the death of Pushyamitra. But according to generally accepted chronology his rule ended in 148 B.C. (according some 151 B.C.) and his son Agnimitra succeeded him in the same year.

Agnimitra was Viceory of Vidisa during the reign of Pushyamitra and reduced Vidarbha to submission to Pushyamitra's suzerainty. He is the hero of the playwright Kalidasa's *Malavikagnimitra*. For eight years he ruled over the Sunga dominions, but no events of this period are known. Unless the copper coins bearing the inscription *Agnimitrasa* in Brahmi scripts, discovered at Panchala can be ascribed to him no evidence of his time has been found.

Agnimitra was succeeded by Sujyeshtha who ruled for seven years. No information about his period is available. He was in his turn, succeeded by Sumitra in 133 B.C. Sumitra has been identified with Vasumitra, Pushyamitra's grandson who led the escort with one hundred princes, guarding the sacrificial horse let loose by Pushyamitra and when an advance column of Merander's cavalry seized the horse, he defeated them. After his accession to the throne he, already a middle aged man, lost his vigour and martial spirit of his youthful days and gave himself up to ease and pleasure. This offered an opportunity to the forces of disintegration and disruption of the empire which began to raise their ugly heads. According to Bana Sumitra, i.e., Vasumitra met with the tragic end of life being assassinated by one Mitradeva or Muladeva, while he was enjoying a concert. 'Muladeva or Mitradeva was the lord of Kosala' who after killing his suzerain made himself fully independent. According to N. K. Sastri "this was the first secession from the empire" and with this loss the Sunga hold on the west of Magadha was lost. Kosala was not the only part of the empire to secede. We come across coins of rulers of Panchala, Kausambi and Mathura of about this period which presupposes that these areas also tore off from the Sugna Empire about this period. The Sugna empire was thus reduced to only Central Indian Territories and Magadha.

According to the Puranic list the next three kings were Andhraka, Pulindaka and Ghosha. But scholars are of opinion that these names were inserted in the list due to some confusion of the editor of these texts. In fact, these three were not Sunga kings. Vasumitra was succeeded by Vajramitra in 123 B.C. and not by Andhraka. Nothing is known of the reign of Vajramitra. He was succeeded by Bhagavata in 114 B.C. From an inscription of a fragment of a stone pillar of Bhagavata discovered at Bhilsa one Gautamiputra is credited with the setting up of a flag-staff in the honour of God Vishnu in the most important temple at Bhilsa. At Besnagar, a place two miles away from Bhilsa, on a Garuda Pillar there is an inscription which refers to the setting up of this pillar in honour of Lord Vishnu by Heliodorus, a Greek, who was sent by the Greek king Antialcidas of Taxila, in the fourteenth year of king Bhagavata. The Garuda Pillar set up by a Greek shows the friendly relations between the Indo-Greek kings in the Punjab and the Sungas, but also the vitality of the Indian culture that influenced the highly civilised Greeks who became devotees of Indian gods. Bhagavata ruled for 32 years and was succeeded by Devabhuti in 82 B.C.

According to Bana Devabhuti was of dissolute nature, fond of women's company. He was murdered at the instance of his minister Vasudeva, by the daughter of a female attendant disguised as a queen. Devabhuti ruled for ten years before he was assassinated in 73 or 72 B.C. The curse that had descended on the Sungas with the murder of Brihadratha by Pushyamitra pursued the dynasty and it also met with the same fate of a tragic end at the instance of another traitor regicide. Vasudeva after contriving the murder of his master ascended the throne and founded the *Kanva* or Kanvayana dynasty. The Sunga dynasty was not, however, totally swept out. Vasudeva permitted the Sunga kings to rule in obscurity in the corner of their former dominions.

Importance of the Sunga Period of Indian History

Dr. H. C. Raychaudhuri observes that "The rule of the emperors of the house of Pushyamitra marks an important epoch in the history of India in general and Central India in particular".

(*i*) The Greek dynasties on the borderland of north-western India sought to emulate Alexander in invading India after the fall of the imperial Mauryas and by renewed incursions they threatened to submerge whole of Central India. But they received a check at the hands of the Sungas and had to revert to the friendly and peaceful policy during the whole of the Sunga period, of their Seleukidan precursors.

(*ii*) Pushyamitra's rule is important not only for stemming the tide of foreign (Yavana) invasion but also for arresting the disintegration of the Magadhan empire which throughout the century of Sunga rule extended upto Bhilsa in central India and perhaps upto the banks of the Indus.

(*iii*) The Sunga period saw the beginning of the Brahmanical Hinduism as is exemplified by two horse-sacrifices at the time of Pushyamitra, which after a few centuries reached full development under the Guptas. The exaggerated stories of the cruel persecution of the Buddhists by Pushyamitra have been refuted by historians by pointing out that pro-Buddhist officers were allowed to serve under the Government and the Buddhist monuments at *Bharut*, *Sanchi*, etc. remained undemolished; on the contrary the railings of *Sanchi Stupa* had been added to under the Sungas. Punishment to the treacherous Buddhists who may have sided with Greeks was well deserved. The Sungas were orthodox Hindus no doubt, but there is nothing to show their intolerance to Buddhists or any other religious sect.

(*iv*) The inscriptions discovered at Vidisa and Ghosundi testify to the growing importance and prevalence of *Bhagavata* religion. Although the Sungas did not indulge in missionary activities on behalf of Hinduism, the influence of *Bhagavata* religion spread on the Greeks as is exemplified by the setting up of a Garuda column by a Greek named Heliodorus at Besnagar.

(*v*) In both art and literature the Sunga period left impress of its genius on the history of India, comparable to the glory of the Guptas. Vidisa (Besnagar) grew into an important centre of ivory and stone-carving. The ornamental stone gate at the *Sanchi Stupa* was the work of the artists of Vidisa. Foucher remarks that "it was the ivory workers at Vidisa who carved, in the immediate vicinity of the town, one of the monumental gates of Sanchi". Rockcut *stupa* at Bharut is the most famous monument of the Sunga period. "They (the Sungas) were responsible for the fine gateway railings which surround the Sanchi *Stupas* built by Asoka." The gate and railings of the Sanchi *Stupa* stand even today as excellent specimens of lithic ornamental art of the Sunga period.

The Sunga period also witnessed a revival of literature specially in central India. Gonarda was the birth place of Patanjali, the greatest literary genius of the period. His *Mahabhashya*, a commentary on Panini's grammar is a celebrated piece of Sanskrit literary work. This period also saw the development of Sanskrit language which gradually reached the peak under the Guptas.

II. THE KANVAS (75—30 B.C.)

The plot which killed the dissolute Sunga king Devabhuti brought the contriver of the plot Vasudeva, his Brahmana minister, on the throne of Magadha. Vasudeva's dynasty came to be known as Kanva or Kanvayana after the name of his gotra.

The chronology of the Kanva dynasty is a matter of controversy. According to Dr. Bhandarkar the Kanva dynasty should be regarded as contemporaneous with the Sungas. But the distinct testimony of the *Puranas* and Bana prove that the *rois faneant* of the Sunga stock who lingered to rule in a corner of the former Sunga empire have not been considered as the Sunga kings the last of whom, Devabhuti, was killed by Vasudeva.

Vasudeva was succeeded by three of his descendants and the entire dynasty comprising the rule of four kings covered a total period of forty-five years. Vasudeva was succeeded by Bhumimitra, Narayana and Susarman. According to Dr. Smith the short period of forty-five years covered by four reigns indicates that the times were disturbed and the succession to the throne was often affected through violent means.

Although in the Puranas it is mentioned that the Kanvas would keep the neighbouring kings in subjections and would rule righteously, nothing really is known about the reign of any of the Kanva kings.

Magadha after the Kanvas

Dr. Raychaudhuri observes that very little is known about the history of Magadha proper after the fall of the Kanvas and the veil of obscurity is not lifted till the rise of the Guptas. It is, therefore, difficult to reconstruct the history of Magadha in the intervening period of nearly three hundred years.

A number of copper coins have been discovered in Rohilkhand with names ending with 'Mitra', such as Agnimitra, Jethamitra, Bhumimitra as also Bhadraghosa. These kings have been identified with the Sunga and Kanva kings of the same name. But these identifications although plausible are not definite. It is not known in what relation these *Mitra* kings stood with the families of the Sungas and the Kanvas. The kings with names ending with *Mitra* seem to have been replaced eventually by the Scythian Satraps both in Pataliputra and Mathura, and the Scythians themselves were ultimately supplanted by the Naga and the Gupta kings. It may, however, be concluded that some of the *Mitra* kings might have ruled in Magadha after the fall of the Kanvas. In any case, it will be reasonable to hold that a large number of independent states flourished in Northern India during this period.

CHAPTER TEN

POST-MAURYA DYNASTIES (IN SOUTHERN INDIA)

I. KALINGA UNDER KHARVELA

In ancient times the country of Kalinga comprised the modern Puri and Ganjam districts as well as parts of Cuttack district of Orissa. At times it also included the present day Telegu-speaking area of the South. Kalinga was conquered by the Nandas but it threw off the Nanda suzerainty before the Mauryas came to power. Asoka conquered it and probably divided into parts for administrative convenience, one part with its headquarters at Tosali and the other at Samapa.

In the first century B.C. Kalinga became one of the strongest powers in India under Mahameghavahana of the Chedi clan. "It is not improbable that some of the Chedi princes migrated from Madhyadesa or Magadha to Kalinga where they carved out a principality, which ultimately became a mighty empire."

But the history of Kalinga after the Mauryas is extremely obscure. It is not known when Kalinga threw off the yoke of Magadha. From an inscription in the Hatigumpha cave in the Udayagiri hill in Orissa, some details of the achievements of the mighty Chedi King Kharvela have been found. Kharvela is described as the third generation of the *rajavamsa* of Kalinga also described as *Chedi-rajavamsa.* The descendants of this family also used the epithets *Arya* and *Mahameghavahana.* It is supposed from the use of name of *Mahameghavahana* as an epithet, that they were descendants of *Mahameghavahana.* This raises the presumption that *Mahameghavahana* was the founder of the Chedi royal house of Kalinga. Now when we relate it to the Hatigumpha inscription, we come to the conclusion that Kharvela was third generation of *Mahameghavahana*, i.e., the latter was the grandfather of Kharvela.

Manchapuri cave of the Udayagiri Hill has two storeys. The lower one was constructed by a King Vakradeva, who belonged to the Arya Mahameghavahana family. The upper storey was constructed by the chief queen of Kharvela. From this, it is supposed that Vakrádeva was the second generation of the Kalinga lineage and therefore probably the father of Kharvela.

Kharvela: His Date: His Career

There is a sharp controversy among the schools of historians about the date of Kharvela. K. P. Jayaswal and Sten Konow placed him in the first half of the second century B.C. But R. P. Chanda, H. C. Raychaudhuri and B. M. Barua place him near to 25 B.C., i.e., the end of the first century B.C. The Hatigumpha inscription does not mention any date, but on paleographic grounds the inscription cannot be placed earlier than the beginning of the second century nor later than the first century B.C. Although it is not possible to definitely fix the date of Kharvela, it is not impossible to place Kharvela's time within narrower limit by considering certain historical events.

In the Hatigumpha inscription there is mention of three invasions of Northern India by Kharvela. In one of these, he overran Southern Magadha striking at Barabar hills and Rajagriha and on another (3rd) occasion he compelled the Magadha King *Bahasatimita* who stands for Sanskrit name *Brihatsvatimitra and not Brihaspatimitra* as is usually supposed to fall at his feet. According to Jayaswal and Sten Konow, *Bahasatimita* was none else than Pushyamitra Sunga. But N. K. Sastri remarks that "It is out of the question that these events happened during the heyday of Sunga glory, i.e., 184-123 B.C." N. K. Sastri remarks that the repeated inroads referred to in the Hatigumpha inscription "could only have been possible either immediately before the accession of Pushyamitra or after the collapse of the Sunga Power".

There are other evidences which show that Kharvela was not a contemporary of Pushyamitra, and therefore did not belong to the first half of second century B.C.

One decisive piece of evidence is that on hearing of the advance of Kharvela's armies to Rajgriha, a Greek invader hastily retreated to Mathura. The Greeks once marched into the Ganges valley and proceeded as far as the metropolis of Pataliputra. This invasion is referred to in *Mahavasya* "as an event of recent past". Further, from the *Yugapurana* it is learnt that the "viciously valiant" Greek had to beat a hasty retreat on account of a deadly war that had broken out among themselves. The Greek ruler who had to beat a hasty retreat due to the news of Kharvela's exploit or due to war breaking out among the Greeks, must have been Demetrius, who has been named *Dimita* or *Dimata*. The war among the Greeks must have been due to the appearance of Demetrius' rival Eucratides. The invasion of Demetrius has been placed before the accession of Pushyamitra (variously 187, 185, 184 B.C.). The third and the last invasion of Pushyamitra of Northern India took place in the 12th regnal year of Kharvela. This shows that Kharvela must have ascended the throne some time before Pushyamitra. Kharvela certainly did not invade Magadha in the heyday of the Sunga rule. This puts the date of Kharvela little before 200-196 B.C.

Further, reference to Rathikas, Bhojakas as independent ruling power in the Hatigumpha inscription shows the period to be near to Asoka's time rather than to the later Maurya period, for in Asoka's inscriptions also these peoples are referred to. This brings the period of Kharvela to the beginning of the second century B.C.

As has already been mentioned Dr. Raychaudhuri, R. P. Chanda and B. M. Barua place Kharvela near the end of the first century B.C. (25 B.C.). Their arguments are based on the grounds (1) that identification of Dimita with Dimetrius, son of Euthydemus, is conjectural, for the part of the inscription where this name occurs is damaged. It is suggested that he might have been an Indo-Greek King other than Demetrius. (2) Likewise the identification of *Bahasatimita* (Brihaspatimitra) with Pushyamitra is hopelessly unconvincing. (3) The most important evidence in respect of Kharvela's date is supplied by the Hatigumpha inscription where there is the reference to Kharvela's enlargement of the aqueduct which was excavated by one of the Nanda Kings three centuries earlier, in the fifth regnal year of Kharvela. This is based on the interpretation of the sentence *Nandaraja-tri-varsha-Sat-odghatila* (excavated three hundred years before by a Nanda King). If this interpretation is accepted we take it that the aqueduct was excavated near about 324 B.C. when the Nandas were overthrown then the date of Kharvela comes to C. 24 B.C. (324—300=24 B.C.). This fits in well with the probable date of Kharvela. Some scholars take the expression *tri-varsha-sat* to mean 103 years. This brings the date of Kharvela's fifth regnal year to 221 B.C. (324—103=221 B.C.). Kharvela was the 3rd generation of Chedi family. In that case independent Kalinga must have been founded during the rule of Asoka (273-236 B.C.) which is absurd, for Kalinga was an integral part of the Maurya empire under Asoka.

(4) From the paleographic point of view the Hatigumpha inscription of Kharvela is definitely later than that of Besnagar inscription of the end of the second century B.C. and must have belonged to first century B.C. This is also borne out by the improved poetic (Kavya) style used in the inscription at Hatigumpha. The scholars of Indian art are of the opinion that the sculptures of the Manchapuri cave excavated during the time of *Mahameghavahana* "are considerably posterior to the sculpture of Bharut" belonging to the Sunga rule.

(5) Again Kharvela's adoption of *Maharaja* which was like *Maharajadhiraja,* was used by the Indo-Greek rulers during the first half

of the second century B.C. It is suggested that a king of Kalinga living not far away from the Indo-Greek kings, certainly would have come under the influence of the Indo-Greek method of using royal epithet of this kind at a later date.

(6) We also know that Kharvela's army invaded the city of Krishna within Satakarni's Kingdom. This Satakarni seems to have been none other than the Satavahana King Satakarni I who belonged to late first century B.C. This also points to the end of first century B.C. to be Kharvela's date.

Thus we can at best mark the upper and lower limits of Kharvela's time as first half of the second century B.C. to the last quarter of the first century B.C.

Kharvela's Career and Achievements

Kharvela the third ruler of the dynasty of Mahameghavahana of the Chedi clan was a great conqueror and at the same time an efficient and a beneficent ruler. He has been rightly regarded as "one of the most remarkable figures of ancient Indian history".[1]

In Hatigumpha Prasasti of Kharvela himself, detailed records of the events of his life and work are preserved. As was customary for a young prince, Kharvela spent the first fifteen years of his life in games befitting princely status but he was one of the very few princes who from his boyhood received thorough instruction in all branches of learning such as Law, Finance, Accounting, Currency, Administration and Royal Correspondence.

At the age of fifteen, according to some writers, sixteen, Kharvela was consecrated as *Yuvaraja,* i.e., heir apparent or Crown Prince. As the Crown Prince he shared the responsibilities of administration of the kingdom and was anointed king when he was twenty-four. He assumed the titles of *Maharaja, Kalingadhipati, Kalinga-Chakravartin* which meant he claimed the honour and status of a universal ruler.

As was customary with all powerful kings, Kharvela soon after his accession, launched upon a career of conquest. In the second year of his reign he sent a large army to the west "without caring for Satakarni" who ruled over the country on the west of Kalinga and carried his arms upto the bank of the river Krishna. The phraseology that he sent the expedition without caring for Satakarni apparently means that the expedition was in the nature of a challenge to the Satkarni, the Satavahana King. The progress of Kharvela's army upto the river Krishna (*Kannabemna*) struck terror into the city Rishikanagara. The extent of the advance made by Kharvela's

[1] Age of Imperial Unity, p. 213.

army cannot be definitely determined as the identity of the river *Kannabemna* with Krishna and city *Rishikanagara* with *Assikanagara* and *Musikanagara* is very much controversial. Rapson and Barua identify the river *Kannabemna* with the Wainganga with its tributary Kanhan and the city as Assika in the Godavari Valley. K. P. Jayaswal, however identifies the river *Kannabemna* referred to in the Hatigumpha inscription as modern river Krishna and the city as Musikanagara. The city is identified by others as Rishikanagara.

There is, however, no reference to any conflict between Kharvela and Satakarni nor is there any reference to Rishikanagara forming a part of the Kingdom of Kalinga. This made some scholars to suggest that Kharvela and Satakarni perhaps were mutually friendly and Kharvela's army passed through the territories of Satakarni without difficulty. But in the Hatigumpha inscription, the expedition is referred to as one of great successes and the victory was celebrated with elaborate festivities which included dancing, drama, musical concert, etc.

In the fourth year of his reign Kharvela occupied the capital of a prince named Vidyadhara and also subdued the ruling chiefs of Bhojakas of Berar and Rashtrikas of the adjoining regions of East Khandesh and Ahmednagar.

In the eighth year of his reign Kharvela destroyed *Govathagiri*, a hill fortress, in the Barbar hills and attacked Rajagriha which struck terror into the heart of a Yavana king who retreated to Mathura.[1]

In his eleventh regnal year Kharvela destroyed the city of Pithuda, Sanskrit Prithuda, the capital of the king of Masulipatam. He threatened the rulers of Uttarapatha, in the next year, and defeated the king of Magadha named *Bahasatimita*.[2] He watered his horses and elephants in the river Ganges. To avenge the humiliation of Kalinga during the time of the Nandas and the Mauryas, Kharvela carried away much booty from Anga and Magadha together with certain Jaina images "originally taken away by a Nanda king from Kalinga". In the same year Kharvela proceeded with his army against the Pandya kingdom of Far South and defeated him.

Kharvela was no mere military general of great distinction, he was a great, efficient and benevolent ruler also. His expedition both towards the north and the south made a deep impression upon his contemporaries although we have no clear picture of the extension the kingdom of Kalinga received under him. That he was a great conqueror is borne out in the inscription of his queen. However,

---

[1] The identity of this Yavana king has been discussed earlier, *ante*. p. 165.

[2] For discussion the identity of Bahasatimita, see *ante*. p. 166.

we cannot rule out in some measure exaggeration in the Hatigumpha Prasasti although his ability as a military leader and his carrying Kalinga to the pinnacle of glory cannot be denied.

In his welfare measures for his subjects may be mentioned the extension of the aqueduct originally excavated by a Nanda king three centuries ago. This served as a great irrigation canal. He brought the waters of a canal from Tanasuli to his capital.

He also spent large sums of money for the welfare of his subjects. He himself was a great master of music and he often entertained his people by arranging musical performances, dancing, drama, etc.

Kharvela was a great builder. In the ninth year of his reign he built a "Palace of Great Victory" (*Mahavijaya Prasada*) in commemoration of his victories in the north. In the very first year of his reign Kharvela repaired the walls, gates and houses of the capital city of Kalinganagara which had been destroyed by a terrible cyclone. He also restored all the damaged gardens of the city.

He was a devout Jaina. Both he himself and his chief queen patronised the Jaina ascetics making liberal provisions for their maintenance, construction of their dwelling places and also offered them silk clothes. Although an ardent Jaina, Kharvela was not a bigot and he repaired the temples of all gods and "what is still more significant, emulated Asoka by showing equal honour to all sects".[1] The very purpose of the Hatigumpha inscription is to record the construction of residential chambers for the Jainas on the Udayagiri hills and the building of a columned hall for the congregation of the Jaina monks. "This grand building was adorned with sixty-four panels of sculptures, and had cost a sum of twenty-five hundred thousands of the current coins."[2]

According to K. P. Jayaswal the last line of the Hatigumpha inscription mentions the convening of a council of Jaina monks by Kharvela, which compiled an authentic version of the Jaina canonical texts—"the sevenfold Angas and sixty-four letters". According to Dr. D. C. Sarkar, Kharvela, a devout Jaina, "excavated a number of caves in the *Kumari Parvata,* i.e., Khandagiri hill" and is also supposed to have built a monastery called *Pabhara* not far removed from the Udayagiri hill caves.

"Kharvela's career appears to have been meteoric. His achievements dazzle us like a flash of lightning, which soon disappears."

---

[1] Comprehensive History of India, Vol. II, p. 115.

[2] Idem.

End Of The Mahameghavahanas

The end of the Chedi Dynasty of Kalinga, i.e., the Mahameghavahana rulers, is obscure. We have no information about any son or successor of Kharvela. There is, however, reference to a prince named Vadukha who is said to have excavated one or two caves on the Udayagiri hill.

Not long after the rule of Kharvela the kingdom of Kalinga seems to have been split up into small principalities. Despite lack of detailed information about the Kalinga kingdom after Kharvela, the fact remains that the Kalingas played an important role in the diffusion of Indian culture in lands beyond the seas, obviously *Suvarnabhumi.* Ptolemy refers to the *apheterion* near a city in Kalinga wherefrom vessels bound for the "Golden Land" sailed for the open sea.

II. THE SATAVAHANAS

Most impressive attempt at political and cultural unity of India in ancient India was made by the Mauryas. Next Great attempt was made by the Satavahanas. "In more senses than one", remarks N. K. Sastri, "it is the heir to the Maurya empire in the Deccan. But it is also part of the general Jaina and Hindu reaction to the Buddhist state of Asoka". In contradistinction to the dynasties of the North, the Mauryas, the Sungas, the Kanvas and the Kushanas, the Satavahana empire endured for 400 years in unbroken continuity both dynastically and administratively.

The sources of the Satavahana period are much limited. Only seven inscriptions from eastern Deccan and nineteen from western Deccan, mostly non-official and short, for so long a period with thirty ruling monarchs, constitute a very meagre source of information, to say the least. Again most of these inscriptions are Buddhist inscriptions of a donative nature and do not supply materials for the history of the Dynasty. Considerable part of the Satavahana empire which covered modern Hyderabad remains unexplored and even excavation of Maski, Paithan and Kondapur has not made any remarkable discovery.

The numismatic evidence, that is, evidence derived from the coins of the period, contribute more information than the epigraphic sources. A very large number of coins have been discovered in western Deccan, eastern Deccan and Madhya Pradesh. Expert numismatists like Cunningham, Rapson, H. R. Scott, Bhagwanlal Indraji, F. W. Thomas, etc. have culled much information from these coins.

The literary evidence is more or less disappointing. Puranas are the only important literary source about the genealogical as also chronological framework of the Satavahanas but as a result of long process of transmission by means of perishable materials has led to interpolations rendering them untrustworthy unless corroborated by epigraphic or numismatic evidence. Gunadya's *Brihatkatha* supposed to have been written at the Court of a Satavahana king has not reached us except in very small fragments in later commentaries and versions whose relation to the original is estimated differently by different writers. The work named *Lilavai* which purports to be a treatment of the activities of king Hala's reign is not trustworthy in its major parts. The kings from the 9th to the 16th and from the 18th to 22nd out of thirty kings remain thoroughly obscure due to the missing pieces of the Puranic lists. Thus much of the history of the Satavahanas remain obscure and a matter of imagination.

Satavahana Chronology—A Puzzle

The chronology of the Satavahana rulers is very much controversial and the starting point of the rule of the dynasty has been variously given by scholars as between 40-30 B.C., that is, the latter part of the first century B.C. and as 235 B.C.

According to the *Puranas* the founder of the Satavahana dynasty was Simuka, misspelt as Sisuka, Sindhuka and Sipraka in the *Purunas.* In the Puranas it is mentioned that the *Andhra Simuka* would assail the Kanvayanas and Susarman, and destroy the remains of the Sunga Power and would "obtain the earth". From this statement it is obvious that Simuka was the contemporary of Susarman who flourished in the first century B.C. (40-30 B.C.).

Again in the Puranic lists ten rulers of the Sunga dynasty which came to 137 years after the accession of Chandragupta Maurya, ruled for 112 years and their last king Devabhuti was overthrown by the *Kanva* dynasty which ruled for a total period of 45 years, and its last king Susarman was overthrown by the Andhra (i.e., Satavahana) Simuka. This also brings the date of Simuka to 30 B.C.[1]

Further, the *Nanaghat* inscription of Nayanika, Simuka's daughter-in-law, according to R. P. Chanda is of a time later than the Besnagar inscription of Bhagavata, the last but one king of the line of Pushyamitra. This brings the date of Simuka to the first century B.C.

Again R. D. Banerjee on good grounds takes *ti-vasa-sata* of Hatigumpha inscription to mean 300 years and not 103 years. This

---

[1]Chandragupta's accession about 324 B. C. Maurya Dynasty's rule 137 Years + 112 years of Sunga rule + 45 years of Kanva rule, i.e., 137 +112+45=294 years. 324 B.C.–294 years=30 B.C.

means Kharvela and his contemporary Satakarni I flourished 300 years after Nandaraja which brings the date of Kharvela and his contemporary Satavahana ruler Satakarni I 24 B.C. This contention is also supported by palaeography of the Nasik, Sanchi and Nanaghat inscriptions and is in conformity with the unanimous evidence of the *Puranas*.

Rapson, Smith, Gopalachari do not subscribe to the above view. They rely on a less unanimous statement in the *Puranas* that the Satavahana rulers, i.e., the Andhras, ruled for a total period of 460 years. They place Simuka towards the close of the 3rd century B.C. and the Dynasty's end they place in the 3rd century A.D., i.e., from 235 B.C. to 225 A.D. This brings the starting point of the reign of Simuka very close to the death of Asoka.

It may be pointed out that the *Puranas* differ in their statements regarding the duration of the Andhra (Satavahana) rule and the names of the kings given by them are not unanimous. The duration of the rule has been variously given as 300, 411, 412, 456 and 460 years and the number of rulers as 19 in some version, 30 in others.

But Dr. Raychaudhuri is of the opinion that the total duration of the Satavahana rule of all the lines is really more than 400 years and if the starting point of the rule of the dynasty is placed towards the end of the first century B.C., the end of the Satavahana rule will come in the fifth century A.D. and remarks that "the *Puranas* are right in assigning to the entire line of 30 kings a period of about four centuries and a half".[1] This brings us to C. 235 B.C. as the starting point of Satavahana rule.

Rise Of The Satavahanas

Origin : There is a sharp controversy about the identification of the Satavahanas. In the Puranas the Satavahanas have been mentioned as *Andhras* or *Andhra-bhrityas*. Dr. Smith, Rapson, Bhandarkar who based their arguments on the use of the expression *Andhra* in the Puranas are of the opinion that the Satavahanas were *Andhras*. But the term *Andhra-bhrityas* has led some scholars to mean "Andhras who were originally servants of some other power such as the Maurya or the Sunga".[2] Some other scholars are of the opinion that the Satavahanas were not Andhras (Telegu), but the servants of the Andhras were of Kanarese origin,[3] and that they at first owed allegiance to some Andhra kings. Dr. D. C. Sarkar in *The Age of*

---

[1] H. C. Raychaudhuri : *Political History of Ancient India*, p. 409 fn.
[2] *Age of Imperial Unity*, p. 193.
[3] *Idem.*

Imperial Unity remarks that "Neither of the interpretations appears to be satisfactory, although it is probable that the predecessors of the Satavahana emperors were feudatories of the Kanvas".[1] According to Dr. Sarkar the expression *Andhra-bhritya* used in the Puranas did not actually mean the Satavahanas who were according to most of them Andharas but dynasties which were subservient to the Satavahanas but became independent after the latter's downfall. According to yet another group of scholars, the name Andhra came to be applied to the kings of the Satavahana rulers in later times when they lost their western possessions and became purely Andhra power ruling over the territory at the mouth of the river Krishna.[2]

Mr. O. C. Ganguly points out that in the text of *Brihat-desi* a clear distinction has been indicated between the Satavahanas and the Andhras.[3]

Dr. Sarkar draws our attention to two expressions used in most of the Puranas, namely, *Satavahanakula* meaning family, and *Andhra-jaitya* meaning "belonging to Andhra race". "The Puranic testimony", remarks Dr. Sarkar, "may be reconciled with epigraphic evidence, if it is believed that the members of the Satavahana family, i.e., the descendants of a prince Satavahana, were Andhras by nationality".[4] In support of this contention Dr. Sarkar also refers to the author of *Suttanipata* commentary where Asmaka and Mulaka—two places in the heart of the Satavahana kingdom who calls them *Andhaka* (Sanskrit *Andhraka*) *rajjyas*.

We cannot, however, avoid the conclusion that *Satavahana, Andhra,* Andhra-bhritya still remain controversial in regard to their mutual identity.

Original Home

We have already seen that Dr. Smith, Rapson, and Bhandarkar took the Satavahanas as Andhras and Dr. Smith draws our attention to the reference to the Andhra people to be found in Megasthenes' account and even earlier in the *Aitareya Brahmana* as a Dravidian people who occupied the deltas of the Godavari and the Krishna rivers. According to Megasthenes the Andhras had an army only second in strength to that of Chandragupta Maurya. According to Burgess the capital of the state is believed to have been *Sri Kakulam* on the lower course of the Krishna. The nation was evidently independent.[5]

---

[1] *Age of Imperial Unity*, p. 193.

[2] H. C. Raychaudhuri : *Political History of Ancient India*, p. 412.

[3] *Age of Imperial Unity*, p. 193.

[4] *Idem.*

[5] V. A. Smith : *The Early History of India*, pp. 217-218.

Dr. Sukthankar depending on epigraphic evidence such as the copper plate inscription of the Pallava king Siva-Skandavarman, suggests that a good portion of the modern Bellary district of the Madras Presidency was the original home of the Satavahana family. Dr. H. C. Raychaudhuri is, however, of the opinion that the Satavahana territory according to the Vinaya Texts was laid on the southern portion of Madhydesa which means northern Deccan and according to Hatigumpha inscription western Deccan. In later period the Satavahana rule became confined to Andhra or eastern Deccan. This is also borne out by the finds of Satavahana inscriptions of the later period in eastern Deccan although enough of them have been found in western Deccan. According to Raychaudhuri the original capital of the Satavahanas was *Pratisthana,* i.e., modern Paithan in Hyderabad. H. C. Raychaudhuri's view is also borne out by the finds of coins.

Dr. D. C. Sarkar remarks, "The suggestion that the Andhras originally inhabited the Vindhyan region and the adjoining part of the Deccan is probably supported by their association with the Pulindas who were another Vindhyan tribe". When the literary, epigraphic and numismatic evidences are considered together we come to the conclusion that the original home of the Satavahanas was in south India, most probably in western Deccan with Pratisthana as their capital.

Political And Administrative History Of The Satavahanas

Simuka : The Puranas mention Simuka as the founder of the Satavahana Dynasty who ruled for eighteen years. About Simuka's ancestry nothing definite is known. In the *Nanaghat* inscription he is named as *raja* Simuka-Sata-Vahana. The Puranas credit Simuka with having overthrown Susarman of the Kanva Dynasty. But N. K. Sastri points out that "there seems to be some error on the part of the ancient editors of the Purana texts, as the Andhra Dynasty had been founded about two centuries before the overthrow of the Kanvas. Simuka and Susarman could not, therefore, have been contemporaries". According to him as well as Dr. Gopalachari, Simuka was almost contemporaneous with the Mauryas and the ruler who overthrew the Kanva Dynasty in Magadha must have been a Satavahana king of much later time. A proper chronological scheme would make Andhra Simuka the immediate successor of Asoka. In his *coup d' etat* against the Maurya empire Simuka allied himself with other *Andhra-bhrityas* as well with the Bhojas and Rathikas, and in the end assumed independent status and regal title.

If we accept the above view, then we cannot but reject the contrary view expressed by Dr. D. C. Sarkar that "the region which

Simuka conquered from the Sungas and Kanvas may have included the district round Vidisa, which was probably the capital of the later Sungas".[1]

According to the Puranas Simuka ruled for 23 years. The Jaina legends mentioned that Simuka caused Jaina and Buddhist temples to be repaired and patronised these two religions in order to obtain the support of these two powerful communities in the west. He is said to have 'turned wicked' in the sense that he began to favour the Buddhists, more than the Jainas. He was dethroned and killed.

Krishna

According to the Puranas Simuka was succeeded by his brother Krishna and has been identified with Kanha *raja* of the Satavahana family. The Nasik inscription tells us that a high official of Nasik at the time of Kanha caused a certain cave to be excavated.

Satakarni I

Krishna or Kanha was succeeded by Satakarni I, who has been variously called a son, a nephew of Krishna. The name of Satakarni appears in the Nanaghat inscription of Nayanika, in the Sanchi inscription as also the Indian literature and on coins inscribed with the legend Sri-Sata. All these names are identified with the name of Satakarni I except that referred to in the Sanchi inscription about which there is a controversy.

Satakarni entered into a matrimonial alliance with *Angiya* family by which he became the sovereign of the whole of Dakshinapatha. He seems to have "controlled eastern Malwa" and performed *Asvamedha* sacrifice. His conquest of eastern Malwa is implied by coins and Sanchi inscription when read with reference to the Puranic statement. From the Mauryas Satakarni I conquered western Malwa and Anupa—the territory immediate south of western Malwa. In the disintegration of the Maurya empire and the confusion caused by the Greek conquests Satakarni succeeded in building up an empire which is borne out by the two *Asvamedha* and one *Rajasuya* sacrifices that he held. He assumed the title of *Dakshinapathapati*, i.e., the Lord of Deccan. These sacrifices marked the revival of the Vedic religion in the Deccan after a long spell of Buddhist ascendancy.

In the *Hatigumpha* inscription there is mention of Kalinga king Kharvela's defying Satakarni. But N. K. Sastri points out that synchronism of the dates of Kharvela and Satakarni is not so certain as

---

[1] *Age of Imperial Unity*, p. 196.

Rapson and some other scholars have supposed it to be.[1] From the same inscription we know that the dominions of Satakarni I abutted on the western border of Kalinga and a different interpretation of the inscription that has been given is that Kharvela and Satakarni were on *friendly* terms.

However, there is hardly any doubt that Satakarni exercised sway over the regions of the Upper Deccan and parts of Central and Western India. The northern Konkan as also Kathiawar may have been within the Satavahanas empire of Satakarni I. Dr. H. C. Raychaudhuri observes that "Satakarni seems to have been the first prince to raise the Satavahanas to the position of paramount sovereigns of Trans-Vindhyan India. Thus arose the first great empire in the Godavari Valley which rivalled in extent the power of the Sunga empire in the Ganges Valley and the Greek empire in the land of the five rivers. According to the evidence of Indian as well as classical writers the capital of Satavahana empire was at Pratisthana, the modern Paithan on the north bank of the Godavari in the Aurangabad district of Hyderabad".[2]

Successors Of Satakarni I

The eventful reign of Satakarni I was rather short and he is said to have fallen in battle. He left his two surviving sons, Vedasri and Saktisri, both minors. His queen Nayanika assumed the government of the kingdom as regent. She governed the kingdom with the help of her father Tranakayiro Kalalaya and caused the excavation of the Nanaghat cave to serve as a rest-house for the caravan merchants from Paithan to Kalyan and inscribed the long Nanaghat record in the cave. Sculptured *rilievo* figures of Simuka, Satakarni I, Nayanika, five princes as also of Tranakayiro were there in the cave and perhaps were wrought during Satakarni's reign.

The period intervening between the regency of Nayanika and the rise of Gautamiputra Satakarni is very obscure and our information is no better than a confused mass of irreconcilable lists of rulers given by the Puranas. Other sources which corroborate the names in Puranic lists are those of Apilaka, Kuntala-Satakarni and Hala. But they do not seem to be the main line of the Satavahana family, they belonged to different branches of the Satavahanas. This obscure period witnessed a temporary eclipse of the Satavahana power due to the encroachment of the Sakas.

[1] N. K. Sastri : *Comprehensive History of India*, Vol. II. p. 303.

[2] H. C. Raychaudhuri : *Political History of Ancient India*, p. 417.

Yet the only relief in the otherwise gloomy picture of the period is the career of Hala.

Hala

Among the early Satavahana rulers Satakarni I was the greatest in war, Hala was definitely the greatest in peace. He is mentioned not only in the Puranas but in *Saptasati, Lilavai, Abhidhana Chintamani* and *Desinamamala*.

Hala's reign was marked by an exuberance in literary activities. His time saw the raising of the Marathi Prakrit from vulgar provincial dialect to an elegant literary language. The brilliant flowering of literature during Hala's reign was the result of long years of victory, conquests and commercial prosperity that the early Satavahana rulers accomplished. "A splendid Court attracted poets and kept them within its glittering orbit."[1] The lighter mood of the period is noticed in the production of profane literature. The most celebrated composition of the time is *Sattasai* or *Gathasaptasati* which is an anthology of 700 verses in Marathi Prakrit and in Arya metre. It is a collection of witty, frivolous and sentimental verses but some are highly philosophical and some again deal with love affairs.

Hala himself is credited with compilation of the anthology. It is suggested that he worked on a previous anthology compiled by certain Kavivatsala and unified and embellished it. This anthology has undergone many more changes at the hands of subsequent editors and Bana refers to it by saying that, "Satavana made an immortal refined treasure (Kosa) of song adorned with fine expression of characters like jewels".[2] The *Saptasati* had considerably influenced the development of Prakrit language but also that of Sanskrit.

The short reign of Hala was not without its military glory. The military events of his reign constitute the theme of the work called *Lilavai*. It is stated therein that Commander-in-Chief of Hala, Vyayanamda led a successful campaign in Ceylon and Hala led a military campaign into eastern Deccan. But scholars doubt the historical truth of these legends.

The Satavahana ascendancy came to a halt due to the foreign invasion that convulsed the north-western India. The Satavahana rulers had fight with the Greeks, the Sakas and the Parthians but the details of the struggle are unknown. The Saka chief called the western Satraps of Malwa and Kathiawar peninsula dispossessed the

---

[1] N. K. Sastri : *Comprehensive History of India*, Vol. II. p. 305.

[2] N. K. Sastri : *Comprehensive History of India*, Vol. II, p. 305.

Satavahanas of their dominions in Malwa, the north-western parts of the Deccan and occupied their important city of Nasik.

After about half a century of stress and tribulations and obscure existence under foreign rule the Satavahana power rallied itself and effected a total recovery in the reign of Gautamiputra Sri Satakarni.

The Later Satavahanas

I. *Gautamiputra Satakarni* : Gautamiputra Satakarni was the greatest of the Satavanaha rulers who achievements inaugurated a happy and fruitful century of Satavahana rule after the long spell of obscurity and ignominy due to the foreign invasions. "We have a wealth of materials about Gautamiputra Satakarni's rule in the Nasik *Prasasti* inscribed by his mother *devi* Balasri, years after his death which is in the nature of a funeral oration by a disconsolate mother."

Gautamiputra Satakarni restored the fortune of the Satavahana dynasty which seems to have been submerged beneath a wave of Scythian invasion. First sixteen years of Gautamiputra's reign seem to have been spent in preparation for an all-out attack upon the Kshaharata power, i.e., Sakas of the Kshaharata dynasty. He inflicted a crushing defeat upon the Saka chiefs of Malwa and Kathiawar peninsula. He thereby not only recovered his ancestral dominions in the Deccan, but also conquered large territories in Gujrat and Rajputana.

His military scccess has been described in Nasik *Prasasti* of his mother Queen Gautami Balasri or *devi* Balasri wherein he is described as a unique Brahmana who totally uprooted the Kshaharata dynasty and extirpated the Sakas, Yavanas, that is, the Greeks and the Pahalvas, i.e., the Paithians. He is also described as the lord of many countries including Northern Kankan, Anupa and Kukura. He totally defeated Kshaharata ruler Nahapana and having driven him out of Maharastra struck coins in his own name and put them into circulation.

Under Gautamiputra Satakarni the Satavahana empire became a vast and formidable power. The empire comprised not only the Satavahana provinces of Eastern Malwa, Western Malwa, the Namada Valley, Berar, Northern Maharastra, Northern Konkan but also Western Rajputana, Surashtra. Gautamiputra has been styled as the Lord of the Vindhyas meaning the central Eastern Vindhyas as well as Satpura hill, Western Vindhyas and the Aravalli, Travancore hills, Eastern and Western Ghats, as well as other mountain ranges encircling the peninsula of South India. Gautamiputra's epithet tri-Samudra-toya-pita-vahana, i.e., one whose chargers drank waters of the three seas in the east, west and south, that is, the Bay of Bengal, Arabian Sea and Indian Ocean shows the vastness of his empire.

Gautamiputra Satakarni is described as "a handsome person with a charming and radiant face with beautiful gait and with muscular and long arms". He is described as obedient to his mother, reluctant to hurt even his offending enemy, of good manners, a repository of all virtues and good fortune and fountain of good manners. As a King he was "obeyed by the circle of all Kings". He was solicitous of the welfare of his subjects with whose woes he sympathised, helped all people, high or low, levied taxes justly and prevented intermingling of four castes, in order to prevent the growth of sub-castes. The poor, weak and the suffering came in for his immediate attention.

Gautamiputra was great in war but was greater still in peace. He combined his military genius with statesmanship and with a resolute sense of public duty. He was instructed in all branches of learning that make an efficient ruler. He based his administration on the twin foundations of *Sastric* injunctions and humanism. Towards the end of his reign Gautamiputra either due to his military preoccupations or illness shared the responsibility of administration with his mother *devi* Balasri.

He was the first Satavahana King who adopted the vedic metronymic Gautamiputra which was followed by his successors. There are three Vedic *gotras,* Vasistha, Gautama and Mathara followed by the Satavahanas. Satakarni's metronymic was derived from Gautama. The adoption of metronymics of only three referred to above was the result of cross-cousin marriages among the Satavahanas.

Gautamiputra Satakarni appears to have lost most of the districts he had conquered from the Kshaharatas to the Kardamakas who were another dynasty of the Sakas. The Junagarh inscriptions of Rudradamana corroborate the loss of territories by Gautamiputra to the Kardamakas. The same inscription shows that most of the territories which Gautamiputra had conquered from Nahapana came under the possession of Rudradamana.

Some scholars suggest that Gautamiputra Satakarni was identical with Vikramaditya of Indian tradition. But this is not acceptable because Gautamiputra Satakarni was of Pratisthana and Vikramaditya of Ujjaini and there is nothing to show that Gautamiputra had assumed the title *Vikramaditya,* nor had he founded any era known as *Vikrama-Samvat.*

II. VASISTHIPUTRA PULUMAYI II

Gautamiputra Satakarni bequeathed his empire to his son Vasisthiputra Pulumayi who ruled for twenty-eight or twenty-nine years.

Pulumayi's inscriptions have been discovered at Nasik, Karle in the Poona district. and at Amaravati in the Krishna district.

We have seen that towards the end of his rule Gautamiputra Satakarni had lost the northern provinces of the empire, but Pulumayi compensated the loss by extending the Satavahana empire in the land upto the mouth of the river Krishna. This is borne out by his Amaravati inscription and a number of coins. During Pulumayi's reign the Satavahana empire also extended over the Bellary district and this new conquest was named as Andhrapatha and Satavahaniya districts. Discovery of Pulumayi's "ship with double mast" coins on the Coromondal coast raises the presumption that his empire extended in the south and he paid attention to naval power, maritime trade and colonisation. In commemoration of his conquests Pulumayi founded the new city called Navanagara and assumed the title *Navanagarasvami*. He also assumed the title of *Maharaja* in *Dakshinapathesvara*.

From the Nasik and the Karle inscriptions we come to know of his having made a donation of a village to the monks of the Vahuraka caves.

III. SUCCESSORS OF PULUMAYI

Pulumayi was succeeded by Sivasri—Satakarni who was certainly identical with Vasishtriputra Sivasri-Satakarni of the coins found in the Krishna and Godavari districts. He was probably a brother of Pulumayi II and married the daughter of the Saka Satrap (i.e., Viceroy or Governor) Rudradamana I. Sivashi-Satakarni was succeeded by Siva Skanda Satakarni and Yajnasri Satakarni. We do not know anything abcut Siva Skanda Satakarni.

IV. YAJNASRI SATAKARNI

Yajnasri Satakarni was a powerful ruler under whom the Satavahana power revived. From the distribution of his coins in Krishna and Godavari districts of the Madras State, Chanda district of Madhya Pradesh, Berar, Northern Konkan, Baroda, Sopara and Kathiwar as well as from his inscription at Nasik, Kanheri and Chinna-Ganjam in Krishna district, etc. it is concluded that Yajnisri Satakarni was a great king who had ousted the Scythian rule not only from Aparanta but probably also from parts of Western India and the Narmada Valley. This must have been facilitated partly due to the struggle between Jivadaman, Rudrasinha I, the rulers of those areas and the rise of Mahakshatrapa Isvaradatta. Yajnasri Satakarni was the last great king of the family and after him the empire began to fall into pieces and the empire gave rise to a number of separate[1] principalities under different princes of the royal blood.

V. SATAVAHANA DECLINE

The successors of Yajnasri Satakarni according to some of the Puranas were Vijaya, Chandrasri and Pulumayi IV. Although some coins of these rulers have been discovered yet their identification remains somwhat controversial and the events of their reigns remain controversial.

According to some of the Puranas 19 kings of the dynasty ruled for 500 years, according to others 30 kings ruled for 456 years. Whatever might have been the actual length of the rule, the Satavahanas ruled for an unusually long time. This long rule led to decrepitude of the imperial government. It has not been possible for any imperial house to keep the reins of government together for so long a period by producing capable successors without break.

The Satavahana may be credited with enduring for a usual length of time in the history of India and fall into pieces due to the rise of the different dynasties such as the (i) Abhiras, who established a kingdom in the north-western Deccan which perhaps included northern Kankan and Southern Gujarat, (ii) the Ikshakus who occupied the Andhra proper between the mouths of the Krishna and the Godavari, (iii) the Bodhis over north-eastern Deccan, (iv) Chutas over South-Western Deccan, (v) the Brihatphalayanas in the Masulipatam region, and (vi) the Pallavas in the reign round Kanchi, (vii) but the most powerful of the new independent principalities was that of the Vakatakas.

POLITICAL, SOCIAL, ECONOMIC, RELIGIOUS AND CULTURAL LIFE UNDER THE SATAVAHANAS

Our information about the political, social, economic and religious life during the Satavahana rule is derived from inscriptions, coins as well as literature of the period. The official records of Gautamiputra Satakarni and Pulumayi and some Buddhist records throw a flood of light on the polity of the vast Satavahana empire.

Political: The Satavahanas had a monarchical system of administration but the kings did neither assume any honorific indicating divine right of the kingship nor did they exercise absolute authority. Their powers and rights were limited by the laws as embodied in the Hindu Dharmasastras as well as by the long standing customs

[1] *Advance History of Ancient India*, p. 110.

of the country. The king was at the top of the administration, he was the Commander-in-Chief of the army and would personally lead the army to the battle field. The monarchy was hereditary and what was very special about the Satavahanas was the absence of any bloody struggle among the successors to the throne. No fratricidal war, no partition of the dominions between the heirs marred the succession to the Satavahana throne. The eldest son was not necessarily consecrated as heir apparent, i.e., Crown Prince nor was there any instance of association of the Crown Prince in the actual administration with the king. The royal princes were, however, appointed as viceroys. In case of minority of the king, the brother of the deceased king or the queen mother would function as the regent. The regency of the queen mother Nayanika is an instance in point.

The Satavahana empire comprised feudatory principalities as also areas under the direct control of the king. The latter were divided into *Janapadas* each of which was divided into *Aharas,* i.e., districts. Every *Ahara* was in charge of an *Amacha,* that is a district officer or governor who would be transferred from one district to another from time to time. The *Amachas* were appointed by the king. Each *Ahara* was divided into several *Gamas,* i.e., villages and a *Gamika,* i.e., gramika or village officer was appointed in each village. Other officials besides the viceroys, governors, gramikas, were the Chamberlains (*Mahatarakas*), Store-Keepers (*Bhandargarikas*) Treasurers (*Heranikas*), Registration Officers (*Nibamdharakas*), Gatekeepers (*Pratiharas*), Envoys (*Dutakas*), etc.

Social: The Society under the Satavahanas was divided with reference to the offices held and duties performed by the people. The first class comprised the *Mahasenapati, Mahabhojas* and *Maharathis.* This first class of officials comprised the highest class of the society. Thert were also feudatory chieftains in charge of *Rastras,* i.e., principalities and districts. In north Konkon we come across officers called *Mahabhojas* and *Maharathis* in Western Ghats. According to Rapson these officials were connected with the royal family by blood or by caste.

The second social class comprised officials like *Amatyas, Mahamatras* and *Bhandagarikas* and non-officials like merchants, head of caravan traders, head of tradeguilds, etc.

The third social class was composed of the physicians, scribes, cultivators, druggists, goldsmiths, etc.

The fourth and the last social class included the carpenters, gardeners, blacksmiths and fishermen.

The mercantile people and the cultivators were divided into *Grihas, Kulas* or *Kutumbas* meaning families at the head of each of which there was a *Grihapati* or *Kutambin*, i.e., the head of the family who occupied a position of authority in the family.

One speciality of the Satavahana period was craft-guilds. There are references to guilds of the oil-pressers, artisans, potters, corn dealers, weavers, bruisers and bamboo-workers. The existence of guilds indicate corporate life of the time. The *Srenis* were not simply craft-guilds or trade-guilds but they acted as bankers and accepted deposits for which they paid interests. There are instances of permanent endowments made to the guilds. Saka governor Usavadatta made two such permanent endowments, i.e., deposits to guilds making provision for his new robes and other for food necessaries. It is interesting to note that a governor of the eminence of Usavadatta deposited his money in permanent endowments in the guilds for he considered that his provision for robe and food would be more secure if he deposited his money with the guilds rather than in the imperial treasure, for empire might be destroyed any time but the guild would continue to function despite political change. Interests on deposits varied from 9% to 12% per annum.

Economic

The economic condition of the Satavahana period has to be viewed from two sandpoints, namely, the economic condition of the government and of the people. "The government lived from hand to month."[1] The Satavahana administration was very simple and did not entail heavy expenditure. True, the constant warfare required considerable spending on the army, yet the expenditure on day to day affairs being not very heavy, the need for taxing people heavily did not arise.

The sources of revenue of the government were the proceeds from the royal domain, salt monopoly, ordinary and extraordinary taxes on land and income from Court-fees and fines. Many taxes including assignments to soldiers and officials were paid in kind.

On the evidence of Pliny, Ptolemy and the *Periplus* we come to know that the period from Pulumayi II to the reign of Yajnasri Satakarni saw brisk commercial intercourse with the countries in the South-East Asia and colonisation of those countries. It goes without saying that commerce with the South-East Asian countries preceded Hindu colonisation of Sumatra, Java, Malaya and Indo-China. The causes behind the twin movement of commerce and colonisation were doubtlessly the peace and progress as also royal encouragement

[1] N. K. Sastri : *Comprehensive History of India*, Vol. II, p. 318.

which followed extension of the Satavahana empire. Commercial relations were not limited to the South-East Asian countries but extended to western countries like Rome. The Roman need for luxury articles like spices, fragrant wood, sandals, resins, aloes, camphor, benjoin and metal like gold lay behind the brisk commercial relations with the western countries. In the maritime commerce the harbours and ports along the entire coastal tract from Kaveripaddinam in the south to Tamralipti in Bengal took part, although South India had a major share in it.

From the Periplus we know that ships from western countries sailed across the Red Sea and following the Arabian coast reached upto Kane. Thence some ships reached Broach (*Barygaza*) and Malabar (*Lymrika*). The most important seaports of the time were Sopara and Kalyan. The ports were both the outlets and inlets for export from inland countries particularly Paithan, Nasik, etc. and distribution of the imports to eastern and western Ocean.

The commercial relations opened the way to cultural relations. "The inner impulse of Aryan culture far and wide" was a potent factor in the spread of Indian cultural influence to countries of the west and particularly those of South-East Asia.

As the Satavahana administration was based on Sastric injunction and humanism, the poor, weak and the suffering received special attention.

Religious

The Satavahana period is characterised by a unique spirit of toleration in matters of religious beliefs. The Satavahana rulers were Brahmanical Hindus who relied on the Vedas and Hindu Dharmasastras. They held *Asvamedha*, ***Rajasuya*** and many other sacrifices. But they seem to have been eclectic in their religious beliefs. They tolerated and actively patronised Buddhism which flourished without any hindrance throughout the Satavahana period.

The Satavahana kings worshipped a variety of Hindu gods and goddesses. In the *Saptasati* of King Hala there is mention of the worship of gods and goddesses like Siva, Krishna, Indra, Gauri. Personal names were also indicative of their worship of different gods and goddesses. For instance, we often come across names like Sivapalita, Sivadatta, etc. which show they were fond of god like Siva. Vaisnavism was also prevalent as we know from names like Vishnupalit, Venhu, Hari, etc. Siva's vehicle, the bull, was also adored. This we can gather from the names such as ***Nandini, Rishavadatta, Rishavanka,*** etc. Serpent worship may have been in vogue, for there are references to ***Sarpa Naga,*** etc.

Under the Satavahanas, Buddhism made a rapid stride. The Buddhist caves and epigraphs at Nasik, Bhoja, Badsa, Kuda in western Deccan, Pitalkhora and *Stupas* at Bhattiprolu, Aramavati, Goti, Ghanta Sala, etc. testify to the predominance of Buddhism. The Karle *Chaitya* constructed during the Satavahana period was "the most excellent in Jambudvipa (India)". The Buddhist objects of worship were the sacred tree, empty throne, foot prints of Buddha, the *Trisula* emblem. Obviously the *Hinayana* form of Buddhism was prevalent, but towards the end of the Satavahana period *Mahayana* form of Buddism and worship of the image of Buddha came to replace the *Hinayana* System.

The Buddhist Church under the Satavahanas had numerous sects chief of which were *Bhadayaniyas, Dhammottariyas* and *Mahasamghikas*. There was no rivalry among these sects and one sect is known to have donated a pillar to a different sect.

A large number of Buddhist teachers called *Sthaviras, Mahasthaviras, Charakas*, etc. moved about in the empire of the Satavahanas enlightening the people in the Law of the Master (Buddha). In eastern Deccan monks, nuns, lay men flocked round the teachers who were well-versed in the Buddhist religious text *Vinaya* and *Dhamma*.

All caves so far discovered in the Deccan were dedicated to the Buddhists and were excavated under the Satavahana rule. The Buddhist caves were of two types, the *Chaityagrihas*, i.e., the temples and *Layanas*, i.e., residential quarters for the *Bhikshus*.

It is a matter of great interest to know that a large number of foreigners embraced Buddhism and Brahmanical Hinduism during the rule of the Satavahanas. The Yavanas (Greeks), Pahlavas (Parthians), Sakas, etc. were these foreigners. Rudradamana embraced Brahmanical Hinduism and a Greek ambassador Heliodrous adopted Vaishnavism. Dr. Bhandarkar mentions that in the cave inscriptions of the time references are there to the gifts made by the Yavanas to the *Chaityas*. At Karle cave two such names found are those of *Singhdhvaja* and *Dharma*, at the cave at Junar the names of *Isila, Chitra* and *Chandra* are found. This shows they turned Buddhists and adopted Hindu names.

Culture

If the Satavahana period was great in administration, economy, social life, and religion, it was no less eminent in cultural activities.

Under the Satavahana ruler Hala, the poet-king, there was a literary exuberance. It was during his rule that the Marathi Prakrit was raised from a vulgar dialect to an elegant literary language. The Satavahana Court under him attracted poets and men of letters round it.

The most important work of the time of Hala was the *Gathasaptasati*, an anthology of 700 verses of diverse nature, from light and profane to most thoughtful and philosophical. Hala himself was a poet and is credited with composition of verses. Hala caused the collection of all great poets and wise men. *Gathasaptasati* exercised a deep influence on the development of Prakrit as also Sanskrit languages and literature. Gunadhya's *Brihatkatha* seems to have been composed during this period. A Prakrit work *Lilavai,* a romance, is said to have been the work of the period.

The Satavahana period is remarkable for the excavation of numerous caves and chaityas. The Nasik, Karle, Bhoja, caves and stupas studded with inscriptions while furnishing us with a very important source of information also testify to the development of stone-cutting art.

From the information supplied by foreign sources we know that the merchant marine reached a high pitch of development. The find of a coin with the double mast ship inscribed on it leaves us in no doubt that the skill of ship making had highly developed under the Satavahanas.

Considered from the different aspects of life during the unusually long Satavahana rule we may conclude that the period of peace and prosperity that followed the conquests led to an alround development of the political, social, economic, religious and cultural life under the Satavahanas.

The Deccan After The Satavahanas

With the dismemberment of the Satavahana empire there arose in the Deccan a number of independent principalities under different branches of the Satavahana imperial line. But they were gradually ousted by other dynasties such as the Vakatakas, Abhiras, Bodhis, Ikshakus and Bhrihatphalayanas.

I. THE VAKATAKAS

The founder of the Vakataka dynasty was Vindhyasakti about whose ancestry and original home nothing definite is known. From his name it is presumed that he ruled over territories near about the Vindhya region. The Puranas credit Vindhyasakti with a reign of 96 years and his son Pravarasena I with 60 years. The latter was succeeded by his four sons. The Puranas also associate Vindhyasakti with the *Yavanas* called the Kilakilas. But the authenticity of the details given in the Puranas has been questioned by scholars but the descriptions given in the Puranas seem to indicate that Vindhyasakti ruled over Eastern Malwa. It is suggested that Vindhyasakti strengthened his position and extended his power across the Vindhyas at the expense of the latter Satavahanas. But most of the records of the descendants of Vindhyasakti have been found in the Madhya Pradesh and Berar and the adjoining regions of the Deccan while a few records of one of their feudatories have been discovered in Bundelkhand. All this shows that the Vakataka Kings had their headquarters in the Nagpur District of the Madhya Pradesh and the Akola District of Berar, and Bundelkhand being ruled through a viceroy or a feudatory. It is suggested, therefore, that the Vakatakas were a feudatory dynasty of the latter Satavahanas, who became powerful and independent with the decay of the Satavahana power. Some scholars suggest that the Vakatakas extended their power over Central India and when the Gupta emperors advanced towards Central India, the Vakatakas transferred their headquarters to the Deccan.

Some other scholars reject this view of Central Indian home of the Vakatakas and hold that their original home was the Deccan, for these is a reference in an early inscription at Amaravati to the name Vakataka. But again there is a controversy and it is said that the reference in the Amaravati inscription is a person named Vakataka and not to the Vakataka Dynasty.

The Puranic account refers to Vindhyasakti, his son and grandson as also the end of the Vakataka rule in Central India before the second quarter of the fourth century A.D. It is also known that Vindhyasakti's great-grandson, Prithivisena I, was more or less a contemporary of Samudragupta since Prithivisena's son married the daughter of Chandragupta II. Then again, the latest reference to the Vakatakas is to be found in the records of the Vishnukundins where it is mentioned that Madhavavarmana I of the Andhra country married a Vakataka Princess. From all this some scholars are of the opinion that the Vakatakas ruled from about the middle of the third to the middle of the sixth century A.D.

The founder of the Vakataka dynasty, Vindhyasakti, was a Brahamana. In the Ajanta inscription he is credited with the conquest of countries and with great liberality as a ruler.

Vindhyasakti was succeeded by his son *Maharaja* Haritiputra Pravarasena. His achievements are narrated in the records of his family. This is the only Vakataka king who is described in the records as *Samrat*. From the Puranas it is known that he performed *Asvamedha* sacrifice. His performance of Asvamedha as well as *Agnishtoma, Yotishtoma, Brihaspatisava*, etc., proves that he was a devout Brahmanical Hindu. From all this, it is supposed that Pravarasena was the founder of the Vakataka empire extending from Bundelkhand in the north to the Hyderabad in the south. Pravarasena probably died about the end of the fourth century A.D.

II. THE ABHIRAS

The Abhiras are usually supposed to have been a foreign people who entered India along with the Sakas or shortly before them. In the Puranas, the Abhiras are referred to as the successors of the Satavahanas. In Patanjali's Mahavasya the Abhiras are mentioned as Sudras. As to the location of the Abhira country there is a controversy. According to the *Puranas* the Abhira dominions lay in the north-west region of the Deccan and may have included northern Konkan as far north as Broach. *Periplus* and Ptolemy, however, refer to Abhira country as between the lower Sindhu Valley and Kathiawar.

In early epigraphic records the Abhiras are referred to as generals of the Saka *Mahakshatrapas* of Western India. An inscription belonging to Rudrasimha I, the Abhira general Rudrabhuti, son of general Bapaka, is credited with the excavation of a tank. One of the Abhira's son named Isvaradatta adopted the title *Mahakshatrapa* and issued coins in his name.

We know of only one Abhira king who may be, in all reasonableness, considered a successor of the Satavahanas in the north-western Deccan. He is Raja Mathariputra Isvarasena, son of Sivadatta. In the Nasik inscription he is referred to have made two investments of 1,000 and 500 *Karshapanas* in the trade guild for the purpose of providing medicines for the sick monks living in the monasteries of the Nasik hills. King Isvarasena is regarded as the founder of the Abhira Dynasty and doubtlessly, he flourished after death of Yajnasri Satakarni.

Isvarasena's inscriptions prove that his dominions comprised the Nasik region in northern Maharastra. The exact extent of his kingdom is, however, not known. The Abhiras continued to rule as late as the fourth century A.D. when, according to Chandravalli inscription, they came in conflict with Kadamba King Mayurasarman. In the Allahabad inscription of Samudragupta the Abhiras are mentioned among the list of tribes subdued by the Gupta emperor. The Abhira territories later on passed to the possession of the Traikutakas.

III. THE BODHIS

The Bodhis held sway over some parts of north-western Deccan. Their coins closely resemble those of the Saka satraps of western India and it is presumed by scholars that they were under the Saka sphere of influence. Bodhi or Sribodhi was perhaps the founder of the Bodhi Dynasty. Some of the coins of the Bodhi kings show a tree surrounded by railings. From this it is supposed by some that the tree was Bodhi tree and the names of the kings Bodhi or ending with Bodhi is because of their Buddhist faith. But this is not accepted by many scholars. From their coins the names of three other kings are known to us, e.g., Sivabodhi, Chandrabodhi or Srichandrabodhi, and Virabodhi or Virabodhidatta. How these three kings were related or how the rule of the dynasty came to an end is still obscure.

IVi. THE IKSHVAKUS

The territories about the mouths of the Krishna and the Godavari districts which were in possession of the main branch of the Satavahana family seem to have passed to the control of the Ikshvaku family which overthrew the Satavahanas. It is not certain whether the Ikshvakus who overthrew the Satavahana main branch were related to the ancient Ikshvaku family of Ayodhya who might have migrated to the Deccan.

The founder of the Ikshvaku family that had overthrown the main Satavahana rule appears to have been Santamula I. He performed *Asvamedha* sacrifice, perhaps to celebrate the overthrow of the Satavahanas. The Ikshvakus originally acknowledged the suzerainty of the Satavahanas before overthrowing them.

In the Puranas the Ikshvakus have been referred to as Sriparvatiya Andhras and they ruled from the city of Vijayapuri situated in the Nagarjunikunda Valley in the Nallamahur range, the ancient name of which was Sriparvata. We have no records of the reign of Santamula I nor have we any idea about the extent of his kingdom. He was a staunch Brahmanical Hindu and is known to have celebrated *Asvamedha* as also *Vajapeya* and some other Vedic sacrifices. It appears that there was a short-lived revival of Brahmanical Hinduism under Santamula I after the Satavahana leanings towards Buddhism. But soon after Santamula's rule, his successors began to lean towards Buddhism.

There are epigraphic evidence that Santamula's eldest daughter was married to Mahasenapati-Mahatalevara Pukiya family whose territory comprised parts of Nellore. Another daughter was given in marriage to Mahasenapati-Mahadandanayaka of the Dhanaka family. Another family known as the Hiranyakas was related to the Ikshvakus. This family perhaps dwelt in Hiranyarashtra which comprised parts of Nellore and Cuddapah.

The next king of the Ikshvaku dynasty was Mathuraputra, Virapurushdatta. The Ikshvakus favoured cross-cousin marriage as appears from the metronym adopted by them. In fact, Virapurushdatta married the daughter of his father's sister. Three of his queen were daughters of his father's sisters. He seems to have also married Mahadevi Rudradhara Bhattarika, daughter of the king of Ujjaini. He is mentioned to have given his daughter in marriage to Chutu-Satakarni of the Kuntala line of the Satavahanas.

At Amaravati, Jaggayyapeta and Nagarjunikonda records of Virapurushdatta's reign have been discovered. From these records we know of his donations to some Buddhist establishments. The records of Nagarjunikonda refer to benefactions of some female members of Virapurushadatta's family.

Virapurushadatta was succeeded by his son Santamula II. An inscription found at Gurzala in the Guntur district mentions the name of *Maharaja* Ruhipurushadatta connecting him with Virapurushadatta. According to Dr. D. C. Sarkar, it is not unlikely that he was the successor of Santamula II.

The independent rule of the Ikshvakus in the lower Valley of the Krishna seems to have terminated by the end of the third century A.D. But they lingered as a local power even after the Pallava conquest of Andhrapatha.

V. THE BRIHATPHALAYANAS

Only one king of Brihatphalayana Dynasty named Jayavarman is known to us. He styles himself as *Rajan* in his Kondamudi grant but as *Maharaja* on the seal on the grant. He is described as a devout worshipper of *Mahesvara* and as belonging to Brihatphalayana *gotra*. According to some scholars the reference to an order of Jayavarmana from camp of victory at Kudura was the headquarters of the district of that name, but according to others Kudura was the capital of the Brihatphalayana Dynasty.

Nothing is, however, known of the predecessors or successors of the Brihatphalayanas King Jayavarmana or about his relations with the Ikshvakus, Satavahanas of the Pallavas. It is supposed that kings of the Brihatphalayana Dynasty before Jayavarmana acknowledged the supremacy of the Satavahanas and later of the Ikshvakus. The Brihatphalayanas and the Ikshvakus were subdued by the Pallavas of Kanchi.

CHAPTER ELEVEN

THE YAVANAS (BACTRIAN GREEKS)

In the ancient Indian Hindu vocabulary the term *Yavana* stood for the Greeks. India experienced a second Greek invasion after the first one by the Macedonian Greek Alexander when the Maurya Empire had fallen into pieces. Alexander's invasion of India was a passing phase of her history the results of which were not of a direct and far-reaching character. But its indirect consequences were many and one such was the infiltrations aid incursions of the Bactrian Greeks in the north-western India.

Although the coming of the Bactrian Greeks into India is called an invasion yet its character was different from the adventurist nature of Alexander's invasion and K. M. Panikkar would like to call it no invasion but infiltration. He would term the coming of the Bactrian Greeks, the Parthians, the Sakas and the Kushanas as infiltration on the ground that their entry into India was in the nature of a migration rather than that of adventure. Yet, it may be pointed out that the distinction between invasion and infiltration is too fine to make much material difference for these foreigners did not penetrate India peacefully. They were conquerors whose amalgamation with the inhabitants of India was so complete that they lost their separate identity.

When the Mauryas had fallen on evil days and the Sungas were coming to power, the north-western and northern parts of India were conquered one after another by Greek rulers who were virtually the successors to the empire of Alexander in the easternmost part of his empire.

Bactria, modern *Balkh,* old Persian *Bakhdhi, Bakhal* or *Bakhli* comprised the vast tract of land which was bounded on the south and the east by the Hindukush on the north by the river Oxus and on the west by modern regions of Merv and Herat. Thus it comprised greater part of modern Afghanistan.

ANTIOCHUS I

On Alexander's death, Seleucus secured for himself a large slice of Alexander's Asiatic dominions with Syria as his Capital. Alexander had left a considerable number of Greek and Macedonian population behind in Bactria. Antiochus I, son of Seleucus became a joint-ruler with his father and was placed in charge of Bactria (293 B.C.). Two years later on the death of his father (291 B.C.) he became sole king. Bactria was now under Governor Diodotus, and the adjoining province of Parthia was under Governor Arsaces.

Antiochus II

Antiochus I Theos was succeeded by his son Antiochus II Soter. According to Justin both Diodotus I and Arsaces revolted against Seleukidan rule and became independent.

Diodotus I : Diodotus II

Diodotus died soon after and was succeeded by his son Diodotus II who reversed his father's anti-Parthian policy and entered into an alliance with Arsaces. Antiochus' successor Seleucus tried to reconquer Parthia but the alliance between Bactria and Parthia stood Arsaces in good stead and the independence of both Parthia and Bactria was saved.

When Diodotus died is not exactly known to us. But when Antiochus, king of Syria, proceeded with a large force to recover the Provinces of Bactria and Parthia, Euthydemus I was on the throne of Bactria. It is supposed that Diodotus II was dethroned and killed by Euthydemus who according to some writers, was related to Diodotus.

Euthydemus

Euthydemus was involved in a long-drawn war with Antiochus III and finding his very existence in stake he proposed an honourable peace with Antiochus. It was impressed on Antiochus that Euthydemus was not a rebel, on the contrary, he put to death Diodotus and his children who belonged to the rebel family. Further, if Syria and Bactria would be engaged in continued warfare the Scynthians would destroy both the countries. These arguments had good effects on Antiochus III who sent his son Demetrius to finalise the terms of the treaty. Antiochus was very much impressed, he recognised the independence of Bactria and cemented the friendship with Euthydemus who gave his daughter in marriage to Demetrius.

Antiochus III

After making peace with Bactria, Antiochus III proceeded in an invasion of India and having crossed the Hindukush and entered into the Kabul Valley and encountered one 'Sophagosenus, king of the Indians'. From the Indian sources we do not know who this *Sophagosenus*, i.e., Subhagasena was. According to the Tibetan historian, Taranath, he was connected with Virasena, king of Gandhara, who was the great-grandson of Asoka. Antiochus was long absent from his capital in his not very decisive conflict with Parthia and Bactria and the threat of the expanding Roman Empire necessitated his return to Syria. He accepted a token submission of Subhagasena and quickly returned to his Capital leaving the formidable Bactrian power with a fresh lease of independence. Subhagasena gave Antiochus ample supplies for his Forces and made over to him a number of war elephants but a large sum he promised to pay remained unrealised as Antiochus left in a hurry for his home which was in danger. His dream of reconquest of the lost provinces of the Seleukidan Empire thus remained unrealised.

We have no literary source to know whether Euthydemus carried his army towards the south beyond Hindukush but numismatic evidence seems to prove that parts of Arachosia and the provinces to its north, Paropamisus and Aria, were conquered by him. It has been suggested by Gardner that the Bactrian Greek conquests in these regions were made under the auspices of Demetrius, the young and valiant son of Euthydemus who probably ruled jointly with his father towards the end of his rule. However, nothing can be said with certainty.

Under Euthydemus Bactria attained great prosperity as has been proved by numerous coins with his name and devices, made of gold, silver, copper, etc. Many of the coins of Euthydemus are masterpieces of numistic art and technique. Some of these with his figure show him to be a well-built man of strong individuality and firmness of character.

Demetrius

Demetrius, son of Euthydemus, about whom Polybius speaks in glowing terms who was sent by his father to finalise the terms of peace with Antiochus III and who made a deep impression on the latter, played a prominent part in the contemporary history of India and Bactria. It was Demetrius who after Alexander the Great, succeeded in carrying Greek arms into the interior of India. His invasion was the first in the series of the Greek invasions which resulted in permanent settlement of foreign invaders in a substantial portion of north and north-west of India. India's really intimate and prolonged Greek contact began with Demetrius.

Graeco-Roman chroniclers like Strabo, Polybius, Justin, etc., have devoted pages to the career of Demetrius. In the Indian tradition although there is no clear mention of him yet a probable reference is found in the grammar of Patanjali and the Mahabharata in both of which mentions one Dattamitra, king of the Yavanas. Much of the information obtained from the literary sources has been corroborated by the numerous coins of his time some of which bore legends both in Greek and Indian Prakrit, written in Greek and Kharosti characters prove beyond doubt that these were meant for circulation in his Indian possession.

Demetrius appears to have succeeded as the sole ruler of Bactria in his full manhood when Bactria was already a prosperous country. He was then 35 years of age with sufficient practical knowledge and experience of diplomacy, administration, etc., as his father's deputy.

Political condition of the extreme north of India at the time was such that it invited the attention of the powerful neighbour Bactria. Demetrius crossed the Hindukush with a large army. His passage through the lands between the Hindukush and the Indus was facilitated due to their dependence and friendship with Bactrian Kingdom. Demetrius conquered portions of the Punjab and Sind and probably founded cities there for the purpose of effective administration of the newly conquered territories. One of such cities has been referred to by Arrian and Ptolemy. While Arrian calls it Saggala, Ptolemy refers to it as Sagala which has been identified with Sakala, i.e., modern Sialkot in the Punjab. During his Indian advance, Demetrius, like Alexander, settled Greek garrisons to protect his rear and flanks. These were called *Demetrius* as Alexander's were called *Alexandrias*. These garrisons of Demetrius became the nuclei of several later Bactrian Greek settlements when their rule was confined to their Indian conquests only.

The exact extent of Demetrius's advance into India is very much controversial and the information supplied by the Greek and the Indian texts have been interpreted in different ways. Strabo, basing his statement on Apollodorus remarks that the expansion of the Bactrian Kingdom in India was the work of both Demetrius and Menander, and that they conquered more nations than Alexander succeeded in conquering. According to Strabo the Bactrian Chiefs, Menander and Demetrius conquered *Patalene*, i.e., the Indus delta, Saurastra (*Saraostos*), Cutch or Sagardvipa (*Sigerdis*). They extended their empire as far as *Seres*, that is, the land of the Chinese and Tibet in Central Asia, and *Phryni*, a Central Asian tribe. In one passage Strabo states that "those who came after Alexander advanced beyond the Hypanis to the Ganges and Palimbothra (Pataliputra)".[1]

[1] Vide : N. K. Sastri : *Comprehensive History of Inida*, Vol. II, p. 153.

The Indian texts like *Yuga Purana* and Patanjali's *Mahabhasya* mention places such as Saketa (Oudh), Madhyamika (Modern Nagari in Rajasthan), Panchala (Rohilkhand), Mathura as conquered by the Greeks. But neither the Greek nor Indian source gives us the places conquered by Menander and Demetrius separately. As Dr. J. N. Banerjee points out the Bactrian conquests were attributed to Menander by some scholars but subsequent researches have proved that it was Demetrius who had carried the Greek arms into the interior of India. According to W. W. Taru, both Apollodotus and Menander advanced into India under Demetrius. Menander came in by the great road across the Punjab and the Delhi passage to the Ganges and the Mauryan Capital Pataliputra; and Apollodotus down the Indus to its mouth and "whatever might be beyond". These two conquering forces were to converge on the centre of India and complete the circuit round northern India. According to him (Taru) Demetrius was the chief guiding factor in the enterprise and was helped by the other two who first acted as the sub-kings under Demetrius and later on succeeded him in different parts of India as independent kings. Taru's arguments, plausible though, are not corroborated by any literary evidence "what is apparent from available evidence" remarks N. K. Sastri "textual as well as archaeological, in the fact, that of these Demetrius held alone Bactria as well as India, whereas the other two held sway in India only; their respective coin types leave no doubt about this".[1]

However, Demetrius' hold over Bactria was soon jeopardised and it became difficult for him to have effective control over so vast an empire from Bactria. The very extension of his dominion in India proved suicidal to him. In his absence in Bactria Eucratides whose antecedents are very little known and who is described by Justin as a leader of "great vigour and ability organised the Bactrian rebellion against Demetrius, put himself at the head of the rebels and made himself thus king". To accomplish all this, there is no doubt, that Eucratides had a prolonged struggle against Demetrius and the memory of which is still preserved in the fragments of classical texts as well as in coins and commemorative medallions. It is also supposed by some writers that after having lost Bactria to Eucratides, Demetrius lived in India for the rest of his life. But nothing is known about the last days of Demetrius.

Demetrius' association with India is borne out by archaeological as well as literary evidences. His coins with Greek legends on the obverse and Kharosti on the reverse may be referred to in this

[1] N. K. Sastri : *Comprehensive History of India*, Vol. II, p. 155.

regard. Scholars have identified *Dattamitra* referred to in the Mahabharata with Demetrius. In *Malakagnimitra* Kalidasa also refers to invasion of India by the Greek at the time of Pushyamitra Sunga and the defeat of the Greeks at the hands of Vasumitra, son of Agnimitra and a general of Pushyamitra, on right bank of the river Sindhu.

Eucratides

From the scanty references to the career of Eucratides in Strabo's and Justin's writings we know of his having overthrown Demetrius. Strabo mentions him to be the lord of a thousand cities but does not say whether the cities were in India or Bactria. Justin says he reduced India to subjection. This subjection of India probably means the land on the Sindhu. From Justin's remark it will not be unreasonable to suppose that some of the thousand cities referred to by Strabo were in India. But as Dr. D. C. Sarker points out Eucratides' success in India was only partial and only temporary in regard to some of the areas. There is evidence to show that he had a series of fight with the princes of the house of Euthydemus who held possession of some parts of India and Afghanistan. From the re-striking of some copper coins of Apollodotus by Eucratides raised the presumption that the former was defeated by the latter. From these coins scholars think that Apollodotus Soter was actually ousted from the *Kapisa* country. It is also possible that Eucratides had to fight with a number of the champions of the house of Demetrius after the latter's death.

Numismatic evidence suggests that Heliocles was the son and successor of Eucratides and there are commemorative coins issued by Eucratides to celebrate his son Heliocles' marriage with Laodice who was the daughter of Demetrius by his wife who was daughter of Antiocus III.

According to Justin Eucratides had to fight not only with Demetrius, the champion of his house but also with the people known as Sogdians, i.e., the people of Sogdiana or the Bokhara region. Prolonged warfare told upon the health of Eucratides and totally exhausted he could ill afford to resist the attack of the Parthian king, Mithridates I who annexed two of Bactrian districts to his territory.

Justin mentions that when Eucratides was on journey homeward he was murdered by his son Heliocles. There is, however, a difference of opinion among scholars about the name of Eucratides' murderer. According to Cunningham Apollodotus was the murderer, but researches have proved that he could not have been the murderer and Heliocles is generally accepted as the regicide.

Heliocles

Heliocles is almost unanimously regarded as the successor of Eucratides. Our knowledge about his reign is probably the haziest. We have, however, two distinct groups of coins of his time, one of Attic (Greek) standard with only Greek legend and the other of bi-lingual type with both Greek and Indian languages. A careful scrutiny of his coins has convinced scholars that Heliocles had given up the Attic standard coins and adopted the one in imitation of his father's coin in Greek and Indian languages, after he had lost control on Bactria and his possessions were confined to Indian territories.

The anti-Bactrian policy initiated by the Parthian King Mithridates I who had occupied two districts of Bactria, was pursued with all vigour and according to a Roman historian Orosius Mithridates conquered all peoples between the Hydaspes and the Indus. This Hydaspes was not the Jhelum but the Medus Hydaspes, a Persian Stream. Thus the Parthian power seems to have extended from East Iran to the Indus. Strabo also mentions that the nomadic tribes *Asii-Asiani, Saraucae-Sacae* drove the Greeks out of Bactria. These tribes have been identified with the Yueh-chi and the Sakas.

Even if the above identifications are held doubtful, the fact remains that the Bactrian Kingdom was lost to the Greeks due to the invasions of the Parthians and the northern nomads. Heliocles, the last of the Greek Kings at Bactria, had to fall back into Kabul Valley and India. The Greek rule in these regions of Afghanistan and north-western India was characterised by internecine wars among various princes belonging to the houses of Demetrius and Eucratides. More than 30 names of the Indo-Bactrian Greek rulers have been found from coins. But history of this large number of rulers is very obscure. Barring three of the rulers, namely, Apollodotus, Menander and Antialcidas about whom we have some evidences, the existence of others is proved by their coins only.

INDO-GREEK RULERS

Apollodotus

We have already come across the names of Apollodotus and Menander while discussing the Indian conquests of Demetrius. They ruled in regions South of the Hindukush and were perhaps related to the house of Euthydemus. The classical writers have mentioned Apollodotus twice in association with Menander. Some scholars suggest that he was perhaps the younger brother of Demetrius and might have been appointed along with Menander in conquering India. The extent of the territories ruled by Apollodotus is not known for certain but from the *Periplus* we know that his territory extended from Kapisa and Gandhara and from western and southern Punjab to Sind and perhaps to the port of Barygaza (Broach). The *Periplus* also mentions that the coins, of both Apollodotus and Menander, were simultaneously in circulation at Broach. The very large number of the coins of Apollodotus discovered in wide expanse of territories show that he ruled over a vast kingdom.

Menander

Strabo calls Menander, the greatest of the Indo-Greek Kings. According to *Milindapanha*, a Pali work in the form of a dialogue with *Milinda* (i.e., Menander), he was a mighty Yavana King of Sakala, modern Sialkot in the Punjab. The dialogue was between Menander and an erudite Buddhist scholar and monk named Nagasena in which Buddhist Metaphysics and Philosophy are discussed. Milinda was an intelligent and acute questioner and being satisfied by the answers of Nagasena was so impressed that he became a convert to Buddhism. There is no doubt about the identification of Milinda with Menander. The classical writers like Strabo, Plutarch, Justin and Trogus mention Menander as a great personality.

The contemporary Buddhists held a very high opinion about him. Nagasena writes : "As a disputant he was hard to equal, harder still to overcome, the acknowledged superior of all the founders of the various schools of thought. As in wisdom so in strength of body, swiftness and valour there was found none equal to Milinda in India. He was rich too, mighty in wealth and prosperity, and the number of his armed hosts knew no end." The unqualified praise lavished upon a foreign ruler shows the great esteem the alien monarch inspired in minds of the Indians.

W. W. Taru's contention that Menander, belonging to a ruling house was not likely to adopt the creed of his subject people is not acceptable to scholars. There have been cases besides that of Menander, where the Greeks adopted Indian creeds. It was Menander alone who had left so deep an impress on the Indian mind that he was remembered with respect long after his time even during the eleventh century A.D. when Kshemendra in his *Avadanakalpalata* makes a respectful mention of his name.

In the *Milindapanha* we have some interesting details about Menander. He is said to have been born in the village of Kalasi in the *dvipa* (island) of Alasanda, i.e., Alexandria, which was 200 yojanas away. The Pali work informs us that the King used to be attended by a large number of his Yonaka (Greek) courtiers when he met Nagasena.

Milindapanha also gives us a description of the capital of Menander. The country of the Yonaka, i.e., Greek King Menander, was a great centre of trade, a city that was called *Sagala*, i.e., Sakala (Sialkot) situated in a delightful country well watered and hilly, abounding in parks, gardens, groves, lakes and tanks, a paradise of rivers, mountains and woods. Wise architects prepared the lay out of the capital and its people did not know of any oppression since all enemies and adversaries had been put down. The defence of the City was strong, with many strong towers, ramparts and beautiful gates. The royal citadel is in the midst of the city which was walled and moated. The streets were well-laid and there were cross-roads, squares and market places. Costly merchandise of many varieties filled the shops. The city had hundreds and thousands of magnificent and very tall mansions. Streets were thronged by people, elephants, horses and carriages. Society had four classes of people—the Brahmanas, nobles, artificers and servants. People showed respect to the master of all creeds. The shops dealt in Benares *muslin*, Kotumbara stuffs and clothes of other varieties. Sweet smell would issue from the markets where fragrant flowers and perfumes were on sale. Jewels were there in plenty, guilds of traders displayed their goods in the market.

We, however, cannot ascertain the exact nature of the relation of Menander with the house of Euthydemus. N. K. Sastri is of the opinion that in spite of what has been said about his royalty in the *Milindapanha*, Menander was a commoner perhaps related to the family of Euthydemus by marriage.

It is suggested that Menander's dominions comprised Kabul Valley of Afghanistan, north-west India, Punjab, Sind, Kathiawar and Rajputana and perhaps parts of modern Uttarpradesh. It is also supposed that Menander had crossed the *Hyphanis* coast and reached the *Isamus*. The Hyphanis has been identified with the Beas and the *Isamus* with Prakrit *Ichchumai*, a river of Panchala that runs through Kumayun Rohilkhand and the Kanauj region. The hold of Menander over Peshawar is borne out by Kharosti inscriptions discovered in the Bajaur tribal territory.

Under Menander Sakala became a shelter for the Buddhists who were persecuted under the rule of Pushyamitra Sunga.

According to Rapson the fame of Menander as a great and just ruler was not confined to India. Plutarch, writing two centuries after the death of Menander, described how after his death in camp the cities of his dominions contended for the honour of preserving his ashes. Rapson rightly points out that, "It is thus as a Philosopher and not as a mighty conqueror that Menander, like Janmejaya, King of the Kurus and

Janaka, King of Videha, in the Upanishads, has won for himself an abiding fame".

Strato-I : Strato-II

At the time of his death in a camp, he was most probably engaged in warfare with some adversary, whose name is not known to us. He was succeeded by Strato-I who was a minor and the mother of the minor King worked as regent. Menander's death adversely affected the fortunes of his dynasty and some parts of his dominions were lost almost immediately. Strato ruled for a long time and was succeeded by his grandson Strato-II and a large number of his silver coins have been discovered.

Antialcidas

Antialcidas was another name that found prominence in the Indian epigraphic record at Besnagar. The inscription records the erection of *Guruda-dhvaja*, i.e., a column erected in honour of Lord Vasudeva, with a figure of *Garuda* as the capital by a Greek from Taxila named Heliodorus who had been sent by King Antialcidas as an ambassador to the court of the King *Kaustiputra* Bhagabhadra of the Sunga dynasty at Vidisa or Besnagar. This inscription testifies to the friendly relations that subsisted between the Yavana, i.e., Greek King of Taxila and the Sunga King of Vidisa, as well as to the adoption of *Vaishnavism* by the Greeks.

It is supposed that Antialcidas belonged to the Eucratides family and to have succeeded Eucratides in the Kapisa region as he issued coins with the image of the city divinity of Kapisa with which Eucratides himself restruck the coins of Apollodotus. In some of the coins found at Taxila, Antialcidas was associated with a senior ruler named Lysias who was probably his father. The rule of Lysias seems to have intervened between the reigns of Heliocles and Antialcidas. It is sometimes suggested that Antialcidas, Lysias, Heliocles ruled simultaneously in different provinces like Taxila, Kapisa and Pushkaravati yet Dr. D. C. Sarkar points out that Antialcidas was the latest of all as he was a contemporary of King Bhagabhadra of Vidisa to whose Court he had sent an ambassador. According to Dr. D. C. Sarkar he sought friendship of Bhagabhadra against Menander.

Hermaeus

Hermaeus was the last of the Kings of the Greek Dynasty of Eucratides. His kingdom was in the upper Kabul Valley which was surrounded by his enemy countries. The Sakas lay on the east, the Pahlavas, i.e., the Parthians on the west and the Yueh-chis on the north.

Naturally, Hermaeus was hard put to the job of maintaining the security of his small kingdom. His neighbouring Greek dominions of Puskaravati and Taxila had already been occupied by the Sakas and it was his turn to be dispossessed. To cope with the situation he married Calliope who was related to Hippostratus of his rival house and sought to put up a united defence. But all this was of no avail and the barbarian blow to his Kingdom was soon to descend. The contention of some earlier scholars that the final blow to Hermaeus' Kingdom was administered by the Kushana (Yueh-Chi) king Kujala Kadphises is no longer accepted as correct. Some scholars also thought that Hemaeus sought the Kushana help in order to ward off the Parthian onslaught and the Kushanas who came as friends ultimately destroyed the King whom they came to help. But according to N. K. Sastri and others Hemaeus was overthrown by the Parthians or the Pahlavas and not the Kushanas. This is also borne out by the evidence of the coins. The Parthian King Gondophernes overthrew the Indo-Bactrian rule in India.

Dr. J. N. Banerjee considers that the second Greek conquest of India was more important than the first conducted by Alexander. Two centuries of cultural contact between the Greeks and the Indians was of immense consequences upon both sides. It was not merely a case of the Greek civilisation influencing the already highly developed Indian civilisation, but the reverse was equally true. Religious ideals and ideas of the Indians had been adopted by the Greeks. We have seen how Nagasena's answers to the searching intelligent questions of Menander made a deep impression upon the latter and he became a convert to Buddhism. The Pali work *Milindapanha* gives us the details of the deep religious and philosophical influence of Buddhism upon Menander. Heliodorus was the Greek ambassador who became a worshipper of Vishnu and set up a *Garuda* column in honour of the deity at Besnagar. A great officer named Meridark Theodorus enshrined the relics of Buddha in the ancient country of Udayana, i.e., Surat Valley. There must have been more Greeks who became converts to Indian religions.

The Greeks also adopted the Indian way of life and living and gradually got identified with the sons of the soil. A second Theodorus, perhaps a descendant of Meridark Theodorus mentioned above caused a tank to be excavated at Udayana, in honour of all beings. In a stone relief depicting two wrestlers with a name *Minandrasa* below is *Kharosti* gives us a glimpse of Graeco-Indian secular life of the time.

In the realm of art the Bactrian Greeks made notable contributions. Die-cutters' art reached perfection in Bactria and the skill with individual portriats on coins were incised and made the coins of the time the very best of the world. Although the degree of excellence had somewhat deteriorated after the Greeks settled in India yet the art was sufficiently potent to remodel indigenous currency. It was during Bactrian Greek occupation of India that the foundations of the Hellenic School of art of Gandhara were laid which reached its flowering during the Saka-Pahlava as also the early Kushana rule in India.

Chapter Twelve

THE SCYTHIANS (SAKAS)

In the inscriptions of the Persian emperor Darius-I we come across one of the oldest references to the Scythians or the Sakas. They were divided into three branches. In the Nakshi Rustam inscriptions the three branches of the Sakas who have been mentioned as vassals of the Achaemenid emperor, were *Saka Somavargah* meaning the Sakas of Haumavarka branch, Saka *Tigraxauda*, i.e., the Sakas with pointed helmets and Saka *Tyetirojraya*, the sakas beyond the Sea. Herodotus also mentions some of these Sakas forming one of the various national contingents that composed the expeditionary forces of Xerxes. Herodotus tells us that "the Sacae or the Scyths, clad in trousers, had on their heads tall stiff caps rising to a point. They bore the bow of their country and the dagger ; besides which they carried the battle-axe or *sagaris*. They were in truth Amyrgian Scythians, but the Persians called them *Sacae* since that the name which they gave to all Scythians".

Two of the branches of the Sakas, it appears, lived in contiguous regions if not in the one and the same place, which is supposed to have been Drangiana-Seistan Territory, that is *Sakasthana*, modern Seistan. The third branch who have been identified by Rapson with the Sakas of Europe dwelt on the north of Black Sea. The Sakas were nomadic tribes who originally belonged to Central Asia. In the middle of the second century B.C. there was a displacement of tribes in Central Asia and under pressure from other nomadic tribes, the Sakas were compelled to move to south and south-eastwards. For the early history of the Sakas and the tribes like Hiung-nu, Wu-Sun, Yue-chi, Saiwang and Ta-hia we are indebted to the Chinese annalists.

The Sakas were ousted from their original home by the Yue-chi, and they migrated to the south and fought against the Greeks of Bactria. Most of the Sakas then settled in valley of the river Helmund and set up small settlements there. One of the settlements is known as *Sakastan* or Seistan, another settlement was in the Jaxartes (Syr Daria) Valley.

References to the Sakas in the Indian texts of the Pre-Christian era, such as in the *Mahabhasya* leave little doubt that the Sakas at the time of Panini were living with the Yavana, i.e., Greeks outside the limits of Aryavarta. "Saka infiltration into the extreme north-western and western borders of India some considerable time before the beginning of the Christian era is extremely likely—perhaps even when the Bactrian Greeks were ruling in these regions".[1] The Indians obtained first knowledge of the Sakas from these border settlements and the Puranas, Jaina literature occasionally refer to these people. In the *Ramayana* there is reference to Saka settlements along with those of the Kambojas and the Yavanas in the extreme north-west beyond Sakala, Capital of the Madra people.

According to Dr. J. N. Banerjee the Sakas came into India by an indirect route. After crossing the Hindukush they entered the northern borders of Gedrosia wherefrom they entered into the Indus region through the Bolan Pass and not through the Khyber Pass. It is supposed that many of the Saka Kings were contemporaneous with the Indo-Greek rulers. The Saka rulers seem to have copied the type of the coins issued by the Indo-Greek Kings. The reason for the choice of indirect route for immigration into India by the main Saka branch was due to the resistance offered by the Greeks under Hermaeus and his predecessors in the Kabul Valley.

The Saka influx into India after the Yue-chi occupation of Bactria mainly followed the southerly and south-westerly directions, receiving checks from the Indo-Greeks and the Parthians. The Scythians, that is, the Sakas made their way into the lower Indus Valley, later known as Indo-Scythia. This view is expressed by Cunningham and some other Scholars. P. Gardner on the other hand holds that the Sakas first entered into Kashmir and the Punjab through the Karakoram Pass and then spread into the Indus Valley. N. K. Sastri points out that the contention of Cunningham is hypothetical, for the difficult terrain mentioned by him was unsuitable for the migration of an entire people, the route being used chiefly by the pilgrims and caravan traders. The Chinese evidence shows that a branch of the Sakas came to India by direct route from Wakhan to the Indus and further to Kashmir and Udayana. N. K. Sastri, therefore, points out that "in all probability there were two ways, direct and indirect, taken by the Saka immigrants into India". This is vouchsafed by numismatic and epigraphic evidences. Early epigraphic evidence also appears to support the theory that Seistan region was the original home of the Sakas wherefrom they entered into India.

On numismatic evidence scholars have identified two or more lines of the Saka Kings ruling over northern, north-western and western parts of India. Some of these Saka Kings are also known from the Kharosti and Brahmi inscriptions. But none of these has, how-

[1] *Comprehensive History of India,* Vol. II, p. 189.

ever, been mentioned in any Indian or foreign literature. Two main royal lines of the Scythians known from their coins are those of Manes in the Punjab and the adjoining areas and Vonones and his associates in Kandahar (Arachosia).

I. VONONES

The Parthian King Mithridates-I conquered eastern Iran and the adjoining parts of India. The capital of the Parthian dominions was Ctesiphon. When the Sakas fell upon the Parthians, the struggle became so serious that two of the Parthian emperors lost their lives at the hands of the Scythians, i.e., Sakas. The life and death struggle of the Parthians with the Scythians naturally led to the loosening of grip of the central government over the provinces ruled through governors. This offered opportunities to the establishment of independent of semi-independent states in the eastern part of the Parthian empire under the leadership of governors of Parthian or of mixed Scytho-Parthian origin.

In eastern Iran the local governor was Vonones who took advantage of the weakness of the central government and made himself independent. The name Vonones is Parthian but his brothers adopted Persian and Scythian names.

Dr. Smith is of the opinion that both Vonones and Maues were Parthians. But Rapson rejects the view of Smith and points out that the Parthian features in their names were due to the long association of Scythians with the Parthians.

Vonones after assuming independent status took the title *Great King of Kings* after the fashion on the Parthian rulers. Vonones seems to have ruled southern Afghanistan besides eastern Iran. Southern Afghanistan and the eastern parts of his dominions were ruled by him through his Viceroys. The exact date of his rule, however, is not definitely known. One interesting feature of Vonones' coins is that his own name is given on the obverse in Greek and of the viceroy on the reverse in Kharosthi. Some times two subordinate rulers' names are likewise associated.

Vonones seems to have ruled conjointly with his brother or step-brother Spalahora and his nephew Spaladagama. Spalahora and his son Spaladagama probably ruled over south Afghanisthan. On the early coins of Vonones another name appears as a ruler. His name is Spalirises who might have been a brother or a step-brother of Vonones who might as well have served as a joint ruler.

Spalirises's later issue of coins of the type "Zeus enthroned" is taken by scholars as indicative of his succeeding Vonones. Some of the coins of Vonones were also restruck into "Zeus enthroned" type coins. This led some scholars to think that Vonones was overthrown by Spalirises. Spalirises also restruck some of the coins jointly issued by Spalahora and Spaladagama, perhaps after overthrowing them presumably because they did not offer their allegiance to the usurper Spalirises.

In this way Spalirises made himself supreme in eastern Iran and Southern Afghanistan. The Scythian chiefs who were ruling over eastern Afghanistan were feudatories of the Parthian rulers but with the success of Vonones they became vassals under him. But there was exception in the time of Spalirises. When Spalirises deposed Vonones and assumed sovereign power, the Scythian chiefs of eastern Afghanistan declared themselves independent. The earliest of these Indo-Scythian independent rulers was Maues or Moga. Dr. D. C. Sarkar is of the opinion that there are reasons to believe that Vonones was the founder of an era which later on came to be known as *Vikrama-Samvat.*[1]

II. MAUES (MOGA)

Soon after Spalirises had overthrown the suzerainty of Vonones, Maues or Moga severed his relationship with the *Great King of Kings* of east Iran and extended the Saka suzerainty in large parts of north-western India and himself assumed the title of *Great King of Kings.* Maues ruled from 20 B.C. to 22 A.D. Numismatic evidence suggests that Maues ruled over territories from eastern Afghanistan to Gandhara. Occupation of Gandhara by Maues drove a wedge between the two Indo-Greek Kingdoms in the north-west of India. Dr. D. C. Sarkar mentions that Maues extended his authority upto Mathura in the east. A dated copper plate inscription found at Taxila, capital of Maues, mentions the enshrining of some relics of Buddha in a *Stupa* and the construction of a *Sangharama* by one Patika, son of Liaka Kusuluka, a vassal chief and gives the date as 78. Whether it had any relation to the *Vikrama-Samvat* of late time is not known for certain.

Azes-I

Maues was succeeded by Azes. The exact nature of the relationship between Maues and Azes is not known. It has been suggested, that Azes was the son of Spalirises and was a joint-ruler with his father in south Afghanistan. This will mean that Azes became ruler of the Kingdom of Maues by conquest or there must have been some relationship between him and Azes which made him the successor of Maues.

[1] Vide : *Age of Imperial Unity,* p. 125 fn.

It is said that Azes not only ruled over the dominions of Maues but also extended his sway by extirpating the house of Euthydemus. From some coins which had been jointly issued by Azes and Azilises with the title of *Great of the Great Kings* for both and showing Azes as the senior ruler with Greek legend on the obverse and Azilises on the reverse with Kharosthi it is supposed that the latter was probably the son of Azes. There are again some coins which put Azilises as the senior on the obverse and Azes as the junior joint-ruler on the reverse. Scholars take this Azes as a second ruler of the same name. Azes was succeeded by Azilises.

Azilises & Azes-II

Azilises was the son of Azes-I and for sometime he was a joint ruler with Azes. But on the death of Azes he became the ruler. Azilises was succeeded by his son Azes-II. Under Azes-II, the Saka Kingdom of Maues' house was reduced to central and western Punjab only. By his time the Saka rule in this area became weak and could not withstand the onslaught of the Parthian Gondophernes, King of Arachosia. Gondophernes overthrew Azes-II and brought a large part of north-western India under his sway. It is suggested by Dr. S. C. Chatterjee that natural calamities like earthquake and pestilence had weakened the Sakas under Azes-II the advantage of which was taken by Gondophernes.

CHAPTER THIRTEEN

THE PARTHIANS (PAHLAVAS)

I. GONDOPHERNES

Gondophernes appears to have been originally a Parthian Viceroy of Arachosia under the Parthian under the *Great King of Kings* Orthagenes. Gondophernes was associated with a subordinate ruler named Guda or Gudana whose name sometimes appear in the coins of Orthagenes. Gondophernes after acquiring independent status gradually extended his power on all sides and became an emperor. From some of his coins it is supposed that he occupied Drangiana, that is eastern Iran. He restruck some of the coins of the Parthian emperors Orodes-I and Artabanus-III from which it is thought that he had also conquered certain districts of the Parthian emperors.

In the north he overthrew the last Greek King Hermaues of the upper Kabul Valley despite the assistance the latter received from Kujula Kodphises, the Kushana King. This is borne out by the evidence of the Chinese historian Fan-ye. According to him the upper Kabul Valley was conquered by the Parthians before its conquest by the Kushanas. The success of Gondophernes in the Upper Kabul Valley was short-lived as it was occupied by Kujula Kadphises. Numismatic evidence also shows that Kujula Kodphises also extended his sway over southern Afghanistan. But Gondophernes' success over the Sakas of India was more spectacular. Discovery of a record of his reign at Takht-i-Bahi in the Yusufzai territory in the Peshawar district as also the tradition that a Parthian of the name Pharaotes ruling in Taxila in 43-44 A.D. point the rule of Gondophernes in Gandhara. When Apollonius of Tyana visited Taxila in 43-44 A.D. a Parthian Pharaotes was ruler there.

Gondophernes' association with his nephew Abdagases as also with Sapedana and Satavastra and his military governors Aspavarman, son of Indravarman and Sasa shows that perhaps during Gondophernes' life time, the allegiance of the governors to him was more or less formal.

The name of Gondophernes is associated with the Christian apostle St. Thomas who, according to Christian tradition visited the Court of Gondophernes and converted him into Christianity. The genuineness of the story is questioned by sober historians and Dr. Smith calls it a myth. It may, however, be accepted that the Christian apostle visited the Court of the Parthian King Gondophernes.

Successors of Gondophernes

Abdagases, successor of Gondophernes, was for sometime a subordinate ruler under Gondophernes, who was his uncle. This is proved by the discovery of joint-type coins. The rule of Abdagases was very short. He was succeeded by Pacores who also ruled for a very short time. But he maintained imperial status throughout his time. He was succeeded by another king named Sanabares. But he does not seem to have any connection with India proper. The end of the Parthian rule in India is marked by small silver coins found by Sir John Marshall from the Sirkap site of Taxila. But with the end of the Parthian rule the foreign domination of India did not end. The Kushanas succeeded to the empire of the Parthians.

The Saka Satrapies

The Sakas called their local governors or rulers as Satraps or *Kshatrapas*. This was derived from a Persian term meaning Provincial Governor. The Sakas followed the system of stationing two Satraps, one senior and one junior, in every province. The senior Satrap was called *Mahakshatrapa* and the junior as *Kshatrapa*. The relation between the two Satraps was in the nature of the relation between the King and Viceroy. During the Saka rule there were many Satrapal houses in different parts of the Saka dominions in India. These may be grouped into (i) Northern Satraps of Taxila and Mathura, and (ii) Western Satraps of Maharastra and Ujjaini.

Northern Satraps of Taxila

The earliest known Saka Satrap of Taxila is Liaka Kusalaka. He is mentioned in the copper plate inscription found at Taxila. He was originally a Satrap of Maues of Gandhara over Chhahara and Chukhsa. It has not been possible to identify Chhahara but Chukhsa has been identified with modern Chach in the north-west of Taxila. The two districts, it has been suggested, were adjacent to each other. According to Dr. D. C. Sarkar Liaka probably belonged to the Kshaharata family.

Laika's son was the *Mahadanapati* Patika. There is no numismatic evidence to show that Patika was a joint ruler with his father. He is said to have enshrined the relics of Buddha. Patika seems to have been a Mahakshatrapa with Mevaki Miyika as his subordinate.

Northern Satrap of Mathura

Mathura capital of the ancient *Mahajanapada* Surasena, was the headquarters of the Satrapal family of the Sakas from the time of Maues. Mathura was the easternmost Satrapy of the Saka dominions. There are many coins and inscriptions dealing with the history of the Satrapy of Mathura. From the coins it is known that Hagamasha and Hagana were the earliest Satraps of Mathura. But there are some coins which mention Hagamasha as the sole ruler. Dr. D. C. Sarkar writes that "The earliest Scythian Kshatraps of Mathura seems to have been Ranjuvula who first ruled as a Kshatrapa, and then as Mahakshatrapa jointly with his son Sondasa as Kshatrapa".[1] According to Smith Hagamasha and Hagana were succeeded by Rajula or Rajuvula. The controversy apart, we know the name of Ranjuvula from both numismatic and epigraphic evidences. Ranjuvula is not only called Mahakshatrapa but also as *Apratihata Chakra Kshatrapa.* Rajuvula appears to have ruled over territories from the Punjab to the Gangetic Doab as is proved by the findspots of his coins.

Sodasa as we have already seen was a Kshatrapa ruling jointly with his father and became a Mahakshatrapa after his father's death. He has been described as a Yuvaraja as the Indian Crown Prince is called as also as Kshatrapa before he became a Mahakshatrapa. This shows that the Sakas were being gradually Hinduised which became all the more evident under his successors. Sodasa's rule must have been confined to Mathura and the surrounding regions, for his coins have been found at Mathura, Padham and Sankisa, all in this belt of U.P.

Sodasa was succeeded by Sivadatta and Sivaghosa and ruled over Mathura for a comparatively short time until, perhaps after a short interregnum this region was conquered by the Kushanas. The adoption of names like Sivadatta and Sivaghosa is indicative of the gradual Hinduisation of the Sakas. This must have been facilitated by the fact that they chose Mathura, a great religious and cultural centre of the Hindus, as their headquarters.

The Western Satrapies

The western Satrapal houses like those of the north had two distinct groups. The Saka families that ruled in Maharashtra region belonged to Kshaharata family, while those ruled in the Ujjaini region belonged to the Kardamaka family.

[1] *Age of Imperial Unity,* p. 134.

The Western Satraps of Maharashtra

Bhumaka: The earliest known western Satrap of the Kshaharata clan is Bhumaka. We have no detailed information about the rule of Bhumaka. On the basis of a number of coins of Bhumaka found usually in the coastal regions of Gujarat and Kathiawar and also sometimes in Malwa it is supposed that these areas were ruled over by him. His coins had bi-lingual legends in *Kharosthi* and *Brahmi, Ksharosthi* later on fell into disuse. "It is likely", remarks N. K. Sastri, "that during the Kushana overlordship of northern and western India, Bhumaka was entrusted with the task of administering the westernmost conquests of the Kushanas. On the other hand, he may have been already ruling there as the Satrap of the Pahlavas when the Kushanas made themselves masters of this region".[1]

Nahapana

Bhumaka was succeeded by Nahapana about whom our sources of information are not only his coins but several of his inscriptions recording the pious endowments and benefactions of his son-in-law Ushavadatta and one of his ministers Ayama. It has not been possible to know the exact nature of Nahapana's relations with Bhumaka, and although Nahapana is quite a well-known figure in the history of India his chronological position in the Satrapal line remains a matter of great controversy among the scholars. His coins bear no date and a few of his inscriptions refer to years bteween 41 and 46 of an unspecified era. But some of his coins which have been discovered show that these were restruck by Gautamiputra Satakarni with his own name that raises a strong presumption that they were contemporaries.

Nahapana was the greatest Satrap of the Bhumaka line. He is credited with the conquest of Maharastra from the early Andhra rulers. He ruled over Broach, Maharastra, Ajmer and Pushkara. Both eastern and western Malwa were within his dominions. From the *Periplus* it is known that northern Konkan was included in Nahapana's dominions. From the same source we know that the capital of Nahapana was one of the two cities of the same name—Min nagara. Dr. Bhandarkar identifies Mandasa as the capital Min nagara of Nahapana. Coins and inscriptions show that Nahapana used the titles of *Raja* and *Kshatrapa* during the major part of his career adopting the title of Mahakshatrapa only towards the end of his rule. It is suggested that Nahapana ruled virtually as an independent ruler acknowledging a

[1] *Comprehensive History of India,* Vol. II, p. 274.

nominal suzerainty of the Kushanas. At the zenith of his power Nahapana conquered parts of Southern Maharastra from the Satavahanas, but the latter reconquered the areas during the rule of Gautamiputra Satakarni. Jaina work *Avasyakasutra* niryukti also refers to frequent attacks made by the Satavahanas on Broach which they conquered in the end.

Nahapana, by all appearances, enjoyed a pretty long reign which continued upto 124 A.D. Traditions current even in the eleventh century A.D. refer to the possession of immense wealth by Nahapana.

Nahapana appears to have become thoroughly Hinduised. He visited Pushkara and many other places of Hindu pilgrimage and made gift of cows and gold to the brahmanas. His wife also made a gift of a cave in order to earn religious merits.

Nahapana's son-in-law Ushavadatta appears to have played an important part in the administration of Nahapana. He was the commander-in-chief of Nahapana and it was he who conquered eastern and western Malwa and extended Nahapana's dominion. On behalf of the government, he undertook various public utility work such as construction of Ferry-ghats, remitted ferry tolls and built cave-dwellings for the Buddhist monks.

The Bhumaka line of Satraps belonged to the Kshaharata clan. But, with the end of Nahapana the Kshaharata line of Satraps became virtually extinct.

Western Satraps of Ujjaini

The western Satraps of Ujjaini belonged to the Kardamaka line, the earliest member of which was Yasamalika. The name Yasamalika is a Scythian name. The Kardamaka Kshatrapas of Ujjaini were the greatest rivals of the later Satavahana empire. In Bana's *Harsha-Charita* Yasamalika has been described as a Saka King, which indicates that the Satraps of Ujjaini were virtually independent rulers. The name Kardamaka was derived from the river named Kardama, in Persia.[1]

Chastana was the son of Yasamalika and started his rule, according to Prof. Dubreuil from 78 A.D. According to Dubreuil Chastana was the founder of the Saka era. But this view has been universally rejected, for the date of Chastana according to most of the scholars was 130 A.D. Raichaudhuri, Rapson and Bhandarkar are of the opinion that Chastana was the viceroy of some Kushana King. The use of *Kharosthi* script on his coins, instead of Greek on the obverse and

[1] H. C. Raichaudhuri : *Political History of Ancient India*, p. 505.

Kharosthi on the reverse also lead to the conclusion that Chastana was a viceroy.

On the evidence of an inscription we come to know that Chastana ruled conjointly with his grandson Rudradamana, son of Jayadamana. It is supposed that Jayadamana predeceased his father Chastana.

RUDRADAMANA I

Rudradamana was, by common consent, the greatest of the Satraps of Ujjaini. Fortunately we have a wealth of information about him from his Junagarh inscription. From the date given in the inscription it has been possible to fix him near about 150 A.D. During the time he ruled conjointly with Chastana and recovered many of the places earlier occupied by the Satavahanas of the Deccan.

Rudradamana's rival Satavahana ruler was none else than Gautamiputra Satakarni, the lord of the Deccan whom he had defeated twice and at least Gautamiputra had been won over by Rudradamana who gave his daughter in marriage to him or to his son *Vasisthiputra* Pulamayi. Rudradamana also defeated the *Yaudheyas* described as a brave warrior republican clan of eastern Punjab by Panini.

Rudradamana ruled over an extensive dominion comprising East Malwa, West Malwa, North Kathiawar, Saurashtra or South Kathiawar, Sabarmati region, Sindhu, Cutch, Lower Indus, North Konkan, Eastern Punjab, West Vindhyas and Aravali, etc. These are territories mentioned in his inscriptions as within his dominions.

In his Junagarh inscription there is reference to the reconstruction of the Sudarshana Lake which had existed from the time of the Mauryas and which burst its dams as a result of a very strong cyclone. The embankments of the lake were also repaired spending a huge amount from his treasury, without oppressing his people of the Province by Taxes or forced labour.

Rudradamana held his court at Ujjaini which is referred to by Ptolemy as the capital of his grandfather and appointed a Pahlava named Suvisakas as his viceroy in the provinces of Anarta and Surashtra.

The Great Kshatrapa is said to have become famous by studying grammar, polity, music, logic, various sciences, etc. The civilised character of his government was marked by his order prohibiting killing of men except in battles. The King was helped in his work of administration by a body of able state officials who were endowed with the qualifications of ministers. The officers were divided into two sections, viz., the Counsellors (*Matisachiva*) and the Executive Officers (*Karma-Sachiva*).

The royal busts on his coins show Rudradamana to be a man of vivacious and cheerful disposition, marked by signs of strong vigour and personality. The Junagarh inscription attributes to him a beautiful body characterised by most excellent marks and signs. Rudradamana left his mark as one of the most outstanding personalities of ancient Indian history and he ruled for a long time.

Successors of Rudradamana

Rudradamana-I was succeeded by his son Damaghsada-I after whom there were two rival claimants for succession. They were Jivadaman and Rudrasimha-I. The struggle was decided in favour of the latter.

Rudrasimha was followed by his son Rudrasena-I. According to some scholars Rudrasimha was succeeded by his brother Jivadamana. Rudrasena-I is regarded as the third Satrap of the line after Rudradamana. The next Mahakshatrapa was Rudradamana-II. We have references to *Kshatrapa* Bhartrivarman and his son Visvasena. But in what relation they stood to the *Mahakshatrapa* Rudradamana-II is not known. Rudrasimha-III was the last of the member of the Kardamaka Satrapal family of Ujjaini who ruled upto 388 A.D. and was killed by Chandragupta-II of the Gupta imperial.

Administrative Machinery of the Scynthian-Parthian Period : Its Cultural Achievements

The administrative set up of the Scytho-Parthian epoch of the Indian history was not a mere improvisation of military upstarts but a highly developed system developed on mature thinking of political theorists and practical statesmanship. The influence of the political thinking—*Arthachintakas* on the Indo-Scytho-Parthian polity is evident. The ablest princes of the time assiduously studied the science of polity and appointed ministers and officials of special merits and arrangements were made to train the princes before their occupation of the throne. Abstention from oppression of the people by unjust taxation, forced labour, etc., looking after the well-being of the people of the *Janapadas* and *Puras* as well as of the country side clearly show that the principles of good government mentioned in the science of polity (*Arthasastra*) were strictly adhered to.

That there was no breach with the past in the matter of administration is proved by the use of the names like *Mahamatras, Rajjukas, Sancharin*, etc., of the officials. At least in southern India the Maurya machinery of government appears to have not ceased to exist although it is not to be supposed that the entire administration was a replica of the Maurya constitution.

The foreign conquerors of north-west India brought with them their knowledge of political systems of the countries through which they had passed. For instance the Persian system of government by Satraps was introduced in the northern, western and southern India. There were also officials with the Greek titles of *Meridarch*, *Stratogos*, etc., functioned simultaneously with officials with Indian designations like *Amatyas*, *Mahasenapati*, etc.

The system of tribal republics which existed in India during the times of Buddha, Alexander, etc., were not extinct even during the Scytho-Parthian epoch. Inscriptions testify to the existence of such communities which took aggressive role against the neighbouring kings. The Indo-Scythian Kings could not extirpate the republican clans, but they did destroy many monarchies in northern and western India. The great rulers of the Scythian age adopted dignified titles like *Chakravartin*, *Adhiraja*, *Rajatiraja*, *Devaputra*, etc. In southern India such titles were of somewhat religious nature, such as *Dharma-Yuvamaharaja*, *Dharma-maharajadhiraja* etc. The queens were likewise invested with titles like *Agra-mahishi*, *Mahadevi*, etc.

One of the most remarkable features of the Scythian age was the system of *Dvairajya*, i.e., Diarchy in northern, western and southern India. The ruler ruled conjointly with the Crown Prince or a near relation who occupied a subordinate position and often stationed in a province. The general administration was divided into central, provincial, district and village administration. Besides the Counsellors and the Executive Officers of the ruler, there were other important Court officials, such as, the royal physician and the royal scribe, the commander-in-chief, the great judge, etc.

The Chief sources of revenue were *bhaga*, *bali*, *sulka*, etc. ; less scrupulous kings used to levy oppressive taxes, forced labour and exact benevolences. The *dutas* were a very important class of officials in the foreign department.

During this epoch the big dominions in northern and western India were split up into smaller provinces ruled by *Mahakshatrapas* and *Kshatrapas*.

The cultural impact of the Graeco-Scytho-Parthian influx can be seen in the coins struck during the period. The coins had bi-lingual legends, the Greek on the obverse and *Kharosthi* on the reverse. The representation of the ruler on coins or in inscriptions was extremely vivid and admitted of our forming a clear idea about the personality of the ruler depicted in them.

In art and architecture there was no breach since the time of the Yavana rule in the north-west and the continuity of the art and architecture in those regions, particularly at Gandhara helped the emergence of the celebrated Gandhara school of art under the Kushanas. In architecture the main feature was simplicity. There was no dearth of cities and towns but architecture did not leave any impression of special excellence. The royal palace at Sirkap may be cited as an instance. The Buddhist caves and the temple of Taxila were, however, specially noted for ornamental work.

A very interesting feature of the different peoples who entered India during the post-Mauryan period was their gradual adoption of Hindu religion, names, etc. The Sakas and the Pahlavas became ultimately thoroughly Hinduised. Intermarriage between the families of the Saka-Pahlavas with Indian families like the Satavahanas, etc. point to the gradual assimilation of the outlanders into the Hindu socio-religious fabric.

CHAPTER FOURTEEN

THE KUSHANAS

Sources

Despite many gaps that still exist in our knowledge about the rise and fall of the Kushanas, we have a wealth of historical materials about this period and the Kushanas are much better known to Indian history than their immediate predecessors the Pahlavas and the Sakas. Evidences—numismatic, epigraphic and literary—partly indigenous and partly foreign as also sculptural and architectural remains make the task of the historians rather baffling, particularly because of the conflicting testimony offered by them.

About the migration of the Yue-chi tribe from the Kan-su and Ning-hsia regions, west of the Huang-ho river in China to India, we have Chinese source of information. Among the foreign literary sources, reference may be made to the Chinese historian Pan-ku's *History of the First Han Dynasty* (*Tsien Han-shu*), history of the later Han dynasty (*Hon Han-shu*) by Fan-ye, chronicle of Ma-twan-lin, account of Chang-kien, the Chinese ambassador to Bactria, account of Chinese traveller Hiuen-Tsang, etc.

Indigenous literature like the epic, the Puranas, Kalhana's *Rajatarangini*, *Asvaghosa's Buddhacharita*, Kumaralata's *Kalpana-mandika*, Nagarjuna's *Madhyamikasutra* threw a flood of light on the history of the Kushanas.

The numismatic evidence about the Kushana period is of great importance in the reconstruction of the history of the Kushanas. The coins struck by the Kushana kings only help us in determining their chronology but also give us a clear idea of their religion. From the distribution of their coins an idea of the expanse of the Kushana empire can be had. The extent of the Roman influence on the Kushana currency can as well be understood from the coins of the time.

We have a large number of inscriptions of the Kushana period. A few *Kharosthi* inscriptions are assumed by some scholars to contain reference to the first Kushana. The *Takht-i-Bahi* inscription of the time of Gondophernes makes reference to prince Kopa who has been identified with Kujula Kadphises. In the *Panjtar* inscription where *Maharaja Cushana* is mentioned, could not be anybody other than Kushana King Kujula Kadphises. There is also another interesting document of the early Kushana period recovered at 'chir tope' near the site of the city of Sirkap. In the silver scroll inscription there is mention of *Maharaja Rajatiraja Devoputra Kushana.*

Archaeological remains like *Stupas*, Chaityas, sculptured figures, palaces, etc. furnish us with important source material for the period. The remains of Purushapura, the specimens of Gandhara art, Amaravati art, etc. not only speak of the cultural and artistic excellence of the time but also indicate the extent of foreign influence.

Origin and the Rise of the Kushanas

On the basis of the Chinese sources it has long been held by scholars that the Kushanas were a branch of the Yue-chi who conquered Bactria and also expelled the Sakas from the Bactrian border land towards the south. In early second century B.C. the Yue-chi were living in Kan-su and Ninyhsia regions south of the river Huang-ho. They were expelled from their homeland by the Hiung-nu, another tribe about the first quarter of the second century B.C. The Yue-chi divided into two unequal hordes, the lesser horde came to be known as the little Ye-chi and the large horde as great Yue-chi. This larger group trekking westward vanquished a number of Saka tribes on the upper courses of the river Hi and settled there for about three decades before a part of this group was subjugated by another nomadic tribe called Wu-sun, the remaining people withdrew further west and settled in the north of the river Oxus. When the Chinese ambassador Chang-kien visited Bactria, he found these people dominant in the rich and fertile country north of the Oxus. Ta-hia, i.e., the people of Bactria seem to have been subjected to the rule of the Yue-chi. The Yue-chi, in course of time gave up their nomadic life.

It is generally held that the Kushanas were a section of the Yue-chi and this inference is based on the annals of the earlier and later Han Dynasties—the *Tsian Han-shu* and *Hou-Han-shu.* But there is a little discrepancy between the relevant statements in these two Chinese annals *Tsien Han-shu* by Panku and *Hou Han-shu* by Fan-ye, written at different times. While in the former work it is said that the Ta Yue-chi subjugated the Ta-hia country which was divided into five *hi-hous*, i.e., districts, each under a chief, the other work mentions that the Yue-chi divided the Ta-hai into five districts *hi-hous.* It has been pointed by some scholars that the Yue-chi found the Ta-hia country divided into five districts each under a small chiefs "which were of Sai origin" definitely prove that the Yue-chi subjugated the Sakas. Some other scholars are of the opinion that because of Yue-chi divided the Ta-hia country into five district *hi-hous* which were under small chiefs of Saka origin shows that the Yue-chi themselves were Sakas. This interpretation that the Kushanas did not belong to the Yue-chi stock was first propounded by the Japanese scholar Kuwabara Jitzue and was accepted by Karlgren, Sten Konow, Haneda Toru, Paul Pelliot, etc. W. W. Taru, however, vehemently rejects the theory and asserts that the Kushanas were a branch of the Yue-chi. The older view that the Kushanas belonged to the Yue-chi stock commends itself for the simple reason that both the Chinese annals of Panku and Fan-ye agree to the major point that the Yue-chi came to occupy Ta-hia region which was later on aggrandised.

The latest attempt to solve the problem relating to the nationality of the Yue-chi and the Kushanas has been made by the American scholar Maenchen-Helfen. He asserts that there is, in fact, no real discrepancy in the two Chinese annals, and that the Kushanas were among five hi-hous as such were feudatories of the Yue-chi king. Maenchen-Helfen's opinion rests on a skilful appraisal of all available historical and linguistic data affecting the ancient composite tribe.

Now if we turn to Fan-Ye's annals *Hou Han-shu* we find that the Kushanas (Kueishuang) was one of the five district *hi-hous*. After more than hundred years the Chief of the Kushana group named Kiu-tsiu-kio (Kujula Kadphises) attacked and annihiliated the four other chiefs and made himself lord and then invaded Parthia, Kabul, Kipin, Pota and became the complete master of the area. Kui-tsiu-kio died at the age of eighty and his son Yen-Kao-tchen succeeded him and in his turn conquered India, apparently the kingdom of Taxila and established there a chief for governing it. "From this time the Yue-chi became extremely powerful. All other countries designated them Kushana after their king, but Han retained the old name, and called the Ta Yue-chi."

The Yue-chi (Kushanas) seem not only to have imbibed many cultural traits of the Sakas, but also to have absorbed a large Saka ethnic element much in the same way as the Sakas of another region appear to have incorporated an appreciable quantity of Parthian traits during their long sojourn in eastern Iran, before they invaded India.

THE KUSHANA KINGS

I. Kujula Kadphises (c 15-65 A.D.)

Kiu-tsiu-kio mentioned in the annals of the later Han dynasty has been identified by scholars with Kujula Kadphises who was the first Kushana king about whom we know definitely. He was originally the Chief of one of the divisions of the Yue-chi who ultimately succeeded in bringing other divisions to subjection and made himself the sole monarch of the Yue-chi nation.

There is a good deal of controversy about the date of the first Kushana king. At first it was suggested that the Indo-Greek king who sought the help of the Kushana chief against the Parthians and eventually allowed some position to his barbarian ally both in administration and territory was none other than Kujula Kadphises. After sometime the Indo-Greek king Hermaues disappeared from the scene, either by death or forcible removal and the Kushana chief became paramount in Kabul region.

Rapson has demonstrated the untenability of this view basing his argument on the numismatic evidence that Kujula Kadphises could not have succeeded Hemaues and these two were separated by a long gap of time.

On the basis of the Takht-i-Bahi inscription Sten Konow suggests that Kujula Kadphises was not a chief in c 45 A.D. far less the master of all the five Yue-chi tribes. The Chinese account of the aggrandisement of power by Kui-tsiu-kio corroborated by Pantiar inscription bearing the date 122 corresponding to 64 A.D. wherein there is mention of *Maharaja Cushana* refer to none other than Kujula Kadphises. Konow further suggests that the Kushana dominion extended during Kujula Kadphises' time upto Taxila. The Taxila scroll of 78 A.D. which mentions Maharaja Rajatiraja Devaputra Kushana is according to Sir John Marshall and Sten Konow none else than Kujula Kadphises.

Dr. H. C. Raichaudhuri and Dr. D. C. Sarkar do not accept the view of Sten Konow in placing Kujula Kadphises to so late a period. They point out the *Maharaja Rajatiraja Devaputra* Kushana mentioned in the Taxila scroll was not a king of the Kadphises of king, it was a title adopted a Kushana group of kings. Dr. Smith places Kadphises-I between 40 and 70 A.D. But according to Dr. R. K. Mukherjee and Dr. D. C. Sarkar Kadphises-I ruled from 15 to 65 A.D. This view is corroborated by the numismatic evidence.

According to Dr. Smith Kujula Kadphises-I wrested Kabul valley from the Parthians, made himself master of Gandhara and Bactria, as also extended his sway upto Taxila. Thus his empire extended from the borders of Persia to the Indus.

Many coins bearing the name of Kadphises-I have been discovered. In the earlier coins there is no royal title in the legend but in coins issued later royal title appears. From this it is presumed that he may have begun his career as a vassal of the Greek king Hermaues with whose assistance perhaps he had brought the other four divisions of the Yue-chi to subjection. But this view is very much controversial.

The epithets adopted by Kadphises-I, namely *dhramathida* and *Sachadharmathida* meaning "established in true faith" may indicate that he was a worshipper either of Buddha or Siva. One of the coins of Kadphises has a figure on it which the numismatists interpret as Buddha seated in the conventional posture. But the figure has also been taken to represent Siva by some scholars. Kadphises' coins with a diademed head on its obverse shows the Roman influence, for it was a close imitation of the coins of emperor Augustus or his successor Tiberius. Kadphises was succeeded by his son Kadphises-II, also known as Wima Kadphises.

Kadphises-II (65-75 A.D.)

Dr. Smith assigns to Kadphises-II (Wima Kadphises) a period of rule from 70 A.D. to 110 A.D. But Dr. R. K. Mukherjee, Dr. H. C. Raichaudhuri, Dr. D. C. Sarkar and others do not accept Smith's view as correct. They fix his reign from 65 A.D. to 75 A.D. Sten Konow and Sir John Marshall's opinion that Kadphises-II came to the throne in 78 A.D. from which the Saka era (Sakabda) is counted is also considered untenable by modern scholars, for this view has not been corroborated by any independent evidence.

In a statute discovered nine miles north of Mathura the name of Kushana King Wima appears on the inscription reading *Kushanaputra shahi Vema takshama.* The word *takshama* is an old Persian word meaning strong. From the inscription it is known that "Vema the strong scion of the Kushana race". This *Vema* is identified with Wima Kadphises-II. This gives us an indication of the personality of Kadphises-II.

Kadphises-II was a valiant warrior and a successful conqueror. As a prince he conquered Gandhara as the lieutenant of his father. On ascending the throne Kadphises resumed his father's policy of conquering Indian territories and from the Chinese annals we know that he carried his arms into the Punjab, a considerable part of the Gangetic Valley and probably upto Benares. He had also conquered Mathura. His empire thus comprised the entire territories from the borders of Persia upto Mathura and probably upto Benares. He appointed a governor to rule over his Indian conquests on his behalf.

According to Dr. V. A. Smith, the Chinese General Pan-chao led his victorious army to the boundaries of the Roman empire and forced the kings of Khotan, Kashgarh and others to buy peace by timely submission. Kadphises-II was naturally alarmed and in his effort to establish peaceful relations with China proposed marriage with a Chinese Princess. This assertion of equal status by Kadphises was taken as an insult and the envoy sent by Kadphises was arrested by General Pan-chao. Kadphises sent an army of 70,000 cavalry under the command of his viceroy named Sic. The difficult terrain through which Sic passed caused much exhaustion to his army which was also decimated. The result was defeat of Kadphises' army. Kadphises was obliged to agree to the term of paying tribute to the Chinese emperor.

Kadphises-II opened up path of commercial intercourse with China and Rome. It was he who had sent an embassy to the Roman emperor Trajan. He issued gold coins of Roman weight and standard besides an extensive number of copper coins. Some gold coins of Kadphises-II were issued in imitation of the Greek coins. The great influx of Roman gold through commerce accounted for the economic prosperity under Kadphises-II. Indian spices, silk, gems were much in demand in Rome. Pliny bitterly complained against drainage of Roman gold to India. In order to stop the drainage of Roman gold to India, import of Indian goods was banned in Rome by legislation.

Kadphises-II became a zealous convert to Pasupata or Mahesvara creed. He is supposed to have been converted to Saivism some time before his formal accession. This is presumed from the fact that the reverse device of his coins almost invariably consists of Siva with a long trident and some times accompanied by a bull. His coins not only indicate his religious belief but also accession to great power for the obverse of his coins depicts him as the *Lord of the Worlds*, the *Great King, King of Kings*, etc.

There is a difference of opinion as to the succession to the Kushana throne after Kadphises-II. Some scholars suggest a period of conflict and confusion soon after the death of Kadphises and Kanishka-I had to suppress the disorder before accession. Dr. D. C. Sarkar, however, remarks that "it is not altogether impossible that the issuer of the *Soter Megas* coins was the semi-independent governor of the Indian possession of Wema and is mentioned in the Panjtar inscription of A.D. 65, and that Kujala Kara Kadphises, probably identical with the Kushana ruler mentioned in the Taxila inscription of A. D. 79, was the governor's son and successor". According to him for a short period after the death of Wema, Kujula Kara and probably also his father towards the end of his life ruled independently. Some nameless coins of the period have also been taken by Dr. Sarkar and some other scholars to justify the contention that there was a period of turmoil when the local governors assumed independence and even extended their influence over Kabul and Kandahar region. They were ultimately overthrown by Kanishka-I.

KANISHKA

His Date

There is a sharp controversy about Kanishka's date centering round two points (1) whether the Kanishka group preceded or succeeded the Kadphises group, and (2) whether Kanishka started his rule in 78 A.D. or later or earlier.

(1) Cunningham was the first writer to sponsor the theory that Kanishka's era started from 58 B.C. which came to be known afterwards as *Vikrama Samvat:* Cunningham, however, gave up this theory later on, but Fleet and after him Kennedy held this view with all earnestness. As a corollary of the above contention it follows that Kanishka group of kings preceded Kadphises group of kings.

But on a careful analysis of the archaeological and numismatic evidences scholars have come to the conclusion that there can be no doubt that the Kanishka group of kings did not precede but followed the Kadphises group of kings.

In support of this view scholars point out if the series of coins issued successively by alien rulers of India upto Vasudeva-I, are carefully studied it will be evident that the coins of the Kadphises kings were issued immediately after those of the Sakas and the Parthians.

Again, the coins of Kanishka and Huvishka, although differ in some details, they seem to be largely prototypes of Wima Kadiphises.

It must also be noted that the practice of issuing bilingual and by scriptural coins introduced by the Indo-Greek kings was continued throughout the Saka-Pahlava period upto the time of Kadphises. The continuity of the practice without break till the time of Wima Kadphises was broken only at the time of Kanishka who gave up the practice of issuing bilingual coins. The legend of his coins was Greek but most of them were not, however, in Greek. Hurishka and Vasudeva followed the practice of Kanishka. Thus we find that while there was a continuity in the method of the striking coins followed upto Wima Kadphises from the line of the Indo-Greeks a different method was followed and continued by Kanishka and his successors. These two different sequences when compared leave no doubt that the Kushana group followed Kadphises group of kings.

Turning to the second point, we find that scholars like Sir John Marshall, Sten Konow, Vincent Smith, Van Wijk and some other scholars are of the opinion that Kanishka began his rule in the first quarter of the second century A.D., some time between 125 to 128 A.D. which lasted for about a quarter of a century. But Ferguson had held long before that Kanishka started his first regnal year in 78 A.D. and inaugurated an era from that date which came to be known as the Saka era (Sakabda) which is still current in different parts of India. Ferguson's view has been supported by scholars like Oldenberg, Thomas, Rapson, R. D. Banerjee, Dr. Raichaudhuri and others. One of the latest scholars to support the view that Kanishka started his rule in 78 A.D. which was also the beginning of an era is Van Lohuizen-de Leeuw.

It has been argued against the above view held by most of the scholars, that if we agree that Kadphises-I reigned about 50 A.D. and Kanishka about 78 A.D. then we are left with only 28 years roughly for the two reigns of Kadphises-I and Kadphises-II which is a very short span for two reigns. But when we remember that Kadphises died at the age of eighty, his son Kadphises-II must have ascended the throne at pretty old age. This makes accession of Kanishka in 78 A.D. quite tenable.

Marshall, Sten Konow and others who are of the opinion that Kanishka ruled in the first quarter of the second century A.D. is directly against the evidence of Junagarh inscription of Rudradamana. Dr. Raichaudhuri draws our attention to the fact that it is clearly mentioned in the Junagarh inscription that Rudradamana held sway over the lower Sindhu region in the first half of the second century A.D. The South Bihar (*Sui-Bihar*) inscription of Kanishka mentions lower Sindhu area as within the dominions of Kanishka. Obviously, both Rudradamana and Kanishka were not rulers over the same region simultaneously. This proves the untenability of the view that Kanishka ruled in the second century A.D. There is also no evidence to show that there was the inauguration of any era in the second century A.D.

Dr. Majumdar's contention that Kanishka was the founder of *Traikutaka-Kalachuri-Chedi* era of 248-249 A.D. is absolutely untenable in view of the Chinese evidence that An-Shi-Kao who lived during the second century A.D. translated a work *Margabhumi-sutra* written by Sangharaksha, chaplain of Kanishka. This precludes placing Kanishka in the third century A.D. as Dr. R. C. Majumdar has done. Dr. R. G. Bhandarkar's view that Kanishka ascended the throne in 278 A.D. is untenable on the same grounds.

Thus most of the scholars are of the view that Kanishka started his rule in 78 A.D. which was also the year from which the Saka era is counted.

It has been contended by some scholars that if the era was founded by Kanishka why should it have been named *Saka era* and not Kushana era after all the Kushanas were not Sakas. But it may be pointed out that the close association of the Yue-chi people of which the Kushanas were a branch, with the Saka-Pahlava made them a composite people with a composite culture in which the contributions of the Sakas was quite large. Further, the Kushanas were not Greeks but some of Kanishka's coins bore Greek legend on them. It is therefore no conclusive argument to say that since the era was called *Saka era* Kanishka could not be its founder. Likewise the contention that the Saka era was not followed in northern India although Kanishka was a ruler of the north is untenable. Facts are, however, otherwise. This era was abandoned temporarily during the Gupta rule when it was confined to the south where its use was spread by the Jainas. But with the end of the Gupta rule the Saka era came back into use and continues to be used even today in different parts of India.

Thus after an analysis of evidences, literary, numismatic as well as epigraphic, the balance of arguments remains in favour of placing the Kanishka group of kings after the Kadphises group of kings and fixing 78 A.D. as the starting point of Kanishka's rule, and also the beginning of the era known as *Saka era* or *Sakavda.*

His Conquests: Extent of His Empire

Kanishka was alone among the Kushana kings who has left a name cherished by tradition and famous in India as well beyond her limits.

At the time of accession to the throne Kanishka's empire comprised Afghanistan, large part of Sindhu, portions of Parthia and the Punjab. He appears to have not forgotten to avenge the defeat of his predecessor Kadphises at the hands of the Chinese general Pan-chao. He also played the part of a conqueror in the early years of his reign. Dr. Smith credits him with the conquest and annexation of the Kashmir Valley. "He certainly showed", remarks Smith, "a marked preference for that delightful country. Here he erected numerous monuments and founded a town, which although now reduced to a petty village, still bears his honoured name".[1] We have, however, no details about the war with the king of Kashmir. *Rajatarangini* refers to three kings Hushka, Jushka and Kanishka who are described as decendants of Turuksha ruler and were given to acts of piety and built monasteries, *Chaityas* and similar other structures.

According to tradition Kanishka penetrated into the interior of India and attacked Pataliputra, the capital of Magadha. It is said that he carried away Asvaghosh, a Buddhist tradition, after the capture of Pataliputra and Buddhist Philosopher Asvaghosa fell into the hands of Kanishka who took the saga with him. Asvaghosa was indeed one of the luminaries that graced the court of Kanishka. We may, therefore, conclude that at least a part of Magadha including Pataliputra was conquered by Kanishka.

Kanishka seems to have waged war against the western Satraps of Ujjaini. Numismatic evidence proves the inclusion of Malwa in his empire. Sylvan Levi, D. C. Sircar and Rapson suggest that the western Satrap Nahapana who ruled over Kathiawar, Malwa and Sourashtra had been a vassal of Kanishka. Some scholars hold that it was Chastana who was defeated by Kanishka and was compelled

---

[1] Smith : *The Early History of India*, p. 275

to hand over a part of Malwa to him. According to Dr. Smith, Kanishka also waged war against the Parthians. Kanishka also conquered Kashgarh, Khotan and Yarkhand. He is credited with defeating the Chinese and thereby avenging the defeat of his predecessor Kadphises II at the hands of the Chinese general Pan-chao and compelled the Chinese to surrender hostages to him.

From the Chinese source as also from Buddhist traditions we come to know Kanishka conquered Kajangal in the Rajmahal hills in Bengal, some parts of Malda, Murshidabad, Bogra, Midnapur, etc. But in absence of any other evidences to support the indirect evidence furnished by the find spots of the coins of Kanishka it is difficult to come to any definite conclusion with regard to the inclusion of Bengal in Kanishka's empire.

Kanishka's empire comprised vast tacts of land extending from Afghanistan, and Khotan, Yarkhand, Kashgarh, etc. in Central Asia to Benares, and perhaps to parts of Bengal. His empire included Gandhara, Peshawar, Oudh, Pataliputra, Mathura. Inclusion of Kashmir is borne out by both the Chinese and Buddhist evidences. The western Satrapies seem to have been under his suzerainty. According to Hiuen TSang "Kanishka Raja of Gandhara in old days having subdued all the neighbouring provinces and brought into obedience the people of distant countries, governed by his army a wide territory even to the east of the Tsung-ling mountains". All this proves that Kanishka's sway extended beyond the borders of India. The Buddhist tradition and Kanishka's own inscriptions are ample testimony to the vast expanse of his dominions within India. Selection of Purushapura, i.e. Peshawar, proves that Kanishka's imperial possessions spread far towards the west and north.

Administration

Kanishka was a mighty conqueror, but no less was his ability as an administrator and he was even mightier in peaceful pursuits and in his solicitousness of the welfare of the people. For an effective and efficient rule of the empire he resorted to the system of Satrapies and appointed *Mahakshatrapa* Kharapallana and *Kshatrapa* Vanaspara in the eastern part of the empire. The northern part was ruled by General Lala as *Mahakshatrapa* with Vaspasi and Laika as *Kshatrapas*. The seat of the Central Government was at *Purushpura* or Peshawar. This practice of rule through Great Satraps and Satraps was the continuation of the system followed by the Sakas and the Pahlavas.

We find a conscious emulation of the methods of Asoka by the Kushana king Kanishka. He pursued the policy of propagating Buddhism both within India and outside India. It was in connection with his missionary activities that he established close relationship, religious cultural and commercial, not only with China, Tibet and Central Asia but also with Rome and influx of gold from China and Rome in particular. The prosperity of the empire attested by the fine gold coins struck by Kadphises I appears to have increased under Kanishka. The unmistakable influence of Rome on the Indian coinage of the time could be noticed.

From the *Periplus* we know that gold and silver specie constituted one of the imports of Barygaza, i.e., Borach, a port on the eastern sea board of India. Swell has also mentioned to huge hoard of Roman coins of the first five Roman emperors discovered in the Madras Presidency. The very name *dinara* of gold coins seems to have close affinity with the Roman *denarius* and *dramma* for silver coins has been adopted from the Greek *drachma*.

Kanishka assumed epithet like *Shaonaus Shao*, as found on his coins, was an adaptation of the Parthian title *Basileos Basileon*. From *Shaonaus Shao* the letter *Shaahan Sha* was derived.

Religion

As it is customary for the Buddhist writers to depict a person wicked before conversion and turned into saint after conversion to Buddhism. Kanishka has been described by them to be devoid of the sense of right or wrong before his conversion. This view of the Buddhist writers has not been accepted by most of the scholars who think that it is an attempt on the part of the Buddhist writers to glorify Buddhism.

Before conversion to Buddhism Kanishka was a believer in many gods, Persian, Greek, Hindu, etc. This is proved by the figures imprinted on his coins. The exact date of conversion of Kanishka is, however, not known. The conversion is supposed to have taken place after some years he had been on the throne. It is supposed that after his association with the Buddhist philosopher and Saint Asvaghosha, he must have come under his influence. Asvaghosha must have won the heart of Kanishka so completely that the latter gave up his allegiance to his previous gods and got converted to Buddhism. Here is a second instance of a great conqueror and emperor being converted to Buddhism and taken to the policy of peace and brotherliness in place of the policy of military conquests.

Kanishka was a close copy of Asoka. What is specially noteworthy about Kanishka is that he was the only foreigner who became a convert to an Indian religion and turned into zealous missionary. In his missionary activities we find him to an emulator of Asoka whose footsteps he tried to follow closely. We renovated the old monasteries which were in a state of disrepair and built many a new one. He endowed the monasteries with liberal money grants for the maintenance of the monks who dwelt in them. Kanishka caused the construction of a number of *stupas* in the memory of Sakyamuni. He also sent missionaries for the propagation of Buddhism to China, Tibet, Japan and Central Asia. The sculptors, painters, as well as the architects of his time also became active propagandists of Buddhism. The celebrated *Chaitya* it Peshawar constructed under his orders excited the wonder and appreciation of travellers down to a late period and famous sculptures therein included a life-size statue of himself.

During his time there arose disputes about Buddhism, among 18 schools of Buddhism prevalent at that time, as we know from the Tibetan historian Taranath. It became necessary to restore the disputes and to that end Kanishka convoked the Fourth Buddhist Council to which was attended by 500 monks. There is a controversy with regard to the venue of the Council. According to some it was held at *Kundavana* in Kashmir but others hold that it met at Jullundur in the Punjab. In the Council the entire Buddhist literature was thoroughly examined and commentaries on the three *Pitakas* were prepared, which were compiled in *Mahavibhasha* which is the greatest work on Buddhist Philosophy. This voluminous work is considered to be the encyclopaedia of Buddhism. The decisions of the Council were inscribed in copper plates and deposited in a stupa built for the purpose, packed in stone chests. Vasumitra acted as the President and Asvaghosha as the Vice-President of the Council.

Buddhist Council

The period of Kanishka saw the transformation of the *Hinayana* form of Buddhism into *Mahayana* form. In the *Hinayana* form the worship of Buddha was only by relics like footprint of Buddha, an empty seat of Buddha, that is, some sort of symbol used to be placed in front of the worshipper. There used to be no figure or image of Buddha to worship. This needed great concentration of mind on the part of the worshipper and the method was very subtle and could be followed by persons of great self-control, and of deepest religious bent of mind. This method of proceeding along the Path of Buddhist religion was called *Hina-Yana,* i.e., lesser vehicle, i.e., subtle mode of transport in the path of religion. But during Kanishka's time worship of the image of Buddha came into use. It became easy to concentrate by keeping as visible representation of Buddha in form. This was a greater and easier method hence called *Mahayana* Buddhism. In the *Hinayana* form of worship emphasis was laid on good action but in *Mahayana* system worship of Buddha and *Bodhisattvas* was emphasised. The use of Pali as the language of the Buddhist religious books was now replaced by Sanskrit.

Art and Learning

Kanishka's patronage of art and learning marked the beginning of a cultural renaissance which was to reach its peak and flower under the Guptas A large volume of Sanskrit literary works both religious and secular, was produced during the period. Asvaghosha, the greatest Buddha Philosopher, saint and literary figure of the time adorned the court of Kanishka. He was a versatile genius whose contributions to the cultural life of the time centred round poetry, philosophy, drama, music. *Buddhacharit* and *Sutralankar* are his two most famous works. *Buddhacharit* on the life of Gautama Buddha in Sanskrit verse has been regarded as a Buddhist epic. Another great Buddhist writer of fame who adorned the court of Kanishka was Nagarjuna. He was the greatest exponent of *Mahayana* Buddhism. Charaka, the celebrated master of the science of medicine, was the court physician of Kanishka. Mathara, a politician of great acumen, was a minister of Kanishka. Besides these worthies, the Greek engineer Agesilaus and many others "played a leading part in the religious, literary, scientific, philosophical and artistic activities of the reign". It is of great interest to know that Nagarjuna in his celebrated work *Madhyamikasutra* expounded the theory of relativity in its preliminary form.

Another celebrity that adorned the court of Kanishka was Vasumitra who presided over the Fourth Buddhist Council held during the reign of Kanishka.

Kanishka was also a great builder and a patron of art and architecture. The works of architecture, art of sculpture of his time are found in Mathura, Peshawar, Taxila and Amaravati. The Sirsukh city in Taxila with its hall, buildings and monasteries was built by him. Statues, sculptures, monasteries added to the beauty of the city. The Gandhara school of art was the product of Graeco-Roman-Buddhist school of art and sculpture. Totally indigenous art also flourished during his reign at Amaravati. The ornamental sculpture depicted in the Amaravati medallion bear testimony to the excellence of purely Indian style uninfluenced by any foreign art. At Mathura find of Kanishka's headless statue is an example of the massive sculptural art of the time.

Estimate of Kanishka

Kanishka happens to be one of the few kings in history who came in as a conqueror and won an empire but was conquered by the religion, language and culture of the country of his conquest. He was an intrepid warrior, a mighty conqueror but what was more he was equally great as an administrator. If he was great in war and administration he was greater still in the arts of peace. He was a great patron of art and literature. He built a vast empire which extended from Central Asia to Mathura, Benares and probably to parts of Bengal but he gave it an administration which brought peace and prosperity to the country and the people, which conduced to pursuit of religion, art, architecture and literature. Before his conversion to Buddhism he was eclectic in his religious belief and was a polytheist. After becoming a Buddhist he became an ardent missionary of the *Mahayanism.* He rendered a great service to Buddhism by convening the Fourth Buddhist Council which resolved the disputes that arose among the Buddhists about Buddhist religion. He was a great patron of Buddhism as his predecessor of the Maurya Dynasty Asoka. Like Asoka he sent missions for propagation of Buddhism in China, Japan, Tibet, Central Asia, etc.

He patronised the Buddhist philosophers like Asvaghosha, Basumitra, Nagarjuna, Political scientist like Mathara, medical scientist like Charaka, engineer like Greek Agesilaus.

He was a great patron of art and architecture. The city of *Purushapura,* his capital, Taxila, Mathura were beautified by monasteries, stupas, etc. The tall Chaitya at his capital with its sculpture forced the admiration of visitors even after long time.

The beneficence of his rule was seem in the prosperity of the people resulting from the influx of huge quantity of gold by way of trade with foreign countries like China, Rome, etc.

Kanishka has been likened to Asoka as a conqueror, preacher. But although he was definitely a lesser personality than Great Asoka, he was the nearest emulator of Asoka in his spirit of toleration of other religions, patronage of Buddhism, and missionary zeal. He, however, was not an apostle of non-violence as Asoka had been yet he had initiated a cultural renaissance which reached its zenith under the Guptas. Kanishka's reign constituted a brilliant epoch in the history of ancient India and the darkness that descended on the Indian History after the fall of the Mauryas was lifted during his reign. Kanishka rightly deserves a place among the best rulers of the ancient history of India.

Kanishka's Successors

Kanishka was succeeded by his son Vasishka. He is supposed to be the son Kanishka. His inscriptions have been found in the Mathura district of U.P. and in Bhopal State in Central India. There has been difference of opinion with regard to the identity of Vasishka, Vajishka, Jushka. If he is identified with Vajishka, father of

Kanishka II, and Jushka, founder of Jushkapura in Kashmir as mentioned in Kalhana's *Rajatarangini* then Kashmir must have also been included in his dominions. His only two inscriptions dated 24 and 28 corresponding to 102 and 106 A.D. discovered at Mathura raise the presumption that he ruled for four years only.

He was succeeded by Huvishka or Hushka who was credited with the founding of the city called Hushkapura. He ruled from 106 A.D. to 138 A.D. He is supposed to have ruled conjointly with Kanishka II, son of Vasishka. The confusive maze is of suggestion and counter-suggestion about the relations between the successors of Kanishka. After a conjoint rule with Huvishka, Kanishka II became the sole ruler after the death of Huvishka and assumed the title of *Kaisara*, i.e., Caesar in imitation of title of the Roman emperors. According to some Kanishka II predeceased Huvishka.[1]

Kanishka II was succeeded by Vasudeva I. This was a purely Indian name and denotes the complete naturalisation of the Kushanas in India. He appears to have ruled between 138 A.D. and 126 A.D. The religious eclecticism of Huvishka and Kanishka II as notified from their coins is less evident under Vasudeva I. He became a worshipper of Siva. Most of his coins represent the figure of Siva with the bull Nandin although his name Vasudeva indicates his nearness to Vaishnavism. There is no clear evidence of Vasudeva's extent of empire. It is suggested that in all probability his rule did not extend much beyond a portion of modern U. P. His rulc, perhaps, came to an end soon after 176 A.D. for no coin subsequent to this date has been discovered. With his death the Kushana empire melted away.

It is nearly impossible in the present state of our knowledge to form a clear idea of the history of the Kushanas after the death of Vasudeva I. There are neither archaeological nor literary evidence for the period. There are only coins that give us an inadequate idea. After Vasudeva I we come across Kanishka III, Vasudeva II. It appears that Kanishka III succeeded after Vasudeva II. From the coins it is supposed that Kanishka III and Vasudeva II lost their hold on the interior of India and their rule was confined to north-western and northern India. The final break up of the Kushana power seems to have been complete during the rule of Vasudeva I's successors.

The downfall of the Kushana Empire

The Kushana empire went the way of all other empires in history and fell victim to decay and fall, the inexorable law of Nature.

Kanishka's rule saw the Kushana empire reach its meridian but it did not take too long to reach its final setting. Huvishka was the

---

1 *Comprehensive History of India*, Vol. II, p. 246.

last Kushana King under whom the Kushana empire did not suffer any diminution. But from Vasudeva's time decadence set in and as it happened with most of the empires, centrifugal forces began to gain momentum and different parts of the empire fell off from it and the weakness was taken advantage of by foreign invaders. The break up of the empire into fragments after a period of splendid unity must have been hastened by a terrible plague which started in Babylonia, and stalked the Roman empire, Parthia and India.[1]

The final break up of the empire was complete during the weak successors of Vasudeva. It is true that the Kushanas who had become totally Indianised, adopted Indian social customs, religion and culture yet the ruling houses dispossessed by them were not reconciled to their rule and as soon as the Kushana rulers showed signs of weakness, the Indians rose in revolt. The Yaudheyas the Kunindas, the Madras, the Arjunayanas, the Nagas, Padmavati, Achhatra and Kantipuri and Maghas pulled down the mighty edifice.

The Yaudheyas threw off the Kushana allegiance in the south-eastern Punjab where they had been ruling before they were brought under the Kushana suzerainty. The Kunindas made themselves independent in the Sutlej Valley of the Punjab and most probably joined hands with the Yaudheyas in expelling the Kushanas from the eastern Punjab. The Madras or the Madrakas made themselves independent in the region between the Ravi and the Chenub. The Arjunayanas also regained their independence after the collapse of the Kushana power.

In the territory below the confluence of the rivers Jhelum and the Chenab extending towards the Ravi the Malavas who had once put up a brave resistance to Alexander later migrated to the Vidhya plateau where they overthrew the Kushana suzerainty and became independent till the rise of Samudragupta.

From the Allahabad Pillar inscriptions and the Puranas we come across the names of the Naga rulers of northern India. These princes were Nagadatta, Nagasena, Ganapatinaga. Their two different families were ruling at Mathura and at Padmavati in the Navwar district of Gwalior. A third family was ruling at Kautit near Mirzapur in the Uttar Pradesh. According to Altekar the title *Bharasiva* was adopted by the Nagas who were worshippers of Siva. The Naga kings of Padmavati possibly raided the Kushana territories and temporarily held sway over the Ganges Valley.

The Maghas of Kausambi originally belonged to Rewa in the Vindhya Pradesh but in course of time they extended their sway over Kausambi and the neighbouring regions. They were originally feuda-

[1] V. A. Smith: *Early History of India*, pp. 288-289.

tories of the Kushana kings but later they became independent as their coins prove. They remained independent rulers before Kausambi was annexed by Samudragupta to his empire.

Thus was the Kushana empire broke into pieces and its different parts fell off from the empire. The weak successors, however, continued to rule in the northern and north-western parts of India and parts of Afghanistan. But with the rise of the Sassanian power in Iran under Ardeshir I there began expansion of the Sassanian power in the east. Ardeshir I came as far as Khorasan whereupon the Kushana king who was still ruling in the north-west of India and beyond sent his envoy and acknowledged the suzerainty of Ardeshir. But in course of time the Sassanian power spread over parts of western and central India and Bactria and the whole of north-western India became provinces of the Sassanian empire. An attempt at regaining independence by the Kushanas appears to have failed. There is no doubt that the rising empire of the Sassanians administered a staggering blow to the declining strength of the Kushanas who were ruling in northern, north-western parts of India and beyond.

Some remnants of the Kushana rule lingered for sometime more in local areas of some parts of the Punjab, Kashmir, north-western province, etc. This is proved by numismatic evidence. They took a new name and were known as *Kidara*. It is difficult to determine the period of their rule, but under the presence of the Gupta emperors of India and the Sassanians the remnants of the Kushana power faded away.

Achievements of the Kushanas: A Review

The abundance of coins and inscription as well as of literary evidence make it somewhat easy to have an idea of the overall condition of India under the Kushanas and to estimate the achievements of the period.

The dark age that commenced upon the downfall of the Maurya empire and the political unity which the labours of Chandragupta and Asoka gave to India, was broken by the intruding Indo-Greek Parthian and the Scythians ended with the triumph of the Kushanas. The darkness was lifted and lost political unity was re-established. The Kushana empire embraced most of northern India, north-western India and beyond, upto Central Asia. The Kushana empire was the second great Indian empire, the first being that of the Mauryas.

Administration

The Kushanas were foreigners who got Indianised. The administrative system under them was, therefore, a mixture of both foreign and Indian elements. Government by the system of Satrapies was the foreign elements in the Kushana administration and the use of the names like *Satraps* for Governors and Viceroys, *Strategos* for the military governors, *Meridarch* for district officers, while manifested it, the use of the names such as *Mahasenapati*, *Amatyas*, etc. showed the Indian element in the administration. It is of interest to note that the areas in the north-west which were under the Bactrians. Parthians and Scythians before coming under the sway of the Kushanas were placed under officers with foreign designations whereas officers with Indian designations were placed in charge of territories in the interior. The Indo-Greek system of conjoint rule was also followed as we understand from Kanishka II and Huvishka's joint rule. The Satraps—senior and junior—were called *Mahakshatrapas* and *Kshatrapas.* The Kushana kings assumed titles *Mahisvara, Devaputra, Kaisar, Shahnu Shah,* etc.

For administrative purposes the empire was divided into Rashtra, Ahara, Janapada, Desa or Vishaya. There appears to have been no Assembly or Council of Ministers. The king appears to have been the supreme head of the state in all matters, religious and secular. Under the Kushanas there was a spirit of toleration prevalent all over the country.

Society

Although the society, generally speaking, retained the original four-fold division into Brahmanas, Kshatriyas, Vaisyas and Sudras, but the rigidity of the caste-system under the Kushanas does not seem to be so exclusive as to preclude foreigners from entering the Hindu Society. The Kushanas, an outlandish race, gradually became thoroughly Hinduised. This shows the basic virility of the Hindu Society and culture.

Religion

The Kushanas were of the Yue-chi origin and were foreigners who were eclectic in their religious belief to begin with as we understand from the numismatic evidence. But they later became either Buddhists or worshippers of Siva or Vishnu. While Kaniska became an ardent follower of Buddhism, took measures for propagation of the religion even in foreign countries like China, Tibet, Japan etc. some of the Kushana kings, it seems from their coins, honoured Greek, Sumerian, Elamite, Zoroastrian and Mithraic deities. Some again, for instance, Kadphises II was a Saiva and Vasudeva perhaps a follower of both Vishnu and Siva.

Kanishka as a Buddhist emulated his royal predecessor Asoka of the Maurya Dynasty and not only sent missionaries to outside countries but also took steps to resolve the disputes among the followers of Buddhism with regard to Buddhist doctrines. He summoned the Fourth Buddhist Council which thoroughly examined the whole Buddhist literature and prepared voluminous commentaries on the three Buddhist Pitakas. The commentaries were collected in *Mahavibhasha*, regarded as the Buddhist encyclopaedia. Mahayanism now became the dominant form of Buddhism.

The Kushanas followed a policy of toleration and Brahmanical Hinduism, Jainism and Buddhism flourished side by side under their rule.

Art, Sculpture and Architecture

The Kushana period witnessed a remarkable development in art, sculpture and architecture. The Gandhara School of Art and Sculpture marked a happy blending of the Graceo-Romano-Buddhist style and techniques. The distinguishing features of the Gandhara Sculpture owed their origin to Greek and Roman styles yet the art essentially was Indian in spirit. "The Gandhara artists had the hand of a Greek but the heart of an India."[1] The most remarkable contribution of the Gandhara School of art is to be seen in the evolution of the image of Buddha, perhaps in imitation of the Greek God Apollo. Images of Buddha and Bodhisatva illustrating the past and present lives of Buddha were executed in black stone. The figures show an excellent idea of human anatomy that swayed the artists. These works of art offer a striking contrast to similar art that we witness elsewhere in India. "The smooth round features of the idealised human figures, draped in transparent and semi-transparent cloth closely fitting to the body and revealing its outline"[2] were due to the influence of the Hellenistic art of Asia Minor and the Roman empire.

The images of Buddha pertaining to the Gandhara school centres of which were Gandhara, Jalalabad, Hadda and Baniyan in Afghanistan, Peshawar and Swat Valley, were more animated and anatomically perfect than those found in other parts of India. While the former are more beautiful physically and accurate in anatomical details as such more realistic, the Indian art and sculpture which produced the images of Buddha were more idealistic giving a spiritual and sublime expression to the images. The technique of the Gandhara school of art of the Kushana period spread through China to the Far East and influenced the art of China and Japan. The Gan-

---

[1] *Advanced History of India*, p. 228.
[2] *Ibid.*, p. 227.

dhara art, according to V. A. Smith, was based on the cosmopolitan art of the Asia Minor and the Roman empire.

There were also purely Indian schools of art in India during the period of the Kushanas. There were the schools of art at Amaravati, Jagayyapeta and Nagarjunikonda. In the Amaravati human figures are characterised by slim, blithe features and have been represented in most difficult poses and curves. The technique of art reached a high standard of development. Plants and flowers, particularly lotuses, have been represented in the most perfect, lifelike manner.

Two *Chaityas* and a *Stupa* discovered at Nagarjunikonda are the relics of the indigenous school of art and show a high standard of development. The limestone panel of figures depicting the nativity of Buddha is an excellent piece of sculpture of the Kushana period which was entirely indigenous.

Architecture of the Kushana period was not so remarkable as the sculpture of the period. There were beautiful temples, monasteries, *Stupas* which indicate considerable development during the period although the technique of architecture did not attain the standard of excellence of sculpture. The famous tower of Kanishka at *Purushapura* (*Peshawar*) was one of the wonders of the world. Much of the architectural specimens of the period perished with time.

Caves hewn in solid rock with pillars and sculptures, hundreds of which have been found in different parts of the Kushana empire show a great improvement upon the technique of excavation that was in use during the time of Asoka. A *Chaitya* with rows of columns on two sides was a fine work of art of sculpture and architecture. The *Chaitya* at Karle is an excellent illustration.

Fa-hien who visited India during the rule of Chandragupta II (5th century) was struck with wonder to find a large number of *Stupas, dagobas* (small stupa), *Chaityas* and images of Buddha carved out of stone during the Kushana period.

There has been a sharp difference of opinion about the celebrity, and the extent of influence of the Gandhara art upon the Indian art during the reign of the Kushanas. Modern scholars think that "The Gandhara School of sculpture has attained a celebrity perhaps beyond its merits". According to some European scholars, the Gandhara School of art was the only school in Ancient India which can claim a place in the domain of art. There are others who are of the opinion that the source of subsequent development of Indian art as well as of the Far East was the Gandhara School of art which developed as a result of a happy blending of the Graco-Romano-Buddhist art.

But despite the foreign influence upon the school of Gandhara art, scholars like Havell, Will Durant, R. C. Majumdar and others are of the opinion that the influence, Hellenistic and Roman, upon the Indian art which was the Gandhara School of art was technical but spirit and the subject matter of the art was purely Indian.

R. D. Banerjee's view that the Gandhara art influenced the Indian art for nearly five centuries to follow is untenable on the ground that there were indigenous schools of art at Amaravati, Nagarjunkonda, etc. where there was no influence of Gandhara School of art. The influence of the Gandhara art failed to penetrate into the interior of India and had no influence on the later development of the Indian art. But the Gandhara School of art achieved a grand success in becoming the parent of the Buddhist art of Eastern and Chinese Turkestan, Mongolia, China, Korea and Japan.

Literature

The Kushana period witnessed a remarkable development of literature and Sanskrit language. Under the patronage enjoyed by the scholars and Buddhist philosophers of the time a massive development in secular and religious literature took place. A large number of standard works in Sanskrit language were written during the period. Asvaghosha's *Buddhacharita*, *Saudarananda Kavya*, *Vajrasuchi*, *Sariputta Prakarana*, Vasumitra's *Mahabibhasa*—regarded as the Buddhist encyclopaedia, Nagarjuna's *Madhyamika-Sutra* in which the theory of relativity was propounded, Charaka's work on medicine, etc. contributed to the fund of human knowledge. Under the Kushanas the royal court became a seat of luminaries mentioned above as also of the Political Scientist Mathara, Greek engineer Agesilaus, etc.

Economy

The Kushana period saw an all-round development. In the field of economy the peace and tranquillity ensured by the efficient rule of the early Kushana rulers, absence of internal revolt and external invasion, conduced to an unprecedented economic prosperity. Commercial relations with Eastern and Western countries led to an influx of gold. India had a brisk trade with Rome and China wherefrom gold poured in due to the balance of trade that India had. Such was the huge amount of gold that came from Rome into India for the export of spices, silk, muslin, gems, etc. to that country that Pliny lamented over the drainage of gold to India. Historian Momsen also refers to the heavy drainage of Roman gold to India for imports from India. The Roman government ultimately had to ban imports from India by passing a law. Sea-borne trade used to be conducted through ports in the Western and South Indian coasts, particularly from Broach.

The coins of the Kushana were mostly of gold and to some extent of copper. The coins depict the foreign influence—Roman—on the currency system. The eclecticism of the Kushana kings can as well be understood from the representation of deities—Iranian, Elamite, etc. on the coins. The Kushana coins also had representations of Brahmanical deities on them.

From the cultural point of view the Kushana period marked the beginning of a renaissance which was to reach its peak and flower under the Guptas. The cultural renaissance which saw its beginning under the Kushana rulers was the result of the impact of diverse foreign influences, Hellenic, Roman, Parthian, Scythian on the Indian culture. The happy blending of these diverse influences gave a new life to the Indian culture which was for a time became somewhat disturbed by foreign invasions. These diverse influences found opportunities to settle down during the peaceful rule of the Kushanas and led to the beginning of a cultural renaissance.

CHAPTER FIFTEEN

THE GUPTA EMPIRE

Disintegration in the Post-Kushana Period

The fall of the Kushanas and the Andhras was followed by a period of political disintegration and for about a century India was divided into a large number of independent States whose struggles and varying successes formed the main features of this period. For some time no great political power emerged in India. During the third century and early part of the fourth nothing definite is known about the dynasties that ruled over northern India except those of the Punjab. The imperial city of Pataliputra, however, continued to be a place of importance as far late as fifth century but little is known of the dynasty that ruled there in the 3rd century. V. A. Smith, therefore, remarks, "The period between the extinction between the Kushana and Andhra dynasties about A.D. 220 or 230, and the rise of the imperial Gupta Dynasty, nearly a century later, is one of the darkest in the whole range of Indian history".[1]

We have already seen how the local chiefs of different dynasties, such as the Nagas, Yandheyas, Malavas, Kunindas, etc., had torn the Kushana empire into pieces.

The Nagas

The most important of the local chiefs were the Nagas. They were a non-Aryan tribe of ancient India who worshipped serpent. Epigraphic and numismatic evidences show that the Nagas lived in different parts of India. In the Post-Kushana period the Nagas flourished at Vidisa, Kautipura, Mathura and Padmavati. According to the Puranas seven Naga kings ruled in Mathura after the downfall of the Kushanas. These rulers might have originally vassals of the Kushana kings.

From numismatic evidence we come across the name of Maharaja Ganendra or Ganapa at Padmavati. This king has been identified with king Ganapatinaga who was defeated by Samudragupta. We came across another king Nagasena in Bana's *Harshacharita*.

---

[1] Smith: *Early History of India*, pp. 291-292.

In the Puranas we come across the names of nine Naga kings of Padmavati, three of them might have been Bhavanaga, Ganapati Naga and Nagasena. Bhavanaga is also mentioned in the Vakataka records. He is described as belonging to the family of *Bharasivas* who were Siva worshippers.

The most important contributions of the Bharasivas was, according to Jayaswal, the foundation of the tradition of Hindu freedom and sovereignty. According to him the Bharasivas re-established Hindu sovereignty in Aryavarta. "They restored the imperial throne and the national civilisation and gave a new life to their country. They revived *Asvamedha* after a lapse of some four centuries." Jayaswal is also of the opinion that the Nagas were the founders of modern Hinduism and the edifice was reared by the Vakatakas and elaborated by the Guptas.

Jayaswal's view is not accepted by modern scholars as an exaggeration of the achievements of the Nagas. Further contention is not corroborated by any independent evidence. The fact, however, remains that the Nagas were local chiefs in different parts of India and made themselves independent when decadence set into the Kushana rule.

That there were other Naga rulers in other parts of India is proved by the testimony of Harisena's Allahabad inscription where there is reference to Nagadatta, Nagasena, Nandi, etc., who are supposed to have been Naga rulers.[1] Achyuta of Ahichhatra is also believed to be a Naga king. Marriage of Chandragupta II with Kuveranaga who is mentioned as *Naga-Kulotpanna* leaves us in no doubt that the princess belonged to the Naga lineage.

The Maghas of Kausambi

From epigraphic and numismatic evidences we come across names of Bhimsena, Pothasri, Bhadramagha, Sivamagha, Satamagha, Vyayamagha who seem to constitute the dynasty called the Magha Dynasty. They originally belonged to Rewa and Vindhya Pradesh but in course of time extended their authority over Kausambi and the adjoining regions. From the Bandhagarh inscription it is found that Bhimsena was the first member of this Dynasty. He seems to have ruled in Rewa and parts of Allahabad district. His dates fall in the period of the imperial Kushanas and in all probability he was a feudatory of the Kushana emperor. He was succeeded by his son Kautsiputra Pothasri. His father did not strike any coins in his

[1] H. C. Raichaudhuri: *Political History of Ancient India*, p. 535.

name as he was a feudatory chief. But Pothasoi minted coins in his own name and it is presumed that he assumed independent status when Vasudeba I was on the Kushana throne.

Pothasoi seems to have ruled conjointly with his son Bhadramagha. The next ruler was probably Sivamagha. Two other Magha rulers are known from the coins. These were Satamagha and Vijaymagha. The line of succession of the Magha rulers has not been definitely known to us. Probably the last mentioned two rulers had been last of the Maghas before they were conquered by Samudragupta.

The other ruling tribes which shook off the Kushana suzerainty taking advantage of the weakness of the successors of the imperial Kushanas were the Yaudheyas, Kunindas, Kulutas, Madrakas, Aryunayanas, and the Malavas about whom reference has already been made.

The Foundation of the Gupta Dynasty

The source materials for the reconstruction of the history of the Gupta Dynasty are as varied as numerous. Besides epigraphic, numismatic and literary evidences of indigenous nature we have evidences of Chinese travellers for the Gupta period.

EPIGRAPHIC

Among the epigraphic evidence, Harishena's Allahabad Pillar inscription is the most important. It gives us a narrative of the imperial conquests of Samudragupta. The Eran and Bhitari inscriptions give us the details about Samudragupta's nomination of his successor Chandragupta II. Dr. Fleet's valuable work *Corpus Inscriptionum Indicarum*, a compilation of the inscriptions of the Gupta Kings from 360 to 466 A.D. and 484 to 510 A.D. gives us an extremely valuable source of information about the Gupta Kings.

Eran inscription (Stone No. 2) of Samudragupta's time contains record of Samudragupta's power and achievements. Bhitari inscription of Skandagupta mentions his fight with the Huns and the Pushyamitras. This inscription also records the exploits of Samudragupta.

The Udaygiri Cave inscription, Sanchi, Mathura and Gandhara stone inscriptions of Chandragupta II Vikramaditya's time furnish us with religious attitude of the Gupta monarchs. Junagarh rock inscription, Indore copper plate inscription give us information about Skandagupta's reign. There are other minor stone inscriptions which also supply some details about one or the other ruler of the Gupta Dynasty.

NUMISMATIC

A number of coins belonging to the Gupta rulers have been discovered, from which most valuable information has been gathered about the taste, religious beliefs, etc., of the Gupta monarchs as also the currency system of their time. Allan's work named *Catalogue of the coins of the Gupta Dynasty* makes a systematic and chronological study of the coins of the Gupta Kings. Samudragupta caused coins with his parents Chandragupta I Kumaradevi's images struck, which obviously was commemorative in nature. We have also a variety of coins of Samudragupta depicting him as an archer, lion-slayer, playing on a lyre, etc. He also issued *Asvamedha* type coins. The varieties of the coins of Chandragupta II Vikramaditya such as Chhatra type, Lion-Slayer type, Conch-type, archer type, similarly the Asvamedha type, tiger-slayer type, elephant rider type coins of Kumaragupta give us some idea of the personal prowess, taste, etc., of the Kings. Coins were by and large made of gold. Chandragupta II, however, issued some silver coins. The legends on the coins sometimes had poetic merit.

Seals

A number of seals of different officers as well as of the queens and brothers of the rulers have been discovered. Mahadevi Dhrubhasvamini, queen of Chandragupta, Govindagupta, Viceroy of Vaisali and officers of different status, high and low, affixed seals to authenticate their orders. These seals throw an interesting light on the gradation of State officials as well as on the provincial administration.

Monuments

Monuments of the Gupta period illustrate the existence of different centres of art and architecture of the time. Mathura, Benares, Nalanda were the important centres of art and architecture. The seated Buddha image belonging to the Benares school of art, now preserved in Saranath Museum, is a masterpiece of sculptural art of the Gupta age. Temples of the Gupta age give us a fair idea of architectural technique and religious beliefs of the people. The temples of Vishnu, Siva, Durga, Buddha, Bodhisvatta, Jaina, etc., show the different religious sects living at that time although the Gupta period marked a Hindu revival. From a temple at Udayagiri it appears that Ganga and Jamuna rivers were deified and worshipped as goddesses.

Literature

Literature was by far the most important sources of our information for the Gupta period. Out of eighteen, five *Puranas*, namely, *Vayu Purana*, *Matsya Purana*, *Brahmanda Purana*, *Bhagavat Purana* and *Vishnu Purana* are important with regard to the Gupta period. Scholars like Kirfel, Pargiter, Jayaswal have demonstrated the trustworthiness of the Puranas with regard to the dynastic list of the Guptas, the extent of the Gupta empire, in different provinces, etc. The *Puranas* also give us a clear idea of the dominions of the Guptas which were under direct imperial rule and the areas under Gupta suzerainty.

Besides the *Puranas* which are an important source of information for the Gupta period the *Dharmasastras*, the *Smritis* of Vyasa, Pulastya, Harita, Pitamaha, etc., which were probably written during the Gupta Period furnish us with considerable historical information. *Kamandaka Nitisara* was a political treatise meant to be followed by the King. The work was written probably by Sikhara, the Chief Minister of Chandragupta II. It was based on principles comparable to Machiavellian ideas.

The poetic-dramas (*Kavya-nataka*) like *Setukavya*, *Devi Chandraguptam*, *Mudrarakshasa*, *Kanmudi Mahotsava*, etc., give us an idea of the political condition of the Gupta period. *Devi Chandragupta* of Vishakhadatta, the author of *Mudrarakshasa*, is a political drama and like the latter gives us much historical information. The drama *Mudrarakshasa* refers to contemporary events leading to the founding of the Gupta Dynasty. It is a treatise giving political and diplomatic guidelines which also throw light on religious condition of the time and spirit of toleration that characterised the Gupta rule. We get a list of the peoples and tribes during the reign of Chandragupta II, such as the Sakas, Kiratas, Yavanas, Kambojas, Parasikas, Gandharas, Maghas, etc.

Accounts of Foreign Travellers

The Chinese traveller Fa-hien who visited India during the time of Chandragupta II left an account about India which is called *Fo-Kuo-Ki* which means *Record of Buddhist Kingdoms*. Although the primary purpose of Fa-hien was to collect Buddhist manuscripts and legends, yet he has incidentally left details of the Social, economic and religious condition of the people of the time.

I-Tsing, another Chinese pilgrim, who visited India in the seventh century mentions a Gupta King Sri Gupta who built a temple at Mrigasikhavana. This Sri Gupta is taken by scholars to be the founder of the Gupta Dynasty.

ORIGIN AND FOUNDATION OF THE GUPTA DYNASTY

It has not yet been possible to disentangle the controversy about the origin of the Guptas. Our source of information is too meagre to admit of any definite conclusion and origin of the Guptas still remains obscure.

The Sunga and the Satavahana records refer to the name *Gupta* but it is far-fetched to connect these *Guptas* with the imperial Gupta who flourished in the Fourth Century A.D. Nor is it reasonable to identify Chandrasena of *Kaumudimahotsava* with Chandragupta I, of the imperial Guptas. K. P. Jayaswal has identified the Guptas as Jats but this has not been accepted by scholars. Dr. H. C. Raichaudhuri's argument based on the claim of Prabhavati Gupta, Chandragupta II's daughter, that she belonged to Dharanagotra as her husband's gotra was different, that the Guptas might have been related to the queen Dharini, the Chief Queen of Agnimitra of the Sunga Dynasty is rejected by R. C. Majumdar as highly hypothetical. Dr. S. Chatterjee in his *History of Northern India* remarks that in *Panchobh* inscriptions there occur names of Kings ending with the surname *Gupta*, who claim themselves as of Kshatriya origin and it is probable that the Gupta Kings were Kshatriyas.

But the veil of obscurity about the origin of the Guptas has not been lifted as yet because of the different suggestions made by different scholars which remain highly hypothetical.

If the origin of the Guptas remains obscure and has given rise to a variety of problematic suggestions, the original home of the Guptas also remains equally controversial and no definite conclusion has been reached as yet.

According to Allan and some other scholars the Guptas were rulers of a principality near *Pushpapura* which has been identified with Pataliputra. The *Vayu Purana*, *Vishnu Purana* and *Bhagata Purana* refer Magadha as the original Gupta territory and extended along the river Ganges up to North-west Bengal. K. P. Jayaswal on the other hand thinks that the Guptas were feudatory chiefs under the Naga Dynasty and originally belonged to the Allahabad region.

There is yet another opinion. Dr. D. C. Ganguly pointed out that the original home of the Guptas was Murshidabad in Bengal and not Magadha. He relies on the statement of I-Tsing who visited India in 672 A.D. that 500 years before his time, that is the second century, a Chinese traveller Hui-lun visited Nalanda and found that Maharaja Sri Gupta built a temple *Mrigashikhavana* for the Chinese priests and endowed twenty-four villages for its upkeep. It was 40 Yojanas to the east of Nalanda. Dr. Ganguly thinks 40 Yojanas along the course of the Ganges to the east from Nalanda would bring one into Murshidabad and identifies the Gupta King who built the temple as the founder of the Gupta Dynasty. But Fleet and other scholars do not agree to the identification *Maharaj*

Sri Gupta with *Maharaj* Gupta, for while the latter flourished in the third century A.D., the former as referred by I-Tsing flourished in the second century A.D. But Allan ultimately accepted the view of Dr. Ganguly.

Dr. R. C. Majumdar on the other hand points out that in the picture of *Stupa* found in Nepal there is a label *Mrigasthapana Stupa of Varendri*. From this it is clear that it was Varendia, the original home land of the Guptas. Thus we find there are two opinions that the original home of the Guptas was Murshidabad, i.e., *Radha* and that it was *Varendri*, i.e., North Bengal.

Now if we consider Dr. S. Chatterjee's suggestion that the temple referred to by I-Tsing which was 40 Yojanas, i.e., 240 miles east of Nalanda was in Malda and not in Murshidabad, our problem is somewhat solved. According to Dr. Chatterjee 240 miles east of Nalanda along the courses of the Ganges will bring one to Malda in *Varendri* but not to Murshidabad in *Radha*.

But there remains yet another problem. According to the Puranas as also Allan the original home of the Guptas was in Magadha and it is also accepted that the Gupta empire included Bengal. This would mean that the Guptas were originally the rulers of a small principality near Pataliputra in Magadha and gradually rose into prominence and extended their sway upto Bengal. Conversely, the Guptas, as we find from the reference to *Mrigashikhavana* temple might as well have originally belonged to Bengal and extended their sway over Magadha. These are still in a conjectural stage and no definite conclusion can be reached at this stage of our knowledge.

The Gupta Rulers

From the evidence of Hiu-lun referred to by I-Tsing as also from inscriptions we come across the names of the first three Gupta Kings. *Maharaja* Sri Gupta was the first Gupta ruler but we do not know who were his immediate successors. Two names which appear in inscriptions are those of Maharaja Gupta and his son *Maharaja* Ghatotkacha.[1] In the Gupta records Ghatotkacha has been described as the son and successor of Sri Gupta. In the records of Prabhavati Gupta, daughter of Chandragupta, this Ghatotkacha is mentioned as the founder of the Gupta Dynasty. But with the next King Chandragupta I we find a marked difference in the title assumed by him from those adopted by his predecessors. When Sri Gupta, Ghototkacha, etc., assumed title of *Maharaja* Chandragupta I was the first King to adopt the more dignified title of *Maharajadhiraj*, i.e., King of Kings. This makes a difference. It seems Chandragupta was a King of a higher status than

[1] H. C. Raichaudhuri: *Political History of Ancient India*, p. 529.

his predecessors who it has been suggested might have been feudatories and Chandragupta I was the first full sovereign of the Gupta rulers and was the real founder of the Gupta Dynasty. But this difference in titles is not very conclusive testimony since in the *Riddhapur Plates* Chandragupta I and even Samudragupta are called *Maharajas*. Dr. Raichaudhuri is of opinion that Chandragupta I was the first independent sovereign of the line. He ascended the throne in 320 A.D., the initial year of the Gupta era.

CHANDRAGUPTA I

With the accession of Chandragupta I, the history of the Gupta gets a continuity and assumes a political purpose which were absent from the time of fall of the Kushanas.

Historians like Dr. Raichaudhuri, Dr. Smith, and some others have attached undue importance to the matrimonial alliance of Chandragupta with Kumaradevi, the Lichchavi princess. The union of the Gupta and the Lichchavi houses has been invested with a diplomatic wisdom by them which is not accepted by other scholars. Raichaudhuri thinks that Chandragupta I "Like the Great Bimbisara he strengthened his position by a matrimonial alliance with the powerful family of Lichchavis then controllng portions of Bihar and perhaps even Nepal. The Lichchavi princess Kumaradevi must have brought to her husband's family an enormous power and prestige." The importance of the Lichchavi marriage is supposed to be also borne out by the coins cf Chandragupta with the image of *Laxmi* with the legend *Lichchavayah* meaning the blessings of Lakshmi were due to the Lichchavis. It is also suggested that Chandragupta was raised by his Lichchavi marriage from the status of a local chief to that of a sovereign as his assumption of his title of *Maharajadhiraja* proved. Chandragupta also struck coins in conjointly with his name and that of his queen Kumaradevi. Further, his son Samudragupta took pride in describing himself as the son of the daughter of the Lichchavis. Dr. R. D. Banerjee's opinion is also very much akin to those of Dr. Raychaudhuri and Dr. Smith. Dr. Banerjee thinks that Chandra-Gupta I's accession to strength due to the Lichchavi marriage helped him to liberate Magadha from the Scythian occupation. But liberation of Magadha by Chandragupta is not corroborated by any other evidence.

Dr. R. C. Majumdar, Allan. and some other scholars do not, however, accept the above view of Dr. Smith and Dr. Raichaudhuri. According to them the pride of the Guptas in their Lichchavi blood was due to the fact that the Lichchavis were an ancient lineage rather than to the material advantage derived from the marriage.

According to Dr. Majumdar the Lichchavi marriage gave Chandragupta I political advantage, not social, nor material advantage any importance. According to Dr. Majumdar undue importance has been attached to this marriage by Dr. Smith and Dr. Raichaudhuri. In fact, the Lichchavis were the ruling clan of Vaisali in the sixth century B.C. but the time of the Guptas they ruled over Nepal Valley. Again there is nothing to show that the Lichchavis might have been ruling over two adjoining regions and the marriage at best might have added to the power and prestige as a result of the unity of two kingdoms.

The Puranic verse, *Anu-Ganga-Prayagamcha Saketam Magadhamstatha Etan Janapadan Sarvan Bhokshyante Guptavamsaja*, which means that the Gupta dynasty would enjoy *Prayaga* (Allahabad) on the Ganges, *Saketa* (Oudh), and *Magadha* (South Bihar), has been taken by Allan and Pargiter to refer to the dominions of of Chandragupta I. From the list of the conquests of Samudragupta it appears, these might have been within the dominions of Chandragupta I. According to Allan Vaisali was one of the earliest conquests of Chandragupta I. But Vaisali (North Bihar) was neither conquered by Samudragupta nor occupied by Chandragupta through Lichchavi marriage as the Lichchavis at the time of the Guptas ruled over region between Vaisali and Nepal. In the Allahabad inscription of Samudragupta there is reference that Samudragupta's empire extended to the borders of Nepal. From this we may presume that North Bihar was within Samudragupta's dominions and may have been included in his time.

According to the evidence of the drama *Kaumudimahotsava* Chandrasena usurped Magadha from King Sundarvarman who was ruling there and died in defending Pataliputra. Dr. R. K. Mukherjee identified Chandragupta I with Chandrasena and observes that after accession to strength as a result of Lichchavi marriage Chandragupta I conquered Magadha. Dr. R. C. Majumdar thinks that the identification of Chandrasena with Chandragupta I is extremely far-fetched and unacceptable as historical truth.

Lack of reference to Pundravardhana, i.e., North Bengal, as a conquest of Samudragupta, in the Allahabad inscription has led Prof. Radhagovinda Basak to suggest that Pundravardhana was within the dominions of Chandragupta I. Prof. Basak would have his believes that Chandra of Merherauli Iron Pillar near Delhi was none else than Chandragupta I. This suggestion has been rejected by scholars.

It is, therefore, highly uncertain whether the extent of the dominions suggested by different scholars, to have belonged to Chandragupta, is historically correct. The only reasonable conclusion that may be arrived at from the evidences referred to above and by following the process of elimination of the conquests under Samudragupta referred to in the Allahabad inscription, is that Chandragupta I ruled over Bihar, North Bengal, Oudh. We have no evidence as to the inclusion of Allahabad in his dominions.

Chandragupta I was the founder of the Gupta imperial Dynasty and he is credited with the founding an era known as Gupta era dating from 319 A.D. according to some scholars and 325 A.D. by others. An important act of Chandragupta I was his summoning an assembly of his councillors and the members of the royal family in whose presence he nominated Samudragupta to succeed him. This choice of his successor with the concurrence of the councillors and the members of the royal house which ensured a peaceful and smooth succession, gave the dynasty by far the greatest of the emperors. Some authors, however, basing their view on the evidence of some coins of Kacha suggest that he was the eldest brother of Samudragupta and preference given to Samudragupta in matters of succession perhaps led to rebellion by him. But his is not certain.

SAMUDRAGUPTA

Samudragupta, son of Chandragupta I and the Lichchavi princess Kumardevi, was declared successor to the Gupta throne in presence of the councillors and members of the royal family raises the presumption that Samudragupta was not the heir-apparent. From Harishena, author of the Allahabad Pillar inscription indicates that the assembly was held in tense atmosphere and Chandragupta's selection of Samudragupta as his successor caused disappointment among a section of the royal family. We must not also lose sight of the fact that Samudragupta was born of the Lichchavi queen Kumaradevi and this might have been one of the causes of his selection as the successor, besides the capabilities of Samudragupta. In fact, Chandragupta embraced his son and "in accent surcharged with emotions" declared "Thou art worthy, rule this world". The presumption that Samudragupta was not the eldest son of Chandragupta I is raised by the fact of the declaration in full court selecting Samudragupta as the successor as also by some coins issued in the name of Kacha who, it has been suggested, was the eldest brother of Samudragupta. Even if we agree to this view, there seems to have been no rebellion of any serious nature and had there been any rebellion by Kacha it must have been put down by Samudragupta easily. Some historians identify Kacha with Samudragupta himself, but it is by no means certain. The tense atmosphere in the assembly where Chandragupta I declared Samudragupta as his successor, and the disappointment in a section of the royal family have been due to supersession of the claim of a better legal claimant.

Samudragupta was great as a warrior, a conquerer, a Statesman, and a ruler. He was no less great as a man. Fortunately we have the eulogy contained in the Allahabad Pillar inscription of the court Poet Harishena which gives us considerable details about the conquest, rule and personality of the monarch although the sequence of events of the reign is difficult to follow due to damages of the inscription in parts. There are also a large number of coins of the time of Samudragupta which also supplement our knowledge of the reign and personality of the King.

Samudragupta was a thoroughgoing imperialist, an Indian Napoleon who turned his arms against northern, central, and southern India and built a vast empire through conquests. Harishena in his panegyric classified Samudragupta's conquests into four categories geographically: (i) Nine Kings of Aryavarta or the Gangetic plain, (ii) Chief of the forest tribes of Central India, (iii) Eleven Kings of the South, and (iv) Rulers of the frontier Kingdoms and republics.

A number of rulers, nine of whom are specifically mentioned in the Allahabad *Prasasti* felt the brunt of Samudragupta's aggressive policy. Samudragupta appears to have been a true follower of Kautilyan Machiavellism: "Whoever is superior in power shall wage a war. Whoever is possessed of necessary means shall march against his enemy." His campaigns against the Kings of Northern India was ruthless war of extermination. He defeated and crushed them and annexed their territories to his dominions of these nine Kings of north, Ganapati-naga and Nagasena were of the Naga family who set up three Kingdoms at Padmavati, Mathura, and Vidisa. Achyuta and Chandravarman were Kings of Ahichchatra (near Bareilly) and Western Bengal (in Bankura) respectively. The Kingdoms of five other kings whose names are mentioned cannot be identified. They are Rudradeva, Nagadatta, Matila, Nandin, and Balavarman.

But from the mention of the frontier Kingdoms and republics, it is possible to get a fair idea of the dominions which were under his direct rule. These frontier Kingdoms and tribal states which paid taxes, rendered obedience and obeyed orders of Samudragupta are well known to us. These were Samatata (South-east Bengal), Kamrupa (upper Assam), Nepal, Davaka (Nowgong district in Assam, or Dacca ?) and Kartripura (Kartarpur in Jullundar district). These were Tributary Kingdoms mentioned as situated on the frontiers of Samudragupta's dominions. Tribal territories which are mentioned as situated on the frontiers as feudatories, were the Malavas, Arjunayanas, Yaudheyas, Madras or Madrakas, Sanakanikas, Abhiras, Prarjunas, Kakas.

If we consider the position of the tributary States on the frontiers of Samudragupta's dominions, we can get a clear idea of the extent of his empire in the north. Towards the east it included Bengal, except its South-eastern extremity. In the north it ran grazing the Himalayan foot hills. Towards the west it extended to Madra or Madraka in the Punjab and probably included the eastern districts between Lahore and Karnal. From the Punjab, the boundary ran along the Yamuna upto Chambal and then southwards upto Bhilsa and Jubbulpore, and to the Vindhya range. The *Atavi rajyas*, i.e., forest Kingdoms of Central India were also within his dominions.

The northern conquests must have been completed and the conquered territories absorbed in the dominions under Samudragupta's direct rule before he undertook invasion of the Southern Kingdoms, a task as Dr. Smith remarks "which demanded uncommon boldness in design, and masterly powers of organisation and execution". In his Southern campaigns he defeated King Mahendra of Kosala in the Mahanadi Valley, Vyagraraja of Mahakantara (forest region of Jeypore in Orissa), Mahendra of Pishtapura (Pithapuram in Godavari district), Hastivarman of Vengi (Pedda-Vengi near Ellore), Ugrasena of Palakka (Nellore District), Vishnugopa of Kanchi (Conjeevaram), Damana of Erandapalla and Kuvera of Devarashtra. Four others Kings Mantraraja of Kaurala, Svamidatta of Kothera, Nilaraja of Avamukta, and Dhananjaya of Kusthalapura cannot be identified. Although some of the Kings of the south cannot be identified, yet it is presumed that Samudragupta proceeded along the Eastern and southern parts of Central India to Orissa and thence along the eastern coast upto the Kingdom of the Pallavas and probably beyond Madras.

Samudragupta was not without the genius of statesmanship. He captured the Kings of the Kingdoms of the South after defeating them. But he foresaw the practical difficulty in absorbing their territories within his dominions and to bring them under his direct control. Samudragupta's farsightedness prompted him not to absorb his South Indian conquests to his dominions. He set the Kings of the Southern Kingdoms free allowing them to rule over their own Kingdoms as his feudatories The wisdom of this step is borne out by the fact that there was no permanent annexation of these southern States ; "the triumphal victor admitting that he only exacted a temporary submission and then withdrew". According to Dr. Smith Samudragupta must have despoiled the rich treasures of the South, and came back with golden booty.

Samudragupta's supremacy was acknowledged by the powerful rulers in the western and north-western frontiers of India, such as the Sakas of Western Malava, the Kushanas of Western Punjab and Afghanistan referred to in the Allahabad inscriptions is *Daivaputra-*

Shahishahanushahi. We have no details about the military campaign in these areas, nor have we any clear idea of the exact nature of Samudragupta's relations with these rulers. They, however, attended Samudragupta's Court, gave their daughters in marriage to the imperial family, used imperial coins as their currency. Discovery of coins with names as Samudra and Chandra as also use of Gupta coins by the Scythian rulers of the frontier Kingdoms indicate exercise of Gupta sovereignty over those areas.

Now, to summarise the extent of his empire in full, we find the dominions under the direct control of Samudragupta in the mid-fourth century A.D. comprised all the most populous and fertile countries of the Northern India extending from the Brahmaputra on the east to the Jamuna and Chambal to the west, and from the foot of the Himalayas in the North to the Narmada in the South. On the borders of these wide limits there were the frontier Kingdoms of Assam and the Gangetic delta as also those on the Southern slopes of the Himalayas; free tribes of Rajputana and Malwa which were attached to the empire by bonds of subordinate alliance. The Kingdoms of the south overrun by Samudragupta were compelled to acknowledge his suzerainty. The empire of Samudragupta was by far the largest that grew in India since the days of Asoka and the emperor of an empire so vast naturally commanded the respect of foreign powers.

His Foreign Relations

Samudragupta, a hero of hundred battles by virtue of his military genius, statesmanship and personal prowess built up an empire which was both a source of terror and strength to the frontier Kings. The Kushana Kings referred to as *Daivaputra-Shahi shanushahi* of the north-west and Afghanistan sought to win the great favour of the great emperor Samudragupta giving personal attendance to his Court, entering into matrimonial alliance with his family and soliciting imperial charters confirming them in the enjoyment of their territories. It is obvious that the Saka chiefs of north-west held a sort of a subordinate position to the emperor and probably sought his help for the Sassanian invasion as also to tide over economic crisis.

From the Ceylonese source we know that the Buddhist King Siri Meghavarna of Ceylon who was a contemporary of Samudragupta sent two monks, one being his own brother, to visit Bodh Gaya. But the monks met with scant hospitality while in India and on return complained to Meghavarna their difficulty in getting any place in India where they could stay in comfort. Meghavarna in order to ensure that pilgrims coming from Ceylon might find adequate and comfortable accommodation in India sent a mission to Samudragupta along with presents of precious stones and other valuable gifts requesting permission for building a monastery for the Ceylonese pilgrims in India. Samudragupta was pleased to consider the gifts as a tribute and granted permission as requested. Similar interpretation might as well have been given to the friendly overtures by the frontagers and mentioned by the Court Panegyrist as token of subordinate status. A splendid convent was built by Meghavarna towards the north of the Holy Tree at Bodh Gaya.

From the inscriptions discovered at Malaya it is presumed that the South-east Asian Hindu colonies such as Champa, Cambodia, Sumatra, Java, etc., maintained friendly relations with Samudragupta.

As it was customary with the Hindu rulers of ancient India, Samudragupta performed horse sacrifice (*Asvamedha*) after completion of his campaigns. This rite was revived after a long period of time and perhaps that the last King before him to perform *Asvamedha* sacrifice was Pushyamitra. The revival of this rite indicates revival of Brahmanical Hinduism besides its importance as a mark of imperial status assumed by Samudragupta.

Personal Accomplishment of Samudragupta : His Estimate

Court-poet Harishena has lavished praise to Samudragupta in his Allahabad *Prasasti* inscribed on an Asokan Pillar, which even when allowance is made for the possible exaggeration of a panegyrist gives us a faithful picture of the personality and achievements of the great emperor. He was not merely the first soldier of his age but a Statesman of no mean order. He was a great warrior, but greater still as a man of culture. He was not one entirely thirsting for conquest and battle. "He appears to have a gentler and more civilised side, being described in the eulogy as a lover of poetry and music." He was a patron of learning, a celebrated poet and a musician. These attributes are not merely the exaggeration of the court panegyrist. This is borne out by his coins representing the emperor as playing upon a lyre. He had a tender heart that could be easily won over. Support of the poor, the helpless and the afflicted kept him busied. He has been likened to Varuna, Indra, Dhanada, etc. He earned the title of the King of poets *Kaviraja* for his poetical compositions. He was a veritable God on earth. We are further told that he possessed a noble heart beloved of his father and the people at large. He was a devout Brahmanical Hindu but he was tolerant of other religions as has been illustrated by his granting permission to Meghavarna to construct a convent for the pilgrims from Ceylon. V. A. Smith has described him as *Indian Napoleon* but he was brilliant as general and statesman and also possessed many qualities of head and heart better suited to a life of peaceful pursuits and which mark him as a versatile genius. The Buddhist records prove his catholicity in religious views which is illustrated in his appointing Vasubandhu as his minister.

It is doubtless that Samudragupta was a striking personality, almost unique in the history of India and ushered in a new age. His coins show him as a man of great prowess—the prowess of a tiger. "The artistic execution of the gold coins of Samudragupta fully illustrates the wonderful progress of art which forms such a distinctive feature of the Gupta period and justifies its designation as the Classical Age in India."

Immediately after his accession to the throne Samudragupta plunged into war following the principle that "Kingdom-taking is the business of Kings".[1] An ambitious monarch as he was Samudragupta cannot be expected to have rest contented to remain within his own borders. His ambition was to establish an empire controlled from the Capital at Pataliputra and including the entire sub-continent".[2] Thus political unification of India, as was achieved by the Mauryas, must have been consciously or unconsciously influencing Samudragupta's aim.

He was a statesman who clearly saw the impracticability of absorbing the distant southern Indian States in the dominions under his direct rule. He played the part of *Dharmavijayin* in regard to the Southern States and rest contented with a formal recognition of his suzerainty by them while retaining their independence for all intents and purposes. The wisdom of this policy was demonstrated by the failure of any ruler of northern India to have a permanent hold over the south. Samudragupta broke the power of the tribal republics in the north-west which had disastrous consequences during the rule of the later Guptas when the Huns invaded north-western India and these tribal territories could no longer act as buffers for the Gangetic Valley.[2]

Samudragupta was not a ruthless conqueror, on the contrary he tempered his military campaign with moderation and "restored the Kings fallen from their high estate, to wealth and fortune".

He realised the need for religious toleration as a state policy and although he was a Brahmanical Hindu who held *Asvamedha* sacrifice, he did not hesitate to allow Buddhists to build convent in his country nor did he show any bias against the Buddhists being appointed to high posts of the State. Vasubandhu, an important Buddhist of his time, was his Prime Minister.

---

[1] Smith: *Early History of India*, p. 298.

[2] *Ibid.*, p. 138.

Samudragupta was a patron of art and literature. He himself was a poet and a great connoisseur of poetry. The Allahabad inscription mentions his munificence which "removed the eternal discord between good poetry and plenty".[1] His coins illustrated wonderful progress of art during his period.

Samudragupta's variety of coins give us some idea of his physical appearance, his power, wealth, grandeur and an insight into his remarkable personality. His personal appearance so far as we can judge from his coins symbolise both the martial and peaceful pursuits of the King. His tall stature, good physique, fully developed chest indicate the bold, determined yet magnanimous mind he possessed. His reign considerably developed the cultural renaissance initiated by the Kushana and which was to reach its fullness under Chandragupta II his successor. After long five centuries of political disintegration and domination India was again near the "Highest watermark of moral, intellectual and material progress. It was the Golden Age which inspired succeeding generations of Indians".[2] The pinnacle was reached under his successor Chandragupta II, Vikramaditya.

Successors of Samudragupta

RAMAGUPTA

From literary evidence such as Visakadatta's *Devi Chandragupta* and other literary works, as well as inscriptions of later period we come across a romantic episode which is of much interest but of little credibility. From these evidences we know that Ramagupta, son of Samudragupta, had succeeded his father. His queen was Dhruvadevi. In a conflict with the Sakas, Ramagupta was besieged and was placed in an extremely desperate situation. To save his people besieged with him he agreed to make over queen Dhruvadevi to the Saka King as a condition for the lifting of the siege. Ramagupta's brother, Chandragupta II, protested against this dishonourable agreement. He resorted to a stratagem and went in disguise of queen Dhruvadevi and killed the Saka King. This saved both the empire and honour of the Guptas. Chandragupta ultimately got rid of his elder brother Ramagupta by killing him and succeeded to the throne. He also married Dhruvadevi, his elder brother's widow.

This episode is not accepted as historical, for there has been not a single reference to the name Ramagupta in any one of the numerous coins of the Gupta period. Without any positive contemporary evi-

[1] *The Classical Age*, p. 14.

[2] *Ibid.*, p. 16.

dence it is difficult to accept it as true, although there may have been some elements of truth in it.

CHANDRAGUPTA II

Of the many sons of Samudragupta we definitely know of one son born of his chief queen Dattadevi whose name is Chandragupta II. It is held by some scholars that there is a reference in an inscription of Skandagupta that his grandfather Chandragupta was selected by Samudragupta as his successor. But this view is regarded as uncertain as it is based on doubtful interpretation of an expression in Skandagupta's inscription. If we accept this as correct then Chandragupta II was the immediate successor of Samudragupta. It may be noted that Samudragupta himself was chosen by his father Chandragupta I as his successor. On the other hand if we accept the evidence of Vishakadatta and later literary works and inscriptions then Ramagupta was the immediate successor of Samudragupta.

According to V. A. Smith before Samudragupta "passed away he had done his best to secure the peaceful transmission of the Crown by nominating as his successor, from among many sons, the offspring of his queen Dattadevi, whom he rightly deemed worthy to inherit a magnificent empire".[1] It customary for scholars to give greater credence to the succession of Samudragupta by his son Chandragupta II who also took the title *Vikramaditya* (Sun of Power).

Chandragupta II was the valiant son of a valiant father and inherited the military genius, the imperial dignity and the cultured mind of his father Samudragupta. Like his father, he also used his marriage relations as a principle of foreign policy and for strengthening his power. As Dr. Raichaudhuri mentions, matrimonial alliance occupies a prominent place in the Gupta foreign policy". Chandragupta II married Kuveranaga, a Naga Princess and the daughter Prabhavati, from this marriage was given in marriage to Rudrasena II, the Vakataka King of Berar and the adjoining territories. Dr. Smith points out that the Vakataka King occupied such a strategic geographical position in which "he could be of much service or disservice to the northern invader of the dominions of the Saka satraps of Gujarat and Saurashtra. Chandragupta adopted a prudent precaution in giving his daughter to the Vakataka prince and so securing his subordinate alliance". Premature death of Rudrasena made Prabhavati the regent of her two minor sons Divakarsena and Prabhakarsena. This naturally all the more increased the influence of Chandragupta II on the Vakataka Court.

[1] Smith: *Early History of India*, p. 309.

From an inscription of Kakusthavarman, a Kadamba ruler of Kuntala, we learn that he gave his daughters to the Gupta rulers. Bhoja and Kshamendra also refer to the sending of an embassy to Kuntala by Chandragupta II. Thus Chandragupta copied Samudragupta's policy of entering into matrimonial alliance with ruling houses for deriving political advantages.

Chandragupta's chief opponents were the Saka rulers of Gujarat and Kathiawar. A Saka official, Sridharavarman, had set up an independent Kingdom in Malwa. These Saka rulers were known as the Western Satraps. According to Dr. Smith, difference in race, creed and manners led to Chandragupta II's hatred for the Sakas. He desired "to suppress the impure foreign rulers of the West".[1]

Smith also states that Chandragupta Vikramaditya was an orthodox Hindu specially devoted to the court of Vishnu, and although tolerant of Buddhism he must have found peculiar satisfaction in violently uprooting the Saka chieftains who probably cared little for caste rules. Whatever might have been the motive, Chandragupta's one major considerations must have been to liquidate the Western Satraps who were a potential danger to the Gupta empire. Chandragupta's desire to "conquer the whole world" as we know from the Udaygiri cave inscription of Virasena-Saba, was perhaps the special reason for his desire to annex the territories of the Western Satraps. The details of his campaign are lacking. The campaign was a prolonged one and on the evidence of Udaygiri inscription of Virasena-Saba, that of Sanekanika Maharaja, a feudatory chief and the Sanchi inscription of Amrakardava we know that Chandragupta had to stay for a long time at Eastern Malwa after he had conquered it before he succeeded in completely uprooting the Saka ruler Rudrasimha III and annexing his Kingdom in the Saurashtra and Kathiwar regions. This military achievement was of immense consequence to the Gupta empire, for it extended the borders of the empire to the Arabian Sea. According to Dr. Smith "The annexation of Saurashtra and Malwa not only added to the empire provinces of exceptional wealth and fertility, but opened up to the paramount power free access to the ports of the western coasts, and thus placed Chandragupta II indirect touch with the Sea-borne commerce with Europe through Egypt and brought his court and subjects under the influence of the European ideas which travelled with the goods of the Alexandrian merchants". The success of this campaign against the Western Satrap also liquidated the almost three centuries of foreign domination in north-western India.

---

[1] Smith: *Early History of India*, p. 309.

On the evidence of Mathura pillar inscription Dr. Bhandarkar suggests that Mathura and its neighbouring areas were wrested from the Kushanas by Chandragupta II. But this view of Dr. Bhandarkar is regarded as incorrect in as much as it was Samudragupta who had extirpated the Naga Kings and extended his empire in the West upto Eran.

In the Mehrauli iron pillar inscription, i.e., the iron pillar near Kutub Minar at Delhi, of a King named Chandra, it is mentioned that he fought against a confederacy of powers in Vanga. Although there is no conclusive proof that this King Chandra was Chandragupta II, many scholars accept this identity. If we hold this view then we will have to take the inscription to mean that Chandragupta II defeated Vanga (Bengal) as also conquered Vahlika which is identified with Balkh at Bactria. According to Kalidasa Vanga denoted the regions between the Bhagirathi and the Padma. But on the basis of the Allahabad inscription we know that Samudragupta was recognised by Samatata, i.e., a part of Bengal as its suzerain.

It is considered by some scholars as possible that the Kushana rulers of the north-west who had been subdued by Samudragupta had thrown off the yoke of the Gupta empire necessitating their subjugation by Chandragupta. Similar reason may have as well induced Chandragupta to conquer Vanga, i.e., Samatata. We are, however, not sure whether it was the motive of aggressive imperialism that led to Chandragupta's campaign against Samatata.

Under Chandragupta II there was a remarkable change in the currency system. His predecessors issued only gold coins but Chandragupta II issued gold, silver and copper coins. The obverse of the silver coins were imitation of the coins of western satraps although the reverse, the usual *Chaitya,* was replaced by the bird Garuda, symbol of Vishnu. These coins were perhaps meant for circulation in the countries conquered from the western Satraps. There were nine varieties of copper coins with the image of the King on the obverse and Garuda on the reverse. Like Samudragupta's gold coins those of Chandragupta II were of equal fineness and brilliance and throw considerable light on Chandragupta II's imperial grandeur and prowess. There are, however, certain significant variations in the types of coins of Chandragupta II and of Samudragupta. While Samudragupta's coins depicted him as tiger-slayer and also as playing on lyre, Chandragupta's coins represent him as lion-slayer and as holding a flower instead of the lyre with the legend *rupakriti.* While it is supposed by scholars that the lion-slayer type coins denoted his conquest of lion-infested Gujrat, those with flower in hand represented his intellectual and artistic sense. There are other types of coins such as the King standing with his hand on the hilt of his sword and with a dwarf attendant with an umbrella. This is interpreted as his status of universal sovereignty, the dwarf representing his feudatories. Likewise his coins representing him riding on a horse depicted his personal prowess. A coin attributed to Chandragupta by some scholar which shows him standing in front of a deity, probably Vishnu and stretching his arm for receiving Prasad in the form of sweetmeats.

Fa-hien, the celebrated Chinese pilgrim who travelled into India through the Gobi desert and the hilly terrains of Pamir, Khotan and Ghandhara and lived in India for ten years during the reign of Chandragupta II has left a very interesting account of contemporary India. He was a Buddhist pilgrim who came for pilgrimage and to study Buddhist religion. He did not, unfortunately, record anything about the political condition of India of the time. He did not even mention the name of the emperor in whose wide dominions he lived at least for five years. But whatever he recorded about the life of the people is of immense value. On many of his coins he is described as Vikramaditya and in some later records he is represented as the Lord of Ujjaini and Pataliputra. His valiance in killing the Saka Chief earned for him the titles of *Sakari* and *Sahasanka.*

The Chinese traveller Fa-hien came to India by land route as described above, stayed in India for ten years (400-411 A.D.) and left by sea route embarking at the Tamralipti port. He spent three years in speaking and writing Sanskrit and in copying out the Buddhist disciplines. He came to Inda to collect Buddhist texts which were then unknown in China. He had four other Chinese with him but none of them has left any account about India.

During his travel through Central Asian countries he saw numerous Buddhists studying Indian language and Buddhist texts. In Khotan he saw thousands of Buddhists of *Mahayana* school. In *Gomati Vihara* alone he saw more than three thousand monks and as many as fourteen other monasteries in Khotan. In Afghanistan there were both *Mahayana* and *Hinayana* Buddhists. In Kashgarh he saw about a thousand Hinayana Buddhists.

Fa-hien visited Gandhara, Taxila, Peshawar, etc. and saw numerous Buddhist monuments. In Mathura he came across ten thousand Buddhists and twenty monasteries. He also visited places connected with the life of Buddha, such as Lumbini, Vaisali, Bodh Gaya, Gaya, Nalanda and Rajagriha.

Fa-hien referred to the area forming the heart of Chandragupta II's dominions as the Middle Kingdom. He observed that the people in this area were numerous and happy. Such was the general contentment that they were not required to register their household nor attend the Court of any magistrates or obey their rules. Cultivators who cultivated the royal demesne had to pay a part of the gain from it to the government. The Government was most efficient and enlightened. The people had fullest liberty of movement and could live at a place to move to any other of their choice. The mode of punishment was ordinarily very simple and light, the normal punishment being levy of fines. The King governed without any physical punishment or decapitation. In cases of repeated attempts at rebellion the offender's right hand was cut off. Trade and commerce flourished and the people followed various arts and crafts. Fa-hien saw signs of wealth and luxury of the people and great contentment of the people. All this indicated most satisfactory economic condition of the people. Although Chandragupta was a follower of Vishnu the life of the people was largely influenced by Buddhistic ideas of non-violence. Garlic, onion, meat, etc., were not taken by the people. Intoxicant liquor was not permitted to be sold in the open market. The only exceptions were the Chandalas.

Such was the contentment and prosperity of the people in general that theft was unknown, gold left on road could be recovered after days; no body would touch it. Highways was safe for travellers and merchants. Charitable institutions by the road sides as also along out of the way roads were built by the people. These were homes of charity where the travellers and wandering monks found food and shelter. Rooms with beds on matresses, food and clothing were provided for resident monks. Pagodas in honour of Moggolan, Ananda, Sariputta and also in honour of Abhidhamma, Vinaya and the Suttas were built. Fa-hien also mentioned that the rich people instituted free hospitals for poor and helpless patients, orphans, widows and the crippled. Doctors attended them, food and medicine were supplied free, according to needs of the patients.

Fa-hien was struck with wonder to see the city of Pataliputra and the palace of Asoka. He was so much impressed by the beauty of the palace which must have been then more than six hundred years old that he remarked that the halls and pillars must have been constructed by spirits. Near an Asokan *Stupa* Fa-hien saw two monasteries inhabited by *Mahayana* Buddhist monks. Fa-hien found the city of Gaya desolate and Bodhgaya jungle-infested. Kapilavastu and Kushinagara were also deserted cities.

The administration was highly tolerant of all religions and religion was not considered a bar to administrative appointments. Virasena-Saba, minister of Chandragupta, was a follower of Siva while his general Amrakardava was a Buddhist. Fa-hien also mentions that

King's body-guards and attendants were paid regular salaries. In buying and selling *Cowrie* was in use. Dr. Raychaudhuri remarks that Fa-hien seems to have not come across the gold coins of the time which were used in cases of large transactions. Fa-hien evidently refers to small transactions with *Cowries* which he had occasion to make.

Estimate of Chandragupta II Vikramaditya

Dr. V. A. Smith remarks that "Little is known concerning his (Chandragupta II) personal character, but the ascertained facts of his career suffice to prove that he was a strong and vigorous ruler, well qualified to govern and augment an extensive empire".[1]

As Dr. R. D. Banerjee points out, Chandragupta II raised the Kingdom left by his father to the status of an empire. He became the master of northern India and became the unquestionably the paramount sovereign of India. "Like Akbar and Shivaji, he was brave to the point of rashness, which is proved by his adventure in disguise with chosen band of followers in the city or camp of the Scythian King." He was an ambitious ruler and an excellent general and succeeded in Kathiawar in his dominions.

Samudragupta had extended the dominions of the Guptas, Chandragupta extended it further but what he did more was to consolidate the Gupta empire. "The brilliant intellectual revival, manifested in arts, science and literature, which distinguished the Gupta age" was largely the contributions of Chandragupta II. The name *Classical Age* or the *Golden Age* by which the Gupta period is denoted was the result of the contributions of Samudragupta and more of Chandragupta II, to the culture and civilisation of the age. (See Separate Section—Gupta Golden Age.)

Chandragupta, not without reason, loved to use high sounding epithets like *Vikramaditya, Sahasanka, Sakari*, etc., which proclaimed his martial prowess and was fond of depicting himself on his coins in combat with a lion as did the old Persian emperors. His use of the titles *Vikramaditya* and *Sakari* has led scholars to identify him with Vikramaditya of legend.

He was a devout Vaishnava but not a bigot, for his catholicity in religious matters transcended all barriers of personal religion. The Buddhist Amrakardava was his general, Saiva Virasena Saba and Sikharasvamin were his ministers.

---

[1] Smith: *Early History of India*, p. 309.

Identification of Chandragupta II with *Sakari Vikramaditya* means that his court was adorned by *nine gems* including Kalidas, Varahamihira. But all of the luminaries did not live at the same time. If Samudragupta is known more for his wars of conquests, his son Chandragupta is remembered for things other than war, "for his patronage of literature and the arts—Kalidasa, the Sanskrit poet, being a member of his Court—and for the high standard of artistic cultural life".[1] Dr. Mazumdar remarks "Samudragupta, the victor of a hundred fights, is a hero of history. Chandragupta II, who brought to maturity the new era of political greatness and cultural regeneration won a place in the heart of his people".[2]

KUMARAGUPTA I

Chandragupta II was succeeded by his son Kumaragupta I sometimes between 413 and 415 A.D. Bhilsa inscription puts the date of his accession at 415 A.D. and his last date in his silver coins in 455 A.D. Kumaragupta, therefore, had a long reign of 40 years. He was born of Chandragupta's Queen Dhruvadevi.

The Gupta empire had reached its zenith when Kumaragupta ascended the throne. Kumaragupta himself does not seem to have conducted any military campaign. At least, there is no such evidence, but there is no doubt that Kumaragupta maintained his grip over the whole empire and kept it undiminished during his long rule for forty years. Kumaragupta also performed *Asvamedha* sacrifice and assumed the title *Mahendraditya.* He also used numerous variants of this name such as *Mahendrakalpa, Mahendrasimha, Mahendrakumar, Asvamedha, Mahendra,* etc.

A large number of records of the feudatories and Viceroys of Kumaragupta have come to light, which give us a fair idea of the administrative machinery, strength and stability of the government. From these epigraphic records it is learnt that Chiradatta was the viceroy, a governor of Pundravardhana Bhukti corresponding to North Bengal. Prince Ghatotkacha Gupta was the viceroy of Eastern Malwa. Bandhuvarman ruled at Dasapura. He is referred to as a feudatory in the Mandasor inscription. In an inscription of 436 A.D. Kumaragputa is stated to be the ruler of whole earth bounded by Sumeru and Kailash (Himalayas) in the north, the Vindhyas in the south and the two oceans on the east and the west.

In matters of religious toleration, there appears to be no change

---

[1] Romila Thapar : *A History of India*, 1, p. 140.

[2] *Classical Age*, p. 23.

of the traditional Gupta liberalism. This is borne out by the fact that people worshipped diverse gods and goddesses as they chose. We have references to the worship of Vishnu, Siva, Sakti, Jina, Buddha, Surya, Kartikeya, etc. Endowments were made to the Brahmanas for helping them to perform their religious rites.

Like his predecessors Kumaragupta also issued coins of various types such as Asvamedha type, lion-slayer, tiger-slayer, Peacock-rider, Elephant-rider types. For the use of Western India Silver coins were issued. The obverse legend of these coins is *Jayati Diwan Kumarah* and on the reverse is *Sri Asvamedha Mahendra.* The distribution of his coins indicate the vastness of his empire and in Satara district alone more than one thousand coins have been discovered.

The long reign of Kumaragupta was both peaceful and prosperous but towards the end of his reign there came the first signs of a new invasion from the north-west. Besides, the prevailing peace of the empire was distributed by an unidentified people. According to Fleet the invading people belonged to the *Pushyamitra* tribe. But the Bhitari inscription on the basis of which Fleet identifies the invaders as the *Pushyamitras,* is not accepted by other scholars as the inscription is damaged where the name of the invading people is mentioned. According to H. R. Divakar the name should be read as *Yudhyamitrams.* There is, however, reference to a people named *Pushyamitras* in the *Vishnu Purana.* The *Puranas* associate the *Pushyamitras* with the inhabitants of Melaka in the Narbuda region. Reference to warlike activities of Melaka is also found in the inscriptions of the Vakatakas. From the Bhagat Plate of the Vakataka King Prithisena II, Narendrasena was the leader of the Pushyamitras. But it has been pointed out that Narendrasena possibly could not lead such an invasion for he himself was in a difficult situation due to the invasion of Bhavadattavarman. From the Junagarh inscription of Skandagupta we come to know that Skandagupta fought against hostile kings who raised their hoods "like so many serpents". The reference is taken by scholars to the invasion of the Pushyamitras whom Skandagupta as a prince had successfully warded off. Thus the fortunes of the Guptas threatened by enemies were saved.

Dr. R. C. Majumdar remarks that although the reign of Kumaragupta is generally regarded as uneventful and void of interest and importance, yet certain significant details are usually overlooked. From the numerous inscriptions only a reference to a solitary military campaign is found at the final stage of his reign, and there is no doubt that his long reign saw a peaceful and stable government over the undiminished vast empire extending from the western (Arabian) and the eastern (Bay of Bengal) Seas. The fact of the defeat of the Pushyamitras at the hands of the Prince Skandagupta towards end of his reign and the warding off of the Huna invasion soon after his death testify to the continued efficiency of the imperial army over the long forty years of Kumaragupta's rule. The modern historians have been rather unusually niggardly in their praise of Kumaragupta than he actually deserves. It will be unfair not to credit him with maintenance of the vast expanse of the empire in tact for long forty years, and to keep it in peace and prosperity without allowing the imperial administration as well as the army to weaken.

SKANDAGUPTA

Problem of Succession : In the midst of triumph of Prince Skandagupta over the Pushyamitras, Kumaragupta I, the old and aged emperor, breathed his last, even before Skandagupta's return to the capital. The official record describes how Skandagupta "reported his victory over the enemies to his mother who received him with tears". Skandagupta, the hero of the nation, came to the throne in 455 A.D.

There are good grounds to believe that Skandagupta's succession to the throne was not a peaceful one. The question of succession remains a ticklish problem with the scholars. In the Bhitari Seal Purugupta is mentioned as the son and successor of Kumaragupta I. But Smith, Raychaudhuri, Allan, etc., are of the opinion that Skandagupta was the immediate successor of Kumaragupta. Thus we find there were two successors and the question is which of them came first. Dr. Majumdar observes "there was a struggle between him (Skandagupta) and his half-brother Purugupta, son of the Chief Queen of Kumaragupta. Probably Skandagupta's mother was queen of an inferior rank and this gave an advantage to his rival (Purugupta). But Skandagupta triumphed in the end". Allan, Smith and Raychaudhuri are of the opinion that Skandagupta died childless and was succeeded by his half-brother Purugupta. This contention is also supported by Dr. Majumdar. That Skandagupta was the immediate successor, although after a struggle is borne out by Skandagupta's own official record where it is mentioned that the "Goddess of Sovereignty, of her own accord selected him (Skandagupta as her husband, having in succession discarded all other Princes".[1] According to Dr. Majumdar Skandagupta had to fight for his claim with one or more rivals. He observes "It is probable, for example, that taking advantage of Skandagupta's absence in a distant campaign, his step-brother Purugupta ascended the throne immediately after his father's death, but was soon removed when Skandagupta returned from his victorious campaign."

[1] R. C. Majumdar: *Ancient India*, p. 327.

This is, however, a probable view and cannot be regarded as historically unquestionable. There are various other views expressed by different scholars but the consensus is in favour of regarding Skandagupta as the immediate successor of Kumaragupta who was in his return succeeded by Purugupta.

War of succession or not, Skandagupta after his accession to the throne did not find much breathing time, for he had been faced with a sea of troubles. The danger of the Pushyamitra invasion was just averted, but he had to fight with hostile kings some of whom are described as *mlechas* in the contemporary records. In the first half of the fifth century, that is, during the reign of Kumaragupta I, the first signs of a new invasion from the north-west were noticed. A branch of the Huns known as white Huns or Epthalites had occupied Bactria in the fourth century and were threatening to cross the Hindukush which they did when Skandagupta came to the throne. They conquered Gandhara and set up a king there, "who was cruel and vindictive and practised the most barbarous atrocities".[1] He proceeded further towards "the heart of India and became a great menace to the Gupta Empire".[2] Skandagupta had earlier, as the crown prince, saved the empire against the Pushyamitra menace, but the danger was now much graver one. He was now a man of mature years and ripe experience, and proved equal to the task and succeeded in inflicting a crushing defeat on the barbarian. So decisive was the victory that for nearly half a century the Gupta empire was safe from their inroads. "It was a great achievement for which Skandagupta may well be drawn in history as the saviour of India."[3] It will be easy to realise the full significance of this great event when we recall what the Huns had done to the mighty Roman empire and what the branch of the Huns even after their defeat at the hands of Skandagupta had done to Persia. They carried fire and sword, completely overwhelmed Persia and killed their king. After this Great exploit Skandagupta justifiably assumed the title of *Vikramaditya* in imitation of his grandfather Chandragupta II.

In the Balaghat Plates there are references to Vakataka Narendrasena who had established influence over Kosala, Mekala, Malwa. But there is no reference to his actual occupation of these areas. On the contrary we find in the Junagarh inscription that Skandagupta "deliberated days and nights before making up his mind who could

---

[1] H. C. Raychaudhuri: *Political History of Ancient India*, p. 579.

[2] *The Classical Age*, p. 26.

[3] *Idem.*

be trusted with the important task of guarding the lands of Surashtra".[1] This shows that for a time the Vakatakas spread their influence in that region with the help of the local lords which worried Skandagupta. He appointed wardens in Central India and Surashtra—the vulnerable parts of the empire and appointed Parnadatta as one of these wardens in Surashtra. There is no doubt, according to Dr. Raychaudhuri that Surashtra, Gujarat, Malwa, etc. were under Skandagupta's rule during his life time.

The last years of Skandagupta's reign was tranquil, but the military campaign against the Pushyamitras, Huns and perhaps also against the Vakatakas put a heavy strain on the resources of the empire. This is evident from the deterioration of purity of gold coins which were comparatively few and mostly of one type. But this did not stand in the public utility work. The Girnar inscription near Junagarh refers to the repairs of the *Sudarshana Lake* originally constructed by Chandragupta Maurya for supply of water to irrigation canals had burst its dams due to excessive rainfall during Skandagupta's time, but was promptly repaired by Parnadatta, Governor of Surashtra, and his son Chakrapalita, the local magistrate. The same lake had burst its dams once again three hundred years before and the damage was repaired by the Saka Chief Rudradamana.

From the inscription of Parnadatta we come to know that Skandagupta's empire which extended from the Bay of Bengal to the Arabian Sea was strong and united, under the vigorous administration of a benevolent ruler. The Junagarh inscription shows Skandagupta took special care in selecting his Governor and officials. Besides Parnadatta, he appointed Sarvanaga as the district officer of the Gangetic Doab and Bhimvarman as that of Kosam region.

Like his predecessors, Skandagupta also followed the policy of toleration in religious matters. He was himself a worshipper of Vishnu but did not interfere with the religious beliefs of his officers or subjects. Bihar Pillar inscription mentions the construction of a circle of temples dedicated to Skanda and the Divine Mothers such as Chandi, Chamunda, Maheswari, Vaishnavi, Kaumari, etc. There is also a reference to the construction of a temple for Sabita, the Sun God by two Kshatiriya merchants.

On the evidence of *Aryamanjusrimulakalpa* Jayaswal remarks that Skandagupta was "the best—a wise justice-loving King". Historians have regarded Skandagupta one of the greatest if not the greatest of the great Gupta Emperors. He alone had the honour of defeating the Huns, three lakhs of whom attacked India, and saving

---

[1] *The Classical Age*, p. 27.

India from the menace for almost half a century to follow. In 467 A.D. Skandagupta died with the supreme satisfaction of leaving the mighty empire he had inherited from his predecessor.

Skandagupta's Successors

Purugupta : Skandagupta was succeeded by his half-brother Purugupta, son of Kumaragupta I, by his queen Anantadevi. In the official genealogy of the later Gupta emperors Purugupta is shown as the immediate successor of Kumaragupta I and the name of Skandagupta is omitted. This might have been due to accession of Purugupta immediately after Kumaragupta's death before Skandagupta had returned from his successful campaign against the Pushyamitras. But in the struggle for succession Skandagupta emerged victorious and it was after his death that Purugupta got the opportunity to ascend the throne. He must have been an old man then and ruled for six years only from 467 to 473 A.D.

Narasimhagupta Baladitya : From both epigraphic and numismatic evidence names of several kings are known whose exact position in relation to the Gupta family has not been known with certainty. According to Raychaudhuri Purugupta was succeeded by his son, Narasimhagupta Baladitya, in 473 A.D. He is identified with Baladityagupta who has been mentioned by Hiuen-Tsang as the King who imprisoned the Hun Chief Mihiragula or Mihirakula. Dr. Raychaudhuri, however, is of opinion that the conqueror of Mihirakula was a different Gupta Ruler.

KUMARAGUPTA II

In 474 A.D. we come across the name of Kumaragupta II, son of Narasimhagupta Baladitya. According to R. C. Majumdar he "might have been a son of Skandagupta". We also come across the names of several Gupta kings in the coins and inscription who ruled about the same time. The presumption is that they were "rival factions contending for the throne during the period immediately after Skandagupta's death. But we have no definite knowledge of the events of the period".[1]

There has been a considerable divergence of opinion among the historians about the line of the succession of the Gupta kings. In this book the list of succession given by Dr. H. C. Raychaudhuri has been followed.

Kumaragupta's reign appears to have terminated in 476-477 A.D. The reign of Skandagupta's successor—Purugupta, Narasimhagupta Baladitya and Kumaragupta II covers only ten years from A.D. 467 to A.D. 477.

---

[1] *Classical Age*, p. 29.

BUDHAGUPTA

Budhagupta, son of Purugupta and his chief queen Chandradevi, ascended the throne in 477 A.D. and ruled for nearly twenty years. It is suggested that there were internal troubles before he came to the throne. But he appears to have succeeded in establishing himself firmly on the throne and restoring peace and order all over the empire. A large number of inscription have been discovered which refers to Budhagupta. In one inscription Budhagupta is mentioned as *Paramadaivata-Paramabhattaraka-Maharajadhiraja-Sri Prithvipati*. In his silver coins, Budhagupta describes himself as *Avanipati* meaning lord of the world. From these titles it may be reasonably presumed that he ruled over a vast empire. From the records of Budhagupta's Governors of Malwa and Bengal it is learnt that under Budhagupta the solidarity of the empire was undisturbed at least to a very large extent of its expanse. But signs of decline of the imperial authority in the outlying provinces began to manifest themselves in his time portending the break-up of the empire at no distant future.

General Bhataraka of the Maitraka family, governor of Surashtra with his capital at Valabhi made the governorship hereditary in his family. Bhataraka and his son Dharasena who succeed him assumed the title *Senapati*, i.e., Governor. But the next Governor, a younger son of Bhataraka, named Drona Simha, assumed the royal title of *Maharaja* and although he paid nominal homage to the paramount ruler, i.e., the Gupta emperor, he was well on the way to complete sovereignty. Likewise the Governors of north Bengal at earlier times called themselves *Uparika*, now assumed the title of *Uparika Maharaja*, the Governors of Malwa now took the title of *Maharaja*. All this doubtlessly indicate that although the Gupta empire might have theoretically remained without substantial diminution its power and prestige were on the decline. In Bundelkhand region *Maharaja* Hastin issued land grants making a general reference to the Gupta sovereignty, but without mentioning the name of Budhagupta, which shows the near independent status of the family. This family had another branch ruling over an adjacent Kingdom with Uchchakalpa as its capital. King Jayanatha of this family ceased to owe any allegiance to the Gupta sovereignty towards end of the reign of Budhagupta.

In he north and east of Bundelkhand, a dynasty called Panduvamsa was rising into prominence and by the end of the fifth century, i.e., at Budhagupta's reign King Udayana of this family threw off the allegiance to the Gupta sovereignty. Another branch of this family is mentioned in a copper plate grant at Rewa State made itself if not wholly, at least partially independent of Guptas.

From two copper-plates found at Allahabad and Rewa State we

come across *Maharaja Lakshmana* who ruled during the reign of Budhagupta with his capital at Jayapura, not yet identified assumed *de facto* independence. Similar was case with *Maharaja* Subandhu who issued land grant from the ancient town of Mahishmati on the river Narmada without any reference to Budhagupta.

In this way outlying provinces of the empire were gradually moving towards complete independence although outwardly suffered no diminution, and its authority was still acknowledged as far as the Bay of Bengal in the east and the Arabian sea in the west, and the Narmada in the South.

Circumstances, both internal and external, caused the decline that set in. The struggle for the throne after the death of Kumaragupta II and Skandagupta had sapped the vitality of the empire. From outside, the Vakataka King Narendrasena appears to have established suzerainty over Kosala-Mekala-Malava which raises the presumption that the Gupta empire was invaded from the South. The Huns whose invasion had been warded off by Skandagupta, reappeared probably during Budhagupta's reign although we are not certain about the date. Thus the mighty edifice of the Gupta empire began to show fissures which gradually developed into wide chasms and the imposing imperial fabric fell into parts not in distant time.

Our information about the part played by Budhagupta is rather scanty. Under him the outward structure of the Gupta empire remained more or less in tact, and he was the last Gupta emperor to enjoy sovereignty over a vast expanse of territories. Yet, the empire was passing through a very critical period and the empire was soon to fall apart after his death.

TATHAGATAGUPTA : BALADITYA

Death of Budhagupta was a signal for internal dissensions which led to the partition of the empire. The renewed Hun invasion made matters worse. The sequence of events and the line, of succession during this period are difficult to pursue. From different sources different names have been found and historians have drawn different lines of succession.

According to Beal's *Life of Hiuen T-Sang* Budhagupta was succeeded by Tathagatagupta and after him Baladityagupta. Dr. H. C. Raychaudhuri accepts this line of succession. Dr. R. C. Majumdar, basing his opinion on certain official documents places Narasimhagupta, brother of Budhagupta, as the latter's successor ; and Narasimhagupta was succeeded by his son. But there are other names such as Vinayagupta and Bhanugupta. Vinayagupta's solitary record has been found in Tipperah district in Bengal. It is suggested by Dr. Majumdar that is dominion was probably confined to Bengal. Bhanugupta's inscrip-on has been found at Eran (modern Saugar district in Central India) 'hich refers to a great battle fought by him in accompaniment of his assal Goparaja, in which the latter lost his life. Dr. Majumdar hinks that reference to two rulers, Vainyagupta and Bhanugupta, as imultaneously ruling leads to the conclusion that in the western part of the empire Bhanugupta ruled, while the eastern part was under Vainyagupta.

The famous battle fought by Bhanugupta along with the vassal Goparaja, according to Dr. Majumdar, is a reference to a battle with Toramana, the Hun Chief. But all this is more or less conjectural. t is not known for certain if Bhanugupta could recover Eran region completely from the hands of the Huns, who had taken possession of t. In spite of the high praise bestowed on him for his exploit in lefeating Toramana, son of Mihiragula or Mihirakula, fact remains that forces of disintegration were at work and convulsed the empire which was hastening its downfall.

THE HUNS

The scourge of the Gupta empire was the barbarians called the Huns. We would rather turn our attention to the Huns, here, who administered a mortal blow to the Gupta Empire.

The Huns are known to have been living on the Chinese border. They came in conflict with the Yue-chi, a neighbouring nomadic tribe, which led to a displacement of races, and the Scythians and Kushanas pushed into India about the first century of the Christian era. Later the Huns also began migrating towards the west and divided themselves into two branches, one moved towards the Volga and the other to Oxus. The branch that moved towards the Volga played havoc with the Roman empire. The branch that moved towards the Oxus valley became very powerful during the fifth century A.D. They are called Ephthalites after the name of the ruler's family. The Greeks called them White Huns. In 484 A.D. the Huns became extremely powerful under their chief Akhschounwar and defeated and killed Firuz, the Sassanian ruler of Persia and occupied Persia. The Huns built up a vast empire with their main capital at Balkh.

Towards India they occupied Gandhara after crossing the Hindu-kush but their further progress into India was checked by Skandagupta about A.D. 464. But either at the end of the fifth or beginning of the sixth century A.D. the Hun Chief Toramana conquered a large part of western India and penetrated as far as Eran, i.e., Saugar district of Madhya Pradesh. The Hun conquest must have taken place not long after Budhagupta's time, if not towards the end of his reign.

We have no definite evidence about the Huns, yet we come acro two names Toramana and Mihirkula who are generally taken as Hu Chiefs. Toramana coins testify to his foreign origin and to his ru over parts of U.P., Rajputana, Punjab and Kashmir. Dr. Majumda suggests that Toramana was probably connected with the Hun rulin family of Gandhara. According to a Jaina work *Kuvalayamal* Toramana got converted into Jainism and lived on the bank of th river Chandrabhaga, i.e., Chenab.

Toramana was succeeded by Mihirgula or Mihirkula. Accordin to Hiuen T-Sang Mihirkula's capital was Sakala, i.e., Sialkot and h ruled over India. *Rajatarangini* refers to the Mihirkula as a ver powerful ruler of Kashmir and Gandhara, who conquered Souther India and Ceylon. Rajatarangini's reference to Mihirkula's inhuma cruelty agrees to the narrative of Hiuen T-Sang but the period assign- ed to his rule in Rajatarangini is too remote to possibly be accepte as a historically reliable source. From the Chinese ambassador Sung- Yun to the Court of Hun King at Gandhara, i.e., Mihirkula, the Hun King, according to this Chinese source, was cruel and vindictive and perpetuated most barbarous activities. He worshipped Demon and did not believe in the law of Buddha. He had 700 war elephants and was constantly with war. Sometime later a Greek named Cosmas in his *Christian Topography* wrote that "Higher up in India, that is fur- ther to the north, are the White Huns. The one called Gollas (Mihir- gula) when jointly to a war takes with him no fewer than two thousand elephants and a great force of cavalry. He is the lord of India, and oppressing the people, forces them to pay tribute". He calls the river Indus as river Phison and remarks that this river separates all the countries of India from the Country of the Huns. Dr. Majumdar thinks that Sung-Yun, the Chinese ambassador, visited the court of Mihirkula. In the interval between the time of Sung-Yun and Cosmas the Hun suzerainty must have been extended over Indian kings for Comas calls him "Lord of India". Hiuen T-Sang also remarks that Mihirguala subdued whole of India. It is presumed that Mihirkula was a powerful ruler who, according to an inscription dated A.D. 530 extended his sovereignty upto Gwalior. It appears from all accounts that Mihirkula was a powerful king who overran a large part of northern India. But Hun ruler Mihirkula was not destined to enjoy his sovereignty for long. He was checked and defeated by Yasho- dharman.

In the Mandasor inscription Yashodharman claims that respect was paid to him even by the powerful king Mihirkula "whose head had never (previously) been brought to the humility of obeisance to any other save (the God) Sthanu (Siva) and embraced by whose arms the mountain of Snow (the Himalayas) falsely pride itself on being styled as inaccessible fortress". Reference to the mountain of snow indicates that he ruled over Kashmir and the adjoining regions. He must have been advancing into the interior of India when he was defeated by Yashodharman, a local Chief of Malwa. But this defeat did not destroy the power of Mihirkula and soon after Yashodharman's death he reappeared in the scene.

This time he had to face Narasimhagupta Baladitya. But long account of praise of Baladitya who defeated Mihirkula, Dr. R. C. Majumdar considers, it an overstatement. The only provisional conclusion that may be arrived at is that Baladitya defeated Mihirkula which crushed the Hun supremacy in India. The Huns no doubt existed in small principalities even after this defeat but they no longer appear to have been any disturbing element in the Indian history.

In the coins of the late Guptas there is reference to the defeat inflicted upon the Huns by the Maukhari King Ishanvarman. Dr. Majumdar thinks that the Maukhari King fought as a feudatory of the Gupta emperor Baladitya in the latter's campaign against Mihirkula. It is true that the Maukharis issued coins in imitation of the Hun Kings and ruled over the territories which formerly were under the Huns. But the Maukharis did not have any war against the Huns independently.

The collapse of the Hun political power was not simply caused by the defeat and death of Toramana and his son Mihirkula but it was mainly due to the crushing blow it received from the confined forces of the Turks and the Persians in the Oxus region which was the central authority of the Huns. The groups of Huns that continued to live in India were gradually absorbed in the Indian Society.

Mihirkula was a Siva-worshipper as is indicated by his coins. In the Gwalior inscription there is mention of Mihirkula's causing Sun Temple to be built. He might as well have been a worshipper of the Sun. But there are evidences of his persecution of the Buddhists.

The short rule of the Huns in India was not without significance. While politically the Hun invasions were largely responsible for the downfall of the Gupta empire, their stay in India after they had lost their political power, introduced a new racial element in the Indian society. They married Indian wives and gradually got absorbed in the Hindu Society. The origin of the Rajputs can be traced from the Huns. Dr. Smith mentions that of the thirty-six Rajput clans one was called by the name *Hun*. Havell also points out that the numerous ramifications of the Rajput clans of the present day are the result of the assimilation of foreign elements by the Indo-Aryan society.

Culturally the Huns were a very backward people, cruel and ruthless. Their invasions of India proved to be destructive of works of art, monasteries, temples and monuments. They destroyed many specimens of Gupta art, burnt valuable records, proved themselves to be a curse to the cultural life of the time. As Havell remarks, "The strong infusion of Hun blood lowered the high ethical standards of Indian Tradition and favoured the growth of many of the vulgar superstitions which were never countenanced by the Philosophers and spiritual teachers of Aryavarta." The Huns were also responsible for importing despotism in the political life of India. According to Havell "Despotism was of Tartar or Mongolian creation; and most probably the Indians borrowed it from the Mongoloid Huns".

YASHODHARMAN

The Hun invasions under Toramana and Mihirkula must have contributed in large measure to the disintegration of the Gupta empire decline of which had started under Budhagupta. Centrifugal forces had already been in action under him and the feudal chiefs and viceroys, high State official and royal princes gradually began to assume power and authority, ultimately helping them to become fully independent. From the inscriptions of the time it is known that it was a period of unrest and disruption. The Huns from the north-west and the Vakatakas from the Deccan invaded the Gupta empire.

Malwa had been experiencing troubles due to the invasions of the Huns and the Vakatakas. The hold of the Guptas over that region, naturally became weak. A local chief Yashodharman took full advantage of this weakness and assumed independent authority and became sufficiently powerful to stem the tide of the Hun invasion by defeating the Hun chief Mihirkula and to defy Gupta suzerainty.

Very little is known of the early life and career of Yashodharman. According to some scholars Yashodharman had some connection with family of the feudatory chiefs who were ruling in Malwa or parts of it. But till his rise into prominence we practically know nothing about him. About his military achievement, however, we have records inscribed in duplicate on two stone pillars at Mandasor. From this *Prasasti* we know that Yashodharman's suzerainty was acknowledged over the vast area bounded by the Himalayas in the north, Mahendragiri in the Ganjam district in the South, the Brahmaputra in the east and the Arabian Sea in the west. He is credited with conquering territories which were conquered neither by the Guptas, nor by the Huns. The Hun chief had to pay respect to his feet. All this naturally raises the presumption that Yashodharman was the undisputed master of Northern India but Dr. Majumdar remarks that "we should hardly be justified in regarding Yashodharman as one sole undisputed monarch of Northern India". But he concedes some truth in the assertion made by the eulogist in the Mandasor inscription and says that "we can well believe that he defeated Mihirkula" and that he rose into distinction and earned popularity by defeating the Hun chief Mihirkula and stemming the tide of the Hun inroads into the interior of India. This must have added to his power and prestige which enabled him to expand his dominions at the cost of the Gupta empire. It has not been possible from the available evidence to determine the limits of his dominions. In any case he could not finally annihilate the Gupta empire nor could he destroy the power of Mihirkula. It was Baladitya, the Gupta monarch, who finally crushed the power of Mihirkula. "Yashodharman", remarks Dr. Majumdar, "rose and fell like a meteor between A.D. 530 and 540, and his empire perished with him".

Other Feudatories

The assumption of independence by Yashodharman was a signal for other feudatories of the Guptas to assume independent status. Of these, the Maukharis and the latter Guptas were specially important. They played an important part in Indian history later on. The Maukhari's who ruled as feudatories of the Guptas in Bihar and U.P. gradually rose into power and strength, and ultimately founded an independent kingdom. The latter Guptas who were distinct from the imperial Guptas but related with them and were at first feudatories of the Guptas but like the Maukharis ultimately became independent in Malwa and Magadha.

Likewise Vanga, i.e., South and East Bengal shook off the suzerainty of the Guptas, the gradual process as in the cases of other feudatories. Vinayagupta, a feudatory of the Guptas in East Bengal, assumed the title of *Maharaja* and later made himself independent. That the Vanga assumed independence is testified by the assumption of the title *Maharajadhiraja* by the ruler of Vanga and striking of gold coins as did the Gupta emperors.

Gauda, i.e., West Bengal also assumed prominence at that time and a Maukhari Chief claims as having defeated them. The latter Guptas are also credited with defeating the people who lived on the sea shore. According to Dr. Majumdar, the reference is to the people of West Bengal.

We may conclude that the example of Yasodharman was imitated by other feudatories and there was legend, "Yasodharman himself was probably the first victim to perish in the conflagration that his own action had brought about".[1]

[1] *The Classical Age*, p. 41.

The Gupta Administration

There is a sharp difference of opinion as to whether the Gupta administrative system was originated by the Gupta rulers themselves or was a continuation of the traditional system of administration that descended down the years from the time of the Mauryas. According to Dr. R. D. Banerjee the inscriptions of the Gupta emperors do not show any trace of the retention of the old Maurya official terms. But Dr. R. N. Sabtore, the Gupta administration, was not genuinely original; it was founded on the historical traditions of the past although improved and adapted to suit contemporary conditions. The Gupta administration assumed a very imposing form due to the vastness of its structure comprising the (i) King, (ii) Council of Ministers, (iii) Great Assembly, (iv) Feudatories, (v) State departments, (vi) Bureaucracy from Centre down to villages.[1]

Dr. R. C. Majumdar also observes that "The Imperial Guptas continued the traditional machinery of bureaucratic administration with nomenclature mostly borrowed from earlier times".[2]

During the Gupta period monarchy was the prevailing form of government but there were a few republics still in existence in the Punjab and Rajasthana such as, the Madras or Madrakas in the Central Punjab, Kunindas in the Kangra Valley, Yaudheyas in South-eastern Punjab, the Arjunayanas in Agra-Jaipur, the Malavas in Central Rajasthan. In Central India there were the Sanakanikas, Prarjunas, Kakas and the Abhiras. But by the beginning of the fifth century A.D. these republics disappeared.

Much information about the Gupta administration has been found in the account of the Chinese pilgrim Fa-hien, contemporary inscriptions and the royal rescripts. Administration was divided into two parts: the Central Government and the Provincial Government.

Central Government: King

The Gupta emperor was at the top of the administration of the entire empire. From the Allahabad inscription we find that the emperor is described as *Achintya Purusha*, that is incomprehensive Being, *Dhanada-Varunendrantaka -sama*, i.e., equal to Kuvera, Varuna, Indra, Yama, also as *Loka-dhama-deva*, i.e., God on earth etc. Thus the king was regarded as a divinity. But the Gupta kings did not claim any infallibility; on the contrary, they had to respect the elders, study the art of government and cultivate righteousness. Haughty,

---

[1] R. N. Sabtore: *Life in the Gupta Age*, p. 318.

[2] *The Classical Age*, p. 251.

tyrannical or irreligious ruler was held in contempt. An ideal king was to be both physically and mentally fit for doing the duties of administration.

The Yuvaraja or the Crown Prince would help the king in his administrative work and had his separate civil and military establishment and could even issue orders to the Provincial governments with the consent of the king. Where the king was old, the Crown Prince carried the major burden of administration.

The Gupta emperors assumed high-sounding titles such as *Maharajadhiraja*, *Prithvipala*, *Paramabhattaraka*, *Paramesvara*, etc. The emperor had diverse powers which may be enumerated as *political*, *administrative*, *military* and *judicial*. Politically all powers emanated from the king. He was the highest executive and in that capacity appointed all governors and important civil and military officers. All of these appointees had to work under the direct orders and supervision of the king. He was sometimes his own commander-in-chief and all lands within the empire were his property. Unclaimed property would escheat to the king. He was also the highest judge. They also nominated their successors in some cases. For instance, Samudragupta was nominated as his successor by Chandragupta I and likewise Kumaragupta I nominated Skandagupta as his successor. Such nominations were, however, not the rule. Succession to the throne was hereditary.

Limitations to the Powers of the King

The Gupta King was the repository of all powers of the State no doubt, but this did not mean that he was a tyrannical despot. He was theoretically the unquestioned authority over all departments of the government but in practice his powers were limited by the (i) traditional ideal of Kingship which meant honouring the age-old customs and solicitousness for the well-being of the people. (ii) The Council of Ministers, that is, *Mantriparishad*, the high ministers, etc. also put a check in the powers of the king. Although it was perfectly within the rights of the king to either accept or reject the decision of the Mantriparishad or of the high ministers, yet it will be reasonable to conclude that the king would not normally go against the decision of the Mantriparishad or the high ministers. This is evident from the existence of an officer named *Kanchuki* or Chamberlain who was a liaison between the King and the Mantriparishad. There was a special class of officers called *Amatyas* who had to keep the king in touch with the decisions of the Council of Ministers.

The Council of Ministers, i.e., the Mantriparishad at times acted as the Council of Regency. There was possibly a Great Assembly[1]

[1] R. N. Sabtore: *Life in the Gupta Age*, pp. 318-319.

which was consulted by the king on special occasions. Such an assembly was summoned by Chandragupta I when he declared Samudragupta as his successor. In the Great Assembly members of the royal family, the councillors and the counsellors, i.e., the Mantrins were summoned.

State Officials

Among other high officials at the centre we have references to *Mahabaladhikrita* (Commander-in-Chief), *Mahadandanayaka* (General), *Mahapratihara* (Chief door-keeper), *Sandhvigrahika* (Minister of Peace and war or foreign minister), *Mahasvapati* (Chief Cavalry Officer), *Mahapilupati* (Chief Officer-in-Charge of elephants), etc. Kalidasa refers to three ministers, namely, the chief Minister, Minister of Finance, Minister of Law and Justice. According to Kalidasa the ministers were expected to be experts in their respective duties.

The Gupta emperors employed a vast number of officers for the efficient administration of the empire. They continued the traditional machinery of bureaucratic administration with nomenclature mostly borrowed from the Maurya times.

Apart from the high officials referred to above the Gupta emperors employed a large number of officers to carry on the administration of the country with efficiency. The link between the Central and Provincial government was maintained through officials called *Kumaramatyas* and ayuktas. We have come across officers called *amatyas* during the Maurya period. The name *Kumaramatyas* who belonged to the class of high imperial officers and to personal staff of the emperors—the Crown Prince and other—must have been the creation of the Gupta emperors. The origin of the *Ayuktas* may be traced to *Yutas* of Asokan inscription. *Ayuktas* were some times entrusted with the task "restoring the wealth of the kings conquered by the emperor and sometimes placed in charge of districts or metropolitan towns".[1] Among other civil officers the more important were the *Rajapurusha, Rajanyaka, Kanchuki, Rajamatya Mahasamanta.*

The revenue department of the Gupta administration was not separated from the Police administration. The important officials of these departments were the *Upasika, Chauradharanika, Dasaparadhika, Dandika, Dandapashika, Kothapala, Angaraksha,* etc.

Mahakshapatalika was probably the Great Keeper of Records. High officials like *Kumaramatya, Upasika, Dandapashika,* etc., each

[1] *The Classical Age,* p. 350.

had his separate *Adhikarana.* If we take the term to mean "a court" as Dr. Sabtore has done, then it is probable that these officers also performed judicial duties. Kalidasa refers to *Dharmasthana, Dharmadhikaras* which most probably were judicial courts.

Punishment during the Gupta rule was very lenient. There was no system of capital punishment. Criminals were fined in proportion to the nature of the crime committed. Even in cases of repeated attempts at wicked rebellion only the right hand of the offender was cut off. In cases of theft the thieves when caught were handed over to the guards called *Rakshinas.*

It may be pointed out here that the testimony of Fa-hien to the effect that the Gupta emperor ruled "without decapitation" is not borne out by literary evidence. Vishakadatta in *Mudrarakshasa* describes how Charudatta was condemned to death for murdering Vasanatasena and led in a procession to the *Vadhyasthana,* i.e., place of execution. In the same work there is also description of how Arthapala was condemned to death for stealing by a very cruel method of crushing under the feet of an elephant. Scoring out of eyes, trial by ordeal of fire, etc., were also mentioned in the literature of the time.

Administrative Divisions

From epigraphic records of the Gupta period we come to know of the administrative divisions of the Empire from the apex to the base. The empire was divided into provinces called *Bhuktis, Pradeshas* and *Bhogas.* We have references to Ainikina Pradesha, Nagarabhukti, Tirabhukti, Pundravardhanabhukti, Uttaramandalabhukti.

Provinces were divided into *Vishayas* which were again subdivided into *Vithi* under which there were unions of villages called *Pethaka* and *Santaka.* Smaller divisions of a village were called *Agrahara* and *Patha.*

Provincial Administration

Provinces called *Bhuktis, Pradeshas* and *Bhogas* had been placed under officers variously known as *Uparikas, Goptas, Bhogikas, Bhogapati,* etc. In some cases Princes or *Rajaputras* were also appointed as governors with such title as *maharajaputra devabhattaraka,* a prototype of *Kumara* viceroys of Asoka's time.

Province which was divided into districts called Vishayas were ruled over by officers called *Kumaramatyas, Vishayapatis* or *Ayuktas.* The special characteristic of the Gupta administration was the principle of decentralisation. The district officers, as we know from the inscriptions, were nominated by the provincial governors, although in exceptional cases such appointments might be made by the emperor himself.

There are references to a host of provincial officers who had the provincial governor in carrying on the administration efficiently. These officers were heads of different branches of military and civil administration of the Province. At the head of the Provincial army was the *Baladhikaranika*, the officer-in-charge of the Police administration was *Dandapashika*. Likewise Audrangika was the tax-collector, *Vinaya-sthitisthapaka* was the officer-in-charge of law and order. *Pustapala* (record keeper), Tadayukta (Treasury Officer) were other important provincial officers.

The District Officer called *Vishayapati* was assisted in his administrative work by *Saulkikas* (Tax-Collector), *Gaulmika* (Officer-in-charge of forts and forests), *Dhruvadhikaranikas* (Land Revenue Officers), *Mahattaras* (Village elders), *Gramikas* (Village Headmen), *Bhandagaradhikrita* (Treasurer), *Ralavataka* (Accountant), etc. The district archive was called *Akshapatala* which was under an officer called *Mahakshapatalika*. There are also references to *Lekhakas* (writers), *Karanika* (clerks), etc.

A number of inscriptions from North Bengal refers to the association of popular element in the provincial, district and village administration as well as in the municipal administration in towns. The business of sale of the government land was carried out by the prince-viceroy, the district officer in cooperation with the Municipal Boards, District office, and at other times by the *astakuladhi Karana* with the village headman, house-holders, etc. What was actually the *astakuladhikara* meant is not clear but it is said to have been headed by the village elders.

In cities and towns the Municipal Board consisted primarily of four members : the President of the Guild, the chief merchant, chief artisan and the chief scribe. This special aspect of association of popular element with local administration was one of the boldest and unique experiments of the Guptas. The seals recovered at Vaisali probably indicate the functioning of District and Municipal Boards functioning in North Bihar under the Guptas. The evidences of North Bengal inscriptions and of the Vaisali Seals raise presumption that similar arrangements existed also in other provinces.

The Gupta Emperors realised the need of showing generosity to certain conquered States both monarchical and republic. This is due to their political far-sightedness that distant conquests were not made integral part of the dominions under their direct rule. These states were allowed to retain their independence under the Gupta imperial suzerainty. We have seen how Samudragupta left a number of conquered States in a position of subordinate independence. In later times similar instances were not wanting. The *Parivrajaka-Maharajas* ruling in the region now called Bundelkhand issued landgrants recognising the suzerainty of the Gupta Emperors. It may, however, be mentioned that the status of feudatories varied and the quantum of their independence differed according to their relative strength in comparison with the imperial authority.

Details of judicial administration during the Gupta period are lacking except in so far as there are references in the account of Fa-hien. We have already seen that the traditional powers of the emperor included highest judicial function. This is also borne out by Katyayana. We have also noted the high officials of different grades had some judicial function to perform in their Adhikarana.

The sources of revenue of the Guptas have been recorded in different inscriptions of the time. An important source of revenue was landtax (*Udranga*). According to Fleet *Uparika* was a tax levied on cultivators who had no proprietory right on land. Fines realised from the offenders, salt tax, tax on sale and purchase, tax on the produce of the mines. Some villages were granted exemption from payment of taxes and forced labour. From this it may be deduced that forced labour was resorted to at that time.

From what we have known about the administration of the Gupta empire we may unhesitatingly conclude that the Gupta administration was well organised both at the Centre and the Provinces. The Central administration was linked up with the village administration through a hierarchy of officials. One special characteristic of the Gupta administration was the decentralisation of the government. The administration of justice was a happy blend of law and humanity.

The Gupta kings were followers of Vishnu and his consort Lakshmi. But there are references to their worshipping gods like, Siva, Devi (Durga) and Kartikeya. There was no sectarianism among the Gupta rulers. Surya cult appears to have become popular during the Gupta period and the Gupta rulers patronised the Surya cult as is evident from the Indore copper plate of Skandagupta. According to Dr. Dikshitar the Gupta emperors were followers of orthodox Hinduism and their religious beliefs cannot be described by sectarian definition as Vaishnavism, Saivism, etc. The Gupta rulers were tolerant of other religions such as Buddhism, Jainism, etc. and even made endowments to the Buddhists. Chandragupta II endowed a Buddhist *Vihara* at Sanchi for the maintenance of the Buddhist Bhikshus.

The Gupta Culture

More than two centuries of Gupta supremacy may be easily regarded as the most glorious epoch in Indian history. The period saw a wonderful outburst of intellectual activity in art, science and literature which has been variously called Gupta Golden Age, Classical Age as well as the Periclean Age of Indian history. It was Barnett who remarked that "The Gupta period is in the annals of classical India almost what the Periclean Age is in the history of Greece". Dr. V. A. Smith compares Gupta cultural achievements with those of the Elizabethan period of English history.

"Politically, the Gupta age was one of integration in the history of India. After more than three centuries of political disintegration and foreign domination northern India rallied herself to political unity under the far-sighted, a man of culture and a patron of arts and letters, he (Samudragupta) became the symbol and architect of a mighty creative urge among the people which, while drawing vitality from tradition and race memory, took on a new shape and power",[1] which found expression in succeeding generations in an intellectual and symbols of tremendous national upsurge. Life was never happier, our culture never more creative than during the Golden Prime of India".[2]

In a stagnant civilisation intellectual horizon seldom gets a chance of expansion and creative urge ceases to exist. It is through interaction of diverse cultures that newer and more virile culture emerges. The series of foreign invasions and foreign domination for about three centuries resulted in a comingly cultures which assumed a new shape and power. This new vitality was to be witnessed in the outburst of intellectual activity during the Gupta age.

Conquests of Samudragupta and Chandragupta II and the consolidation of the empire brought about that imperial peace which made possible the progress of culture and civilisation. The new era of political greatness reached maturity under Chandragupta II and the cultural regeneration that followed won the hearts of the people.

Added to these was the liberal patronage extended to scholars and litterateurs by the Gupta emperors. Coins of Samudragupta contain illustration of his love of fine arts music, while the couch type coins of Chandragupta II suggested his artistic and intellectual temperament.

The Gupta period witnessed political unity and prosperity which combined with the great patronage extended to Sanskrit literature

---

[1] *Classical Age*, pp. xi-xii.

[2] *Ibid.*, p. xv.

and learning resulted in the flourishing of every branch of knowledge. In fact, this period produced the best authors in almost all branches of literature as well as in sciences like Astronomy and Mathematics. This is borne out by the fact that dramatists and poets like Kalidasa, Bhavabhuti, Bharabi and Magha, prose writers like Dandin, Subandhu and Bana, grammarians like Chandra, Vamana and Bhartrihari, philosophers like Gandapada, Kumarilbhatta and Prabhakara, rhetorician like Bhamaha, lexicographer like Amara, astronomers like Aryabhatta, Varahamihira and Brahmagupta flourished during this period.

Dr. V. A. Smith who compares the Gupta period with the Elizabethan age of the English history aptly remarks that as the brilliance of Shakespeare alone outshone all the lesser authors of the time in England so did Kalidasa outshone all other lesser lights of contemporary India. Again even if Shakespeare were not born the Elizabethan age would have gone down in history as a gloden age of English literature, similarly even if there were no works of Kalidasa, the Gupta age would still be regarded as a golden age of literature. Such had been the variety and volume of literary and scientific work done by scholar in the Gupta age.

At one time it was held by some scholars including Maxmuller that the Gupta period saw a revival of Sanskrit language and literature. This view has been now discarded as incorrect. For the Sanskrit language and literature had never been altogether eclipsed in the ages preceding that of the Guptas. Its influence continued to exist without break despite use of Prakit during the Maurya period. During the Kushana period Asvaghosa wrote in Sanskrit. Bhasa in his *Pratima Nataka* used Sanskrit. Thus it is evident that Sanskrit continued to be used without break during the periods preceding the Gupta age. The Allahabad inscription and the Mandasor inscription show a highly developed poetic style which could not have been attained except through a continuous process of progress. Hence to say that the Gupta age witnessed a revival of Sanskrit is not factually correct.

During the Gupta period full development of the Puranas and the final phase of the Smriti literature were reached. Probably, the Epics, the Ramayana and the Muhabharata, also took their present shape during the Gupta period. The Puranas, eighteen in number, were written long before the Gupta Age, originally seems to have meant "old narrative". Some of the eighteen Puranas, particularly the *Vayu Purana*, had been written down in its existing form during the Gupta period. The *Puranas*, like the Epics, were originally composed by bards. Later on these fell into the hands of the Brahmanical priests who added a good deal of new matters to them and took more or less a sectarian character. The importance of the *Puranas* was great in the development of Hinduism and cannot be over-estimated for they give us an insight into the Hindu mythology, idol worship, Hindu theism, Pantheism, Love of God, Hindu Philosophy, Superstitions, Ethics, etc. According to Pargitar the *Puranas* were originally composed in literary Prakrit but were re-written in Sanskrit later on.

Dr. Hazra has shown that different sections of the *Puranas* dealing with orthodox rites and customs were added to some of the different *Puranas* at different stages of the Gupta period.

Some of the Dharmasastras which definitely belonged to the Gupta Period were *Smritis* of Katayana, Devala, Vyasa. It was during the closing years of the Gupta Age, that *Bhasya*, i.e., commentaries on different *Smritis* began.

The principal systems of Philosophy of the period were those of Isvarakrishna's *Sankhya-Karika*, which expounded *Sankhya* system of Philosophy, a work called *Paramarthasaptatic* written by Vasubandhu was a criticism of Shasti-tantra. Gandapada better known as Siddhasena Divakara was the *Paramguru* (teacher's teacher) of Sankara and the first systematic exponent of monistic Vedanta. Bhartihari's work *Vakyapadiya* of this period has a great affinity with those of Sankara.

Kalidasa was the most brilliant luminary in the literary firmament of the Gupta age who shed enduring lusture on the secular Sanskrit literature. He was the greatest poet and dramatist that ever lived in India and his works have been enjoying a unparalleled reputation and popularity through ages, which remain undiminished even today. Unfortunately we have no definite idea about the time in which he flourished nor any knowledge about his life. Scholars differ as to the date of Kalidasa but the general opinion is in favour of regarding him as the court poet of a Gupta Emperor, most probably Chandragupta II Vikramaditya, tradition ascribes *Nabaratna*, i.e., nine gems of literature with King Vikrama of whom Kalidasa was the most resplendent. But most scholars think that all the nine gems could not have been Kalidasa's contemporaries. Dr. Smith says, "Although, it is difficult to fix the dates of the Great Poet's career with precision, it appears to be probable that he began to write either late in the reign of Chandragupta II or early in the reign of Kumaragupta II. The traditional association of his name with Raja Bikram of Ujjain is thus justified by sober criticism".[1] A close study of his works shows that Kalidasa "was a pious Brahmin of Ujjain and a liberal Saiva by belief, who had acquired a knowledge of the various branches of Brahmanical learning".[2] He was familiar with *Sankhya*,

[1] Smith: *The Early History of India*, p. 302.
[2] *Ibid.*, p. 303.

Yoga, Dharmasastras, Kamasutra, Natya-Sastra, Vyakarana, Jyotih-*sastra,* even fine arts, music and painting. "His versatile genius, his acquaintance with Court etiquette, his shrewdness, his modesty, not without a due sense of self-respect, and his poetic talent are very well reflected in his works which are all permeated with a feeling of ease and contentment, perfect satisfaction with the existing order of things".[1]

The greatest and best work of Kalidasa is his drama *Sakuntala* which is considered not only the best in Sanskrit literature, but is the literature of the world. Two of his earlier works were *Malavikagni-mitram* and *Vikramovarsiya.* Two of his epics *Raghuvamsa* and *Kumarasambhava* and his lyrical poem *Meghaduta* "are universally regarded as gems of Sanskrit poetry". "Kalidasa is unquestionably the finest master of Indian poetic style"[2] and both in drama and poetry he stands unsurpassed and unrivalled even today. He is inimitable in the use of the metaphor and simile.[3]

Two other remarkable dramatists that flourished during the period are Sudraka, author of *Mrichchakatikam* (*The Little Clay Cart*), and Visakadatta, author of *Mudrarakshasa.* Visakadatta is also supposed to have been the author of another remarkable drama named *Devi-Chandraguptam.* Bharavi, author of *Kiratarjuniyam* and *Sisupalbadha* also flourished during this age. Dr. Smith states that "the Laws of Manu, as we now know the book, may be dated from about the beginning of the Gupta period".

Evolution of the fables as a form of Sanskrit literature reached its fullness during the Gupta period and its best example in *Pancha-tantra.* The author was Vishnusarma. The book not only earned wide popularity all over India but became a distinct part of the world literature through its translation in more than fifty languages and with about two hundred versions. In India three versions can be traced in (i) *Brihatkathamanjari and Kathasaritsagara,* (ii) *Tantra-khyayika,* and (iii) *Hitopadesa.* Another work of fable form belonging to the period is Gunadya's *Brihatkatha* written in *Paisachi* prose. Among the romantic story writers mention may be made of Dandin who is supposed to have flourished during this period. His *Kavya-darsa* and *Dasakumarcharita* demonstrate his power of characterisation and daring realistic scenes of life in easy style full of wit and

---

[1] Smith: *The Early History of India,* p. 302.

[2] *Ibid,* p. 307.

[3] Upama Kalidasasya
Bharavechartha Gauravam
Nishade Padalalityam
Maghe Santi Trayoguna.

humour. Varahamihira was a great versifier who used a large number of Sanskrit metres in his *Brihat-Samhita* and *Brihat-jataka*.

Although lexicography in India can be traced back to Vedic texts, yet lexicon in the real sense of the term can be noticed for the first time in Amar's *Namalinganusasana* usually called the *Amarakosa*. He was also responsible for beginning contributing to medical lexicons like those of Dhanvantari.

In the field of sciences the Gupta age is adorned by the illustrious names of Aryabhatta and Varahamihira. Varahamhira in his *Panchasiddhantika* preserved the account of five astronomical works of his time some of which, according to scholars, indicate a knowledge of Greek and Roman astronomy. The fair works preserved in Varahamihira's work *Panchasiddhantika* are Romaka Siddhanta, Paulisa Siddhanta, Vasistha Siddhanta, Paitimaha Siddhanta, and Surya Siddhanta.

From Varahamihira we come across the names of several other astronomers of the time such as, Lata, Simha, Pradyumna, Vijayanandin, and the famous Aryabhatta. Brahmagupta was another great astronomer and mathematician of this age. He anticipated Newton in the theory of gravitation.

Aryabhatta, besides havnig been an astronomer, was one who first treated Mathematics as a distinct discipline and dealt with different branches of the subject including algebraic identities. He was also the first to hold that the earth is a sphere rotating on its axis and that eclipses were the shadow of earth falling on the Sun or the Moon. Aryabhatta's unique contribution was the system of decimal now used all over the world.

Besides the subjects mentioned above, there were other fields in which the period witnessed a remarkable development. Vatsyayana in his *Kamasutra* dealt with the art of love. Likewise works on subjects like architecture, music, dancing, painting, etc. were also produced during this period.

Harishena, the general and foreign minister of Samudragupta, was also the royal panegyrist who was responsible for composing the Allahabad *Prasasti* inscribed on an Asokan Pillar at Allahabad in poetic form.

The Gupta Art & Architecture

In art, architecture, sculpture, painting and terra-cotta the Gupta period witnessed unprecedented activities and development all over India.

In architecture the period marks a parting of ways. While the period saw the culmination and exhaustion of the earlier tendencies and movements in architectural types it ushered in a new age which is particularly noticed in the architectural style of the temples. In fact, it initiated a creative and formative period for the foundation of a typical Indian temple architecture.

In the rock-cut architecture, the conventional types reached their culmination. The rock-cut caves mostly Buddhist, but also Hindu and Jaina, had the conventional two parts: the proper shrine called the *Chaitya* and the monastery, i.e., the *Vihara* or *Sangharama*, saw the culminating point of development. The most notable of these are to be found in Ajanta, Ellora, Aurangabad (Hyderabad), and Bagh (Central India). Brahmanical rock-cut shrines although lesser in number than those of the Buddhists, were not rare either. Reference may be made in this connection to the Udaygiri series of shrines near Bhilsa in Bhopal State. The shrines are both rock-cut Brahmanical shrines and are also to be found at Badami in the Bijapur district. Jaina caves are to be found at Badami as also at Aihole.

Structural buildings in altogether new style was initiated. Formerly structural buildings, temples, etc., were constructed of perishable materials like wood, bamboo, etc., but during this age with the application of principle of architecture and pre-planning the Indian architects began to build monuments in permanent materials like bricks, dressed stones, etc. Contemporary epigraphic evidence refers to the building of numerous temples and cities with lofty edifices with the new materials. Flat-roofed temples, temples with *Sikharas*, rectangular temples, circular and square temple survive today as specimens of the new architectural style and system. Sanchi temple, Parvati temple, Meguti temple, Baigram temples may be mentioned in this connection. The temples at Sanchi, Tigawa, and Eran are the best preserved among the structural temple of the period. The most well-known *Sikhara* temple is that of Dasavatara at Deogarh. Brick temple of Bhitargao in Kanpur may be referred to as one of the new structural temples built with the new material, bricks.

The allied art of sculpture of the Gupta period had human figure as its pivot. At Mathura and Amaravati human figures of men and women around whole at Sanchi and Bharut vegetal world find predominance. The art of this period "indicates a deeper qualitatively meaningful transformation of human figures". The vegetal life also shows transformation. The most noteworthy features of the Gupta art are its elegance, simplicity of expression and its spiritual purpose. Gupta art are its elegance, simplicity of expression and its spiritual purpose. "A largeness of conception endows the human figure with a mental and physical discipline that discards the earthiness of Mathura and sensuousness of Vengi and elevates it to a state of experience of either a subtle spiritual or deeper rational or a sturdier and more vital existence. The face is lit up with this experience which is *wisdom* itself, which the eyes with drooping eyelids, instead of looking out into the visible world, seem to look within where every thing is at rest in contemplative concentration".[1] It may be mentioned that the Gupta plastic conception had its birth at Mathura and spread to Sarnath, Sravasti, Prayag, and other places. At Sarnath the plastic conception of Mathura school with all its elegance reached perfection in figure of seated Buddha in *Dharma-Chakra-Pravahthana* attitude. The perfection is also noticed in a few specimens found in the figures of Siva, Kartikeya, etc., at Malwa, and partly noticed in the *Durga-mahishamardini* and bust of Siva at Bhumara.

The Siva-Parvati relief at Kosam and the Ramayana panels at Deogarh are, however, good specimens of art although less refined and different in connection and elegance from the Sarnath School. Yet these are more homely and closer to day to day life. Reference may be made, in this connection, to similar homely specimens in the Brahmanical bas-reliefs at Chandimau. The quality of the Aihole reliefs is rather mediocre both in composition and plastic execution.

The art of painting, including terra-cotta and clay modelling, assumed a secular character during this period and became more popular than stone sculpture. Vatsayana's work *Kama-sutra* includes painting as one of the sixty four *Kalas*, i.e., arts and Yasodhara, commentator of Vatsyana refers to *Shadanga*, i.e., Six limbs of art: distinction of types (rupabheda), ideal proportions (pramanas), expression of mood (bhava), embodiment of charm (Lavany-yojana), points of view (Sadrisya) and preparation of colours (Varnakabhanga). All this and other references prove the intellectual ferment of the Gupta period and the detailed thinking about the theory and technique of painting.

The best specimens of painting of the period are to be found on the walls of the Ajanta caves, Bagh cave in Gwalior, Settannavasal temple at Puddukkottai and at Badami. Incidents of life of Buddha were the subject matter of the Gupta painters. The painting 'Dying Princess' in one Ajanta cave has earned the admiration of Burgess, Fergusson, Griffiths and many others. The Gupta art of painting has been praised by art critics for its brilliance of colour, richness of expression and delicacy of execution.

The artists of the Gupta age were experts in casting metals and making of copper statues. The wrought iron pillar at Delhi made at the time of Samudragupta is a marvel of metallurgical skill of the Gupta period artists.

Dr. R. D. Banerjee rightly remarks that "Gupta art is really a

---

[1] *The Classical Age*, p. 522.

renaissance due to the transformation of the ideals of the people of northern India in the fourth and the fifth centuries. This transformation was based on an assimilation of what was old, an elimination of what was exotic and foreign, and finally a systematic production of something entirely new and essentially Indian.

The coins of the Gupta period while furnish us with a lot of historical information show the artistic temperament, valiance, personality of the Gupta emperors. Both the gold and silver coins of the time give us a clear impression of the deveolpment of the currency system as well as the fineness of the coins and artistic representations of figures both human and religious on them.

Socio-Economic condition under the Gupta

According to Dr. K. N. Ghosal the Gupta Age was a period of Brahmanical reaction against ascendancy of Jainism and Buddhism. The age-old division of the society into four fundamental *varnas* seems to have shown a tendency towards intensification with the supremacy of the Brahmanas. The Buddhist and the Jaina reforms movement and the predominance received a direct check due to the Counter-Reformation by Brahmanical Hinduism. On the evidence of Varahamihira's *Brihat-Samhita* we know that different quarters were assigned to cities for the Brahmanas, Kshatriyas, Vaisyas, and the Sudras. But in spite of this stratification of the four *Varnas* according to the Smriti law, there were instances of Brahmanas and Kshatriyas adopting occupations of the lower *varnas*, that is, of the Vaisyas and Sudras and the Vaisyas and Sudras adopting the occupations of the higher *varnas*, that is, of the Brahmanas and Kshatriyas. There are also examples of inter-marriages between *varnas*. In the Sanskrit literature of the period there are mentions of Brahmanas and Kshatriyas marrying daughters and even female slaves of courtesans. Smriti laws were thus followed not with unexceptionable rigidity.

Apart from the age-old four varnas there were numerous other mixed castes. *Chandalas* occupied the lowest rank in the society and they had to live outside the towns or villages. The Smriti laws laid down strict rules for avoiding pollution of other classes of the society by their contact. Fa-hien bears testimony to the residence of the Chandalas outside the boundaries of towns and how they had to strike a piece of wood as a warning to others to keep away from them, when they would come to towns or market places. There were aboriginal tribes like the *Sabaras*, *Pulindas*, *Kiratas*, etc., who lived in forests of the Vindhyas, far removed from the Aryan society and practised reprehensible rites as offering human flesh to their deities and live on hunting.

Slaves

In the Gupta Age there were certain changes in the Smriti laws about slaves. Katyayan puts greater emphasis with regard to the application of the rules of slavery to the higher classes of the society and in this respect he is more categorical than Yajnavalka and Narada. According to Katyana a Brahmana could not be reduced to slavery. He also modifies the earlier rules relating to slavery by prescribing that in case of apostasy which a Kshatriya or a Vaisya was to be made a slave, a Brahmina was only to be banished. Sale or purhase of a Brahmana women was to be *ipso facto* annulled. According to Katyana a free woman marrying a slave would become a slave herself, but a child born of a free man and a slave woman would become free from slavery. The drama *Mrichchakatikam* also bears out the rules of slavery referred to above.

Marriage : Position of Women

During the Gupta period the older Smriti laws relating to marriage remained practically unaltered. There was, however, a tendency to lower the marriageable age of girls and it was enjoined that girls must be given in marriage before attainment of puberty. Vatsayana's view was, however, at variance with the Smriti laws of marriage. From his work it appears that marriage both before and after attainment of puberty by girls was prevalent at that time. According to Vatsayana a young man could marry a girl of his choice by courtship or even by trickery and violence. Girls choosing their own husbands, i.e., *Svayan-bara* as prescribed by the Smriti laws is also mentioned by Vatsayana.

Brahmanical sacred law had from a long time before the Gupta period prohibited study and utterance of the Vedic *mantras* by women. But on the evidence of Vatsayana it is learnt that girls of high families, daughters of nobles and Princess acquired knowledge of the *Sastras*. Vatsayana mentions a long list of subsidiary branches of knowledge recommended for women.

Again referring to the qualifications of a good wife Vatsayana says that she should be sufficiently educated to frame family budget and regulate domestic expenditure. The virtues of a Hindu wife Vatsayana explained in greater details than in the *Smritis*, are self-restraint and service as also household management. She ministers to the comforts of her husband at table, attends religious festivals, observes fast along with him. She serves her father-in-law and mother-in-law and obeys their commands. All these qualities remain as the hallmark of Hindu wives down to the present day.

During the Gupta Age the widows were required to follow the rules prescribed by the Smritis from earlier times. The widows had to live a life of strict celibacy, but according to Brihaspati she had to burn herself in the funeral pyre of her husband. In the Gupta Age the widow followed the earlier Smriti laws and lived a life of purity, fasts and vows. She was also allowed to inherit her husband's property. According to some writers the custom of Sati was highly praised while others condemned it. On the whole it may be said that during the Gupta Age the widows lived a chaste and pious life prescribed by the Smritis. Widow remarriage was not forbidden although held in disfavour.

The system of female courtisans (ganika) was also prevalent during the Gupta period as of old and in certain temples *Devadasis* were retained. In the temple of Mahakala at Ujjain such girls were present during Kalidasa's time.

The trend towards denigrating the status of women in society which began previously continued during the Gupta Age. Yet there were certain changes for the better. For examples, women's right to property was recognised along with women molested by robbers and other anti-social persons. Women also exercised public rights as is exemplified by Prabhavati-Gupta's ruling over the Vakataka Kingdom. Use of veils by women of high social standing while appearing in public seem to have been prevalent under the Guptas.

Literature of the Gupta Age as also the account of the Chinese traveller Fa-hien point to the high standard of living during that period. There are other evidences which prove the luxury and wealth of the people of the time. Jewels were used not only by the members of the royal family but also by others. Ornaments of various types, for the head, forehead, neck, ears, forearms, arms, waist, fingers, legs were in use. Garments of men and women had two distinct parts, for the upper and the lower parts of the body. Women had their bodices, petticoats, and winter cloak reaching the feet. From *Amarakosa* we come to know that high standard of cleanliness and comfort was maintained during the Gupta period. Scented hair oil, hair lotion, perfumes, etc., were presumably in use, for the formulas for their preparation are found in Amarakosa.

Rice, wheat, barley, pulses of different kinds, butter, oils, molasses, coarse sugar, fish, meat and liquor were taken as food and drink by the people of the time. Fa-hien's remark that killing of animals, drinking wine, eating onions and garlic were unknown in the *Middle Kingdom*, i.e., the dominions under the direct rule of the Gupta emperor was an exaggeration. But it gives us a general impression of the Buddhistic influence on the life and habits of the people of the

People seem to have believed in omens, portents, spells and divination. Common people believed in superstitions. But intelligent and educated people, the kings and princes were above all such superstitious beliefs.

Contemporary literature gives us a picture of the gay life of the townsmen during the Gupta period. Works, both poetic and prose, describe the splendour and magnificence of many of the well-known cities and towns of the period. The nature of life was one of refined Epicureanism. Houses consisted of two parts, outer one for the males and reserved for "their amorous enjoyment", and the inner one for the women of the family. A garden of trees and flower plants was attached to every house. Pet birds, domestic animals were also kept by the householders of the city. The townsmen had their periodical enjoyments since as the *Samajas, Ghatas*, i.e., assemblies, social gatherings, public sports, drinking parties, etc. Every fortnight or every month the people assembled at the temple of *Saraswati*, the goddess of learning and arts.

During the Gupta period a highly cultured urban life was evolved. Even in daily life "a high and refined, delicate and elegant art of toilets and cosmetics" could be noticed. Doing of hair and scenting of the face, body and dress with *aguru* incense and other perfumes and powders and paste were prevalent. "Indeed whatever was done to beautify the body and the soul during this period was raised to the standard of lalitakala or fine art in which simplicity, delicacy, refinement and elegance were the main watch words."[1]

In the field of economy, the Gupta period witnessed a great progress in agriculture, industry, trade and commerce and banking. Agriculture was both intensive and extensive. Epigraphic evidence of cultivation that it was not easy to find or follow, uncultivated or unsettled land even for the purposes of charitable grant. Grant of massive plots of land was an impossibility and small plots in different parts would be included in such grants if made. So great importance was attached to agriculture that grant of lands to educational institutions would require the institution to keep adequate labour and draught animals for cultivating the land given as grant.

In the Gupta Age there were guilds of various types. Guilds, called Srenis, were there for industry, trade and banking. We have references to guilds of merchants, artisans, traders, bankers, oilmen, weavers, etc., as well as federation of guilds of the same kind as federation of artisans' guild or of the bankers' guilds.

The guilds used to receive deposits as trustees and pay stipulated

[1] *The Classical Age*, p. 583.

amount to the beneficiaries. There were also irrevocable endowments to guilds for the benefit of *Viharas* and temples. These institutions were maintained out of the endowments made to the guild.

Extensive number of coins of gold, silver, and copper of the Gupta period reveal the fineness of the coins as well as the development of the currency system of the time.

Public utility works like the repair of dams, for example, of the Sudarsana lake, digging of wells, tanks, reservoirs of drinking water, lakes, building of temples with halls, causeways and laying of parks and gardens were undertaken during the Gupta Period.

Among the industries of the time mention may be made of textile industry which produced Silk, muslin, calico, linen, wool clothes. Amarakosa refers to various qualities of cloth, coarse and fine, cloth meant for making male and female garments. Dresses, both stitched and unstitched, were made at that time. Benares, Mathura, Pundra, i.e., North Bengal were specially noted for silk cloth and rare type of cotton cloth.

Metallurgy was also highly developed during this period. The iron Pillar of Chandra at Delhi is illustrative of this development. For manufacture of different medicine use of bowls and instruments of gold, silver, lead, copper, and bronze is recommended by Charaka. Ornaments of gold and silver with pearls and jewels set skilfully in order to have best colour effect and brightness. Ivory was in extensive use for manufacture of furniture, seals, etc. The specimens of sculpture and architecture of the time indicate a high degree of excellence attained in the stone-cutters' job at that time.

Trade and commerce, both maritime and over land, used to be carried on with Ceylon, Indo-China, etc. A good deal of the material prosperity and high standard of living was due to the brisk trade, particularly carried on from the ports on the western and eastern coasts of India. Tamralipta was one of the most important ports for export of commodities to Ceylon and South-East Asian countries.

Religion

Religious movement during the Gupta period shows a positive swing towards concrete from abstract. The Vedic pantheon and sacrificial worship receded into the background and ceremonial worship of the images of Brahma, Vishnu, and Mahesvara (Siva) as well as other gods such as Surya, Kartikeya, Saraswati, etc., became popular. Temples, sometimes very magnificent ones, were erected for the gods and goddesses mentioned above. But the old ideas of sacrificial worship of the Vedic Hinduism were retained by a progressively dwindling number of orthodox votaries. The transformation that took place in the Brahmanical religion led to the evolution of a new pantheon whose history and glory are told in the Puranas.

The characteristic features of the religious life of the period were, *first*, wide prevalence of the images of gods. The idea that was current is that "worship and meditation are possible only when the Supreme Being is endowed with form". Thus iconographic evolution was a distinct trait of the period.

Secondly, another important characteristic feature of the period was the spirit of toleration among the followers of different religious sects. "One aspect of this tolerant spirit was the attempt to establish the unity of different gods like Vishnu and Siva and to combine in a single iconographic motif the attributes of different gods. The very idea of the trinity of Brahma, Vishnu and Siva is an evidence of the same spirit, which is further displayed by regarding Buddha as an incarnation of Vishnu".[1]

What was true of the Brahmanical Hinduism was also true of Buddhism and there was transformation of the austere moral code of the Mahayana Buddhism into Vajrayana and later approach of Buddhism nearer and nearer to new Hinduism helped Buddhism to be gradually absorbed by Hinduism. But the failure of Jainism to adapt itself to new ideas and environment prevented it from acquiring that popularity which Buddhism acquired within and without India.

During the Gupta period the religious condition in India assumed a complex character due to the prevalence of various religious sects side by side. But this at least proved the great spirit of religious toleration that characterised the period.

Some scholars, among whom Dr. Keith is most prominent, remark that the Gupta period signified a revival of Brahmanical Hinduism. But this view is only partially correct for although since the time of Asoka Buddhism became the predominant faith and continued to be the state religion for major part of the time, Hinduism did not vanish. It was only pushed into the background. But with the coming of the Sungas to power Brahmanical Hinduism regained its position of pride and Pushyamitra who was a Brahmana himself celebrated *Asvamedha* sacrifices thereby reviewed the Brahmanical religion. This was also the case with the Kanvas and the Andhras. Even before the Guptas, the Nagas popularised Brahmanical religion by holding ten *Asvamedha* sacrifices. But under the Gupta rulers Hinduism staged a fullest come back through the patronage it received from them. Yet it will be a mistake to think that there was any Hindu reaction since the Gupta rulers extended toleration to other religions and religious sects.

[1] *The Classical Age*, p. 373.

Later Guptas

It was after the reign of Skandagupta that decline of the Gupta empire began till by the middle of the 6th Century A.D. (550 A.D.) the Gupta empire became extinct. Under Skandagupta's successors Purugupta, Narasimhagupta Baladitya, Kumaragupta-II, Vishnugupta, Budhagupta, Tathagatagupta, Bhanugupta etc., the Gupta empire broke up and on ramified parts different rulers related to the Gupta were ruling. Although the Gupta empire broke up small families related to the Guptas were found to rule in some parts as local rulers upto the eighth Century A.D. The last King of the Gupta dynasty was Jivitagupta-II.

CAUSES OF THE DOWNFALL OF THE GUPTA EMPIRE

In the fourth century when the Roman empire in the West was declining, in India the Gupta empire, noted for its exceptional cultural advancement and dissemination, had emerged. Not since the days of the Mauryas had India been a united political power before the emergence of the Guptas, but in the fifth century decline had set in the Gupta empire and it tottered to its fall by the middle of the sixth century.

The Gupta empire which was built by the labour and genius of Samudragupta and Chandragupta-II and which had reached the highest watermark of cultural achievements under Chandragupta-II was on its decline from the end of the fifth century. The causes of the decline and break up of empires in India, whether the Maurya, Sultanate or the Mughal empire, show a family likeness. The Gupta empire also had similar causes behind its decline and fall. From the contemporary historical sources the causes of the fall of the Gupta empire may be mentioned as (i) the internal dissension in the royal family, (ii) rebellion of the feudatories, (iii) assumption of independence by the Provincial Satraps, (iv) foreign invasions, (v) lack of military and administrative abilities on the part of the later Gupta rulers.

(i) Decline of the Gupta empire had set in, for all practical purposes, during the reign of Skandagupta. True, he had successfully constrained the Pushyamitra and the Huna menace but the jolt that the imperial fabric had received, loosened the enduring grit of the empire. While the forces of decay were at work, the princes of the royal blood engaged themselves in mutual conflict in furtherance of their selfish gains and even began to take sides with the struggle between the local rulers. All this denigrated the power and prestige of the Gupta empire which was soon parcelled out between the princes, local rulers, and high officials. Skandagupta's wars to save the empire from external attacks had heavily told upon the finances of the government and the proof was found in the debasement of the gold coins of his as also in the lesser number of gold coins issued during his reign.

(ii) Removal of strong rule at the centre, and distinctly after Budhagupta brought the centrifugal forces in action and Kathiawar, Bundelkhand, North Bengal became virtually independent. The process of disintegration once set in began to run its course and when external invasions further weakened the empire break-up of the empire was simply a question of time.

(iii) With the growing weakness of the central authority due to struggle for succession among the princes of royal blood and personal inefficiency of the rulers, the feudatories of the Gupta empire began to raise the standard of rebellion and eventually tore off their local areas from the Gupta empire. Yasodharman, a feudatory of the Gupta empire in central India with his capital at Mandasor, was valiant soldier and a capable ruler who earned the fame of warding off the Huna invasion. He naturally made himself independent of the Gupta emperor and carved out a large dominion by conquest of northern India. His example emboldened other feudatories who began to follow his foot-steps and made themselves independent. The Maukharis set up an independent Kingdom in Uttar Pradesh, the Maitrakas who were military governors of the Gupta emperors at Valabhi made themselves independent. A branch of this dynasty made itself independent in western Malwa. In the sixth century, that is, about the same time when other parts of the Gupta empire were falling off South, West and East Bengal shook off Gupta sovereignty.

(iv) The greatest scourge of the Gupta empire was the external invasion. Samudragupta in his statesmanship realised that the Vakatakas would be either of great service or disservice to the Gupta empire and therefore left them unmolested during his Deccan campaign and Chandragupta-II went one step further to strengthen his power by entering into a marriage alliance with the Vakatakas. But the prudent policy pursued by Samudragupta and Chandragupta-II was forsaken by the later Gupta rulers and during the reign of Budhagupta, Vakataka King Narendrasena invaded and exercised a great influence over Malwa-Kosala-Mekala and his orders were obeyed there. Malwa and Gujarat had later on been conquered by the Vakatakas.

The Vakatakas were not the only invaders from outside. The Huns had administered the most shattering blow to the Gupta empire. Although their invasion during the reign of Skandagupta had been successfully warded off yet the Huns reappeared and carried on devastation in north-western and western India and Gandhara, Punjab, Malwa and Gujarat passed under their control. Their progress towards Central India was successfully checked by Yashodharman of Mandasor. The Hun Chief Mihirkula was abjectly defeated at his hands. The last defeat of the Huns was at the hands of Narasimha-Gupta. The common opinion that the Hun invasion was the principal cause of the break up of the Gupta empire, has been refuted by Dr. R. C. Majumdar. According to him "There is a general belief among historians that the Hun invasion was the principal cause of the downfall of the Gupta empire. But it is difficult to subscribe to this view. The gates of India were successfully barred against the Huns throughout the fifth century A.D. In spite of temporary successes, first of Toramana and then of Mihirkula, the Huns never counted as a permanent factor in Indian politics save Kashmir and Afghanistan which lay far beyond the frontiers of the Gupta empire. So far as evidence goes, the death-blow to the Gupta empire was dealt not by the Huns but by ambitious chiefs like Yasodharman".[1] But it cannot be denied that the repeated Hun invasions had shaken the Gupta imperial fabric violently enough thereby making it possible for Yasodharman and other feudatories to administer the death blow to it.

(v) One of the contributory factors leading to the downfall of the Gupta empire was the competition among both the civil and military officials for furthering their own interest when foreign invasions had thrown the administration out of gear. Lack of discipline and sense of duty contributed the weakness of the administration which was certainly one of the contributory factors.

(vi) The Gupta emperors like Samudragupta, Chandragupta, Skandagupta were patrons of Hinduism in a militant form. Celebration of *Asvamedha* is a point in illustration. But later Guptas had Buddhist leaning and even their names like Budhagupta, Tathagata-gupta, etc., exemplified this. This transformation in religious attitude had its repercussion on the policy of the government and what had actually happened to the intense Buddhistic attitude of mind of Asoka, could be seen to some extent at least among later Gupta rulers. If the story of Hiuen T-Sang that Baladitya who had taken Mihirkula prisoner set him free at his mother's behest, thereby leaving the enemy unharmed is true, it must be said that this was a misplaced kindness which in a king desirous of maintaining the integrity of his empire and defending it against external invasion was a sign of weakness.

[1] *The Classical Age*, p. 44.

All these factors combined to accomplish the break up of an empire so vast in expanse and so advanced in culture.

Foreign Impacts on the Guptas

Dr. V. S. Smith rightly points out that the "contact or collision of diverse modes of civilisation is the most potent stimulus to intellectual and artistic progress". The Gupta period saw an unprecedented cultural excellence in the Indian history due to its contacts with civilisations, both of the east and the west. The conquest of Malwa and Surashtra during the reign of Chandragupta-II opened up communication between India and western countries which facilitated reception of European ideas. The result of the impact of foreign contacts can be noticed in the coins of the Gupta kings in which imitation of the Roman coins is obvious.

The astronomy of Aryabhatta was undoubtedly influenced by the Alexandrine School of astronomy. Varahamihira's *Surya Siddhanta* appears to have been equally influenced by the Greek and Roman astronomy.

In art and literature, Dr. Smith rightly observes, it is difficult to measure the impact of the foreign influence. The sculpture of the Sleeping Vishnu at Deogarh has a close resemblance with the Graeco-Roman works represented by the Endymion at Stockholm. Prof. Basham endorses the view but he remarks that the Indian sculpture of the Gupta period represents Greek spirit in Indian form.

In the intellectual and artistic output of the Gupta period the influence of the Roman is suggested by Dr. Smith.

According to Mr. Keith there was close relation between Indian and Greek mathematical science. "Some critics have thought that Chinese ideas may be traced in the Ajanta frescoes and they may be right".[1]

All this is but one side of the picture. The Indian culture when it had attained fullness under the Guptas transcended its physical limits and through commercial relations spread into the South-East Asian countries like Sumatra, Java, Bali, Combodia, Anam, Borneo, etc. During the Gupta period we find many rulers in these countries who bore Indian names. In these countries Indian religion, social and cultural life, language and script had spread. Between the second and the fifth centuries Indian colonies were established in the countries of South-East Asia and continued to exist for a period of a thousand years.

---

[1] Smith: *Early History of India*, p. 324.

CHAPTER SIXTEEN

THE MAUKHARIS AND THE PUSHYABHUTIS

Maukharis of Kanauj

The Maukharis belong to a very ancient family. There is reference to the Maukharis in Panini's work. A clay seal of the Maukharis has been found at Gaya belonged to the Maurya period. Reference to a Maukhari general is found in an inscription dated 239 A.D., discovered at Kotah in Rajputana. Four stone inscriptions of different Maukhari families have been in this area, which indicate existence of seven Maukhari families during the third century. The Maukharis claimed descent from Asvapati, mentioned in the *Mahabharata* as the King of Madra in the Central Punjab.

From epigraphic evidence we come to know that two groups of Maukhari Kings ruling in South Bihar and U.P. early in the sixth century A.D. The founder of one group of rulers was Yajnavarman who was succeeded by his son Sardulavarman and Anantavarman. The rulers of the second group were Harivarman. Adityavarman, Ishwaravarman, Ishanavarman, Sarvavarman, Avantivarman, and Grahavarman were feudatories to the Guptas and ruled early in the sixth century A.D. They are referred to as *Samantas* or Samantachudamani.

Harivarman, the first of the second line of rulers, assumed the title of *Maharaja* and it is presumed that he perhaps had assumed an independent status. He is described in his inscriptions as one who had carried on extensive military campaigns and brought other kings under subjection. The Maukhari history becomes definite from the time of Ishanavarman. One of his inscriptions dated A.D. 554 coincides with the downfall of the Gupta empire and he must have come to power before this date. Ishanavarman claims to have defeated the Andhras, Sulikas and the Gaudas, and assumed the title of *Maharajadhiraja*. It is, therefore, probable that Ishanavarman was the first full-fledged independent Maukhari king. It is, however, not possible to determine the limits of his dominions with certainty. From the findspots of his coins it is presumed to be present Uttar Pradesh, parts of Orissa, and Bengal.

The later Gupta rulers had protracted conflict with the Maukharis and King Ishanavarman was defeated by Kumaragupta and probably also by Damodargupta. Ishanavarman was succeeded by Sarvavarman and the latter by Avantivarman.

From Bana's *Harshacharit* we come to know that Avantivarman was succeeded by his son Grahavarman who later married Rajyasri, daughter of Prabhakarvardhana, the Pushyabhuti king of Thaneswar. Grahavarman was not, however, destined to rule for long. Devagupta, a Gupta king of Malwa, who was an ally of King Sasanka of Gauda, defeated and killed Grahavarman and carried away Rajyasri as captive. Rajyavardhana was also killed by Sasanka, ally of Devagupta and the throne of Thaneswar also fell vacant. It was at this juncture, the throne of Kanauj, that is of the Maukharis, was united with that of Thaneswar and Harshavardhana became the king of the United Kingdom.

Another State that arose out of the ashes of the Gupta empire was that of Thaneswar under the Pushyabhuti family. This state was destined to play more important part than the Maukharis of Kanauj and Maitrakas of Valabhi, etc.

Pushyabhutis of Thaneswar

Prabhakarvardhan : The first three kings of the Pushyabhuti dynasty were mere names and do not seem to have exercised any power. Prabhakarvardhana, the fourth king, extended his dominions at the expense of his neighbours and that he had built up a powerful dominion is clear from his assumption of imperial title: *Paramabhattaraka Maharajadhiraja.*

Prabhakarvardhan's sovereignty probably extended to the whole of the Punjab and Malwa. After a busy aggressive career Prabhakarvardhana died in A.D. 604 and he was succeeded by his eldest son Rajyavardhana. He had given his daughter Rajyasri in marriage with the Maukhari King Grahavarmana.

Prabhakarvardhana's career synchronised with those of two other rulers who had established powerful Kingdom in Bengal and Assam. They were Sasanka King of Bengal and Bhaskaravarman of Kamrup.

Under Prabhakarvardhan the Kingdom of Thaneswar was well on the road to imperial expansion. He conquered Malwa, north-west Punjab from the Huns and Rajputana from the Gurjaras. He was related through his maternal side to the Gupta imperial dynasty and ambition for building an empire was but natural for him in whose veins ran the Gupta imperial blood.

In 604 A.D. when the Huns attacked the Kingdom of Prabhakarvardhana, the latter sent his eldest son Rajyavardhan against them. Rajyavardhan defeated the Huns and established a reputation as a military commander.

Prabhakarvardhan gave his daughter Rajyasri in marriage with Grahavarman, the Maukhari King of Kanauj. Alliance between the two families, namely, the Pushyabhutis of Thaneswar and Maukharis of Kanauj greatly strengthened the power and position of Prabhakarvardhan. Sasanka, King of Bengal, sought to counter this accession of strength of Prabhakarvardhan by contracting a friendly alliance with Devagupta of Malwa, for Sasanka who himself was aspiring after imperial expansion foresaw a conflict with the House of Thaneswar. Thus towards the end of the reign of Prabhakarvardhan there were two political leagues in northern India, one under the leadership of the House of Thaneswar and the other under Sasanka of Bengal. In 605 A.D. Prabhakarvardhan died rather suddenly and was succeeded by his eldest son Rajyavardhan.

RAJYAVARDHAN (605-606 A.D)

Hardly Rajyavardhan ascended the throne, the Bengal-Malwa league took the initiative to attack Kanauj. Devagupta, ally of Sasanka, took the Maukhari capital of Kanauj by surprise, defeated and killed Grahavarman and took his wife Rajyasri prisoner. The news of the defeat and death of Grahavarman came as a shock and surprise to Rajyavardhan who immediately marched against Devagupta of Malwa with a force of 10,000 cavalry to take revenge for Grahavarman's death and imprisonment of Rajyasri. The promptness with which he proceeded against Devagupta had its advantage and resulted in complete defeat of the latter. On his return march to Kanauj Rajyavardhana was killed by Sasanka, King of Bengal and an ally of Devagupta. An unresolved mystery surrounds round the episode of the death of Rajyavardhana by Sasanka. According to Bana, author of *Harshacharit*, Rajyavardhan was treacherously murdered by Sasanka. But from two grants of Harshavardhan, the death of Rajyavardhan is referred to as the sequel to a duel between him and Sasanka. On the basis of the evidence of Bana as also according to Hiuen T-Sang it is held by some scholars that "Rajyavardhan was allured into confidence by false civilities on the part of Sasanka, the King of Gauda, and then weaponless, confiding and alone despatched in his own quarters". Dr. Majumdar is of the opinion that partisans of Rajyavardhan ascribed his death to foul treachery on the part of Sasanka but there is reason to believe that "this is a perversion of truth for party purposes". Dr. Majumdar also remarks that "our sole authorities Banabhatta and Hiuen T-Sang were both hostile to Sasanka and cannot be looked upon as impartial".[1] But their statements differ in respect of the circumstances under which the treachery was acted by Sasanka. Further, from almost a contemporary inscrip-

[1] *The Advanced History of India*, p. 166.

tion of Harsha it is learnt that Rajyavardhan "gave up his life in the mansion of his foe owing to his adherence to a promise". From these divergent views and statements it is difficult to arrive at any definite conclusion about the manner of the duel and eventual death of Rajyavardhan. Dr. Majumdar remarks "certain it is, Rajyavardhan failed in his enterprise and lost his life".[1]

Dr. R. D. Banerjee points out that Bana's mention of the death of Rajyavardhan as a treacherous murder has been followed by many of the modern historians. But two grants of Harshavardhan describe the event as the result of a duel between Rajyavardhan and Sasanka.[2] However, the mystery about Rajyavardhan's death remain still unravelled.

The death of Rajyavardhana in 606 A.D. brought his younger brother, Harshavardhan, on the throne of Thaneswar. This was approved by the royal court at the suggestion of Bhandi, a member of the Royal Court. The death of Grahavarman of Kanauj had also left the throne vacant there, the throne of Kanauj was also offered to Harshavardhan. Thus the two Kingdoms came under one King and Harsha became ruler of both Kanauj and Thaneswar.

HARSHAVARDHAN (A.D. 606-647)

Lack of historical materials that embarrasses the historian in reconstructing the history of the latter half of the sixth century is no longer felt for writing the history of the seventh century. The source materials for the reign of Harshavardhan are diverse and numerous, both indigenous and foreign. Our knowledge about the period of Harshavardhan is, therefore, more precise than what we possess about any earlier Indian ruler except Asoka.

The invaluable description of India recorded by Hiuen T-Sang during the rule of Harshavardhana "reads like a Gazetteer in the scope of its enquiry and its wealth of details". The life of Hiuen T-Sang by his friend Hwui-li translated by Beal in his *Life of Hiuen T-Sang*, the official Chinese historical works are of immense importance as source of materials for the reign of Harshavardhan.

Bana's *Harshacharit* contain a considerable historical information about Harshavardhana and his time. The information furnished by the above sources when combined with that furnished by inscriptions, coins, and other sources give us a knowledge surpassing in fullness and precision that is available for any other period

[1] R. C. Majumdar: *Ancient India*, p. 251.

[2] R. D. Banerjee: *Prehistoric Ancient and Hindu India*, p. 199.

except that of the Mauryas. Dr. Smith remarks "His personal characteristics and the details of his administration, as recorded by men who knew him intimately, enable us to realise him as a living person who achieved greatness by his capacity and energy."

When in 606 A.D., on the death of Rajyavardhan, Harshavardhan, a youth of 16 or 17 years of age, was called upon to occupy the throne ; he was reluctant. But he was constrained by the nobles to accept vacant throne.

Immediate task before him was the rescue of his sister Rajyasri. Information reached him of the escape of Rajyasri. According to Bana, as the tragic news of the murder of Rajyavardhan reached Harsha he took a vow to take revenge against Sasanka, the King of Gauda, the killer of Rajyavardhan. "I swear", said Harsha, "that unless in a limited number of days, I clear this earth of Gaudas...... then I will hurl my sinful self like a moth, into an oil-fed flame". According to Bana Harsha was not simply to exterminate Gauda but decided upon world-wide conquest. He also caused a proclamation to be issued all over India asking all kings to either accept his over-lordship or to be prepared for war with him.

Hardly Harsha had proceeded in his march against Sasanka, a messanger from Bhaskaravarman, King of Kamrupa, with its Capital at Pragjyotisha came and reported that as his master was a devotee of Lord Siva and does homage to him alone, it would not be possible to do homage to any earthly king and offered to enter into a perpetual alliance with Harshavardhan. An alliance was entered into between the two parties when within a few days Bhaskaravarman personally met Harshavardhan. The alliance was of great benefit to both Harshavardhan and Bhaskaravarman, for it was an added strength to Harsha against his enemy Sasanka and a measure of safety to Bhaskaravarman against his powerful neighbour Sasanka.

After Harsha had continued his march for a few days Bhandi who was returning with the remnant of Rajyavardhan's army informed him of the release of Rajyasri from confinement and her taking shelter in the Vindhya forest and the numerous search parties sent to find her out had not yet returned. Harsha left Bhandi in charge of his army and went to search out his sister. In the Vindhya forest he met Rajyasri who after a few days' wandering was about to mount a funeral pyre. She was persuaded to return with Harsha.

Bana's narrative abruptly ends here. But in Hiuen T-Sang's account it is stated that Harshavardhan and his two predecessors were rulers of Kanauj. He, however, refers to the fact that the ministers at the instance of Po-ni, usually identified with Bhandi, the great minister, invited Harshavardhan to ascend the throne of Kanauj, on

Rajyavardhan's death. Hiuen T-Sang mentions a romantic story that Harsha sought the oracle of a statute of Avalokitesvara Bodhisatva on the bank of the Ganges. The Bodhisatva advised Harsha not to ascend the throne actually and not to use the title of Maharaja. Thereupon Harsha became King of Kanauj assuming the title and style *Rajaputra Siladitya.* Chinese work *Fang-Chih* represents Harsha as a joint ruler with his widowed sister. Dr. Majumdar thinks that Harsha probably administered the government of Kanauj in the name of his sister to begin with, later openly assumed the crown and sovereign rights over Kanauj.

Hiuen T-Sang's story has been regarded as absurd by modern historians, for Harsha did not come to occupy the throne of Kanauj on the death of his brother-in-law. The only implication of Hiuen T-Sang's narrative is that at the instance of Bhandi Harsha was invited to rule over Kanauj presumably because Grahavarman did not leave any heir to succeed him and Rajyasri perhaps did not agree to undertake the responsibility of ruling the country. Thus, on Harshavardhan's assumption of the rule of Kanauj, both the thrones of Kanauj and Thaneswar were united under the same ruler.

His Conquests

Harsha was a great warrior and carried on a series of military expedition which made him the most powerful ruler in northern India. The Chinese traveller Hiuen T-Sang mentions that Harsha "went from east to west subduing all who were not obedient, the elephants were not unharnessed, nor the soldiers unhelmeted". He proceeded in his military campaigns with 5,000 war elephants, 20,000 cavalry and 50,000 infantry.

After rescuing Rajyasri Harsha rejoined his army but what was the outcome of his campaign against Sasanka of Bengal is not known, for Bana's narrative does not continue after Harsha's finding of his sister in the Vindhya forest. R. S. Tripathi amusingly enough fills in the gap by introducing an imaginative story that Sasanka "beat a masterly retreat" on the approach of Harsha's army considering that discretion was the better part of valour. That Harsha could not make much headway against Sasanka is evident from the absence of any reference in Bana's narrative and from the fact that Sasanka was known to have ruled over Bengal, south Bihar, and Orissa till 619 A.D.

Manjusri Mulakalpa, a Buddhist chronicle, mentions of the defeat of Sasanka at the hands of Harsha who forbade the former to move out of his capital. Dr. Majumdar is of opinion that no reliance can be placed on this vague and obscure statement of the medieval Buddhist chronicle.

We have, however, no systematic or chronological reference to the military campaigns of Harsha, for Hiuen T-Sang's account makes only general and rather vague reference to his expeditions. However, Harsha's military campaigns may be considered under four distinct phases, namely, his conflict with (i) Kingdoms of Valabhi and Gurjara, (ii) Chalukya Kingdom, (iii) Sind, (iv) Eastern countries such as Magadha, Gauda, Odra, and Kongod.

(i) At the time of Harsha Valabhi was a powerful and independent Kingdom and exercised supremacy over northern Gujarat and a part of Malwas. From a Gurjara inscription at Broach, there is reference to Harshavardhan's over-powering the lord of Valabhi. This proves that there was a conflict between Harshavardhana and the Kingdom of Valabhi. The King of Valabhi at that time was Dhruvasena or Dhruvabhatta. But the identification is not, however, definite. According to some scholars, Dr. R. C. Majumdar, for instance, thinks that Harshavardhana gave his daughter to the King of Valabhi and thus the hostilities between the two, ended in sweet relationship and Valabhi had not to accept Harsha's suzerainty. Dr. D. C. Sarkar, on the other hand, maintains that the King of Valabhi had to recognise Harsha as his suzerain. According to some other scholars Harsha did not fare well in his conflict with the King of Valabhi and that was why he had to enter into a matrimonial alliance with him. From Hiuen T-Sang's account and an inscription of Dhruvasena, the Maitrakas of Valabhi ruled over Malwa and north Gujarat as independent ruler.

(ii) Harshavardhan's war with Pulakeshin-II, the Chalukya King of the south, was a memorable event both for the Chalukya Kingdom and Harsha. According to Hiuen T-Sang, Harsha although succeeded in defeating kings of many countries failed to defeat Pulakeshin-II. Harsha, according to Hiuen T-Sang "gathered troops from the five Indias, and summoned the best leaders from all countries, and himself gone at the head of the army to punish and subdue those people, but he has not yet conquered their troops". Obviously Harsha took an aggressive attitude towards Pulakeshin but suffered defeat at the latter's hand. The successors of Pulakeshin regarded defeat of Harsha as a matter of great pride but also mention that after defeating Harsha Pulakeshin took the title Paramesvara. The successors of Pulakeshin and some modern scholar's assertion of a crushing defeat of Harsha notwithstanding, there is no evidence to prove where battle was actually fought and Dr. Smith's opinion that Pulakeshin-II who guarded the passes of the Narmada so effectively that Harsha compelled to retire accepting the river Narmada as the dividing line between his Kingdom and that of Pulakeshin-II. In the Aihole inscription the Latas, Malavas and the Gurjaras are referred to as feudatories of Pulakeshin as such it is doubtful if the Narmada could be the boundary of his kingdom towards the South.

(iii) It may be remarked that Harsha's attempt at conquest of Valabhi and Chalukya Kingdom ended in a failure. He was also not successful against Sind. Sind was hostile to Prabhakaravardhan also. It is suggested by Dr. Raychaudhuri that Harsha might have led a campaign against Sind but Hiuen T-Sang leaves no doubt that Sind was a strong and independent Kingdom even when he visited it. Bana is also not very explicit about the outcome of the conflict for he rhetorically remarks that Harsha "pounded the King of Sindhu and appropriated his fortune".

(iv) On the evidence of *Life of Hiuen T-Sang* we learn that when early 643 A.D. Hiuen T-Sang had been to Kamrup at the invitation of Bhaskaravarman, Harsha had completed the subjugation of Kongod and Orissa, and was halting at Kajangal near Rajmahal. This proves that Harsha must have led victorious campaigns towards the east and conquered the territories mentioned above and all the intervening regions. From the Chinese encyclopaedist Ma-twan-lin, we learn that Siladitya assumed the title of the *King of Magadha* in 641 A.D. Harsha must have conquered Magadha after the visit of Hiuen T-Sang, for when he was in Magadha during the year 637-638 A.D. the ruling King was Purnavarman who revived the Bodhi tree at Gaya which was cut down by Sasanka. This corroborates Harsha's occupation of Magadha after Hiuen T-Sang's visit to that country and Ma-twan-lin's statement that Harsha assumed the title of the *King of Magadha* in 641 A.D.

According to Hiuen T-Sang Harsha had brought *five Indias* under his allegiance. Five Indias which have been identified as the Punjab, Kanauj, Bihar, Orissa and Bengal. Dr. Majumdar is, however, doubtful if Harshavardhan had even got possession of territories east of the Bhagirathi or north of the Padma river. But there is evidence that Bhaskaravarman, King of Kamrup, probably occupied this area or a considerable portion of it. Dr. Majumdar, however, concedes that "we cannot altogether exclude the possibility that Harsha was suzerain of Bengal for a short time and it was not till after his death that Bhaskaravarman gained the same position".

K. M. Panikkar is of opinion that "Nepal and Kashmir were also within this 'Harsha's empire. While his authority in north of Vindhyas was complete, Harsha's arms met with a definite set back when he advanced towards the south".[1]

From the contemporary records we learn that Harsha led an

[1] Panikkar: *A Survey of Indian History*, p. 77.

expedition against Kashmir and brought the tooth relic of Buddha from there. But there is no reference to the time when he did so.

Extent of Harshavardhan's Empire : A Critique

There is a great divergence of opinion about the extent of Harshavardhan's empire. According to some scholars Harsha's empire comprised Thaneswar, Kanauj, Ahichhatra, Sravasti, Prayag, etc. According to Hiuen T-Sang Magadh and Orissa were also within his empire. In the Advanced History of India, it is remarked that "The emperor's army had overrun the whole of northern India, from the snowy mountains of the north to the Nerbudda in the south, and from the Ganjam in the east to Valabhi in the west". Dr. R. C. Majumdar also holds that the whole of northern India was within Harsha's empire. We have already mentioned that Panikkar thinks a modern biographer of Harsha, that Harsha's empire extended from Nepal and Kashmir to the Vindhyas. Another biographer of Harsha, Ettinghansen, also holds the same view.

It has also been pointed out that Kamrup was a subordinate ally of Harshavardhan. In some south Indian inscriptions Harshavardhan has been referred to as Sakalauttarapathanath, i.e., Lord of whole northern India.

Dr. R. C. Majumdar states that there has been an exaggerated notion about the extent of Harsha's empire on the basis of Bana's Harshacharit and Hiuen T-Sang's account. The contention that whole of northern India was under Harsha, Dr. Majumdar points out, "would not bear a moment's scrutiny. For, Kashmir, Western Punjab, Sindh, Gujarat, Rajputana, Nepal, and Kamrup were certainly independent states in his day".[1]

After a detailed discussion of the political condition of India and the status of differnt Kingdoms during the time of Harsha, Dr. Majumdar comes to the conclusion that Harsha's Kingdom originally comprised Thaneswar and Kanauj was later united with it. He also added some territories both in the north and the west. "It may be said to have comprised the Eastern Punjab and Uttar Pradesh. Towards the close of his reign, he had annexed Magadha and even pushed his conquests as far as Orissa and Kongod. It is not definitely known, however, whether the last two with the intervening territory were ever incorporated in his dominions"[2]

It becomes quite obvious that this limit of Harsha's empire was far less wide in expanse than what is generally believed. The findspots of his coins and inscriptions also corporate this view. In the present

---

1 R. C. Majumdar: *Ancient India*, p. 265.

2 *The Classical Age*, p. 113.

State of our it is difficult to agree to the view that Harsha exercised his sovereignty over whole of northern India.

Administration under Harsha

Harshavardhan's administration was personal government without despotism. He believed that constant exertion by the king himself was the secret of administrative efficiency. From Hiuen T-Sang we come to know that the Harsha was indefatigable in his activities as a king. A day was too short for him, such was the task he would perform.

For the control of his extensive empire Harsha relied on his personal supervision executed with untiring energy rather than upon the services of the bureaucracy. He was constantly on the move of punishing the wrongdoer and rewarding the meritorious. It was only during the rains when travelling was impossible in those days that he would stop going to different parts of his empire. His itinerary was a big affair, for like the Mohgul emperors he would have a very extensive number of camp followers all marching beat of the drum.

From the evidence of Hiuen T-Sang and Bana, we may doubtless come to the conclusion that Harsha was a ruler of versatile ability and wonderful personality. Like his predecessor Fa-hien, about two centuries earlier, Hiuen T-Sang was highly impressed by the benign character of the government.

Theoretically the government of Harsha was an autocracy but a considerable measure of autonomy was left at different levels down to the village and the most characteristic feature of his government was the cooperation of the central government with popular bodies. It was, therefore, a government which was a mixture of autocracy and popular elements.

The empire was divided into provinces (*Bhuktis*), provinces into districts (*Visayas*) and the districts into village (*gram*). The government had two parts: the central government and the provincial government.

The emperor was the supreme head of the State. He was assisted by a Council of Ministers. The Council seem to have enjoyed the power of choosing the king when the normal line of succession was disturbed or when the throne fell vacant without an heir-apparent. We know how the Chief Minister, Bhandi, convened a meeting of the Council of Ministers and after deliberating on the suitability of Harsha being placed on the throne and what is more important that the people at large would trust him that Harsha was called upon to ascend the throne after it had fallen vacant due to the death of Rajyavardhan. That the Council of Ministers also exerted its influence on the king in his dealings with foreign potentates is evident from the fact that Rajyavardhana accepted the invitation of Sasanka to meet him and got himself killed. Beal remarks that "Owing to the fault of his ministers, he was led to subject his person to the hand of his enemy". Harsha had a well-organised Secretariat through which the orders of the government were acted upon. Besides minister-in-charge of foreign relations and war, Commander-in-Chief, Chief Commandant of war elephants, there were keeper of Records, and high officials of the state called Mahasamanta, Maharaja, Paramatara, Rajasthaniya, Kumaramatya, Uparika, Visayapati, etc. The top ranking civil service was manned by *Kumaramatyas*. It was from the *Kumaramatyas* that Ministers, district officers, and secretariat officers were appointed. According to Hiuen T-Sang high officials were assigned portions of land, and their maintenance was the responsibility of the cities assigned to them. Lower grade officers were, however, paid in cash or assignment of land. Bana enumerates the high officials each of whom was in charge of a department.

Harsha was a great warrior and quite in keeping with the royal tradition of ancient India, maintained a huge army for military conquests. From Hiuen T-Sang we learn that his army comprised 5,000 elephants, 2,000 cavalry, and 50,000 infantry but with acquisition of more territories he raised the strength of the army to 30,000 cavalry, 7,000 elephants, and 600,000 infanьry. Dr. R. C. Majumdar remarks that "The Statement of Hiuen T-Sang is certainly open to grave doubts". But great attention paid to the cavalry by Harsha, is borne out by Bana.

The system of provincial government, by and large, continued to be as it had been under the Guptas. The high officials already mentioned above, such as the Mahasamantas, Maharajas, were officers who were hereditary local chiefs. Other provincial officers were the Kumaramatyas, Uparikas, etc. Visayapati was the district officer and Gramika, the village officer. The central and provincial government maintained keeper of records called *Karanika.*

Revenue

The royal revenue was derived from three kinds of taxes, namely. the *Bhaga*, *Bali*, and *Hiranya*. The major source of revenue was the *Bhaga*, i.e., the land tax. The term *Bhaga* means 'Share'. *Bhaga* was one-sixth share of the produce of the land taken as revenue. Tax paid in cash realised from the merchants and farmers was called *Hiranya*. The nature of the tax called *Bali* is not very clear, but it is supposed to be an extra tax. Besides these major sources of revenue, there were ferry tax, customs duties, etc. Taxes on merchandise, i.e., customs, were levied with reference to the weights or measures of the merchandise. Forced labour was resorted to, but it was paid for. The burden of taxation, we learn from Hiuen T-Sang, was light.

According to Hiuen T-Sang the crown land was divided into four parts, the income of first part was used for the affairs of the State, that of the second part for payment of officers, the third part for rewarding men of genius, and the fourth part for grant to religious communities.

Penal System

We learn from Hiuen T-Sang that the number of criminals and rebels was too small but should any law be broken, any crime committed or any rebellion staged, the offenders used to be punished severely. For certain officers' mutiliation of limbs, such as cutting off the nose, ears, etc. of the offender and turning him out of the city is to live a forlorn life in the jungles for the rest of his life. For certain offences only small fines were imposed. There was no system of repression for exacting confession from the offenders. For some kinds of offences trial by ordeal was resorted to.

Character of the Administration

Hiuen T-Sang speaks well of the character of Harshavardhan's administration. It is mentioned as a very generous administration and absolutely non-interfering with the lives of the people. But Dr. Altekar does not think that the administration of Harsha was as efficient as that of the time of the Mauryas or of the Guptas. Hiuen T-Sang's eulogy of Harshavardhan's administration is, according to Dr. Altekar, is rather unjustified. In fact, Hiuen T-Sang himself had fallen in the hands of robbers and lost much of his belongings and narrowly escaped with his life. Yet, after taking all things into consideration, it must be conceded that Harshavardhan's administration is not a model one from the point of view of efficiency, it was sufficiently solicitous of the welfare of the people and was based on benign principles.

Religion

One distinctive feature of the Pushyabhuti family was that the kings had their individual preferences in regard to religion. While Prabhakarvardhan was worshipper of the Sun, Rajyavardhan was a Buddhist and Harshavardhan was eclectic in matters of religion and worshipped Siva, Sun and Buddha. Harshavardhan appears to have been deeply impressed by the religious ideas of Hiuen T-Sang and by listening to the latter's discourses on Mahayana Buddhism. Harsha himself turned in favour of Mahayanism.

Kanauj Assembly

In order to take full advantage of Hiuen T-Sang's presence and mastery over the laws of Buddhism and for the spread of this religion Harsha summoned an Assembly at Kanauj in A.D. 643. The Assembly was attended by 3,000 Hinayana and Mahayana Buddhist monks, same number of Brahmanas and Nigrodhas, and nearly 1,000 scholars from the University of Nalanda. Hiuen T-Sang presided over the Assembly and the discussion took place on Mahayanism. Many kings including the King of Valabhi from the extreme west and the King of Kamrup from the extreme east attended the Assembly.

The centre of attraction of the Assembly was the great shrine erected for the purpose on the bank of the Ganges wherein a golden image of Buddha equal in height with Harsha was installed and was kept in a 100 feet high tower. Smaller images of Buddha, 3 feet in height, was carried every day in solemn procession of twenty kings and three hundred elephants. The canopy was borne by the King Harsha himself. The King as he proceeded on the procession scattered pearls, golden flowers, and other precious substances in honour of *Buddha Religion* and the *Order* (Buddha, Dharma, and Sangha)—the three jewels of Buddhist religion. Harsha bathed the image of Buddha with his own hands and carried it on his shoulder to the western tower and offered it gems and thousands of silken robes. After dinner the Assembly sat in a religious disputation.

Harsha heard that Hiuen T-Sang's life was in danger at the hands of rival theologians, particularly because of Harsha's manifest partiality towards him, a proclamation prohibiting all from touching the Master of Law, i.e., Hiuen T-Sang on pain of instant execution. But all who would desire to profit by his instructions need not have to be afraid of this proclamation. As a result no one entered into the disputation.

It was on the occasion of the ceremony at Kanauj that an attempt on the life of Harsha was made by a fanatic, armed with a dagger but the assassin was promptly apprehended. It transpired that the assassin was instigated by the Brahmins who resented excessive royal favour to the Buddhists. Five hundred Brahmins were put under arrest, confession was extorted and some of the leaders were executed and about five hundred were exiled.

It becomes evident that during the time of Harsha there was not only bitter animosity between the Hinayana and Mahayana Buddhism which was all the more accentuated due to Harshavardhan's support of Mahayanism but there was also a great ill-feeling evoked in the minds of the orthodox Hindus when they noticed manifestly partial treatment towards Buddhism upon whom royal favour was being lavished.

Prayag Assembly

After the Kanauj Assembly, Harsha invited the Chinese pilgrims to accompany him to the *Moksha Parishad*, another Assembly, at Prayaga on the confluence of the Jumna and the Ganges. Eighteen royal dignitaries and about half a million people attended this Assembly. Harshavardhan had been holding such Assemblies every five years for the past thirty years and this Assembly held in 643 A.D. was the sixth in the series.

The religious ceremony was of an eclectic nature. On the first day an image of Buddha was installed in a temporary hutment built on the sands and a large quantity of costly clothes and other valuables were distributed among the people. On the second and third days images of the Sun and Siva were similarly honoured, but distribution of gifts was only half of what had been distributed on the first day.

On the fourth day gifts of 100 gold coins, a pearl, and a cotton cloth besides food, perfume, flowers, etc. were given to each of ten thousand religious persons of the Buddhist order. The next twenty days the Brahmans received royal gifts followed by similar distribution of gifts for ten days to the Jainas and other sundry religious sects. This was followed by distribution of gifts to mendicants from distant parts, the poor, destitute, and the orphans. The ceremony lasted for long 75 days. Hiuen T-Sang states that by this all the accumulation of the past five years was exhausted except the war elephants, horses, and other military accoutrements. Hiuen T-Sang mentions that "Besides these the king freely gave away his gems and goods, his clothing and necklaces, ear-rings and bracelets, chaplets and neck-jewel and bright head jewel, all these he freely gave without stint. All being given away, he begged his sister (Rajyasri) for an ordinary second hand garment, and having put it on he paid worship to the Buddhas of the ten regions".

After the Assembly at Prayaga Hiuen T-Sang was permitted to depart. He was offered various gifts which he declined to accept; only he agreed to receive three thousand gold and ten thousand silver pieces to cover his arduous journey.

Religious Condition

Here we may pause for a brief review of the religious condition of the time of Harsha. It goes without saying that the great spirit of religious toleration he practised marked the Maurya and the Gupta periods. As Dr. R. K. Mookerji points out, Harsha's anxiety to preach Mahayana Buddhism was his personal religion and his manifest particularly to Mahayana Buddhist period was open to hostility.

Brahamanical Hindiusm was, it may be pointed out, the predominant religion. Bana refers to followers of Krishna, Kapila, Kanada, Nyaya, and the Upanishada among the Brahmanas. There were also a large number of Siva worshippers. Hiuen T-Sang saw numerous Hindu temples consecrated to Vishnu, Siva, Surya in Kanauj, and a hundred temples at Banares, mostly of Siva. At Multan he saw a Surya temple. Likewise he saw many important monasteries of the Buddhists named after important Buddhist monks. There were also quite a number of Jaina monks living in Jaina monasteries. Thus while the general religious condition of the country was one of religious cosmopolitanism, Harsha's too much leaning towards the Mahayanism in preference to Hinayanism gave rise to religious animosity as we have seen on the occasion of the Kanauj Assembly.

Authorship and Patronage of Learning

Harshavardhan was equally great in both peace and war. He was himself a poet of great skill, remarkable for originality and learning. Bana's praise of Harsha as a poet and man of learning has been corroborated by the Chinese pilgrim I-T-Sing. Harsha is credited with the authorship of three dramas, *Nagananda*, *Ratnavali* and *Priyadarsika.* He was also a great calligraphist. I-T-Sing tells us that Harsha was a great patron of learning and the learned. He was responsible for causing the compilation of the poetic works of the learned men of his court. Five hundred poetical compositions on the previous lives of Buddha had been compiled and presented to him. It is known as *Jatakamala.* Jayadeva, the celebrated poet of *Gitagovinda,* mentions Harsha as a poet comparable to Kalidasa and Bhasa, although there is exaggeration in the statement. Dr. Smith remarks that his play *Nagananda* "is considered to rank among the best works of Indian theatre". The greatest ornament of the literary circle of Harsha's court was the Brahman Bana who composed the *Harshacharit* and *Kadambari.* Harsha was a great patron of learning. Jayasena, Haridatta, and many other scholars of the time received his patronage and encouragement. The revenue of a fourth part of the Crown was spent for the maintenance of the learned and places of learning. The University of Nalanda enjoyed the liberal patronage of Harshavardhan. Education was widely special among the Brahmanas and the Buddhist monks. The learned were held in great esteem by the government.

After enjoying a long reign Harshavardhan died in A.D. 646 or early in A.D. 647.

Estimate of Harsha

The reign of Harshavardhan constitutes and marks an epoch in the history of India. Harsha forces our admiration as a great ruler, a brave warrior, and an able military strategist and above all as a patron of Arts and letters. He was a man of noble impulses and was one of the best monarchs and distinguished personalities that India had produced in the ancient times.

Harsha sat upon throne of Thaneswar at a critical period of the history ; it was also critical from the point of view of the royal family. Rajyavardhan had been killed by enemy, Grahavarman of Kanauj, husband of Rajyasri, was defeated and killed. Rajyasri, sister of Harsha, was herself taken prisoner. Sasanka, king of Gauda and the leader of the Sasanka-Devagupta alliance, was posing a serious danger to the kingdoms of Thaneswar and Kanauj. Harsha not only surmounted these difficulties but succeeded in making Thanesvar the most powerful kingdom of northern India and raising it to the status of an empire.

As a conqueror and a military genius, he had many successful military campaigns to his credit. He suffered occasional defeats no doubt, the most humiliating being that at the hands of Pulakesin II. But he was decidedly the unquestioned master of northern India, and the kings who did not acknowledge his suzerainty at least stood in awe of the great conqueror. Unity of the two thrones of Thanesvar and Kanauj under Harsha must have facilitated the increase of his strength and power.

As a ruler he has been praised by Hiuen T-Sang for the indefatigable manner of his work, forgetting even his food and sleep for the well-being of his subjects. His itinerary all over the empire in all seasons except the rains, kept him in touch with his subjects which facilitated his work for the good of the people and kept the imperial administration alert and in good trim.

Dr. R. K. Mookerjee remarks that as a conqueror and administrator, as one solicitous of the well-being of his subjects Harsha "combined in himself some of the attributes and characteristics of Samudragupta and Asoka". Other historians have also praised Harshavardhan in a somewhat different strain. K. M. Panikkar states that "Harsha has often been compared to Asoka, but there is no similarity between them except of the most superficial kind. The only point of comparison is perhaps that they were both patrons of Buddhism...... A more suitable parallel then that of Asoka is Akbar...... Like Akbar again, Harsha was a military monarch for greater part of his reign. In spite of obvious shortcomings Harsha was without doubt an enlightened monarch and deserves to be considered among India's greatest rulers...... There is no doubt that Harsha, the ruler, the poet, and the religious enthusiast, will ever have an honoured place in Indian history."

Rawlinson, however, has an unqualified praise for Harsha whom he mentions as "a remarkable man and stands besides Asoka and Akbar among the greatest rulers that India has produced. Soldier and administrator, unwearied in his efforts for the good of his subjects, pious and merciful, a patron of literature and himself a poet and dramatist of distinction, he stands forth on the page of history, a bright and fascinating figure".

"Harsha distinguished himself both in the arts of peace and war. He could wield the pen as well as the sword" (Majumdar). If he had built up an empire by his military campaigns, he had himself had contributed to the literary achievements of the period by writing three dramas, *Nagananda, Priyadarsika,* and *Ratnavali* and was a patron of learning and the learned. The luminaries of his court were Banabhatta, Mayura, and other men of literature. Harsha had a part of his revenue marked for the support of men of intellectual eminence. Education was widely diffused under his reign and the great Nalanda University became a centre of culture, education, and seat of Buddhist Philosophy under his patronage.

Banabhatta and Hiuen T-Sang who have left pompous, rhetorical exaggeration about Harsha's personal qualities and activities may not be accepted to us fully. Yet after making due allowances for such fulsome praise, we cannot deny that Harsha was "a ruler of versatile ability and wonderful personality".[1] In his religious activities although he was eclectic yet we miss that measure of complete toleration during his time, which had characterised the Maurya and the Gupta Ages.

Some scholars are of the opinion that Harsha was the last Hindu ruler who attempted to build an empire. Dr. R. C. Majumdar refutes such opinion by saying that "It would be wrong to assume, as many have done, that Harsha was the last great empire-builder in Hindu period and his death marked the end of all successful attempts to restore political unity of northern India. Several empires, which did not compare unfavourably with his, rose and fell in northern India during the next five centuries, and some of them, like the Pratihara empire, were not only bigger but also more enduring".[2]

---

1 *The Classical Age,* p. 117.

2 *Ibid,* p. 113.

By common consent Harshavardhan was decidedly one of the most remarkable rulers and an admirable personality of Hindu India.

RELATION WITH CHINA

Harshavardhana appears to have been very much impressed by what he had come to know of the Chinese emperor's power and prestige from Hiuen T-Sang. He felt encouraged to send a Brahman as ambassador to the court of the Chinese emperor in A.D. 641. The Chinese emperor reciprocated by sending an embassy under Liang-hoai-King with a letter, who reached Harsha's court in A.D. 649. In Ma-Twan-Lin's encyclopaedia historical work, he even is described in the following way: "In (641) Siladitya assumed the title of King of Magadha and an ambassador with a letter to the emperor. The emperor, in his turn, sent Lian-hoai-King as an envoy with a royal patent to Siladitya with an invitation to him to submit to the authority of the Chinese emperor. Siladitya was full of astonishment and asked his officers whether any Chinese envoy ever came to his country since time immemorial. 'Never' they replied in one voice. Thereupon the king went out, received the imperial decree with bended knees, and placed it on his head."

Ettinghausen has taken this as signifying a condition of utter helplessness on the part of Harsha who perhaps was in trouble and sought the help of the Chinese assistance, hence assumed that submissive attitude. Dr. R. C. Majumdar considers such a conclusion drawn by the Chinese chronicler Ma-Twan-Lin as wholly unwarranted, for it is absurd to believe that Harsha could expect any material assistance from such a distant country as China, obviously almost unknown to him before Hiuen T-Sang met him. The whole confusion was due to the invariable practice of the Chinese chroniclers to represent the customary presents from the envoy of a foreign country as tributes.

In the same year (A.D. 643) a second embassy came to Magadha under Li-y-Piao and Weng-hiuen-Tse. This embassy carried with it the reply of the Chinese emperor to Siladitya and was received with great honour. Wang-hiuen-Tse returned to China in A.D. 645. In the meantime Hiuen T-Sang had also reached China. Presumably after hearing the details about India and emperor Harsha from Hiuen T-Sang, Wang was at once sent again to Harsha's court in 646 A.D. This was the third Chinese mission to India, but when it reached India Harsha was already dead. Arjuna, a minister of Harsha, had usurped the throne in the meantime. He massacred the Chinese Mission and looted the presents brought by it for Harsha. Wang-hiuen-Tse obtained military assistance from Srong-tsan-Gampo who was related to the Chinese emperor and defeated Arjun in a battle near Trihut and took him as prisoner to China. Trihut remained under Tibet for some time.

Wang-Hiuen-Tse again visited India in A.D. 657 to offer robes to the Buddhist Holy places.

Hiuen T-Sang

The most celebrated of the Chinese pilgrims who visited India, was Hiuen T-Sang. He is variously called *The Master of Law, Prince of the Pilgrims,* and *Present Sakyamuni,* etc. The material and reliability of the facts of his work have made his work one of the most important documents we possess on the life of India at that time. He visited India during A.D. 630 and A.D. 644.

In those days the Chinese were not permitted by the Chinese government to freely leave China, permission would be necessary for it. Hiuen T-Sang having been refused permission to leave China for a visit to India, he secretly left his country, passed through Tashkhand, Samarkhand, and Balkh in Central Asia and reached Gandhara in 630 A.D. From Gandhara he reached Kashmir and after staying there for two years he came to Punjab and began an itineracy to places connected with the life of Buddha, such as Kapilavastu, Benares, Bodhgaya, Kushinagar, etc.

At the Nalanda University Hiuen T-Sang stayed for long five years studying Buddhist philosophy. Nalanda at that time was the most important centre of studies in Buddhist and Hindu *Dharmasastras.* Hiuen T-Sang received his lessons from Silabhadra, Acharya of the Nalanda University.

Hiuen T-Sang visited Kamrup on the invitation of the King and therefrom came to the court of Harshavardhan who invited him to his Court. On listening to the masterly discourses on *Mahayana* Buddhism Harsha became an ardent follower of *Mahayanism.*

The Chinese pilgrims also visited the Deccan and the Western-ghats. He described the Chalukya King Pulakesin II and Harsha as the two greatest kings of southern and northern India respectively. While at the court of Harshavardhan, Hiuen T-Sang attended the great Kanauj Assembly held in his honour as also the quinquennial Assembly at Prayaga, at the request of Harsha. After the Assembly at Prayaga had been over, he left for home (A.D. 644) with the permission of Harsha who deputed King Udhita to escort him upto the frontier. Laden with numerous images of Buddha made of gold, silver and sandal wood, 657 volumes of Buddhist manuscripts and 150 relics of Buddhas body he proceeded to his home country. He was deposited more than once on his way home, he succeeded in carrying the above materials with him. He reached China in 645 A.D. and on hearing of his experience in India and about emperor Harsha, the Chinese emperor sent Wang-Hiuen-Tse for a second time as an ambassador to the Court of Harsha with various presents (A.D. 646). Wang reached India when Harsha was already dead.

Hiuen T-Sang has left an account of his travels in India which although dealt with Buddhism in India, is replete with details about the life and condition of India prevalent at that time which according to Dr. R. K. Mookerjee "reads like a Gazetteer in the scope of its enquiry and its wealth of details". On reaching China, Hiuen T-Sang abided the rest of his life in translating the manuscripts that he had taken from India.

Hiuen T-Sang's account, translated by Beal, gives us a wealth of information—political, social, economic, and religious aspects of India of the time of Harshavardhan. Importance of his work lies in the fact that the details are acquired on his own first hand information. There are certain statements here and there which have been questioned by modern scholars, yet by and large his account is a faithful narration of the condition of India of the time. It is of particular importance coming as it does, from a foreigner, to find words of praise for the administration, economic and social condition of the time.

We may attempt a resume of the account left by Hiuen T-Sang about India.

Administration

As regards the administration under Harshavardhan, Hiuen T-Sang observes that it was founded on benign principles and the Executive was simple. The people were not required to register themselves, nor were they subjected to forced labour. The *Khas* lands, i.e., the Crown land was divided into four parts. The income of the first part was ear-marked for the affairs of the State, that of the second part for paying the ministers and other officers of the Crown; of the third part for rewarding men of genius and of the fourth for giving alms to religious communities. Taxes were light and services required for the people were also very moderate. Those who cultivated the royal demesne had to pay a sixth part of the produce as revenue. Merchants and traders travel from place to place in pursuit of their business and had to pay customs, tolls, ferry charges on their merchandise. Labour required for the public works was exerted no doubt, but was paid for.

Crimes and rebellions were very few in number, and fewer of them were really troublesome. Law breakers were punished with fines.

There was no corporal punishment but the offenders were thrown out of the protection of the State. In cases of violation of rules of morality or justice, or when a man was guilty of dishonesty or was wanting in respect to the parents, the offenders' nose and ears were cut off and he is expelled from the city to wander in the jungle for the rest of his life. Extortion of confession by torture was not resorted to. In case where the offender was obstinate and would not admit his fault trial by ordeal was resorted to.

Hiuen T-Sang mentions that Harsha was indefatigable in his administrative duties and would often forget his food and sleep in doing his work. Except in rainy season he would be constantly on move visiting different parts of his empire, punishing the evil-doers and rewarding the meritorious.

Hiuen T-Sang mentions that at first Harsha's army comprised 50,000 infantry, 2,000 cavalry and 5,000 elephants and was subsequently raised to 600,000 infantry, 60,000 elephants and 100,000 horses. This statement of Hiuen T-Sang has been doubted by modern scholars.

According to Hiuen T-Sang all transactions of the government were recorded. He refers to Harsha as a great patron of the University of Nalanda where he (Harsha) built a magnificent *Vihara* and a bronze temple.

Society

Hiuen T-Sang tells us that caste-system dominated the Hindu Society. While the Brahmanas performed religious duties, the Kshatriyas comprised the governing class, the Vaisyas were engaged in trade, commerce and industry, the sudras did the work of cultivation and menial work. About the Brahmans and Kshatriya Hiuen T-Sang remarks that the Brahmanas and the Kshatriyas were cleanly and wholesome in their dress, and lived in a homely and frugal way. The rich merchants were very particular in their cleanliness. They braided their hairs, pierced their ears. They mostly went about barefooted, a few wore sandals. All people, Brahman, Kshtriyas, Vaisyas, etc., washed before eating, never used left over food of the previous meals. Metal vessels were washed clean after every meal. They washed their hands and mouth after every meal.

About the general nature of the people Hiuen T-Sang remarked that they were naturally light-minded, but were upright and honourable. In money matters, they were without craft and in the administration of justice they were judicious and considerate. "They are not deceitful or treacherous in their conduct, and they are faithful to their oaths and promises and their rules of government, there is remarkable rectitude, while in their behaviour there is much gentleness and sweetness."

No inter-caste marriage was permissible and marriage within one's own caste was prohibited upto certain degrees of relationship. There were certain restrictions in taking of food by different castes. Purity of diet was strictly observed. Onions and garlics were rarely used. Widow marriage was not permissible. The rite of *Sati* was prevalent and Queen Yashomati burnt herself to death after the death of her husband Rajyavardhan.

Economic

Hiuen T-Sang was very much impressed by the economic prosperity of India. He mentions that the people of India had a high standard of living. The main source of the economic life was agriculture. The soil was very fertile and the produce was abundant. Besides cereals which constituted the staple food, various fruits and vegetables were produced. Main food of the people consisted of wheat, parched grains, sugar, milk, ghee, and on occasions fish, veneson, mutton, etc. Flesh of certain birds and animals as also beef were forbidden as food. Gold and silver coins, cowries and pearls were in circulation as medium of exchange.

About the industries, Hiuen T-Sang remarks that the art of making fine silk cloth, woollen and cotton fabrics had reached a high degree of excellence at that time. Of the various textiles, a mixed cloth called *Kausiya* was made of silk and cotton. Kasuma or linen cloth was manufactured from cotton, flux, and jute. Blankets were also manufactured from wool.

Gold ornaments were manufactured for the king and the grandees. Rings, bracelets, tiaras, neckchains, etc., were manufactured with great skill.

Industries had their guilds. The Brahmans, however, did not take part in the industrial activities and the Sudras were confined to agriculture.

Towns and Cities

Hiuen T-Sang mentions that the towns and villages had wide and high walls with inner gates. The streets and lanes were tortuous and the roads winding. Thoroughfares were dirty. Stalls with signboards were arranged on both sides of the streets. Butchers, fishermen, dancers, scavangers, etc., had to live outside the city. There people had to keep to the left side of the road while coming in or going out of the towns and cities. Walls and buildings of the towns and cities were built of bricks and tiles. Towers, balconies and belvederes were made of bamboos and wood. "Different buildings have the same form as those in China". Walls of buildings were smeared with mud, or lime mixed with cowdung for purity. The monasteries were constructed with extraordinary skill. Three-storied tower at each of the four corners was built and beams and projecting heads were carved with great skill into different shapes. Doors, windows, and the walls were painted profusely. In the centre of the monastery was a hall, high and wide. Hiuen T-Sang tells us that many new cities came into prominence while the old ones were on the decline. Pataliputra had ceased to have its former glory and Kanauj took its place. He saw hundreds of monasteries and two hundred Hindu temples in Kanauj itself. The City of Kanauj had "lofty structures, beautiful gardens, tanks of clear water and museum of varieties collected from strange lands". Sravasti, Kapilavastu had been in ruins. Prayaga became prominent as a town. Nalanda, the seat of learning, both religious and secular, and Valabhi were places with a Buddhist learning.

Learning and Religion

Learning during this period was diffused through monasteries. While religious works were written on paper of leaves, the Vedas were transmitted orally and not reduced to writing. Brahmi scripts were used. Sanskrit was the language of the learned and grammar was strictly followed in the use of this language. Education of a person lasted from the age of 9 to 30 years of age. About Nalanda, where Hiuen T-Sang himself had studied for five years, where eminent scholars held disputations and one who would distinguish himself by refined language, subtle investigation, logic and deep penetration, would highly be honoured and one who would fail in his argument and knowledge would be publicly disgraced.

Hiuen T-Sang mentions that the general nature of life was largely influenced by Buddhism. He had noticed numerous Buddhist monasteries and about 200 Hindu temples in Kanauj itself. He also mentions the eclectic nature of Harsha's religion and describes how he honoured Buddha, Surya and Siva at Prayaga. That the period was not free from religious animosity is proved from Hiuen T-Sang account. There was bitter animosity between the two great sects of the Buddhist Church, i.e., the Hinayanists and the Mahayanists but also between the Buddhists and the Brahmanical Hindus. From Hiuen T-Sang it is known that Mahayana doctrine was more predominant than Hinayanism.

Hiuen T-Sang's account is not only an excellent source of information about India of the time but significant for the praise contained in it from the pen of a foreigner who saw things himself and therefore a matter of pride for India.

Banabhatta's Harshacharit

The most brilliant luminary in the Harsha's Court was his Court-poet Brahman Banabhatta. He was the author of the *Harshacharit* which is an eulogistic history of the reign of Harsha and a very reliable source of our information regarding the reign of the monarch, excluding of course the pompous rhetorics used by the poet.

The initial chapter of *Harshacharit* is devoted to the life and family of Banabhatta himself, chapters second to fourth to the ancestry of Harsha and the history of Thanesvar, and the rest is devoted to Harsha's military campaigns and the different religious sects living in the Vindhyas.

Bana's work gives us an idea of the political, social, economic, and religious life of the time and helps us considerably in the task of reconstruction of the history of the reign of Harshavardhan. His work has been translated into English by Cowell and Thomas. About the merit of the work of Banabhatta, Cowell and Thomas remarks that "The Court, the camp, the quiet village and still more quiet monasteries and retreats, whether of Brahmanas or Buddhists, are all painted with singular power". *Harshacharit* supplements as well as corroborates the work of Chinese traveller Hiuen T-Sang.

Bana's narrative, however, abruptly ends with the recovery of Rajyasri from the Vindhya forests. From Bana we know of Harsha's determination for world-wide conquests and the issue of a proclamation to all kings of India to either accept his allegiance or to be prepared for a fight with him. We are also told how Bhaskaravarman of Kamrup negotiated a friendly alliance and not one of vassalage. About Harsha's determination to make the earth Gaudaless within a specified time but no reference to Harsha's success against Sasanka of Gauda has been referred to by the poet.

Despite the usual exaggeration of a royal panegyrist while praise of his master had been done, the work of Banabhatta in essential parts is reliable and where he is corroborated by the foreign traveller Hiuen T-Sang, it is unassailable.

Nalanda

Nalanda was the seat of learning and culture during the reign of Harshavardhan and continued to be so long after Harsha. I-tsing who visited India after Hiuen T-Sang compared Nalanda with the best of the Chinese Universities. The Nalanda monastery was founded by one of the later Gupta Kings, in the 5th century A.D. It received patronage not only from the Indian King, but being a centre of learning where specially Buddhist philosophy was taught as also the Vedic Philosophy, logic, grammar, medicine, received patronage from foreigners. Originally started as a Buddhist monastery, Nalanda soon outgrew its limits as a seat of Buddhist learning and became a seat of learning of various subjecs, giving it the real character of a University.

The Nalanda University had a very vast campus with magnificent buildings. There were eight colleges in it, one of which was built by King Balaputradeva of Sumatra. On the inscription of Yasovarmadeva there is eloquent praise of grandeur of the buildings of the Nalanda University. According to Hiuen T-Sang the University campus was enclosed by a wall made of bricks. The eight colleges were built in a row and one gate opened into the great college from which eight other halls were separated. There were Priests' chambers which were of four stages. "The stages have dragon projections and coloured caves, pearled pillars, carved and ornamented, richly adorned balustrades, and roofs covered with tiles that reflect the light in a thousand shades."

The students were provided with all kinds of facilities expected in a University. There were three great libraries in the University, namely, the *Ratnasagara*, *Ratnadodhi*, and *Ratnaranjak*. Hiuen T-Sang who studied in the University of Nalanda for long five years saw more than 10,000 students and teachers there. The students and teachers came from all over India as well from countries like China, Japan, Korea, Tibet, Ceylon, Sumatra and other countries of South East Asia.

The Nalanda University did not only attrack scholars in large numbers particularly from the Buddhist countries but sent out scholars to outside countries like China, Tibet, etc. Santarakshit, Padmasambhava, Buddhakirti, Sthiramali, Kamalasila went to Tibet while Kumarajiva, Paramartha, Subhakara, and Dharmadeva went to China. They were responsible for the spread of Buddhism in those countries.

Some of the most famous teachers at Nalanda were Nagarjuna, Anga, Aryadeva, Vasubandhu, Dinnaga, Silabhadra, Silrakshit, Dharmapala, Jinamitra, Prabhamitra, Chandrapala, etc. Atisadipankar had been a student and later a teacher at Nalanda before he was sent to Tibet at the request of the Tibetan King for the purpose of reforming Buddhism there. A huge number of scholars of great ability and learning were there whose fame had spread far and wide. The students and teachers discussed subjects of studies and they found the day to be too short and spent day and night in scholarly discussion for perfection of their knowledge.

Nalanda had the true character of a university for it stood for freedom of knowledge and welcomed knowledge from all quarters, religions and sects. Admission to this University was restricted by selection test and the percentage of rejection of intending candidates was as high as 80%. According to Hiuen T-Sang, Nalanda University was joined by learned scholars for attaining perfection.

The expenses of the University was met from rich endowments made to it by Indians and foreigners and the liberal patronage it received from the Indian royal houses, such as the Guptas, Harshavardhana, and the Palas. The University had vast agricultural lands, dairy farms from which supplies of rice, milk, butter, etc. came.

The Nalanda University was not only a residential University but it had *Viharas* affiliated to it as is evident from the find of seals inscribed with *Sri Nalanda-Mahavihara-Arya-Bhikshu-Samghasya,* that is, "of the Governing Body of the august University of Nalanda. Seals had *Dharmachakra* inscribed on them. Likewise *Viharas* or Colleges also used seals mentioning the fact of their affiliation to the Nalanda University. Obviously association of the name of the Nalanda University was by itself a great honour for colleges of the time.

When I-Tsing visited India in the last quarter of the seventh century, he found the Nalanda University equally great and important centre of learning. He found more than 3,000 resident students at Nalanda. It had then 200 villages under it for meeting the expenditure of the University. He mentions that the rules of the monastery of Nalanda were very strict. Nalanda University continued to be the most important centre of learning upto the twelfth century A.D. and its end came in the wake of the end of Buddhism in India.

CHAPTER SEVENTEEN

GENERAL REVIEW

I. ECONOMIC FACTORS IN POLITICAL HISTORY

A. Economic Factors in the Growth and Decline of Magadhan Imperialism

For the period of Magadhan imperialism our sources for the economic history are Kautilya's *Arthasastra* and the Smritis. The *Arthasastra* mentions that the powers of the king were of three categories: the strength of heroic valour, the army, and the treasury. According to him, the Treasury is the source of the army, while the army is the means of acquiring and preserving both itself and the treasury.

According to the traditional principles of taxation prevalent in India from the time long before the period of Magadhan ascendancy, the taxes should be fixed by the king in such a way that he himself and the producer, that is, the taxpayer may participate in the result. Both from Kautilya and Manu we come across another principle: a king must follow in respect of taxation. The king while must not grant advances or remissions to the cultivators in an excessive quantity he must not take more than what was legitimately due to him, even though he might be in straitened circumstances. The broad fact that was recognised at the period under review was that the State revenue ultimately depended on the production of wealth by individuals and whatever would tend to diminish the latter was bound to react on the former. Thus the fundamental principle of taxation of modern times appears to have been followed in classical antiquity in India, namely, that the wealth produced by the subjects is the source of the State revenue. Among the qualities of a good treasury mentioned by Kautilya, Kamandaka, and Somadeva the most important was that it should be capable of supporting expenditure and meeting the unforeseen emergencies. As a corollary to the above empirical rules, was the injunction that king should increase the funds of the State day by day.

We may now turn to look at the application of the empirical

rules mentioned above relating to the State finances during the Magadhan epoch of the many factors that contributed to the greatness of the Magadhan Kingdom which acquired the first imperial status under the Mauryas, material resources played a very important part, although the strategic position, the character, and the spirit of the people gave life and efficiency to it.

The outstanding achievement of Mahapadmananda was completion of the political unity of northern India and raising Magadha from a local Kingdom to the Status of an empire. "Northern India, by virtue of its fertile soil and favourable climate, its magnificent waterways and its extensive coast line must have from the first enjoyed exceptional opportunity provided by nature for economic prosperity. Under the strong and centralised administration of the Nandas trade and industry could not but advance greatly. In particular, the needs of their exceptionally wealthy Court, to which later traditions bear witness, and their organised administration heralding that of the Mauryas must have given a great impetus to industrial and commercial effort".[1] Thus the opportunities offered by northern India for economic prosperity under the Nandas while were taken full advantage of by them, the economic prosperity in its turn provided opportunities for the Mauryas to raise Magadha to the first greatest imperial power in ancient India.

Let us now turn our attention to the various sources of revenue that made for the strength of the treasury which made the army and the administration strong. The vast army of the Maurya emperors was responsible for the political unification of India under them and the army and the Court administration and efficiency depended on the able and judicious management of the country's economy. We may recall Kautilya's dictum that it was not on the amount that the government could extort from the people that the quality of administration rested, but on what the people could pay to the government with ease keeping enough for their sustenance. Obviously the imperial house of Magadha from the time of Mahapadmananda the *Treasury* was kept systematically strong. The economic life was largely controlled by the State.

The various sources of the revenue, i.e., Treasury, were: (1) Agriculture: The land revenue was the main source of the income of the State. The economic prosperity of the Nanda and the Maurya times was rendered possible by the abundance of India's agri-

---

[1] K. A. Nilkanta Sastri: *Age of the Nandas and Mauryas*, p. 260.

cultural resources. Megasthenes bears it out. According to him vast plains of great fertility are all intersected by a multitude of rivers. The soil bears on its surface all kinds of fruits and it has underground, numerous veins of all sorts of metals—gold, silver, copper, iron, and other metals. The land revenue reached a remarkably high level.

The principal branch of land revenue was the king's share of the produce of the soil called *Bhaga*, assessed at various rates from one-fourth to one-twelfth part of the produce. Under Asoka it was one-eighth. Other levies on agriculture were *Bali*, an undefined cess above *Bhaga*, and may be compared with *abwabs* of the Mughal revenue system in India. The third levy was called *Kara*, i.e., a property tax ; next was the *Vivita*, i.e., a tax on the Pastures. *Rojju* was a cess payable for survey and settlement and lastly, *Chorarajju*, a cess for police administration, i.e., *Chowkidari* tax. From Kautilya and the Smritis we came to know that elaborate arrangement for survey of land was there and the revenue of different types of land varied.

There were state farms which were ploughed and sown under supervision of the king's stewards by slaves, convicts of free labourers. Fields left uncultivated by the king's stewards were let out to tenants who shared half or one-fourth of the produce according to the labour or cattle provided by them. They were in the nature of bargadars, i.e., sharing of crops. The royal farms let out to cultivators, if irrigated, would be liable to water-rates.[1]

There were model farms run by the government for improvement of agriculture in the country. "Seeds of various crops to be grown were collected here. Government had its own flower, fruits and vegetable gardens and undertook cultivation of commercial crops like cotton (*Karpasa*) and jute (*Kshauma*)."[2]

There were landless agricultural labourers, slaves, and other ordinary labourers for wages who worked on the royal farms or on the fields of the peasant proprietors.

The village cattle and domestic animals comprised cows, buffaloes, goats, sheep, asses, pigs, dogs, etc. The State maintained cattle farms, stud-farms, and had necessary staff for the purpose such as *go-palaka* (cowherd), *dohaka* (milker), *manthaka* (churner), etc. The

---

[1] U. N. Ghosal : *The Hindu Revenue System*, pp. 44-45.

[2] R. K. Mookerji : *Chandragupta Maurya and His times*, pp. 198-199.

cattle farms reared calves, steeds, draught oxen, stud-bulls, buffaloes, etc.

(1) **Trade and Industry:** Considerable development for trade and industry is noticeable during this period. There are references to 18 standard handicrafts in the Jatakas, in epigraphic and the literary records.

There were handicrafts like wood cutting, stone-cutting, painting, ivory-working, smithy, jewellery, confectionery, pottery, weaving, bow and arrow making, etc. Magasthenes mentioned that gold, silver, copper, and iron mining were very important industries of the time. There were smaller crafts such as the tanners, butchers, fishermen, musicians, hunters, trappers, etc. Localisation of industries was also there. The village of potters, iron-smiths, carpenters, etc. referred to in different records point to the localisation of industries in those days.

The State had monopoly in many industries which entailed heavy investments and needed pioneering. The mining industry was nationalised for its supreme importance to the Statute as primary source of its wealth. The government worked the mines of gold, silver, diamond, gems, precious stones, and other inferior metals like copper, led, iron, bitumen. Manufacture of salt was also a government monopoly. The system was worked through granting of licences to private lessees. Manufacture of arms and armaments, boats and ships, minting of coins, etc., were in the hands of the government.

Needless to say, a large amount was earned by the government from this source. The entire trade was not in the hands of the government. A large field of industry was occupied by Private Industrialists.

That an active encouragement of trade and industry was a state policy under the Nanda-Maurya period is illustrated from the above as also from the construction of trade routes and arrangement for their security. The State also took special care to protect the artisans and merchants.

The State earned considerable revenue from tolls, transit duties, customs, etc. In Arthasastra there is mention of *Sulka* (toll), *dvaradeya* (gate-duty), duty on *Sura* (liquor), duty on weights and measures as also on market. Rates of duties on imported goods was generally one-fifth of the value. Tolls were levied on both exports and imports. In Arthasastra a distinct schedule of rates is laid down for specific classes of goods.

Among the sources of revenue were also included the revenue

from the forests, game forests, elephant-forests, etc. Although we have no specific information about the revenues derived from the forests yet from Kautilya's description of the duties of the Superintendent-in-Charge of forests, we get the idea that he was not only to collect forest produce but also arrange for its being turned into commodities. The proceeds of the sale of the forest products and manufactures from them brought a good revenue to the state. Fines for theft of forest produce or poaching for games made up a good revenue item.

There were also miscellaneous receipts from levies on cattle and a fee in the nature of inheritance fee. There were taxes on hunters, artisans, craftsmen, traders, labourers, etc. Besides all these, the king could replenish his treasury at times of emergency by levying extra-tax.

When we remember the principle of taxation followed by the State at that period, the long list of various taxes, cesses and levies did not amount to any heavy burden on the people for the State realised what the people could pay with ease not what the State could extort with force.

The economic prosperity, therefore, was one of the major factors for the growth of Magadhan imperialism and conversely the growth of imperialism with its extremely efficient revenue administration, economic policy led to economic prosperity to an unprecedented scale. The touch of modernism in the Nanda-Maurya economic policy, for instance, State participation in costly and pioneering enterprises, State monopoly in mining, forest and similar other industries of national importance, model farming run by the State, etc., conduced to the growth of the Magadhan imperialism which marked an epoch in the history of ancient India.

But the system of finance is not by itself helpful unless there is efficient revenue administration. From Arthasasastra we come to know of two high officials called *Samarharta* and *Sannidhata* who were vested with immediate control of whole financial administration. They combined finance with other functions. For instance, *Samarharta* combined certain functions of police and criminal justice with those of finance. He had to keep watch, through spies, on the conduct of cultivators, hermits, merchants and superintendents, and also to bring to book persons living by underhand means by either punishing them with fines or banishing them. In his financial functions he had to look after seven specified constituents of State income and expenditure, to raise revenue, increase the income and diminish the expenditure.

Sannidhata was in charge of the construction of government buildings, and depositing various articles in the royal store house. Erection of storehouse, royal treasury, armoury, jail and the courts of justice, etc. to receive money, gems, articles of great as well as small value, etc. Below the *Samarharta* and *Sannidhata* there were the *Adhyakhas*, i.e., Superintendents. There were diverse clas ses of superintendents each in charge of a specific financial duty, such as Accounts Officer, treasury, mines, mint, metals, salt, gold, agriculture, forests produce, toll and octroi, shipping, royal merchandise, trade, etc.

The scientific revenue system and efficient revenue administration during the Nanda-Maurya period showed the characteristics of an advanced economy. But during the rule of the successors of Asoka with the dissolution of the Maurya dominion, the country lost her political unity and even the large kingdoms that arose during Post-Asokan period were poor substitutes for the vanished empire. The successive foreign invasions dislocated trade and industry, at least temporarily. The economic decline had already set in even before the end of the rule of Asoka. The contemporary canon law discouraged participation of the Brahmanas in agriculture and industry. The Brahmanical Smritis looekd upon agriculture and industry and to a less extent trade with disfavour. According to Smritis, trade was the best of occupation of the Vaisyas. "A Brahmana or a Kshatriya even in distress must avoid agriculture".[1] Again a large number of agricultural, pastoral, industrial and commercial occupations are placed under social, religious and even legal disabilities under Smriti Law. "A person making a sea-voyage, for instance, is excluded from Sraddha".[2] The Buddhist and the Jaina canons were equally unfavourable to economic progress. The Buddhist monks were forbidden to cultivate land. The Jainas went so far as to forbid even laymen to engage in agricultural operations or certain types of industries and trades. "The canon laws by condemning agriculture and a number of basic occupations, must have retarded the application of capital and enterprise to their development. The free movement of labour and capital was restricted by the association of specific trades and industries with particular castes and sub-castes." Both Brahmanical and Buddhist and Jaina canon law discouraging all attempts to improve material condition of the people brought about a set back in the economic progress of the country. The economic progress which was one of the major

---

[1] *Comprehensive History of India*, Vol. II, p. 450.

[2] *Idem.*

factors in the development of Magadhan imperialism and its retardation partly contributed to its decline.

B. Economic Factors in the History of the Imperial Kushanas

The successive foreign invasions after the fall of the Mauryas dislocated trade and industry for some time. "And according to all accounts, the country soon recovered and advanced towards economic progress. In the first century A.D. the expansion of India's trade with Roman World ...... brought about a marked development of India's agricultural and industrial production."[1]

The period that intervened between the fall of the Maurya empire and the rise of the Guptas was covered by a succession of foreign rule and till we reach the period of the imperial Kushanas our knowledge about the economic condition and revenue administration is fragmentary and imperfect. But some inscriptions, the *Periplus*, Roman coins, etc. give us valuable, though indirect information in this regard.

The occupation of north-western India by non-Indian peoples was advantageous to the merchants since it led to trade with regions which had as yet been untapped. "The Indo-Greek Kings encouraged contact with western Asia and the Mediterranean world".[2] Under the Saka-Parthian-Kushana rule, particularly under the Kushanas, the Indian economy registered a remarkable progress and the peace and contentment of the people became manifest in the cultural progress of the time. During this period central Asia was brought into the orbit of the trading activities of the Indian merchants and their commercial contacts gradually extended to China. Again the Roman demand for spices and other Indian luxuries took the Indian traders to South-East Asia and brought the Roman traders to southern and western India. The result was the prosperity of India, particularly of the merchantile community all over India. This is borne out by inscriptions, charitable donations and literature of the time. The *Periplus* gives a long list of Indian Sea ports through which seaborne trade with foreign countries was conducted. The progress of trade and commerce does not, however, suggest that agriculture had decreased despite certain prohibitions put by the Brahmanical, Buddhist, and Jaina caninical laws in the pre-

[1] *Comprehensive History of India,* Vol. II, p. 456.

[2] Romila Thapar : *A History of India,* Vol. I, p. 109.

ceding age. That the age of the imperial Kushanas was one of great economic prosperities is also borne out by the huge influx of Roman gold into India through commerce, which was lamented over by the Roman writer Pliny.

Reference must be made to the guild system which continuing from the Maurya period became a more important factor to the economic and urban life of the time for it organised production, shaped public opinion, set standard of quality and above all saved manufacturers from individual competition and offered security to the artisans. Besides the guilds, there were workers' bodies which used their own seals and emblems. There are instances where guilds made donations to religious institutions, built caves and stupas. The ivory workers' guild of Vidisa carved the stone sculpture on the gateways and the railings round the Sanchi Stupas. Another important fact worth mentioning is that the guilds acted as bankers, financiers and trustees.

Localisation of industries took place because industries were organised in areas where raw materials were available in abundance. Silk, cotton and woollen textiles, iron, copper and lead mining, gold, silver, precious stones mining, musk, salt collection, production of saffron, spices, sandal wood, etc. were the main economic activities of the time, besides production of cereals and commercial crops.

Barbaricum on the Indus delta, Barygaza, Tamralipti were important ports through which export and import trades were conducted. From Ethiopia came the African ivory and gold for Indian muslin. In the island of Socotra the Indian rice, wheat, textiles and female slaves were exchanged for tortoise-shells. Countries in the Persian gulf received Indian copper, teak, sandal wood, ebony and sent to India pearls, purple dye, wine, textiles, dates, slaves, etc. Barbaricum imported topaz, coral, resin, frankincense, glass, silver, gold plate, wine and exported variety of spices, turquoise, lapis-lazuli, muslin, silk-yarn, indigo, etc. Barygaza (Broach) was the oldest and largest port on the western coast of India and handled the bulk of the trade with western Asia. Likewise Tamralipti handled the bulk of the trade with South-East Asia from the eastern Indian countries.

The economic impact of the brisk trade carried on with foreign countries which led to an unprecedented influx of gold was to be seen in the prosperity of the Kushanas as also of the people in general and the contact with foreign countries through commercial relations led to exchange of ideas which contributed to the cultural excellence of the time.

II. CHIEF FEATURES OF THE SOCIETY (4th CENTURY B.C. TO 6th CENTURY A.D.)

(A) **Social and Socio-economic Divisions:** During the Nanda-Maurya period, the Fourfold order of society which was the most characteristic feature of the Aryan way of life, i.e., the *Varna* and *Asrama*, continued as the dominant feature of the society. Our sources of information for the social condition of this period are many and varied, consisting of religious literature, foreigner's account, and epigraphic records. Divergence of opinions among these different sources although create some confusion, yet it is possible to draw a reliable and comprehensive picture of the period from the late fourth century B.C. to the sixth century A.D. The Society was divided into four *Varna*, that is, castes, the Brahmanas, Kshatriyas, Vaisyas, and Sudras.

Duties of the different castes enumerated in the *Dharmasastras* have been analysed by Kautilya in an inimitable manner. The Brahmanas had to do the duties of study, teaching, worship, work as priest, give gifts, accept gifts. The Kshatriyas had to study, worship, give gifts, accept the profession of arms, protect living beings. The Vaisyas had the duties of studying, worshipping, giving gifts, doing agricultural work, cattle-rearing, and trading. The Sudras' duties were menial work for the upper three castes, production of wealth by their labour, arts and crafts. It may be noted that while study, worship and giving gifts were enjoined for the upper three castes, the lowest caste, the Sudras, had to go without education, self-improvement through worship or even to make gifts, but production of wealth, arts and crafts were their duties which required physical labour and acquisition of artisans' skill.

The Brahmanas were assigned the highest status and dignity by the Brahmanical canon law. *Manu Samhita* gives highest status and supremacy to Brahmanas but at the same time laid stress on their acquiring superior knowledge and qualifications on which their superior status vested. The Brahmana was to fill the highest offices of the state and society by working as teacher, priest, judge, prime minister, assessor, as member of Dharma Parishad, legal commission, etc. A Brahmana would lose his status if he violated the rules relating to food, profession, livelihood, etc. prescribed for him. Similar rules were also prescribed for other castes as well.

The Sudras had menial service as "his portion in life". The Sudras were not permitted to hear sacred texts nor were they eligible for sacraments. Manu, however, did not deny the right of learning to the Sudras. It does not escape notice of a very casual observer that the lot of the Sudras was an unenviable one.

We may now turn our attention to the doctrine of rise and fall in caste status as advocated by Manu and Yajnavalka after Gautama. If a Brahmana marries a Sudra woman, and a daughter is born of this union and that daughter marries a Brahmana and in this way daughter after daughter marries Brahmanas for seven generations the seventh generation will be Brahmana. Conversely, if a Brahmana who marries a Sudra woman and a son is born of this union, and the son marries a Sudra woman and in this way if son after son marries Sudra woman then from the seventh generation the son becomes a Sudra. The same rule applied in cases of Kshatriya and Vaisya marriage.

K. A. N. Sastri remarks that "The period intervening between the downfall of the Imperial Mauryas and the rise of the Gupta emperors marks a crisis in India's social history". On the one hand Asoka's imperial propaganda had given Buddhist an all-India character and spread it into East and South-East Asia. In the course of this religious movement within the fold of the Indian Society, the situation became somewhat complicated due to the influx of foreigners of altogether alien and cultural standards, the first reaction of which was gloomy forebodings of universal decay and dissolution of the social fabric which can be noticed in the contemporary Brahmanical works. "And yet in this age of seeming social collapse were sown the seeds of great revival." Brahmanism, far from being engulfed by onrush of the waves of foreigners, found in some of the ruling houses of the northern and southern India patrons who upheld the Brahmanical society and its religious practices. This also strengthened the Brahmanical society to meet its two rivals Buddhism and Jainism. At the same time the problem created by the settlement of foreigners in India was solved with great rapidity with which the Brahmanical society assimilated these foreign elements completely into its fold.

Another significant social development of this period was the increase in the number of mixed castes. We have already seen how the Brahmanical society solved the problems of intermarriage and social status of the offspring of intermarriage between the different castes of the fourfold social orders. But intermarriage between the traditional Brahmanical four castes and the Yavanas, Sakas, Chinas, Pahlavas, etc. gave rise to many more mixed castes or social unity.

It becomes clear, therefore, that while the traditional fourfold division of castes continued to exist during the period under review, many mixed castes grew up as a result of intermarriages. This proves that caste-system had not been become rigid or petrified although it was showing signs of hardening, and had not reached the stereotyped form as we see in today.

The Buddhist and the Jaina texts even in the epics give a different picture of the caste-system. According to these, one does not become a Brahmana by birth, but by education and conduct. In the *Mahabharata* as also in the Buddhist texts the son of a Brahmana is a Brahmana even when his mother be a Kshatriya or Vaisya. According to the Buddhist and the Jaina texts Kshatriyas are superior to the Brahmanas and among the four castes, the Kshatriyas are given the first place. In these texts the superiority of the Brahmanas is challenged and this is due to the fact that although in theory the priestly power is higher than royal power, in practice the king always gets the upper hand. The Buddhist texts also show that caste was not rigidly tied to craft. Kshatriyas were seen to work as potters, basket-makers, cooks, and garland makers, whereas Vaisyas worked as tailors, potters, etc. Brahmanas worked as physicians, traders, policemen, hunters, menials of kings, etc. Both the Buddhist and Jaina texts describe a normal Brahmana as one serving the society as a hermit, or a rishi and living in forest. The first class Brahmanas are described as persons who served as the king's priests, as ministers, ambassadors and military officers. From all this it is clear that the Buddhist texts and even the epics did not believe in the rigid caste structure of the Brahmanical social system.

Megasthenes enumerates seven classes or castes into which the whole population of India was divided : Philosophers, Husbandmen, Herdsmen, Artisans, Military, Overseers or Spies, Councillors or Assessors, and remarks that no one was allowed to marry out of his caste or exchange one profession for the other.

This division of the Indians into seven castes is contrary to the age-old fourfold division of castes and must have been due to his confusing the professional classes with *castes*.

In conclusion we may say that during the period from the fall of the Maurya and before the rise of the Guptas the Hindu Society became something like a federation of castes and sub-castes whose members sometimes inter-marry, more frequently in earlier than in later ages, but which nevertheless retained their separate identity".[1] The caste was not, however, altogether static, for new sub-castes arose from migration, fusion, and inter-marriage.

---

1 *The Age of Imperial Unity*, p. 551.

By the early decades of the Gupta Age a strong Brahmanical reaction appears to have set in against the Buddhist and Jaina ascendancy. There was an intensification of the social division into four *Varnas* and pre-eminence of the Brahmanas. The reform movement started by the founders of Buddhism and Jainism lost its momentum and a Counter-Reformation movement by the Brahmanical Hinduism became a strong force. The problem of social fitment of the foreign hordes was solved by the barbarians adopting Indian social manners and faith and orthodox Hinduism meeting the problem by conceding the foreigners the status of Kshatriyas.

The age-old division of the society into four *Varnas* continued to be the keynote of the society under the Guptas and there is no doubt that rules relating to the duties of the different *Varnas* and their mutual relation were generally observed.

Anuloma and *Pratiloma* marriages, that is, the marriage of a Brahmana with a woman of an inferior caste and that of a woman of a superior caste with man of an inferior caste, respectively, took place during the Gupta period. Both from Smriti Law in the Gupta Age and accounts of Chinese travellers the Brahmanas appear to have retained social status assigned to them by the old Smriti Law. Even in punishing a Brahmin offender no capital punishment and confiscation of property were permissible.

As in the preceding age there were not only numerous mixed castes during the Gupta period, but also *Chandalas* who occupied the lowest stratum in the mixed castes and did the meanest work, such as claiming unclaimed dead bodies and doing the duties of hangmen. The *Chandalas* were not to move about in towns or villages at night and in the day time they had to move with distinguishing marks in order that pollution of other classes might not take place by their contact. They had to live outside the limits of villages. The beginning of untouchability may thus be traced from earliest times and continued to show signs of rigidity with the passage of time. Further removed from the *Chandalas* were the Pulindas, Sabaras, Kiratas, etc. who lived in the hills and forests of the Vindhyas. They were given to outlandish practice, such as offering human flesh to deities, living on hunting, partaking of meat and wine.

Caste System

The existing institution of caste is peculiar to India and is "the most vital principle of Hinduism", dominaing the Hindu social life, manners, moral and thought. Dr. Apte very aptly remarks that "The elaborate institution known as the caste system among the Hindus in

India may almost be said to be without a parallel in the world" although there is hardly a country in the world where some kind of social gradation is not met with.

Dr. V. A. Smith defines a caste as a "group of families internally united by peculiar rules for the observance of ceremonial purity, especially in the matters of diet and marriage". One caste is distinguished from the other by a common origin, name, tutelar deity, occupation and ceremonies, as also by homogeneous caste-group.

There has been a good deal of controversy among the scholars about the origin and development as also about the interpretation of various phrases and words in the *Rig Veda* relating to caste. There are also various speculations in later Brahmanical literature about the origin of castes. From the famous *Purusha-Sukta* we learn that the *Brahmanas* were created out of the head, the *Kshatriyas* from the arms, *Vaisyas* from the thighs and the *Sudras* from the feet of the Creator, the primeval *Purusha.* But this theory has been rejected by many scholars, according to whom the caste-system was developed later. The transition of the Aryans from the caste-system during the *Yajur-Veda* time was the result of further migration of the Aryans from the Punjab to the east.

Dr. Apte refers to a scientific explanation of the caste-system accepted by some scholars. Ceaseless fight of the Aryans with, and the conquest of, aborigines led to the merger of petty tribes into centralised kingdoms. Thus emerged the powerful king while the lesser tribal chiefs and princes were reduced to the status of nobles. The kings needed armed forces for resisting external invasions by other tribes or for quieting revolts. The nobility was drafted into the army. This gave rise to the warrior class, the Kshatriyas. The people afforded protection from the warrior class settled down to peaceful life devoted to agriculture, trade, industry, etc. They constituted the third class, the *Vis* later called the *Vaisyas.* Side by side there grew up a distinct community of the priest. To begin with the petty kings and princes could offer sacrifice for himself and his people. But with the growth of large kingdoms the hands of the kings were full of administrative and military duties, at the same time rituals became more elaborate and complicated. This gave rise to a hieratic order, comprising more intellectual and educated elements who would be free from distractions of war or peace and faithfully perform sacrifices and rituals. This was the genesis of the priestly class, i.e., the Brahmanas.

The fourth class, i.e., the Sudras, were the defeated aborigines absorbed as slaves. In the *Rig Veda* they were mentioned as *dasyus* and *dasas*. According to Dr. Apte, the development of caste-system in a rigid form did not take place till the time when the Vedic Aryans had settled down in Madhyadesa or Brahmavarta.

The above view is not accepted by some scholars mainly on the ground that there are references to the threefold, even fourfold division of castes in the *Rig Veda* itself. The existence of similar division of society among the Iranians has been pointed out by these scholars and raises the presumption of the development of hereditary caste-groups among the Aryans in the Rig Vedic period. The Iranians had the fourfold division of society such as the priests, warriors, agriculturists, and artisans which resembles very closely the fourfold division of the Aryan Society as Brahmanas, Kshatriyas, Vaisyas, and the Sudras. But this similarity between the Iranian and Indo-Aryan divisions of society does not conclusively prove that these were identical.

From the early post-Vedic Age in Grihya-Sutras and Dharma-Sutras we find that the fourfold division of Society with the rules of rites and ceremonies, manners and customs continued to exist as of old. The *Varnasrama*, i.e., the four stages of life enjoyed for the Brahmanas, Kshatriyas, and Vaisyas are also found in Kautilya's *Arthasastra*. In the Dharma-Sutras highest status and dignity are claimed for the Brahmanas. Highest offices of the State such as the priests, ministers, judges, members of *Mantri Parishad*, etc. were reserved for the Brahmanas. A Brahmana enjoyed immunity from capital punishment.

The caste rules relating to food, marriage, and professional work were more rigidly applied during the post-Vedic period upto the end of the Maurya Age. The *Sudras* had to render menial service. But Manu did not deny the right of education and of teaching by the Sudras. But on the whole the life of the Sudras was unenviable. The most significant development during this period was the rise of numerous mixed castes due to inter-marriage between castes as also to the influx of the Yavanas, Sakas, Chinas, Pahlavas, etc.

Despite the predominance of the Hindu caste-system, the Jaina and the Buddhists did not go by the caste order. They placed the Kshatriyas at the top of the caste-order.

In the period that intervened between the fall of the Mauryas and the rise of the Guptas the fourfold caste-system received a shock due to the influx of the barbarians and it seemed that there would be a collapse of the social system. But with the patronage of the Brahmanical system by the ruling house, in northern and southern India there was a revival of Brahmanism which reached its crowning triumph under the Imperial Guptas. The fourfold caste-system continued to exist with growing rigidity although inter-marriages were permissible. The caste-system acquired a permanent character and influenced the social customs, law, and social ideals. All the same the institution of castes was not altogether static as it became later on and continues even today.

Slavery

Slavery in India is as old as the Vedic times. The Buddhist canonical texts as well as the Smritis mention different classes of slaves and their status. The Buddhist texts distinguish slaves of different classes as (i) Slaves by birth, (ii) Slaves by capture in war, (iii) Slaves by purchase, and (iv) Slaves by choice. Kautilya in his *Arthasastra* for the first time mentions certain rules governing the status of the slaves. In the Smritis also we have various rules regarding the status of slaves. According to Manu and Narada slavery could be acquired in different ways, by birth in the master's house, by capture in war, by purchase, accepting slavery for food, by gift, by inheritance from ancestors, by release from heavy debt, by voluntary surrender of freedom, for apostasy from asceticism, by connection with a female slave, and by various other ways. In the *Mahabharata* also there is mention of temporary slavery of the defeated foe. In the *Mahabharata* and *Milindapanha* sale of wife and children presumably into slavery is mentioned as a recognised custom. But sale of wife or child is condemned by both Manu and Yajnavalkya. Enslavement of an adulterous wife is prescribed as one of the modes of punishment to such a wife.

Yajnavalkya and Kautilya lay down the principle that slavery shall be in the descending order of castes. Kautilya specifically mentions that no Aryan could be reduced to slavery under any circumstances.

About the rights of the slaves while the Smritis are silent about their right to acquire, inherit or bequeath property, Kautilya allows such rights under certain circumstances.

About the emancipation of the slaves, both Yajnavalkya and Narada lay down that (i) a slave who saves the life of his master is forthwith freed and becomes entitled to a son's share of the master's property, (ii) persons captured and sold by robbers as slaves or those who have been forcibly enslaved are to be freed by law, (iii) persons who accepted slavery for food are to be freed on payment of the expenses, (iv) payment of ransom would emancipate those who are captured in war and converted into slaves. There are other ways in which slaves can earn freedom.

The laws relating to slavery mentioned in the Smriti Law of the Gupta Age developed the earlier Smriti Law regarding slavery. Katyayana, for instance, repeats Yajnavalkya and Narada and specifies that a Brahmana can never be reduced to slavery. According to Katyayana a free woman herself becomes a slave by marrying a slave, but a female slave bearing a child to her master is immediately emancipated. The drama *Mrichchakatikam* of the Gupta period both supplements and confirms the rules relating to slavery mentioned above.

The slaves in ancient India received benign treatment at the hands of their mastery. Megasthenes' remarked that "all the Indians are free and not one of them is a slave. The Indians do not even use an alien as slave and much less a countryman of their own". But from various contemporary evidences the remark of Megasthenes appears to be incorrect. His statement may be regarded as correct in respect of any particular region, but not for whole of India. Or else it may be interpreted to mean that the treatment of the slaves at time was so liberal that Megasthenes was led to believe that there was no slavery in India.

Prof. Rhys David's remark is relevant in this context. He remarks that "For most part the slaves (in India) were household servants, and not badly treated and their number seems to have been insignificant". Dr. Apte justly concludes that "Such mild treatment, which offered a striking contrast to the system of slavery with which Megasthenes was familiar, probably led him to believe that there were no slaves in India".[1]

The Indian caste-system has been subjected to adverse criticism due to its obvious demerits. It has been suggested that it shuts off the Indian from free association with the foreigners rendering it difficult for the Indians to understand and the foreigners and *vice versa*. Dr. V. A. Smith says that it is easier for a foreigner to attain full sympathy of the casteless Burmese than an Indian Chitpavan or Nambudripad Brahmana so much veiled by caste-system.

It is often an unpleasant experience of history, polished foreigner to find his touch polluting a high-caste Hindu. Within India even caste-system has broken up the Indian society into a thousand parts. The institution of castes has hindered coöperation between peoples politically, economically, and socially. Poet Nazrul Islam has in his poems has castigated the caste-consciousness of the Hindus.[2] Conditions of modern life have often come in conflict with the caste-rules. It is noticed that despite considerable laxity in practice, the

1+2 *The Age of Imperial Unity*, p. 571.

sentiment of class exclusiveness persists even today in full strength. Of course there are varying degrees of the sentiment. With the spread of education and movement by eminent Indians, such as Ramkrishna, Vivekananda, Nanak, Kabir, Sree Chaitanya, the Brahmo Samaj, Arya Samaj, etc., as well as with the growth of national feeling the intensity of caste-system is in the process of being reduced.

But caste-system is not without its merits. Critics of the institution of castes have overlooked the fact that an institution which has forced its way through centuries, from the Himalayas to Cape Comorin, must have merits to justify its existence and universal prevalence in India. Caste-system has to be considered as an integral part of Hinduism, and of Hindu social and economic systems. It is intimately associated with the Hindu philosophical ideas of *Karma*, rebirth, and the theory of *Svata*, *Raja*, and *Tama gunas*.

But the chief merit of the caste-system is the stability and solidarity that it gave to the Hindu Society. Caste-system as an institution has been the main "agent in preserving the Hindu ideas of religion, morals, art and craftsmanship".[1]

Foreign Elements in Population

While the institution of caste-system in India reveals the conservative aspect of the Hindu Society it has its refreshingly liberal aspect that may be noticed in its liberality. During the period under review, foreign invaders like the Greeks, Bactrian Greeks, Parthians, the Sakas, and the Kushanas invaded India and barring the followers of Alexander a small number of whom remained in north-western India, others came into India never to return. They settled in India and were finally absorbed by the Hindu Society and no trace of their individual identity or characteristics remained. From a good number of inscriptions we find the gradual transformation of these barbarian hordes into thorough-going Hindus by adoption of languages, manners and customs, religion, etc., of the Hindus, and finally through matrimonial ties they were incorporated into the Hindu Society. This transformation is best illustrated by the Western Satraps whose early outlandish names, such as Ghsamotika, Chastana, Nahapana, etc., were gradually replaced by their successors' names in the purely Indian fashion, such as Rudrasena, Visvasena, Rudrasimha, Vijaysena, and the like. Gradually their barbaric language and religion were also replaced by Indian languages and Indian religion. They became devotees of Hindu gods, adopted Sanskrit as their language. The

1 V. A. Smith: *Oxford History of India*, p. 68.

process of transformation became complete through their marital relations with Brahmanical royal dynasties and other Hindu families. In this way they became an integral part of the Hindu Society.

It may be pointed out that the Yavanas and other foreigners who settled in India, instead of upsetting the traditional social order, or destroying the accepted canons of morality and conduct were themselves completely absorbed into the indigenous social system. "Quite unmistakably, the captive India captured her captor"—aptly remarks N. K. Sastri. The process of Indianisation may be cleanly traced from the second century B.C. when Demetrius contrary to Hellenistic customs struck coins with bi-lingual legends, Greek and Prakrit with Kharosthi script. With the adoption of Indian script went acceptance of Indian religions. There are inscriptions of recording dedications of Buddhist relics by pious Greek donors. The Greek ambassador, Heliodorus, at the Court of Vidisa erected a column in honour of Vasudeva. The example of the Greeks who considered all non-Greeks as barbarians, in adopting Indian religion and social customs was followed by the Sakas, Parthians, and the Kushanas. While the Saka and Kushana rulers became great patrons of Indian religions other ordinary foreigners were contented with adoption of Indian religions and social canons of conduct and morality. The writers of Smriti met the new element in the Hindu Society by according the foreigners the status of the Kshatriyas.

If the Hindu Society absorbed the foreign elements that came into India, the Brahmanical and Buddhist missionaries by their propaganda all over Asia brought many of its peoples within the pale of Indian culture. The Hindu missionaries and the merchants "raised the people in the Far East from their primitive barbarism to a high state of progress and refinement.[1]

Family Life : Marriage

The use of the term *Kula* in the Vedic literature, meaning system of individual family comprising several members, proves the existence of family in India in the Vedic times. From the *Upanishads* and *Brahmanas* the absolute control of father over the sons and daughters and other inmates of the family is proved. Relation between the father and the children was of deep affection. Families were sometimes large enough and included grandfather, grandmother as well as great-grandsons. Adoption was resorted to in absence of natural sons, but also to add to a specially qualified member to the

[1] R. C. Majumdar: *Ancient India*, p. 203.

family. Among relations of the family are mentioned cousins, nephews, wife's brothers, etc.

During the period under review family system characterised the society. Unquestioned obedience to the father was considered the highest of duties of sons and daughters. Great veneration was shown to all elders in the family, next to father in respect, was the elder brother. Relation between the family and the wife's parents, husband's parents, brothers and sisters was one of great affections and respect. There is, however, dearth of instances of the mother-in-law or the daughter-in-law taking refuge in nunnery to escape from tyranny of the other members of the family.

While conjugal fidelity and ideal relationship between the wife and husband formed the most distinguishing characteristic of the Hindu family instances of lack of conjugal fidelity were not small either. Megasthenes and Manu mention this aspect of the moral lapse of the society. But this was not, however, the general picture.

The family life was adversely affected by Polygamy and inter-marriages. The first wife was usually a girl of the same caste of the bridegroom, but other marriages might not be within one's own caste. Megasthenes states that the Indians married many wives, some for pleasure, some for having more children, and some to bring in willing helpmates. This is also corroborated by the Smritis.

Wife of the same caste with the husband, enjoyed special privilege and status of sons and in the matter of inheritance would depend on the status of the mother. It is supposed by scholars that this inequality in treatment must have disturbed the peace of the family and adversely affected the relation between members of the family. Needless to say, introducing wives of different nature and habits led to the degradation of the cultural life of the family and supersession of wives on flimsy grounds.

As to polyandry, i.e., one wife having more than one husband we have the instance of Draupadi in the *Mahabharata* as also an instance of a girl married to the entire family in *Apastamba*, but the extent to which this practice was followed is highly debatable. But this practice is to come across in Kumaun even today.

From Vatsyayana we get an idea of the family life of the Hindus during the Gupta period. The most important person of self-restraint and household management made for the happiness of the family life and these remain as the hall mark of Hindu wives down to the present day. Where the woman is the only wife, she ministered to his comfort at table, shared the fasts and vows with her husband, attended festivities, religious ceremonies along with her husband. She was not be puffed up in prosperity, would serve her mother-in-law and father-in-law and did what they would command her to do. She would not laugh aloud, speak sweet words. In absence of her husband she would wear only sober dress and would not wear ornaments except those signifying her married state. Besides attending to her husband and husband's parents, she would attend to the relations and friends of the family. We get more or less a picture of the family life in the Hindu Society today from the Vatsyayana and other Smriti writers.

Marriage

Rules relating to marriage in their fundamental aspects continue more or less unaltered from the Vedic times uptill the present day among the Hindus. During the Vedic Age marriage did not normally take place before attainment of puberty and was banned within the circle of agnates and cognates upto certain degrees. Marriage within the same *gotra* was forbidden. Brothers or sisters were not to marry before their elders. Widow remarriage was allowed and polygamy undoubtedly prevailed. Sale of daughter for marriage was not unknown but was looked upon with disfavour. There were also marital relations between the higher castes and the Sudra men and women. In *Atharva Veda* there are references to *Sati*, i.e., immolation of the wife in the husband's pyre.

During the post-Vedic Age marriage between the same caste was preferred. As in the previous age, marriage with the same gotra was prohibited and also with certain degrees of relationship. Though forbidden by Manu the Southerners married the daughter of maternal uncle. The *Dharma-Sutras* and the institutes of Manu refer to eight different kinds of marriages. These are: (i) *Brahma*, that is marriage negotiated by the father of the girl and dowry is given at the time of marriage, (ii) *Daiva*, that is marriage of a daughter given by the father to the priest; (iii) *Arsha*, that is marriage given by the father of his daughter in return for a cow and a bull, (iv) *Prajapatya*, where the father gives the daughter citing a mantra uniting them in marriage, (v) *Asura*, where takes the girl on payment of wealth to the girl and her Kinsmen, (vi) *Gandharva*, voluntary union of the girl and her lover, (vii) *Rakshasa*, where the girl is abducted and married forcibly, and (viii) *Paisacha*, where the girl is seduced while sleeping or by doping. The last form of marriage is universally condemned and the seventh is condemned in case of the Kshatriyas. Megasthenes states that in Indian marriage a pair of oxen is given as gift. This shows that the 3rd form, i.e., *Arsha* marriage was the most popular in the 4th century B.C.

According to some scholars the *Prajapatya* marriage in which the husband and wife are united by citing *mantra* forbids the husband to marry any other wife. *Brahma* marriage also enjoins the husband and wife to remain inseparable in the spheres of love, wealth, and religion. "On the whole this spirit pervades the first four forms of marriage, which are regarded as a religious sacrament and no mere contract.[1] The other forms of marriage were also held.

Nearchus states that the Indians "marry without either giving or taking dowries, but the women, as soon as they are marriageable, are brought forward by their fathers and exposed in public to be selected by the victor in wrestling or boxing or running or by some one who excels in any other manly exercise". This is perhaps a reference to *Svayamvara* marriage which used to take place after puberty when the girls were well-developed and grown up. But there was a tendency in the Sutra texts to lower the marriageable age of the girls. Gradually child marriage was coming into vogue, but marriage at mature age was not at all uncommon. In later Smritis it is laid down that girls should be given in marriage before their attaining puberty. This was perhaps due to the anxiety to maintain the bodily purity of girls. It is suggested by some writers that marriage before puberty applied to the Brahmanas. This is also borne out by the literary evidence of the time.

Rules relating to marriage laid down in the older Smritis remained materially unaltered during the post-Maurya and the Gupta periods. From Vatsyayana we come to know that girls were given in marriage during this period both before and after they attained puberty. Marriage within the same caste was preferred while marriage within certain degrees of relationship was prohibited as in the previous age. Hiuen T-Sang also bears out this. Persons uniting themselves in love according to canonical rites with girls of the same caste is according to Vatsyayana is blessed and receives public approval. Making love to girls of higher caste or with married woman is prohibited. But love with woman of lower caste who are sufficiently pure, or with harlots or with re-married widows appears to be neither condemned nor approved. Obviously inter-marriage between different castes was put under greater restrictions than laid down by the earlier Smritis. Vatsyayana forbids *Pratiloma* marriage and puts *Anuloma* marriage on the same low status as marriage with harlots.

---

1 *The Age of Imperial Unity*, p. 560.

During this period, negotiated marriage through parents was held precious as in the time of Smritis. Vatsyayana quotes *Apastamba Grihya-Sutra* and emphasises that happiness depends on the choice of the girl. After selection of the girl any of the four kinds of marriages mentioned in the Smritis, namely, *Brahma, Prajapatya, Arsha,* and *Daiva* is to be performed. Courtship marriage is also referred to Vatsyayana and he gives details about different forms of courtship. *Svayamvara* marriage mentioned in the Smritis is also prescribed by Vatsyayana.

In the literary works of the Gupta Age repeated references to *Gandharva* marriage are met with. From literature of the time illustrations of great repugnance felt for selection of husbands by the maidens out of love are found.

Status of Women

As with the caste-system, we notice a retrograde movement in the position and status of women during the period under review. With the lowering of the marriageable age of women and extreme emphasis laid on physical chastity of women and unquestioned obedience to her husband led to progressive deterioration of her status and position. But this downward movement, however, did not reach its lowest stage during the post-Vedic period. Gone were the days when Indian women participated in highly philosophical subjects and even composed verses and entered into disputations on Sastras.

Megasthenes states that the "Brahmanas do not communicate a knowledge of Philosophy to their wives". But there were exceptions and Megasthenes also remarks that some women did pursue Philosophy. Thus the spirit of the time was to gradually relegate the women to an unequal and inferior status to men.

It may be mentioned that two completely different pictures about the status and position of women are found during this period. In one, women are represented as fickle, quarrelsome, and untruthful—a veritable pot of poison. She must, therefore, remain under control all throughout her life, in girlhood under the control of her father, in youth under the control of her husband and in old age under the control of her son. In another, woman is represented as the glory of the home and the symbol of prosperity, the better half of her husband and the friend, philosopher, and guide of her husband. She is, therefore, worthy of all attention and respect "As a mother she is superior to ten fathers, superior to anything else on earth".[1]

---

[1] *The Age of Imperial Unity*, p. 562.

In the older Smritis as well as in Manu and Yajnyavalka it has been enjoined in strongest terms that women should be honoured by their male relatives. Women were given precedence along the road in the same way as the king and the *Snataka*, that is, one who had completed his education. Newly wedded women and the pregnant women were to be fed before all other inmates of the household. Manu also declares that the gods are pleased with those household where women are held in honour. A husband who would cast off his wife who is not guilty of any crime should be punished by the king. Manu and Yajnyavalka lay down that mother, wife, and other female relations are persons whose faults should be borne without resentment. Mother should be shown highest reverence just as one does to his father and the teacher. Again a wife was to worship her husband as God even if he were devoid of qualities or destitute of virtues. Manu, also at the same time, lays down that the husband has absolute rights over the wife and could even inflict corporal punishment on her and discard her forthwith if she said anything disagreeable to him. Thus we find a sort of a contradiction in the rules of treatment of women.

With growing importance attached to physical chastity of women there was gradual discouragement of widow remarriage, divorce, etc., and greater encouragement to the system of *Sati*. Upto the time of Kautilya remarriage of women was permissible where the husband was dead, or has become an ascetic or gone abroad after waiting for a specified period. But Manu and Yajnyavalka forbid widow remarriage. Narada, however, permits it. Thus there seems to have been no strict uniformity in regard to the woman's right to remarry. Narada even permits a married woman to leave her husband if it becomes known only after marriage the he has blemishes, and take to another husband. This was an early form of divorce.

The tendency to relegate women to inferior status is also noticed in the Brahmanical canon law forbidding Vedic Study, even utterance of Vedic mantras by women long before the Gupta Age. Yet there were exceptions and Vatsyayana mentions instances of princesses and daughters of nobles acquiring knowledge of Sastras. In the Gupta Age the move towards relegating women to inferior status continued which had begun in the post-Vedic Age. But certain striking changes took place during the Gupta Age in woman's right to property.

Earlier Yajnyavalka introduced for the first time the right of widow to her husband's property in absence of any son. Women were also entitled to own and bequeath their *Stridhana* or special property. But that the lot of the widows was very hard has been borne out by all literary evidences. Unmarried girls were also allowed the right to share the property of the deceased father along with their brothers.

In the Gupta Age Katyayana gave increased recognition of the woman's right to property. Another important rule in *Arti* and *Devala* is that women molested by robbers or others were allowed to regain their social status.

That women exercised the right to share public administration is proved from the account of Megasthenes who mentions that the Pandaean nation was governed by females. The Satavahana queen Nayanika, we know, acted as regent during the minority of her son. Queen Prabhavati Gupta, daughter of Chandragupta II, also ruled the Vakataka Kingdom as the regent of her minor son. Likewise princess Vijayabhattarika was a provincial governor under Chalukya King Vikramaditya I.

From Patanjali we come to know that women worked as spear-bearers. But Megasthenes gives us a better and direct example of women bodyguards of Chandragupta Maurya. Kautilya also bears out this when he refers to the custom that when the King would get up from bed shall be received by women troops.

References to use of veil by women while coming before their elders like father-in-law or women of high families appearing in public with veils, are found in the both secular and canonical literature of the period. The custom of *Purdah* probably continued under the Guptas.

As in Athens, the Indian courtesans (ganika) were given great honour. The instance, *Amrapali*, may be mentioned in this contest. Kautilya also bears it out when he states that a prostitute, noted for beauty, youth and accomplishments should be appointed superintendent of the prostitutes on a salary of 1000 *pana* per annum. They were also appointed to the royal household on high salaries.

Education

The highly developed intellectual life that was responsible for the composition of the vast mass of Vedic literature must have had a well-planned system of education. The *Guru* of the Vedic times formed the backbone of the educational system. Study of Vedic Philosophy was not forbidden in case of the women.

In the post-Vedic period the Dharma-Sastras carried on the Vedic traditions and practices of education which had its own ceremonies and rituals such as *Vidyarambha*, *Upanayana*, etc. Manu calls *Upanayana* as *Brahma-Janma*, a sort of a rebirth hence a *dvija*.

The pupil had to live a life of discipline in the house of the *Guru*, i.e., preceptor, as a *Brahmachari*. Normally no fee was paid to the teacher. According to Manu no fee was to be paid to the teacher. A teacher charging fee was condemned. Admission to study was guided by the principle of fitness of the pupil. Mostly pupils studied day and night and would even read in the light from burning cowdung for want of oil. But there were also pupils who found study irksome and uninteresting and would discontinue. Transgression of the rules of discipline would entail dismissal by the teacher. Sometimes, students would change teachers and schools but this practice was looked with disfavour and such pupils would be derisively termed as *Tirthakaka*, i.e., crow which does not stay at the same place of pilgrimage for long.

A teacher was held in great esteem and would become famous to those students who from distances of hundreds of miles would come to study. Teachers were of two kinds : *Upadhyayas* who took to teaching as a profession for livelihood and taught the Vedas and *Acharyas* who taught the Vedas, Kalpa-Sutras and Upanishads without any fee. The pupils after completion of study would, however, present the teacher with field, gold, cow, shoes, umbrella, clothes, etc.

A definite system of education was evolved by the people of the time. Kautilya lays down eagerness to listen what the teacher said (*Susrusa*), grasping by the ear (*Sravana*), understanding what the teacher said (*grahana*), retention of what was learnt (*Dharana*), discussion (*Upapoha*), acquisition of full knowledge of the lessons learnt from the teacher (*Vijnana*), and comprehension of the underlying truth of what has been learnt (*Tattvabhinivesha*). It was the common idea that "The student learns a fourth from his *Acharya*, a fourth by his own intelligence by himself, a fourth from his fellow-pupils, and the remaining fourth in course of time by experience".[1]

The knowledge of writing had in the meantime greatly improved which introduced a great change in the system of education. The oldest alphabet called *Brahmi* was used in most of the records of Asoka and from this script various scripts used all over India were derived. The Achaemenian conquerors introduced the *Aramaic* in the Punjab, from which was derived the *Kharosthi* alphabet, written from right to left. But this script went out of existence by the fourth century A.D.

Teaching was mainly oral. The Buddhist sacred books were committed to memory and were not written. Similar was the case

---

1 *The Age of Imperial Unity*, p. 584.

with Brahmanical canon literature. This was probably due to the growing desire of the Brahmanas to withhold the sacred *mantras* from the people and to retain the privilege exclusively for themselves. But the great mass of literature in the 4th or even in the fifth century B.C. and the extensive use of writing for administrative purposes during the time of Asoka leads invariably to the conclusion that books were much more extensively used than is now commonly believed. Lesser use of books in teaching was probably due to the desire to impart knowledge in a way that might develop personality and power of comprehension in the pupils and to make instruction less bookish.

Subjects of study included besides Vedic literature, the *Dharma-Sastras*, i.e., *Smritis*, *Itihasa* and *Purana*, Economics and allied subjects, dialectics, politics (*Dandaniti*). Three Vedas and Economics are referred to by Kautilya as four important subjects of study.

The Princes had to study the four subjects referred to by Kautilya as important and also to receive military training including its operational aspects. Besides they had to study *Purana*, *Itivritta* (History), tales (Akhyana), illustrative stories (Udhaharana), Dharma Sastra and Arthasastra. Milindapanha mentions a long list of subjects for the study of the Brahmanas, such as, the Vedas, Puranas, Itihasa, Lexicography, Prosody, Phonology, Verses, Grammar, Etymology, Astronomy, Astrology and the Six Vedangas. They must also acquire the knowledge of interrputing signs and omens, study the eclipses of the Sun and the Moon. Thus the Brahmanas had to become the top class in the society by well-deserved merit by acquisition of diverse knowledge.

The Kshatriyas had to acquire knowledge of the art of war, of horses, elephants, chariots, bows, rapiers, documents, currency. The Vaisyas and the Sudras had to learn husbandry, merchandising, and care of the cattle. King Minander (Milinda) is said to have acquired knowledge of nineteen arts and sciences.

Instruction was given in all subjects by Brahmana teachers. Even instruction in agriculture was also imparted by them. From Narada Smriti we come to know of rules relating to admission to an industrial school. Elaborate rules relating to industrial education, training and apprenticeship, etc., leave no doubt that the highly developed handicrafts were the results of India's rich training.

Science of medicine was also taught and Taxila was the seat of medical education. The texts speak of the method of preparation of medicine from roots, leaves, fruits, gums, lime, etc. Operation of diseased limb, bandages, compressing of swollen parts of the body, etc., were all known.

Centres of studies were the Brahmanical *Asrama* and the Buddhist *Vihara.* A full-fledged *Asrama* had a prayer hall, department of Vedic studies, department for the study of politics, economics, department of military studies, department of astronomy, department of botany, department dealing with transport and conveyance, and department of military organisation, methods of forming patrols, battalions and armies. The Principal of the *Asrama* was called *Kulapati*, a teacher of 10,000 pupils.

The Buddhist Vihara had two classes of teachers, *Upadhyaya* and *Acharya.* The duties of the teacher and the pupils were the same as in the Brahmanical system. The Buddhist *Vihara* education was imparted to students living collectively in spirit of brotherhood and democracy, the Brahmanical *Asrama* was a home which hardly called for any organisation to deal with large number. What was absent in the Buddhist system was the domestic touch of the Brahmanical system.

In the post-Maurya period including the Gupta Age there was no appreciable change in the educational system that prevailed in the preceding age. From Bana we learn that the former Brahmanical system of living with the *Guru* was in vogue. In fact, Bana himself returned from the home of his *guru* at the age of fourteen. Even during Harsha's time, i.e., in the seventh century the system was prevalent, as we know from the evidence of Hiuen T-Sang.

The teacher-pupil relation has been elaborated in the Buddhist works which lay down the same nature of discipline as prescribed by the Brahmanical texts. The Chinese traveller, I-TSing, also corroborates it. The discipline that was insisted on the pupils both in the Brahmanical and Buddhist texts has been mentioned by I-TSing. The pupil had to rub the teacher's body, fold his clothes, sweep his yard and the apartment, bring water for the teacher. The teacher on the other hand would nurse the pupil in his illness, supply him medicine and look after him as he would do for his son. In the Buddhist *Viharas* or monasteries Buddhist texts were taught.

There were centres of advanced studies in Buddhist monasteries and the Nalanda Vihara in Magadha became the most renowned of them, all for the magnificence of its establishment and the intellectual pre-eminence of its inmates. "Owing its foundation to six successive generations of the Gupta kings, it housed a population of several thousands" who were maintained out of the income of the vast landed properties donated to it. In the seventh century Hiuen TSang admired its resident monks for their learning that rivalled Nalanda was Valabhai in Kahtiawar during the seventh century. The curriculum of studies was the same as had been followed in the preceding period, and referred to above. There were the eighteen branches of learning including sciences.

Let us now examine the extent to which women were allowed to share in the system of education. During the Vedic period we have instances of accomplished women who studied Vedic Sastras. Apala, Ghosa, Gargi, Visvavara, etc., may be mentioned in this connection. But during the period of the Smritis there was a tendency to give the girls in marriage before they attained puberty. This interfered with their education. Study of Sastras and mantras was forbidden in case of the women. But there are also indications of two classes of women, the *Brahmavadini* who remained lifelong students of sacred texts and *Sadyodvaha* who prosecuted studies till their marriage. Buddhist and Jaina texts also refer to women of *Brahmavadini* class who remained unmarried to prosecute their studies all throughout their life. Most of the Buddhist nuns who were maidens composed songs which are preserved in the *Theragatha.* From the Jaina text we come across Jayanti, daughter of the King of Kausambi, who remained unmarried all throughout her life for study of philosophy and religion. Thus, although the Brahmanical sacred law denied to women the Vedic study, even utterance of the mantras, there were many instances of women who devoted their whole life to the study of Sastras and philosophy and many who prosecuted studies upto the time of their marriage. In the Gupta Age as well we have good grounds to believe that girls of high families had sufficient opportunities for acquiring proficiency in general learning. In Vatsyayana's *Kamasutra* there are references to princesses and daughters of nobles "whose intellect is sharpened by the knowledge of the *Sastras*". There were also female teachers as we know from *Amarakosa,* a work of the Gupta period. *Upadhyayi* was a female teacher who taught Vedic *mantras.*

We may, therefore, safely conclude that despite the prevalent tendency in the *Smriti* Law to deny study of Sastras by women and the practice of giving girls in marriage in very young age before attainment of puberty which prevented acquisition of learning by girls, female education did not suffer completely. Acquisition of knowledge of Sastras as well as general knowledge by women continued during the period under review in certain classes of the Society.

General Life

A country so vast in expanse as India, with a great multiplicity of races the general character of the life of the people varied in all ages. During the period under review, i.e., 4th century B.C. to 6th century A.D. social life on the whole had become richer in content, more comprehensive in outlook and much wider in range.

Due to the Jaina and Buddhistic influences there was a greater emphasis on asceticism. Yet the common people had a tendency towards enjoyment of all good thngs of life. Literature and sculpture of the period show the vivacious side of the life, full of bustle and activity, joy and humour.

Singing, dancing, performing art, entertainment, the buffoonery, mimicry, etc., as well as gardening, heraldry, singing bards, etc., characterised the lighter side of the life. Hunting, wrestling, boxing, chariot-races, archery competition, etc., were the more valiant side of amusements. Festive assemblies such as *Utsava, Samaja, Vihara* were held and dainty dishes and intoxicants were served. Meat was one of the major delicacies that were served on such occasions. We know of Asoka's prohibiting the *Samajas* for entertainments.

It may be mentioned that even before Asoka's propagation of his moral code and his *Dharma* the people of India had a high sense of morality. Megasthene's remarks are worth quoting: "Truth and Virtue they hold alike in esteem. Hence they accord no special privileges to the old unless they possess superior wisdom." Adherence to truth, confidence in people's honesty and mutual good relations characterised the social life of the people. This made the social life so easy and cordial that seldom people went to the law court. The Greeks were struck by the fact that the Indians preserved the memory of their ancestors not by erecting monuments, but by songs in praise of their virtues. This shows that the Indians set great store of virtues. Death was no terror for them as life was regarded no more than a mere illusion. Need for maintaining balance in life was fully recognised, and *dharma, artha, Kama* and *Moksha,* i.e., religion, wealth, happiness and salvation, were regarded as the four ends of life.

In spite of the emphasis on the spirit of *Ahimsa* (non-violence) by the Jains and the Buddhists and Asoka's enforcing laws in this regard, fish, meat including beef were extensively taken by the people. Kautilya recommends that the State should preserve forests for animals and birds and also maintain a slaughter-house. Articles of food consisted of rice, beans, *tila,* honey, rice-milk, molasses, fruits, milk, curd, ghee, butter-milk, butter, etc., besides fish and meat. Various kinds of liquor were used. Drinks were made from grape-juice, honey, various fruits, etc. Kautilya directs that drinks should be sold to men of well-known character and in small quantities. According to Megasthenes the Indians did not drink except at sacrifices. Manu prescribes serious punishment for those who manufactured liquor. But this orthodox Brahmanical rule did not conform to actual practice.

There were cities and big buildings no doubt, but the common people lived in dwelling houses made of brick, stone or wood, straw and leaves. Roof and the walls were plastered on both sides. Walls were coloured. There were windows and shutters. Walls were often decorated with paintings and engravings. Verandahs, covered terraces, living room, retiring room, etc., comprised the dwelling house. Hygienic arrangements were kept in view in the construction of privies, screens, varieties of chairs, cushioned, straw-bottomed, cane-bottomed, pedestals, bedsteads, beds comprising mattresses, etc., were the furniture used in the period preceding the Gupta Age. Mosquito-curtains, filters for straining water, flower-stand, mosquito-fans were also used.

Costly utensils such as bowls made of benyl, gold, copper, glass, silver, tin, bronze, with some of them painted and jewel-set were extensively in use. All these give us an impression of a high standard of living.

The literature of the Gupta period points to the continuity of the high standard of living that prevailed in India in the preceding centuries discussed above. Needless to say that there were striking differences among the habits and temperaments of the people in different regions of the country. Vatsyayana bears out this. Hiuen TSang who visited all parts of India except the far South in the seventh century gives us an account of the Ganga and the Brahmaputra regions. According to him people of these regions were "remarkable for qualities of honesty, courage, love of learning and so forth, those of north-western India and of the Deccan plateau as well as people of the extreme north, east, west and south were generally of contrary disposition". The people praised by Hiuen TSang were those of Taxila, Nagar, Poonch, Satadru, Matipura, Ahichchatra, Kanauj, Prayaga, Kausambi, Varanasi, Vaisali, Magadha, Kajangala, Pundravardhana, Kamrupa, Karnasuvarna, Maharastra, Valabhi, Dravida, etc. The people about whom his attitude was one of rather condemnation were those of Gandhara, Lampa, Jalandhara, Nepal, Andhra, Chola, Broach, Surat, Ujjaini. People of Kashmir, Udayana, Tamralipti, Kongod, Kalinga and Sind were of mixed character. This general characterisation certainly applied to people of the Gupta Age as well. From Fa-hien and other sources we come to know that generally the Indians were marked by exceptionally high degree of honesty. The Brahmanas and the Kshatriyas were distinguished for their honesty, purity and charity. Indians, according to Hiuen TSang, were habitually benevolent and charitable. The needy and the seek were provided with food and medicine by private individuals also, besides the arrangements made by the State.

Literary evidence of the Gupta period bears out the luxury in which the kings and queens down to the ordinary people lived. *Brihat Samhita* and *Mrichchakatika* testify to the lavish magnificence of women of higher station of life. *Kadambari* gives us a description of the luxury of the kings' bath and toilette. Ornaments were worn by both males and females and *Amarkosa* gives a long list of ornameants then in use from head to foot. Women used bodices and petticoats and during winter they used cloak-like garment covering the body upto the feet. In *Srinagarasataka*, a work attributed to Kalidasa makes mention of social gatherings called *gosthis* which were also attended by good poets.

The gosthis were of the nature of Samajas of the preceding age.

Toilette and personal hygiene and cleanliness were of high standard as before. Teeth-stick was used by all. Perfumes, hair-lotions, perfumed hair oils, sandal-paste, camphor were used for bodily embellishment.

In the Gupta Age the food and drink did not materially vary from wheat and barley. These were the cereals used. Pulses of three kinds, butter, ghee, oil, molasses, coarse sugar. fish, meat, etc., were extensively taken as food. People were addicted to intoxicating liquor. Fa-hien's remarks that killing of animals, drinking of wine, and eating of onions and garlic were not known in Madhyadesa, was an exaggeration and might have been the case with a limited region. Any way, Fa-hien's account gives us a faithful picture of the habits, manners, etc., of the Indians of the time. Hiuen T-Sang who visited India in the seventh century must have seen what must have been the continuation of the preceding age. According to him cakes, parched gram, milk, sugar, mustard oil, fish, flesh of goats and sheep were the common articles of food. Taking of some kinds of meat was forbidden. Eating of onions and garlic would lead to loss of caste. Intoxicating liquors of various qualities would be drunk by different classes of people.

Magical incantation and spells which are as old as the Vedas continued to exist in one or the other form throughout the period upto the Gupta Age. The Mahayana Buddhists had evolved a kind of protective spells during the Fourth Century A.D. which acquired great popularity. The literature of the Gupta period proves that belief in portents, spells, omens, etc., was prevalent at that time. Literary evidences of the Gupta period points to the fact that the kings and princes and the inelligentsia rose above popular superstitions. The city life of the period was one of indulgence and Epicurean enjoyment.

The *nagarika*, i.e., the citizen of the city after finishing his education would become a householder and his house was furnished in a manner indicative of high-taste and elegance. The house with attached garden with flowers and tame birds was decorated elegantly. The *nagarika* took bath every day, chewed betel, applied collyrium to his eyes and lack-dye to his lips. The *nagarika* would hold periodical entertainments in the *Samaja*, social gathering and drinking party. There are various references in contemporary literature which point to the gay, merry life of the *nagarika*. "The high level of Gupta urban culture evolved also a high and refined, delicate and elegant art of toilets and cosmetics."

CHAPTER EIGHTEEN

ECONOMIC CONDITION (4TH CENTURY B.C. TO 6TH CENTURY A.D.)

During the Maurya-Scythian era of Indian history there was an all-round development of agriculture, industry, and trade. The economy of the time was built on both private enterprise and state control and management. Our sources of information are Kautilya's *Arthasastra*, Megasthenes, *Periplus of the Erythrean Sea*, and few other Greek writers.

I. AGRICULTURE

Agriculture was the backbone of the rural economy and the main stay of a large part of the people of the country. A village which was a collection of families numbering from 30 to 1000 had been surrounded by a stockade, outside which lay the arable field of the village. Land was divided into small holdings which were cultivated by their owners themselves or by hired labour. There were large, very large holdings as well. Landless labourers and slaves were employed for cultivation of land where the owner did not or could not cope with the work of cultivation. Every village had its pastures which was used by all alike. Ditches for irrigation were excavated on a cooperative basis. Kautilya gives us a clear idea of the different kinds of lands that every village possessed. These were (i) cultivated land, (ii) fallow land, (iii) high and dry ground, (iv) land sown with crops, (v) grave, (vi) fruit plantations, (vii) forests, (viii) sugar-cane plantation, (ix) pastures, (x) land covered by roads.

Among the agricultural produce were rice of different varieties, wheat, sesame, pepper, pulses, linseed, mustard, vegetables, fruits like plantain, pumpkins, gourds, sugar-canes, grapes, etc. For the purposes of agriculture draught animals were necessary. The state, therefore, maintained cattle-studs and reared draught oxen, buffaloes, stud bulls, etc. The importance of cattle-breeding was recognised as a means to agricultural development. Agriculture depended mainly on rainfall.

Irrigation was the concern of the State and it was an important source of revenue, for water-rates were charged for supply of water for irrigation. We have already referred to cooperative irrigation resorted to by the holders of cultivable land.

The great importance of agriculture in the economy of the time becomes clear from the *Jatakas* where it is stated that "the distressing sight of sturdy peasants leaving at home their empty barns, and swelling the ranks of landless agricultural labourers to toil as hireling on the estates of royal capitalists" is a sign of social decadence.

The State derived a great part of its revenues from the variety of levies on agriculture and agricultural produce. *Bhaga* was the State share of the produce, *Bali* was the cess over and above *Bhaga*, *Kara*, i.e., tax levied on property periodically, *Vivita*, a tax on pasture, Rajju, a tax for survey and settlement, *Chorarajju*, a chowkidari tax.

The State had a large part of the agricultural land of the country directly in its own hands, in its vast crown estates. These were let out on condition of revenue payment. The state did not interfere in the enjoyment of these lands so long as revenue payments were made regularly.

The State used to run model farms where seeds were collected of various crops, fruits, and vegetables. The State also maintained flower, fruit, and vegetable gardens and raised commercial crops like jute, cotton, hemp, etc.

In the Age preceding the Gupta period India had developed an advanced system of agriculture, industry, and trade. The development of agriculture in the Gupta era seems to have continued on the traditional lines. In spite of the richness of the soil and availability of abundant water, Indian agriculture was dependent mainly on rainfall. From Varahamihira's *Brihat-Samhita* we know how careful forecasts of excessive, sufficient, and scanty rainfall were made in light of astronomical and meteorological data. Arrangements on the part of government for irrigation are illustrated by the construction of *Sudarsana Lake*, which had burst its dam due to a storm and was restored by a local Governor of Skandagupta in 455-58 mentioned in Junagarh Rock inscription. Amarakosa gives us the names of various agricultural implements and the details about agricultural operations.

Amarakosa and *Brihat-Samhita* refer to the different agricultural produce of the time: rice of different varieties, wheat, barley, peas, lentils, oilseeds, such as mustard, sesame, linseed, ginger, pepper, vegetables, medicinal herbs, sugarcane, etc. The agricultural crops and the fruits of trees and plants during this period were as remarkable as in the preceding centuries. The most prized fruits of the time, as of the past, were mangoes, melon, cocoanut, plantain, jackfruit, apple, tamarind, oranges, pomegranates, etc.

In the Smriti law certain rules were laid down for the encouragement of agriculture and deterrant punishment was prescribed for destruction of agricultural fruits, flowers, dams, roots, etc. Cultivators neglecting cultivation used to be fined and on the other hand one who turned waste land into arable land would be allowed to enjoy its produce for a period of seven or eight years.

II. INDUSTRY

The Nanda-Maurya-Scythian era saw a remarkable progress in industry. Our sources of information are the *Mahabharata*, Kautilya's *Arthasastra*, Megasthenes, *Periplus*, and *Smriti*. Numerous arts and crafts and occupations are not only referred to in the literature and inscriptions but also in the sculpture of the period. The main industries and handicrafts were those of weaving, wood-cutting, smithy, jewellery, ivory-working, confectionery, pottery, making of bows and arrows, etc. On the evidence of Megasthenes, we learn that gold, silver, copper and iron mines were worked. Making of furniture, carts, chariots, wooden buildings, and sea-going vessels were also important industries of the time. Costly skins and furs were valued industries in the north-western Himalayas and Eastern India in the time of Kautilya. Finest ivory work was produced by the ivory workers of Vidisa. Ivory workers of Vidisa were employed for engraving the ornamental sculpture of the Gates of the Sanchi Stupa. Ivory was used for making hair-combs, dice, ornamental sword-hilt, etc.

Textile industry continued to be in the same flourishing condition in Maurya period during the period from/after the fall of the Mauryas and rise of the Guptas. From the Brahmanical, Jaina and Buddhist works of this period that refer to the variety of textile fabrics manufactured during this period as during the Maurya period, referred to in Kautilya's *Arthasastra.* Silk, wool and different kinds of cotton linen were extensively produced. According to Kautilya Vanga, East Bengal was famous for fabrics of *dukula* (a kind of a plant), linen, and cotton. Pundra, that is, North Bengal was also famous for *dukula* and cotton fabrics. Vatsya, Konkon, Kalinga, Kausambi, Mysore were renowned centres of cotton industry. The *Periplus* mentions several centres of cotton manufacturers which agree to the list given in Kautilya's *Arthasastra.* Muslin in large quantities was produced in Kalinga, Argaru, etc.

While Arthasastra furnishes us with a wealth of materials about diverse subjects its information about mining and metallurgical industries during this period is scanty. According to Pliny, India had neither brass nor lead but exchanged these for precious stones, pearls, etc. India imported copper, lead, tin from foreign countries through Barygaza (Broach), and Malabar ports during the latter half of the First Century A.D. "On the other hand, according to the testimony of the *Periplus*, the manufacture of Indian iron and steel was so advanced in quality and quantity that they were exported from Kathiawar and the inland areas to East Africa". The *Acharanga* Sutra refers to bowls made of iron, tin, brass, etc.

According to *Periplus*, during the first Century A.D., pearl fisheries were operated off the coasts in Pandya and Chola countries. According to Pliny India was the greatest producer of most costly gems. He gives a long list of gems that India produced and called India a "gem-bearing" country.

Kautilya mentions various metallic ores extracted in India in those days, such as gold, silver, copper, lead, tin, iron, and a metal called *Vaikrintaka*, which has not been identified. He also refers to the knowledge of the Indians in technical sciences dealing with the art of smelting metals. This shows that the remarks of a Greek writer that although India was rich in gold and silver mines they were inexperienced in the arts of mining and smelting and followed too primitive a way in these regards, are unfounded.

In Kautilya's *Arthasastra* there is reference to the manufacture of weapons of war such as bows and arrows, swords, spears, axes, etc.

There were also lower crafts (*hina-seppas*) like those of manufacture of dyes, drugs, perfumes, pottery, rush-weavers, tannery, butchery, etc.

We learn from Kautilya that there was a considerable state-control both in trade and industry. "The State had a monopoly of industries which depended upon risky, costly, and pioneering enterprise." Mines were nationalised and these were the main sources of State revenue. The State worked the mines of gold silver, diamond, gems, precious stones, copper, lead, tin, iron, and bitumen. State also worked the oil fields, explored the ocean for pearls. It held monopoly of salt and granted licences to private lessees for working the salt fields. Minting of coins was also a state monopoly. The Mint Master received from the public bullion and struck it into coins on payment of a small fee. Convicts were employed by State to collect pearls from the seas and to work in the Prison factories. State had spinning houses for manufacturing cotton, silk, jute and wool yarn, as well as factories for manufacture of clothes of all kinds, blankets, curtains, ropes, etc.

During the Gupta Era different branches of industry were maintained in the same high level as in the preceding age. There was of course greater abundance of raw materials and much improvement in the skill and enterprise of the artisans and craftsmen during this period.

From the literature of this period we come across a large variety of clothes manufactured and used. These were of cotton, silk, wool, linen, and barks of trees. In the seventh century the textile industry continued to be of equally high standard and the varieties then in use have been referred to in the Bana's *Harshacharita*, Rajyasri's marriage garments comprised *Kshauma* (linen), badara (cotton), dukula (bark-silk), *lala-tantu* (spider silk), *amsuka* (muslin), netra (shot-silk), etc. Hiuen T-Sang also refers to the Indians clothing materials as silk, cotton, linen, wool, goat's hair, etc. *Amarakosa* also gives a variety of names of the wearing materials and refers to bleached and unbleached silk. From Ajanta frescoes we come across four distinct types of wearing, gold and silver brocades, dyed muslins, spotted muslins, etc.

Of the different centres of textile manufactures, Banaras was the producer of the best silk clothes. Pundra, i.e., north Bengal, Kamrupa, Mathura were other centres of cotton and silk textile manufacture.

From *Amarakosa* we come to know of the manufacture of leather-fur, leather-bottle for containing oil, leather boots and shoes. Ivory work also was highly developed and put into various uses. Ivory seals of the Gupta period have been found at Bhita near Allahabad.

Mining of metals, such as gold, silver, copper, iron, etc., was going on as usual. There was also an abundant influx of gold from the Byzantine empire in exchange for Indian goods. Copper, tin, and lead were also imported from abroad.

In the Ajanta frescoes metallic mirrors have been traced by scholars. The iron pillar of King Chandra at Meherauli in old Delhi which belongs to his period is a wonderful specimen of polished cast iron and it has not undergone any corrosion despite exposure to weather for centuries.

The art of jewellery maintained the high standard of manufacturing excellence during the period which was attained during the previous age. In the *Brihat-Samhita* there is mention of twenty-two jewels which were in abundant use, such as sapphire, ruby, emerald, pearl, coral, beryl, amethyst, moon-stone, topaz, azure, opal, conch-shell. Diamond was also in great use at that time. These jewels were also exported to foreign countries. Varahamihira mentions varieties of diamond and seven sources from which these are obtained. All these sources are Indian. Some of these place names from which diamond thus available have also been mentioned by Ptolemy; pearls, and jewels were extensively used in making ornaments.

TRADE : INLAND AND MARITIME

Foreign Trade : From the 4th century B.C. Indian Trade and maritime activities had been highly developed. Alexander's invasion (327-325 B.C.) resulted in close contact with the Hellenic world. Embassies were sent to the Maurya court by the Greek rulers of Syria and Egypt. Asoka had sent missioneries to five Greek Kingdoms. These relations with the Hellenic world encouraged Trade relation between India and these countries. In fact, a good part of the State revenue was derived from the traders. *Sulka*, i.e., tax on merchandise constituted an important source of royal revenue. There was a large number of foreigners living in the metropolis during the Maurya period, many of them were traders. In the first century B.C. there was a close contact between India and Rome. During the early centuries of the Christian era India had commercial intercourse with China, Hellenic world, Ceylon and South-East Asian countries. These are recorded in *Milindapaṇha* and Nagarjunikonda inscriptions.

Indian traders and merchants carried the products of various industries from one end of India to the other in bullock carts. At times hundreds of bullock carts formed into caravans and traversed the country from one end to the other. The roads being infested with robbers, the traders would engage on payment protection force for security. Commodities would also be carried to ports and harbours for export to foreign countries.

From the old Pali texts we come to know of several main trade routes. Growth of industry is dependent on facilities of cargo movement. In ancient India, therefore, there was particular recognition of this important pre-condition to growth of trade and commerce. Some of the more important trade routes were, one that ran from Sravasti to Rajagriha with twelve halts including those at Vaisali and Pataliputra with a single crossing of the Ganges at Patna, another route linked Sravasti to Paithan with six halts and numerous crossing of rivers and one route led towards Sind and to Sauvira.

Caravans are known to have moved overland towards east and west as well as across the deserts requiring many days to cross the Rajputana desert only by the coolness of night. The old Grand Trunk road passed from Rajagriha through Banaras, Saketa, Sravasti, Taxila and the frontiers connecting India with Central and western Asia.

By the time of Chandragupta Maurya a Royal road linked up Pushkaravati in the north-west frontier with Pataliputra, the Maurya capital. According to Megasthenes the length of the road was 10,000 stades, i.e., 1156 miles.

Periplus gives us precise indications of the trade routes during the first century A.D. Two Trade-routes one from the terminus of the Maurya Royal Road to Minnagara, capital of Indo-Scythia and its capital Barbaricum; another joined Kashmir, Hindukush and Kabul countries with Brygaza. Ujjaini was also linked up with this port. To this famous port Barygaza routes from the Deccan marts of Tagara in Hyderabad and Pratisthana, that is, Paithan, were linked up.

Transports used for the purpose of trade were litter, horse carriage, bullock-carts, camels, and asses.

Coastal Trade

Simultaneously with the overland Trade coastal trade from eastern and western coasts was carried on. From Chola port, we are told by *Periplus* country boats sailed upto Malabar while large vessels sailed upto the mouth of the Ganges. A complete list of the names of the chief marts can be had from the *Periplus* and *Geography* of Ptolemy. Some of the more important ones were Barygaza, Supara, Muziris, Nelcynda, Poduca, Soptma, Tamralipti, Paloura, etc. *Milindapanha* also refers to Barygaza, Kaveripattanam, Vanga, i.e., Tamralipti, Barbaricum, etc.

Policy of friendship begun between India and the Hellenic world from the time of Chandragupta and followed during his successors created most favourable condition for the expansion of Indian trade with the West. Trade route between India and the Hellenic World was conducted both by land and sea. The most important land-route led from Taxila *via* Kapisa, Bactria, Hekatompylos and Ecbatana, another land-route connected the lower Indus Valley *via* Seistan and Carmania to the same terminus.

The Sea route was through west Indian ports through the Persian Gulf and Ports of South Arabia. The Indian exports to Egypt were ivory, tortoise-shell, pearls, unguents, dyes, indigo, iron, wood, etc. During early Saka-Pahlava era, the Greek mariners making use of their discovery of monsoons undertook direct voyages successively to the Indus delta and Gujarat coast and the Malabar ports. In the last quarter of the first century A.D. the Western merchants sailing from the Egyptian Coasts would reach Indian port Muziris, i.e., Cranganore in the South in forty days.

Indian trade with Rome reached its peak during the rule of Emperor Augustus (29 B.C.). Isidore of Chararx in his *Parthian Stations* gives a detailed itinerary of the caravan route from Antioch in the West to the valley of the river Helmund on Indian border. Roman maritime trade with India in the early Christian era was conducted in large ships from the Egyptian Coasts. Tamil works also refer to *Yavana* merchants' colony in the coastal cities. Recent excavations at Arikamedu near Pondichery have brought to light the remains of a Roman trading station there. Fragments of Roman pottery and hoards of Roman imperial coins have been found on other sites in South India. The Arab merchants also carried on trade with the Indian ports in their own ships.

From the literary evidences we come to know that the export to foreign countries, particularly Rome, comprised agricultural products like rice, wheat, sesame-oil and sugar, forest products like teak, sandal-wood, black-wood, ebony, etc.; animals like lions, apes, tigers, monkeys, birds, specially parrots, ivory, shell of hawk-bill turtles, etc. Long-pepper, black-pepper, cinnamon-leaf, various other spices were exported to Rome.

Fine quality cotton textiles as also coarser varieties were exported to Arabia, East Africa, and Egypt. Indian iron and steel were exported to Somali coasts and Alexandria.

Such was the hugeness of the quantity of gold that Rome had to pay to India for the Indian merchandise that Emperor Tiberius in 22 A.D. wrote to the Roman Senate complaining that the country was being drained of its treasures for baubles. Pliny complained a little latter of the huge amount of gold paid to India annually for Indian products which were sold at one hundred times more than their original costs. Such was the abundance of the influx of the Roman gold coin in India that the Kushana emperors restruck the Roman coins in their names.

Indian commercial relations with Ceylon and countries of South-East Asia, particularly *Suvarna dvipa,* go back to centuries before the Christian era. In the second century A.D. a regular sea route was in operation from the eastern India Sea Border. Another route linked up upper Ganges regions with *Suvarna bhumi or Suvarnadvipa.* Through Commerce Indian Kingdoms had begun to be set up in Malayan Peninsula, Cambodia, and Champa from the first century A.D. The friendly relations between these colonies and the mother country led to increased commercial intercourse between them.

As early as the second century B.C. India had trade relations with South-West China through overland route by way of upper Burma and Yunnan. About 128 B.C. Chinese ambassador Chang-Kien while visiting Bactria was surprised at Indian textiles and bamboos in the market there. In the first century A.D. the Chinese historian writing about the Chinese traders travelling in foreign ships for buying pearls, beryl, rare stones, etc. visited India as also other countries and made purchases in exchange for gold and Chinese Silk. In the same century there was a regular trade by overland route between India and China. Chinese raw silk, silk yarn, silk cloth, etc., were the main merchandise that came from China. In the second half of the first century A.D. sea route to China was in use and from the second century onwards we have evidences pointing to the use of sea route to Tonkin by the Indians.

The peace and order established all over the empire under the strong arm of the Gupta rulers led to expansion of inland trade and commerce. Coinage of gold and silver issued in extensive number by the Gupta emperors helped the growth of trade. Merchants and traders of the Gupta Age conducted trade both by overland and sea routes. Amarakosa makes references to markets, shops as well as to merchants travelling by boats. In the Gupta site at Bhita rows of shops along the high street and side street have been discovered. From the records of this period it is learnt that import and export trade was conducted through sea ports. Cosmos writing in the early sixth century A.D. mentions a number of important trading stations of which are *Sindhu*, *Orrhotha*, *Sibor*, *Calliana*, and five marts on the Malabar coasts. The names of the ports have not all been identified. Among the most flourishing among the ports of the time was Tramralipti. Even during the time of the visit by Hiuen T-Sang and I-tsang, Tamralipti, because of its happy geographical situation, became the emporium of vast trade of Eastern India and the port where voyagers from China, Indonesia, and Ceylon came for trading with Eastern India and left for home.

Most significant development in the economic history of Eastern and Southern Asia during the third decade of the sixth century A.D. was the inter-oceanic trade reaching from China through Indonesia and the east coast of India upto Ceylon and extending thence along the west Indian coast to Persia and the Homevite country (in Arabia) and Adula (the port of Assum, the capital of Ethiopian Kingdom).[1]

According to Cosmos also merchandise from China, Indonesia and South India was carried to Ceylon and thence to western lands. We are also told that merchant ships from India, Persia, and Ethiopia often visited Ceylon. During the Gupta Age also several overland routes connected India with China. Both Fa-hien and Hiuen-T-Sang testify to the great north-western route running by way of Central Asia and Bactria to the passes of Suleiman range, thence to the interior of India. A more difficult route ran across the Karakoram range and Kashmir and connected India with China. A third route led from Tonkin through Kamrupa across Pundravardhana to Magadha.

India's principal articles of trade were agricultural products, forest produce, gems and pearls, diamonds, etc., textiles and metals. Among agricultural products long pepper, black pepper, cinnamon,

---

[1] *The Classical Age*, p. 598.

Cardamom, and other spices occupied the first place. Among the forest products were sandal-wood and images of Buddha carved out of sandal-wood, medicinal plants, etc. Pearls, corals, diamonds, silk and ivory were also important articles of export. A variety of cotton brocades and cotton fabrics were exported to China. This is stated by Cosmos. Indian iron was an important item of export. Among the imports were Chinese silk, horses from Arabia and Persia, ivory from Ethiopia, Copper from the *mlechcha* countries, that is, countries of the Western Mediterranean, sapphire from Ceylon, etc.

Organisation of Trade and Industry

Trade and industry during the Maurya-Scythian period had developed organisations of their own among persons of the same trade or industry, which compared favourably with the *guilds* of the Medieval Europe. The Indian guilds were called *Srenis*. Organisation of industrial guilds can be traced back to the period of the early Buddhist literature. The *Jatakas* refer to eighteen *Srenis*. In the Arthasastra we come across references to types of industrial organisations and other associations called *samgha* and *Sreni*. In both Manu and Yajnavalka the rules and customs of the *Srenis* and other associations were put on the same level with those of regional caste and family customs.

Almost every industry had its guild which laid down rules and regulations for the guidance and conduct of it's members in order to safeguard their interests. The law of the land recognised these rules and regulations. The guild had its constitution with a President or a Headman and an Executive Council. The executive officers at the head of the guilds were called *Jethakas*.

The guilds acquired in course of time great prestige and power and the heads of the guilds were members of the Court. Sometimes guilds were found to maintain trained armies which were used during fights between different guilds. The king could, in times of need, requisition the services of the armies of the guilds.

Epigraphic evidences of the first two centuries of the Christian era show that one of the important functions of the guilds was to act as the trustees of various pious and charitable endowments. Cash or property was deposited by pious donors in perpetuity with the guilds in return for interests on the deposits. Many donors to the guilds were foreigners.

People also deposited money with the guilds on condition that the interest accruing to the deposits should be spent for some specified purposes. Sometimes guilds became centres of learning and culture.

Guilds were both industrial and commercial. The industrial type of guilds were those of weavers, potters, makers of hydraulic engines, oil-makers, brazers, bamboo workers, etc. The business guilds were organised on the principles of joint-stock companies. There were Traders' League, Union of Traders, Traders' *Corner*, Traders' *Trust* were also prevalent in those days. The Traders' guilds were sometimes of the nature of Trusts. Smriti works mention business by partnership.

From the facts referred to above it is proved beyond doubt that a keen business instinct characterised the society and trade, commerce and industry, and commerce flourished in ancient India to a very high degree.

During the Gupta Age the guilds and partnerships were developed in a much greater extent. In the later Smriti works there were laws which dealt with the violation of agreements which related to groups, i.e., *Sreni*, *Puga*, and *Naigama*.

Srenis were guilds of artisans and traders referred to in the preceding age, which continued during the Gupta Age with greater efficiency. Puga has been defined variously by different authors. According to Katyayana these were groups of merchants, etc. *Naigama*, according to the same author, were groups of inhabitants of the same town. But in *Amarakosa* the term applied to merchants.

During the Gupta period, the trend was to enhance the status and position of the guilds. According to the late Smritis the guilds and other associations were to be headed by high executive Officers called *Adhyakshas* who were assisted by two to five persons called *advisers*. The *adhyakshas* had the power to punish wrongdoers by reprimand, censure or being excommunicated. The judgements passed by the high executive officers, that is, the *adhyakshas* in discharge of their duties were respected by the king. The guilds had to follow the opinion of the advisers. The king had the right to intervene and settle disputes between the chief executive officers and the groups.

The guilds entered into compacts in order to preserve their rules, customs, and usages in tact. These compacts or conventions were enforced by the king wherever necessary. The rules or conditions of the convention or compact had to be obeyed by the individual members and where these were in conflict with the order of the king, the king's order was to be obeyed. Extreme punishment for disobedience was excommunication or banishment of the offending member.

The members of the guild had certain specific rights and duties. They were not to carry arms, nor enter into mutual conflict. One who would injure common interest or insult those who were learned in the Vedas was to be banished. One who would commit heinous crime or cause a split in the guild or destroy property of groups was to be brought before the king and destroyed. All members were to have equal share in gains as well as in debts.

From the clay seals discovered at Basrah and Bhita of the Gupta times it is believed that industrial and trading guilds or groups entered into conventions or compacts with individuals, obviously for industrial or trading benefits.

From the Indore copper plate inscription of Emperor Skandagupta we come to know of the perpetual endowment of a sum of money by a Brahmana to the local guild of oilman for daily supply of fixed quantity of oil to a Sun temple. The guilds thus performed the functions of bankers. There are instances where kings and princes made endowments to the guilds for regular performance of acts of charity or piety. Partnership as a business organisation is treated in the later Smritis on the lines of the older Smritis. It is mentioned that the income of each member should be in proportion to his share, or according to the agreement. The proportion of profit sharing has been mentioned by Katyayana and Brihaspati in the following order: apprentice, advanced learner, expert and teacher as 1 : 2 : 3 : 4. A document issued by a partner with the approval of other partners shall be binding upon all of them. Conversely a partner putting the organisation to loss due to his action without consent of others must make good the loss. An unscrupulous partner should be expelled. Such were the organisational discipline and rules of business organisation of that period.

Labour and Wage

From sources—epigraphic, literary and classical as also the accounts of the foreign travellers—we can easily understand that the economic development from the Nanda-Maurya period down to the Gupta Age and even seventh century A.D. there was a clear realisation in India that wealth of the country was related to the exploitation of natural resources and the utilisation of skilled and unskilled man-power.

It goes without saying that the problem of labour is directly related to production and wages to profit. Compared to profits derived during the period under review wages were low. This was natural in a generally capitalist system of production.

Hired labour was used for agriculture, animal husbandry, industry and trade as also for domestic services. Hired labour was divided into three grades: (i) the soldiers, (ii) cultivators, (iii) porters and domestic servants. Employment of labourers might be on daily basis, or fortnightly, three or six monthly or annual basis. Wages were paid either in cash or in kind.

Use of forced labour belonged, as in the previous age, almost exclusively to the State. Slaves were mostly employed by the public as personal attendants.

Labour laws were laid down in the later Smritis following the lines of Manu and Yajnavalkya. Hired labourers guilty of treachery in the performance of the work of his master forfeited his wages and was liable to be sued in the court of law. Labourers who received wages but failed to do his work was forced to pay double the amount of the wages received as fine to the king and refund the wages to the master. Failure to complete the work for which an agreement or a contract was entered into was punished with a heavy fine. On the other hand, the master who failed to pay wages to the labourers on completion of the work was forced to pay the same by the king and pay a fine. According to Katyayana a servant was not liable for the loss due to theft, fire or flood. A master who would abandon his sick servant was liable to a fine. Workmen who would be required to work overtime were paid extra wages. A workman engaged as herdsman who would let animals of his master to be lost, killed or maimed was liable to pay a heavy fine. If the animals in his charge would cause loss to the field of others he would be liable to a fine. Similarly a washerman was not to use, hire or pledge his employer's clothes. The weavers and metal workers were required to conform to standard and not to decrease the materials in the process of manufacture.

Another important factor concerning labour was its mobility. There are references to the movement of artisans and skilled labourers from one region to another for better prospect or for avoiding slump at home. Further skilled labourers were also invited from one area to another. For instance, the sculptors from Mathura were invited to Sravasti and Saranath for carving stone images. In the Gupta period the silk weavers who had formed into a guild migrated from Gujarata to Mandasor. Merchants also migrated from one region to another for better opportunities. The Pratihara inscription from Gwalior mentions emigration of Nagabhatta of the Vanik-varkhata caste from Anandapura.

Medium of Exchange: Currency and Banking

In the pre-Maurya era India had silver and copper coins as medium of exchange. Gold *rishka* although in use as a medium of exchange did not possess all the characteristics of proper coinage in the early period. In Manu we have reference to silver coin of 32 *ratis*, i.e., 58.56 grams, called *purana* or *dharana*. Copper coin of 82 *ratis*, i.e., 146.4 grams was known as *Karshapana*. In South India the name *Karshapana* was used for gold and silver coins also. The Buddhist texts use *Kahapana* for a coin. There are references to varieties of coin in the Buddhist texts. There are *nikkha* and Suvarna of gold, bronze and copper coins are mentioned as *Kamsa*, *Pada*, *Masaka* and *Kakanika*. 5 *masakas* were equivalent to 1 *pada*.

The most noteworthy feature of the economic development of the Maurya-Scythian period was the use of coins as common currency. The old barter system was gradually replaced by exchange in precious metals. From Herodotus we know that India paid 360 talents of gold dust or ingots to the Persian emperor as annual tribute in the 6th century B.C. This was soon followed by use of metal of regular shape, weight, and fineness guaranteed by competent authority. This marked the beginning of a common currency system. The coins were issued by the rulers only. Figures on the coins were marked by a punch, hence came to be generally known as *punch-marked* coins. There were, however, no names or legends on such coins.

It is with the coming of the Bactrian Greeks that names and portraits of the rulers issuing the coins began to be put on the coins, generally the image of the king on the obverse and of a deity on the reverse and were executed with great artistic skill. Needless to mention that the Indian currency system was largely influenced by the foreigners who ruled over parts of India. The huge influx of Roman and Chinese gold into India as well as from *Suvarnabhumi* was an important factor in the development of Indian currency. The Graeco-Bactrian coins, the Roman coins influenced the system of coinage of the Sakas, Pahlavas, and the Kushanas and through them the coinage of later Indian rulers. The Indian rulers not only copied the form, character, weight, and fineness of the foreign coins, particularly the Roman, but even used foreign names like *dinara* (denarius) and *dramma* (drachma). Circular coins bearing superscription of the ruler in whose name these were issued were the result of the influence of the West, though this system did not take root except in the case of the Gupta coinage.

Thus we may conclude that punch-marked coins served as Indian currency till the end of the Maurya period and later gradually under foreign influence Indian currency began to use coins of regular form, weight, and fineness with names of the rulers issuing them. It is very much likely that smaller transactions were carried on with cowries all throughout the period under review and continued down to the 18th century A.D.

Banking as an institution in the modern sense is not mentioned anywhere in our sources of information. But the basic principle of banking which is trust, was fully realised during the Nanda-Maurya period down to the Gupta Age and beyond. The existence of credit and banking facilities as a part of the economic life in Ancient India is proved by literary and epigraphic evidences. We have numerous references to the functioning of guilds in the capacity of banks by accepting deposits of money and other endowments for performing specific duties in return or payment of interest.

Inscriptions of Saka Ushavadatta mention two weavers' guilds in Nasik accepting permanent deposits on condition of payment of interest of 1 per cent and .75 per cent per month. From a Brahmi inscription of Mathura of the second century A.D. during the time of Huviska, we know that a foreigner from Badakshan in Central Asia deposited 500 *Puranas* each in two guilds for daily feeding the Brahmanas and distributing some stuff to the poor in lieu of interest.

From records belonging to period preceding the Gupta Age, we come to know of endowments made by princes and private individuals to guilds to perform certain acts of charity or piety as specified by the donors. There are also instances where kings put their fortunes into the guilds for these were considered safer than ever the royal treasury. During the Gupta Age we have instances of the Emperors making perpetual endowments to guilds for the performance of some specific duty. For instance, from the Indore copper plate inscription we come to know of a certain Brahmana making an endowment to a local guild of oilmen to supply a fixed quantity of oil for a Sun temple. The guild invested the endowment for earning profits for meeting the expenses of the supply of oil to the temple and certainly to some extent for its own profit. The guilds were rendering the services of bankers from the early times till the tenth century A.D.

Functions of the Bankers were also done by individual creditors who loaned out money on interest. This was in the nature of *Mahajani* System. Manu and Yajnavalkya were followed by later Smriti writers like Nada, Brihaspati, Katyanana, etc., in laying down the rules of interest. There were different rates of interests for secure and insecure loans. The rates of interest mentioned by different Smritis were different. Interest at the rate of Rs. 1.25 per month mentioned both by Nanda and Yajnavalkya is definitely very high. If the loan was not repaid on demand the interest might be raised to 5 per cent. But it was also laid down that accumulated interest could not be more than the principal. As money lending helped people to better their economic prospects through profitable investments, the profession of money lending was accepted in the economic life of Ancient India.

State Control over Trade and Industry

In the *Arthasastra*, we have references to the traditional State policy in relation to trade and industry. Active encouragement of trade and industry was contemplated as a duty of the State by Kautilya. With regard to trade, the king was enjoined to secure trade routes from obstruction by officers, frontier guards, as well as by thieves, robbers, and animals. The king was also to cause construction of trade-routes and foundation of market-towns. The *Arthasastra* also describes the measures a king had to take for saving the people against the merchants and artisans. "Kautilya characterises merchants, artisans, and some other specified classes as thieves in fact, though not in name." The rules detailed in the *Arthasastra* for dealing with cases of short weight and measure as well as various other ways that merchants and artisans might injure the interests of the people clearly point to the strict paternal care of the State for the people. Similar measures are prescribed for the security of the people against the trading classes. It is mentioned in the Arthasastra that only old wares of proved ownership should be sold and mortgaged under the supervision of the market Superintendent. While a graduated scale of fines was laid down for the traders that gave short weights or measures, a fixed profit of 5 per cent for home grown commodities and 10 per cent on foreign goods was permissible.

During the Maurya period the State Policy as recommended in the *Arthasastra* in relation to trade and industry was followed. Construction of roads was put under the charge of a class of officers called *Agronomoi* by Megasthenes. Again in the cities the *City Commissioners* were divided into six boards, the fourth Board was in charge of sales and barter. There was also the Superintendent of weights and measures.

Goods were not to be sold where these were produced, but in appointed markets where the dealers had to register the quality and price of the goods. The Superintendent of Commerce fixed the wholesale prices. Traders had to get licence for their Trade. Foreigners had to take out a passport in addition to his professional licence.

As in trade, so in industry the State control during the Nanda-Maurya period was quite extensive. The State provided for the security of industrial classes. Injury to artisans or damage to agricultural implements were punished by the State.

The State had monopoly of industries which were costly, risky or required pioneering enterprise. Mines were a nationalised industry. There were gold, silver, diamond, precious stones, copper, lead, tin, iron, and bitumen mines which were worked by the State. The State also explored the ocean in search for pearls, mother-of-pearl, conch-shell and coral. Oilfields yielding mercury and other minerals were worked by the State. Manufacture of salt was also a Government monopoly and it was done through farming out salt-beds to lessees. A special officer looked after the Government business in pearls, conch-shells, corals, diamonds, and precious stones. Another special officer was in charge of gold and silver. State had also monopoly of manufacture of wines, liquors and their sale. Arms and armaments, building of boats and ships were State monopoly. Minting of coins was done by the State.

The Government also had its own cotton, oil, sugar, dairy and agricultural industries besides private enterprises in these. There were State spinning and weaving houses, State warehouses.

In the post-Maurya and the Gupta periods although the traditional economic activities continued yet we have no information as to systematic State control of industries and trade by the State. Manufacture of arms and armaments, minting of coins, construction of roads, collection of ferry-charges, tolls and customs were, however, there as no Government could leave these in private hands.

Problem of the Origin of Feudalism in Socio-Economic Set-up

In recent years there has been a tendency among some scholars to identify the origin of feudalism in the later Gupta period. Romila Thapar refers to an inscription of the later Gupta period in which "The Gupta monarch had Surashmichandra as his feudatory who in return had Mantrivishnu as his sub-feudatory. This hierarchy is frequently described in the inscriptions of the later Chalukyas".[1] Basing her argument on this, she remarks that it "is one of earliest evidences of the beginning of feudal hierarchy". Thapar also argues that although there was difference between the Indian System of land tenure and European feudalism, "the difference is not so significant as to preclude the term feudalism for conditions prevailing in India during the period (800-1200 A.D.)".[2]

But before attempting to trace the origin of feudalism in India from the later Gupta period, it is necessary to discuss at some length

[1] Romila Thapar: *A History of India*, Vol. I, p. 242.

[2] *Idem.*

what the term *feudalism* denoted in Western Europe from which the term had originated. Further, it has to be determined if the Indian feudatories like Samanta, Mahasamanta were the Indian version of their European counterpart.

There is no doubt that central principle of feudalism as it originated in the West was land tenure on condition of military service. But it was also a social and economic system which grew up from various sources under the pressure of the barbarian invasion. In the West feudalism grew from the bottom and reached the apex and gave it a pyramidal shape. The king was last to be feudalised. Later the theory developed that the king was the owner of all lands. The tenants-in-chief who were his immediate under-lords had to hold their tenure in return for military service, paying homage to the king, making payments to him on certain specified occasions, such as marriage of the king's son or daughter, pay an inheritance fee and wardship when the tenant-in-chief would die leaving a minor son to succeed him. The economic aspect of feudalism was manorial system. The tenant-in-chief would have his manor within which he was the supreme lord. He allowed the serfs to cultivate strips of lands allotted to each of them in return for certain duties and he had his own acreage which he got cultivated by employing labourers whose work was supervised by the lord's officers. The lords, i.e., the tenants-in-chief appointed sub-tenants by following the system of sub-infeudation on same terms and condition as they received land from the king. The sub-tenants let out their acres to serfs who were tied to the soil.

Thus *feudalism* as we understand the term in the European context had the following main features ; (i) it arose as a defensive measure against the invasions of the barbarians, (ii) it began from the bottom and at the ultimate stage reached the apex, i.e., the king, (iii) it was a land tenure based on military service, (iv) its economic aspect was Manorial System, (v) it entailed certain specific payments on certain occasions, (vi) Oath of fealty bound the tenant-in-chief with the king, the sub-tenants with the tenant-in-chief his overlord, (vii) in it, the lowest stratum was composed of the serfs who were a sort of landed slaves.

But landlordism in ancient and medieval India does not bear any material resemblance with the Western feudalism and should not be confused with it. In India feudatory States formed out of conquered kingdoms of princes and local chiefs were not feudal estates. The feudatory States were in the nature of tributaries and not feudalised States. Further here is no trace of sub-infeudation by the tributary States on any contractual basis. The apparent structure may be found to resemble the feudal structure such as the king, feudatories and smaller estate holders but the Indian system did not contain the essence of the Western feudalism. For there was no question of any formal oath of fealty to be taken by the feudatories, simply acceptance of suzerainty of the overlord would be enough. But this was not necessary in the case of sub-lords or estate holders. They were not required to accept any formal suzerainty of the overlord.

The Indian landlordism which has been likened by some scholars with Western feudalism was neither born as a measure of safety, nor was it based on any specific military service which was the essence of feudalism of the West. The underlords of the feudatories likewise were not bound by any bond of military service. The military help requisitioned from time to time by the king from the feudatories was by virtue of the authority of the suzerain over his tributaries. The Indian cultivators were not the villeins, nor were they tied to the soil. There were slaves and free labourers who could be employed by the small land-owing cultivators to assist them in agricultural work. According to Dr. D. C. Sircar "In India the king was never the actual owner of the land under permanent tenants".[1] This virtually takes away the very basis of the feudal character from the Indian landlordism. The remark of R. Thapar that "The basic requisites of a feudal system were present in India" is not borne out by available evidences except in the *Amara* tenure in the Vijaynagar Kingdom.

According to Thapar the relationship of the feudatories to the king was subordinate and the feudatories conquered.

Problem of the Origin of Feudalistic Elements in India

In recent years there have been attempts by scholars to find out origins of feudalism in the Indian political, social, and economic set up of Ancient India.

Feudalism, as we understand in the European context, had its origin in the fifth century A.D. and continued till the middle of the 15th century when rise of strong national monarchy in different European countries proved the end of feudalism. Of course some remnants and annoyances of feudalism still continued to exist for quite some time in some of the countries.

The origin of the feudalism in Europe lay in the need of self-defence among the people who had lands of their own, when in the fifth century the imperial rule at Rome became powerless to render protection to different parts and localities in the face of barbarian

---

[1] D. C. Sircar: *Landlordism and Tenancy in Ancient and Medieval India*, p. 33.

invasion. As the system was essentially a measure of self-defence military service constituted the very central principle of feudalism. Lesser landlords sought protection from the bigger landlords who had more power and means to protect the locality against barbarian attacks. This voluntary surrender to the bigger lords meant surrender of the landed proprieties by the lesser lords on condition of retaining possession of the same but getting the bigger lord's protection in times of danger and rendering military service to the bigger lord for a specific number of days, usually forty days in a year. The lesser lord had to be bound to the bigger lord by an oath of fealty. He had also to make certain payments such as payment at the time of lord's daughter or son's marriage, an inheritance fee when his son would succeed on his death and wardship if the son was a minor. The system when became fully developed by the process of the big lords appointing high born persons who had entirely frittered away their patrimony or became landless for other reason, as sub-lords. In this way there were a double process through which Western feudalism became fully developed. Ultimately the king who was, in theory, the owner of all land of his dominions, became feudalised by recognising the big lords as his tenants-in-chief on similar condition on which the lesser lords had accepted the bigger lords as their suzerain. Ecclesiastics with vast landed property were no exception. They also became tenants-in-chief and appointed sub-tenants by following the system of sub-infeudation. The tenants-in-chief had to render military service to the king on specific number of occasions (40 days a year), do him homage, pay fees and charges as did the lesser-lords to their suzerains. Besides, the tenants-in-chief had to pay for ransoming the king if he would be taken prisoner in war. Below the tenants-in-chief came the lesser lords who came to be known as sub-tenants who rendered similar services, as already referred to above. The economic aspect of feudalism was Manorial System where the lords, tenants or sub-tenants would parcel out their acres into strips and disributed them among the serfs who were landed slaves tied to the soil. The lord had a portion of the land usually one-third under his direct possession which he got cultivated by the serfs under supervision of his own officers. He ran the flour mill, wine-press, oil mill, etc., the products of which were sold to the serfs. The life of the serfs was miserable, all work and suffering. Socially, the possession of land was the determinant of status and prestige. The life of the lords was one of luxury and abandon. This was in short, what Feudalism meant in Europe.

If we take the term feudalism in the sense it carried in European history during the Middle Ages, we will perhaps make an initial mistake. It will be better if it is borne in mind that the Indian feudalism although structurally resembled European feudalism it vastly differed from in many aspects from other types of feudalism, European or others.

Prof. R. S. Sarma is of the opinion that tendenices towards feudalisation of the administrative and political mechanism of India may be traced to post-Maurya and the Gupta periods. He also points out that traces of this system were also to be found in the Dharmasastras and the epics. Romila Thapar while pointing out that although Indian feudalism differed from other types of feudalism and that the Indian feudalism did not emphasise the aspects as did the European feudalism, yet "the difference is not so significant as to preclude the use of the terms feudalism for conditions prevailing in India during this period (800-1200 A.D.)"[1] According to Thapar, basic requisites of feudalism existed in India.

Thapar's main arguments are : (i) Feudatories who had been conquered in war were allowed little scope for independent action although some of the feudatories were permitted to sub-infeudate their territories without obtaining permission from the king. Thus a feudal hierarchy grew up. A certain Gupta king had Surashmichandra as his feudatory who appointed Matrivishnu as his sub-jugator. Such hierarchy is met, Thapar points out, in the inscriptions of latter Chalukyas.

(ii) That the feudatories besides payment of their dues had to maintain a specified number of troops for the king, and had other obligations like attendance at king's court on certain occasions.

(iii) That the *Sudras* carried out work of cultivation and they "in effect were almost tied to the soil".

It may be pointed out that R. Thapar's arguments are least a labourious attempt to almost equate Indian landlordism with feudalism as we understand the term in European context. Dr. D. C. Sircar rightly remarks that "landlordism of ancient and medieval India.... should not be confused with feudalism". He points out that in India the king was never the owner of the land under permanent tenancy, but in feudalism the basic principle is king's ownership of all lands in his kingdom.

Thapar's argument that the feudatories were left without much independence of action is not borne out by facts of history. Samudragupta's feudatories in South India were allowed to retain their auto-

[1] Romila Thapar: *A History of India*, Vol. I, p. 242.

nomy only, accepting his suzerainty and payment of tributes, obedience to him and attending his court on certain special occasion. The solitary instance of Surashmichandra does not explain the general character of landlordism in Gupta India. From numerous charters discovered all over India it is proved that grants of land were made to Brahmanas and temples without stipulating any obligation whatsoever. Obviously the priestly class was unsuitable for military obligation. But even where military obligation was a condition of the land grant, the system was extremely limited. This again could be seen in South India in the late medieval time. Except the *Amara* tenure of the late medieval period of the history of South India "there is absolutely no mention of obligations having resemblance with these of feudal type even in such records".[1]

As to Thapar's next argument that the feudatories had to maintain a special number of troops for service of the king is equally unrelated to facts. It is true that early Indian rulers sometimes granted Jagirs for the maintenance of their officers but the latter were not under any feudal obligations. Further, we know from Arthasastra that the rate of the salary of the infantry was 500 *panas* a year.[2] We also know that the Gupta emperors had regular army under their pay. This is borne out by the existence of the office of the treasurer of the War Department (*Ranabhandagaradhikarana*) mentioned in the clay seal, discovered at the site of ancient Vaisali by Theodore Block.[3] Both in the central and provincial governments under the Guptas the military finance was separate from the civil finance. It may as well be mentioned that the huge influx of bullion into India through foreign trade did not require payment of the officers and the soldiers by land grants, there was abundant supply of coins in the country during that period.

Thapar's third argument that the *Sudras* carried out the work of cultivation and were more or less tied to the soil is also not factually correct. To be tied to the soil would presuppose the System of villeinage which was the most inhuman aspect of Western feudalism. In the Maurya-Scythian period we find that agricultural work was carried out by (i) landless agricultural labourers (*Vishti*) who worked as domestic servants on the basis of free food and a little wage, (ii) ordi-

---

[1] D. C. Sircar: *Landlordism and Tenancy in Ancient and Medieval India*, p. 33.

[2] U. N. Ghosal: *Hindu Revenue System*, p. 209.

[3] *Ibid.*, p. 258.

nary labourers (*Karmakaras*) who worked for wage, (iii) the slaves, (iv) the agriculturists proper or peasant proprietors.[1] R. K. Mookerjee states that the arable land of the village that is the *Gram Kshetra* was distributed among individual holdings usually small enough to be cultivated by their owners, and with the help of hired labourers if necessary. The idea prevalent at that time was that "peasants leaving at home their empty barns and toiling as hirelings on the estate of royal capitalists" was "a symptom of social decadence".[2] Obviously, the peasants could leave their land at their choice which the *villeins* could not. There has been no reference to the cultivators tied to the soil in any epigraphic or literary records. On the contrary in *Manu Smriti* it is mentioned that "Land made fit for cultivation is to be settled *on rent* with its cultivator for life". Megasthenes who in his *Indica* dealt with the husbandmen in details does not refer to their being bound to the soil. On the contrary he found them to be so important to the natural life that even in times of war they were not in any way disturbed.

In the Gupta period also we have no reference to the *Sudras* being tied to the soil. On the contrary there are numerous instances of Brahmanas and Kshatriyas adopting the occupations of the classes below them and the Sudras and Vaisyas following those of the classes above them. The Smritis mention cultivation of land and rearing of animals among the traditional occupations of the Vaisyas.[3]

Lastly, the accounts of the Greeks and the Chinese as well as indigenous evidences show that the general condition of the people, the vast majority of whom lived a life of contentment. These are not facts which permit equating the Indian cultivators with the serfs of the Western Europe.

It may, however, be mentioned that *Amara* tenure of the late Medieval South India was a near approach to feudalism. Under this tenure the landlords under the Vijaynagar emperors were responsible for the supply of foot-soldiers, horses and elephants to the king in times of need for the enjoyment of the estates held under *Amara* tenure. The *Amara-nayakas*, as the feudatories were called, followed the process of sub-infudation and gave their hand in smaller estates to subordinate holders.

The occasional land grants made by the rulers during the early history of India to their feudatories called *Mahasamanta*, *Mahamanda-*

---

1 *Vide*: R. K. Mookerji: *Chandragupta and His Times*, p. 199.

2 *The Age of Imperial Unity*, p. 595.

3 *Comprehensive History of India, Vol. II*, p. 432.

lesvara and lesser feudatories called *Samanta, Raja, Ranaka,* etc., did not by themselves account for the origin of feudalism. These were tendencies which may be called *feudal* in nature. In late medieval history of India, however, there were tenures as we have discussed above which assumed more or less feudal character and reached its culmination in their own way during the Mughal period. In the period under review it is difficult to trace the obligations of feudatories for neither in the *Smritis* nor in any other source there has been any reference to these. But in the contemporary literature, Prof. R. S. Sarma points out, some trends are noticeable in this regard.

CHAPTER NINETEEN

ART AND ARCHITECTURE (3rd CENTURY B.C. TO 7th CENTURY A.D.)

I MAURYA-SUNGA-KANVA PERIOD

The earliest relics of India in varied fields of art and architecture have been left behind by the chalcolithic civilisation of the Indus Valley. The relics discovered at Harappa, Mohenjo-daro, and other sites in the Punjab, Sind, Baluchistan, and further north and east clearly prove that these belong to the domain of high art with a long period of experience and tradition behind them. These express fully and significantly a highly developed, sophisticated culture-ideology of an urban people. Like the Indus civilisation itself, the Indus art and architecture had reached the creative climax of a tradition. Although there were evidences of affinities between the Indus Valley art and architecture with those of the contemporary Mediterranean world, yet in their essential qualities and character they were Indian and the Indian art and architecture of the historical period had a link with them.[1]

A long gap intervened between the Indus Valley civilisation and the third century B.C. when we "once more come across the vestiges of a flourishing artistic culture".[2] Absence of artistic or architectural relics cannot be taken to mean that the highly developed traditions of the earlier age died out altogether. The only reasonable explanation is that either these remain undiscovered yet, or they perished because these were made of perishable materials like wood, etc. "Though the link between the Sindhu Valley and Maurya art is missing and a complete hiatus separates the two, literary evidence leaves no doubt that the activities of both architects and sculptors continued during the intervening period".[3]

Cities and Architecture

Buddhist *Mahaparinibbanasutta* testifies to the existence of cities with large buildings even before the time of Buddha, but practically nothing has survived of these cities. We also learn from the Greek

---

[1] N. K. Sastri: *Age of the Nandas and Mauryas*, p. 342.

[2] *The Age of Imperial Unity*, p. 483.

[3] *Idem.*

authors that cities on the banks of rivers were made of wood and those on more commanding position, not so much exposed to floods, were built of mud or bricks. Obviously the important nature of the building materials account for the absence of relics of such cities except the boundary wall of Rajagriha constructed of massive blocks of unhewn stones.

Buddhist literature, Kautilya's *Arthasastra,* and *Milindapanha* mentioned cities with, and their municipal organisations. Milindapanha gives the details of layout and plans of cities.

Palaces

It was from the Maurya period that we have references to cities and visible relics of art and architecture. More or less a clear idea of the architecture of the Maurya period may be had from the description of the Maurya capital city of Pataliputra. Dr. Spooner has unearthed fragments of huge wooden palisade of the city. The Greek writers describe the grandeur of Chandragupta's capital city of Pataliputra as one which neither the palaces of Susa nor Ecbatana could vie with. The Chinese traveller Fa-hien visiting Pataliputra several centuries afterwards was struck by its grandeur although it was then in a dilapidated condition. Excavation at Kumarahar has unearthed the remains of the Maurya palace which give us an impression that the palace was an aggregate of buildings the most noteworthy part of which was the large pillared-hall. Fragments of stone pillars have also been discovered and these, from their very smooth polish raise presumption that Asoka was responsible for the construction of the pillared-hall.

In his description of Chandragupta's palace the Greek ambassador Megasthenes mentions that the palace had a garden in its front where tamed birds, fish ponds, etc., added to the attraction of the pleasure garden. It may be mentioned here that besides Pataliputra, there were similar other cities which must have been specimens of similar town-planning and architectural skill. These were Kausambi, Ujjaini, Taxila and Pundranagar.

It is often remarked that Indian art is the hand maid of religion, and it is essentially true of Indian architecture and other formative arts. The artistic achievements of the Maurya period may be classified under the heads *Stupas, Chaitya-halls, Pillars, Caves, Palaces* and *Sculpture.*

Stupas

We have already referred to the palace architecture of the Maurya period. In *Mahaparinibbana Sutta* Buddha is mentioned to have enjoined Ananda to erect a *Stupa* over the relics of his body at the crossing of four highways. Jainas also erected *Stupas.* It may be easily understood that the tradition of erecting *Stupa* was older than Buddha and Mahavira. *Stupas* were solid domes of bricks or stone masonry. Their size and dimensions varied from very small structures, less than a foot and in higher diameter, called votive *Stupas* to very large ones built by Asoka who is credited with erecting 84,000 *Stupas*, large and small. The famous *Stupa*, it may be noted, have underwent additions and alterations in later times.

A *Stupa* is a plain and simple structure with a hemispherical dome placed on a low circular base with flights of steps, and surrounded by a passage for circumbulation, occasionally fenced by railings as in the caves of the *Sanchi Stupa* and the *Stupa* at *Bharut.*

Another structure that acquired greatest celebrity in Asia was the relic tower or pagoda which the Kushana King Kanishka created in Purushapura, i.e., Peshawar, his capital. It consisted of "a basement in five stages (150 feet), a superstructure of carved wood in thirteen stories (400 feet) surmounted by an iron column from thirteen to twenty-five gilt copper unbrellas (88 feet) making a total height of 638 feet". Chinese pilgrim Fa-hien describes it to be of incomparable beauty, and that "tradition says that this was the highest tower in Jambudvipa".[1]

In the ancient Gandhara region quite a number of *Stupas* have been discovered which bear the traditional plan and structure of the *Stupas.* The *Stupas* in the post-Christian era in particular, in the Gandhara region were heavily ornamented.

Stupas were also erected in South India, most important of these being in Amaravati, Bhattiprolu, Jaggayyapeta, Ghantasala, Nagarjunikonda, etc.

Chaitya-hall and Caves

The *Chaityas* are a variant of the *Stupas.* The *Chaitya-hall* is a shrine which occupies the altar and serves as a place of congregation. Traces of Chaitya halls have been found at Sanchi, Saranath, Sonari, etc. After Asoka *Chaityas* were excavated in the body of the rocks. The convenient physical structure of the Indian rocks gave a special encouragement to rock-cut architecture and *Chaitya-halls* were excavated in the rock-cut caves. The *Chaitya-halls* in their fully developed form resembled Christian Church. Asoka caused the excavation of Sudama (Nyagrodha) cave for the Ajivikas but it was after his time that rock-cut caves became more common.

[1] *The Age of Imperial Unity*, pp. 491-492.

The rcok-cut caves at Barabar hills, the most important of them being the Lomasa Rishi cave , is, however, supposed to have been of the Maurya period. Asoka's grandson, Dasaratha, also excavated cave dwellings for the monks. The interiors of the caves, "burnished like mirrors are wonderful monuments of patient skill and infinite labour".[1]

Pillars

Very few specimens of Maurya art during the reign of Asoka have reached us, but of them the most beautiful and characteristic specimens are furnished by his Stone Pillars. About thirty to forty pillars were erected as his command. Monolithic columns, weighing nearly fifty tons prove the extraordinary skill of the engineers and stone-cutters of Asoka's time.

Sculpture

Sculpture under the Mauryas flourished under the patronage of the Court, especially during the reign of Asoka. The best specimens of sculpture during the period are represented by the majestic animal capitals found near Vaisali, Lauriya, Nandangarh, Rummindei, Saranath, Sanchi, and at other places. The capital is monolithic and divided into three parts, by an inverted lotus, abacus, and a crowing sculpture in the round. The surface is chiselled and shows that Mauryan workmanship can clearly be traced. The Bhakira pillar is the first specimen with its crude and clumsy workmanship which improved through experience to reach culmination in the artistic effort reached in the Lauriya-Nandangarh column and the wonderful lion-capital of Saranath. Figure of elephant carved out of rock at Dhauli in Orissa "shows much more sense of creative form and is artistically far superior". Carved figures of animals like bull, horse, etc. also show close observation and realistic vision of the workmen of the time.

It is held by some scholars that the Maurya art impetus originally came from outside from Iran and Achaemenid emperors. But one relevant point has to be borne in mind that while the Achaemenid columns were monolithic, the polish, the inverted lotus called the **Persepolis** bell, etc., point to Achaemenid and Hellenistic artistic infuence on Maurya art. But whatever might have been the origin of inspiration, "the Mauryan column has never been surpassed in later Indian art".

[1] Iegge: *Fa-hien*, p. 77.

In the post-Maurya period the bas-relief on the railings of Bharut, Bodh Gaya, and Sanchi, as also the friezes of Khandagiri and Udayagiri caves closely follow on the art of the Mauryas. Spiritually and formally the Sunga-Kanva art was opposed to Maurya art and stood for different motive and direction. The bas-reliefs of Bharut, Bodh Gaya, Sanchi, Amaravati, etc., provide an illuminating commentary on the contemporary Indian life and attitude to life. These bas-reliefs were **charana-chitras** translated into stone.

Although depicting high technical skill, Asokan caves were neither very large nor richly carved. But in the next period the large caves at Bhoja, Kondane, Bedisa, Junnar, Nasik, Ajanta, Ellora in the west and in Udayagiri and Khandagiri in Orissa in the east depict a considerable development in style but also in fine ornamental sculpture which ranks very high in artistic development.

Another noteworthy development of art in this post-Maurya period is to be noticed in the ornamented gateways of the Sanchi *Stupa*. The sculpture represents the scenes in the life of Gautama Buddha, Sylvan Scenes, groups of ordinary and extraordinary animals, processions, etc. The gateways and railings of the Bharut *Stupa*, the railings and stupa itself at Amaravati were also decorated with fine sculptures. In variety and in ornamentation the sculptures of this period have not been surpassed by the whole history of art.

The artists of the Sunga-Kanva period seem to have a special knack in depicting figures in all conceivable shapes, positions, and attitudes. If in Bharut the figures show the great efforts of the artists Bodh Gaya distinctly shows the figures as work of better skill, more free and lively. "Gaya was a step forward from Bharut."[1] The ornamental reliefs of the Sanchi gateways are in the continuous line of evolution of Bharut and Bodh Gaya. The ornamental sculptural reliefs of the four gates depict the contemporary Indian life "in all its mundane love and delight, pageantry and grandeur, peace and beauty, idyllic romanticism and violent struggle".[2] The reliefs also depict the episodes of the life of Buddha. The Sanchi artists appear to have been more engrossingly interested in the life in this world and the human figures carved by them are more harmonious, free, happy yet not as sensuous as is Bodh Gaya. An extensive representation of fauna and flora depicted the naturalistic feelings of the Sanchi artists.

In Udayagiri and Khandagiri in Orissa contain numerous sculptured friezes and panels although fall under the art generally called

[1] *The Age of Imperial Unity*, p. 513.

[2] *Ibid.*, p. 514.

art of Madhyadesa, nevertheless depict a local or provincial style. Manchapuri Cave relief in Udayagiri and Anantagumpha reliefs in Khandagiri are characterised by vigorous movements and robust vitality. The long friezes of the Ranigumpha and Ganesagumpha which belonged to a date probably not earlier than early second century A.D. are equally provincial in outlook but much more advanced in conception and execution.

In western India Bhoja and Karle rock-cut reliefs were conceived from the roots of aboriginal, almost primeval and executed with great vitality. The Bhaja reliefs "were ethnically conditioned" yet they are aboriginally Indian.

Karle reliefs, a century later, although touched by the plastic exuberance of Bhaja was vigorously disciplined. The human figures, male and female, were heroic specimens of humanity, strong, self-assured and animated.

Painting and Terracotta

Brahmanical and Buddhist literature contain numerous references to art of painting. Painting had already acquired a long tradition by the time of the Mauryas. Mahabharata refers to Chitralekha a gifted portrait painter, *Vinaya Pitaka* mentions Amarapali engaged many painters to paint her walls with figures of kings, traders and merchants seen by them and seeing the portrait of Bimbisara she fell in love with him. We have references to king Prasenjit's pleasure hall containing *Chitragara*, i.e., portrait galleries. Besides portrait and mural paintings, we find mention of *lepya-chitra*, *lekhya-chitra*, and *dhuli-chitra*. From literary records we come to learn that from very early times paintings, both secular and religious, were considered an important form of artistic expression.

No specimen of ancient painting has reached us. The earliest example of painting that we come across consists of a row of human figures painted in yellow and ochre in the ceiling of the Jogimara cave in the Ramgarh hills in the Surguja State. There is also another band of large aquatic animals *makara* painted in the same yellow and ochre. From the remains of the murals show that human figures which are depicted in three-quarter people are lively and rythmical. From the similarity in garments of the human figures depicted in the Jogimara and the early reliefs of Sanchi, it is believed by scholars that the former belonged to the middle of the first century B.C.

After another century and half, the Indian mural paintings on the walls of Ajanta caves represented the next and more developed phase of the Indian painting. The very scanty specimens of the

Ajanta phase of paintings that have been preserved show that the work is mature and belongs to contemporary Indian plastic art. In the fulness of composition and aesthetic effects only the Amaravati reliefs can perhaps vie with these paintings.

Terracotta represents the artistic expression of the humbler folk to whom stone was not easily available and more expensive. A large variety of terracotta work has been found at sites like Pataliputra, Buxar, Taxila, Mathura, Vaisali, Ahichchatra, Kausambi, Banaras, Mahasthan, etc. Terracotta made of clay and sand were shaped and modelled by hand or mould. These contained representations for religious purposes, for decoration, seals, children's toys, amulets, etc. Terracotta art of India although did not acquire the dignity of sculpture was an important vehicle of human expression.

A few of the terracotta plaques discovered belonged to the Maurya period. Generally these were baked to various shades, black, grey, ochre or red. In the Sunga-Kanva period majority of the terracotta work consisted of female figures, richly dressed, well-disciplined body, magnificently modelled busts and elaborate hair-dressing.

Terracotta of Saka-Kushana period exhibit a great variety of ethnic types and nomadic factions. Musicians, horsemen, etc., have been represented with a good deal of ethnic touch during this period.

II. INDO-BACTRIAN-SAKA-PAHLAVA-KUSHANA PERIOD

During this period the north-west India became the meeting ground of the East and the West. The effect in art and sculpture was seen in the rise of the Gandhara school of art with Peshwar as its Centre. This region was under the rule of the Greeks for long before the Kushanas held sway over it. Gandhara art which reached culmination under Kanishka during the second century A.D. covered the regions of Jalalabad, Hadda and Barriyan in Afghanistan, the Swat Valley, and Peshwar. As Dr. Smith points out the Gandhara school of art was based on cosmopolitan art of Asia Minor and Roman empire. A large number of Graeco-Roman craftsmen seem to have been employed in the execution of the Gandhara art. According to N. R. Roy the Gandhara art covered the period from first century B.C. to the fifth century A.D. It is difficult to precisely fix the period of the Gandhara art but there is no doubt that it began to flourish long before Kanishka and continued long after him. Much of the best work of this school was executed during the reign of Kanishka and Huvishka.

Dr. Kramirst observes that the Gandhara represented an eastward expansion of Hellenic civilisation mixed with Iranian elements.

Sir John Marshall is of the opinion that mix-up of the Iranian and Hellenistic elements took place in Bactria and its neighbouring countries after Alexander the Great had colonised them. He is also of the opinion that the hybrid art was introduced into India as a result of the friendly intercourse between the Greek world and the Mauryas, or as a result of the subsequent invasions of India by the Bactrian Greeks, Scythians, Parthians, and Kushanas who must have been influenced by the Graeco-Iranian culture. The Hellenistic influence was, however, more prominent. Buddha was transformed into the likeness of Apollo and Bodhisvatta's flowing drapery giving a sense of Greek realism. The starving Buddha of Lahore exemplifies the decadent Greek realism. Yet, the Gandhara art, though represents, Graeco-Roman-Iranian influences, with a Greek overtone, yet in its content and subject matter it continued to be Indian. In the first century A.D. we notice a degeneration in the Gandhara art, the figures became shorter, stumpy and treated in a rough manner. This must have been due to the Saka-Kushana influence from Mathura. But there was a distinct revival in the third century onwards, of the artistic excellence that characterised the Gandhara art of the first century A.D. and it was the revived art that was spread to Central Asia and China.

Opinions vary as to the influence of Gandhara art on the Indian Art as a whole. According to Havell the influence of the Hellenic art on Indian art was confined to technical aspects only and was in no way a spiritual or intellectual force. In fact, the spiritual centre of Buddhist in Mahayana form was Magadha, which received Kanishka's patronage. Will Durant also of the opinion that Gandhara art had but little influence on the sculpture form of the Indian art. Dr. R. C. Majumdar remarks that the Gandhara art failed to penetrate into the interior of India and had no share in the later development of the Hindu art of Amaravati, Bharut, and Mathura. Outside India, however, the Gandhara school achieved spectacular success and became the parent of the Buddhist art of Chinese, Turkistan, Mongolia, China, Korea, and Japan.

R. D. Banerjee and Paul Mason-Oursel hold that the Gandhara art had influenced all other schools of Indian art as well as those of Central Asia, China, Korea, Japan, etc.

But as Rene Grousset and others point out that the Gandhara art bears no comparison with the school of Sanchi or with the schools of art under the Guptas and Palhavas in their inspirations, sincerity, emotion, and spontaneity.

It has to be added that both schools of Mathura and Amaravati flourished under the lavish patronage of the Scythian kings. The portrait statue of Kanishka added a novel feature to the sculptural art

In the Deccan Jainism obtained royal patronage. Many rulers, their ministers, and chieftains showed definite inclination to Jainism. The Ganga Kings of Mysore were associated with Jainism. Likewise the Kadamba rulers of Vaijayanti are often regarded as of Jaina persuasion. About the Chalukyas of Badami there is no definite evidence of their Jaina and Kirtivarman mentions a few Jaina teachers. Although it is difficult to know precisely the position of Jainism in South India during the early centuries of the Christian era, yet from the Jaina tradition as well as literary works it shows that Jainism was in a prosperous state in South India during the Gupta and the post-Gupta periods.

The growth of Jaina doctrines is neither easy to trace nor was it very rapid. We do not know what exactly the preaching of Mahavira was and what additions were actually made. As Brahmanical philosophy, Jaina thought, has remained very much conservative. Jacobi has demonstrated how the original Jaina philosophical tenets have not changed in the course of centuries.

We have already discussed that Mahavira was no founder of a new religion but in reality he was a reformer of an existing religion. While Parsvanath taught only four vows, Mahavira taught five. Confession of sin was his own innovation. "Apart from these reforms in ethical teaching, it is difficult to ascertain what additions Mahavira made to the ontological and psychological system of his predecessor."[1] It is likely that Mahavira was responsible for the codification of the unsystematic mass of beliefs into a set of rigid rules of conduct of monks and laymen.

As a result of different schism only minor changes were effected in superficial details. The schism which led to division of community into Svetambara and Digambara sects also did not mean much important dogmatic change. Jaina system did not undergo any fundamental change in later days.

But the Jaina sacred literature called *Agama* underwent several alterations. Such has been the nature of alteration in the Jaina canon that the original version when the Jaina community was not split into Svetambaras and Digambaras is not available. The one version claimed by the Svetambaras as original took its present form after about a thousand years of the death of Mahavira and in all probability not the original Jaina canon.

Both the Svetambara and the Digambara Jainas postulate the original Jaina canon to consist of twelve *Angas* and that the last *Anga*

---

1 *The Age of Imperial Unity*, p. 420.

includes fourteen *Purvas*. Apart from *Acharanga* and *Sutrakritanga*, it is difficult to say the extent to which the other *Angas* contain the original form. *Bhagavata Sutta*, however, contains to some extent the original contents.

According to Jaina Philosophy the world consists of two eternal, uncreated, co-existing yet independent categories, the *Jiva*, i.e., conscious and *Ajiva*, the unconscious.

In Jainism *Jiva* means life which could inhabit in a plant, an animal or a human body. It is born and reborn, it knows and feels. Its highest endeavour is to free itself from bondage.

The *Ajiva* or the unconscious is, according to Jainism, the entire world *minus* the *Jivas*. It includes not only *matter* but also time, space, virtue and vice, etc.

The Jainas do not recognise God or Creator and man's emancipation from sufferings does not depend on the mercy of God. Man is the architect of his own destiny and by living an austere life of purity and virtue he can escape the evils of life. "The best life was the life of renunciation. It was thus the shortest way to salvation."[1] Jainism is thus a moral code than a religion in the modern sense.

Vaishnavism

Vaishnavism is a theistic religion of which Vishnu is worshipped as the supreme God. Origin of Vaishnavism may be traced to Rigveda. In Rigveda, however, Vishnu is associated with Sun, but it is difficult to say if Vaishnavism had developed into a theistic sectarian religion in the Vedic times. It was in the fifth century B.C. that Vaishnavism, that Panini in his Ashtadhyayi Vasudeva, is mentioned as an object of *Bhakti*, i.e., devotion. In the fourth century B.C. Megasthenes mentions that the people of Mathura region held Heracles in special honour. Heracles was the Greek name for Vasudeva-Krishna.[2] Vasudeva-Krishna, the hero of the Jadava clan, was deified and was styled Bhagavat. In the second century B.C. we find the deification of Vasudeva complete and the Greek ambassador Heleodorus created a pillar at Besnagar in the honour of Vishnu, the God of Gods.

Vasudeva, i.e., Vishnu is identified with Rama as well as Krishna. In north India he is adorned more under the name, Krishna, but in the South a number of great temples has been dedicated to him. In Travancore, however, he is worshipped under the name, Padmanabha.

---

[1] *The Age of Imperial Unity*, p. 425.
[2] *Ibid*, p. 432.

In the *Bhagavata Purana* there is mention of 22 incarnations of Vishnu. *Bhaktamala* gives the number as 29 and *Panchatantra* gives 39. But most commonly ten incarnations are mentioned, the first five being *mina* (fish), *Kurma* (tortoise), *Varaha* (boar), *Nri-Singha* (Man-Lion), and *Bamana* (dwarf). The sixth incarnation is Parasurama. The seventh incarnation of Vishnu is Ramachandra. Krishna is also regarded as an incarnation of Vishnu and in fact was completely identified with. Buddha is also accepted as an incarnation of Vishnu. The last incarnation is Kalki.

In the *Chhandogya Upanishad* there is a reference to Krishna, son of Devaki and disciple of sage Ghora, and the religion associated with Ghora and Krishna is supposed to have been based on *Bhakti*. *Chhandogya Upanishad* mentions virtues like asceticism (*tapas*), charity (*dana*), simplicity (*arjava*), non-injury (*non-violence*) and truthfulness (*Satyavachana*) to be inculcated in this religion. Interestingly, the same virtues have been extolled by Krishna in the *Gita*.

The first step in the evolution of Vaishnavism was the identification of Vasudeva-Krishna with God Vishnu of the Veda. This identification was complete by the time *Bhagavat Gita* was composed and from that time Vasudeva cult or Bhagavata religion came to be known as *Vaishnava* religion.

The next step in the evolution was the identification of Vasudeva, Krishna and Vishnu with a deified sage named Narayana. In *Taittiriya Aranyaka* Narayana, Vasudeva, and Vishnu have been regarded as the one and the same. Here Narayana is also identified with Hari.

It has already been mentioned above that Panini, Megasthenes referred to the worship of Vasudeva, but lack of reference to the worship of Vasudeva in the Buddhist texts or in Asokan inscriptions, raises the presumption that Vasudeva worship had not become very prominent by that time and perhaps remained confined to Mathura region and neighbouring areas. In the second century B.C. we have the information from a Besnagar inscriptions of the erection of *Guruda dhvaja* at Besnagar in the honour of Vishnu. Another Besnagar inscription of the first century B.C. refers to the erection of *Garuda column* of an excellent temple of Bhagavat, i.e., Vasudeva. *Garuda* is the *Vahana*, i.e., the vehicle of Vishnu.

From both epigraphic and literary evidences we come to know of the spread of *Vaishnavism* outside Mathura to western India and northern Deccan. A Satavahana inscription at Nanaghat shows that some people in the first century B.C. regarded Vasudeva as an equal to Indra and other gods. But another Satavahana inscription of the second century A.D. shows that the Satavahana claimed himself to be equal of Rama and Kesava, that is Vasudeva-Krishna. In the same century an inscription at Krishna district begins with an adoration to Vasudeva. All this shows the growing importance of the worship of Bhagavat Narayana in South India.

Representation of Vishnu by image cannot be traced before the beginning of the Christian era. A deity with four arms and holding a *Chakra* in one is found inscribed on the coin of a Panchala King named Vishnumitra. In a seal, identified by Cunningham as that of the Kushana King Huvishka, represents Vishnu with *Sankha, Chakra, Gada,* and a ring like object instead of *Padma.* Some coins of Huviska bear the figure of a four-armed God name *Ooshna,* obviously Vishnu. The adoption of the name Vasudeva by Huvishka's successor who had one of his important centres at Mathura, the original centre of Vasudeva cult, is an added proof of the Bhagavata learnings of the Kushanas.

The best exposition of the Bharata doctrine is to be found in *Bhagavadgita,* also called simply the *Gita.* The *Bhagavadgita* holds a unique position in the Indian religion and literature. It imparts lesson in philosophy, religion, ethics, etc. At a moment of psychological crisis Arjuna became pessimistic and was almost reluctant to fight with his own Kinsmen ; and he was about to withdraw from the sinful fratricidal battle. Krishna who served as Arjuna's charioteer dissuaded him from the cowardly course of withdrawing from the battle field and his advice and teaching to Arjuna in this connection formed the subject-matter of *Bhagavadgita.* "It is this specific situation involving a moral dilemma which gives a perennial charm and universal appeal to the poem."[1] The *Gita* also teaches the doctrine of rebirth. The theory of *Avatarvad,* i.e., incarnation is also mentioned in the *Gita* and Krishna is regarded as *Purushottama* or Perfect Man. When piety, i.e., *dharma* diminishes and impiety, i.e., *adharma* raises its ugly head, says Krishna in the Gita, He is born and protects the righteous and punishes the sinful. The most reassuring spirit expressed in the Gita is the rise of an *Avatara* when the world is faced with a moral crisis is the message of the Gita.

The spirit of toleration is another very heartening message of the Gita where it states that all roads to salvation lead but to Lord Krishna, i.e., God. The roads of salvation mentioned therein are through *Jnana,* i.e., knowledge, ***Karma,*** i.e., action, and *Bhakti,* i.e., devotion.

Jnana or knowledge is incomparable in its purifying power and

[1] *The Age of Imperial Unity,* p. 441.

removes the intellectual fog, trains the mind, and cleanses the soul for attainment of final emancipation.

Karma-Yoga in the Gita means sacrifice of *sense* pleasures. This sacrifice is nothing but self-restraint and self-surrender. A *Karma-Yogin* surrenders to God whatever work he does, and does not think of the result. It is a complete surrender.

The *Bhakti-Yoga* is the way of love and worship or an emotional attachment to God as distinguished from knowledge or action. *Bhakti* is according to the *Gita* the royal road to *moksha* (salvation). A true Bhakta may be a *Karma-Yogin*, but in the midst of his activities if he keeps his mind steadfastly on God.

During the Gupta period we find Vaishnavism receiving royal patronage under Chandragupta II who was a devout follower of Vaishnavism. He assumed the title *Parama-Bhagavata*, a title which his successors also followed to assume. Samudragupta did not, however, assume the Vaishnava title of *Parama-Bhagavata*, but from his claim to be have been an incarnation of the Inscrutable Being and his adoption of the emblem of *Garuda-dhvaja* prove beyond doubt that he was also a *Vaishnava*. The patronage of *Vaishnavism* by the imperial Guptas was the cause of the growing importance of the new religious creed during the Gupta Age. From the end of the fourth century A.D. this religion gradually grew in popularity all over India and many royal families in different parts of India assumed the title of *Parama-Bhagavata* or *Parama-Vaishnava*.

During the Gupta Age *avatara* worship became popular. This is testified by the epigraphic records of the period from the 4th to the 8th century A.D. Kalidasa (c. 400 A.D.) in his *Raghuvamsa* gives the description of Vishnu on the coil of the Great Serpent (*Anantanaga*) in the ocean of milk with Lakshmi massaging his feet, as is mentioned as have been born as Rama, Dasaratha's son, for the destruction of sinful Ravana. In his *Meghaduta*, Kalidasa refers to the foot-prints of Raghupati, i.e., Rama on the Ramagiri. This incarnation of Vishnu, that is, Rama is worshipped even today along with Sita and Lakshmana in the temple at Ramtek. Worships of Rama in the sixth century A.D. is borne out by Varahamihira who formulated the rules for making Rama's image. In the Junagarh inscription of Skandagupta worship of the *Bamana* avatar, i.e., Dwarf is referred to. Likewise *Varaha*, *Nri-Sinha* avatars were also worshipped.

There are evidences of the existence of differences among the Vaishnavas during the Gupta period. It is illustrated in Harshacharita, not long after the Gupta period by mentioning two types of

Vaishnavites, namely, the *Vishnu-Bhaktas*, i.e., devotees of Vishnu and *Vishnu-bheda*, i.e., a sect of the Vishnu worshippers.

One important feature of Vaishnavism during the Gupta period is the concept of *Sri* or Lakshmi, wife of Vishnu. A second wife of Vishnu was supposed to be the Earth called *Vashnavi*. It is supposed that the Sankhya doctrine of Purusha and Prakriti influenced the concept of Lakshmi and Vishnu, as also that of the Devi and the Siva.

Saivism

The cult of Siva goes back to the Pre-Aryan period of Indian history. From the evidence so far available the earliest form of Siva was the *Pasupati* of the Indus civilisation as also stones discovered there of the shape of Siva-ling or the phallus. In the Rig Veda Siva is represented as *Rudra*, the god of Natural violence and destruction. In the Yajurveda the Rudra is given a long string of epithets and is given the name Sankara and is begged to be propitious. He is described as patron of the violent and the unruly, his haunts being mountains, deserts, and uncanny places, but he is also described as the patron of craftsmen, huntsmen, and the lord of hosts of spirits. He is also regarded as a great cosmic force who dwells in the flowing streams, in billows and tranquil water. He becomes in a sense a representative of all forces, good and evil, and is on the way to became an All-God.

In the Atharva-Veda he is conceived as a lord of spirits and animals. He is described as the lord of beasts and birds, natural elements, in fact, of everything animate and inanimate. It was out of the concept of all pervasiveness that the character of Siva grew.

In the *Mahabharata* reference is found of Pasupata along with the systems of Sankhya, Yoga, Pancharatna, and the Veda and it is stated that consort of Uma, namely, Pasupati, i.e., Siva, son of Brahma revealed *Jnana* called Pasupata.

The Saivas believe that Siva was the first preceptor of their doctrine. According to *Vayu Purana* Mahesvara is said to have mentioned to Brahma that he would incarnate himself as a *brahmachari* named Nakulin when Vishnu would be born as Vasudeva. He is also mentioned to have said that he would make Kushika, Gargya, Mitruka, and Rushta as his disciples. The *Linga* Purana gives the same legend but calls Nakulin as Lakulin and among the disciples Kaurushy in place of Rushta. From epigraphic source as well we find mention of a teacher of Saivism named Lakulin or Nakulin who was regarded by his followers as an incarnation of Siva. Likewise in inscription dated 971 in the Natha temple near that of Ekalinga near Udaipur it is mentioned that Siva was born in Bhrigukachha (Broach) as a man bearing a lakula, i.e., club in his hand. Thus from various sources we find Lakulin to be the person who taught Saivism. According to Bhandarkar he flourished in the second century B.C. but the Mathura inscription of Chandragupta II places him in the second century A.D.

Nakula's four disciples were the founders of four different schools of Pasupata, i.e., Saivism. According to the Pasupatas Mahesvara, i.e., Siva, taught five methods for the release of the *Jiva*, i.e., life from bondage. There are *Karya*, *Karana*, *Yoga*, *Vidhi*, and *Duhkhanta*, i.e., effect, cause, path, rule, and end of misery. The acquisition of these fivefold knowledge is regarded as essential for release from the bond of life.

Karya-Karana, i.e., relation of cause and effect is a highly abstruce philosophical concept. *Yoga* is the path to connect the individual soul with God. *Vidhi*, i.e., the rule which takes the aspirant to the proximity of Dharma, i.e., the Lord. *Duhkhanta*, that is, the final deliverance from sorrow.

Megasthenes' account is the earliest historical record of Siva worship. He mentions two Indian deities worshipped by the Indian as Dionisus and Heracles who are identified with Siva and Krishna respectively. Patanjali in his *Mahabhashya* in the second century B.C. refers to *Siva-Bhagavatas* as also two images of Siva and Skanda which were sold by the Mauryas for raising money. The Maurya King Jalauka, successor of Asoka, was also a Saiva. In the early Christian era some of the Kushana rulers also adopted *Saivism*.

The epics the Ramayana and the Mahabharata as also the Puranas refer to the family of Siva, his consort Uma, daughter of Himavat. All this shows the growing popularity of Saiva cult.

That the supremacy of Siva was not recognised by the worshippers of other gods is evident from the story of Daksha who refused to recognise Rudra, that is, Siva as a god worthy of propitiation and did not invite him in the sacrifice performed by him. This legend at least testifies to the growing popularity of Saiva cult and the opposition is created in the non-Saiva religionists.

From the earliest times Saivism was gaining in popularity in South India and in the literature of the Sangama period refers to Siva as the greatest God. Writer, Nakkiran, compares the Pandya King of his time to Siva who is described as having long braid of matted hair, having a bull as his ensign and mentioned as the God of creation, of death, and destruction.

Siva has been worshipped from the earliest times as Pasupati, with an image in human form as also in phallic, i.e., linga form. In the Mahabharata we find references to the orthodox Brahmins rather unwilling to worship Siva in the linga form. It may be noted that while the emblem of Siva—the linga—was realistic in appearance in early times it gradually underwent a modification due probably to the aversion of a section of the people to such realism. In the medieval times the linga moved away from its original realistic form and Havell Ven goes to the extent of suggesting that the linga was modelled on votive Stupas of the Buddhists.

In the Gupta Age when there was a Hindu revival, although most of the Gupta rulers became Vishnu-worshippers, Saivism also flourished along with other forms of Hinduism. This was possible due to the non-sectarian and tolerant attitude of the Gupta rulers. Kumargupta who was a follower of Vaishnavism also favoured Saivism for he worshipped Skanda (Siva) as well.

The *Vayu Purana* and *Matsya Purana* which are devoted to Siva are assigned to the Gupta period. Patronage of the rulers is an index of popularity of a religion. In this context like the early Kushana kings, Saivism as a religious cult not only received patronage from some of the Gupta rulers but even Huna King Mihirakula became a patron of Saivism and was a devout Saiva. King Sasanka of Bengal, some kings of the Pushyabhuti family of Kanauj, the Maitraka rulers of Valabhi were devout Saivas. King Harsha also in his eclecticism honoured Siva.

In South India the great rival of Saivism at this period was Jainism. The Pallava King Mahendra I (600-630 A.D.) was originally a Jaina and followed a policy of persecution of the Saivas and other non-Jaina religionists. But later he came under the influence of Saint Appar and was converted into Saivism. It was due to the devotional poetry that the leading Saints of the Saiva cult of this period flowed led to a great upsurge of Saivism in the South. There were as many as sixty-three canonical saints of Saivism and many of these saints called *nayanars* or *adiyars* flourished during this period. A body of Saiva literature that grew up during this period testifies to the growth of Saivism, the most noteworthy of the works being Tirumular's *Tirumandiram* which is a highly abstruse work on Siva doctrine full of mysticism.

The image of Siva was being worshipped besides anthropomorphic form by Siva's emblem Linga from a long time past. During the Gupta Age the same spirit which was already there of subduing the realism in the form of the linga continued. Yet it may be noted that in some seals of the Gupta period found at Bhita the Siva *linga* is depicted in its older aspects.

Images of Siva in human form during the Gupta Age show a bewildering multiplicity. One specimen preserved in Calcutta Museum, found at Kosam, bearing the inscription of Skandagupta represents Siva and Uma in standing posture. Likewise rock-cut shrines at Ellora (8th century A.D.) have a variety of images of Siva in human form. Similarly besides the lingas, there is a great variety of Siva images in human form in the South India as well as in other parts of the country.

OTHER RELIGIOUS SECTS

Brahma

During the Vedic Brahmana period Prajapati was regarded as the creator of gods, men, and demons. Later he was identified with *Brahma* the infinite and impersonal, Absolute of the Upanishads and the Vedanta. But gradually worship of Prajapati fell into disuse and a new name in place of Prajapati was adopted, it was *Brahma* and gave him the first place in the Hindu Trinity, namely *Brahma, Vishnu, Mahesvara.*

Surya

From the Vedic times worship of *Surya*, i.e., the Sun can be traced. It came down through ages with slight modifications and in the 3rd century B.C. Sun worship became very popular. The Greek writers refer to Sun god and the Kushana rulers issued coins with the name and image of the Sun. The infiltration of the Persian Sun worship into India and Multan is supposed to have been the original Seat of Sun temple although the fact is not incontrovertible. The Puranas narrate the introduction of the Solar cult into India from *Sakadvipa*, i.e., Eastern Iran. The *Brihat-Samhita* also refers to the foreign features of *Sun God* which are to be noticed in North Indian specimen of god. Sun worship did not penetrate Southern India and in later times when it spread in a limited way into the South it was uninfluenced by the Persian innovation and imitated also in certain areas of norhern India.

Uma or Durga

Saivism did not develop an elaborate *avatarvad*, i.e., incarnation theory as did Vaishnavism. Siva was regarded as the head of a family each member of which is even today a cult object. A Saivite owes religious allegiance to one or other of the members of Siva's family. In one of the *Samhitas* Ambika was described as the sister of Rudra, later came to be regarded as his wife and was given the title Great Mother. The Great Mother became great object of veneration in the Sakta cult and she was called by various names such as Uma, Parvati, Haimavati, etc. These names are also to be found in *Taittiriya Aranyaka* and *Kena Upanishad*. During the Kushana period, the figure of Uma is represented in the coins of Huvishka either with her consort Siva or alone. The popular belief was, and even today, is that Siva and Uma are bound by marital relations. In *Bhismaparva* and *Virataparva* hymns the new name of Uma was coined and she is called Durga. Durga gives victory and is also *Mahisasuramardini*, i.e., one who killed the demon who took the form of a buffalo. Later she has been given various epithet such as Chandi, Kali, Kapali, Kumari, Mahakali, Karali, Katyayani, Vijaya, etc. In the Durga *Saptasati* and *Markandeya Purana*, she is extolled for saving gods from the Mahisasura demon. Her name is also glorified in other Puranas as well. The family of Siva and Uma comprising Ganesa, Kartikeya, Lakshmi, and Saraswati are also worshipped with varied importance in different parts of the country. Each of these members was the object of an independent cult. This is proved by the literary as well as numismatic data.

Karttikeya was worshipped for vigour, Ganesa for bounty. The latter is still counted as one of the major gods. He is giver of success (Siddhi).

Lakshmi

In early coins, sculptures and carvings of Sri or Lakshmi has been represented as either standing or sitting cross-legged on a lotus and two elephants bathing her by water poured from jars held by them from two sides. At Bharut four representations are seated and the rest standing have been found. Goddess Lakshmi is regarded as beauty, i.e., *Sri*, and is the goddess of hope, faith, modesty and fortune. She is also represented as seated or standing on lotus with a lotus in hand.

The worship of Lakshmi became widespread from the third century B.C. to first century A.D. Lakshmi representing plenty is mentioned in the Rigveda, the Ramayana, and the Mahabharata and the tradition of her being the goddess of fortune and this tradition has travelled down the ages.

Lakshmi had come to be regarded as Rajalakshmi, the Fortune-giver of the king and would stay with her bounty for the king so long as the king practised virtues and protected his subjects. Lakshmi is also referred to in literature and coins as city goddess as in the case of Rajagriha, Kapisa, Ujjaini, etc. The Gupta Kings also represented Lakshmi in the coins as goddess of fortune.

Naga Cult

There were numerous other cults and objects of worship from the earliest times and it is difficult make out their different methods of worship.

From the Vedic times, serpent as cult-object has penetrated into all major Indian sects. All through the centuries down to the present times Snake worship has persisted. Even at the Indus Valley during Mohenjo-daro period Snake has been associated with a figure in *Yogic* posture which anticipated serpent's association with the Saiva cult. In Panchala *Adi Naga* was the presiding deity. The coins of Agnimitra and Bhanumitra snake has been represented on the reverse. In later Samhitas and Sutras the Nagas, i.e., Serpents are supposed to be of semi-divine origin and fit to receive adoration and worship. In the Kushana period veneration to serpents is attested by tradition, folk-lore, and literature. The growing importance of the Naga cult is borne out by the fact that only Saivism, but also Vaisnavism, Buddhism, and Jainism accorded the serpent a position, although subordinate, in their religious systems. Siva, Durga, even Ganesa, and Surya wear Snakes.[1] The Vaishnavas adopted the snake in a different fashion. Garuda, the carrier (*Vahana*) of Vishnu, was hostile to the snakes but later snake was taken in a friendly way and the coil of *Ananta Naga* became the seat of Vishnu. In imitation of the hood of Ananta Naga, the figure of Baladeva in Mathura and the adjoining regions is furnished with the hood of the Naga. The Snake, Naga Basuki or Basuki, is regarded as the associate of Varuna, lord of waters. Serpent cult still continues to exist in different parts of India.

Secular Literature: Gupta Renaissance

The Gupta Age witnessed an unprecedented development in Sanskrit literature and learning, which alone has marked the period as most significant in Indian history.

After the political disintegration, foreign invasions and rule during the post-Maurya period, India rallied herself into a political unity and prosperity under the Guptas which resulted in the flourishing of Sanskrit literature in all its branches. But the most significant developments took place in secular literature.

The most brilliant luminary that shed lusture on the Sanskrit literature of the Gupta Age was Kalidasa. The greatest poet and dramatist that India ever produced was Kalidasa whose works have enjoyed high popularity and reputation down the centuries. Many

[1] *The Age of Imperial Unity*, p. 472.

legends and anecdotes have gathered round his name which although not of much historical value, at least prove the great popularity his name enjoyed. Kalidasa is usually regarded as one of the nine gems associated with the King Vikramaditya. Most scholars regard Kalidasa's association with Vikramaditya of Ujjaini as a historical fact, although they feel that all the scholars comprising the nine gems could not have been contemporaries. The general opinion is that Kalidasa lived at the Court of Chandragupta II, Vikramaditya, not King Vikramaditya or Bhoja or Dhara, as held by some scholars

The best known of Kalidasa's works is his drama *Sakuntala*. This play has been regarded as not only the best in Sanskrit literature, but one of the best in the world literatures. The theme of the play was taken from the *Mahabharata* but Kalidasa breathed a style and spirit into it which made the play so neat and immortal. Kalidasa's genius as a playwright, his mastery in delineating sentiments, constructing the plot and characterising the dramatic personae revealed his dramatic genius and poetic gift. His work has elicited highest praise and admiration in the whole literary world.

His other plays Malavikagnimitra, Vikramorvasiya, his lyrical poem Meghaduta, his two epics Kumara-Sambhava and Raghuvamsa, his lesser poem Ritusamhara, etc., have made Kalidasa unquestionably the finest master of Indian dramatic and poetic styles. His skill in use of *simile* has become proverbial.[1]

"His charming and graceful diction, the refinement of his language and sentiments, his minute observations of man and nature, his innate sense of beauty, his masterly use of metaphors and other figures of speech, his elevation of thought and suggestiveness of expression have immortalised him and as has been aptly expressed, his works will endure so long as human beings retain taste for great literature."[2] In the literary world—in drama and poetry—Kalidasa is not only unsurpassed but even unrivalled. He has been very aptly compared to Shakespeare of Elizabethan England and if one Shakespeare would have been enough to make Elizabethan Age immortal in literature, one Kalidasa would have been enough to make the Gupta Age immortal in literature.

But among Kalidasa's successors in the field of drama was Bhavabhuti. Of his three plays, two were based on the *Ramayana* and the third is a social drama. In depicting pathos and tenderness Bhavabhuti is said to have even surpassed Kalidasa. Bharavi, the author of *Kiratarjuniya*, an epic, and Magha, the author of *Sisupalavadha*, rivalled Bharavi in every respect. Bharavi is noted for his

[1+2] *Ibid*, p. 307.

diction, while Magha combined the metaphors of Kalidas, diction of Bharavi, and the rythmic beauty of Nishad.[1]

Bhatti, the author of *Bhattikavyam* or *Ravanavadha*, flourished during this age. In this work he has illustrated the rules of grammar and *alankara*, i.e., rhetoric.

Among the fables and romances the only work that strictly belongs to this period is Brihatkatha of Gunadhya written in *Paisachi* Prose.

Varahamihira was himself a great versifier who used a large number of classical Sanskrit meters in his *Brihat-Samhita* and *Brihat-Jataka*. He has illustrated about 60 meters in the former work.

The Gupta Age also has given us a rich harvest of works on various scientific subjects. Lexicography in India is as old as the Vedic age, but lecon in the real sense of the term we come across in Amara's work usually known as *Amarakosa*. His predecessors in this type of work were Vyadi, Dhvanantari, Vararuchi, Katyayana, Vachaspati, etc.

Chandragomin evolved a system of grammar called *Chandra* which was free from the Brahmanical element. His work contains 3,100 aphorisms. The other form of grammar called *Jainendra Vyakarana* was a condensation of Panini's *Ashtadhyayi* and Katyayana's *Varttikas*.

Varahamihira who lived in the sixth century A.D. preserved in his work *Panchasiddhantika* some of the contents of five astronomical works which were regarded as authoritative at that time. These five works or *Siddhantas* are *Paitamaha*, *Romaka*, *Paulisa*, *Vasishtha*, and *Surya*. *Paitamaha Siddhanta* belonged to pre-scientific period. But the remaining four indicate knowledge of Greek and Roman astronomy. The name *Romaka Siddhanta* is indicative of this. In Varahamihira we come across the names of other astronomers such as Lata, Simha, Pradyumna, Vyayanandin, and Aryabhata. Of the works of these astronomers a few works of Aryabhatta named *Aryabhatiya*, *Dasagitika Sutra*, and *Aryashtasata* have reached us. Aryabhata was first to treat Mathematics as an independent subject and dealt with evolution and involution, area and volume, equation and algebraic identities, etc. He was also first to hold that the eatrh is a sphere and rotates on its axis and that eclipses were not the eating of the Sun or Moon by Rahu but the shadow of the earth falling upon them. But these views were rejected by Varahamihira and Brahma-

1 *"Upama Kalidasasya, Bhave, Cha Arthagauravam Nishade Padalalityam, Maghe Santi Trayo Gunah."*

gupta. The other revolutionary feature of Aryabhata's Mathematics is his system of decimal which was unknown to the peoples of the world then but in use now throughout the world. Aryabhata occupies a high place of honour among the Indian astronomers.

There were also many works on Horoscopes during this period among which *Bhrigu-Samhita*, *Jataka-Sutra*, *Minaraja-Jataka*, *Javana-Jataka*; etc. Texts on various subjects are like architecture, music, dance, paintings, etc.

From the above details it is evident that the secular Sanskrit literature covered a wide range of subjects during the classical Age. Some important sciences such as Grammar, Mathematics, Astrology, Astronomy reached an unprecedented development during this period. This period is also singularly fortunate to have a galaxy of litterateurs who by their contributions made the period the Golden Age of Hindu learning and literature covering almost every branch. This period procuced the very best of authors in almost every branch of literature. "This is evident from the fact that dramatists and poets like Kalidasa, Bhavabhuti, Bharavi, Magha, prose writers like Dandin, Sambhu and Bana, rhetoricians like Bhamaha, grammarians like Chandra or Chandragomin, Vamana and Bhartrihari, lexicographer like Amara, Philosophers like Gaudapada, Kumarila, and Prabhakara, and astronomers like Aryabhata, Varahamihira, and Brahmagupta, all flourished during this period which may, therefore, aptly be described as the Golden Age of Sanskrit Literature."[1]

The literary exuberance of the period was the result of the political unity and prosperity brought about by the Gupta ruler and their enthusiastic patronage of Sanskrit literature. The contacts with foreigners that came into India between the fall of the Maurya empire and the rise of the Guptas led to the widening of the mental horizon of the Indians which gave rise to a virile, literary, and scientific productivity which won the period the name Classical Age or Golden Age

It was customary at one time for the scholars to regard the spurt of literary activities of the Gupta Age as a revival or renaissance of the Sanskrit literature. The basic spirit of renaissance or revival is a re-birth, a re-awakening after a period of mental stupor, the one that had taken place in the West in the fifteenth century. But use of the term revival or renaissance in regard to Sanskrit literature in the Gupta Age will be technically incorrect. For there was no forgetfulness of the past nor any cessation of literary activities prior to the Gupta Age. Sanskrit literature was never eclipsed before the

---

[1] *The Classical Age*, p. 291.

Gupta Age and its influence and activities continued in the centuries preceding the Gupta Age. Bhasa, Asvaghosa's works as well as the Allahabad Pillar inscription of Samudragupta and the Mandasor inscription of Vatsabhatti show that Sanskrit language and literature had already reached maturity early in the fourth century A.D. What the Gupta Age saw in Sanskrit literature was a Sanskrit literary exuberance, a short of an efflorescence. But it cannot be called a revival or renaissance.

CHAPTER TWENTY

BENGAL FROM EARLIEST TIMES TILL 1202 A.D.

When the Vedas were composed, the Aryan habitations did not extended beyond Bhagalpur. Bengal naturally did not find any mention in the Vedic hymns. It was in the Aitareya Brahmanà, however, that there is an indirect reference to the people of Bengal. It is mentioned that the peoples living on the frontiers of the Aryan dominions were *dasyus* among whom the people known as the *Pundras* were also there. The Pundras have been identified, on the basis of epigraphic evidence, with the people of Bogra district in Northern Bengal. According to some scholars, there is a reference to *Vangas* in the Aitareya Aranyaka. But the identity of Vanga with Bengal has been questioned by many modern scholars.

There is, however, four clear references to the *Vangas* in the epics and the *Dharmasutras*. In the *Bodhayana Dharmasutra* there is reference to Aryavarta lying between the Himalayas and the western Vindhyas covering the riparian areas of the Ganges and the Jumna. This area was the most sacred of all. Next in sanctity was the regions covered by Malwa, East and South Bihar, South Kathiawar, the lower Indus Valley and the Deccan. The outermost region which was outside the pale of the Vedic culture, hence not sacred, comprised Arattas of Southern Punjab and Sind, *Vangas* of Central and Eastern Bengal and the Kalingas of Orissa. The peoples of the first two regions referred to above has to undergo expiation if they would live in the places referred to in the last regions.

In the epics, however, the *Vangas* were no longer regarded as sacrileges and impure barbarians. In the *Mahabharata* Bhima is mentioned as making a whirlwind campaign in the land, later known as Bengal. After defeating and killing the King of Monghyr, Bhima attacked the King of Pundras who ruled over his Kingdom on the banks of the river Kosi. Next he marched against the Kings of the *Vangas* and then brought to subjection the Kings of Tamralipti, Karvata and the rulers of *Suhmas*, the modern Hooghly district. There is also reference to Pra-Suhmas who are supposed to have lived in some regions in West Bengal in the neighbourhood of the Suhmas. In the *Tirtha Yatra* section of the *Vanaparva* of the epic there is men-of this period. During the Kushana period beautiful *Stupas* were constructed at Amaravati, Jagayyapeta, and Nagarjunikonda. The striking difference between those *Stupas* and those of the northern India has had to the classification of these *Stupas* and figures as belonging to a new school called Amaravati School.

Kushana period is, however, not much rich in architecture as in sculpture. Yet the famous tower of Kanishka at *Purushapura*, i.e., Peshawar, his capital, was one of the wonders of the world of the time. Besides, there were number of beautiful temples and monasteries constructed during this period and a large number of *Chaityas* was also constructed during this period. A *Chaitya* was a fine work of art with a Central hall for worship. The *Chaita Caves* at Nasik, Bhaja, Bedsa, Karle and others have already referred to.

The Gupta Art

With the Gupta period begins the classical phase of the Indian Art. "In one respect, it is an age of culmination and ultimate exhaustion of earlier tendencies and movements in architectural types and forms. In another, it marks the ushering in of a new age, which is particularly connected with the formative age, with immense possibilities for the future, an age associated with the foundation of the typical style of Indian temple architecture".[1]

Sculpture

As a result of the efforts of preceding several centuries, the techniques of sculptural art had reached perfection during this period and definite types were evolved and the ideals of beauty were executed with masterly precision. A highly developed aesthetic sense, an intelligent grasp of the aims and ideals and a masterly execution characterised the sculpture of this Age. The standard reached during this period did not only remain models of Indian art for all time to come, but served as models of sculptures of the Malayan peninsula, Sumatra, Java, Champa, Cambodia, and even Celebes.

The main object of the Gupta sculpture was human figure. Greatest contribution of the Gupta art was the evolution of perfect types of Buddhist and Brahmanical divinities. A large number of the images of Buddha have been unearthed at Sarnath near Benares; one among these has been regarded by common consent, the finest in the whole of India. Stone and bronze images of Siva, Vishnu, and other Brahmanical gods have been discovered at Deogarh and other places.

---

[1] *The Classical Age*, p. 471.

There were sculpture, human and animal figures, also in the preceding age at Mathura, Amaravati, and other places. Vegetal patterns were also worked out. But during the Gupta period, "a deeper qualitatively meaningful transformation of human figure takes place, and here, too it is the vegetal life that causes this transformation".[1]

As the inner movement of life finds its fullest expression naturally the Gupta artists invariably adopts youth to represent their artistic conception. The largeness of their conception "endows the human figure with a mental and physical discipline that discards the earthiness of Mathura and the sensuousness of Vengi" and raises it to a rational and spiritual existence.

From the specimens that have reached us of the Gupta period, the artistic conception of the time seems to have its birth at Mathura. "The Mathura laboratory used to export its products to Sravasti, Prayag, Sarnath, and presumbly to other places as well. The practice continued in the fourth century as well and we find Mathura artists and Mathura inspiration working at Kasia, Bodh Gaya, and also at Sarnath".[2] The process and experience that Mathura and Sarnath went through had influenced the Gupta sculpture.

The art of metal casting reached a wonderful degree of development during this period. The Nalanda copper image of Buddha, bronze image of Buddha found at Sultanganj and the iron pillar at Meherauli in Delhi belong to the Gupta period.

Architecture

"Compared with sculpture, Gupta architecture, to judge by the extant remains, must be regarded as poor." Rock-cut caves which represented an important aspect of the Indian architecture of the earlier period persisted during the Gupta Age. Two conventional types of rock-cut arhcitecture were *Chaitya* hall, i.e., shrine proper and *Vihara*, i.e., monastery. Of the twenty-eight caves at Ajanta five belonged to the pre-Gupta period while twenty-three belonged to the Gupta Age. For the twenty-three only two are *Chaitya* caves and the rest are all *Viharas*. Apart from Ajanta, other places where notable groups of caves have been found are Ellora, Aurangabad in the State of Hyderabad and Bagh in Madhya Bharat.

The cave halls which were constructed during this period although not far removed from the earlier prototypes in general plan, there was

---

[1] *The Classical Age*, p. 522.

[2] *Ibid.*, p. 523.

a great difference in ornamentation. The decorations and motifs belonged to a different school of thought and were far richer than others. Another noteworthy innovation was that figurine sculptures covered every possible space of the interior as well as the outer walls.

The *Viharas* were constructed in the nature of cells in rows. About twenty *Viharas* belonged to the period under discussions. The Central halls of the *Viharas* were supported by pillars. There is at least one example of a two-storied cave at Ajanta. The technique of construction, decorative sculpture, etc., show that Indian architecture attained its perfection in Ajanta.

The *Vihara* caves at Bagh in Madhya Pradesh are closely related in plan arrangement to those at Ajanta. The Bagh series comprises nine caves excavated by A.D. 600. Highly ornate porch, ornamental feature inside monastic hall, and its extraordinary appearance are not found in any other caves of the time.

The rock-cut caves art of Aurangabad comprises twelve excavations, one of the series is *Chaitya* cave and the rest are *Viharas.* The Aurangabad artistry excelled in figurine sculptures and figures of men and women show striking individuality and characterisation.

Ellora excavations cover a mile in a low ridge of hills overlooking a vast plain. These have three series of caves—Buddhist, Brahmanical and Jaina. The most important of the caves are two double-storeyed monasteries, called *Don Thal* and *Tin Thal. Don Thal* is a cave for it is in fact a three-storeyed monastery, the bottom floor remaining long hidden under accumulated debris.

Rock-cut Brahmanical shrines were also not rare during this period. The earliest of these being those at Udayagiri. The Udayagiri shrines consist of rock-cut as well as stone-built caves. Two caves at Udayagiri contain inscriptions belonging to the reign of Chandragupta II, dated 401 A.D.

The next phase of rock-cut Brahmanical shrines are to be found at Badami in Bijapur district. These belonged to the early Chalukya Dynasty. Three of the shrines belong to Brahmanical faith, one of them bears inscriptions dated in Saka year 500, that is, A.D. 578 and supplies 4 valuable data for dating the other caves.

The Brahmanical caves at Ellora date from 650 A.D. Sixteen of the caves belong to Brahmanical faith. The most important of these being *Dasavatara, Ravan-ka-Khai, Ramesvara, Dhumar Lena,* and the famous *Kailasha* temple. The Elephant cave in the island of Elephanta near Bombay is a Brahmanical cave and similar to the cave of *Dhumar Lena* but less regular and far smaller.

Besides Buddhist and Brahmanical caves, there were Jaina caves excavated during this period. The number of Jaina caves was comparatively very small. Two Jaina caves of celebrity were one at Badami and another at Aihole. Both appear to date from the middle of the seventh century.

Temples

In structural buildings the Gupta Age marked the beginning of a new epoch in the history of architecture. Hitherto before structural buildings were made of impermanent materials like wood, bamboo, etc. and naturally there was limited scope for the application of the principles and plans of architecture in construction of buildings with such materials. But from this period the Indian architects began to built buildings with permanent materials such as dressed stone and bricks and apply their new outlook.

From epigraphic evidence of the period we get a fair idea of the large number of temples erected during this period as also of their beauty and decorations. Hiuen T-Sang who visited shortly after the Gupta period was over bears testimony to the innumerable buildings and temples that had studded the whole country. Most of the buildings and temples of this period have perished but the few that have survived bear stamp of primitiveness and insufficient techniques. Yet because of their bearing upon the future development of Indian architecture and their initiating a new technique of structural building with permanent materials, their importance cannot be underestimated.

Cave excavations were found to be unsuitable for enshrinement and ritualistic worship of images of gods and goddesses. The new movement was, therefore, concerned with construction of structural temples widely different in details of form and general appearance. A wide variety of forms and types gave the architecture of the period its special importance. The varieties of the temples of this period fall under several heads, viz., (i) flat-roofed temples with a porch, (ii) flat-roofed square temples with ambulatory passage around, sometimes two-storeyed and with a porch, (iii) Square temple with a *Sikhara* at the top, (iv) rectangular temples with barrel vaulted roof, (v) circular temples with two roofed projections at four cardinal points.

The fourth and the fifth varieties, that is, rectangular temples with barrel vaulted roofs and circular temples with four projectives bear resemblance to former *Chaitya* halls of the Buddhists and the *Stupa* designs of Andhra country of second to fourth century A.D.

The Durga temple at Aihole belongs to the sixth century A.D. It is a flat roofed temple with *Sikhara* at the top. The temple known as

Maniyar Math—the shrine of Mani Naga at Rajagriha is a peculiar structure made of cylindrical bricks. The temple belongs to the fifth group mentioned above.

There were three other groups of structural temples which may be regarded as the precursors to the medieval Indian architecture. Of these three groups the first is flat-roofed square temples. Temples at Sanchi, Tigawa and Eran are best examples of this group.

The second group is also flat-roofed temples. Its plan is rather novel. It has a sactum in a smaller Square within a large Square which forms the covered gallery for perambulation, i.e., Pradakshina round the inner sactum. The Parvati temple at Nachna Kuthara, Siva temple at Bhumara, Kant Gudi and Meguti temples at Aihole belong to this group.

To near about the same period belong the *rathas* of Mamallapuram, the seaport city founded by Narasimhavarman Mahamalla, south of Madras. These are free-standing separate Monoliths shaped as *rathas*. There are eight *rathas*, the Dharmaraja *ratha*, Arjuna *ratha*, Bhim *ratha*, Ganesa *ratha*, Nakula *ratha*, Sahadeva *ratha*, Draupadi *ratha*, etc. The connection between Arjuna and Dharmaraja *rathas* and the storeyed temples of the Gupta period is unmistakable.

The third group is nothing but elaboration of the first group but its importance lies in its innovation of a *Sikhara*. From epigraphic source we come to know that already in the fifth century A.D. high and lofty towers came into existence. No Sikhara temple can, however, be placed before the sixth century A.D. The most important and representative is *Sikhara* temple in the *Dasavatara* temple at Deogarh in U.P. Another example is the Siva temple at Nachna Kuthara. The brick temple at Bhitargaon and Mahabodhi temple at Bodh Gaya as seen by Hiuen T-Sang are also examples of *Sikhara* temples. The Durga and Hucchimallagudi temples at Aihole are temples with tower at the top.

Painting

The art of painting reached its highest water mark during this period. While the stone sculpture during this age was concerned with religion, painting assumed a secular character. Again sculpture was the work of the professionals only, painting was considered as an essential social and cultural accomplishment not only in the urban areas or among the upper strata of society including princes, nobles of the Court and highborn ladies but also among members of various professional guilds and was practised even by amateurs and ordinary people.

Vatsyana in his *Kamasutra* mentions painting as one of sixty-four *Kalasa*, i.e., arts. Yasodhara, a commentator on Vatsyayana, mentions that during this period an increasing number of professionals and amateurs received regular training in the art of painting; these are as Coomaraswamy translated them as distinction of types (*rupa-bheda*), proportion (*Pramana*), expression of mood (*bhava*), charm (*labanya vojana*), points of view (*Sadrisya*), and preparation of colours (*Varnikabhanga*). A work *Vishnu-dharmottaram* of the Gupta time devotes a chapter to the art of painting. This work mentions the technical details of painting such as how to prepare the ground for mural application of colour, adding high lights and also classification of painting as realistic, lyrical, secular, and mixed. From the literary evidences of the time we can easily understand that "the intellectual ferment of the Gupta culture-period led to serious and detailed thinking about the theory and technique of painting and that it was during this period that the aesthetic canons in respect of the art of painting were formulised".[1] These canons are similar to those of the art of dancing, such as gesture, poses, attitudes, and proportions.

Vishnu-dharmattoram distinguishes different kinds of paintings suitable for palaces, temples, and private houses. The remains of paintings at Ajanta, Bagh, Badami, and Sittannavasal show them to be ecclesiastical in theme and designed to serve religious purposes. "But in inner meaning and spirit, and in their general direction and atmosphere nothing could be more secular or even more courtly and sophisticated"[2]

The royal palaces and houses of the rich were elaborately decorated with mural paintings and were furnished with picture galleries. That the Scytho-Kushana monarchs had also their picture galleries is mentioned by Bhasa.

Fresco-painting on the walls and ceilings of the Ajanta caves have forced unstinted admiration of the whole world. But of twenty-nine caves sixteen contained paintings which survived till the end of the nineteenth century and thereafter most of these have been destroyed and others are gradually crumbling to dust. But whatever remains till today shows an excellent conception executed in brilliant colours with masterly skill. Decorative designs are as graceful as fanciful. These paintings mostly belong to the Gupta Age and depict incidents of the life of Buddha. The paintings captioned, *The Dying Princess* and *The Mother and the Child*, the *Figures of Monkeys*, have won highest admiration.

---

[1] *The Classic Age*, p. 543.

[2] *Idem.*

There are also faint traces of paintings in the Badsa caves supposed to have been painted in the 3rd century A.D. Kanheri and Aurangabad caves belonging to the sixth century A.D. contain faint traces of painting. In the Bagh caves some fresco painting of merits still survive.[1]

The Gupta Age attained an unprecedented height in all the spheres of national life and its cultural achievements gave it a celebrity unsurpassed in subsequent periods of Indian history.

RELIGIOUS DEVELOPMENTS (FROM 3RD CENTURY A.D. TO 6TH CENTURY A.D.)

During the whole period of ancient Indian history there was never any hindrance to the freedom of religious speculation. This freedom which led to the rise of philosophical thoughts of the Upanishads, also had characterised the subsequent periods and led to the rise of new philosophical tenets and religious sects in the sixth century B.C. The Vedic religion had by then lost credit and a twofold reaction began, namely, (i) a movement challenging the Vedic gods and the pre-eminence of the Brahmanas in spiritual matters and (ii) a monotheistic movement which accepted devotion (*Bhakti*) as the only way to please a personal God.

We have already seen how two of the numerous revolutionary religious movements of the sixth century B.C., namely, Jainism and Buddhism had arisen and struck their roots. Two more religious movements were also to follow. These were Vaishnavism and Saivism. Interestingly enough, Jainism, Buddhism, and Vaishnavism were all founded by the Kshatriyas and their origin was in the eastern and western parts of India which were outside Madhyadesha which was the home of orthodox Vedic religion. Saivism also developed as a sectarian religion in western India.

Jainism and Buddhism had no veneration for Vedic gods or for any god whatsoever. But Vaisnavism and Saivism were two theistic religions which centred round two Vedic deities Vishnu and Siva. Jainism and Buddhism, however, possess a common background of Aryan culture and inspired by ascetic ideals and philosophy of the Upanishads. Both may be viewed as a revolt against Brahmanical religion and emphasise self-denial, renunciation and *ahimsas*.

About the life and tenets of Buddha and Mahivira discussion has already been made. Here we shall confine our discussion to the

---

[1] *About Art of Painting During the Gupta Age.*

history of the Buddhist and Jaina movements as well as of the Brahmanical-cults and sects.

I BUDDHISM

In the history of Buddhism we notice four distinct stages of development which helped the religion to become a powerful factor in the culture not only India but also of a large part of the world.

The first stage of the development of the Buddhism movement is marked by the *First Buddhist Council* held by King Ajatasatru soon after the death of Buddha.

This council was convened by Mahakassapa, a distinguished disciple of Buddha, in order to put all scattered sayings of the teacher relating to *Dhamma* and *Vinaya.* The result was the compilation of the two pitakas known as *Sutta Pitaka* and *Vinaya Pitaka.* To what extent Buddhism had developed before the First Council cannot be determined. But the three *jewels* of Buddhism—*Buddha,* *Dhamma,* and *Sangha* remained in the *Sangha* and were growing and Devadatta's attempt to create division in the *Sangha* failed.

Till we reach the time of Asoka, the Nandas Maurya emperors, Chandragupta, and Bindusara were continued to be Brahmanical Hindus, although there is reason to believe that Chandragupta adopted Jainism towards the end of his life. It was Asoka that imperial patronage was fully extended to Buddhism and Buddhism spread not only within India but also beyond India's borders and became a world religion.

The most important events associated into the Buddhist Church were the two Councils, the second and the third, both held during the reign of Asoka according to some scholars. According to this the Second Council was convened under the auspices of Kalasoka or Kakavarna, son of Sisunaga. According to N. K. Sastri traditions do not agree with this identification and this Kalasoka may have been Asoka Maurya. The Second Council was held at Vaisali.

According to Buddhist traditions there arose difference among the followers of Buddha about the ten rules of discipline which the Buddhist of eastern India followed although the westerners protested against that. The then rules were: storing salt for use, taking food after mid-day, over-eating by taking a second forenoon meal, observance of *Upasatha* at different places, to take sanction for an action after it has been done, use of precedents for an act, drinking whey after meal, use of a seat without border, drinking of unfermented palm juice, and acceptance of gold and silver.

A sub-committee with four members from the easterners and the westerners each was formed which declared the ten rules as unorthodox. The easterners called *Vajiputtakas* did not accept the decision and called another Council which they named as *Mahasanjiti* and accepted the ten rules as valid. According to some later texts the difference between the two groups related not only to the rules of the discipline but also to doctrines. According to Dipavamsa the seceding monks made certain changes in the texts of the *Tripitaka* and excluded *Abhidhamma Pitaka* from the sayings of Buddha. The easterners came to be known as *Mahasanghikas* and the westerners as *Theravada*. The *Mahasanghikas* were also known as *Acharyavada*.

This diversion in the *Sangha* began to grow upto its logical conclusion and *Achariyavada* was divided into seven sects while the *Theravada* was divided into eleven sects. But all the eighteen sects were *Hinayanists*. A few sub-sects of *'Achariyavada* group later introduced a new doctrine called *Mahayanism*. The deification of Buddha by certain important sects which branched off from *Mahasanghikas*, i.e., *Achariyavada*, and introduction of Bodhisattva concept were the precursors of Mahayanism.

The next stage of the development of Buddhism was the rise of a large number of monastic organisations and the history of Buddhist monastic organisation ceased to be one and unified. The important of these different monastic organisation compiled their own set of *Pitakas* and passed them as the original saying of Buddha. Despite these differences Buddhist monks belonging to any sect could live in any monastery but gradually dispute arose in regard to *Upasatha* ceremony. Every fortnight this ceremony used to be held and like the Christian *confession*, every monk had to declare that he had not committed any breach of any rule of discipline. But while an *Achariyavada* (*Mahasanghika*) would declare him as pure even after taking a meal in the afternoon, *Theravad* would regard it as impure. Asoka in order to rid the Sangha by dismissing all those were not believers in *Theravad* soon called a Council under the Chairmanship of Moggaliputta Tissa who refuted the views of the non-*Theravadins*. His refutations were compiled under the title *Kuthavattu* which became the fifth book of *Abhidhamma Pitaka* of the *Theravadins*.

The holding of this Council (3rd) by Asoka is not considered authentic by many scholars basing their arguments on Sanskrit traditions and the records of the Chinese travellers. It is, however, conceded that Council might have been a sectarian one meant for the *Theravadins* and Asoka or his ministers had nothing to do with it.

The excess of zeal shown by Asoka for Buddhism led to a reaction and his successors were not favourably disposed towards Buddhism. The reaction against Buddhism reached its climax under Pushyamitra Sunga. But despite this antipathy Buddhism enjoyed great popularity for a time and reached phenomenal development by the beginning of the Christian era.

One of the important factors in the development of Buddhism was the patronage it received from foreign rulers like King Menander. The *Milindapanha* or the questions of King Milinda answered by Nagasena is an evidence of the interest taken by Minander in Buddhism which he helped in spreading in the hilly regions of Hindukush and Sindhu. Other Greek kings also followed Menander's example. The Kushana King Kanishka was a great patron of Buddhism. Although initially disinterested in Buddhism Kanishka later adopted this religion. He was perplexed by the different interpretations of Buddha's sayings by different teachers. He, therefore, convened a Council at Kashmir (Jalandhar according to some) in which Vasumitra was elected chairman. The discussions held in the meeting were compiled in a commentary known as *Vibhashasastras.* This Council was also a sectarian affair and was held by *Sarvastivadins* as the Third Council was of the *Theravadins*

The Fourth Council held during the time of Kanishka marks the great split of the Buddhist Church and its fundamental doctrines. With it emerged *Mahayanism* as a distinct movement of a large section of Buddhists. The beginning of the movement may be traced to a much earlier period as we have already seen.

Buddhism retained its originality for the first hundred years of its existence but after that a new liberal outlook and inauguration of a new movement in interpreting the doctrines and the rules of discipline in a more pragmatic and liberal way are noticed. Emphasis on monastic life was still there, but a new Bodhisvatta ideal was incorporated in the doctrine. The doctrine of Bodhisvatta implied that any one, be he a recluse or a house holder, was entitled to perform certain meritorious deed (*Paramitas*) in order that ultimately he might attain Buddhahood. *Paramita* means the highest acquisition of a particular virtue. These virtues are : liberality (*Dana*), righteousness (*Sila*), forbearance (*Kshanti*), mental strength (*Virya*), mental concentration (*Dhyana*), realisation of truth (*Prajna*), skilfulness in expedients (*Upayakausalya*), vow (*Pranidhana*), attainment of certain power (*Bala*), and knowledge (*Jnana*). Gautama and all other Buddhas had to acquire these virtues in several of their existences before attaining Buddhahood.

Mahayana Buddhism at first began with the *Mahasanghikas* and by the time of Kanishka had become a recognised form of Buddhism. But it led to a formal and clear split in the doctrines and rules of discipline from the time of Kanishka and attained its full glory under the care of Nagarjuna, Aryadaṇa, Asanga, and Vasubandhu. The con tention that Asvaghosa, the contemporary of Kanishka was the earliest exponent of *Mahayana* philosophy is not acceptable to many of the modern scholars.

Nagarjuna and Asanga's masterly exposition of *Mahayanism* made a strong appeal to the intelligentsia, and development of Buddhism as a popular cult all over India and even far beyond its frontiers was due to the growth of *Mahayanism.* Introduction of theism in Buddhist religion by deification Buddha made *Mahayanism* more easily understood by common people as well as foreigners. The pristine Buddhism which went by the name *Hinayanism* was atheism and very much symbolic, therefore difficult of comprehension by common people. This *Mahayanism* meant a greater vehicle in the path of religion and *Hinayanism* a lesser vehicle. Worship of Buddha images gave an opportunity to the masses to satisfy their religious emotions, for they found a visible means for expressing their devotion. They covered India with temples and monasteries filled with images of Buddha in the belief that there would be meritorious deeds both for the donors and the artists.

The rise of *Mahayanism* effected a significant revolution in Buddhism, both in thought and in practice. It is indeed a great vehicle "for its universal sympathy, it invited all to aspire for the highest goal of Buddhahood, its outlook was broad and its aim infinitely great like the infinite sky, its all embracing doctrine of universal emptiness and also of universal compassion, its capacity to accommodate various shades of religious beliefs and popular practices; and its uncompromising intellectualism. All these factors contributed towards its growth and popularity".[1] *Mahayanism* is also called *Bodhisattvayana*, the vehicle for future Buddha. The Mahayanists claim superiority over the Hinayanists "Vasubandhu regarded *Hinayana* as milk and *Mahayana* as the cream of milk".[2]

Mahayanism becomes an infinite inspiration to literary and scholastic activities among the Buddhists. The most famous and important literature of *Mahayanism* is the *Prajna-Paramita* literature.

Emergence and development of *Mahayanism* as a theism and image-worship brought it near to Hinduism. Image-worship and *bhakti*, i.e., loving devotion became the common features of *Mahayanism* and Hinduism. The Bodhisattva like Avalokitesvara, and Manjusri and goddesses like Tara and Harti appear to be similar to Siva, Vishnu, Lakshmi, and Parvati of the Hindu religion. The Gupta period has been regarded as the golden age of Indian civilisation and

[1] Lalmoni Joshi: *Studies in Buddhistic Culture of India*, p. 4.

[2] *Idem.*

it saw allround progress of Indian Culture including Buddhism. Under the Gupta the *Mahayana* philosophy reached its climax.

Besides common practice of image worship in Buddhism and Hinduism, the fact of common patronage, those two faiths received at the hands of the Gupta rulers brought Buddhism nearer to Hinduism. About the middle of the sixth century A.D. Buddha seems to have been accorded the status of an *avatara,* i.e., incarnation of Vishnu in the Puranas. In *Mahayanism* Manjusri, Avalokitesvara, and goddess *Prajna-paramita* assumed paramount position. The cult of Amitava Buddha grew during the Gupta period and it seems to have attracted such eminent philosopher as Vasubandhu. Worship of images of Buddha and Bodhisattvas with elaborate rituals had become a universal practice during the period. The sixth century A.D. reveals two important trends, one was the emergence of the Buddhist version of the science of logic and beginning of intense controversy between the Buddhist and the Brahmanical schools, and the other was the emergence if *Vajrayana.* In the development of the Buddhist version if the science of logic the works of Nagarjuna, Maitreyanath, Asanga, and Vasubandhu had furnished the background. It was Dinnaga who actually put it on a firm foundation and initiated the scientific study or *Pramana,* i.e., means of proof and has been regarded as the *father of Indian Logic.*

Emergence of *Vajrayana* led to gradual transformation of Buddhism into a new faith and the result was the Tantrika Buddhism with which grew popularity of *mantras, dharanis, spells, charms,* worship of many male and female deities, cult of Avalokita and Tara and Buddhism made nearest approach to Hinduism and eventually made it easy for the latter to assimilate Buddhism after about two centuries.

We may now turn of discuss at some length the concept of Bodhisattva about which reference has been made above. The term *Bodhisattva* "means one whose essence is knowledge but is used in the technical sense of a being who is in the process of obtaining but has not yet obtained Buddhahood.[1]

The concept of Bodhisattva emerged out of the idea that a Buddha being so superior to ordinary humans should be born suddenly. He was not an incarnation in the strictest sense. It was, therefore, thought logical to suppose that Buddha was the product of a long evolution of virtue, of good deeds and noble resolutions extending countless ages, culminating in Buddhahood—a being superior to the *Devas,* i.e., gods. The Pali canon although recognises the Bodhi-

[1] Sir Charles Eliot: *Hinduism and Buddhism,* p. 7.

sattva as a type, if rare, yet makes its appearance at intervals, does not suggest that one should try to become Bodhisattva in order to attain Buddhahood.

The concept of Bodhisattva is characteristic of the *Mahayanism* and its doctrine is that man can try and should try to become Bodhisatta with the ultimate object of attaining Buddhahood.

In the Pali canon we come across Arhats, Pacceka, Buddhas, and perfect Buddhas. The ultimate goal of the three being *Nirvana.* A Pacceka Buddha is superior to a Arhat and a perfect Buddha is superior to a Pacceka Buddha from the points of view of intellectual power and omniscience. The virtues of a Bodhisattva were similar to those of Arhat. A Bodhisattva must be strenuous and concentrated, he must cultivate strict morality, patience, energy, meditation, and knowledge. He should also be a *bhakta*—a devotee, adoring all past, present, and future Buddhas. Asanga, however, gives a more technical and scholastic description of the stages that mark the Bodhisattava's progress towards complete enlightenment, that is complete Buddhahood. These stages are : joyful, immaculate, light-giving, radiant, hard to gain, facing transmigration and Nirvana, immovable and good-minded.

The *Mahayana* texts give the minutest details about the duties of a Bodhisattva for completing each of the different virtues called *Paramita* in the process of progress to Buddhahood. Thus virtues are *Dana-paramita, Sila-paramita, Kshanti-paramita, Virya-paramita, Dhyana-paramita, Prajna-paramita.* The virtues have differently mentioned as five, seven, and ten. The *Mahayana* texts refer to the above six. Stress was also laid on two other virtues : *Karuna*, that is, compassion and *Maitri*, that is, love.[1]

Jainism

The career of Mahavira and his contributions to Jainism have been discussed earlier.[2] We have also seen that the Jainas had twenty-four *Tirthankaras* or ford-makers of whom Parsva was the twenty-third and the twenty-fourth and the last was Mahavira. All *Tirthankaras* before Parsva were mythical and Parsva was the first historical person. The historiocity of Parsva has been confirmed by the Jaina canons and Jacobi has adduced strong arguments to prove Parsva's historical existence.

The origin of the religion which came to be known as Jainism

---

1 N. Datta: *Aspects of Mahayana Buddhism and its Relation to Hinayana*, pp. 306-308.

2 See *Ante.*, p. 68 etc.

existed even before Mahavira. The founder of this religion was Parsva but the Jaina traditions preserved only the points where Parsva's religion differed from the religion of Mahavira. "The few differences that are known make Mahavira definitely a reformer of an existing faith, and addition of a vow, the importance of nudity and a more systematic arrangement of its philosophical tenets may be credited to his (Mahavira's) reforming zeal."[1] Mahavira must, therefore, be regarded as a reformer of an existing religion rather than the founder of a new religion. Even Jaina tradition does not make any such claim for Mahavira. The Pali canon also shows that it regarded Mahavira merely as a leader of a religious sect already in existence but not a founder of a new sect.

From the Jaina *Bhagavati* Sutta we come to know that Gosala Manukhaliputta became a pupil of Mahavira in the second year of his monkhood and stayed with him for six years, then there came a breach between the two. Soon after he proclaimed himself a *Jina* and began to live at Sravasti. From the Buddhist source some information may be had of the doctrines of Gosala who became the head of the *Ajivika* sect and a parallelism between Gosala's doctrines and those of the Jainas is noticed. It is probable that the rules about the diets of the Jaina monks have been taken from those of the *Ajivikas.*

Mahavira wandered eight months in a year, resting during the rainy season, preaching his doctrines to all kinds of men. From the Jaina tradition we know that he stayed and preached in places like Champa, Vaisali, Rajagriha, Mithila, and Sravasti. But the list is not exhaustive. During forty-two years of his wanderings he must have covered many more places.

Gosala's *Ajivika* doctrines had very close ties with Jainism and it became the effort of the Jaina canon to refute the *Ajivika* doctrines. But the *Ajivikas* as a sect continued to exist.

Jainism also received royal patronage and Srenika king of Magadha became devoted to Mahavira. Later Jaina tradition, unconfirmed by any other source, mentions that "all kings of north India in those days" related to Mahavira through their marriage with the daughters of Chetaka, maternal uncle of Mahavira. This assured the royal patronage to Mahavira's religion.

From the very start there were signs of dissension in the Jaina religion, Gosala differed from Jainism. His doctrine of fatalism was not acceptable to Mahavira. After Mahavira Jamali struck a note of dissension. There were seven schisms in Jainism but most of these

---

1 *The Age of Imperial Units.*

could not leave any permanent mark. But the last schism split the Jaina community into *Digambara* and *Svetamvara* sects, each claiming greater authenticity.

The spread of Jainism was effected more by the process of migration than by any continuous expansion. The migration took place due to famine of twelve years' duration which caused the spread of this religion. Wanderings of Mahavira included, besides the places mentioned in the Jaina tradition, kingdoms like Kosala, Videha, Magadha, and Anga. According to *Kappasutta* the Jaina monks wandered as far as Anga-Magadha to the east, Kausambi to the south, Sthuna to the west, and Kunala to the north. From the inscription of Kharvela King of Kalinga showed a decided inclination towards Jainism. The numerous Jaina caves in the Udayagiri and Khandagiri in Orissa show that Jainism continued to exist in this part of the country.

Another migration brought Jainism to Mathura. There is a large number of votive tablets, dedicatory inscriptions, arches belonging to first and the second century A.D. which suggest flourishing condition of Jainism in this region. The region round Ujjaini was also a stronghold of Jainism. The story of Asoka's son King Samprati's conversion to Jainism, and the story of Kalacharya of Malwa show that Jainism had spread to the Malwa region.

Junagarh inscriptions of Jayadamana testify to the spread of Jainism in that area.

Extension of Jainism to South India is associated with the migration of Digambaras when there was a great famine in Magadha. According to Digambara tradition Bhadrabahu along with his royal disciple Chandragupta and a large group of followers took shelter in the South. This was how the Digambar Jainism spread into the South with Sravana Belgola in Mysore State as its centre. Svetambara Jaina tradition ascribes the spread of Jainism to the South through a migration from Ujjaini in Malwa. Dr. Ghartage points out that a close scrutiny will show that neither Bhadrabahu nor Chandragupta Maurya had anything to do with the migration to the South. He is of opinion that the first migration was of the sect known as Senayana from Gujarat through Maharastra to Karnataka and thence to the countries to the extreme South, and this is quite probable.

During the six centuries from 300 years B.C. to 300 years A.D. approximately covered by the above discussions, Jainism had taken its roots practically all over India. "Starting from its original home in Magadha, it had slowly spread to different countries like Kalinga to the South-east, Mathura and Malwa to the west, and Deccan and

Tamil lands to the South. At the same time it appears to have lost its hold over Magadha, the land of its origin."[1]

Initially Jainism received royal patronage in the North but the patronage was enjoyed only for a short time, although merchants, bankers in the North continued to extend Jainism their support. But if it had lost royal support in the North it more than compensated the loss by winning support of many ruling houses of the South and during the third to sixth centuries the countries to the South of the Vindhyas became the stronghold of the Jaina religion.

The Gupta imperial age marked a revival of Hinduism and of classical literature. It was an age of decline for both Jainism and Buddhism. The decline was primarily to the loss of royal patronage and it is found that Jainism still continued to be popular among the middle classes. During the reign of Kumaragupta a Mathura inscription mentions dedication of a Jaina image by a lady and another inscription at Udayagiri at Malwa mentions erection of a Statue of Parsva by a private individual. The Kahaum inscription of the time of Skandagupta refers to the setting up of five images of Jaina prophets in the village Kahaum. These records definitely prove that Jainism was practised in such distant places as Mathura, Udayagiri, and Kakubha. But in Bihar and Bengal Jainism had, however, lost much of its influence. In Paharpur copper plate of 478 A.D. There is record of the donation of some land by a private individual and his wife for the maintenance and worship in a Jaina *Vihara* at Vata Gohali which was presided over by nirgrantha Guhanandin of Banares. This vihara was unearthed at Paharpur in the Rajshahi district of Bengal now in Bangladesha.

In the post-Gupta Age there is the testimony of Hiuen T-Sang about the existence of Jainism of both the Svetambara and Digambara sects near Taxila to the west and Vipula to the east, and the Digambaras were very numerous in Pundravardhana and Samatata in the east. The Brahmin writers had a very low estimate of the Jainas. This is proved by the reference to the naked Kshapanaka by Bana in his Harsha-charita and the fun that Dandin made of the conversion of the poor wretch to Jainism. Two Gurjara Kings Jayabhatta I and Dadda II of the seventh century A.D. were given the epithet of *Vitaraga* and *Prasantaraga* in their grants which show that they patronised Jainism. In the early medieval period as well, the presence of the Jainas in Kathiawar and Gujarat is proved by epigraphic and archaeological evidence.

---

[1] *The Classical Age*, pp. 408-409.

tion of the sanctity of the river Karotoya which flowed past Mahasthangarh, i.e., Pundranagara in North Bengal.

In Jaina *Acharanga-sutra* the land of Ladha (Radha) in West Bengal has been described as a pathless country, inhabited by rude people who would set dogs on peaceful monks. In Jaina *Upanga*, however, the Ladhas and the Vangas have been classed as Aryans and latter have been mentioned as in possession of Tamalipti, i.e., Tamluk and the former in possession of Kotivarsha in the Dinajpur district. In *Acharanga-sutra* Ladha has been divided into Vajjabhumi and Subbha, i.e., Vajrabhumi and Suhma.

Reference to Suhma is found in the writings of the early Buddhist writers but not to Vanga. The first reference to Vanga in Buddhist literature is to be found in *Milindapanha.* References to Bengal as mentioned above lacked chronological arrangement.

During the historical period reference to a peoples by historians of Alexander is found in the name *Gangaridai* who as Pliny, Ptolemy and other classical writers mention as the people who occupied the country of the lower Ganges, and tributaries. Both the Jaina and Buddhist texts refer to the contemporaries of the Mauryas in Pundravardhana. That Pundravardhana existed during the Maurya period is also testified by a Brahmi inscription discovered at Mahasthangarh in Bogra district. The Chinese pilgrims who visited India in the post-Maurya period noticed Asokan monuments in different parts of Bengal.

The *Periplus,* Ptolemy's Geography, *Milindapanha* and *Nagarjunikonda* inscriptions give us some details about Bengal during the early centuries of the Christian era. Ptolemy refers to the city of Ganges and distinguishes it from *Tamalites*, i.e., Tamralipti.

From the fourth century A.D. it was possible to reconstruct the history of Bengal and its administrative division with fair certainty on the basis of distinct chronology. Well-known divisions of Bengal such as Gauda, Vanga, Radha, of course, varied in extent during this period.

When Chandragupta I and Samudragupta were marching from victory to victory adding territory after territory to the Gupta empire, Bengal was then divided into a number of independent kingdoms. In his campaign against Aryavarta, Samudragupta is known to have defeated Chandravarman and occupied western and southern Bengal. North Bengal was also under Samudragupta as is evident from an inscription of Samudragupta in which Kamrupa is mentioned as a tributary state of Samudragupta on the northern border of his empire. Samatata (East Bengal) was originally a tribute-paying kingdom of the

Guptas, but later on it was included in the Gupta empire. Thus the whole of Bengal was a part of the Gupta empire during the fifth century A.D. From a few copper plate inscriptions it is known that North Bengal comprised the *Pundravardhana-bhukti* and was under a governor appointed by the Gupta emperor. It is also known that in 507 A.D. Maharaja Vainyagupta ruled over Samatata and later became the Gupta emperor. Of course, the nature of the Gupta rule in Southern and Western Bengal is not known to us.

When as a result of the repeated invasions of the Huns and internal dissension the Gupta empire became weak. Yasodharman made himself the master of the whole of Aryavarta. Advantage was taken of this situation by Southern and Eastern Bengal which tore off from the Gupta empire and set up a strong independent kingdom there. From epigraphic evidence the names of some of the kings of this kingdom have been found, these were Gopachandra, Dharmaditya and Samachardeva. Gold coins with the name of Samachardeva have been discovered. The kings of this dynasty were doubtlessly very powerful monarchs and Dr. R. C. Majumdar is of opinion that whole of South and East Bengal and part of West Bengal were under their rule. In some other coins of this period have been discovered different parts of Bengal in which we come across the names of two more Kings, namely, Prithuvir and Srisudhanyaditya. But it is difficult to determine if all the Kings named above belonged to the same dynasty.

But there is no doubt that Gopachandra was the oldest of all these Kings. He is supposed to have ruled for at least eighteen years and Dharmaditya for three years and Samachardeva for fourteen years. According to Dr. Majumdar these three Kings must have ruled between A.D. 525 and A.D. 575. However, our knowledge about these Kings and their rule, as also about their mutual relationship are not known to us, although the copper plate inscriptions of their time leave no doubt that they were very powerful Kings.

About the fall of this Kingdom no details are available. Kirtivarman VI, the Chalukya King, has been mentioned in his *Prasasti*, i.e., eulogy that he conquered Anga, Vanga, Kalinga and Magadha during the last quarter of the sixth century A.D. Chalukya invasion must have been, therefore, the reason for the break-up of the Kingdom although the rise of the Kingdom of Gauda must have been the major cause.

KINGDOM OF GAUDA

During the rule of the later Gupta parts of North and West

Bengal were under them. It was at about that time this area came to be known as Gauda, and although under the suzerainty of the later Gupta rulers, Gauda developed into a principality of great strength and fame, the Maukhari King Ishanvarman is said to have defeated the Gaudas and compelled them to take shelter on the sea coast. Obviously the invasion and defeat of the Gaudas was an episode in the prolonged enmity between the Maukharis and the Guptas, since Gauda was under the Guptas. Sarvavarman and Avantivarman, successors of Ishanavarman, probably conquered parts of Magadha, and according to some scholars, it was after this, that the Guptas left both Magadha and Gauda, and shifted to Malva. But whatever might have been actual history, upto the end of the sixth century, Gupta King Mahasenagupta's rule extended over Gauda, Magadha and spread upto the Brahmaputra river.

But the prolonged hostilities between the Maukharis and the Guptas, invasions of the Chalukya from the South and Tibet from the north made the later Gupta rulers too weak to keep control over Magadha and Gauda, and withdrew to Malava. Advantage of this political situation was taken by Sasanka who set up an independent Kingdom in Gauda.

Sasanka

Among the Kings of Bengal, Sasanka was the first fully sovereign ruler and he occupies a prominent place in the history of Bengal. The exact time and date when Sasanka had ascended the throne of Bengal is, however, not definitely known. In the Rohtasgarh inscription there is mention of one Sri Mahasamanta Sasanka. From this it is presumed that Sasanka was originally a Mahasamanta, that is, Feudatory Chief. But whether he was a feudatory under the Maukharis or the Guptas is not known. But the fact that Mahasenagupta of the later Guptas was in possession of Gauda and Magadha during the sixth century A.D. raises the presumption that Sasanka was a feudatory under the Guptas. In 595 A.D. Mahasenagupta took refuge in the court of Prabhakarvardhana. The name of the mother of Prabhakarvardhana was Mahasenagupta. From this it is inferred by some that as a result of the Kalachuri invasion Mahasenagupta took refuge at the court of Thaneswar that is his sister. However, it is generally agreed that it was from the ashes of the Gupta empire that the independent kingdom of Gauda took birth. Sasanka was in endless struggle with the Maukharis of Kanauj and the kingdom of Kamrup. This also points to the conclusion that it was as the successor to the Guptas that Sasanka was locked in a continuous struggle with the houses of Kanauj and Kamrup. Some historians are of the opinion that the name of Sasanka was Narendragupta and he was a scion of the Gupta dynasty. But this opinion is unacceptable to most of the modern historians.

Bana and Hiuen T-Sang have described Sasanka as the king of Gauda and his capital has been named as Karnasuvarna. But the actual site of his capital has not been determined. It is supposed to be a place now called Rangamati, six miles away from Behrampore.

Before the rise of Sasanka the Mana dynasty became a powerful independent kingdom between Midnapore and Gaya district in Bihar. Later this dynasty occupied Orissa. Sasanka defeated Shambhujas or his successor and occupied Dandabhukti, that is Midnapore, Utkal, i.e., Orissa, and Kangod, i.e. South Orissa. The kings of Sailotbhava dynasty accepted the overlordship of Sasanka and continued to rule over Kangod i.e., South Orissa. The kingdom of Vanga, comprising south and eastern Bengal also recognised the supremacy of Sasanka. But nothing can be definitely said about this. Sasanka did not only make Gauda an independent and sovereign country but extended its dominions upto Ganjam towards the south, the whole of Bengal, Magadha and Varanasi. When Sasanka proceeded against the Maukharis, the Pushyabhutis of Thaneswar opposed him, for the Mukhari king Grahavarman was the son-in-law of Prabhakarvardhana. Sasanka had a friend and ally in Devagupta of Malava. Devagupta was inimically disposed towards Grahavarmana. As Sasanka proceeded against Kanauj after having conquered Varanasi, Devagupta also was on his march against Kanauj. In the meantime Prabhakarvardhana had died and his eldest son Rajyavardhana was on the throne of Thaneswar. The joy of succession to the throne was soon marred by the news that Grahavarman, husband of Rajyavardhan's sister, Rajyasree, had been defeated and killed by Devagupta who put Rajyasree in a prison. Rajyavardhana placed the charge of his kingdom in the hands of his brother Harshavardhana and proceeded against Devagupta and for the release of Rajyasree. Sasanka in the meantime also was on the march for Thaneswar. In the encounter between Rajyavardhana and Devagupta, the latter was defeated and killed but as he was proceeding towards Kanauj he met Sasanka on the way. In the battle with Sasanka Rajyavardhana was defeated and killed.

The defeat and death of Rajyavardhana at the hands of Sasanka gave rise to various conflicting stories. Among these one mentioned on Bana's *Harsha Charit* and Hiuen T-Sang's narrative deserves mention. According to Bana Sasanka invited Rajyavardhana to his camp and finding him alone killed him. In Hiuen T-Sang's narrative it is mentioned that Sasanka on the advice of his ministers invited Rajyavardhana to his camp and done him to death. It was because he was advised that so long as an honest and pious king like Rajyavardhana would be alive there would be no prospect for the greatness of the kingdom of Gauda. In the inscription of Harshavardhana it is mentioned that Rajyavardhana lost his life in the camp of his enemy in order to keep truth. From such conflicting statements it is difficult to find out the truth. Further, that in order to tarnish the character of Sasanka who was the enemy of Rajyavardhana and Buddhism, it is possible that Bana, the Court panegyrist, and Hiuen T-Sang might have exaggerated the incident. That Sasanka behaved in a treacherous manner is not mentioned in any one of the narratives. For all this, the modern historians are reluctant to stigmatise Sâsanka as a treacherous killer of Rajyavardhana.

On hearing the news of the death of Rajyavardhana, Harshavardhana as we know from *Harsha Charit*, promised to clear the earth of Gaudas, otherwise he would burn himself to death. Thereafter he proceeded with a large force against Sasanka, but on the way he came to learn that his sister Rajyasree had fled from the prison of Devagupta and taken shelter in the Vindhyas. He left the charge of his army to Bhadi, his General, and left in search of Rajyasree. In the meantime Bhaskarvarman of Kamrup being fearful of the growing strength of Sasanka entered into a friendly alliance with Harshavardhana. Whether Harshavardhana succeeded in defeating Sasanka in any battle is not mentioned any where except in *Manjusreemulakalpa*, a Buddhist book, in which it is mentioned that Harshavardhana defeated Sasanka. In this book the reference has been made in the nature of forecast. Further, the statement of Hiuen T-Sang that Sasanka oppressed the Buddhists, cut the Bodhi tree, constructed a Hindu Temple by the side of Bodh Gaya as a result of which sins he died of various diseases is also to be found in *Manjusreemulakalpa*. It is difficult, according to modern historians, to accept these as true. These were nothing more or less than the prevalent stories among the Buddhists. There is a significant reference in the Buddhist books, that Harshavardhana did not receive proper respect in the barbarian country under Sasanka and returned. This statement does not show that Harshavardhana was successful against Sasanka. Further, there was not a single word in Bana's *Harsha Charit* about Sasanka's defeat at the hands of Harshavardhana. This significant omission is enough to prove that Harshavardhana was not successful against Sasanka.

That Harshavardhana was not much successful against Sasanka is also proved by three inscriptions of Sasanka himself. One of these inscriptions is dated 699 A.D. which shows that he was in possession of his territories till 619 A.D. In that inscription it is mentioned that a king of the Sailotbhava dynasty of South Orissa was feudatory of Sasanka. According to Dr. R. C. Majumdar, till his death in 637, Sasanka's dominions comprised Gauda, Dandabhukti, Magadha, Utkal, and Kangod. Thus even if Harshavardhana remembered his oath of clearing earth of the Gaudas within a limited number of days he could not do any harm to Sasanka.

Sasanka was a worshipper of Siva. Even if it is agreed that he was not tolerant of other religions, his oppression of the Buddhists was not borne out by facts. Hiuen T-Sang's account gives out this truth. For, from Hiuen T-Sang we come to know that Karnasuvarna and in other parts of Sasanka's kingdom he saw Buddhism prevalent. If Sasanka oppressed the Buddhists how could Buddhism could be found to exist in all parts of his dominions including his capital ?

Estmate of Sasanka

In the history of the Bengalees and Bengal, Sasanka occupies a place of respect. It was he who for the first time mooted the idea of a Bengali Empire in the Aryavarta and his idea was largely successful during his life time. He made Gauda independent from the overlordship of the Guptas and made it a sovereign state. He spread his authority all over Bengal including Dandabhukti, i.e., Midnapore, as also over Magadha, Utkal, Kongod, Baranasi. For a time he staked his claim over Kanauj and Thaneswar, but was not successful. Harshavardhana could not do him any harm during his life time. Sasanka was a diplomat of no mean ability. He entered into friendly alliance with Devagupta of Malava against Maukharis of Kanauj. The portrayal of character of Sasanka in Buddhist books and Hiuen T-Sang's account is not the correct picture of his character. Modern researches have revealed some aspects of Sasanka's character which are at variance with those given out by the Buddhist books and Hiuen T-Sang.

CHAPTER TWENTY-ONE

BENGAL UNDER THE PALAS AND THE SENAS

Matsya-nyaya in Bengal : The political condition of Bengal after the death of Sasanka was one of disorder and confusion. Hiuen T-Sang came to visit Bengal immediately after death of Sasanka and he found Bengal divided into five principalities, namely, Kajangal, Pundravardhana, Karnasurvarna, Samatata and Tamralipti. Utkal and Kangod although had been parts of Bengal had become independent.

In *Manjusreemulakalpa* there is a clear reference to the total disruption in Bengal after the death of Sasanka. Manab, son of Sasanka, ruled over Bengal for eight months five days and rulers who arose in different parts of Bengal likewise ruled for very short time. Taking advantage of the situation Bhaskarvarman of Kamrup conquered Gauda and Harshavardhana conquered Utkal and Kangod. When Harshavardhana was camping at Kajangal near Rajmahal, Bhaskarvarman came to see him with twenty thousand war elephants and thirty thousand warships. The kingdom of Bengal was broken up in this manner soon after the death of Sasanka. After Harshavardhana's death Bengal was being invaded by neighbouring kings repeatedly. The king of Tibet, the later Guptas, the kings of the Saila dynasty, Yasovarman of Kanauj, Harshadeva of Assam, and Lalitaditya of Kashmir invaded Bengal one after another. Vatsyaraj of Gurjara also invaded Bengal.

The conquest of Bengal by Yasovarman of Kanauj was the subject-matter of his *Gaudabaho* written by Bakpatiraj, the court poet of Kanauj. Yasovarman had also conquered the kingdom of Vanga, that is, northern and eastern Bengal. Of course Yasovarman's authority in these areas was very short-lived. It is needless to stress that due to internal disorder and external aggression condition in Bengal became desperate. The small local rulers were mutually at war, the stronger was oppressing the weaker, the more powerful was attacking the less powerful. There was veritable matsya-nyaya, that is, the logic of the fishes prevailing in Bengal. As the larger fish devours the smaller ones so the more powerful or bigger local lord was occupying the territories of the smaller and the weaker ones. Internecine conflicts, lack of law and order made the condition of the common people unbearable. In this intolerable circumstance the leading persons of Bengal met and by common consent placed one named Gopal on the throne of Bengal in (Cir.) 750 A.D.

THE PALAS

Gopala Cir. 750-770 A.D.: The establishment of the Pala rule in Bengal during the middle of the eighth century A.D. was landmark in the history of Bengal. From that time it is possible to write the complete history of Bengal on the basis of historical materials.

By electing Gapala to the throne of Bengal the leading persons of Bengal of that time had given proof of their sense of nationalism and patriotism. By placing a capable man like Gopala on the throne of Bengal they gave proofs of their far-sightedness, self-lessness and their solicitousness for the well-being of the people of the country.

Gopala ascended the throne of Bengal with the good will and the willing allegiance of the people of Bengal. Although we know of his father Bapyat and grand-father Dayitvshnu from his inscription, yet the manner in which reference has been made to them raises the presumption that they were commoners.

Gopala's first task was the removal of lawlessness and disorder from the country which he did without delay and thereby fulfilled the expectation of the people of Bengal. His reign was occupied largely by war for bringing about peace and to ward off foreign invasions. His efforts were crowned with success and Bengal enjoyed a period of peace and prosperity under him. He founded the Pala dynasty of Bengal. Although much is not known about his reign, it is believed that he brought whole of Bengal under his sway. The exact length of his reign is also not definitely known.*

Dharmapala Cir. 770-810 A.D.: Dharmapala, the second ruler of the Pala dynasty, was the real founder of the power and supremacy of the Palas. He came to the throne about 770 A.D. and during his long reign of thirty-two years he made Bengal the most powerful state in northern India.

Soon after his accession Dharmapala launched upon a career of conquest of Aryavarta in order to establish an empire there. But

---

* "The reign-period of Gapala is not definitely known. According to Taranath he ruled for 45 years but this statement canot be taken without corroboration. According to *Manjusreemulakalpa* his reign-period was twenty-seven years. His accession to the throne may be placed with tolerable degree of certainty within a decade of 750 A.D. and he probably ceased to rule about 770 A.D." *History of Bengal*, (D.U.) Vol. I., p. 103.

the Vatsyaraj, king of the Gurjara-Pratiharas, had become so powerful that it did not become easy for Dharmapala to establish an unquestioned mastery over Aryavarta. When Dharmapala proceeded towards Aryavarta, Vatsyaraja also advanced with his army towards Aryavarta. In the engagement between the two, Dharmapala was defeated. At this point of time Druba, the Rashtrakuta king of the south, also proceeded to establish his sway over Aryavarta and defeated Vatsyaraja completely. Vatsyaraja had to flee for his life. When Dhruba and Vatsyaraja were engaged in war, Dharmapala conquered Magadha, Varanasi, and Prayag. After defeating Vatsyaraja Dhruba proceeded against Dharmapala and defeated him. This defeat, however, did not mean any loss of territory to Dharmapala. Soon after when Dhruba left for the Deccan, Dharmapala found his opportunity to conquer Aryavarta. He waged a number of wars but no details of these wars have been found.

The Tibetan historian Taranath has specifically mentioned that the empire of Dharmapala extended from the Bay of Bengal in the north to Delhi, Jullundhar, and to Vindhyas to the south. Dharmapala had deposed Indrayudh from the throne of Kanauj and placed his own nominee Chakrayudh on it. From the Khalimpur inscription of Dharmapala it is known that he had summoned a *Durbar* at Kanauj which was attended by kings of Bhoja, Matsya, Madra, Kuru, Jadu, Yavana, Avanti, Gandhara, Kira, etc. who endorsed his setting up of Chakrayudh to the throne of Kanauj. This arrangement, however, did not last long. Indrayudh with the help of the Gujara King Nagabhatta II defeated Chakrayudh and Dharmapala and recovered Kanauj.

Dharmapala took the title of Paramabhattaraka Maharajadhiraja which was significant of his sovereign status. He set up his capital at Pataliputra and thereby revived its past glory. Dharmapala did not abide his time in warfare only, he did much for the Buddhist religion and higher education. He caused the construction of the Vikramsila Mahavira which had 107 temples and 6 colleges within it. As many as 144 professors taught different subjects in these colleges. Although a patron of Buddhism, Dharmapala was respectful towards other religions. He donated lands for the construction of Hindu temples. Garga, a Hindu Brahmin, was his minister. He did not allow his religious belief to overcloud his judgement. From the Khalimpur inscription we know that Dharmapala ruled for long 32 years, but Taranath the Tibetan historian puts his years of reign as 60 years. Taranath's statement is not acceptable to modern historians.

Devapala, Cir. 810-850 A.D.: The third king of the line, Devapala is regarded as the most powerful of all the kings of the Pala dynasty. His General Lausena or Labasena is said to have conquered Assam and Kalinga. During his reign there was recrudescence of war with the Gurjara-Pratitaras and the Dravidas. Bhoja I, the Gurjara king, defeated Devapala in a battle. He on the other hand defeated the Rashtrakuta king, Amoghavarsha, in an engagement. The Court poet of Devapala called him the lord of whole land from the Himalayas to Kanyakumarika. But this was indeed an exaggeration of the Court panegyrist. For, from an inscription of his reign, we come to know that Devapala's empire extended from Kamboj in the north to the Vindhyas in the south.

That he had relations with the north-west Indian rulers is doubtless. He appointed one named Vira Sena Saba, a Brahmin of that area, to a high post under him. The fame of Devapala had spread outside India and spread to Sumatra, Java, Malaya, etc. Balaputradeva, king of Sumatra, sent an ambassador to Devapala's court to ask for five villages at Nalanda for the use of the Buddhist monks who could come to Nalanda University for studies. Devapala granted this request. The fame of the Nalanda University during the reign of Devapala had spread far and wide and due to the patronage of Devapala Nalanda became a centre for the study of Buddhist religion and culture. Devapala appointed Indradeva, a great teacher and scholar in Buddhism, as the Chancellor of the Nalanda University.

Like other kings of the Pala dynasty, Devapala was a Buddhist. Due to his patronage, Buddhism which was decaying in northern India saw a period of revival.

Devapala was a patron of art and architecture. He caused the repair of the Buddhist monasteries at Magadha. He also caused the construction of several monasteries at Nalanda and a very large temple at Bodhgaya. He was very much respectful towards education and educated persons. His court was adorned by the Buddhist pundits of various countries. Devapala built a new capital for his empire at Monghyr.

Pala Kings after Devapala: After Devapala the power and glory of the Pala empire did not last. The latter Pala emperors like Vigrahapala, Narayanpala, Rajyapala, Gopala II, and Vigrahapala II were as weak as worthless. As a result under their rule the Pala empire was fast moving towards its fall.

After Devapala, his nephew Vigrahapala, became the king. Vigrahapala was the son of Bakpala, brother of Devapala. As Vigrahapala was given more to the pursuit of religious activities than to administration of the country, there ensued looseness in administration. Ultimately Vigrahapala abdicated his throne in favour of his son, Narayanpala, and gave himself fully up to religious activities.

During the reign of Vigrahapala and the early years of the reign of Narayanpala some places of the Gupta Empire had fallen off from the empire. According to some, Narayanpala ultimately succeeded in recovering all the lost places. Narayanpala was peace-loving and weak-kneed like his father and in fact, during the rule of Vigrahapala and Narayanpala extending for nearly half a century the Pala empire was broken up into pieces due to internal disruption and external attacks. A large part of the Pala empire was occupied by outsiders. During the life time of Devapala the Rashtrakuta and Pratihara kings who came to invade Bengal were defeated but during Narayanpala's rule the Pala empire had not the strength or determination to ward off the attacks of those two powerful houses. In the inscription of Amoghavarsha it is mentioned that Anga, Vanga, and Magdha accepted his (Amogavarsha's) overlordship. From this it may be inferred that the Pala king was defeated at his hands. The Pratihar King Bhoja defeated Narayanpala with the help of Kalachuri and Guhilat kings.

The Pala kings who succeeded Narayanpala such as Rajyapala (Cir. 908-940), Gapala II (Cir. 943-960), Vigrahapala II (960-988) were very weak and worthless, taking advantage of which a hill tribe known as Kambojas attacked the Pala dominions. The details of the Kamboja attack are to be found in the Dinajpur pillar inscription. Wherefrom the Kambojas had come is not known for certain. However, towards the end of the tenth century A.D. the Pala empire reached its lowest ebb. The ninth Pala king, Mahipala, drove out the Kambojas and recovered some of the lost possessions of the Pala empire.

The Second or the Revived Pala Empire

Mahipala I: The greatest achievement of Mahipala was the expulsion of the Kambojas and revival of the Pala Empire. When he ascended the throne, Chandra dynasty was ruling in East Bengal and Sur dynasty was ruling in West Bengal. From the inscriptions found on the bases of the Vishnu image discovered Baghaura and Ganesh image found at Narayanpur, in Comilla, it is known that Mahipala occupied East Bengal within two-three years of his accession. The North and West Bengal also came under his possession. Among the Sur kings of West Bengal, the Adisur famous in folk tales is specially important. On his accession to the throne Mahipala conquered the whole of Magadha, he also conquered Tirabhukti. His empire extended from Varanasi and Mithila to East Bengal.

Mahipala was a patron of Buddhism. In the eleventh year of his reign a large Buddhist temple was caused to be constructed by him at Nalanda. Some Buddhist temples were reconstructed by

Mahipala's relations Sthirapala and Basantapala. During his reign the architecture of Bengal took a new turn in style.

Towards the end of the reign of Mahipala Chedi King Gangeyadeva attacked Mahipala's empire and conquered Tirabhukti. Besides, Rajendra Chola I, king of the Chola kingdom of distant south, came through Orissa, entered Bengal and defeated Mahipala in 1023 A.D.

Pala Kings after Mahipala: After the death of Mahipala I the revived Pala empire was hastening to its fall. His son Nayapala (Cir. 1038-1054), his grandson Vigrahapala III (Cir. 1054-1072) and the latter's son Mahipala II had not the ability to defend the revived Pala empire. Taking advantage of this increasing weakness of the Pala rulers a Chasi-Kaivarta rebellion took place during the reign of Mahipala II. The Chasi-Kaivartas who came from North Bengal rose in rebellion under their leader Dibyok who killed Mahipala and made himself predominant in North Bengal. In folk tales Bidyok or Dibbya was represented as a saint and a patriot. It is said that he saved North Bengal from the oppressive rule of Mahipala II. But in Rama Charit there is no reference to such exploit of Dibyok. In absence of dependable historical materials, it is difficult, according to most of the historians, to regard Dibyok as a saint and a patriot. After Dibyok, his brother Rudrak and after Rudrak his son Bhim became the ruler of North Bengal. Under Bhim North Bengal, i.e., Barendra became a powerful and prosperous kingdom. There is mention of Bhim in Rama Charit. The Kaivarta pillar at Dinajpur even today stands as a monument of the Kaivarta rule in North Bengal.

After the death of Mahipala II his two younger brothers, Surapala and Ramapala, fled from the prison where they were kept confined by their elder brother Mahipala. They went to Magadha and began to rule there as independent rulers. Magadha was presumbly part of Bengal then. First Surapala and then Ramapala ruled there. Ramapala defeated Bhim and recovered North Bengal. In order to enlist the support of the people of the country behind him Ramapala reduced the taxes on the people and made improvement in agriculture. He set up a new capital called *Ramabati* near, perhaps near, Malda and began to make efforts for reviving the greatness of the Pala empire. The King Dharmaraja of East Bengal and king of Kamrupa accepted the overlordship of Ramapala. He deposed the Utkal King Karnaraj after signally defeating him. This involved him in prolonged warfare with Anantavarma Chodaganga. From *Ramacharit* it is known that Ramapala conquered Anga and succeeded in defending his kingdom against the attack of the Chalukyas. After a long reign of 42 years Ramapala died after giving cohesion to the disrupted Pala empire of Bengal. By good government and strong administration the lost glory of Bengal was revived under Ramapala, only to be lost during the weak rule of his successors. Vijaysena seized power from the Palas taking advantage of their weakness.

THE SENAS

Samanta Sen : Hemanta Sen : In the middle of the eleventh century two brothers, Samanta Sen and Hemanta Sen, established a small kingdom at Kasipuri. Kasipuri is believed to be the present Kasiari in the Mayurbhanj district. The Senas are supposed to have come from Karnataka in the south. The Senas were originally feudatories of the Palas but when the Palas had become very weak after Ramapala Vijay Sen, grandson of Samanta Sen, dislodged the Palas from power and seized the throne of Bengal. From that time the Senas acquired an independent status and gradually began to increase their power and territory.

Vijay Sen, Cir. 1095-1158 : Vijay Sen was the first independent and powerful king of the Sen dynasty. How he had defeated the local kings of Radha, the Varma dynasty of East Bengal and the Palas of North Bengal is not known. He was, however, not content with defeating the Palas, he after having conquered major part of Bengal launched upon a career of conquest of North Bihar, Orissa and Assam. It is learnt from *Vallal Sen Charit* written by Ananda, that Vijay Sen entered into a friendly alliance with Chodganga, king of Kalinga. He married Bilasdevi, the daughter of the King of South Radha, which enhanced his power and prestige considerably. Vijay Sen defeated the Yadava dynasty of East Bengal and set up a capital Vijaypur there. Much of the time of Vijay Sen's reign was consumed in warfare. From the Deopara inscription it is learnt that Vijay Sen defeated Naya, Vira, Raghava, Bardhana and other local rulers as also the kings of Gauda, Kalinga and Kamrupa.

During the long reign of Vijay Sen law and order, peace and prosperity returned to Bengal. From the panegyric of Umapatidhar the achievements of Vijay Sena have been known in details.* Vijay Sena saved the people of Bengal from the prevalent disorder that became widespread in the wake of the end of the Pala rule. Vijay Sen was an intrepid soldier, a tactful military general, and a good administrator. He assumed titles like *Prameswara Parama bhattaraka, Mahadhiraj, Arirajbrishavashankar*, etc. which denoted his imperial status.

---

* "The long and memorable reign of Vijay Sen which restored peace and prosperity in Bengal made a deep impression upon its people. This feeling is echoed in the remarkable poetic composition of Umapatidhar preserved on a slab of stone found at Deopara." *History of Bengal* (D.U.) Vol. I, p. 215.

He died after a long reign of sixty (forty according to some) and was succeeded by his son Vallal Sen.

Vallal Sen, Cir. 1158-1179 A.D.: Vallal Sen, son and successor of Vijay Sen, was more interested in internal regeneration and reconstruction than external conquests. Whether he had gone on any military expedition is not known for certain, but during his reign his kingdom was completely secure from external attack. Like his father he also adopted title like *Ariraj Nishankar Sankar* significant of his imperial status. Vallal Sen is famous for introducing *Kulinism* with a view to reorganising the Hindu Society. *Kulinism* was introduced among three upper classes of the society, namely, the Brahmins, the Vaidyas and the Kayasthas. These three classes had to follow certain rules of conduct in social behaviour, marriage, etc. This was done in order to enhance the sense of honesty, justice, sanctity of caste and similar other virtues. Later on the system of Kulinism lost its real purpose and became a corrupt oppressive system. According to tradition Bengal was divided into five parts under Vallal Sen, namely, Vanga, Barendra, Radha, Bagdi and Mithila.*

Vallal Sen was a patron of Tantrik Hinduism and he sent preachers to Magadha, Chittagong, Orissa, Arakan and Nepal for preaching this religion. He was also a patron of learning. He himself was the author of two important books named *Danasagara* and *Adbhutsagara.* The latter book he could not complete which was done by his son Lakshman Sen.

Lakshman Sen, Cir. 1179-1205 A.D.: Lakshman Sen succeeded his father Vallal Sen. According to Mihaj-ud-din, Lakshman Sen was about sixty years old at that time. His capital was at Nadia. He also assumed the title of *Ariraja Madan Shankar* and also called him *Gaudeswar.* But in royal rescripts he unlike his predecessors called him *Parama Vaishnava Parama Narasinha* instead of *Parama Maheswara.* It becomes clear from all this that Lakshman Sen was a Vaishnava. This is also proved from his inviting Jaydeva, the devout Vaishnava to his court. Lakshman Sen conquered Gaya and Mithila and included south-west Bihar in his dominion. He waged war against the king of Garhwal Govinda Chandra and in this connection he marched with his army right upto Varanasi and Allahabad. Lakshman Sen earned fame both as a conqueror and a patron of learning and was comparable to his father in this respect. Court poet Saran and Umapatidhar made reference to a great conqueror without naming him. This was none else than Lakshman Sen himself. Jaydeva, the author of *Geet Govinda,* Dhoyi, author of *Pabanaduta,* poet Saran

* *Ibid.,* p. 217.

and philosopher Halayudh graced the court of Lakshman Sen. Lakshman Sen completed the unfinished work of his father named Adbhut Sagar. Some of the slokas included in the Sanskrit book Sadukti Karnamrita were composed by Lakshman Sen, his father and grandfather.

Towards the end of the twelfth century Ikhtiyar-ud-din Mohammad bin Bakhtiyar Khalji was entrusted by Kutbuddin Aibak to conquer Bengal and Bihar. Ikhtiyar-ud-din made a sudden attack on the capital of Lakshman Sen who being incapable of defending himself against this sudden attack he left Nadia for East Bengal where he and his successors ruled as independent kings for some time more.

Minhaj-ud-din described Lakshman Sen as a very powerful *Rae*, i.e., king. In his *Tabakat-i-Nasiri* Minhaj has related a story about the conquest of Nadia, capital of Lakshman Sen by Ikhtiyar-ud-din Mohammad bin Bakhtiyar Khalji. It is said that when Lakshman Sen came to know of the conquest of Bihar by Ikhtiyar-ud-din, his ministers advised him to leave Nadia. But Lakshman Sen did not listen to the cowardly advice of his ministers. Many of his ministers and well-to-do subjects, businessmen left for East Bengal, Assam, etc. One day at noon when Lakshman Sen was taking his meal Ikhtiyar-ud-din with eighteen horsemen appeared before the gates of the royal palace of Nadia. His main contingent was following him but fell behind as they could not keep pace with Ikhtiyar-ud-din. As Ikhtiyar-ud-din took Lakshman Sen by surprise, the latter finding resistance impossible left the palace through the backdoor for East Bengal. The modern historians do not take this story of Mihaj in its face value. For it is unthinkable that Lakshman Sen would not make any preparation for the defence of his capital even after coming to know of the conquest of Bihar by Ikhtiyar-ud-din. Even if Minhaj's story is taken as true, the fact that Lakshman Sen continued to live in Nadia even after the advice of his ministers to leave and actual leaving of Nadia by many of the ministers and businessmen, shows the determination and sense of patriotism of Lakshman Sen. He was surprised by Ikhtiyar-ud-din and finding defence impossible in the circumstance, he left Nadia. Minhaj has been fair in characterising Lakshman Sen whom he called not only a powerful king but also a liberal and kind-hearted ruler. It may be mentioned here that Nabin Chandra Sen, Dwijendralal Roy have not properly characterised Lakshman Sen in their works. They have done an injustice to him by calling him a cowardly king.

ADMINISTRATION, SOCIETY, ECONOMIC CONDITION, CULTURE UNDER THE PALAS AND THE SENAS

The long reign of four hundred years of the Palas in Bengal

is in itself significant, for seldom a dynasty had such a long lease of life. From the historical materials at our disposal it is not possible to reconstruct a full history of the Pala administration, but it may be reasonably presumed that a long reign of four hundred years must have led to the evolution of a highly developed administrative system. From the contemporary inscriptions, grants, literature, etc., it has been possible to draw a general picture of the Pala administration. The administration was divided into two parts, the Central and Provincial :

(i) Central : At the head of the Central Government, for the matter of that of the state was the king. The Pala kings in imitation of the Gupta rulers assumed high sounding titles like *Parameswara*, *Paramabhattaraka*, *Maharajadhiraja*, etc. Appointment of Prime Minister by the Pala kings was an innovation for heretobefore no Indian king had appointed Prime Minister. The post of the Prime Minister later on became hereditary. In the Badal inscription details of the powers of the king and the Prime Minister have been given. In the Pala Central administration there was the system of appointing a various grades and types of officers. Among these officers reference has been found in the Pala royal grants and inscriptions of Amatyas, Angarakshas, Baladhakshyas, Chauradharanikas, Dandikas, Dandasaktis, Dasgramikas, Dutas, Gramapatis, Jyesthakayasthas, Kottapalas, Mahapratiharas, Mahasandhibigrahikas, Senapati or Mahasenapati, Naukadhakshyas, Prantapalas, Rajasthaniyas, Uparikas, Vishayapatis, etc.

The responsibility of administration lay on the king and the officers directly under him. Rajputra, Prime Minister, Mahasandhibigrahika, Rajamatya, Mahakumaramatya, Duta, etc., were such officers. Rajasthaniyas, i.e., the Viceroy or the Regent used to carry on with the work of administration in absence of the king. Angaraksha was the head of the royal bodyguards. The Adhakshyas referred to in Kautilya's Arthasastra were also appointed during the Pala time. The royal elephant and cavalry corps were under their charge.

The charge of the revenue department was in the hands of Vishayapati, Uparika, Dasgramika, Gramapati, etc. Bhaga, Bhoga, Kara, Hiranya, extra-cess etc. were different kinds of revenue that the state earned. Reference to all this is to be found in the contemporary royal grants, gift of lands, etc. Revenue used to be collected through officers in charge of different areas. The officer called *Bhogapati* perhaps realised the tax called *Bhoga*. *Sastha Adhikrita* was the officer who realised one-sixth of the produce of the land. The royal revenue was also derived from tax for keeping villages safe from thieves and robbers, customs duties, ferry toll, fines and forfeitures. Public accounts were checked by Maha-akshapatalika and Jyesthakayastha. Mahadandanyaka was in charge of the judiciary. There were different grades of judicial officers under him.

Senapati or Mahasenapati was the highest general of the army. The army consisted of infantry, cavalry, elephant corps, camal corps. The navy was an important part of the Pala military system. The outlying provinces were under the charge of Wardens of the Marches. Kottapal was in charge of the fortresses. *Mahapratihar*, *Dandika*, *Dandapasika* were in charge of the police force. The existence of a class of officials called *Khola* raises the presumption that the Palas engaged secret police, i.e., spies for collecting secret information.

Provincial Administration : Under the Palas Bengal, Bihar and Assam were under the direct rule of the Pala kings.* For administrative convenience these areas were divided into Bhuktis, Vishayas, Mandals and Patakas. In the royal grants, inscriptions and literature of the Pala time, we have reference to Pundravardhana Bhukti, Danda Bhukti and Bardhaman Bhukti into which Bengal was divided, Bihar was divided into Nagara Bhukti and Tira Bhukti and Assam into Pragjyotishpur Bhukti. The Bhuktis or provinces were divided into Vishayas, that is, districts and Vishayas into Mandalas. The Mandalas were subdivided into Patakas. The details about the administration of these different divisions and subdivisions are not known to us.

With the extension of the Pala Empire a new type of local administration was also functioning. The conquered territories were allowed to be ruled over by their original rulers as Samanta, i.e., feudatories called *Rajan*, *Rajanyak*, *Ranak*, *Samanta*, *Mahasamanta*, etc. These feudatories were under the fullest control of the Pala kings so long as the central administration was strong. But as soon as weak kings began to ascend the throne at the centre many of them became independent. This apart, some of the feudatories, such as Iswar Ghosh, was so powerful that they ruled in practical independence of the Palas.

It goes without saying that the Palas had developed an efficient administrative system. It may, however, be mentioned that much of the Pala administration was a copy of the Gupta administration. The administrative system detailed in Kautilya's Arthasastra is also found to have much influence on the Pala administration. The efficiency of the Pala administration reflected itself in the economic prosperity and culture of that period. The cultural progress which is possible under a life of peace, prosperity and contentment had been ensured under the Palas. The Palas were not only mindful of political, economic and

---

* "The Palas exercised direct administrative control over Bengal, Bihar and Assam". *History of Bengal*, (D.U.) Vol. I, p. 273.

social progress of the country, but also for the development of morality, religion and culture. Patronage of the University of Nalanda, of a large number of poets, men of letters, etc. establishment of monasteries for the Buddhists were proofs of their liberality of mind. The Pala kings were tolerant of others' religions. Most of the Pala kings were Buddhists but they appointed Brahmins as their Prime Ministers as a rule. The general contentment, peace and prosperity of Bengal under the Palas were the results of their solicitousness for the well-being of their subjects.

(ii) Administration under the Senas : Under the Senas, generally speaking, the Pala system of administration was continued. Bhuktis, Vishayas, Mandals, etc. continued to be administrative divisions even under the Senas. Patakas and Chaturakas are names of smallest administrative divisions which appear repeatedly in the inscriptions and literature of the Sena times. This raises the presumption that under the Senas the small administrative divisions like Patakas and Chaturakasa acquired more importance. Among the royal officers Bhuktipati, Mandalpati, Vishayapati occur repeatedly. The Prime Minister of the Palas was now called Mahamantri. The Sena kings used to adopt titles like *Aswapati*, *Narapati*, *Rajaprayadhapati*, etc. There are evidences of the Sena kings making grants of lands to their Queen or Rajmahishi. The *Purohitas* and *Mahapurohitas* were also given land by formal grants which prove that the *Purohitas* or *Mahapurohitas* had acquired much respect and importance. The *Sandhivigrahika* of the Palas took the name of *Mahasandhivigrahika* under the Senas. These apart, *Mahamudradhkrita*, *Mahasarbadhkrita* were new officers appointed by the Sena kings. Likewise the highest judge was called Mahadharmadhyakshya. The military officers also took new names under the Senas. Mention may be made of Mahapilupati, Mahaganastha, Mahabyutpati in this connection. In the copper plate of Iswar Ghosh there is reference to twenty-nine classes of officers under the Senas. In no other time in independent Bengal there were so many different classes or grades of officers. But it must be mentioned that the main structure of the administration of the Palas remained unaltered under the Senas, although changes were effected in detail. The class of officers called *Pradeshtris* mentioned in Kautilya were also appointed during the Sena period. This shows that the traditional Hindu administrative system, that is, the system detailed in Kautilya's Arthasastra had a deep influence on the Sena administration.

Lastly, it has to be mentioned that in the history of Bengal the period of the Sena rule was also one of peace and prosperity. The peace and contentment that led to the cultural activities during the

Pala period continued even under the Senas and the Sena period is also a memorable age in the history of Bengal. In politics, religion, economy, society there was an all-round improvement under the Senas.

Society and Culture under the Palas and the Senas: That politically the Pala Age constituted a glorious chapter of the history of Bengal, nay of India, is agreed on all hands. Not only political field but also in social, economic, literary and cultural activities this period registered a great development. Under the Senas, the political supremacy of Bengal had been somewhat diminished but in social and cultural development this period also was almost equally great.

Social conditions: Hiuen T-Sang describing the prosperity of Bengal and the social habits of the Bengalees one century before the rise of the Palas, was full of praise about the character, courage, honesty and culture of the Bengalees. Hiuen T-Sang was specially pleased at the amiability and love of education among the Bengalees. From the literary sources of the time of the Pala and the Sena rule we come to know that characteristics noted by the Chinese traveller were all present among the Bengalees during the Pala and the Sena rule. From the literary sources we come to know that the Bengalees of the Pala-Sena period were unostentatious, easy-going and simple in their daily life and living. In Sandhyakar Nandi's *Ramcharit* it is mentioned that society had persons who were living a highly moral life and others who were given to debauchery. This is borne out in the writings of Vatsayana. The Sena King Vallal Sen had introduced *Kulinism* among the Brahmins, Vaidyas and Kayasthas in order to maintain the racial purity of these sections of the society. From this it is presumed that conservatism in caste system must have prevailed at that time and marriage between different castes was not permissible. The society then was divided mainly into Brahmins, Baidyas, Kayasthas and Sudras.

Position of women was very high in society. Holding women in high respect was the traditional aspect of the Hindu culture. The praise of the women of the Pala and the Sena period is found in contemporary literature.

The Bengalees partook of food as they do at the present day. Rice, pulses, vegetables, fish, meat, ghee, curd, milk and various preparation from rice used to be taken by them. Sugar and molasses used to be produced in large quantities in Bengal at that time.

In matter of dresses there was no ostentation. The males used dhoti and chaddar as their dress while women used sari. Bodices and a small orna were also used. Sandal paste and camphor were used as perfumes by women. Wooden sandales and sandles made of hides were used by men.

Both the males and the females used to wear ornaments made of gold and silver. Kundala, keyur, bangles, neck-laces, mekhala, rings, nose-studs, anklets, etc., were the ornaments of the time. Ladies of the rich families wore ornaments with jewels-set on them. Married women used vermilion on their forehead.

In social and religious functions dance, songs, music, etc., were a must. There were various religious rites performed all throughout the year as is done today. Games of various types, chess, etc., were the pastimes of the people.

Bullock cart, horse, elephant, palanquin, boats, etc., provided the means of transport at that time. The women of the rich families used to travel in boats and palanquins.

Economic condition: During the Pala and the Sena period the Bengalees lived in villages. Agriculture was the very basis of the economic life of the people. Small industries and cottage industries as well as trade and commerce also were highly developed. While the men engaged in trade and commerce used to live in cities the women of the family would live in villages. People living in towns did so for earning livelihood. Although by far the largest number of the population lived in villages there was no dearth of towns and cities which were wealthy and a large section of the population of such towns and cities were well-to-do financially. The towns and cities had wide roads on both sides of which stood buildings. The royal palace would have a golden pitcher at the top of the building. In *Ramcharit* by Sandhyakar Nandi there is a nice description of the Pala capital *Ramabati* which was studded with temples, stupas, monasteries, gardens, ponds and swimming pools, etc. Trees and creepers of various kinds added to the beauty of the capital city. It was not a speciality for Ramabati. Every town and city had similar decorative trees, ponds and gardens.

During the Pala-Sena period Bengal was famous for small and cottage industrial products. These were exported to Ceylon, Burma, Champa, Cambodia, Java, Siam, Sumatra, China, etc., through the ports of Tamralipti and Saptagram. Bengal had also trade relations with other parts of India and caravans used to travel upto Tibet, Nepal and Central Asian countries by land. Fine cotton cloth produced in Bengal used to be exported to the countries of East and West at that time. In the account of an Arabian merchant Khordadbaha we find how a dhoti made of finest cotton yarn in Bengal could be passed through a fingure ring. From Suleiman, the Arab merchant, we come to know that Bengal used to export horns of rhinoceros to China. In *Abhidhan Rantnamala* there is a reference that tin used to be raised from tin mines in Bengal.

From the above description it becomes clear that under the Pala-Sena period agriculture, small and cottage industries, trade and commerce flourished to a great degree in Bengal.

Literature and Culture : Under the Palas and the Senas there was an unprecedented development in literature and culture in Bengal. Apart from political supremacy established by the Palas and the Senas, their rule constituted a glorious chapter in the history of literature and culture in the history of Bengal and for the matter of that in the history of India.

Literature : Under the Palas and the Senas an unprecedented expression of the Bengali intellect and talent could be seen. The education and literary development during this period was the result of patronage of the Pala and the Sena kings. Vedas, Dharmasastras, Puranas, Ramayana, Mahabharata, Mathematics, Economics, Ayurveda, Grammar, Astrology, etc., were vastly read by both men and women. It was under the Palas that many *Dohas* and folk songs called by the name of *Charyapada* were composed. Lui Pa and Kanha Pa were the most celebrated of the composers of the Doha and songs called *Charyapada*. These were the original form of the Bengali language. Sandhyakar Nandi's *Ramacharit*, Gauda Abhinanda's *Kadambari Kathasagar*, and Halayudh's *Abhidhan Ratnamala* were written during this period. The author of Chikitsa Sangraha, Chakrapani Datta, was the greatest authority in Ayurvedasastra of that age. Srikar was one of the greatest authors of Smritisastra of the period. Jimutabahana, Sridharabhatta enriched this period by their works. Sena King Vallal Sen wrote two books *Dansagara* and *Adbhutsagara*. Under the patronage of the Sena art and literature in Bengal had registered a marked development. The famous poet Jaydev, author of *Geetagovinda*, Dhoyi, author of *Pavanaduta*, poet Umapatidhar, etc., flourished during the Sena rule.

Education : Gopala, founder of the Pala dynasty, constructed the Odantapuri Mahavihara. The Buddhist Philosopher Santi Rakshit enjoyed the patronage of Gopala. He was the greatest exponent of Tantrikism. During the reign of Gapala's son Dharmapala as many as fifty Buddhist monasteries were built. Buddhist philosopher Haribhadra used to teach Buddhist philosophy in these monasteries. One of the greatest achievements of Dharmapala was the establishment of the Vikramsila Mahavihara on the Ganges near Patharghata in Bhagalpur district. There were 107 temples and 6 colleges in this Mahavihara and Buddhajnanpada was the Chancellor of this University or Mahavihara. Prasasta Mitra, Buddhasakti, Buddhajnanpada, Rahulabhdra and other Buddhist philosophers taught Tantrik Buddhism in the colleges of this University. Kamalsila was the greatest annotator of the Mahavihara. Kalyan Rakshit, Prabhakar, Purnavardhan, etc., were the professors who taught Nyaya in the University and there were other professors who taught grammar, logic, and various other subjects. There were altogether 108 professors engaged in teaching different subjects in the Vikramsila University. The students had not to spend anything for their residence, food or tuition, on the contrary they were paid some pocket money to meet their sundry expenses. Those of the students who could show proficiency in the subject of their study would be conferred diploma. Students from different parts of India, Tibet and other countries used to come to Vikramsila for study. Many Sanskrit books were translated into Tibetan in this Mahavihara. Dipankar Srijnan was a professor in Vikramsila. Under Devapala another Vihara known as Sompuri Vihara was constructed. The ruins of this University have been discovered in the Paharpur area of Rajshahi district. Pala King Devapala was also responsible for the establishment of a monastery known as Traikutaka monastry. It was a centre for the study of Buddhism. During the Pala rule the Nalanda University again became famous as a seat of learning and scholars from far and wide used to come to this university for study. The ruler of Sumatra Balaputradeva of the Sailendra dynasty sent an emissary to Devapala asking for the grant of five villages in the vicinity of Nalanda for the residence of the scholars from Sumatra. Balaputradeva's request was complied with. Devapala himself had constructed a monastery at Nalanda. He was a great patron of learning and the learned men.

Art, Architecture and Sculpture: Under the Palas arts of painting, architecture and sculpture were highly developed. Under the Senas as well, architecture registered a great improvement. The art, architecture and sculpture that had developed under the patronage of the Palas and the Senas have been mostly destroyed during the Moslem invasion. Yet some of the specimens that have been found here and there give us a clear idea of the excellence reached in art, architecture and sculpture during that period. The Odantapuri Vihara constructed by Gopala is an excellent specimen of the architectural skill of the time. The first Buddhist Vihara at Tibet was constructed in imitation of the Odantapuri Vihara. In the South-East Asian archipelago copy of the Somapuri Vihara style is largely seen. The Somapuri Vihara had a spacious courtyard and all its four sides buildings, temples, dining halls, etc., were constructed. The ruins of the architectural works of the time of the Palas and Senas have been discovered in many places of Bengal. In the art of painting and sculpture Dhiman and his son Bitapal reached perfection under the Palas. They knew the art of making images with metal. The sculptural remains of the Pala period force our admiration even today. The greatest artist of the Sena period was Sulapani.* During the Pala rule many aquaducts were excavated and some of them exist even today in the Dinajpur district.

Religion: The Pala kings were Buddhists. Buddhism was on the wane in other parts of India at that time, but it was lively in the domains of the Palas. In those parts of India both Buddha and Mahavira were being regarded as Hindu gods. The influence of Saivism and Vaishnavism fell deeply on Buddhism and Jainism and both Buddha and Mahavira Jina were being looked upon as incarnation of Siva and Vishnu. The simplicity of worship in Buddhism which was formerly characteristic of this religion gradually gave place to Hindu rites and rituals as well as mantras in the worship of Buddha. As Tantrikism made a deep influence on Buddhism it became easy for Hinduism to gradually bring it under its fold. With the gradual introduction of Mudra, Mandal, Rites, Brata, formalities, Mantras, Homa, etc., in Buddhist worship, Buddhism gradually got merged into Hinduism. *Manjusreemulakalpa* shows how a good deal of Hinduism had entered into the worship of Buddha. In this way while in other parts of India Buddhism was gradually being mixed up with Hinduism, in Bengal under the Palas Buddhism continued to exist in its real form. Although the Pala kings were Buddhists, they were tolerant of other religions. During the Sena period Hinduism became predominant in Bengal.

Contact with the Outside World under the Palas and the Senas: Under the Palas and the Senas, particularly under the Palas Bengal was regarded as the source of religion, industry, literature, trade and commerce. Bengal was the mistress of Nepal, Tibet, China, Japan, Burma, Ceylon, Java, Sumatra, etc. From Tamralipti and Saptagram a large number of merchant vessels would carry on regular trade with Ceylon, Burma, Java, Sumatra, etc. Many princes and merchants who for one reason or other had lost their fortune would go to Suvarnadwipa, that is Sumatra and other South-East Asian countries to repair their fortune and would come back with ship loads of gold. For this, the region generally came to be known as Suvarnadwipa, particularly meaning Sumatra.

Due to the patronage of the Palas Buddhism had spread to South-East Asian countries like Sumatra, Java, Burma, Japan and

---

*"Sulapani, a Ranaka, chief of the guild (*gosthi*) of *Silpis* of *Varendra*" *History of Bengal* (D.U.) Vol. I, p. 534.

also to Tibet, China, etc. In Devapala's royal rescript there is mention of three kings of the Sailendra dynasty of Sumatra, Java, etc. A Bengali called Kumara Ghosa was the preceptor (guru) of the Sailendra Kings. The king of Sumatra, Balaputradeva, sent an emissary to Devapala asking for five villages in the vicinity of Nalanda for construction of a monastery for the scholars from Sumatra. From all this, it may be presumed that in the Suvarnabhumi, i.e., the South-East Asian archipelago religion and culture of Bengal had spread. Buildings of the style of Sompuri Vihara were constructed in this region.

Commercial and cultural relations with Tibet with India was much older than the Pala period. The king of Tibet, Strong-San-Gampo, was instrumental to the spread of Buddhism in Tibet. Many Buddhist monks came to Nalanda to study Buddhist philosophy. It was at the invitation of the king of Tibet that the Palas sent Ratna Bajra and Atish Dipankar to Tibet to reform the Buddhist religion there. The first Buddhist Vihara in Tibet was constructed after the style of Odantapuri Mahavihara. A brisk trade also was carried on between Bengal and Tibet during the Pala rule.

During the Pala rule the religious and commercial relations between Bengal and China went on uninterrupted. In 973 a professor from Nalanda went to China being invited by the Chinese emperor. Many other Buddhist monks from other parts of India also had gone to China at that time. Likewise a large number of Chinese Buddhist monks came to visit India during the Pala rule; five of them left an inscription at Bodhgaya.

Through Burma, Tibet and China both religious and cultural influences spread to Japan during the Pala rule.

The Sena kings were also great patrons of religion. They were patrons of Brahmanical Hinduism. Vallal Sen sent religious preachers to Magadha, Chittagong, Arakan, Orissa and Nepal for preaching Brahmanical Hinduism.

From the above narrative it will be evident that under the Palas and the Senas in the fields of politics, religion, literature and culture there was an unprecedented development in Bengal. The Senas were last independent Hindu ruling dynasty of Bengal. During the reign of Lakshman Sen the last of the Sena rulers Ikhtiyar-ud-din Mohammad bin Bakhtiyar Khalji defeated Lakshman Sen and occupied his capital at Nadia in 1197. Lakshman Sen withdrew to East Bengal where he and his successor ruled for some time more.

CHAPTER TWENTY-TWO

SOUTH INDIAN KINGDOMS : THE RASTRAKUTAS : CHALUKYAS : THE GREAT PALLAVAS AND THE CHOLAS

The Rastrakutas: The Rastrakutas called themselves descendants of one named Satyaki. But there is difference of opinion about their origin among the historians. According to some they were originally of Dravidian peasant extraction. From some of the inscriptions of the Chalukya kings it is known that the Rastrakutas were feudatories of the Chalukyas. Perhaps their original home was Karnataka and their mother tongue was Kanarese. The founder of the Rashtrakuta power was Dantivarma or Dantidurga. The Rastrakuta King Dantivarma or Dantidurga was contemporary of Chalukya King Pulakesin II. Dantidurga occupied all territories between the Godavari and the Vima. The first authentic date of the Rastrakutas that has been known is 753 A.D. Systematic history of the Rastrakutas is known from this date. Dantidurga is said to have conquered Kalinga, Kosala, Kanchi, Srisril, Malava, Lata, etc. He annexed Maharastra to his kingdom by defeating Chalukya King Kirtivarma.

Dantidurga was succeeded by his uncle Krishnaraja (768-772). He conquered the territories that were still under the Chalukyas and thereby completed conquest of the Chalukya territories. He also occupied Konkan and also defeated King Rahappa. It is not known for certain the name of the country over which Rahappa used to rule. Chalukyaraj Vishnuvardhana IV of Vengi and the Ganga king of Mysore were defeated at the hands of the Rastrakuta King Krishnaraja. Krishnaraja was responsible for the construction of the Kailash temple of Ellora which stands as an excellent specimen of the Rastrakuta art and architecture.* Krishnaraja's eventful career came to an end within a very short time and he was succeeded by his son Govindaraj who ruled for some time as Govinda II. His worthlessness as a ruler and his lack of interest in administration led to his deposition by his brother Dhruva who ascended the throne himself. Dhruva was by far the best ruler of the Rastrakuta dynasty. He ruled for a short span of time but within this short time he entered into a struggle with the Gurjara-Pratihara King Vatsyaraja and defeated him signally. He also likewise defeated the Pallavas of Kanchi and the Pala King Dharmapala of Bengal.

***Early History of India*, V. A. Smith, pp. 444-445.

Dhruva was succeeded by Govinda III his son and with almost equal vigour as of his father. He succeeded in keeping the Gurjara power sufficiently under control. He defeated the great Gujara King Nagabhatta II. It is said that the Pala King Dharmapala and his protege Charayudh sought the help of Govinda III. Govinda III made the Rastrakutas dynasty one of the most powerful dynasties of contemporary India. His kingdom spread upto the Vindhyas and Malava in the north and the river Tungabhadra to the south.

The greatest king of the Rastrakuta dynasty was Amoghavarsha. As a warrior he was, however, no match with his father Govinda III, but he succeeded in defeating the East-Chalukya kings. It was Amoghavarsha who had successfully arrested the progress of the Gurjara King Bhoja I towards South India. He set up a new capital at Malkhed and during his reign Broach became the best port of his kingdom.

Amoghavarsha was a great patron of education and literature. Under his patronage Jinasen wrote an important book called *Parsva Abhyudaya-Jaydhavala, Ratnamalika*—two celebrated works in philosophy, *Sara-Sangraha*—a work in Mathematics were produced during his reign. From the evidence of the Jaina works it is known that Amoghavarsha was converted into Jainism by Jinasena, a Jaina monk. Amoghavarsha spent the accumulated wealth of his predecessors to beautify his kingdom.

Suleiman, an Arab merchant, in his account called Amoghavarsha as one of the four greatest kings of the world, the other three being the Caliph of Bagdad, the king of Constantinople and the emperor of China.

Amoghavarsha ruled for 63 years and he was succeeded by his son Krishna II who in his turn was succeeded by Indra III. Indra III was a powerful king. He defeated and deposed Mahipala. The Rastrakuta Kings Amoghavarsha II, Govinda IV and Amoghavarsha III were weak and worthless kings. The last powerful and efficient king of the Rastrakutas was Krishna III. He had a prolonged struggle with Mahipala the Gurjara king. He also succeeded in conquering Tanjore and Kanchi. In the middle of the tenth century for a time he succeeded in defeating the Tamil kings of Chola kingdom. But towards the end of the same century the Rastrakuta King Kaka* was defeated and deposed by Taila or Tailapa, the Chalukya king of Kalyani. With Kaka's defeat the Rastrakuta power came to an end.

---

* *Early History of India*, p. 446.

The Rastrakuta kings maintained a friendly relation with the Arabs of Sind. When the Gurjara-Pratihara were engaged in fierce struggle against the Arabs, the Rastrakutas were profiting by carrying on trade with the Arabs. By way of this business relation a large number of Arab merchants came to the Rastrakuta kingdom. Suleiman was the Arab merchant and was the most celebrated of them. Suleiman called the Rastrakuta kings as 'Balhara'. The Rastrakuta kings called themselves 'Ballava'. 'Balhara' of Suleiman was obviously a corruption of the expression 'Ballava'.

THE CHALUKYAS

Chalukyas of Batapi: The political history of the Deccan may be said to have begun from the sixth century A.D. with the rise of the Chalukyas. The Chalukyas called themselves as Rajputs who had migrated from the northern India. In later Chalukya inscriptions they claimed to have come from Ayodhya. According to Dr. Smith the Chalukyas were a branch of the Gurjaras and had probably come from Rajputana to the Deccan.* Some historians are of opinion that the Chalukyas were a Kanarese people.†

Pulakesin I was the founder of the Chalukya house of Vatapi. Vatapi was a part of the present Bijapur district of South India. The Chalukyas were an orthodox Hindu dynasty like the Gurjara of northern India. Pulakesin I celebrated the foundation of his kingdom and dynasty by holding *Aswamedha Jajna.*

Pulakesin I was succeeded by his son Kirtivarma. He was the real founder of the Chalukya greatness. He conquered all the places on the northern coast of India and towards the north proceeded upto the Bay of Bengal. Towards the south he conquered the Tamil kingdoms of Chola, Pandya, etc., and Magadha, Anga, Vanga, Kalinga, Dravida, etc. were included in his kingdom. On the western coast he occupied Mysore and parts of Travancore. He dispossessed the Nalas, Kadambas and the Mauryas of Konkan.

Kirtivarma was succeeded by his brother Mangalesh. He conquered a part of the Deccan plateau. During his reign a large rock-cut temple with a vast audience hall was constructed near Batapi or Badami. In his old age he was deposed and killed by Pulakesin II, son of Kirtivarma.

* "There is some reason for believing that the Chalukyas or Solankis were connected with the Champas and so with the foreign Gurjara tribe of which Champas a branch and it seems to be probable that they emigrated from Rajputana to the Deccan." *Ibid.*, p. 440.

† *Ancient India*, R. C. Majumdar, p. 288.

Pulakesin II was the greatest king of the Chalukyas of Vatapi. He defeated Harshavardhana and prevented his progress towards South India. Pulakesin II defeated South Kosala, Kalinga, the Gurjaras of Broach, Gangas -and Latas. Under him the whole of the Deccan plateau came under the sway of the Chalukyas of Vatapi. Hiuen T-Sang described Pulakesin II as the greatest king of South India. Pulakesin II had sent an embassy to the Persian Emperor Khusru II and the latter reciprocated by sending an envoy to Pulakesin's court.

Pulakesin II brought the Tamil kingdoms of Chera, Chola and Pandya under his complete control and occupied Vengi by defeating the Pallavas of Kanchi. But towards the last part of his reign the Pallavas took revenge of their former defeat by signally defeating Pulakesin II

After the death of Pulakesin II the Chalukya power became weak. At that time a branch of the Chalukya dynasty set up a captial first at Pistapuram and then at Vengi and began to rule independently there. They came to be known as the East Chalukyas.

Among the successors of Pulakesin II the names of Vikramaditya I and Vikramaditya II are worth mentioning. Vikramaditya I defeated the Pallavas and thereby avenged the defeat of Pulakesin II in their hands. Vikramaditya I gave the Chalukya kingdom the status of an empire. The greatest achievement of Vikramaditya I was the warding off the Arab invasion of the south. The Chalukya power at Vatapi came to an end in the middle of the eighth century with their defeat at the hands of the Rastrakutas.

The Chalukyas of Vatapi or Vadami were orthodox Hindus. They followed the Vedic rites and practices of religion. Under them art, architecture and sculpture reached a high level of excellence. The Elephant Cave, the Ajanta Caves bear testimony to the Chalukya art and arcihtecture even today. The paintings on the inner wall of the Ajanta Caves force the admiration of the visitors from different parts of the world. In trade and commerce the Chalukyas were particularly well up. They carried on a brisk trade with the ports on the Arabian Sea and held a monopoly business.

Chalukyas of Kalyani : The Chalukya kingdom of Kalyani was formed with the south-western parts of the Deccan. Taila or Tailapa II established this dynasty after defeating Kaka the last of the Rastrakuta king. Taila was the descendant of Vikramaditya II, the Chalukya king of Vatapi. Taila II waged war against Malava. After Taila II Satyasraya, Vikramaditya II, Jaysingha occupied the throne of Kalyani one after another. It was during the reign of Jaysingha that a Saiva preacher preached a new religion called *Lingayet* sect. Jaysingha was a contemporary of King Bhoja and Rajendracholadeva. He was naturally always fearful of these two powerful kings. In fact, Rajendracholadeva defeated him in an engagement.

The next king Someswar established the city of Kalyani. He was defeated by the Chola kings more than once. After Someswar, Someswar II and Vikramaditya VI became kings. Vikramaditya VI instituted an era from 107 called Chalukya Vikramaditya Era. He was the greatest king of the Chalukyas of Kalyani and he succeeded in reviving the Chalukya Power of Kalyani and even occupied a part of Mysore taking advantage of the weakness of the Chola kings. Vikramaditya VI was responsible for the authorship of works on Political Science, Astrology, Judicial System, Medicine, Rhetoric, Chemistry, etc.

Vikramaditya VI was succeeded by Taila III, Someswar VI, etc. At that time Vijjala, the Kalachuri king, occupied the throne of the Kalyani but within a short time the Yadava and the Hoysala took possession of Kalyani.

The Pallavas of Kanchi : There is difference of opinion among historians about the origin of the Pallavas. We have come across Pallavaraj Vishnugopa among the kings of South India whom Samudragupta had conquered but allowed them to retain their kingdoms accepting Samudragupta as their overlord. But nothing is known after Vishnugopa till we reach the end of the sixth century A.D. when Singhabahu or Singhavishnu occupied the Pallava throne and gave a continuity to the Pallava rule. Singhabahu conquered the Chola kingdom as well as many other kingdoms of the south. He even extended his dominions to Ceylon. Kanchi was the capital of the Pallava kingdom.

After Singhabahu, his son Mahendravarma I occupied the Pallava throne. He was engaged in a life and death struggle with the Chalukyas of Vatapi. Pulakesin II was the Chalukya king of Vatapi at that time. In 609 or 610 Pulakesin defeated Mahendravarma I and occupied Vengi from him. Pulakesin had appointed his younger brother ruler of Vengi. This was the faint beginning of the East-Chalukya kingdom of Vengi.

Mahendravarma I was a great patron of sculpture and architecture. During his reign Trichinpalli, Chingelput, northern and southern Aracot were studded with rock-cut temples of extraordinary beauty. These are still extant and force the admiration of visitors. Mahendravarma had constructed a city called Mahendrabadhi and a large aquaduct called Mahendrabapi. He was originally a Jaina but later on became a Saiva.

Next king was Mahendravarma's son Narasinghavarma. He

also waged relentless war with the Chalukyas. He succeeded temporarily in defeating the Chalukyas of Vatapi and in occupying their capital at Vatapi. Under Narasinghavarma Pallava domination was established all over South India. Narasinghavarma took the assistance of the king of Ceylon in defeating the Chalukyas. As a reward for this assistance Narasinghavarma helped the king of Ceylon to become independent of the Chalukyas. During the reign of Narasinghavarma Hiuen T-Sang visited the kingdom of the Pallavas and from his account it is known that the city of Kanchi spread over five to six square miles. The land of the Pallava kingdom was very fertile and there was abundance of agricultural crops, flowers, fruits, etc. The capital city had numerous Hindu, Buddhist and Jaina temples. Large number of Buddhist monks used to live in Buddhist monasteries. King himself was a great patron of sculpture and architecture. It was during his reign that the seven Rathas after the names of the horoes of Mahabharata, such as Judhisthir ratha, Draupadi ratha, Bhima ratha etc. were cut from huge stones at Mahavalipuram.

After Narasinghavarma his son Mahendra II and after him Parameswara II became king at Kanchi. The Pallava King Narasinghavarma II was a great patron of architecture. It was during his reign that the Kailashnath Temple of Kanchi, the temples on the sea coast of Mahavalipuram were built. During his reign Chalukya King Vikramaditya II occupied the Pallava capital Kanchi. Later on with the defeat of the Pallavas at the hands of the Cholas the Pallava Power came to an end and the Pallavas were reduced to small feudatories. The last of the Pallava kings was Aparajitavarma.

In political and cultural fields the Pallavas of Kanchi constituted an important chapter in the history of India. In the southern part of the Pennar and the Tungabhadra they were the first to build up a strong power. Their authority had spread for a time even over Ceylon. In sculpture and architecture the Pallavas rule constituted a landmark in Indian history.

Pallava Art : The excellence that the sculpture and architectural arts had attained in South India can very well be understood from a look at the remains of the temples of the Pallavas. During the Kushana period the indegenous art that had flourished at Mathura and Amaravati continued to develop without any break and reached its peak and flowering under the Pallavas. Some of the excellent specimens of the Pallava art can be seen at Kanchi and Mahavalipuram. Of course the earliest Pallava specimens of art have not survived but what we find at Kanchi and Mahavalipuram are those of the later Pallava times. The Pallava artists made their temples out of large rocks yet their sense of proportion and jewellers' precision with which they performed their task are astonishing. All this bears eloquent testimony to the extraordinarily high standard reached by the Pallava artists.

The Tripurantakeswar and Airabateswar temples of Kanchi, Mukteswar and Kailashnath temples at Mahavalipuram are the best specimens of the arts of sculpture and architecture of the Pallavas. The style and execution of the work force our admiration. The images sculptured on the walls of the temples are excellent specimens both from the points of view of proportion and anatomy.

Draupadi ratha, Arjuna ratha, Bhima ratha, Dharmaraj ratha etc. are rathas i.e. chariots cut-out of massive rocks were stupendous sculptural feats which had been mastered by the Pallava artists. These rathas were based on the tales of the Mahabharata. Many of the temples at Java were built after the fashion of the rathas at Mahabalipuram. The Pallava sculpture and architecture have occupied a position of distinction in the history of Indian art.

Pallava Literature : The Pallava kings were patrons of Sanskrit language and literature. Kanchi, the capital of the Pallavas, was a centre of Sanskrit studies. Poet Bharavi, the author of *Kiratarjuniyam*, was the court poet of Pallava King Singhababu or Singhavishnu. Sanskrit scholar Dandin was the greatest litterateur of that period. Pallava King Mahendravarma was himself a great man of letters.

Religion of the Pallavas : The Pallava kings were Brahmanical Hindus. King Singhababu or Singhavishnu was perhaps a worshipper of Vishnu. Mahendravarma I, the Pallava king, was originally a Jaina but he came under the influence of a Saivite saint Appar and was converted into Saivism. He caused the construction of temples for Vishnu and Brahmma. Towards the end of his reign he became intolerant of Jainism and ordered the demolition of Jaina monasteries. But generally speaking it cannot be said that the Pallava kings were intolerant of other religions. The attitude of Mahendravarma towards the Jainas was something unusual of the Pallava kings. Hiuen T-Sang noticed about ten thousand Buddhist monks and numerous Buddhist monasteries and Viharas of the Mahayana sect within the Pallava dominion. He also mentioned the existence of a large number of Jainas within the Pallava dominion. Thus it may be safely concluded that although the Pallava kings were Brahmmanical Hindus they were not intolerant of other religions.

The Cholas : In the inscription of Maurya Emperor Asoka the Cholas of the far south had been described as an independent people. From the writings of the ancient Greek, Roman and Tamil writers there are references to the maritime activities of the Cholas. But there is no detailed information about the political history of the Cholas.

Karikal was the first historical king of the Cholas. It is said that he had once conquered Ceylon and brought a few thousand labourers from there to his own country. With the help of these labourers he constructed a *bund* in the river Kaveri and built a new capital named Kaveripaddinam.

From the contemporary literature it is learnt that in the 3rd century A.D. the Chola Power became very weak taking advantage of which the Pallavas occupied the Chola dominions. But in the eighth century A.D. the Chola recovered their territories when the Pallavas were defeated at the hands of the Chalukyas and also their former territories. Vijalalaya was the Chola king who made the Chola Power independent during the middle of the ninth century and his son Aditya completed the ouster of the Pallavas and set up the Chola kingdom in fullest sovereignty. It was from the time of his son Parantaka I that systematic history of the Chola dynasty can be found (907).

Parantaka I was an intrepid soldier and a great military strategist. He invaded the Pandya kingdom and occupied its capital Madura. He also invaded Ceylon. It was Parantaka I, who was the founder of the Power and greatness of the house of the Cholas. He was succeeded by a few weak kings during whose reign there was disorder in the Chola kingdom. At last with the accession of Rajaraja in 985 peace and order returned to the Chola kingdom.

Rajaraja was the greatest king of the Chola dynasty. With him began the history of peace and prosperity of the Chola kingdom. During his long reign Rajaraja conquered many territories and made himself the unquestioned master of the Deccan. He defeated the Chera and Pandya kingdoms and occupied Vengi by defeating the East-Chalukyas. With the help of his powerful navy Rajaraja conquered Ceylon and the Malaya. His kingdom spread from present Madras Presidency to Coorg, Quilon, Pandya kingdom, Ceylon, Malabar coasts.

Rajaraja was not great as a conqueror alone, he was equally great as patron of literature, art and architecture. The famous Siva temple at Tanjore was built under his patronage. On the walls of that temple the accounts of Rajaraja's wars have been inscribed. The temple bears testimony to Rajaraja's greatness both at war and peace. He was really a great king and the appellation Rajaraja the Great has been well deserved by him.

Rajaraja was a devotee of Siva but he was tolerant to other religions. He made a liberal gift to the Burmese Buddhist temple at Negapattam.

Rajendracholadevagogaikonda : Rajaraja was succeeded by his son Rajendracholadeva. As a prince he assisted his father in administration of the country and on accession to the throne he adopted the policy of his father of imperial expansion. He sent his invincible navy to the Bay of Bengal and succeeded in occupying Pegu, Andaman, Nicobar etc. for some time. He defeated the Pala King Mahipal I of Bengal and in commemoration of this victory adopted the title 'Gogaikonda'. He also established a new capital of the name of *Gogaikondacholapuram* and decorated this city by constructing a number of beautiful buildings. He excavated a large lake in the middle of the city.

On the death of Rajendracholadeva, his son Rajadhiraj ascended the throne. The major part of his reign was consumed in putting down internal rebellion and wars with Pandya kingdom and Ceylon. In his attempt to invade the Chalukya territory he was killed at the hands of the Chalukya king. Rajadhiraj was succeeded by Adhirajendra. He was as incapable as high-handed as a ruler. The subjects were so dissatisfied at his rule that he had to lose his life at the hands of an assassin. During the rule of Adhirajendra the great Vaishnava philosopher Ramanuj lived at Srirangam within Chola kingdom. Ramanuja did not receive fair treatment at the hands of Adhirajendra who was a Saiva and the policy of persecution that he followed towards the Vaishnavas led Ramanuj to leave Srirangam and take refuge in Mysore. The Chola kings after Adhirajendra were weak and worthless, taking advantage of which Malik Kafur occupied Chola kingdom and thereby brought about the end of the Cholas.

Chola Administration : The Chola administration was as efficient as integrated. From the inscription of Parantaka I the details about the Chola administration can be found. The basis of administration was the village. A large village or a group of villages formed *Kurram*. Every village had arrangement for self-government. A village assembly of the nature of village-panchayat was in charge of the administration of the village. There were officers who looked after the activities of the village assembly. The village assembly had control over all lands belonging to the village. The members of the village assembly would constitute themselves into small committees each in charge of the ponds, gardens, judicial system of the village. Every village assembly had a treasury of its own.

A few large villages or *kurrams* would constitute a district, i.e., *Nadu*, and a few *Nadus* would form a Division or *Kottam*. A few Divisions or *Kuttams* would constitute a Province. There were six provinces in the country which was called *Cholamandalam*.

One-sixth of the produce of the soil was realised as revenue. This apart other taxes had also to be paid. But the total realisation by the state as land revenue, taxes etc. did not exceed more than 4/15th of the income of a person. Land revenue could be paid either by money or by produce of the soil. The currency of the time was *gold Kasu.*

The Chola kings developed a powerful navy for the purpose of developing a maritime empire and sea-borne trade. For the purpose of irrigation a few massive irrigation plans were executed. For the purposes of excavating irrigation canal, public thoroughfares forced labour was used. Royal roads were always kept in good trim.

Chola Art : The Chola art essentially means Chola sculpture and architecture. The Cholas had practically no contribution to the field of painting. In sculpture and architecture the Chola attained the highest water-mark of excellence. The Chola sculpture and architecture were free from any foreign influence and may be regarded as copy and continuation of the Pallava sculpture and architecture.

Most of the Chola kings were patrons of sculpture and architecture. The best specimen of the Chola art of the time is the Rajrajeswar (Siva) temple of Tanjore. This temple was made under the orders of Rajrajeswar. This beautiful temple has fourteen tiers in its top and each tier has been cut-out of a big stone in a circular fashion. On the walls of the temples of Gogaikondacholapuram beautiful images have been sculptured. The main characteristic of the Chola art is its massiveness. The Chola artists have chiselled out beautiful temples from large rocks and executed their work with jeweller's precision. Fergusson, an English historian, aptly remarked that the Chola artists planned like giants and finished like jewellers.

Pandya Kingdom : Nothing is known of the ancient history of the Pandya kingdom. When Hiuen T-Sang visited the Deccan the Pandya country was under the Pallavas. Of course Hiuen T-Sang did not visit the Pandya country. The Pandya King Sundar Pandya was originally a Jaina, later on he adopted Saivism and is said to have followed a policy of persecution of the Jainas.

Later on the Pandya kings were constantly at war with Pallavas, Cholas and Ceylon. In the eleventh and the twelfth centuries the Pandyas were compelled to owe allegiance to the Cholas. It was in the thirteenth century that the Pandya kingdom acquired independence and became one of the important powers of the Deccan. In the same century Marco Polo visited Pandya country twice—once in 1288 and again in 1292. In his account Kayal, the capital of the Pandya kingdom, was a prosperous port and a beautiful city. With the fall of the Tamil Power at the hands of Malik Kafur in 1310, the Pandya kingdom also came to an end.

Chera Kingdom: Nothing is practically known of the Chera kingdom. In Asoka's inscription there is reference to Keralaputra, i.e. Chera kingdom which was then an independent country. But later on it was annexed to Chola kingdom.

Maritime Activities of the Tamil Kingdoms: From the remotest time of history India had commercial and cultural relations with the outside world. During the Gupta Age as also during the post-Gupta period this contact remained undisturbed. But the commercial and cultural relations became more fruitful through the South Intdian countries. In the Periplus written in the middle of the first century A.D. the names of the ports of South India have been given. From the South Indian ports of Muziris, the present Cranganore, Kayal, Korkai and from the northern Indian ports, a sea-borne trade with the Western countries was carried on. In the Greek and Roman accounts there are references to the commercial relations of the Tamil countries of Chera, Chola and Pandya countries with the East and the West. Later on more than one Chola king conquered Ceylon. Karikal the first Chola king had conquered Ceylon and brought a few thousand labourers from there whom he engaged in constructing a *bund* in the Kaveri river and in building a new capital called Kaveripaddinam. Rajaraja the Great, the Chola king also conquered Ceylon, obviously because it had become independent in the meantime, Laccadives and Maldives and built up a maritime empire. He had a large navy which he used for both military and commercial purposes. Rajendracholadeva conquered Pegu from Burma as also Andaman and Nicobar islands. His merchant marine used to constantly carry on sea-borne trade with Burma, Malayan archipelago etc. Kaveripadinam was the greatest port of the Chola kingdom. The best port of the Pandya kingdom was Karikal. Merchants of South India would start with their merchandise for Alexandria, Syria, etc. across the Arabian Sea. The Indian merchandise used to be sent from Alexandria, Syria etc. to the western countries. Later on the Arab merchants began to take direct part in the Indian trade and would come to the South Indian ports for purchase of merchandise, particularly spices.

South India had commercial and cultural relations with the South-East Asian countries like Sumatra, Java, Malay, Borneo etc. From these places Indian merchants ships used to reach China, Japan etc. That South India had commercial relations with China is proved from the extensive number of Roman coins that have been discovered in South India. In the first century B.C. an emissary was sent from the Pandya country to Emperor Augustus of Rome. Evidence of seven other similar embassies has been found.

It goes without saying that in the wake of commerce cultural influence also spread to the South-East Asian countries with which southern India had a brisk commercial relation. In the matter of colonisation of countries in South-East Asia South Indian countries took the lead.

Between the second and the fifth century A.D. Indian colonies were set up in Malay, Cambodia, Annam, Sumatra, Java, Bali, Borneo and even in Philippine islands. In this region the Saivism from South India had spread. Side by side with Saivism Buddhism also had spread in this region. Hindu manners and customs, influence of Sanskrit language had also spread in this region. Chola king Rajaraja the Great had paid a huge amount of money to the Burmese Buddhist temple at Negapattam. From this it is proved beyond doubt that a large number of Burmese used to live in that place. The Pallava and Chola sculpture and architectural style had been imitated at Java, Sumatra and other Indian colonies in South-East Asia. In the temples of these places the South Indian architectural style can be noticed even today.

The South Indian countries held sway over Indian Ocean and Bay of Bengal for a long time. Later on when the Portuguese merchants had seized these areas from the Indian hands the South Indian commercial and maritime supremacy came to an end.